Lecture Notes in Artificial Intelligence 10640

Subseries of Lecture Notes in Computer Science

More information about this series at http://www.springer.com/series/1244

Floriana Esposito · Roberto Basili
Stefano Ferilli · Francesca A. Lisi (Eds.)

AI*IA 2017
Advances in
Artificial Intelligence

XVIth International Conference
of the Italian Association for Artificial Intelligence
Bari, Italy, November 14–17, 2017
Proceedings

 Springer

Editors
Floriana Esposito (iD)
University of Bari
Bari
Italy

Roberto Basili
University of Rome Tor Vergata
Rome
Italy

Stefano Ferilli (iD)
University of Bari
Bari
Italy

Francesca A. Lisi (iD)
University of Bari
Bari
Italy

ISSN 0302-9743   ISSN 1611-3349   (electronic)
Lecture Notes in Artificial Intelligence
ISBN 978-3-319-70168-4   ISBN 978-3-319-70169-1   (eBook)
https://doi.org/10.1007/978-3-319-70169-1

Library of Congress Control Number: 2017959750

LNCS Sublibrary: SL7 – Artificial Intelligence

Printed on acid-free paper

This Springer imprint is published by Springer Nature
The registered company is Springer International Publishing AG
The registered company address is: Gewerbestrasse 11, 6330 Cham, Switzerland

Preface

This volume collects the contributions presented at the XVI International Conference of the Italian Association for Artificial Intelligence (AI*IA 2017) that was held in Bari, Italy, during November 14–17, 2017. The conference is the yearly event organized by AI*IA (the Italian Association for Artificial Intelligence).

The conference received 91 submissions by authors from 18 countries. Each paper was carefully reviewed by at least three members of the Program Committee. The final outcome was the acceptance of 39 papers for presentation at the conference, yielding an acceptance rate of about 40%. The significant effort spent by the community in the review process involved 97 researchers whose commitment and technical quality mainly contributed to the excellence of the body of work presented here.

AI*IA 2017 hosted a significant number of relevant events, starting with the exciting keynotes by Carla P. Gomes, Cornell University (USA), and Peter W.J. Staar from IBM Laboratories Zurich (Switzerland). The conference program also included an unprecedentedly large set of interesting workshops: AIRO, the Workshop on Artificial Intelligence and Robotics; AI*AAL.it, the Third Italian Workshop on Artificial Intelligence for Ambient Assisted Living; AI*CH, the Artificial Intelligence for Cultural Heritage workshop; AI^3, the Workshop on the Advances in Argumentation in Artificial Intelligence; CeX, the Workshop on Comprehensibility and Explanation in AI and ML; MLDM, the 6th Italian Workshop on Machine Learning and Data Mining; NL4AI, the Workshop on Natural Language for Artificial Intelligence; RCRA, the International Workshop on Experimental Evaluation of Algorithms for Solving Problems with Combinatorial Explosion; as well as WAIAH, the Workshop on Artificial Intelligence with Application in eHealth.

Moreover, AI*IA 2017 featured the traditional Doctoral Consortium. Finally, three panels completed the program. Two were organized in collaboration with, respectively, the GULP (the Italian Chapter of the Association for Logic Programming) and AISC (the Italian Association for Cognitive Sciences), and targeted to an audience of experts. Conversely, the third was an educational event open to the public (mainly to students from the last year of secondary school and the first years of university) concerning the impact of AI on society, and proposing a unified view of AI, economy, and ecology.

The chairs wish to thank the Program Committee members and the reviewers for their invaluable work in reviewing, the organizers of all workshops held at the conference, as well as the workshop chairs, the Doctoral Consortium chair, and the industrial liaisons chair for their help in organizing the conference. Moreover, a wishful thanks to the conference sponsors that supported the conference and enabled different important social initiatives (among which student grants and technical awards).

Finally, many thanks to the Organizing Committee for the huge effort dedicated to the conference ideas, economics, and logistics.

November 2017

Floriana Esposito
Roberto Basili
Stefano Ferilli
Francesca A. Lisi

Organization

AI*IA 2017 was organized by the Department of Computer Science, University of Bari Aldo Moro, Italy, and the Italian Association for Artificial Intelligence.

Executive Committee

General Chair

Floriana Esposito   University of Bari Aldo Moro

Program Chairs

Roberto Basili   University of Rome Tor Vergata
Stefano Ferilli   University of Bari Aldo Moro
Francesca Alessandra Lisi University of Bari Aldo Moro

Workshop Chairs

Marco de Gemmis   University of Bari Aldo Moro
Nicola Di Mauro   University of Bari Aldo Moro

Doctoral Consortium Chair

Donato Malerba   University of Bari Aldo Moro

Industrial Liaisons Chair

Giovanni Semeraro   University of Bari Aldo Moro

Local Organizing Committee

Sergio Angelastro   University of Bari Aldo Moro
Andrea Pazienza   University of Bari Aldo Moro
Marco Polignano   University of Bari Aldo Moro
Antonio Vergari   University of Bari Aldo Moro

Program Committee

Luigia Carlucci Aiello   University of Rome-Sapienza, Italy
Giovanni Adorni   University of Genoa, Italy
Davide Bacciu   University of Pisa, Italy
Matteo Baldoni   University of Turin, Italy
Stefania Bandini   University of Milan-Bicocca, Italy
Nicola Basilico   University of Milan, Italy

Gustavo E.A.P.A. Batista	University of São Paulo, Brazil
Federico Bergenti	University of Parma, Italy
Tarek Richard Besold	University of Bremen, Germany
Stefano Bistarelli	University of Perugia, Italy
Stefano Cagnoni	University of Parma, Italy
Diego Calvanese	University of Bozen-Bolzano, Italy
Amedeo Cesta	CNR – National Research Council of Italy
Antonio Chella	University of Palermo, Italy
Federico Chesani	University of Bologna, Italy
Gabriella Cortellessa	CNR – National Research Council of Italy
Tommaso Di Noia	Polytechnic of Bari, Italy
Agostino Dovier	University of Udine, Italy
Aldo Franco Dragoni	Polytechnic University of Marche, Italy
Salvatore Gaglio	University of Palermo, Italy
Marco Gavanelli	University of Ferrara, Italy
Chiara Ghidini	FBK-irst – The Fondazione Bruno Kessler, Italy
Floriana Grasso	University of Liverpool, UK
Nicola Guarino	CNR – National Research Council of Italy
Evelina Lamma	University of Ferrara, Italy
Nicola Leone	University of Calabria, Italy
Antonio Lieto	University of Turin, Italy
Bernardo Magnini	FBK-irst – The Fondazione Bruno Kessler, Italy
Marco Maratea	University of Genoa, Italy
Simone Marinai	University of Florence, Italy
Viviana Mascardi	University of Genoa, Italy
Alessandro Mazzei	University of Turin, Italy
Paola Mello	University of Bologna, Italy
Alessio Micheli	University of Pisa, Italy
Alfredo Milani	University of Perugia, Italy
Evangelos E. Milios	Dalhousie University, Canada
Stefania Montani	University of Piemonte Orientale, Italy
Angelo Oddi	CNR – National Research Council of Italy
Viviana Patti	University of Turin, Italy
Maria Teresa Pazienza	University of Rome Tor Vergata, Italy
Roberto Pirrone	University of Palermo, Italy
Piero Poccianti	Co-operative Consortium of MPS, Italy
Gian Luca Pozzato	University of Turin, Italy
Francesco Ricca	University of Calabria, Italy
Fabrizio Riguzzi	University of Ferrara, Italy
Andrea Roli	University of Bologna, Italy
Silvia Rossi	University of Naples, Italy
Salvatore Ruggieri	University of Pisa, Italy
Alessandra Russo	Imperial College London, UK
Fabio Sartori	University of Milan-Bicocca, Italy
Marco Schaerf	University of Rome-Sapienza, Italy
Maria Simi	University of Pisa, Italy

Eloisa Vargiu   Eurecat Technology Center – eHealth Unit, Italy
Marco Villani   University of Modena and Reggio Emilia, Italy
Giuseppe Vizzari   University of Milano-Bicocca, Italy

Additional Reviewers

W.T. Adrian
M. Alberti
G. Amendola
C. Baroglio
E. Bellodi
L. Consolini
G. Cota
B. Cuteri
A. Dal Palù
R. Damiano
A. Dang
R. De Benedictis
L. Di Gaspero
F. Fracasso

V. Franzoni
A. Ghose
P. Giuliodori
D.I. Hernández Farías
M. La Cascia
L. Lo Presti
D. Magro
J. Mei
E. Mensa
R. Micalizio
M. Mordonini
M. Nanni
S. Nourashrafeddin
G. Oliveri

L. Pedrelli
R. Peñaloza
G. Pilato
G. Prini
R. Pucci
A. Sajadi
F. Santini
M. Torquati
A. Umbrico
P. Veltri
N. Vitacolonna
G. Xiao
J. Zangari
R. Zese

Sponsoring Institutions

University of Bari Aldo Moro
University of Bari Aldo Moro – Department of Computer Science
University of Bari Aldo Moro – Inter-departmental Center for Logic and Applications

Gold Sponsors

Artificial Intelligence Journal (http://aij.ijcai.org/)
IBM (https://www.ibm.com/)

Silver Sponsors

CELI (https://www.celi.it/)

Bronze Sponsors

AILC (http://www.ai-lc.it/)
Babelscape (http://babelscape.com/)
PluribusOne (https://www.pluribus-one.it/)

Contents

Planning and Scheduling

Applications of AI

Using Sources Trustworthiness in Weather Scenarios: The Special Role of the Authority

Rino Falcone[⊠] and Alessandro Sapienza

Institute of Cognitive Sciences and Technologies, ISTC - CNR, Rome, Italy
{rino.falcone,alessandro.sapienza}@istc.cnr.it

Abstract. In this work we present a platform shaping citizens' behavior in case of critical hydrogeological phenomena that can be manipulated in order to realize many possible scenarios. Here the citizens (modeled through cognitive agents) need to identify the risk of a possible critical events, relying of their information sources and of the trustworthiness attributed to them. Thanks to a training phase, the agents will be able to make a rational use of their different information sources: (a) their own evaluation about what could happen in the near future; (b) the information communicated by an authority; (c) the crowd behavior, as an evidence for evaluating the level of danger of the coming hydrogeological event. These weather forecasts are essential for the agents to deal with different meteorological events requiring adequate behaviors. In particular we consider that the authority can be more or less trustworthy and more or less able to deliver its own forecasts to the agents: due to the nature itself of the problem, these two parameters are correlated with each other. The main results of this work are: (1) it is necessary to optimize together both the authority communicativeness and trustworthiness, as optimizing just one aspect will not lead to the best solution; (2) once the authority can reach much of the population it is better to focus on its trustworthiness, since trying to give the information to a larger population could have no effect at all or even a negative effect; (3) the social source is essential to compensate the lack of information that some agents have.

Keywords: Social simulation · Cognitive modeling · Trust · Information sources

1 Introduction

Critical weather phenomena and in particular floods have always created enormous inconvenience to populations, resulting in a huge economic loss for the reference authorities. For instance, [17] reports that in Italy "In the 20-year period from 1980 to 2000 the State set aside 7,400 million euro for flood damage, or roughly one million euro per day". In addition to direct damages, easy to see and to estimate, natural disasters can also cause a series of secondary and

© Springer International Publishing AG 2017
F. Esposito et al. (Eds.): AI*IA 2017, LNAI 10640, pp. 3–16, 2017.
https://doi.org/10.1007/978-3-319-70169-1_1

indirect damages that are very difficult to detect and predict. It could be a psychological damage [11,12] or again an economical loss due to secondary aspects. For instance, taking once again into account the economical aspect, being subjected to a natural disaster could lead to a decrease in tourist flows resulting in a workers' dismissal. Consider that if the population perceives a particular area risky, it will be very difficult to change their mind. A practical case is the one of Umbria (an Italian central region) that in 2016 has repeatedly been stricken by earthquakes. The streets, houses and structures in general reported extensive damages, but this is not all. Looking at the data reported by the local authority, it is possible to notice that the tourism, representing an important source of earnings for the local population, decreased by 35% (http://www.regione.umbria.it/turismo-attivita-sportive/statistiche-turismo-2016). Even if earthquakes are different and present different features, it is still necessary to consider this kind of indirect loss from floods. As [13] reports "self-protective behavior by residents of flood-prone urban areas can reduce monetary flood damage by 80%, and reduce the need for public risk management". Thus if it is true that floods represent a very serious threat both for the population and for the authorities, it is also true that the citizens' self-protective behavior can substantially reduce the problem of direct and indirect damages. This is why local authorities and governments should not just focus on helping people after a disaster, but they should also have the goal of leading the population towards preventive actions that can minimize the future risks. Analyzing in detail the authority's role inside this scenario, it must:

1. Inform the citizens about what is going to happen as soon as it can and with the most reliable forecast.
2. Provide the information in a proper way: for instance [7] analyze the community resilience, that is the capacity to lead itself in order to overcome changes and crisis. They showed that this value positively correlates with how satisfied the community is with respect to the information communicated by the authority. This is an important aspect and it needs to be highlighted, but we are not going to investigate it in our research.
3. Encourage citizens to take self-protective behavior, which can substantially reduce the problem of direct and indirect damages.

By the means of simulations, we are going to investigate the authority's role and how it affects the citizens' choices.

2 State of the Art

The current literature proposes a lot of studies about the risks of critical weather phenomena and floods in particular, but just a few of them focuses on the population's response.

In [13] the authors state that there are basically three main factors determining the damages that a population suffers. The first one is the exposure to floods (frequency, water level, duration and so on) and the second one is the sensitivity, measurable by population density, the economic value of buildings and structures etc. These two parameters tell us how much the potential damage is. The third factor is the adaptation, which describes the ability of people to avoid the potential damage and to limit its extent by the means of adjustment in the system they live. According to them these adaptation measures can reduce monetary damage by the 80%. Starting from this consideration, they propose a socio-psychological model based on Protection Motivation Theory (PMT) to understand why some people take precautionary action while others do not. They tested 157 subjects using a survey to identify the values of the model's parameters. Then they used a regression model to understand how much each of these parameters could explain the citizens' choice to take preventive actions or not. They show that threat experience appraisal, threat appraisal, and coping appraisal correlate positively with protective responses, while reliance on public flood protection correlates negatively with protective responses. Then it seems that the authorities should put more effort in stimulating citizen's prevention measures than in appearing trustworthy for dealing with floods.

In [1] it is shown that it is possible to successfully exploit the collective intelligence of a population in the field of weather forecasts. They created a platform in which human users provide their bets about the future events, allowing them to modify their choice at any time, until a given deadline. In particular, they investigated three betting mechanisms: full transparency, allowing participants to see each other's bets; partial transparency, where participants could just see the group's average bet; no transparency, in which no information on others' bets is made available. Results clearly show that the forecasts' accuracy provided by the collective intelligence was not so far by the one of the meteorological model, especially in the full transparency case. This represents a very interesting example of how to successfully exploit the social source to produce weather predictions. Other interesting works focus on the historical study of the phenomena happened in a given geographical area: how they happened, their intensity and frequency and so on. For instance [2] realized a georeferenced database comprising data about historical natural events occurred in the area Valtellina di Tirano, a mountain area in the Central Italian Alps. Within their study, the authors show that collecting and making use of this historical information is fundamental to identify hypothetical critical scenarios and to evaluate the territorial threats and then to handle future emergencies.

Another kind of simulative works concerning weather forecast uses simulations with the aim of estimating the damages that an event can cause [17,22]. In [17] the authors propose a model simulating critical scenarios and evaluating the expected economic losses. They consider the flood water level as a factor indicating the event magnitude. Given a catastrophic natural event of a given intensity affecting a given area, the model estimates economic losses connected to direct damages as the number and the economic value of the units of each element in the area and on the degree of damage they are exposed. This model needs a good knowledge of the local area and a description of the physical event to produce an output. Clearly it has the limit of estimating just direct damages, but this is absolutely reasonable as indirect damages are not so easy to detect. As far as we know, ours is the first simulative approach trying to model citizens' decision in the case of critical weather phenomena. The classical approach to the problem is that of survey [3, 14], but it has the limit of identifying what the people think they would do, not what they actually would do. Moreover, it does not allow studying a huge set of agents all together. On the contrary, our way to investigate the problem allows showing some interesting outcomes, since you can put in the same world a lot of agents interacting with each other and you can infer what social phenomena emerge. Furthermore, it let us study how the individual parameters influence the problem and what role they have, and what happens if we put them together.

3   The Trust Model

In our view [6] trusting an information source (S) means to use a cognitive model based on the dimensions of competence and reliability/motivation of the source. These competence and reliability evaluations can derive from different reasons:

1. Our *direct experience* with S on that specific kind of information content.
2. *Recommendations* (other individuals reporting their direct experience and evaluation about S) or *Reputation* (the shared general opinion of others about S) on that specific information content [8, 15, 20, 21, 25].
3. *Categorization* of S (it is assumed that a source can be categorized and that its category is known), exploiting inference and reasoning (analogy, inheritance, etc.): on this basis it is possible to establish the competence/reliability of S on that specific information content [4, 5, 9, 10].

Given the complexity of simulations, we chose to use in this paper a relatively simple trust model, focusing just on the first dimension above described: the direct experience with each source. In fact, we use also the categorization analysis for distinguishing the sources on the basis of their different nature. Trust decisions in presence of uncertainty can be handle using uncertainty theory [16] or probability theory. We decided to use the second approach, as in this platform agents know a priori all the possible events that can happen and they are able to estimate how much it is plausible that they occur. We decided to exploit bayesian theory, one of the most used approach in trust evaluation [18, 19, 23], and we based our concept of trust on [6].

In this model each information source S is represented by a trust degree called TrustOnSource, with $0 \leq TrustOnSource \leq 1$, plus a bayesian probability distribution PDF[1] (Probability Distribution Function) representing the information reported by S. The trust model takes into account the possibility of many events: it just splits the domain in the corresponding number of intervals. In this work we use five different events (described below), then the PDF will be divided into five parts. The *TrustOnSource* parameter is used to smooth the information referred by S through the formula:

---

[1] It is modeled as a distribution continuous in each interval.

$$NewValue = 1 + (Value - 1) * TrustOnSource \qquad (1)$$

This step produces the Smoothed PDF (SPDF). We have that the greater the $TrustOnSource$ is, the more similar the SPDF will be to the PDF; the lesser it is, the more the SPDF will be flatten. In particular if $TrustOnSource = 1 =>$ SPDF = PDF and if $TrustOnSource = 0 =>$ SPDF is an uniform distribution with value 1. The idea is that we trust on what S says proportionally to how much we trust S. We then define GPDF (Global PDF) the evidence that an agent owns concerning a belief P. Once estimated the SPDFs for each information source, there will be an aggregation process between the GPDF and the SPDFs. Each source actually represents a new evidence E about a belief P. Then to the purpose of the aggregation process it is possible to use the classical Bayesian logic, recursively on each source:

$$f(P|E) = \frac{f(E|P) * f(P)}{f(E)} \qquad (2)$$

$$f(E) = \int f(E|P) * f(P)dP \qquad (3)$$

where: $f(P|E) = GPDF$ (the new one); $f(E|P) = SPDF$; $f(P) = GPDF$ (the old one). In this case f(E) is a normalization factor, given by Eq. (3).

In other words, the new GPDF, that is the global evidence that an agent has about P, is computed as the product of the old GPDF and the SPDF, that is the new contribute reported by S. As we need to ensure that GPDF is still a probability distribution function, it is necessary to scale it down[2]. The normalization factor f(E) ensures this.

3.1   Feedback on Trust

We want to let agents adapt to the context in which they move. This means that, starting from a neutral trust level (that does not imply trust or distrust) agents will try to understand how reliable each single information source is. To do that, they need a way to perform feedback on trust. We did it through a weighted mean between the old evaluation and the new one:

$$newTrustDegree = \alpha * oldTrustDegree + \beta * performanceEvaluation \quad (4)$$

$$\alpha + \beta = 1 \quad (5)$$

In Eq. (4) α and β[3] are the weights of the two variables.

---

[2] To be a PDF, it is necessary that the area subtended by it is equal to 1.

[3] Of course changing the values of α and β will have an impact on the trust evaluations. With high values of α/β, agents will need more time to get a precise evaluation, but a low value (below 1) will lead to an unstable evaluation, as it would depend too much on the last performance. We do not investigate these two parameters in this work, using respectively the values 0.9 and 0.1. In order to have good evaluations, we let agents make a lot of experience with their information sources.

Here *oldTrustDegree* is the previous trust degree and the *performanceEvaluation* is the objective evaluation of the source's performance. This last value is obtained comparing what the source said to what actually happened. Let's suppose that we have 5 possible events, as in the simulations. The PDF reported by the source is then split into five parts. Suppose that there has been an event e5, which is the most critical event. A first source reported a 100% probability of e5; a second one a 50% probability of e5 and a 50% of e4; finally a third one asserts 100% e3. Their performance evaluations are 100% for Source1, 50% for Source2 and 0% for Source3.

4   The Platform

Exploiting NetLogo [24], we created a very flexible platform, where a lot of parameters are taken into account to model a variety of situations. Given a population distributed over a wide area, some weather phenomena happen into the world with a different level of criticality: there are five possible events, going from the lightest (e1) to the most critical one (e5). The world is populated by a number of cognitive agents (citizens), which need to analyze the situation and to understand what event is going to happen, in order to decide how to behave. To do so, they will exploit the information sources they can access, attributing them a trust value. We associate a correct action to each possible event, respectively a1, a2, a3 a4 and a5. Just the action corresponding to the event is considered as correct, the others are wrong.

In addition to citizens, there is another agent called authority. Its aim is to inform promptly citizens about the weather phenomena. The authority is characterized by a reliability value, expressed in terms of standard deviation, and by a communicativeness value, that represents its ability to inform the wider or narrower population.

4.1   Information Sources

To make a decision, each agent consults a set of information sources, reporting evidence about the incoming event. We considered the presence of three kinds of information sources (whether active or passive) for agents:

1. Their personal judgment, based on the direct observation of the phenomena. Although this is a direct and always true (at least in that moment) source, it has the drawback that waiting to see what happens could lead into a situation in which it is no more possible to react in the best way (for example there is no more time to escape if one realizes too late the worsening weather).
2. Notification from the authority: the authority distributes into the world weather forecasts, trying to prepare citizens to what is going to happen. It is not sure that the authority will be able to inform everyone.
3. Others' behavior: agents are in some way influenced by community logics, tending to partially or totally emulate their neighbors' behavior.

The authority provides its notification as a clear signal: all the probability is focused on a single event. Conversely, the personal judgment can be distributed on two or three events with different probabilities. This can also be true for others' behavior estimation as the probability of each event is directly proportional to the number of neighbors making each kind of decision. If no decision is available, the PDF of the social source is a uniform distribution with value 1.

4.2   Citizens' Description

When the simulation starts the world is populated by a number of agents having the same neutral trust value 0.5 for all their information sources. This value represents a situation in which agents are not sure if to trust or not a given source, as a value of 1 means complete trust and 0 stands for complete distrust. Two main factors differentiate these citizens. The first one relies on their ability to see and to read the phenomena. In fact, in the real world not all the agents have the same abilities. To shape this, we equally divided agents into three sets:

1. *Good evaluators* will quit always be able to correctly detect the events, and then we expect them to rely mainly on their own opinion. They are characterized by a standard deviation of 0.3, which means that their evaluations will be correct 90% of the time[4].
2. *Medium evaluators* can detect the event, but not as good as the previous category. They are characterized by a standard deviation of 0.7, which means that their evaluations will be correct 55% of the time.
3. *Bad evaluators* are not able to understand the events. They are characterized by a standard deviation of 100, which corresponds to a performance of 20% (that is the same of a random choice).

The second difference resides in how easily the authority reaches them. In the real world, in fact, it could be possible that the authority cannot reach everyone, since not all the agents have the same probability to be reached by its information. According to that, we equally divided agents into three categories: class A agents are the firsts to receive the authority's communications; after that, class B agents receive the information, and then class C agents. The class A agents are privileged, as they will always receive the information, but the other agents will probably cope with lack of institutional information.

4.3   The Authority

The authority's aim is to inform citizens about what is going to happen. Ideally it would produces a correct forecast and it would have the time to spread this information through all the population. However this is as desirable as unreal. The

---

[4] In this evaluation we take into account the ability of an agent to inquire further sources that it can access, considering this as its own attitude/ability. This explains the high level of accuracy.

truth is that weather forecast's precision increases while the event is approaching. In our framework the authority is characterized by a standard deviation, determining the accuracy of its forecasts. Given the particular context we are considering, we have that this forecasts become more and more precise as the event approaches. This means that there will be less time for the authority to spread this information: it can reach a lower percentage of the population. According to this consideration, we decided to link the authority accuracy (in term of standard deviation) with the percentage of the population it can reach. In an ideal world it would reach all, but it should at least reach the majority of the population. We let the authority's standard deviation change from the highest value to a lower value, representing a bad performance: from 0.1 (96% of accuracy) to 2 (39% of accuracy). We also consider the citizens' number: the greater is the population, the less time the authority has to inform it (see Eq. 6).

$$ReachedPopulation = 60\% + \frac{StandardDeviation * 40}{\frac{CitizensNumber}{100}} \tag{6}$$

4.4 World Description

The world is made by 32×32 patches, which wrap both horizontally and vertically. It is geographically divided in 4 quadrants of equal dimension, where agents are distributed in a random way. Each quadrant will be affected by an event, so that at the same time we can have different events in the world. These events/phenomena are modeled through the presence of clouds. As already said, there are 5 possible events with an increasing level of criticality, going from e1 (light) to e5 (critical). In each quadrant, each event has a fixed probability to happen: 35% e1, 30% e2, 20% e3, 10% e4, 5% e5.

4.5 Workflow

Each simulation is divided into two steps. The first one is the training phase, in which the agents make experience with their information sources to determine how reliable they are. At the beginning we have in the world an authority and a given number of agents, with different abilities in understanding weather phenomena. The authority spreads its forecasts reporting the estimated level of criticality. This information will reach a given percentage of the population, according to the authority's standard deviation (see Eq. 6). Class A agents are the first to receive this information, then class B agents and class C (if possible). Being just a forecast, its correctness is not ensured. It will happen with a probability linked to the precision of the authority (depending on its standard deviation). However it allows agents to evaluate the situation in advance, before the possible event. During the decision making phase, the agents check their own information sources, aggregating the single contributes according to the corresponding trust values. They subjectively estimate the probability that each single event happens: P(e1), P(e2), P(e3), P(e4), P(e5). In order to minimize the risk, they will react according to the event that is considered more likely to happen. We associate a correct action with each possible event, respectively a1, a2, a3 a4 and a5. Just the action corresponding to the event is considered as correct, the others are wrong. While agents collect information they are considered as thinking. When this phase reaches the limit, they have to make a decision, which cannot be changed anymore. This information is then available for the other agents (neighborhood), which can in turn exploit it for their decisions. At the end of the event, the agents evaluate the performance of the sources they used and adjust the corresponding trust values. If the authority did not reach them, there will not be a feedback on trust but, as this source was not available when necessary, there will be a trust reduction linked to the kind of event that happened: −0.15 for e5, −0.1 for e4 and −0.05 for the others. This phase is repeated for 100 times (then there will be 100 events) to let agents make enough experience to judge their sources. After that, there is the testing phase. Here we want to understand how agents perform, once they know how reliable their sources are. In order to do that, we investigate the accuracy of their decision (1 if correct, 0 if wrong).

4.6 Platform's Inputs

The first thing that can be customized is the *number of agents* in the world. Then, one can set the value of the two parameters α and β, used for the sources' trust evaluation. Moreover, it is possible to set which *sources* the citizens will use in their evaluations: it is possible to choose any combination of them. It is possible to change the *authority reliability*, modifying its standard deviation, which results in a change in it ability to reach the population. Concerning the training phase, it is possible to change its *duration* and determine the *probability of the events* that are going to happen on each quadrant.

5 Simulations

We used the platform to investigate how different authority's behaviors affect citizens' choices and the trust they have in their information sources. We believe in fact that the authority's choices affect not only citizens individually and directly, but also, through a social effect, citizens that do not receive its forecast. To do that, we investigated a series of scenarios, populated by equal populations, but in presence of different authorities. Then we analyze how citizens respond to these changes, measuring their trust values and the choice they make in presence of possible risks. Simulations results are mediated through 500 cases, in order to delete the variability that a single case can have.

Given the framework described above, we analyzed a series of scenarios with the following settings: number of agents: 200; α and β: respectively 0.9 and 0.1; exploited sources: all, self and social, self, social, authority, authority and self, authority and social; authority reliability: going from 0.1 (96% of accuracy) to 2 (39% of accuracy), increasing at regular steps of 0.1; 5. Training phase duration: 100 events; events' probability: 35% e1, 30% e2, 20% e3, 10% e4, 5% e5.

Figure 1 shows how the agents' collective performance changes by varying the authority's standard deviation. The first interesting result is that combining information sources brings almost always to a better performance. This is not true anymore when the authority becomes unreliable. For instance, when its standard deviation is lower than 1.1 exploiting all the sources (blue curve) becomes less convenient than using just the own experience and the social source (orange curve). Interestingly, the authority's standard deviation value guaranteeing the best performance is not 0.1, but 0.2: the agents' average performance increases of 1%. This means that just focusing on the authority performance does not lead to the optimal point. Instead, it is necessary a trade-off between the authority's accuracy and the quantity of agents it can reach.

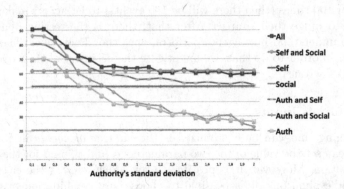

Fig. 1. Agents' average performance using a different source's combination (Color figure online)

Figure 2 shows a more detailed analysis of the case in which agents use all the sources. Good evaluators' performance is weakly influenced by the authority; when this source becomes unreliable, they can still count on their own ability. The same does not stand for medium and bad evaluators, mainly relying on the authority. The agents' categorization based on the possibility to receive the information from the authority provides a very interesting insight. We have that

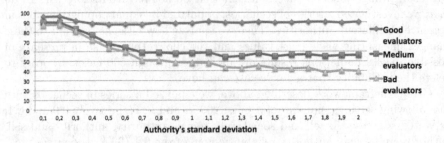

Fig. 2. The average performance of good, medium and bad evaluators

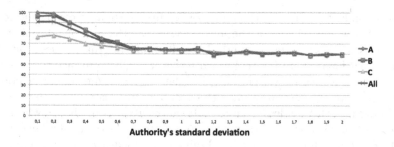

Fig. 3. The average performance of Class A, B and C agents.

class A agents tend to perform better and class C agents have the worst performance (Fig. 3). Again, this effect has a limit, since when the authority's standard deviation reaches the value 0.8 there is no difference in their performances. Concerning the agents' perception of the authority's trustworthiness (Fig. 4), the optimal result seems again to be obtained with an authority's standard deviation of 0.2: from this point forwards, Class C trust in the authority is going to increase, but the other two categories will do the opposite. In fact, even if in the 0.2 case the authority has a lower trustworthiness than in the 0.1 case, it produces a better utility spreading more information and then it is perceived as more trustworthy. From Fig. 4 we can clearly see how giving information to Class C agents represents a waste of resource for the authority: they are not going to use it, as they do not trust the authority. It may not be worth sacrificing the information quality in order to reach them, while it would be definitely better to provide more reliable information to a subset of the population.

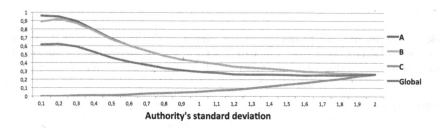

Fig. 4. The average authority's trust evaluation for the categories A, B and C

6   Conclusion

We presented an articulated platform for social simulation, particularly suited for studying agents' choice in presence of critical weather phenomena. To this purpose we realized a Bayesian trust model, used by agents to evaluate and aggregate information coming from different information sources. By the means of a simulative approach we proved some interesting effects, while it would have been very difficult to identify them otherwise. In particular, we were interested in studying the special role of the authority. It has the aim of informing citizens about the incoming events and ideally it would inform all the population with a correct forecast. In the real world however, we have to face the fact that weather forecasts' accuracy is negatively related to the percentage of population that receive the message, since the accuracy increases while the event is approaching and there is less time left: the authority has to choose whether to inform more citizens with a less precise forecast or vice versa. We have shown that the optimal solution cannot be obtained just focusing on the accuracy or on the percentage of the population, but that it is necessary to consider them together. Moreover, the social source (observation of the others' behavior) plays an interesting compensative role. It is true that focusing just on it the agents have a very low performance, but combined in presence of the other sources it guides them towards a higher performance, even if (1) there is just one source and only a few agents can access this reliable source or (2) there are two other sources and one of them is unreliable.

Since we showed that, under bonding conditions for authority's reliability and communicativeness, trying to inform as many people as possible could result in a waste of resources, we are planning to study in the next future the limit point we identified in this work, in which the authority's communicativeness cannot be increased further without lowering the community's performance and how this relates with the social effect. We would like to emphasize that, due to the lack of data on the authority's trustworthiness and communicativeness, the results obtained at this level of abstraction provide general reasoning for guidelines. We analyzed a phenomenon on which real data are not so easy to find, but whose features are almost known. We focused our efforts on trying to model those features even if it is necessary to have real reference data to identify specific results.

Acknowledgments. This work is partially supported by the project CLARA CLoud plAtform and smart underground imaging for natural Risk Assessment, funded by the Italian Ministry of Education, University and Research (MIUR-PON).

References

1. Arazy, O., Halfon, N., Malkinson, D.: Collective intelligence for rain prediction. In: Collective Intelligence 2015, Santa Clara, CA, USA, 31 May–2 June (2015)
2. Blahut, J., Poretti, I., De Amicis, M., Sterlacchini, S.: Database of geo-hydrological disasters for civil protection purposes. Nat. Hazards **60**(3), 1065–1083 (2012)
3. Bronfman, N.C., Cisternas, P.C., López-Vázquez, E., Cifuentes, L.A.: Trust and risk perception of natural hazards: implications for risk preparedness in Chile. Nat. Hazards **81**(1), 307–327 (2016)
4. Burnett, C., Norman, T., Sycara, K.: Bootstrapping trust evaluations through stereotypes. In: Proceedings of the 9th International Conference on Autonomous Agents and Multiagent Systems (AAMAS 2010), pp. 241–248 (2010)
5. Burnett, C., Norman, T., Sycara, K.: Stereotypical trust and bias in dynamic multiagent systems. ACM Trans. Intell. Syst. Technol. (TIST) **4**(2), 26 (2013)

6. Castelfranchi, C., Falcone, R.: Trust Theory: A Socio-Cognitive and Computational Model. Wiley, Hoboken (2010)
7. Cohen, O., Goldberg, A., Lahad, M., Aharonson-Daniel, L.: Building resilience: the relationship between information provided by municipal authorities during emergency situations and community resilience. Technol. Forecasting Soc. Change (2016). http://doi.org/10.1016/j.techfore.2016.11.008
8. Conte, R., Paolucci, M.: Reputation in Artificial Societies. Social Beliefs for Social Order. Kluwer Academic Publishers, Boston (2002)
9. Falcone, R., Castelfranchi, C.: Generalizing trust: inferencing trustworthiness from categories. In: Falcone, R., Barber, S.K., Sabater-Mir, J., Singh, M.P. (eds.) TRUST 2008. LNCS, vol. 5396, pp. 65–80. Springer, Heidelberg (2008). https://doi.org/10.1007/978-3-540-92803-4_4
10. Falcone, R., Piunti, M., Venanzi, M., Castelfranchi, C.: From Manifesta to Krypta: the relevance of categories for trusting others. In: Falcone, R., Singh, M. (eds.) Trust in Multiagent Systems, vol. 4, no. 2, March 2013. ACM Trans. Intell. Syst. Technol. 4(2) (2013)
11. Freedy, J.R., Shaw, D.L., Jarrell, M.P., Masters, C.R.: Towards an understanding of the psychological impact of natural disasters: an application of the conservation resources stress model. J. Traumatic Stress 5(3), 441–454 (1992)
12. Freedy, J.R., Saladin, M.E., Kilpatrick, D.G., Resnick, H.S., Saunders, B.E.: Understanding acute psychological distress following natural disaster. J. Traumatic Stress 7(2), 257–273 (1994)
13. Grothmann, T., Reusswig, F.: People at risk of flooding: why some residents take precautionary action while others do not. Nat. Hazards 38(1), 101–120 (2006)
14. Jia, Z., Tian, W., Liu, W., Cao, Y., Yan, J., Shun, Z.: Are the elderly more vulnerable to psychological impact of natural disaster? A population-based survey of adult survivors of the 2008 Sichuan earthquake. BMC Public Health 10(1), 172 (2010)
15. Jiang, S., Zhang, J., Ong, Y.S.: An evolutionary model for constructing robust trust networks. In: Proceedings of the 12th International Conference on Autonomous Agents and Multiagent Systems (AAMAS) (2013)
16. Liu, B.: Uncertainty Theory, 5th edn. Springer, Heidelberg (2014)
17. Luino, F., Chiarle, M., Nigrelli, G., Agangi, A., Biddoccu, M., Cirio, C.G., Giulietto, W.: A model for estimating flood damage in Italy: preliminary results. Environ. Econ. Invest. Assess. 98, 65–74 (2006)
18. Melaye, D., Demazeau, Y.: Bayesian dynamic trust model. In: Pěchouček, M., Petta, P., Varga, L.Z. (eds.) CEEMAS 2005. LNCS, vol. 3690, pp. 480–489. Springer, Heidelberg (2005). https://doi.org/10.1007/11559221_48
19. Quercia, D., Hailes, S., Capra, L.: B-trust: Bayesian trust framework for pervasive computing. In: Stølen K., Winsborough, W.H., Martinelli, F., Massacci, F. (eds.) iTrust 2006. LNCS, vol. 3986, pp. 298–312. Springer, Heidelberg (2006). https://doi.org/10.1007/11755593_22
20. Sabater-Mir, J.: Trust and reputation for agent societies. Ph.D. thesis, Universitat Autonoma de Barcelona (2003)
21. Sabater-Mir, J., Sierra, C.: Regret: a reputation model for gregarious societies. In: 4th Workshop on Deception and Fraud in Agent Societies, Montreal, Canada, pp. 61–70 (2001)
22. Scawthorn, C., Blais, N., Seligson, H., Tate, E., Mifflin, E., Thomas, W., James Murphy, J., Jones, C.: HAZUS-MH flood loss estimation methodology. I: overview and flood hazard characterization. Nat. Hazards Rev. 7(2), 60–71 (2006)

23. Wang, Y., Vassileva, J.: Bayesian network-based trust model. In: Proceedings of IEEE/WIC International Conference on Web Intelligence, WI 2003, pp. 372–378. IEEE, October 2003

24. Wilensky, U.: NetLogo. http://ccl.northwestern.edu/netlogo/ Center for Connected Learning and Computer-Based Modeling, Northwestern University, Evanston, IL (1999)

25. Yolum, P., Singh, M.P.: Emergent properties of referral systems. In: Proceedings of the 2nd International Joint Conference on Autonomous Agents and MultiAgent Systems (AAMAS 2003) (2003)

Robust Optimization for Virtual Power Plants

Allegra De Filippo[1(✉)], Michele Lombardi[1],
Michela Milano[1], and Alberto Borghetti[2]

[1] DISI, University of Bologna, Bologna, Italy
{allegra.defilippo,michele.lombardi2,michela.milano}@unibo.it
[2] DEI, University of Bologna, Bologna, Italy
alberto.borghetti@unibo.it

Abstract. Virtual Power Plants (VPP) are one of the main components of future smart electrical grids, connecting and integrating several
types of energy sources, loads and storage devices. A typical VPP is a
large industrial plant with high (partially shiftable) electric and thermal
loads, renewable energy generators and electric and thermal storages.
Optimizing the use and the cost of energy could lead to a significant
economic impact. This work proposes a VPP Energy Management System (EMS), based on a two-step optimization model that decides the
minimum-cost energy balance at each point in time considering the following data: electrical load, photovoltaic production, electricity costs,
upper and lower limits for generating units and storage units. The first
(day-ahead) step models the prediction uncertainty using a robust approach defining scenarios to optimize the load demand shift and to estimate the cost. The second step is an online optimization algorithm,
implemented within a simulator, that uses the optimal shifts produced
by the previous step to minimize, for each timestamp, the real cost while
fully covering the *optimally shifted* energy demand. The system is implemented and tested using real data and we provide analysis of results and
comparison between real and estimated optimal costs.

Keywords: Virtual Power Plants · Robust optimization · Forecast
uncertainty

1 Introduction

The progressive shift towards decentralized generation in power distribution networks has made the problem of optimal Distributed Energy Resources (DER)
operation increasingly constrained, due to the integration of flexible (deterministic) energy systems combined with the strong penetration of (uncontrollable
and stochastic) Renewable Energy Sources (RES). This challenge can be met
by using the Virtual Power Plant (VPP) concept, which is based on the idea of
aggregating the capacity of many DER, (i.e. generation, storage, or demand) to
create a single operating profile to increase flexibility through the definition of
approaches to manage the uncertainty.

© Springer International Publishing AG 2017
F. Esposito et al. (Eds.): AI*IA 2017, LNAI 10640, pp. 17–30, 2017.
https://doi.org/10.1007/978-3-319-70169-1_2

We develop a two-step optimization model to be employed in the Energy Management System (EMS) of a VPP. Our EMS decides the optimal planning of power flows for each timestamp that minimizes the cost. The planning decision model is composed by two steps: the first (day-ahead) step is designed to optimize the load demand shift and to estimate the cost, and models the prediction uncertainty using a robust (scenario-based) approach. The second step is an online greedy algorithm implemented within a simulator that uses the optimized shifts from the previous step to minimize the operational real cost, while fully covering the *optimally shifted* energy demand and avoiding the loss of energy produced by RES generators. We propose the following main contributions: (1) a robust optimization approach for planning power flows to minimize the VPP expected cost and to obtain optimized load shifts in presence of forecast uncertainty; (2) the development of a real case study to test the model; (3) an assessment of the quality of our solutions in terms of the Expected Value of Perfect Information (EVPI), i.e. by comparing the actually obtained costs with the optimal expected costs that would be possible assuming perfect information.

The rest of the paper is organized as follows. Section 2 discusses the main approaches proposed in the literature for modeling VPP and for handling uncertainties in energy management problems. Section 3 describes the proposed two-step optimization model for the EMS of a VPP. Section 4 presents how we applied our model to data in a real case study. Section 5 provides an analysis of results. Concluding remarks are in Sect. 6.

2   Related Work

The potential applications of the VPP concept has been recognized in recent literature. For example, [2] shows that the advance of DER in the commercial and regulatory structure of electricity markets in course of liberalization has created opportunities for decentralization of the role of traditional power utilities.

VPPs are one of the main components of intelligent electrical grids of the future, connecting and integrating several types of power sources (both renewable and non-renewable), storage and energy loads to operate as a unique power plant. The heart of a VPP is an EMS which coordinates the power flows coming from the generators, controllable loads and storages. In [12] an EMS for controlling a VPP is presented, with the objective to manage the power flows for minimizing the electricity generation costs, and avoiding the loss of energy produced by renewable energy sources. In general, the EMS can operate by minimizing the generation costs or by maximizing the profits. On the basis of actual energy prices and availability of DER, the EMS decides: (1) how much energy should be produced; (2) which generators should be used for the required energy; (3) whether the surplus energy should be stored or sold to the energy market.

Moreover, DER aggregation can effectively couple traditional peak electrical plants by supporting them with the flexible contribution of consumers to the overall efficiency of the electric system. From this perspective, the EMS of a VPP can develop Demand Side Management (DSM) mechanisms to modify temporal consumption patterns. DSM can provide a number of advantages to the energy system and focuses on utilizing power saving mechanisms, electricity tariffs, and government policies to decrease the demand peak and operational costs instead of enlarging the generation capacity. As an example, [13] proposed an Energy Management System for a renewable-based microgrid with online signals for consumers to promote behavior changes. The integration of renewable sources must be adequately addressed so as to manage uncertainty and to avoid affecting the operational reliability of a power system. Unit commitment (UC) is a critical decision process, which can be formalized as the problem of deciding the outputs of all the generators to minimize the system cost. The main principle in operating an electrical system is to cover the demand for electricity at all times and under different conditions depending on the season, weather and time, and by minimizing the operating cost. The deterministic formulation of this problem may not adequately account for the impact of uncertainty. For this reason, different approaches are used to manage UC under uncertainty [10]: (1) *Stochastic UC*, which is based on probabilistic *scenarios*. The basic idea is to find optimal decisions taking into account a large number of scenarios, each representing a possible realization of the uncertain factors. Stochastic UC is generally formulated as a two-stage problem [16] that determines the generation schedule to minimize the expected cost over all of the scenarios, while respecting their probabilities. The approach usually requires high computational cost for simulations. (2) *Robust UC* formulations, which optimize assuming a well-defined range for the uncertain quantities, instead of taking into account their probability distribution. The range of uncertainty is defined by the upper and lower bounds on the net load at each time period [15]. (3) *Hybrid models* have been proposed in recent years to combine the advantages and compensate the disadvantages [14]. The assessment of uncertainty in the modeling of distributed energy systems has received considerable attention in recent works that apply machine learning techniques for forecasting flexibility of VPP. Many studies have been done on the residential sector using support vector regression and neural networks [6,9] and some methods present promising results however it seems unlikely they may be implemented in real life in particular in the industrial sector. We plan to improve these methods in our model for future works.

We propose an EMS composed of a two-step optimization model for a VPP. Our focus is on modeling renewable sources and load demand uncertainty in the first (day-ahead) step, by proposing a robust optimization with DSM to support DER aggregation by decreasing peak usage of traditional energy generators. The second step is an on-line, greedy, algorithm that receives the optimized demand shifts as input and manages power flows in the VPP and it is necessary to make the whole approach applicable in practice, but should not be considered a major contribution of this work.

3   Model Description

3.1   Robust Approach to Model Uncertainty

We propose a two-step optimization model for the VPP EMS that produces optimized demand shifts (S_{Load}) by assuming as input the predictions for the solar power (P_{fPV}) generation profile, for the demand load profile (P_{fLoad}), and a fixed percentage of allowed demand shift. We use a robust approach to model uncertainty, which stems from (1) prediction errors in the solar power profile; (2) uncontrollable deviations from the planned demand shifts. For each of these quantities, the range of uncertainty is specified via a lower and an upper bound (for each timestamp), which can be obtained for example by estimating confidence intervals. We use these bounds to define a limited number of scenarios to calculate the optimized demand shifts that minimizes the expectation of the daily operating costs.

Then we feed these optimized shifts as input to an online greedy heuristic, implemented within a simulator, that calculates for each timestamp the optimal flows for the diesel power (P_{CHP}), the power exchanged with the storage system ($P_{Storage}$) and the power exchanged with the external grid (P_{Grid}) to supply the *optimally shifted* load demand. Figure 1 shows the proposed EMS model.

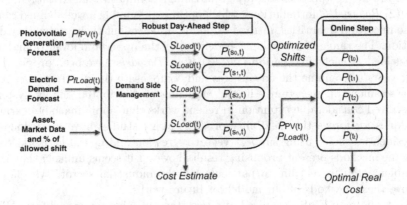

Fig. 1. The two steps of the optimization model for the EMS

In the first step, our objective function minimizes the VPP estimated cost over all scenarios and the whole optimization period (one day):

$$min(z) = \frac{1}{|S|} \sum_{s \in S} \sum_{t \in T} c^s(t) \tag{1}$$

The objective function will be described in more detail in Sect. 3.8. Where t is a timestamp, s is a scenario, and $c^s(t)$ is the (decision-dependent) cost for a scenario/timestamp pair. T is a set representing the whole horizon, and S is the set of all considered scenarios. In detail, those are:

$$S = \{s^{++}, s^{+-}, s^{-+}, s^{--}\} \tag{2}$$

s^{++} is the scenario with the highest values of predicted $P_{PV}(t)$ and $P_{Load}(t)$ (i.e. $P_{PV}(t) + \delta_{PV}(t)$ and $P_{Load}(t) + \delta_{Load}(t)$, where $\delta_{PV}(t)$ and $\delta_{Load}(t)$ define the considered range of uncertainty and are part of the problem input). The other 3 scenarios are easily deducible.

3.2 Modeling of Uncertainties

The diffusion of PV systems, as green and free sources of energy, implies their consideration as basic component of recent VPP. As a side effect, it becomes necessary to consider ways of addressing their uncertainty so as not to compromise the reliability of the system. Also load demand, due to its significant volatility, should be considered as uncertain to avoid that the actual VPP behavior deviates too much from the optimal one.

Formally, we assume that the error for our load demand forecast can be considered an independent random variable: this is reasonable hypothesis, provided that our predictor is good enough. This allows to define our uncertainty range based on confidence intervals. In particular, we assume that the errors follow roughly a Normal distribution $N(0, \sigma^2)$, and that the variance for each timestamp is such that the 95% confidence interval corresponds to 20% of the estimated load. Formally, we have that $1.96\sigma = 0.2P_{Load}(t)$; in practice, this simply means that the δ_{Load} parameters used to obtain our four scenarios is equal to $0.2P_{Load}(t)$ as in [8].

Methodologies for the estimation of hourly global solar radiation have been proposed by many researchers and in this work, we consider as a prediction the average hourly global solar radiation from [11] based on the period of recorded data (summer) in [7]. We then assume that the prediction errors in each timestamp can be modeled again as random variables. Specifically, we assume normally distributed variables with a variance such that the 95% confidence interval corresponds to ±10% of the prediction value. In other words, our δ_{PV} parameter for timestamp t is equal to $0.1P_{PV}(t)$.

The designs of the EMS with its objective function, the power balance constraints, and the dynamic model of the generation units are presented in the next subsections. All problems are modeled via Mixed Integer Programming (MILP) formulations. We first describe the (robust) step 1 and then (i.e. Sect. 3.9) we illustrate the online step of our EMS.

3.3 Modeling of Generator Units

We consider a Combined Heat and Power (CHP) dispatchable generator, with an associated fuel cost. Our approach should decide the amount $P_{CHP}^s(t)$ of generated CHP power for each scenario ($s \in S$) and for each timestamp ($t \in T$).

We assume bounds on $P_{CHP}^s(t)$ given by the Electrical Capability based on real generation data [3, 7]. In our approach we treat CHP decisions in each timestamp as *independent*, because we assume that each timestamp is long enough to decide independently (from the previous timestamp) whether to switch on or off the generator. Therefore, we can model the generated CHP power with:

$$P_{CHP}^{min} \leq P_{CHP}^s(t) \leq P_{CHP}^{max} \quad \forall t \in T \tag{3}$$

3.4   Modeling of Storage Systems

The development of battery systems has increased over the last few years to cover the use of renewable energy sources when they are not available. Our model for the battery system is based on the level of energy stored at each timestamp t as a function of the amount of power charged or discharged from the unit.

$P_{Storage}^s(t)$ is the power exchanged between the storage system and the VPP. We actually use two decision variables: $P_{St_{In}}^s(t)$ if the batteries inject power into the VPP (with efficiency η_d) and $P_{St_{Out}}^s(t)$ for the batteries in charging mode (with efficiency η_c). The initial battery states and the efficiency values are based on real generation data [3, 7]. We use a variable $charge^s(t)$ to define for each timestamp the current state of the battery system:

$$charge^s(t) = charge^s(t-1) - \eta_d P_{St_{In}}^s(t) + \eta_c P_{St_{Out}}^s(t) \quad \forall t \in T \tag{4}$$

More accurate models for storage systems are present in recent literature. For example, [4] optimizes battery operation by modeling battery stress factors and analyzing battery degradation. However, in our work, it is sufficient to take into account the status of the charge for each timpestamp since we assume that each timestamp is long enough to avoid high stress and degradation level of the batteries.

3.5   External Grid

The variable $P_{Grid}^s(t)$ represents the current power exchanged with the grid for each scenario and for each timestamp. Similarly, the total power is defined as the sum of two additional variables, namely $P_{Grid_{In}}^s(t)$ if energy is bought from the Electricity Market and $P_{Grid_{Out}}^s(t)$ if energy is sold to the Market. We assume bounds given by the net capacity from literature [3] based on real data for the maximum input/output net capacity.

$$P_{Grid_{In}}^{min} \leq P_{Grid_{In}}^s(t) \leq P_{Grid_{In}}^{max} \quad \forall t \in T \tag{5}$$

$$P_{Grid_{Out}}^{min} \leq P_{Grid_{Out}}^s(t) \leq P_{Grid_{Out}}^{max} \quad \forall t \in T \tag{6}$$

3.6 Demand Side Management

The DSM of our VPP model aims to modify the temporal consumption patterns, leaving the total amount of required daily energy constant. The degree of modification is modeled by shifts that are optimized by the first step of our EMS. The shifted load is given by:

$$\tilde{P}_{Load}(t) = S_{Load}(t) + P_{Load}(t) \quad \forall t \in T \tag{7}$$

where $S_{Load}(t)$ represents the amount of shifted demand, and $P_{Load}(t)$ is the originally planned load for timestamp t (part of the model input). The amount of shifted demand is bounded by two quantities $S_{Load}^{min}(t)$ and $S_{Load}^{max}(t)$. By properly adjusting the two bounds, we can ensure that the consumption can reduce/increase in each time step by (e.g.) a maximum of 10% of the original expected load.

We assume that the total energy consumption on the whole optimization horizon is constant. More specifically, we assume that the consumption stays unchanged also *over multiple sub-periods of the horizon*: this a possible way to state that demand shifts can make only local alterations of the demand load. Formally, let T_n be the set of timestamps for the n-th sub-period, then we can formulate the constraint:

$$\sum_{t \in T_n} S_{Load}(t) = 0 \tag{8}$$

Deciding the value of the $S_{Load}^{max}(t)$ variables is the main goal of our day-ahead optimization step.

3.7 Power Balance

In general, ensuring power balance imposes that the total power generation must equal the load demand, $P_{Load}^s(t)$, in all timestamps and for all scenarios.

In this work, the load demand that must be satisfied is the *optimally shifted* demand of (day-ahead) step of our model. At any point in time, the overall shifted load is covered by an energy mix considering the generation from the internal sources, the storage system, and power bought from the energy market. Energy sold to the grid and routed to the battery system should be subtracted from the power balance. Overall, we have:

$$\tilde{P}_{Load}^s(t) = P_{CHP}^s(t) + P_{PV}^s(t) + P_{Grid_{In}}^s(t) - P_{Grid_{Out}}^s(t) + P_{St_{In}}^s(t) - P_{St_{Out}}^s(t) \tag{9}$$

3.8 Objective Function

The objective of our EMS is to minimize the operational costs z of the VPP in a time horizon (T). The objective function formulated as:

$$z = \frac{1}{|S|} \sum_{s \in S} \sum_{t \in T} c_{Grid_I}(t) P_{Grid_{In}}^s(t) + c_{CHP} P_{CHP}^s(t) \tag{10}$$

$$+ c_{Grid_S}(t) P_{St_{Out}}^s(t) - c_{Grid_O}(t) P_{Grid_{Out}}^s(t)$$

where $c_{Grid}(t)$ is the hourly price of electricity on the Market and we assumed the same price for c_{Grid_I}, c_{Grid_O} and c_{Grid_S}. c_{CHP} is the diesel price, assumed to be constant for each timestamp.

3.9   Online Step

The online step of our model is designed to obtain the real optimal values for the power flow variables, *assuming that the shifts have been planned using the first day-ahead step of the model*. The on-line greedy algorithm is a restricted version of our MILP model, obtained by: (1) Fixing all the $S_{Load}(t)$ to the value assigned by the step 1; (2) Considering a single scenario, corresponding to the actual realization of the uncertain quantities. (3) Each timestamp is optimized one at time. The MILP model is:

$$P_{CHP}^{min} \leq P_{CHP}(t) \leq P_{CHP}^{max} \quad \forall t \in T \tag{11}$$

$$charge(t) = charge(t-1) - \eta_d P_{St_{In}}(t) + \eta_c P_{St_{Out}}(t) \quad \forall t \in T \tag{12}$$

$$P_{Grid_{In}}^{min} \leq P_{Grid_{In}}(t) \leq P_{Grid_{In}}^{max} \quad \forall t \in T \tag{13}$$

$$P_{Grid_{Out}}^{min} \leq P_{Grid_{Out}}(t) \leq P_{Grid_{Out}}^{max} \quad \forall t \in T \tag{14}$$

$$\tilde{P}_{Load}(t) = P_{CHP}(t) + P_{PV}(t) + P_{Grid_{In}}(t) - P_{Grid_{Out}}(t) + P_{St_{In}}(t) - P_{St_{Out}}(t) \tag{15}$$

$$z = \sum_{t \in T} c_{Grid_I}(t) P_{Grid_{In}}(t) + c_{CHP} P_{CHP}(t) + c_{Grid_S}(t) P_{St_{Out}}(t) - c_{Grid_O}(t) P_{Grid_{Out}}(t) \tag{16}$$

4   Case Study

The model is implemented and tested using real data and our case study is based on a Public Dataset[1]. From this dataset we assume electric load demand and photovoltaic production forecasts, upper and lower limits for generating units and the initial status of storage units.

---

[1] www.enwl.co.uk/lvns.

4.1 Dataset Description

The dataset presents 100 individual profiles of load demand with a time step of 5 min resolution from 00:00 to 23:00. We consider aggregated profiles with timestamp of 1 h and we use them as forecasted load. We can see, after aggregation, that most of the electrical consumption occurs in certain parts of the day by presenting consumption peaks, as expected. This lead to the need of demand side mechanisms to reduce these peaks.

The photovoltaic production is based on the same dataset with profiles for different size of PV units but for the same sun irradiance (i.e. the same shape but different amplitude due to the different size of the PV panels used). We use also in this case the PV production as forecasted production. Most of the aggregated photovoltaic forecast production occurs around midday, with a consequent need of balancing this source of energy to cover periods of high request of energy in the VPP. In Fig. 2 we show forecasted values of load demand, optimized demand shifts and PV production in the case with maximum allowed shifts of 10%.

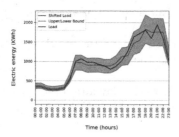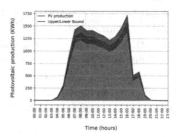

Fig. 2. Scenarios for load demand (left) and for PV production (right) with 10% of allowed shift

The demand electricity hourly prices have been obtained based on data from the italian national energy market management corporation[2] (GME) in €/MWh. The diesel price is taken from the Italian Ministry of Economic Development[3] and is assumed as a constant for all the time horizon (one day in our model) as assumed in literature [1] and from [7].

4.2 Model Comparison

For performing the experiments, we need to obtain realizations for the uncertainties related to both loads and PV generation. Since we have assumed normally distributed prediction errors, we do this by randomly sampling error values according to the distribution parameters. Specifically, we consider a sample of 100 realizations (enough for the Central Limit Theorem [5] to ensure that sample average values will follow approximately a Normal distribution).

---

[2] http://www.mercatoelettrico.org/En/Default.aspx.
[3] http://dgsaie.mise.gov.it/.

For each realization, we obtain a solution and a cost value by solving our two-step approach (robust optimization + on-line algorithm) using Gurobi as a MILP solver. We evaluate the quality of the approach by comparing the costs with those that could be obtained assuming perfect information. This allows us to estimate the Expected Value of Perfect Information (EVPI).

In particular, we consider two different models that make of perfect information: the first is named *Day-ahead Oracle*, and the second the *Day-after Oracle*. The *Day-ahead Oracle* is identical to the robust model, except that only one scenario is considered and *this corresponds to an actual realization of the uncertain variables*. The cost obtained from this model represents the best achievable result for the whole problem, assuming that no uncertainty is present.

The *Day-after Oracle* is designed to obtain the best possible values for the power flow variables, *assuming that the shifts have been planned using the robust optimization approach*. The oracle replaces the on-line greedy algorithm with a restricted version of our MILP model, obtained by: (1) Fixing all the $S_{Load}(t)$ to the value assigned by the robust approach; (2) Considering a single scenario, corresponding to the actual realization of the uncertain quantities. The main difference w.r.t. the greedy algorithm is that all timestamps are optimized simultaneously, rather than one at a time.

It is interesting to investigate the estimated costs of the robust optimization step, and evaluate how accurately it predicts the actual costs from the on-line approach, or the costs of the two oracles.

We refer to the day-ahead oracles as DA, to the day-after oracle as DF, and to the two steps of our model as RS1 (Robust Step 1) and OS2 (Online Step 2).

5 Results and Discussions

The optimal costs from the on-line approach and the costs of the two oracles are shown together in Table 1 for comparison. The inspected variable is the objective function i.e. total daily VPP cost. The comparison is shown also in terms of percentage difference to show the differences among costs by inserting uncertainty and perfect information of inputs. It is possible to notice that the percentage difference between the DA and the DF is relatively small (from 3.79 to 6.99) by changing the percentage of allowed consumption shift. This allows to deduce that the *optimized shifts* in the DA (i.e. by assuming that no uncertainty is present) are similar to the optimized shifts after the introduction of input uncertainty. By comparing the two oracle models with the online step of our model, it can be observed that the optimal costs of OS2 significantly deviate from the optimal oracle costs. From this results we can deduce that our OS2 reduces the quality of the solution by 30% compared to DA (i.e. the best achievable result for the problem, assuming that no uncertainty is present).

We investigated also the parameters of μ and σ over the 100 tested samples and we obtained that for the two oracle models the standard deviations are in the order of 10^{-5} and in the OS2 the data are slightly more scattered (i.e. in order of 10^{-1}) but on average they all have a good stability.

Table 1. Costs and % difference among the three costs with allowed shift of 10%

Shift %	c_{DA} μ (K€)	c_{DF} μ (K€)	c_{OS2} μ (K€)	$c_{DA} - c_{DF}$ diff (%)	$c_{DA} - c_{OS2}$ diff (%)	$c_{DF} - c_{OS2}$ diff (%)
5	347.56	371.86	474.94	6.99	36.65	27.72
10	344.21	366.38	471.28	6.44	36.92	28.63
15	341.43	360.90	468.41	5.70	37.19	29.79
20	339.03	355.59	466.10	4.88	37.48	31.08
25	337.58	350.38	464.67	3.79	37.65	32.62

To estimate how accurately the robust optimization step predicts the actual costs from the on-line approach, we compare in Table 2 the expected optimal cost from RS1 (see Fig. 1) and the optimal real cost given by OS2. We compare (over the 100 realizations) by changing the allowed percentage of shift from 2% to 20%. In the OS2 costs we can see, as expected, an improvement trend by augmenting the percentage of shift (i.e. by relaxing the constraint) and we do not have a significant deviation from the optimal solution of RS1.

Table 2. Difference between expected and real costs of the two steps of our model

Shift %	RS1 (Expected cost (K€))	OS2 (Optimal Real cost (K€))	Difference %
2	471.36	477.19	1.24
5	439.56	474.94	8.05
8	410.82	472.70	11.51
10	401.94	471.28	14.68
12	416.19	470.02	12.93
15	426.34	468.41	9.87
18	420.23	466.24	10.95
20	416.18	466.10	11.99

We assume that every hour the EMS will compute the energy that will be produced/sold/bought by each of the VPP components, as the result of the optimization problem so, in addition to producing the minimum (optimal) daily cost for VPP, our model also generates the optimal energy flows for each timpestamp. In Fig. 3 we show the optimal flows produced by, respectively, the OS2 (left), the DA (center) and the DF (right) in the same realization (over the 100 possible ones) and always in the case of 10% of allowed shift. The following considerations are deducible from the simulation results: in the DA we can see that, by having perfect information, it is possible to acquire energy from the grid in advance (i.e. when the cost is lower) for example in timestamp from 01:00 to 04:00 and to sell energy to the grid in period of highest price on the market

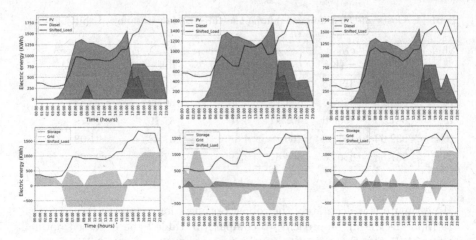

Fig. 3. Optimal energy flows in the VPP for OS2 (left), DA (center) and DF (right) in the same input realization

or when more energy is available from renewable sources; renewable resources are always 100% exploited, because they are convenient in term of costs; around midday the EMS buys (or sells less) energy from (to) the grid rather than using the CHP because it is cheaper; CHP production is thus reduced (and absent in oracle models) during off-peak hours and is fully restored during on-peak hours to cover the load demand; the storage constraints are more strict (i.e. charge of storage for each timpestamp) and for this reason the storage is less used also during peak-periods. In the online step, the exchange of energy with the storage system is never used because, due to the greedy heuristic and the assumption of equal prices, is better to sell energy to the grid rather than to store it for future hours.

6   Conclusion

This work proposes a VPP EMS, a two-step optimization model, that decides the minimum cost energy balance at each point in time considering electrical load, PV production, electricity costs, upper and lower limits for generating units and storage units. The first step models the prediction uncertainty using a robust approach defining scenarios to optimize the load demand shift and to estimate the cost. The second step is an online optimization algorithm implemented within a simulator that uses the optimal shifts produced by the previous step to minimize, for each timestamp, the real cost while fully covering the optimally shifted energy demand. A case study is used to illustrate that the first robust step of our model produces good optimized shifts that do not significantly deviate (in term of costs) from the model with no uncertainty. We compare results conducted over 100 input realizations and we can observe that we have a loss of result quality in the second step developed with a greedy heuristic. We plan to improve this second online step by developing a multi-stage step able to react to unexpected event and by testing our model on real data of a large industrial plant. We plan to apply machine learning techniques to perform the whole range of predictions involved in the activities of a VPP in the industrial sector.

References

1. Aloini, D., Crisostomi, E., Raugi, M., Rizzo, R.: Optimal power scheduling in a virtual power plant. In: 2011 2nd IEEE PES International Conference and Exhibition on Innovative Smart Grid Technologies, pp. 1–7, December 2011
2. Awerbuch, S., Preston, A.: The Virtual Utility: Accounting, Technology and Competitive Aspects of the Emerging Industry, vol. 26. Springer Science & Business Media, Berlin (2012). https://doi.org/10.1007/978-1-4615-6167-5
3. Bai, H., Miao, S., Ran, X., Ye, C.: Optimal dispatch strategy of a virtual power plant containing battery switch stations in a unified electricity market. Energies 8(3), 2268–2289 (2015). http://www.mdpi.com/1996-1073/8/3/2268
4. Bordin, C., Anuta, H.O., Crossland, A., Gutierrez, I.L., Dent, C.J., Vigo, D.: A linear programming approach for battery degradation analysis and optimization in offgrid power systems with solar energy integration. Renew. Energy 101, 417–430 (2017)
5. Bracewell, R.N., Bracewell, R.N.: The Fourier Transform and its Applications, vol. 31999. McGraw-Hill, New York (1986)
6. Edwards, R.E., New, J., Parker, L.E.: Predicting future hourly residential electrical consumption: a machine learning case study. Energy Buildings 49, 591–603 (2012)
7. Espinosa, A., Ochoa, L.: Dissemination document low voltage networks models and low carbon technology profiles. Technical report, University of Manchester, June 2015
8. Gamou, S., Yokoyama, R., Ito, K.: Optimal unit sizing of cogeneration systems in consideration of uncertain energy demands as continuous random variables. Energy Convers. Manag. 43(9), 1349–1361 (2002)
9. Jain, R.K., Smith, K.M., Culligan, P.J., Taylor, J.E.: Forecasting energy consumption of multi-family residential buildings using support vector regression: investigating the impact of temporal and spatial monitoring granularity on performance accuracy. Appl. Energy 123, 168–178 (2014)
10. Jurkovi, K., Pandi, H., Kuzle, I.: Review on unit commitment under uncertainty approaches. In: 2015 38th International Convention on Information and Communication Technology, Electronics and Microelectronics (MIPRO), pp. 1093–1097, May 2015
11. Kaplanis, S., Kaplani, E.: A model to predict expected mean and stochastic hourly global solar radiation I(h;nj) values. Renew. Energy 32(8), 1414–1425 (2007)
12. Lombardi, P., Powalko, M., Rudion, K.: Optimal operation of a virtual power plant. In: Power and Energy Society General Meeting, PES 2009, pp. 1–6. IEEE (2009)
13. Palma-Behnke, R., Benavides, C., Aranda, E., Llanos, J., Sez, D.: Energy management system for a renewable based microgrid with a demand side management mechanism. In: 2011 IEEE Symposium on Computational Intelligence Applications in Smart Grid (CIASG), pp. 1–8, April 2011
14. Zhao, C., Guan, Y.: Unified stochastic and robust unit commitment. IEEE Trans. Power Syst. 28(3), 3353–3361 (2013)

15. Zheng, Q.P., Wang, J., Liu, A.L.: Stochastic optimization for unit commitment, a review. IEEE Trans. Power Syst. **30**(4), 1913–1924 (2015)
16. Zhou, Z., Zhang, J., Liu, P., Li, Z., Georgiadis, M.C., Pistikopoulos, E.N.: A two-stage stochastic programming model for the optimal design of distributed energy systems. Appl. Energy **103**, 135–144 (2013). http://www.sciencedirect.com/science/article/pii/S0306261912006599

Applying Machine Learning to High-Quality Wine Identification

Giorgio Leonardi and Luigi Portinale[✉]

Computer Science Institute, DiSIT, University of Piemonte Orientale,
Alessandria, Italy
luigi.portinale@uniupo.it

Abstract. This paper discusses a machine learning approach, aimed at the definition of methods for authenticity assessment of some of the highest valued *Nebbiolo-based* wines from Piedmont (Italy). This issue is one of the most relevant in the wine market, where commercial frauds related to such a kind of products are estimated to be worth millions of Euros. The main objective of the work is to demonstrate the effectiveness of classification algorithms in exploiting simple features about the chemical profile of a wine, obtained from inexpensive standard bio-chemical analyses. We report on experiments performed with datasets of real samples and with synthetic datasets which have been artificially generated from real data through the learning of a Bayesian network generative model.

Keywords: Classification · Fraud detection · Artificial data generation

1 Introduction

The quality and safety profiles of fine wines represent a peculiar case of the notion of *food integrity*, because of the very high value of a single bottle, and because of the complex chemical profile, requiring therefore specific and robust methods for their univocal profiling/authentication. About one-third of Italy's wine production is Controlled Appellation (DOC and DOCG, now Protected Denominations of Origin [10]). The protection of local and regional wines with designation of origin labels is necessary for authenticity reasons and in order to protect consumers against frauds and speculation. Although specific regulations exist in this matter, and some analytical approaches and protocols are well established for wine tracking and authentication, quality wines are highly subjected to adulteration. This triggers destabilization of the wine market, particularly regarding the quality aspect, with an estimated impact of about 7% of the whole market value. A frequent type of counterfeiting in wine sector, is mislabeling, regarding both the used cultivar of grape and the geographical area of origin, causing an economical impact estimated to be several million of Euros [10].

The detection of adulterations or declarations which do not correspond to the labeling are actually official tasks of wine quality control and consumer protection. Some analytical methods, like stable isotope ratio analysis by nuclear

© Springer International Publishing AG 2017
F. Esposito et al. (Eds.): AI*IA 2017, LNAI 10640, pp. 31–43, 2017.
https://doi.org/10.1007/978-3-319-70169-1_3

magnetic resonance, and isotope ratio mass spectrometry, have been adopted as official methods by the European Community (EC). However, isotope analysis is both time consuming and very expensive to undertake, by requiring a lot of specialization as well. Moreover, these methods require very large data sets when used for the identification of wine and origin. Non analytical approaches like olograms, trasponder systems or QR codes only partially address the problem of wine authenticity. For these reasons, a challenge for wine authenticity is to obtain standard analytical procedures to describe a wine proof-of-identity, which could defend consumers from illegal adulteration practices, as well as from unintentional mislabeling due to mistakes during wine production.

Given a specific set of measured features, obtained from chemical analyses conducted from the data analytic perspective, the main goal of the work is to show that well-established state-of-the-art classification methodologies from machine learning, can be suitably adopted to fulfill the task of controlling specific wine adulterations. The consequence is the generation of an added value to the quality control process of such high-quality wines.

In the paper we will discuss the experience concerning the TRAQUASWINE (TRAceability, QUALity and Safety of wine) project, having as a major goal the authenticity assessment and the protection against fake versions of some of the highest quality (and often top priced) *Nebbiolo-based* wines like *Barolo, Barbaresco* and *Gattinara*. Following Wagstaff's scheme [19], we discuss how data have been collected, how they have been prepared, how suitable classification models have been identified and how the interpretation of the results suggests the emergence of an active role of classification techniques, based on standard chemical profiling, for the assessment of the authenticity of the high-quality wines which were target of the study.

2   The Chemical-Analytical Framework

The TRAQUASWINE project involved both industrial and academic partners in the creation of a network operating in the wine sector, with the aim to trace and authenticate the origin, quality and safety of Piedmont high-quality *Nebbiolo-based* wines. In this context, the main goals of the project were: (1) to define the *chemotype* of Nebbiolo grape and derived wines, identifying molecular markers useful for quality control and wine traceability; (2) to establish a comprehensive analytical approach, based on the exploitation of machine learning techniques for multivariate analysis to chemotype datasets, useful to the traceability and authentication of high-quality *Nebbiolo-based* wines, produced in different area of Piedmont, by diverse wineries.

Chemical parameters and methods were selected by taking into account two main criteria: the economical cost of the analyses (particularly regarding the required instrumentation), and the avoidance of the need of pluri-annual consolidated databases, as often required by classical isotopic methods. An important feature has been the use of data from different origin, by considering different producers, different areas of production, different typology of wine (i.e., commercial wines on the market, as well as "model" wines explicitly produced for the study) and different aging of the product (see [1] for more details).

Considering **data collection**, we organized the study as follows: we selected some of the most valued Nebbiolo-based wines as the high quality classes to be protected from fakes, and in particular *Barolo* (BRL), *Barbaresco* (BRB) and *Gattinara* (GAT); we then selected some control wines we called *Langhe* (LAN) (referring to a specific DOC allowing the blend of Nebbiolo and other grape varieties) and Blend (BLE) (wines that were specifically prepared to model blends for GAT that are not allowed by the disciplinary of production). The goal was to simulate unallowed blends for BRL and BRB in the former case, and unallowed blends for GAT in the latter. We obtained a total of 146 samples of different wine types. In particular, besides the wine types introduced above, we have analyzed samples of *Sizzano* (SIZ), *Roero* (ROE), *Nebbiolo d'Alba* (NEB) and *Ghemme* (GHE), resulting in a total of 9 possible classes.

In addition, we also tested some samples corresponding to wines produced without Nebbiolo grape, and in particular with 100% of some grape varieties partially present in some of LAN commercial wines; we labeled them as NON (*NO Nebbiolo*). We reserved 12 samples of NON wines as additional control wines, to test the response of the learned models with respect to simulated fake wines with the absence of Nebbiolo grape, and with the additional complication that no such a kind of wines have been used in the training of the models.

Regarding the **data preparation** phase, chemical analyses were oriented to characterize wine samples by their phenolic composition [11]. Given the goal of inexpensive procedures mentioned before, two main types of analyses were performed: *spectrophotometric methods*, which include not specific and low-cost assays useful to quantify general class of compounds, and *chromatographic methods*, which are more advanced but require instrumentation which is generally available in the standardly equipped laboratories for quality control. Food chemistry experts have identified 40 parameters of interest that have been measured with the above methods and related instrumentation. Such a set of parameters has been then reduced by means of a feature reduction methodology; in particular, *correlation-based feature selection* with sequential forward/backward search [9] has been performed, resulting in the reduction from 40 to 15 attributes for each sample. Finally, two attributes concerning grape percentage information (that survived the feature selection filter) were removed as well, since they have been considered not generally trustable (or even available), in a real scenario. The final set of features used in the experiments described in the present paper is reported in Table 1[1].

---

[1]   Classification experiments have been performed also with the datasets of 40 and 15 attributes; results are reported in [1].

Table 1. Features names and acronyms

Feature	Acronym	Feature	Acronym
Total Polyphenols	TP	Total Tannins	TT
Peonidin-3-O-glucoside	Pn-3-glc	Malvidin-3-O-glucoside	Mv-3-glc
Delphinidin-3-O-glucoside (perc)	PDn-3-glc	Peonidin-3-O-glucoside (perc)	PPn-3-glc
Malvidin-3-O-glucoside (perc)	PMv-3-glc	Caffeic Acid	Caff
Ferulic Acid	Fer	Kaempferol-3-O-glucoside	Kae-3-glu
Myricetin	Mir	Coutaric Acid (perc)	PCout
cis-Resveratrol	cResv		

3   Data Characterization and Analysis

Starting from the chemical-analytical framework described in the previous section, we have obtained a dataset of 146 records with 13 attributes plus the class; about 22% of the records have a missing value in correspondence of the measured *cResv* feature. From the data analytical point of view, we have considered both *unsupervised* and *supervised* methods as reported in the following.

3.1   Unsupervised Data Analysis

We firstly searched for regularities in the chemical profiles of the available wines through unsupervised data analysis. We considered two different *clustering* algorithms (*EM* and *K-means*) and dimensionality reduction through *PCA*; furthermore, we also considered two different kind of evaluations: a *multi-class evaluation* with respect to the original 9 classes (i.e., wine types), and a *binary evaluation* where important high quality wines (BRL, BRB and GAT) represented the *positive* class and the others the *negative* class. The second kind of analysis has been performed as the emphasis of the study was on the protection of high quality wines with respect to different wines that could be placed on the market as fakes. In particular, we evaluated the following unsupervised algorithms

- for multi-class evaluation: *K-means* with $K = 9$ clusters, *EM* with no predefined number of clusters, *EM* with a predefined set of 9 clusters;
- for binary evaluation: *K-means* and *EM* with a predefined set of $K = 2$ clusters.

The above algorithms have been tested by using both the original set of features available from chemical analyses, and by considering a PCA feature reduction approach. Since the class information is actually available in our application, the unsupervised methods have been evaluated through *external metrics*, measuring how close the clustering is to the predefined benchmark classes [7]. To this end, we have measured the following indices: *Purity, Precision, Recall, Rand index, Fowlkes-Mallows (FM) index* and *F1-measure*. All such indices are values in the interval $[0, 1]$, with 0 representing the worst cluster quality and 1 the best one. In particular, *Purity* measures the accuracy of the assignment of the most frequent class to a given cluster (i.e. a purity index equal to 1 means that every class is perfectly separated in the clusters); *Precision* and *Recall* are the usual measures adopted in the information retrieval setting, and computed by considering the number of possible pairs of the same class present in the same cluster or in different clusters. They are the basis for the computation of the *F1-measure* (the harmonic mean of Precision and Recall) and of the *FM index* (the geometric mean of Precision and Recall). Finally, the *Rand index* measures the percentage of correct decisions made by the clustering algorithm with respect to the ground truth given by the class distribution.

Results of the external evaluation of the different clustering on both the original dataset and the one resulting from PCA feature reduction are reported on Table 2. From such results, we can notice that cluster quality indices are rather poor (except for Purity in binary classification). When no predefined number of clusters is provided, EM clustering produces $nc = 6$ clusters on the original dataset and $nc = 13$ clusters on the PCA dataset (out of 9 actual classes). Finally, we can notice that there is no significant difference between the indices when computed on the original dataset with respect to the PCA dataset (a slight difference can be evidenced when EM does not use a predefined number of clusters, and this can be explained by the fact that we have 6 clusters in one case and 13 clusters in the other one). These experiments suggested us that regularities associated to wine classes should be better investigated through supervised methods.

Table 2. External evaluation of clustering ("nc" number of clusters)

	K-means					EM				
	Original		PCA			Original		PCA		
	nc=9	nc=2	nc=9	nc=2		nc=6	nc=9	nc=2	nc=13	nc=9	nc=2
Purity	0.43	0.71	0.42	0.71	Purity	0.41	0.53	0.71	0.55	0.51	0.71
Precision	0.21	0.59	0.24	0.58	Precision	0.22	0.33	0.59	0.37	0.39	0.58
Recall	0.41	0.52	0.33	0.78	Recall	0.49	0.37	0.52	0.24	0.37	0.52
Rand Index	0.69	0.50	0.75	0.53	Rand Index	0.68	0.80	0.50	0.83	0.83	0.50
F1-measure	0.28	0.55	0.28	0.66	F1-measure	0.30	0.34	0.55	0.29	0.38	0.55
FM Index	0.29	0.55	0.28	0.67	FM Index	0.33	0.35	0.55	0.30	0.38	0.55

3.2   Classification

Concerning supervised methods, we have considered three different classifiers:

1. a Bayesian Network classifier (BN), with learning performed with standard Cooper/Herskovits algorithm [3], allowing a maximum of 3 parents per node;
2. a Support Vector Machine (SVM), based on Sequential Minimal Optimization algorithm (SMO) [14] with a Pearson Universal Kernel having Lorentzian

peak shape [17], and with Platt scaling in order to get a probability distribution over the classes [15][2];

3. a Multi-Layer Perceptron (MLP) with one hidden layer of $n = \frac{f+c}{2}$ hidden units (being f the number of features and c the number of classes).

Multi-class classification has been performed as a *one-agaist-all* approach. Moreover, the evaluation of each classifier refers to a *10-fold cross validation* performed on the obtained dataset (146 records with 13 attributes). To perform our experimentation, we have exploited the WEKA machine learning tool [8]. As mentioned before, the main focus was not on general accuracy (even if definitely an important measure), but rather to check the performance of the classifiers with respect to the classes of high-quality wines (BRL, BRB and GAT) and control wines (LAN and BL), by looking at their possible misclassifications. Table 3 reports the general accuracy and KAPPA statistic of the three classifiers for the considered dataset. Figure 1 reports the prediction statistics with respect to the classes of interest for BN (upper left), MLP (upper right) and SMO (lower left) classifier respectively. For each class, the number of predictions in the different classes is reported in the bar chart, as well as the Matthews Correlation Coefficient (MCC) and F1-measure, with MCC being more significant in our case, since the number of *positive* instances (those of the target class) are much less that the number of *negative* instances (those of all the other classes). We can remark that, concerning control wines (LAN and BLE), classification accuracy is very good, but more importantly, no control wine is misclassified as a high-quality one and vice versa. This holds for every tested classifier; in particular, SMO has the best performance even from the qualitative point of view; indeed, if we consider high-quality wines, we can notice that misclassifications of BRB and BRL just confuse each other (and this is definitely reasonable from the "oeanological" point of view), while GAT has a perfect recognition.

Table 3. Accuracy and KAPPA statistic of the classifiers.

	Accuracy	Kappa
BN	79%	0.75
MLP	82%	0.79
SMO	89%	0.87

To get more insights, we computed, for each classifier, the probability distribution on the predictions that are misclassified, by focusing on the classes of interest. Tables 4, 5 and 6 show the results for classifiers BN, MLP and SMO respectively (predictions performed by the classifier corresponding to the bold-face entries). It can be noticed the very good performance of SMO, that in case

---

[2] The regularization parameter (a.k.a complexity) has been set to 10, since we are dealing with a multi-class problem with 9 different classes, and it is a good practice to set the parameter close to the number of classes [13].

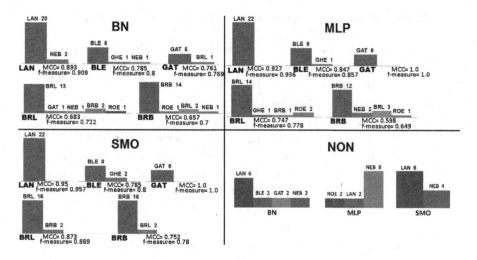

Fig. 1. Predictions of the tested classifiers

Table 4. Probability distribution of misclassifications: BN classifier.

True Ground	Probability distribution of misclassified predictions								
	GHE	GAT	SIZ	NEB	BRL	ROE	BRB	LAN	BLE
LAN	0	0	0	**0.566**	0	0.002	0.002	0.43	0
	0	0	0.005	**0.955**	0	0.001	0.032	0.001	0.005
BLE	**0.611**	0	0	0.002	0	0	0	0	0.387
	0.037	0	0	**0.632**	0.001	0	0	0.015	0.314
GAT	0	0.017	0.001	0.08	**0.893**	0	0.008	0	0
BRL	0.209	**0.419**	0.013	0.004	0.354	0	0	0	0
	0	0	0.001	**0.718**	0.281	0	0	0	0
	0.011	0	0	0	0.481	0	**0.508**	0	0
	0	0	0	0	0.237	0	**0.763**	0	0
	0	0.037	0.051	0.151	0.313	**0.324**	0.119	0.005	0
BRB	0	0	0	0.009	0	**0.991**	0	0	0
	0.072	0	0	0.035	**0.846**	0	0.044	0	0.004
	0	0	0	0	**0.979**	0	0.021	0	0
	0.01	0.012	0.002	**0.611**	0.086	0	0.186	0.009	0.084

of BRB and BRL (the only high-quality wines having misclassifications) shows
a null probability of predicting control wines and in one prediction of BRL (the
second misclassification of BRL) has a 31% probability of predicting the correct
wine (against a 64% probability of confusing it with the similar BRB). Moreover,
predictions on BLE (the only misclassified control wine) show a null or close to
null probability of predicting high-quality wines.

Table 5. Probability distribution of misclassifications: MLP classifier.

True Ground	Probability distribution of misclassified predictions								
	GHE	GAT	SIZ	NEB	BRL	ROE	BRB	LAN	BLE
BLE	**0.471**	0	0.076	0	0.005	0	0	0	0.447
BRL	**0.862**	0.095	0.001	0.001	0.039	0	0	0.002	0
	0.383	0.012	0	0	0.014	0	**0.518**	0	0.072
	0	0	0.21	0	0.064	**0.69**	0.036	0.001	0
	0	0	0.118	0	0.278	**0.59**	0.014	0	0
BRB	0	0	0.025	**0.641**	0.233	0.095	0	0.001	0.004
	0	0	0.014	**0.748**	0	0.233	0	0.001	0.005
	0.004	0.109	0	0.008	**0.543**	0	0.335	0	0
	0	0.041	0.001	0	**0.591**	0.002	0.365	0	0
	0	0.004	0	0.009	**0.878**	0.002	0.107	0	0
	0	0	0.035	0.327	0	**0.626**	0	0.002	0.01

Table 6. Probability distribution of misclassifications: SMO classifier.

True Ground	Probability distribution of misclassified predictions								
	GHE	GAT	SIZ	NEB	BRL	ROE	BRB	LAN	BLE
BLE	**0.99**	0	0	0	0	0	0	0	0.01
	0.747	0	0.059	0.01	0	0	0.002	0	0.182
BRL	0.001	0	0.043	0	0.16	0	**0.795**	0	0
	0.002	0	0.052	0.001	0.309	0	**0.636**	0	0
BRB	0.001	0	0	0	**0.936**	0	0.063	0	0
	0	0	0	0.001	**0.937**	0	0.063	0	0

Finally, we tested the learned classifiers, using the test set TS composed by the instances of NON wines; differently from the wine samples used for training the classifiers, the wine samples in TS do not contain any part of Nebbiolo grape; this implies that acceptable predictions can be those selecting our control wines (LAN and BLE) which are the ones containing parts of the grape varieties contained in the wine samples of TS; in particular, LAN is also a preferred predictions than BLE, because of the way NON wine samples have been prepared. The results are summarized in Fig. 1 (lower right). They show a greater robustness of SMO with respect to other classifiers in the presence of control wines on which the classifier was not trained.

4   Synthetic Dataset

Since a weak point of the study is the limited number of actual wine samples, in order to investigate classification results on a larger dataset, we decided to perform an artificial data generation, starting from the real data we have collected. To this end, we have considered the original dataset of real samples as the base dataset and, for each class (i.e., wine) we have performed the following tasks: (*i*) selection of all the instances of the class; (*ii*) learning of a Linear Gaussian Bayesian Network (LGBN) [6] specific for the class, using the PC learning algorithm [16]; (*iii*) generation of a new data set from the learned model for the current class. The idea is to exploit a generative model, learned from real data, to produce synthetic data by model simulation. We ended up choosing an LGBN model because of two main reasons: the ability of generating continuous features and the modeling of specific dependencies among the features; the adopted learning algorithm is Spirtes et al's PC algorithm [16] that belongs to the class of constraint-based learning algorithms, deriving a set of conditional independence and dependence statements by statistical tests. PC allowed us also to introduce some background knowledge concerning well-know dependencies among the measured features and determined by chemical experts. As an example, Fig. 2 reports the LGBN structure learned for the wine class BRL (features names are reported in Table 1). Conditional probability distributions are linear gaussian distributions with respect to parents.

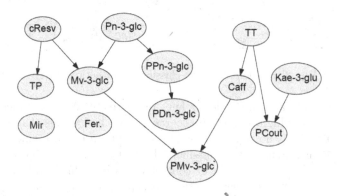

Fig. 2. Structure of LGBN for Barolo artificial dataset

To learn the generative model we exploited the GENIE/SMILE software tool (www.bayesfusion.com), which also allowed us to implement the synthetic data generation from the model. At the end of this process, all the class-specific synthetic instances have been collected together to produce an artificial dataset for supervised learning; in particular, we generated 100 times the number of instances in the base dataset, resulting in a synthetic dataset of 14600 instances. We performed the same set of experiments performed on the real dataset also for the synthetic one. Table 7 reports the general accuracy and KAPPA statistics of the three tested classifiers. The accuracy of all the classifiers is very good, with a high degree of significance as reported by the KAPPA statistics. In Fig. 3 we can inspect the predictions with respect to the classes of interest for BN (upper left),

Table 7. Accuracy and KAPPA statistic for synthetic dataset.

	Accuracy	Kappa
BN	92%	0.90
MLP	90%	0.89
SMO	94%	0.93

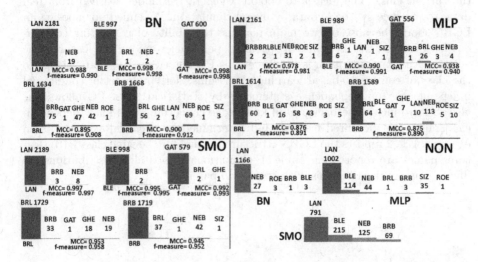

Fig. 3. Predictions of the classifiers, synthetic dataset

MLP (upper right) and SMO (lower left) respectively. We can notice that, in addition to the very high prediction accuracy for each class, also this evaluation confirms that there is no significant confusion between control wines and high-quality wines for all the tested classifiers. In particular, all the classifiers have only a very few misclassification of control wines with high-quality ones (the largest number of such misclassifications is represented by 6 samples of BLE out of 1000, classified as BRB by MLP) with a particular good performance of both BN and SMO. Moreover, by looking at the misclassifications of high-quality wines, we can see that the great majority concerns wines which are not control. In particular, misclassifications of BRB are mainly reported as either BRL or NEB, and misclassifications of BRL are mainly reported as either BRB or NEB. This is really reasonable, since BRB and BRL are very similar wines, both produced with 100% Nebbiolo grape as also NEB wines are. We can then conclude that also for the synthetic dataset, the tested classifiers represent a valuable and viable tool for the goal of the study.

Finally, we produced a synthetic dataset using the test set TS of NON wines; again this was done by learning an LGBN from TS and by generating 1200 synthetic instances. We call this new test set STS. Figure 3 (lower right) shows the results obtained by testing STS on the classifiers learned by using the whole synthetic dataset of 14600 instances as a training set. We can notice that all the tested classifiers identify the vast majority of the synthetic samples as LAN which is the most suitable class for this type of wines. The most robust classifier in this test appears to be the BN classifier, while SMO, which is the classifier best performing on the real data, shows some problems in classifying 125 samples (about 10% of the generated samples) as NEB and 69 samples (about 5% of the total set) as BRB. MLP shows an intermediate situation between BN and SMO. In order to get more insights, we then analyzed the prediction probabilities of the classifiers for each predicted class. Maximum, minimum and average values of such probabilities are reported in Fig. 4 (minimum and maximum values are the extreme points of the segment for each class, while the average values are the middle square points). It is interesting to notice that the 69 predictions of BRB

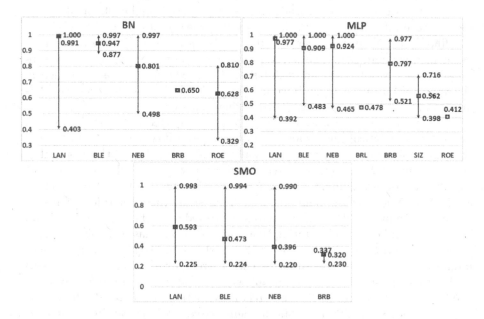

Fig. 4. Prediction probability for NON wines, synthetic test set TST

of the SMO classifier have a very small probability (average probability of 0.32, with minimum probability of 0.23 and maximum probability of 0.337). However, the SMO probability of predicting a NEB wine from dataset TST has an average value of about 0.4, resulting in a moderate average strength of prediction for such a class (that should not be predicted in TST dataset).

In conclusion, by considering the fact that samples in the TST dataset are instances of wines never seen by the classifiers during learning, also the results of the experiments on the synthetic dataset suggest that standard chemical profiling of Piedmont *Nebbiolo-based* wines, coupled with classification techniques, can be a powerful tool to authenticate high-quality and high-value wines, and that state-of-the-art supervised techniques may be really effective in dealing with the recognition of specific features of such wines.

5   Conclusions

In this paper we have reported the results of a study exploiting classification for the authenticity assessment of some high-valued Italian wines. The problem has been addressed without expensive and hyper-specialized wine chemical analyses, and by learning and suitably evaluating different standard classifiers on the resulting chemical profiles. The proposed approach can be regarded as an instance of the 3-phases Wagstaff's scheme based on three fundamental steps [19]: *Necessary Preparation* has involved the definition of the analyses for data collection and preparation, *Machine Learning Contribution* has regarded the selection of a supervised strategy and of a suitable set of classifiers, while *Impact* has concerned the evaluation of the classification results with respect to the study's objectives.

The main weak point of the study has been the limited number of available samples; however, if compared with similar studies, the sample size used in the work is definitely adequate and larger than the usual ones (see e.g., [5, 12]). To partially overcome this limitation, we also tested the classification models by using a synthetic dataset; we started from real data and learned some generative models in the family of Linear Gaussian Bayesian Networks, then we automatically generated from these models some extended artificial datasets.

Concerning related works, several papers are reported in literature, focused on different analytical targets and techniques, where however the complexity of the data analytic task is often proportional to the complexity of the chemical or sensory analyses. Moreover, employed techniques cover essentially all the possible classification or discriminant analysis methods, showing that no "silver bullet" is available in general [2, 18]. Similarly, also in our study there is no clear "winner" among all the proposed classifiers, across the tested datasets; however, a general conclusion can be drawn by stating that state-of-the-art classifiers like Bayesian Networks, Multi-Layer Perceptrons and Support Vector Machines emerge as very promising in this context, both for detecting wrong or illicit blends (not necessarily of low quality, but not compliant with regulations as in the case of LAN and BLE), as well as for avoiding incorrect introductions of unrelated cultivars (as in the case of NON). This suggests that supervised machine learning techniques can be suitably proposed to address the wine quality control issue, even without resorting to complex (and expensive) procedures to generate the needed datasets. Future works will focus on exploiting ensamble learning techniques, and in particular *stacking* [4], in order to evaluate their impact on this specific application.

Acknowledgments. The present work has been funded by Regione Piemonte (POR-FESR grants), as a part of the TRAQUASwine project. We would like to thank M. Arlorio, J.D. Coïsson, M. Locatelli and F. Travaglia for their collaboration.

References

1. Arlorio, M., Coisson, J., Leonardi, G., Locatelli, M., Portinale, L.: Exploiting data mining for authenticity assessment and protection of high-quality Italian wines from Piedmont. In: Proceedings of 21th ACM SIGKDD International Conference on Knowledge Discovery and Data Mining (KDD 2015), pp. 1671–1680. AUS, Sydney (2015)

2. Arvanitoyannis, I., Katsota, M., Psarra, E., Soufleros, E., Kallithraka, S.: Application of quality control methods for assessing wine authenticity: use of multivariate analysis (chemometrics). Trends Food Sci. Technol. **10**, 321–336 (1999)
3. Cooper, G., Herskovits, E.: A Bayesian method for the induction of probabilistic networks from data. Mach. Learn. **9**(4), 309–347 (1992)
4. Džeroski, S., Ženko, B.: Is combining classifiers with stacking better than selecting the best one? Mach. Learn. **54**(3), 255–273 (2004)
5. Gòmez-Meire, S., Campos, C., Falqué, E., Dìaz, F., Fdez-Riverola, F.: Assuring the authenticity of northwest Spain white wine varieties using machine learning techniques. Food Res. Int. **60**, 230–240 (2014)
6. Grzegorczyk, M.: An introduction to Gaussian Bayesian networks. In: Yan, Q. (ed.) Systems Biology in Drug Discovery and Development, vol. 662, pp. 121–147. Springer, Heidelberg (2010). https://doi.org/10.1007/978-1-60761-800-3_6
7. Halkidi, M., Batistakis, Y., Varzirgannis, M.: Cluster validity methods: Part 1. ACM SIGMOD Record **31**(2), 40–45 (2002)
8. Hall, M., Frank, E., Holmes, G., Pfahringer, B., Reutemann, P., Witten, I.: The WEKA data mining software: an update. SIGKDD Explor. **11**(1), 10–18 (2009)
9. Hall, M.A.: Correlation-based feature subset selection for machine learning. Ph.D. thesis, University of Waikato, Hamilton, New Zealand (1998)
10. Holmberg, L.: Wine fraud. Int. J. Wine Res. **2010**(2), 105–113 (2010)
11. Locatelli, M., Travaglia, F., Coïsson, J., Bordiga, M., Arlorio, M.: Phenolic composition of Nebbiolo grape (Vitis vinifera L.) from Piedmont: characterization during ripening of grapes selected in different geographic areas and comparison with Uva Rara and Vespolina. Eur. Food Res. Technol. **242**, 1057–1068 (2016)
12. Marini, F., Bucci, R., Magr, A., Magr, A.: Authentication of Italian CDO wines by class-modeling techniques. Chemom. Intell. Lab. Syst. **84**(1), 164–171 (2006)
13. Mattera, D., Haykin, S.: Support vector machines for dynamic reconstruction of a chaotic system. In: Schölkopf, B., Burges, C., Smola, A. (eds.) Advances in Kernel Methods, pp. 211–241. MIT Press, Cambridge (1999)
14. Platt, J.: Fast training of support vector machines using sequential minimal optimization. In: Schölkopf, B., Burges, C., Smola, A. (eds.) Advances in Kernel Methods, pp. 185–208. MIT Press, Cambridge (1999)
15. Platt, J.: Probability for SV machines. In: Smola, A., Batlett, P., Schölkopf, B., Schuurmans, D. (eds.) Advances in Large Margin Classifiers, pp. 61–74. MIT Press, Cambridge (2000)
16. Spirtes, P., Glymour, C., Scheines, R.: Causation, Prediction and Search. Springer, Berlin (1993). https://doi.org/10.1007/978-1-4612-2748-9
17. Üstün, B., Melssen, W., Buydens, L.: Facilitating the application of support vector regression by using a universal Pearson VII function based kernel. Chemom. Intell. Lab. Syst. **81**, 29–40 (2006)
18. Versari, A., Laurie, V., Ricci, A., Laghi, L., Parpinello, G.: Progress in authentication, typification and traceability of grapes and wines by chemometric approaches. Food Res. Int. **60**, 2–18 (2014)
19. Wagstaff, K.: Machine learning that matters. In: Proceedings of the 29th International Conference on Machine Learning (ICML 2012), Edinburgh, UK (2012)

Collision Avoidance Dynamics Among Heterogeneous Agents: The Case of Pedestrian/Vehicle Interactions

Stefania Bandini[1,2], Luca Crociani[1(✉)], Claudio Feliciani[2], Andrea Gorrini[1], and Giuseppe Vizzari[1]

[1] CSAI Research Center, Università degli studi di Milano - Bicocca, Milan, Italy
luca.crociani@unimib.it
[2] RCAST, The University of Tokyo, Tokyo, Japan

Abstract. The dynamics of agent-based models and systems provides a framework to face complex issues related to the management of future cities, such as transportation and mobility. Once validated against empirical data, the use of agent-based simulations allows to envision and analyse complex phenomena, not directly accessible from the real world, in a predictive and explanatory scheme. In this paper, we apply this paradigm by proposing an agent-based simulation system focused on pedestrian/vehicle interactions at non-signalized intersections. The model has been designed based on the results gathered by means of an observation, executed at a non-signalized intersection characterized by a relevant number of pedestrian-car accidents in the past years. Manual video-tracking analyses showed that the interactions between pedestrians and vehicles at the zebra cross are generally composed of three phases: (i) the pedestrian freely walks on the side-walk *approaching* the zebra; (ii) at the proximity of the curb, he/she slows down to evaluate the safety gap from approaching cars to cross, possibly yielding to let the car pass (*appraising*); (iii) the pedestrian starts *crossing*. The overall heterogeneous system is composed of two types of agents (i.e. *vehicle* and *pedestrian* agents), defining the subjects of the interactions under investigation. The system is used to reproduce the observed traffic conditions and analyse the potential effects of overloading the system on comfort and safety of road users.

Keywords: Agent-based modelling · Simulation · Collision avoidance

1 Introduction

The *"Global Status Report on Road Safety"* by WHO [18] showed that road accidents represent the eighth leading cause of death in the world population: 1.25 million people are killed on roads every year. Pedestrians are some of the most vulnerable road users: the percentage of pedestrian fatalities corresponds

© Springer International Publishing AG 2017
F. Esposito et al. (Eds.): AI*IA 2017, LNAI 10640, pp. 44–57, 2017.
https://doi.org/10.1007/978-3-319-70169-1_4

to 36% of the overall traffic victims in Japan, 23% in the United Kingdom, 16% in Italy and 14% in USA.

To effectively contrast the social cost of traffic accidents it is necessary to make transportation infrastructures safer, but also to design traffic policies able to integrate theoretical knowledge and analytical data within an evidenced-based approach [15]. In this framework, the effort from academic research can support the development of advanced traffic management strategies and design solutions, to enhance the safety of transportation infrastructures and to prevent the occurrence of road fatalities. From a methodological point of view this represents a challenging field of study which requires a cross-disciplinary knowledge (e.g., traffic engineering, traffic psychology, safety science, computer science).

In this context, computer-based systems for the simulation of vehicular or pedestrian traffic have been increasingly reported in the technical and scientific specialized literature, as a support to the activity of engineers and planners in the design of efficient and safe transportation networks. In particular, scientific communities started to incorporate agent-based systems to improve the expressiveness of traditional modelling approaches and to simulate the complex behaviour of traffic dynamics in urban scenarios.

The intrinsically dynamical properties of agent-based models offer indeed a research framework to face the complexity of the future cities [14], offering new possibilities to incorporate and integrate the growing presence of autonomous entities/artefacts both physical (e.g. autonomous vehicles) and virtual (e.g. data coming from heterogeneous sources: social media, distributed sensors etc.).

The development of plausible agent-based systems requires to test the quality of the obtained simulation results against real data [4]. Once validated, the use of simulations can support the activities of decision makers thanks to the possibility to test in advance the effects of different traffic management solutions in a predictive and explanatory scheme. In line with this general approach, the aim of this paper is to present a real case of data collection performed to: (i) collect empirical results about pedestrian-vehicles interactions at non-signalized intersections; (ii) support the development of a heterogeneous agent-based system to simulate the phenomenon.

From pioneering works, several models have been developed and applied for the simulation of pedestrian and vehicular dynamics, including both cellular automata and differential equations based models [8]. These two approaches have, separately and independently, produced a significant impact; efforts proposing instead an integrated model considering the simultaneous presence of vehicles and pedestrians are not as frequent or advanced. With the notable exception of [13], most efforts in this direction are relatively simplistic, narrow (i.e. targeting extremely specific situations [19]), homogeneous for the simulated entities, and they are often not validated against real data [11].

In this paper we present a novel simulation model that allows simulating pedestrian/vehicle interactions at non-signalized intersections. The model has been designed according to the results of a video-recorded observation, which focus on: (i) the level of compliance of drivers to traffic norms (yielding crossing pedestrians); (*ii*) pedestrians' behaviour while deciding to cross (speeds and safety gap evaluation). Thus, the model is based on the overall observed *collision avoidance* dynamics, in the context of interactions among heterogeneous agents and its implications on self-organization dynamics. In particular, we focus on the effects of a variation of the traffic conditions, described in terms of both incoming vehicles and pedestrians, on the performances of the crossing.

2   Data Collection

The video-recorded observation [12] was performed on May 18, 2015 (from 10:45 am, 73 min in total), at a non-signalized intersection in Milan (Italy). The intersection has been selected by means of a preliminary analysis related to the localisation of road traffic accidents. Results showed that this area is characterised by a high number of pedestrian/car accidents in the past years. The observation was performed during the peak hour of the open-air local market which is held every Monday. Weather conditions during the observation were stable and sunny.

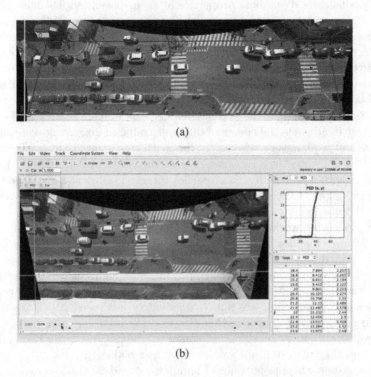

(a)

(b)

Fig. 1. A video frame of the observed zebra crossing with an example trajectory (a). A screen shot from the tracker tool used for data analysis (b).

A first phase of data analysis consisted of manual counting activities to quantify the bidirectional flows of vehicles (1379 vehicles, 18.89 vehicles per minute, 67% cars) and pedestrians (585 pedestrians, 8.01 pedestrians per minute).

The level of performance of the cross-walk has been estimated according to the Level of Service criteria (LOS) [15], which describes the degree of comfort and safety afforded to drivers and pedestrians as they travel/walk through an intersection or roadway segment (see Table 1). The LOS have been estimated by time stamping: (i) the delay of vehicles (time for deceleration, queue, stopped delay, acceleration) due to vehicular and pedestrian traffic conditions; (ii) the delay of crossing pedestrians (waiting, start-up delay), due to drivers' non compliance to their right of way on zebra crossings. Results showed that both the average delay of vehicles (3.20 s/vehicle ± 2.73 sd[1]) and the average delay of pedestrians (1.29 s/pedestrian ± 0.21 sd) corresponded to LOS A.

Table 1. Level of service criteria for two-way stop-controlled unsignalized intersections [15].

LOS	Description	Vehicular Delay [s/veh]	Pedestrian Delay [s/ped]
A	- Nearly all drivers find freedom of operation - Very small delay, none crossing irregularly	< 5	< 10
B	- Occasionally there is more than one vehicle in queue - Small delay, almost no one cross irregularly	5 - 10	10 - 15
C	- Many times there is more than one vehicle in queue - Small delay, very few pedestrian crossing irregularity	10 - 20	15 - 25
D	- Often there is more than one vehicle in queue - Big delay, someone start crossing irregularly	20 - 30	25 - 35
E	- Drivers find the delays approaching intolerable levels - Very big delay, many pedestrians crossing irregularity	30 - 45	35 - 50
F	- Forced flow due external operational constraints - Pedestrian cross irregularly, engaging risk-taking behaviours	> 45	> 50

Then, a sample of 812 crossing episodes was selected from the video in order to assess the compliance of drivers to pedestrians' right of way at non-signalized intersection (see Table 2). The crossing episodes have been selected considering only cases in which one vehicle directly interacted with one or more pedestrians at the side-walk. Moreover, the position of pedestrians is described with reference to the direction of vehicles (either near or far side-walk).

Table 2. Results about the drivers' compliance to the right-of-way of crossing pedestrians.

Type of pedestrian/vehicle interactions	Compliant	Non-compliant
Ped. approaching/waiting/crossing from the near side-walk	191 (46.14%)	223 (53.86%)
Ped. approaching/waiting/crossing from the far side-walk	230 (57.69%)	168 (42.21%)

---

[1] Standard deviation.

Results showed that 48% of the total number of crossing episodes was characterized by non-compliant drivers with crossing pedestrians from the two side-walks. A multiple linear regression[2] was calculated to predict the percentage of non-compliant drivers per minute based on: (i) number of vehicles per minute (18.89 veh/min in average; p = 0.007, significant predictor) and (ii) number of crossing pedestrian per minute (8.01 ped/min in average; p < 0.001, significant predictor). A significant regression equation was found, but only 30% of the values fits the model with $R^2 = .293$ [F(2,70) = 14.526, p < .001].

According to the results presented by [16], the results of the observation show that the non-compliance of drivers is determined by traffic conditions and by pedestrian flows on zebra. Despite the low level of drivers' compliance, no accidents or risky situations have been observed, thanks to the self-organization of the system based on pedestrians' yielding/collaborative behaviour to approaching cars and the observed high level of performance of the cross-walk (LOS A).

A second phase of video tracking data analysis was executed by using the software *Video Analysis and Modelling Tool*[3] (see Fig. 1), which allowed to manually track a sample of 50 pedestrians and 79 vehicles[4]. The data set (including the X, Y coordinates and the associated frames t) was exported for data analysis, aiming at measuring the speeds of vehicles and pedestrians while interacting at the zebra crossing and the safety gap accepted by pedestrians to cross.

Pedestrian speeds have been analysed among the time series of video frames (trend analysis), as characterised by: (i) a stable trend on side-walks, (ii) a significant deceleration in proximity of the cross-walk (decision making) and (iii) an acceleration on the zebra crossing. According to results, crossing behaviour is defined as composed of three distinctive phases (see Fig. 2):

(a) Approaching: the pedestrian travels on the side-walk with a stable speed (Speed MA - CA $\simeq$ 0);

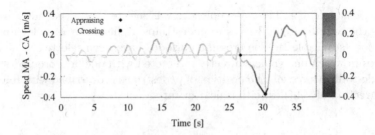

Fig. 2. An exemplification of the trend analysis performed on the time series of speeds.

---

[2] All statistics have been conducted at the p < .01 level.

[3] See www.cabrillo.edu.

[4] The sample was selected avoiding situations such as: platooning of vehicles on the roadway inhibiting a crossing episode, the joining of pedestrians already crossing, and in general situations influencing the direct interaction between the pedestrian and the drivers.

(b) Appraising: the pedestrian approaching the cross-walk decelerates to evaluate the distance and speed of oncoming vehicles (safety gap). We decided to consider that this phase starts with the first value of a long-term deceleration trend (Speed MA - CA < 0);

(c) Crossing: the pedestrian decides to cross and speed up. The crossing phase starts from the frame after the one with the lowest value of speed before a long-term acceleration trend (Speed min).

An analysis of variance (ANOVA) showed a significant difference among the speeds of pedestrians while approaching (1.28 m/s ± 0.18 sd), appraising (0.94 m/s ± 0.21 sd) and crossing (1.35 m/s ± 0.18 sd) $[F(2,144) = 61.944, p < 0.000]$.

The term *safety gap* denotes the ratio between the pedestrians's evaluation of the distance of an approaching vehicle and its average speed (not taking into account acceleration/deceleration trends). The average safety gap accepted by pedestrians corresponds to 4.20 s ± 2.24 sd (average distance of vehicle = 16.83 ± 8.71 sd; average speed of vehicles = 15.93 hm/h ± 7.02 sd). Although pedestrians have the right of way on zebra-striped, 30% of them gave way to at least one approaching vehicle. This result suggested that pedestrians were able to regulate their behaviour, by taking into account their own crossing capacities (walking speed), but also the breaking distance needed by vehicles to stop and the lack of compliance of drivers to traffic norms.

3   Simulation Model

The model presented here extends the work proposed in [7]; for sake of space, we will provide a brief description of its core components, supporting the evaluation of results presented in the next section. For a complete and thorough discussion, we refer to [9]. The model supports the simulation of non-signalized pedestrian crossing by means of heterogeneous agents, namely pedestrians and vehicles. The two types are hosted in different environments, which grant an effective reproduction of the two different but coupled dynamics considered in the simulation.

3.1   The Multi-layered Environment

The overall environment is schematised in Fig. 3(a). Lanes of the road are represented as 1-dimensional continuous edges where car-agents can move only in one direction. The position of a car-agent is described as a point in the edge and there is no real space occupation for them: the physics of the system is ensured by means of the equations that rule their behaviour. Moreover, in order to achieve the results presented in Sect. 4 each edge is defined as toroidal, thus periodic boundary conditions are guaranteed by moving the agent to the beginning of the road once it arrives at its other extreme.

The dynamics of pedestrians is simulated with a rectangular grid of square cells whose side is assumed to be 40 cm, to describe the space occupation of

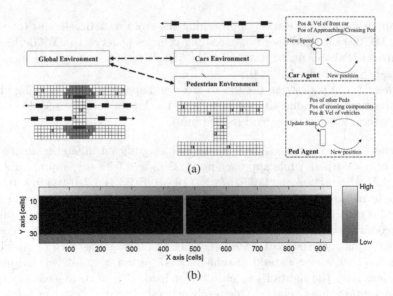

(a)

(b)

Fig. 3. (a) Schematic representation of the environments and agents. (b) Example of a floor field spread in the simulated scenario of the crossing.

pedestrians [17]. Each cell can be occupied by at most one pedestrian-agent, allowing thus to reproduce the range of local densities generally observable. Cells inside the area describing the road lanes are not walkable, while the crossing is represented by cells that are walkable in case of non signalized crossing or while the traffic light is green or yellow[5].

Pedestrian-agents are moving towards their objective by means of discrete potentials called *floor fields* [3]. Each potential is spread from a set of cells describing a target in the environment. The particular scenario of the crossing is designed by means of four origin-destination areas at the corners of the rectangular environment (Fig. 3 shows the bottom-left one), and two intermediate destinations delimiting the extremes of the cross-walk.

Since the dynamics of pedestrians and vehicles influence each other, the different environments are connected by means of a global environment supporting a mutual perception among pedestrians and vehicles. Rules managing the coupled dynamics will be described in the following subsections.

3.2   The Behaviour of Car-Agents

The motion of cars is based on the car-following model by Gipps [10], in which the speed of each vehicle is updated considering, firstly, internal parameters of the agent: (i) maximum acceleration a for each time-step of the simulation;

---

[5] In this particular work we will not show results related to the presence of a traffic light, but the proposed model aims at allowing a general simulation of pedestrian crossing.

(ii) maximum breaking capabilities b; (iii) speed limit of the road v_{max}. The presence of a vehicle ahead of the updating one affects its next speed according to a safe speed v_{safe}. v_{safe} is calculated based on the distance between the two vehicles and their breaking capabilities. In this way, possible collisions between cars are simply avoided in this model since they are not subject of investigation. The update rule of the speed $v_{c_i}(t)$, for a car-agent c_i at time-step t, is then calculated with Eqs. 1, 2 and 3:

$$v_{c_i}(t+1) = \min(v_0, v_1) + |v_0 - v_1| \cdot r \tag{1}$$

$$v_0 = v_1 - \varepsilon\,(v_1 - (v_{c_i}(t) - a)) \tag{2}$$

$$v_1 = \min\left[v_{c_i}(t) + a, v_{max}, v_{safe}\right] \tag{3}$$

where $r \in [0,1]$ is a random number and ε is an additional parameter of the model typically set to 0.4. v_{safe} is calculated according to the Eqs. 4, 5 and 6:

$$v_{safe} = b\,(\alpha_{safe} + \beta_{safe}) \tag{4}$$

$$\alpha_{safe} = \left[\sqrt{2\frac{d_p + g}{b} + \frac{1}{4}} - \frac{1}{2}\right] \tag{5}$$

$$\beta_{safe} = \frac{d_p + g}{(\alpha_{safe} + 1)b} - \frac{\alpha_{safe}}{2} \tag{6}$$

Here b is the maximum deceleration of the car, g is the distance between the car ahead and d_p is the minimum breaking distance $d_p = b\left(\alpha_p\beta_p + \frac{\alpha_p(\alpha_p-1)}{2}\right)$. α_p and β_p are respectively the integer and decimal part of the ratio v_{c_i}/b, which is the number of time-steps required to arrive at a zero speed. This original model by Gipps reliably simulates the physics of vehicular traffic by assuming the duration of a time-step of 1 s. The time window described by the time-step, in fact, represents the time needed by one event to be perceived by the other agents, thus in this case it implements the *reaction time* of car drivers to a variation of the speed of an ahead car, or to the arrival of a crossing pedestrian. By configuring a higher time resolution, that would be plausible for a situation involving pedestrians, this set of rules of the model would generate unrealistic reaction times of drivers, and the physics of the system would no longer be plausible in terms of flows of vehicles in the congested state. To solve this problem, we extended the baseline model with a gap $\hat{g}$ dependent on the assumed reaction time of the agent $t_{reaction}$ and the distance $t_{reaction} \cdot v_{car}$ that it would cover during this time: $\hat{g} = g - t_{reaction} \cdot v_{car}$.

For the simulation presented in the results section, we assumed a duration of the time-step of 0.1 s and a reaction time assigned with a normal distribution with $\mu = 1.1$ s and $\sigma = 0.2$ s, which provides data about the density–flow relation for vehicular traffic in accordance with observations from literature.

Summarizing, car-agents simply accelerate until v_{max} if the road is free; otherwise they adjust their speed to v_{safe} in order to be always able to stop if the vehicle ahead c', moving at speed $v_{c'}$, starts breaking.

The rule defined in Eq. 4 is suitable and it is used also to manage interactions with crossing or approaching pedestrians. The latter are simply considered as obstacles, just as the preceding vehicles: this choice allows employing the same rules managing the braking to avoid car accidents also to prevent accidents with crossing pedestrians.

The overall algorithm that defines the behaviour of car drivers is shown in Fig. 4. Firstly, the agent selects the closest agent ahead and, if any, checks for its type. If it is a car-agent, then the speed is updated as discussed above. If the agent is a pedestrian and is already crossing, then v_{safe} is calculated in order to let the car stop in correspondence of the zebra cross. Given the rules of the interaction also on the pedestrian-agent side, in this case the car-agent will always be able to stop before the crossing. On the other hand, if the pedestrian is approaching or waiting to cross the street, the car-agent will yield to the pedestrian if both there is enough space, according to its current speed, and the car-agent chooses to be *compliant*. For this particular work, the compliance of drivers has been simply modelled in a static way by further differentiating the agent type: car-agents are configured as either *compliant* or not at their generation and they will keep this behaviour for all the simulation run. The probability of generating a compliant car-agent is then assigned to 0.5, in accordance to the observation.

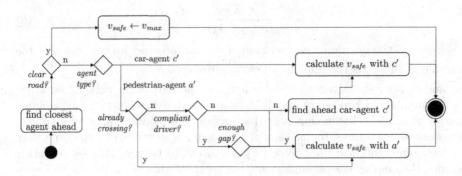

Fig. 4. The decision algorithm of car drivers.

3.3   The Behaviour of Pedestrian-Agents

When activated, pedestrian agents can move in the 8 cells surrounding their position in the grid (i.e. Moore neighbourhood). By considering the assumed side of cells and the time-step duration of the car model, the instantaneous speed of the agent is computable as $0.4/0.1 = 4.0$ m/s, which is rather high for pedestrian walking. A different time-step duration of 0.3 s is then assumed to simulate the pedestrian motion, in order to get a maximum speed of pedestrians of about 1.3 m/s.

To simulate the three phases of behaviour described in Sect. 2, among which a significant difference in the speed of pedestrians is observed, the activation of pedestrian-agents for movement at the beginning of the time-step is managed in a probabilistic fashion, similar to [2]. In particular, the probability to be activated for movement is given by $\psi = \nu_d/\nu_m$, where ν_d is the *desired speed* of the agent and ν_m is the *maximum speed* assumed for the simulation, calculated as explained above. By configuring ν_d and also varying it during the simulation, it is therefore possible to configure differences in pedestrian type (age, gender, etc.), as well as in the phases of behaviour while crossing: when a pedestrian-agent arrives at a certain distance from the zebra, it switches to the appraising phase and it decelerates until it either reaches the curb or it evaluates the crossing to be safe. The algorithm for the movement of pedestrian-agents is then shown in Fig. 5(a).

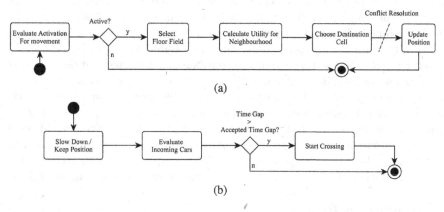

Fig. 5. Algorithms to manage the movement (a) and appraising phase (b) of pedestrian-agents.

The choice of movement is made in a probabilistic way and dependent on a simple utility function similar to the original floor field model [3], computed for cells of the neighbourhood. The function takes into account values of the floor field, possible occupation of cells by other agents and not walkable cells, and it drives pedestrian-agents towards their targets avoiding overlapping with others. In addition, possible conflicts arising from multiple choices of the same destination cell are managed with a random extraction[6] of a winner which will be allowed to move, while the others will keep their positions until their next activation.

A more detailed representation of the pedestrian behaviour by considering proxemics and groups as in [1] has not been considered given the free-flow conditions of the pedestrian environment in the simulated scenario and the focus on the interactions with vehicles. Such level of detail will be necessary for future works, aimed at integrating the proposed model in a multi-scale one able to

---

[6] With equal probabilities among the agents involved.

simulate and optimize microscopic pedestrian and vehicular traffic in urban areas [5,6].

In order to trigger a specific behaviour for the appraising phase, we exploited the intrinsic nature of the floor field generated by the curb close to the zebra crossing: since it indicates the distance from the cells generating it, its low value will trigger a specific set of actions to decide about crossing timing. In particular, when the pedestrian agent perceives the arrival at the curb, it will activate an evaluation summarized in Fig. 5(b). The algorithm is rather simple but it is based on the features recognized with the field-observation previously presented. It is founded on the concept of *time gap*, which describes the time needed by the incoming car-agent c_i to reach the pedestrian-agent position, considering the current speed v_{c_i}. Results of the observation showed that there was no significant difference between the average time gap accepted by appraising pedestrians regarding their age, or regarding the lane of the incoming vehicles (near or far one). As empirically identified, thus, the *accepted time gap* for all pedestrian agents in the simulation has been normally distributed with $\mu = 4\,$s and $\sigma = 2\,$s. In the negative case, the pedestrian will continue slowing down–if it did not reach the curb yet– or keep its position, until either the car starts breaking to yield at the crossing or one of the following cars allows a higher time gap. Note that the compliance of car-agents does not necessarily lead to the crossing of pedestrian-agents and vice-versa: the time gap could be accepted by pedestrian-agents even if the behaviour of the car-agent is set as non-compliant. This particular situation will not lead to a collision since the non-compliant car will start to slow down as well when it will perceive the pedestrian as already crossing (see Fig. 4).

4   Simulation Results

The traditional way to evaluate the plausibility of models in the transportation area includes the generation of the so called fundamental diagram, i.e. a graph depicting the relationship between velocity or flow and the density in the simulated environment. In this context, we need to consider the impact of both vehicles and pedestrians: we chose to vary the vehicular density in a fine grained way and to consider just four situations associated to different pedestrian crossing ratios, respectively (i) no pedestrians, (ii) 2 pedestrians per minute, (iii) 5.52 pedestrians per minute (the arrival rate empirically observed) and (iv) 10 pedestrians per minute. For each value of vehicular density and pedestrian arriving flow, a set of 20 simulations iterations are run to analyse the variability of results. The simulated area is relatively short (around 400 m), but covers a longer space than the observed one and this is configured to accommodate buffer zones before and after the crossing and therefore to allow the generation of different plausible vehicular densities. The speed limit was set to 35 km/h, based on the empirically observed velocities: despite the speed limit of 50 km/h, drivers were not able to approach this velocity due to environmental factors not considered in the simulation, such as other road intersections roughly 150 m before and after the modelled crossing. We also considered a share of non-compliant drivers analogous to the observed one, that is, about 50%.

Figure 6(a) and (b) respectively show the trend of vehicular speed and flow according to vehicular density and pedestrian arrival rate. The baseline result (i.e. no pedestrians) is in line with results generally observed in urban roads, both in terms of speeds and overall flow; as expected, higher pedestrian arrival rates reduce vehicular speed and, consequently, flow.

Figure 6(c) and (d) describe the results of the model in terms of average waiting times (one point in each picture denotes the average result for the whole simulation iteration) respectively for vehicles and pedestrians. This outcome highlights the *levels of service* of the crossing, for either pedestrians and vehicles, resulting from the simulation of each configured scenario. Both diagrams shows a monotonic growing trend of vehicle and pedestrian waiting time at the increase of the density of vehicles in the scenario. Moreover, a growth in the flow of pedestrians leads to a decrease of the level of service of the crossing for

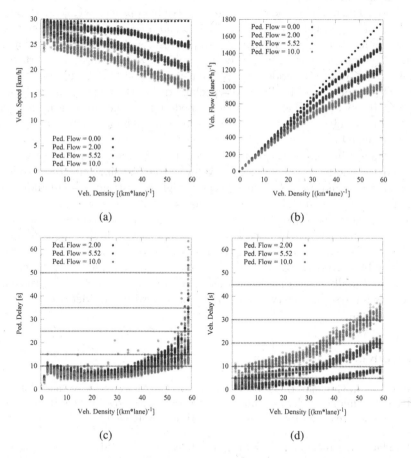

Fig. 6. On the top, fundamental diagrams in the form density–speed (a) and density–flow (b) of vehicular traffic in the investigate scenarios. On the bottom, waiting times of pedestrians (c) and vehicles (d) in relation with the density of vehicles in the simulated scenario (static grey lines marks the transitions between levels of service).

vehicles (Fig. 6(d)); at the same time, the average pedestrian delay is actually lower and with a smoother growth compared to low pedestrian density situations (Fig. 6(c)). The explanation of this phenomenon is due to the fact that pedestrian platooning in the crossing is more probable and, moreover, since it increases the probability that a pedestrian arrives at the curb in a favourable moment (i.e. with an acceptable time gap due to slow or stopped nearby vehicles, or due to very far approaching vehicles), leading vehicles to stop irrespectively of their non-compliant behaviour.

5   Conclusions

The present paper has introduced a model for the simulation of non signalized road crossings in which pedestrian and vehicular traffic meet and require a direct interaction. The model is based on already existing approaches extended to grant the different actors the possibility to interact and coordinate their behaviours. The model has been defined according to the results of an observation that also produced empirical data that has been employed to calibrate and perform an initial validation of the model in a reference scenario. The model improves the results of previous works in this area especially due to the fact that an empirically observed behavioural phase for crossing pedestrians (i.e. appraisal) has been specifically considered and also since non-compliant behaviours by vehicle drivers is now admitted.

Results are in tune with plausible levels of service for this kind of intersection and the model can be used to evaluate the plausible effects of different non-standard situations (e.g. exceptionally high pedestrian or vehicular densities). Future works are aimed, on one hand, at further analysing the model results to identify potential limits not visible in the presented experimentation: for instance, the growth in pedestrian delays in case of high vehicular density and low pedestrian demand seems excessive due to the lack of a cooperative behaviour by driver agents and to an overly careful behaviour by the crossing pedestrian. Finally, some ongoing works are already aimed at enriching the model in order to analyse the safety of crossings with regards to accidents between cars and pedestrians.

References

1. Bandini, S., Crociani, L., Gorrini, A., Vizzari, G.: An agent-based model of pedestrian dynamics considering groups: a real world case study. In: 17th IEEE International Conference on Intelligent Transportation Systems, ITSC 2014, pp. 572–577 (2014)
2. Bandini, S., Crociani, L., Vizzari, G.: Heterogeneous pedestrian walking speed in discrete simulation models. In: Chraibi, M., Boltes, M., Schadschneider, A., Seyfried, A. (eds.) Traffic and Granular Flow 2013, pp. 273–279. Springer International Publishing, Heidelberg (2015). doi:10.1007/978-3-319-10629-8_33

3. Burstedde, C., Klauck, K., Schadschneider, A., Zittartz, J.: Simulation of pedestrian dynamics using a two-dimensional cellular automaton. Phys. A: Stat. Mech. Appl. **295**(3–4), 507–525 (2001)
4. Campanella, M., Hoogendoorn, S., Daamen, W.: Quantitative and qualitative validation procedure for general use of pedestrian models. In: Weidmann, U., Kirsch, U., Schreckenberg, M. (eds.) Pedestrian and Evacuation Dynamics 2012, pp. 891–905. Springer, Heidelberg (2014). doi:10.1007/978-3-319-02447-9_74
5. Crociani, L., Lämmel, G., Park, H.J., Vizzari, G.: Cellular automaton based simulation of large pedestrian facilities–a case study on the staten island ferry terminals. In: Transportation Research Board 96th Annual Meeting, Washington DC, United States, pp. 17–05137 (2017)
6. Crociani, L., Lämmel, G., Vizzari, G.: Multi-scale simulation for crowd management: a case study in an urban scenario. In: Osman, N., Sierra, C. (eds.) AAMAS 2016. LNCS, vol. 10002, pp. 147–162. Springer, Cham (2016). doi:10.1007/978-3-319-46882-2_9
7. Crociani, L., Vizzari, G.: An integrated model for the simulation of pedestrian crossings. In: Wąs, J., Sirakoulis, G.C., Bandini, S. (eds.) ACRI 2014. LNCS, vol. 8751, pp. 670–679. Springer, Cham (2014). doi:10.1007/978-3-319-11520-7_71
8. Duives, D.C., Daamen, W., Hoogendoorn, S.P.: State-of-the-art crowd motion simulation models. Transp. Res. Part C: Emerg. Technol. **37**, 193–209 (2013)
9. Feliciani, C., Crociani, L., Gorrini, A., Vizzari, G., Bandini, S., Nishinari, K.: A simulation model for non-signalized pedestrian crosswalks based on evidence from on field observation. Intelligenza Artificiale (2017, in Press)
10. Gipps, P.: A behavioural car-following model for computer simulation (1981)
11. Godara, A., Lassarre, S., Banos, A.: Simulating pedestrian-vehicle interaction in an urban network using cellular automata and multi-agent models. In: Schadschneider, A., Pöschel, T., Kühne, R., Schreckenberg, M., Wolf, D.E. (eds.) Traffic and Granular Flow'05, pp. 411–418. Springer, Heidelberg (2007). doi:10.1007/978-3-540-47641-2_37
12. Gorrini, A., Vizzari, G., Bandini, S.: Towards modelling pedestrian-vehicle interactions: empirical study on urban unsignalized intersection. In: Proceedings of Pedestrian and Evacuation Dynamics 2016, pp. 25–33 (2016)
13. Helbing, D., Jiang, R., Treiber, M.: Analytical investigation of oscillations in intersecting flows of pedestrian and vehicle traffic. Phys. Rev. E **72**(4), 046130-1–046130-10 (2005)
14. Masthoff, J., Vasconcelos, W.W., Aitken, C., Correa da Silva, F.: Agent-based group modelling for ambient intelligence. In: AISB Symposium on Affective Smart Environments, Newcastle, UK (2007)
15. National Research Council, Washington, DC: Highway Capacity Manual (2010)
16. Varhelyi, A.: Drivers' speed behaviour at a zebra crossing: a case study. Accident Anal. Prevent. **30**(6), 731–743 (1998)
17. Weidmann, U.: Transporttechnik der Fussgänger - Transporttechnische Eigenschaftendes Fussgängerverkehrs (Literaturstudie). Literature Research 90, Institut füer Verkehrsplanung, Transporttechnik, Strassen und Eisenbahnbau IVT an der ETH Zürich (1993)
18. World Health Organization: Global status report on road safety 2015. WHO (2015)
19. Zeng, W., Chen, P., Nakamura, H., Iryo-Asano, M.: Application of social force model to pedestrian behavior analysis at signalized crosswalk. Transp. Res. Part C: Emerg. Technol. **40**, 143–159 (2014)

Smartphone Data Analysis for Human Activity Recognition

Federico Concone, Salvatore Gaglio, Giuseppe Lo Re, and Marco Morana[✉]

DIID, University of Palermo, Palermo, Italy
{federico.concone,salvatore.gaglio,giuseppe.lore,marco.morana}@unipa.it

Abstract. In recent years, the percentage of the population owning a smartphone has increased significantly. These devices provide the user with more and more functions, so that anyone is encouraged to carry one during the day, implicitly producing that can be analysed to infer knowledge of the user's context. In this work we present a novel framework for Human Activity Recognition (HAR) using smartphone data captured by means of embedded triaxial accelerometer and gyroscope sensors. Some statistics over the captured sensor data are computed to model each activity, then real-time classification is performed by means of an efficient supervised learning technique. The system we propose also adopts a participatory sensing paradigm where user's feedbacks on recognised activities are exploited to update the inner models of the system. Experimental results show the effectiveness of our solution as compared to other state-of-the-art techniques.

1 Introduction

Nowadays, smartphones have become an indispensable tool for everyday life, offering a number of features that go beyond the simple calling or messaging capabilities. In order to let the user perform different tasks, these mobile devices are equipped with many sensors that make them real sensing platforms able to extract relevant information. One of the most attractive scenario in which such information can be exploited is Human Activity Recognition (HAR), where data captured by motion sensors, e.g., accelerometer and gyroscope, can be analysed to infer user's current physical activity.

In this context, human activities can be intuitively considered as sequences of recurrent patterns in raw data captured from smartphone's sensors. Many HAR algorithms have been presented in the literature, however their application is frequently restricted to specific application scenarios, e.g., e-health, or their inner behaviour is unknown. For example, one of the most reliable HAR technique is that implemented in the Google APIs for Android, which unfortunately acts as a black-box not providing neither a way to understand what mechanisms are behind it, nor intermediate information to supervise the running of the recognition process.

In this paper we present a framework for real-time human activity recognition using smartphones. In particular, we address a participatory sensing scenario

© Springer International Publishing AG 2017
F. Esposito et al. (Eds.): AI*IA 2017, LNAI 10640, pp. 58–71, 2017.
https://doi.org/10.1007/978-3-319-70169-1_5

where users contribute to the proper functioning of the system by providing (i) their own data through a secure client-server architecture, and (ii) feedbacks on the correctness of the recognised activities.

Such information is exploited to maintain the inner models of the systems updated, so as to recognize even more instances of known activities performed by different users. The core of the HAR module consists in a state of the art machine learning technique, i.e., k-nearest neighbors (K-NN), which showed the best performances both in terms of algorithmic efficiency and recognition accuracy.

The remainder of the paper is organized as follows: related work is outlined in Sect. 2. The system architecture is described in Sect. 3, and the experimental results are shown and discussed in Sect. 4. Conclusions follow in Sect. 5.

2   Related Work

Most of the methods presented in the literature in the area of human activity recognition can be grouped in two main categories: vision and sensor-based.

The former can infer user's activity by analyzing video sequences [3] captured by a number of different devices. Early techniques were based on the extraction of the users' silhouettes from RGB images, however, the cost of image processing algorithms needed for cleaning noisy input data make these approaches usually unsuitable for real-time applications. More recently, the focus moved to unobtrusive devices capable of capturing both RGB and depth information, e.g., the Microsoft Kinect [21,24]. RGB-D data were proven to improve the recognition process allowing for real-time analysis of the observed scene [14]. Some applications have been proposed in the context of ambient intelligent systems aimed to recognize the user activities [11], e.g., for energy saving [10] purposes, or to improve the user experience [20] providing unobtrusive interfaces. Unfortunately, activity recognition through these sensors is quite limited to indoor environments.

Sensor-based HAR techniques analyze information from various sensors located in different parts of the human body. This approach overcomes the limitations of vision-based methods, but *wearable* sensors are reluctantly accepted by the users due to their intrusiveness [25]. Early experiments were performed using only one accelerometer to capture acceleration values on the three axes [28]. However, since a single sensor is not suitable to describe very complex activities, several studies have been presented merging information provided by multiple sensors [13,23]. For example, in [5] the system acquires data from five biaxial accelerometers, worn simultaneously on different parts of the body, to recognize both simple and complex activities. In [6] the use of wearable devices in a e-health scenario is presented. The authors of [4] describe a method to recognize *walking, sitting, standing*, and *running* activities by means of five accelerometers. Other studies tried to improve the performances of their recognition systems by relying on the combinations of heterogeneous sensors, e.g., accelerometers and gyroscopes, microphones, GPS, and so on [19,30].

Over the years, more and more works have focused on HAR using smartphone-based applications. This choice is mainly due to the widespread diffusion of smartphones which exhibited suitable characteristics, e.g., embedded sensors, easy portability of the device, network connectivity, and higher computing power.

In [12] the authors present an approach that combines machine learning and symbolic reasoning for improving the quality of life of diabetic patients. The whole system is based on the recognition of some activities using smartphone sensors in order to trace patients' fatigue and depression while performing the daily routines. The system described in [31] covers a mobile health scenario where neural networks, implemented on Android smartphones, are used to recognize five activities: *static*, *walking*, *running*, *upstairs*, and *downstairs*. The same scenario is addressed in [16], where a fall detection system using accelerometers and magnetometers is proposed. In particular, if a certain threshold value is exceeded, the method is able to recognize falls in four different directions: backward, forward, left and right. In [18], the authors describe an unsupervised learning approach to human activity recognition using smartphone sensors, even when the number of activities is unknown. However, the recognition process is strictly dependent on the number of clusters chosen during the design phase. Thus, distinct activities could be erroneously merged into one, or different instances of the same activity could be seen as unrelated. KAFKA [26] is a system analyzing real-time data collected by inertial sensors mounted on Android devices, i.e. smartphones and smartwatches.

An open framework designed to ease the development of Mobile CrowdSensing (MCS) systems is presented in [8,9]. Mobile Sensing Technology (MoST), available for Android-based devices, provides some activity recognition and geofencing algorithms optimised to meet computational and power constraints of smartphones. Activity recognition is performed by processing raw data captured by on-board sensors, and allows to distinguish between three kinds of activities: *walking*, *running*, and *phone still*. Geofencing aims to find and delimit the geographic area where a certain activity, or event, occurs. This is usually achieved by correlating motion data captured by heterogeneous sensors with geographic coordinates provided by GPS (Global Positioning System) or IPS (Indoor Positioning Systems). The latter can include a number of different algorithms and sensors, for this reason MoST architecture is modular, allowing developers to extend its functionalities by implementing new techniques or considering custom and virtual sensors.

Despite of the efforts made to design efficient frameworks, one of the best performing HAR solution is still that proposed by Google [1] since its API level-1. However, since such a tool is closed source, developers are not able to use intermediate results as part of their systems, nor to provide any feedback to the activity recognition routine.

3   Activity Recognition System

The architecture we propose here aims at automatically inferring the activity performed by the users, in a generic scenario, according to data collected through their smartphones. The system components can be logically divided in three parts (see Fig. 1). The first is responsible for *data collection*, that is for capturing raw data through the smartphone sensors while an activity is performed. The raw values are sent as input to the *features detection* module, where a set of n-dimensional points are extracted to distinguish different activities. Activities are classified using a machine learning algorithm, then user can provide feedbacks on the output of the recognition so as to allow the system to properly perform future classifications.

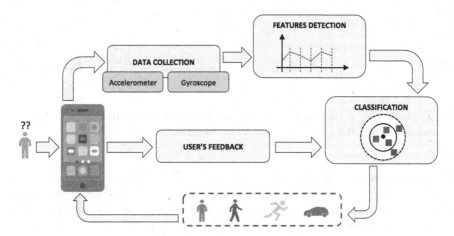

Fig. 1. System overview. The activities performed by the users are captured by means of the smartphone sensors. Collected data are analyzed to detect some relevant features, that are then used for classification. User's feedbacks on recognised activities are exploited to improve the classification process.

Data collection is performed by using the MoST open-source library, simply requiring that the user performs different activities while having its smartphone in the pants pocket. Differently from [18], our system does not take into account the gravity acceleration, allowing the user for holding the smartphone without worrying about its orientation.

In order to understand how the activity patterns change according to accelerometer and gyroscope readings, Fig. 2 shows values of three-axes acceleration (top row) and angular velocity (bottom row) captured while performing *still*, *walking*, *running*, and *vehicle* activities respectively.

As regards the acceleration values, even though these four activities look somehow different from each other, some of them, i.e., *still* and *vehicle* share a similar pattern, whilst others, i.e., *walking* and *running* are characterized by

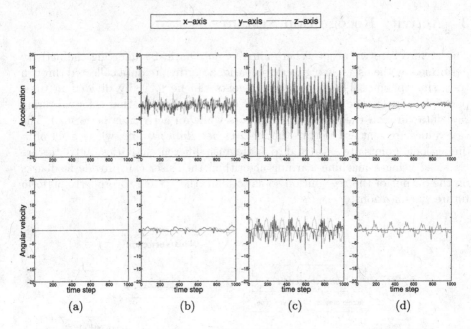

Fig. 2. Three-axes acceleration (top row) and angular velocity (bottom row) for *still* (a), *walking* (b), *running* (c), and *vehicle* (d) activities.

high noise as they are intrinsically associated with a significant user movement. On the contrary, by analyzing the values of angular velocity we noticed that *still* and *vehicle* exhibit distinct patterns, whilst other activities are generally characterized by oscillations of different width and frequency. For this reason we combined data from the two sensors, so as to get the best from both sides.

To ensure real-time activity recognition, the system must be able to process input data within certain time windows in order to extract the features that will be used in the next classification stage. The entire process of feature extraction is shown in Fig. 3.

We define an activity a as the user behaviour observed from initial time t_i to final time t_f. Given that the duration, in seconds, of the activity a_j is denoted by d_j, data captured within this interval is processed into fixed-length windows of $m \times n$ samples, where m is the number of axes along which measurements are performed. In particular, the activity recognition process is based on (X_A, Y_A, Z_A) values provided by the accelerometer, and (X_G, Y_G, Z_G) values from the gyroscope.

Choosing the proper length for the acquisition window is essential because of the impact it could have on the whole system. Short windows may improve system performance in terms of execution time and CPU load, but may not contain enough information to properly capture the characteristics of the activity. Vice versa, long windows may alter the system performances since information about multiple activities performed in sequence might be analyzed within a sin-

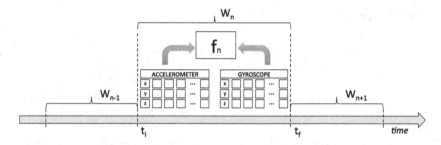

Fig. 3. Feature extraction mechanism. Accelerometer and gyroscope data are processed within the n-th fixed-length time window W_n, in order to obtain the corresponding feature vector f_n.

gle window. Experimental results using windows of different length, suggested us to use fixed-width windows of 3 seconds with no overlap.

In order to obtain a compact representation of input data, feature vectors are built similar to [8] by considering (i) *max value*, (ii) *min value*, (iii) *mean*, (iv) *standard deviation*, and (v) *root mean square* over the three accelerometer and gyroscope axes. Therefore, each feature vector f contains 30 elements, i.e., 15 values of acceleration and 15 values of angular velocity.

The classification process is based on the k-nearest neighbors (K-NN) technique. Given the set of feature vectors $(f_1, f_2, \cdots, f_m)$, the key principle behind K-NN is that an unknown feature point f, projected into a *large* training set of labeled data, would be ideally surrounded by samples of its same class. If this happens, the algorithm could assign to f the same class of its closest neighbor, i.e., the closest point in the feature space. More generally, the set S containing the k closest neighbors of f is selected and the most recurrent class in S is assigned to f.

As mentioned earlier, our system adopts a participatory sensing paradigm [7], which aims at exploiting information provided by a community of users to improve the system performances. To this end, a client/server architecture has been designed, allowing each user to (i) share its own data captured by the smartphone, and (ii) use the same device to leave feedbacks about the recognition process, indicating, every time an activity has been recognized, whether the output class is correct or not. Data sent by the client are analyzed within the server to determine if the models of the different activities need to be updated. In particular, the feature vector f_{new} received from the client is projected into the current feature space, together with the class declared by the user. Then, f_{new} is compared with existing data from the same class, and if they are similar above a certain threshold, the activity models are re-computed and sent back to the client for future classifications.

4   Experiments

In order to evaluate the effectiveness of our framework, several experiments were performed. First, we present a comparison between the results obtained while using the K-NN method, and a classifier based on K-means clustering. Then, the overall performances of the HAR system we propose are compared with two state of the art techniques, i.e., the activity recognition tools provided by MosT and Google.

The experiments were carried out using five different models of smartphones, as summarized in Table 1, equipped with built-in accelerometer and gyroscope sensors. Our application can be installed on any Android device with Ice Cream Sandwich OS or higher.

Table 1. Smartphone models used for the experiments.

Model	CPU	RAM
Galaxy S7 Edge	8 Core 2 GHZ	4 GB
Galaxy S5 Neo	8 Core 1.6 GHZ	2 GB
Galaxy S4	4 Core 1.9 GHZ	2 GB
Galaxy S2 NFC	2 Core 1.2 GHZ	1 GB
Galaxy Note	2 Core 1.4 GHZ	2 GB

The choose of the specific classification algorithm to adopt is mainly dependent on two aspects: its accuracy, and its efficiency in terms of time complexity and memory consumption. For this reason, we firstly compared K-NN with a widely used clustering algorithm that can be adapted to classification.

4.1   Choosing the Classification Algorithm

In the considered scenario, given the set of feature vectors $(f_1, f_2, \cdots, f_m)$, the most common application of the K-means algorithm consists in partitioning the m observations into k sets, $\mathbf{C} = (C_1, C_2, \cdots, C_k)$, so as to minimize the intra-cluster error:

$$E = \sum_{k=1}^{K} \sum_{f_i \in C_k} \|f_i - \mu_k\|^2, \tag{1}$$

where μ_k is the mean value of the k-th cluster C_k.

Nevertheless, K-means can also be used for classification, i.e., supervised learning, according to two different schemes [15]. The first, straightforward, solution is to apply K-means to the whole blended training set and observe how data from k different classes are associated with each of the k centroids C_k. Then, each centroid is marked as representative of a certain class i, with $i = 1, ..., k$, if most of the samples in the cluster associated with C_k belong to i. Classification of a new, unknown, feature vector f is performed by finding its closest centroid and then assigning to f the same class of C_k. The major drawback to this method is that performing K-means on blended data produces heterogenous clusters. i.e., there is no guarantee that all the points in the same cluster represent the same class.

The second approach helps to overcome this limitation by separating the training data in n distinct groups, each containing samples from one of the n classes we want to recognize. The K-means algorithm is applied on each group/class separately, so as to obtain k homogeneous clusters, i.e., all the centroids within a single group represents the same class. Thus, classification can be performed by comparing a new, unknown, feature vector f with the $k \times n$ labeled centroids, and assigning to f the class of the closest one.

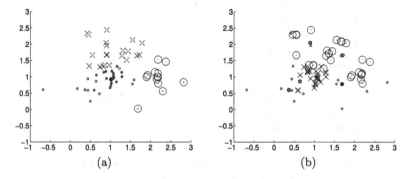

Fig. 4. Examples of k-means classification adopting two different schemes. Data from three classes (red, green, and blue) are classified into three clusters (crosses, circles, and dots) using blended (a) or separated (b) training sets. (Color figure online)

The differences between the two methods are summarized in Fig. 4. Original samples from three classes are represented by red, green, and blue points. As a result of the classification, points are marked as belonging to one of three clusters denoted by crosses, circles, and dots. When using the first scheme, K-means is applied to the whole blended dataset (Fig. 4-a) so that each cluster contains data from different classes, e.g., the cluster denoted by crosses includes red, green, and blue points. On the contrary, the second scheme (Fig. 4-b) is preferable since it allows to apply K-means on each class separately, so obtaining homogeneous clusters, e.g., the elements of the cluster denoted by circles are all greens.

As regards the choice of K, some experiments were conducted to determine the best value for K-means and K-NN.

For K-means, the value of K is simply the number of activities to be recognized, i.e., $K = 4$. In order to find the best value of K for the K-NN algorithm, two techniques for predictive accuracy evaluation have been used, i.e., Resubstitution and Cross Validation. Since we addressed a scenario where limited resource devices are employed, only odd values of K in the range $[3, 9]$ were considered. Experiments showed that best results are achieved with $K = 7$.

Then, tests were performed to compare K-NN with K-means (scheme 2) in terms of *accuracy*, *precision*, and *recall* [29]. Figure 5 shows that slightly better results are obtained while applying the K-NN algorithm. This is mainly due to the incapacity of K-means to distinguish between some similar activities. In particular, as highlighted by the confusion matrices shown in Tables 2 and 3, *still* and *vehicle* activities are frequently mistaken because of their similar acceleration values (see Fig. 2). This error is almost negligible when adopting the K-NN classifier.

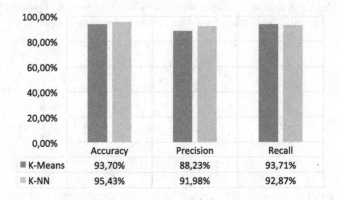

Fig. 5. Accuracy, precision, and recall of K-means and K-NN.

Table 2. K-means confusion matrix.

	still	walking	running	vehicle
still	.87	.03	0	.1
walking	0	1	0	0
running	0	0	1	0
vehicle	.12	.03	.06	.79

Table 3. K-NN confusion matrix.

	still	walking	running	vehicle
still	.97	0	.01	.02
walking	0	1	0	0
running	0	0	1	0
vehicle	0	.01	.02	.97

The next set of experiments were aimed at comparing K-means and K-NN in terms of time of execution and memory consumption. We performed some tests to measure these two parameters while varying the duration of the processing windows. Results are shown in Fig. 6(a) and (b). For the first two cases, i.e., test A and test B, the duration of the window is about 2 min, whereas smaller windows of about 50 s where used for C, D, and E. K-means is generally faster than K-NN, whilst K-NN, independently of the length of time windows, requires almost constant memory consumption.

Thus, since we want the HAR application to be as lightweight as possible so as to prevent the system resources from being consumed more than necessary, we decided to build the classification module on the K-NN algorithm. Such analysis is also confirmed by the results reported in [22].

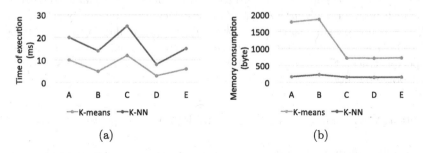

Fig. 6. Time of execution (a) and memory consumption (b) of K-means and K-NN classifiers measured under five different conditions denoted by {A,B,C,D,E}.

4.2 Comparison with MosT and Google

The last set of experiments was designed for comparing the system described in Fig. 1 with two state of the art HAR techniques, i.e., those implemented by the MosT framework and by the Google APIs.

As discussed in Sect. 1, Google does not provide any detail of the algorithms behind their products, thus we treated their recognition algorithm as a black-box. On the contrary, MosT is based on a well known algorithm to efficiently build decision trees, namely C4.5 [27].

Since MosT and Google are able to recognize different types of activities, in order to perform a meaningful assessment two distinct subsets have been defined. More precisely, the class *other* was added to cover the activities not considered in both of the systems alternately compared. Thus, since Google technique is unmodifiable, and it recognizes a greater number of activities than our system, the comparison was based on a subset formed by *still, walking, running, vehicle,* and *other.* On the contrary, even if MosT originally included only *still, walking,* and *running,* we have been able to add the *vehicle* activity obtaining the same set addressed by our system.

Accuracy, precision, and recall achieved by the system we propose as compared to MosT are showed in Fig. 7. MosT results are detailed in the confusion matrix reported in Table 4. As expected, *walking* and *running* are almost correctly classified, whilst the recognition of *vehicle* and *still* is more difficult to perform. This can be explained because MosT considers only accelerometer data, that, as shown in Fig. 2, are not useful enough for discriminating between a still user and one driving at constant velocity. Moreover, decision trees are generally less predictive than other classification approaches, since a small change in the data can cause a large change in the final estimated tree [17].

As regards the results obtained comparing the proposed system with the Google activity recognition tool (see Fig. 7), we can notice that Google performances are quite lower than ours, and this can be explained by referring to the Table 5. In fact, the implementation provided by Google is not able to correctly distinguish between *walking* and *running* activities. In addition, as already discussed, it is not possible to run further experiments, similar to those described for MosT, to analyze how changing the set of activities would impact on the system performance. This represents a further advantages of our system compared with Google method.

Table 4. MosT confusion matrix.

	still	*walking*	*running*	*vehicle*
still	.33	0	0	.67
walking	0	.96	.04	0
running	0	.02	.98	0
vehicle	.43	0	0	.57

Table 5. Google confusion matrix.

	still	*walking*	*running*	*vehicle*	*other*
still	.92	0	0	0	.08
walking	0	.56	.44	0	0
running	0	.45	.55	0	0
vehicle	0	0	0	.91	.09

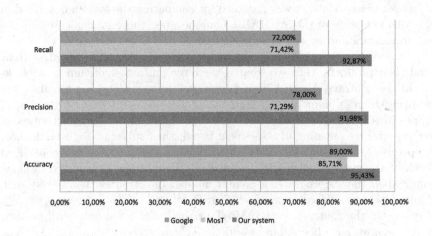

Fig. 7. Comparison between the proposed system, MosT, and Google.

5   Conclusions

In this paper we presented a novel human activity recognition framework based on smartphone built-in accelerometer and gyroscope sensors. The characteristics of four activities, i.e., *still, walking, running,* and *vehicle,* are represented through some feature vectors obtained by processing input data within fixed-length time windows. A K-NN classifier is then applied to recognize the activity performed by the user. Moreover, our architecture includes a participatory sensory module which allows to exploit user's feedbacks on recognised activities to keep updated the inner models of the system as more examples become available.

A set of experiments were run to compare the proposed solution with two state of the art techniques, i.e., the MosT framework, and the activity recognition tool provided by Google. Experimental results showed the effectiveness of our implementation both in terms of accuracy and efficiency.

As future works, we want to introduce a dynamic mechanism to filter out noisy data captured just before or after an activity is performed, e.g., when the user interacts with its smartphone to start or stop the Android application. Moreover, the adoption of variable length detection windows will be investigated.

We also plan to extend the set of activities by including some frequently performed in everyday life, e.g., *stairs down, stairs up, on bicycle,* and so on. This would be very useful in order to design a system that is able to recognize complex activities composed of simple tasks, such as those described in this paper. For example, the complex activity *from home to work,* could be recognized as a concatenation of *stairs down, walking, vehicle, walking, stairs up,* and *still.* In order to improve the user feedback mechanism, we want to investigate the adoption of reputation management techniques, as discussed in [2].

References

1. Activity recognition API. https://developers.google.com/android/reference/com/google/android/gms/location/ActivityRecognitionApi/, November 2016
2. Agate, V., de Paola, A., Lo Re, G., Morana, M.: A simulation framework for evaluating distributed reputation management systems. In: Omatu, S., et al. (eds.) Distributed Computing and Artificial Intelligence. Advances in Intelligent Systems and Computing, vol. 474, pp. 247–254. Springer, Heidelberg (2016). doi:10.1007/978-3-319-40162-1_27
3. Aggarwal, J.K., Xia, L.: Human activity recognition from 3D data: a review. Pattern Recogn. Lett. **48**, 70–80 (2014)
4. Banos, O., Damas, M., Pomares, H., Prieto, A., Rojas, I.: Daily living activity recognition based on statistical feature quality group selection. Expert Syst. Appl. **39**(9), 8013–8021 (2012)
5. Bao, L., Intille, S.S.: Activity recognition from user-annotated acceleration data. In: Ferscha, A., Mattern, F. (eds.) Pervasive 2004. LNCS, vol. 3001, pp. 1–17. Springer, Heidelberg (2004). doi:10.1007/978-3-540-24646-6_1
6. Baretta, D., Sartori, F., Greco, A., Melen, R., Stella, F., Bollini, L., D'addario, M., Steca, P.: Wearable devices and AI techniques integration to promote physical activity. In: Proceedings of the 18th International Conference on Human-Computer Interaction with Mobile Devices and Services Adjunct, pp. 1105–1108. ACM (2016)
7. Burke, J., Estrin, D., Hansen, M., Parker, A., Ramanathan, N., Reddy, S., Srivastava, M.B.: Participatory sensing. In: Workshop on World-Sensor-Web (WSW 2006): Mobile Device Centric Sensor Networks and Applications, pp. 117–134 (2006)

8. Cardone, G., Cirri, A., Corradi, A., Foschini, L., Maio, D.: MSF: an efficient mobile phone sensing framework. Int. J. Distrib. Sens. Netw. **9**(3), 538937 (2013). http://dx.doi.org/10.1155/2013/538937

9. Cardone, G., Corradi, A., Foschini, L., Ianniello, R.: Participact: a large-scale crowdsensing platform. IEEE Trans. Emerg. Topics Comput. **4**(1), 21–32 (2016)

10. Cottone, P., Gaglio, S., Lo Re, G., Ortolani, M.: User activity recognition for energy saving in smart homes. Pervasive Mob. Comput. **16**(PA), 156–170 (2015)

11. Cottone, P., Lo Re, G., Maida, G., Morana, M.: Motion sensors for activity recognition in an ambient-intelligence scenario. In: 2013 IEEE International Conference on Pervasive Computing and Communications Workshops (PERCOM Workshops), pp. 646–651 (2013)

12. Cvetković, B., Janko, V., Romero, A.E., Kafalı, Ö., Stathis, K., Luštrek, M.: Activity recognition for diabetic patients using a smartphone. J. Med. Syst. **40**(12), 256 (2016)

13. De Paola, A., La Cascia, M., Lo Re, G., Morana, M., Ortolani, M.: Mimicking biological mechanisms for sensory information fusion. Biol. Inspired Cogn. Archit. **3**, 27–38 (2013)

14. Gaglio, S., Lo Re, G., Morana, M.: Human activity recognition process using 3-D posture data. IEEE Trans. Hum.-Mach. Syst. **45**(5), 586–597 (2015)

15. Hastie, T., Tibshirani, R., Friedman, J.: The Elements of Statistical Learning: Data Mining, Inference and Prediction, 2 edn. Springer, Heidelberg (2009). doi:10.1007/978-0-387-84858-7

16. Hwang, S., Ryu, M., Yang, Y., Lee, N.: Fall detection with three-axis accelerometer and magnetometer in a smartphone. In: Proceedings of the International Conference on Computer Science and Technology, Jeju, Korea, pp. 25–27 (2012)

17. James, G., Witten, D., Hastie, T., Tibshirani, R.: An Introduction to Statistical Learning: With Applications in R. Springer Publishing Company, Heidelberg (2014). doi:10.1007/978-1-4614-7138-7

18. Kwon, Y., Kang, K., Bae, C.: Unsupervised learning for human activity recognition using smartphone sensors. Expert Syst. Appl. **41**(14), 6067–6074 (2014)

19. Lester, J., Choudhury, T., Borriello, G.: A practical approach to recognizing physical activities. In: Fishkin, K.P., Schiele, B., Nixon, P., Quigley, A. (eds.) Pervasive 2006. LNCS, vol. 3968, pp. 1–16. Springer, Heidelberg (2006). doi:10.1007/11748625_1

20. Lo Re, G., Morana, M., Ortolani, M.: Improving user experience via motion sensors in an ambient intelligence scenario. In: Proceedings of the 3rd International Conference on Pervasive Embedded Computing and Communication Systems, PECCS, vol. 1, pp. 29–34. INSTICC, SciTePress (2013)

21. Manzi, A., Dario, P., Cavallo, F.: A human activity recognition system based on dynamic clustering of skeleton data. Sensors **17**(5), 1100 (2017)

22. Munther, A., Razif, R., AbuAlhaj, M., Anbar, M., Nizam, S.: A preliminary performance evaluation of K-means, KNN and EM unsupervised machine learning methods for network flow classification. J. Electr. Comput. Eng. **6**(2), 778–784 (2016)

23. Paola, A.D., La Cascia, M., Lo Re, G., Morana, M., Ortolani, M.: User detection through multi-sensor fusion in an AmI scenario. In: 2012 15th International Conference on Information Fusion, pp. 2502–2509 (2012)

24. Park, S., Park, J., Al-masni, M., Al-antari, M., Uddin, M.Z., Kim, T.S.: A depth camera-based human activity recognition via deep learning recurrent neural network for health and social care services. Procedia Comput. Sci. **100**, 78–84 (2016)

25. Patel, S., Park, H., Bonato, P., Chan, L., Rodgers, M.: A review of wearable sensors and systems with application in rehabilitation. J. Neuroeng. Rehabil. **9**(1), 21 (2012)
26. Pinardi, S., Sartori, F., Melen, R.: Integrating knowledge artifacts and inertial measurement unit sensors for decision support. In: KMIS, pp. 307–313 (2016)
27. Quinlan, J.R.: C4. 5: Programs for Machine Learning. Elsevier, Amsterdam (2014)
28. Ravi, N., Dandekar, N., Mysore, P., Littman, M.L.: Activity recognition from accelerometer data. In: Aaai, vol. 5, pp. 1541–1546 (2005)
29. Sokolova, M., Lapalme, G.: A systematic analysis of performance measures for classification tasks. Inf. Process. Manag. **45**(4), 427–437 (2009)
30. Subramanya, A., Raj, A., Bilmes, J.A., Fox, D.: Recognizing activities and spatial context using wearable sensors. arXiv preprint arXiv:1206.6869 (2012)
31. Torres-Huitzil, C., Alvarez-Landero, A.: Accelerometer-based human activity recognition in smartphones for healthcare services. In: Adibi, S. (ed.) Mobile Health. Springer Series in Bio-/Neuroinformatics, pp. 147–169. Springer, Heidelberg (2015). doi:10.1007/978-3-319-12817-7_7

A Game-Based Competition as Instrument for Teaching Artificial Intelligence

Federico Chesani[1], Andrea Galassi[1], Paola Mello[1(✉)], and Giada Trisolini[2]

[1] Department of Computer Science and Engineering (DISI),
University of Bologna, Bologna, Italy
{federico.chesani,a.galassi,paola.mello}@unibo.it

[2] Department of Education Studies (EDU), University of Bologna, Bologna, Italy
giada.trisolini2@unibo.it

Abstract. This paper reports about teaching Artificial Intelligence (AI) by applying the experiential approach called "learning by doing", where traditional, formal teaching is integrated with a practical activity (a game competition, in our case), that is relevant for AI discipline and allows for an active and playful participation of students.

Students of the course of Fundamentals of AI at the University of Bologna have been challenged (on a voluntary base) to develop an AI software able to play the game of Nine Men's Morris: at the end of the course, the software players have been compared within a tournament, so as to establish the competition winner. The game has been chosen to let the students deepen the knowledge about AI techniques in solving games, and to apply it in a real, not trivial setting.

The significance and the impact of this approach, from the educational point of view, have been assessed through two questionnaires, a first one focused on the technical aspects, and a second one on the students' opinions about the initiative. The results are encouraging: students declare they felt highly motivated in studying AI algorithms and techniques, and they have been stimulated in autonomously search for extensions and new solutions not deeply investigated during traditional lessons.

1 Introduction

Learning how intelligent systems work and are designed is important for new generations which will grow in a world full of "smart objects". New forms of teaching have to be determined to ease people's approach to Artificial Intelligence (AI), not only in the university context, but also in primary and secondary schools, as well as in the industry. Beside traditional teaching techniques, AI should be approached through tasks people are familiar with, such as games, and through practical experiences.

The "Learning by Doing" concept belongs to the pedagogical approach proposed by Dewey, who founded and supported the so-called "active pedagogy" [4]. In that context, the traditional informative and passive education model was confronted with an active and progressive model based on experiential and

© Springer International Publishing AG 2017
F. Esposito et al. (Eds.): AI*IA 2017, LNAI 10640, pp. 72–84, 2017.
https://doi.org/10.1007/978-3-319-70169-1_6

participatory learning processes. According to Dewey, education should be considered as an active process where the student can interact with the context, and possibly modify it. While in the past the scientific debate considered traditional learning in contrast with Learning by Doing, nowadays it is highly preferred to merge the traditional informative and passive education model with an active and progressive model based on experiential and participatory learning processes. To facilitate the knowledge building processes, active didactic methods should be considered: as Dewey pointed out in [4], it is necessary to promote practical efficiency with awareness and critical thinking, otherwise the experiential learning is reduced to a routine mechanism.

One of the most effective didactic strategies is represented by Dewey's laboratory classrooms, where students can learn by their direct experiences, put in practice their previous knowledge and, at the same time, acquire new skills. In this theoretical context, students have an important and active role: pupils participate actively in the learning processes and expand their own knowledge and thinking by interacting with the environment through the experience. Teachers become facilitators of the learning process by changing their role from an instructive one towards a collaborative and participative role.

Games and game competitions have played an important role in AI progress: beside providing stimulating research problems, games provide also benchmarks for confronting solutions and approaches. Games are also familiar and well-known to the large public audience, that can easily follow successful results without the need of deep AI knowledge. Moreover, many prestigious universities, such as Stanford and Essex, are exploring games and game competitions as a teaching methodology within their university courses. The University of Huelva (Spain) has made a further step, and has completely integrated the *Google AI Challenge* into its AI courses [3]. These experiments have been successful from many perspectives, resulting in an improvement of students motivation and acquired knowledge.

In [17] the author provides an interesting analysis of AI competitions, and lists a number of characteristics that could lead such competitions to success or to failure. Among the many, we report here the following:

- The development should be independent of the programming language and the operating system.
- The game should be fun for human players.
- The code of the competition and of the past years competitors should be open source.
- The rules of the competition should be clear and stable.
- It should be easy to develop a very simple (and probably not competitive) solution.
- A discussion group for technical support, with both participants and organizers, should be run.

We experimented the principles of the "Learning by Doing" approach in an AI course at the University of Bologna: following the AI traditional fondness for game competitions, we proposed the students to compete on the development of a software agent for the Nine Men's Morris game. Students participated on a voluntary base, and teams (upto four members) were allowed. At the end of the course, the software players have been confronted in a tournament, and students have been invited to give a formal presentation about technical choices (with their colleagues as audience).

The Nine Men's Morris game has been chosen because it is a non-trivial challenge, yet master degree students have the needed knowledge to successfully implement a player. Moreover, the game has been the subject of a number of scientific studies: it has been proved that its solution is a draw [6], a well-performing heuristic function has been calculated with genetic algorithms [11], and a strategy that could lead to better results against a fallible opponent has been defined [7].

The development of an artificial player required the students to apply their AI knowledge into a practical implementation. In particular, students experimented with the application of key concepts of AI game solving such as, for example, Minmax algorithm and Alpha-beta pruning, heuristics search, and optimization. Moreover, students were stimulated to investigate other themes such as machine learning, therefore consolidating and expanding their knowledge. The outcomes of this teaching experience have been evaluated through two questionnaires, one focused on the adopted techniques, and a second one focused on how they perceived the experience. The questionnaires answers confirm the success of the experiment and provide useful indications for further challenges.

The paper is structured as follows. In Sect. 2 we outline the educational approaches which may be relevant to this experience. The competition is described in details in Sect. 3, while Sect. 4 contains the discussion about how the entire experience has been evaluated and which have been the results. Finally, Sect. 5 will conclude the paper.

2   Educational Approaches

The didactic perspective of Constructivism [12] is focused on some principles of "active pedagogy", and in particular on *participation* and *social practices*. Constructivism is an epistemological orientation according to which knowledge is acquired through an active building process, culturally situated and socially negotiated: the student actively participates in building knowledge within a participatory context [10]. The process of learning, strongly influenced by social relationships, is considered to be the result of two factors: the *cooperation with others* (social factor) and the *features of the task* (environmental factor). Therefore, acquiring knowledge is the result of a group interaction: the learning of an individual is the result of a working group that is born from the comparison and collaboration of interdependent groups, and of the use of interpersonal communication methods [9].

In this work the adopted didactic strategies focus on integrating an innovative approach, characterised by experiential and collaborative learning, in a traditional education approach. Within and during the traditional course lessons, the students are invited to join a competition that requires them to apply their acquired knowledge, by working alone or in team. In this laboratorial part of the course, students can put in practice their knowledge with the activation of experiential learning processes.

The laboratorial/practical activity guides the students toward simulating certain hypothesis and verifying them: in an artificial context with conditions similar to reality, students can recognize variables and useful elements required to make a decision. In addition, team working allows the students to discuss, share and create new knowledge, by using social and communication skills and by activating other models such as peer tutoring and reciprocal teaching. Moreover, the collaborative learning approach allows students to access their competences and soft skills which are enhanced by teamwork. This concept was described as the Zone of Proximal Development [18], in which students gradually develop the ability to perform tasks autonomously. This aspect is especially relevant to AI field, where applications typically require diversified skills and interdisciplinary knowledge.

Summing up, the didactic strategy based on gaming can improve students motivation and collaboration. Moreover, its effectiveness can be enhanced by including also the competition dimension in the game.

3   Competition Development

In the following we provide a description of the main aspects of the competition. In particular, we introduce the game of Nine Men's Morris, the educational context of the students and the setting of the competition itself.

3.1   Nine Men's Morris

Nine Men's Morris game (also called Mill or Cowboy Checkers) is a ancient [2] two-player perfect information boardgame. Different versions of the game exist, but in this work we follow the rules described in [6].

Both players have 9 checkers, also called stones or men, of the same color (usually black for one player and white for the other one). The game board, illustrated in Fig. 1, presents three concentric squares and four segments which links the squares by joining the midpoints of the sides. The 24 points of the board where lines intersects are the position where the players can place their checkers. At the start of the game, the board is empty and the players have their stones in hand. The players alternate their moves, with the "white" player usually making the first move.

The game develops along three different phases which are determined by the number of checkers that players have in their hands and on the board. The rules for each phase are the following:

1. In the first phase, during their turns the players put a stone on an empty position on the board.

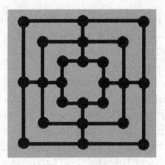

Fig. 1. Nine Men's Morris game board.

2. When all stones are placed, a move consists in sliding a checker along a line into a nearby empty position.
3. When one or both players are left with only three checkers on the board and none in the hand, they can move anyone of their checkers into any empty position on the board.

Players eliminate an opposing checker by "closing a mill", i.e. by aligning three stones along a segment. If there are adversary's stones which are not part of a mill, they must be chosen instead of the ones which are aligned in a mill. To win, players have to remove 7 opposing stones or manages to impede any possible move to the adversary. If a board configuration is repeated, the game is declared a draw (this can happen only during the second and the third phase).

The number of possible board states is included between 7.6×10^{10} and 2.8×10^{11} [6], which is relatively small compared to other classic board games. As a quick comparison, consider that the number of Chess configurations is included between 10^{43} and 10^{50}, while Go complexity has been estimated to be 10^{172} [1].

3.2 Educational Context

The educational context of the students to whom this challenge is addressed is a fundamental factor to take into account. The usefulness of this experience is strictly correlated with the objectives that the AI course aims to achieve, while its success could be also linked to the competences that students already have.

The Artificial Intelligence Course. The goal of the course is to introduce the main concepts and methods of Artificial Intelligence, with a particular emphasis on symbolic systems and problem solving, knowledge representation and reasoning, and computational logic.

The problem solving topic, intended as a search in a state space, is introduced along with the main search strategies. Games, constraint satisfaction problems, and planning problems are chosen as practical instances and deeply discussed in the course both from theoretical and from practical points of view. Regarding games in particular, Minimax-Decision algorithm and Alpha-beta search are introduced, together with some examples related to a number of games. The adopted reference book within the course is [14]. During the course, the design and the implementation of some practical AI systems based on procedural and declarative programming languages (Prolog in particular) are also stressed. Moreover, seminars on specific AI topics are planned: to cite few, an introduction to genetic algorithms, and an overview of Natural Language Processing and Understanding.

The course is the first experience about AI for the Master students in Computer Engineering, and is intended as preparatory course for the Intelligent Systems course, where Machine Learning techniques are introduced together with applications of problem solving techniques in scheduling, planning and optimization. Therefore, no strong prerequisites are required: the student is gradually introduced to the fundamental notions of the AI. However, basic notions of a high level programming language are required, to successfully understand case studies and applications presented during the lessons.

Classroom lessons are interleaved by some practical activities in the laboratories. For example, an activity focuses on the use of the software library AIMA[1], a collection of AI algorithms implemented in different programming languages such as Java, Lisp and Python. Moreover, autonomous AI projects are welcomed and promoted by suggesting ideas and possible case studies. Further details about the course are available on the university website[2].

Bachelor Degree Background. Most of the students who attend the Artificial Intelligence course hold a bachelor degree in Computer Engineering from the University of Bologna. Hence, the majority of the students already have a background knowledge about object oriented programming and about principles and patterns of software engineering. Moreover, students who attended the bachelor degree are also proficient in topics like concurrent programming, computer networks, and information systems and databases. The computer science-related courses in the bachelor degree comprise traditional lessons (held in classrooms), as well as laboratory sessions, where students reinforce the acquired knowledge and apply it on practical experiences, for example by programming in languages such as C, Java and C#.

3.3 Competition Description

The competition is presented to the students during the course lessons, usually in the last weeks of March or the first ones of April. Students are required to "register" for the competition within one month from the presentation in the course, and they are allowed to withdraw at any moment. Such freedom in

---

[1] http://aima.cs.berkeley.edu/code.html.

[2] http://www.engineeringarchitecture.unibo.it/en/programmes/
course-unit-catalogue/course-unit/2016/385372.

the competition registration/withdraw is meant to avoid adding an additional stress factor to the students, and instead propose the competition as a further opportunity. To encourage the participation, a small reward is granted on the final course grade: a bonus of 2 points out of 30, which means upto 6.67% of the final grade. To encourage teamwork without imposing limitations (some students might prefer to work alone), a competition team can be made of 1 up to 4 students. The deadline for the project submission is usually at the end of May, after which students are required to prepare a presentation that will be given to the classmates. The total time available for working on the project is therefore of 8–10 weeks, plus one additional week for the presentations. Students are strongly encouraged to communicate with the competitors, and to share knowledge between the teams: moreover, the presentation given in front of the class mates serves as a further chance for discussion and confrontation.

The software structure of the competition is quite simple: a Java program acts as referee of the game, while two other programs act as players. The referee communicates to the players with TCP protocol, sending them the state of the game in the form of a Java object and asking them the move they intend to make in the form of a textual string. Students are provided with the referee software, along with some classes representing the problem, the game state, as well as an example player (which is simply a text-based interface for playing). The AI software player should be capable of playing the game, i.e. to read the game state provided by the referee, and to send back the chosen move. For each turn the players have a maximum time limit to provide the move to the referee (currently, 60 s), otherwise they are declared defeated.

The competition is organized as a round-robin tournament: each player has to play against all the other players twice, once with white checkers and once with blacks. When all the matches have been played, the final result of each match is published on the website of the course, along with the winner of the competition. Records of the matches, along with a brief description of the players and their compiled code is maintained on the competition website[3]. The competition is run by academic staff in a controlled environment for sake of fairness.

The competition has been held for three years consecutively (academic years 2014/2015, 2015/2016, and 2016/2017). The number of participants has been 17, 27 and 19, respectively, while the number of teams has been 7, 10 and 8.

Table 1. Team composition

Group members	♯ groups
1	3
2	10
3	8
4	4

---

[3] http://ai.unibo.it/mulinochallenge.

Table 1 shows the number of teams w.r.t. the number of participants: clearly, students generally preferred to work in teams.

4   Educational Experience Assessment

In this section we introduce and discuss the results of the competition. Students were asked to answer two questionnaires. In the qualitative questionnaire students provided their feedback on a number of different aspects related to the usefulness, impact, and organization of the competition. The technical questionnaire is focused more on the technologies adopted by the participating teams. The former questionnaire aims to capture the perception of the students about the competition, while the latter one aims to spot AI techniques and solutions that were not covered in the course but used anyway within the competition, thus pointing towards a certain degree of autonomy and maturity of the students. We have also compared the exam marks of students who have participated to the challenge and students who have not.

4.1   Evaluation of Students Opinions

At the end of the competition, the participating students have been asked to answer a qualitative questionnaire of 20 questions, 18 of which are based on a five-level Likert scale (1 = strongly disagree; 5 = strongly agree), one question requires a numeric estimate and one question simply asks for suggestions. Table 2 shows the questions, that have been strongly inspired by the questionnaires used in [3]. Figure 2 reports average and standard deviation of the answers to the 18 questions based on the Likert scale.

The questionnaire is divided into the aspects of interest for this study: (i) if the experience has enhanced or increased the students' knowledge (Q1–Q5); (ii) if the competition has stimulated the students (Q6–Q10); (iii) if it has enhanced skills which are not strictly related to AI (Q11–Q15); and (iv) how much it has been difficult to take part in the competition (Q16–Q19). Answering the questionnaire was not mandatory, only 36 out of 63 students filled it.

Students agree that this experience has improved their knowledge about AI concepts (both new and already known) and problem solving, while are neutral about how it has influenced their programming languages knowledge. Students' motivation has resulted to be stimulated by competing in a challenge, indeed their feelings about the course have been improved by this experience, even though they were already high. Students' skills have been positively influenced by the competition and their perception of the value of sharing information has increased. Despite the mixed feelings about the difficulty of the experience and the amount of hours spent for it, students agree that this challenge has been well organized and, more importantly, has been a satisfying experience.

It is worth noting the quite important standard deviation of the amount of hours that students have dedicated to the project. A possible explanation would take into account the number of members in a team: it is likely that a student

Table 2. Student's quality questionnaire

#	Knowledge	Avg	SD
1	The experience enables the consolidation of theoretical concepts on AI	4.36	±0.63
2	The experience allows new concepts on AI to be acquired	4.42	±0.76
3	The experience allows to discover new ways to solve problems	4.17	±0.73
4	The experience allows new concepts on language programming to be acquired	3.14	±1.11
5	My ability to apply knowledge in practical and real problems after the challenge is positive	4.17	±0.83
#	Interest/Motivation	Avg	SD
6	My general assessment for the course before the experience is positive	4.11	±0.74
7	My general assessment for the course after the experience is positive	4.47	±0.60
8	The result obtained in the challenge influences learning on AI	3.69	±1.05
9	The result obtained in the challenge influences interest and motivation	3.97	±1.09
10	Competing in a challenge promotes motivation and interest	4.58	±0.72
#	Personal Skills	Avg	SD
11	The value of sharing information before the challenge is positive	4.00	±0.88
12	The value of sharing information after the challenge is positive	4.19	±0.70
13	The challenge serves to better understand personal skills	3.97	±0.93
14	The experience allows knowledge on work organization to be acquired	3.83	±0.93
15	The experience allows knowledge on cooperation and teamwork to be acquired	4.19	±0.91
#	Workload/Difficulty	Avg	SD
16	The difficulty and workload of this practice/experience is high	3.36	±1.13
17	How many hours have you spent working on this project?[a]	38.41	±25.09
		38.83	±24.11
18	The general assessment on development and organization of this practice is positive	4.06	±0.74
19	My general assessment for this practice/experience is positive	4.31	±0.81
#	Suggestions		
20	How could this experience be improved?[b]		

[a] Five answers, such as "Enough", did not express a quantifiable amount of time, therefore they have not be taken into account. For 3 answers which indicated an interval, such as "20–30", we have considered the mean value of the interval.

Four answers used different time units, such as days. We have not considered these answers in the first line. In the second line we have considered them estimating 4 h of work for each day.

[b] Obviously this question does not have associated values.

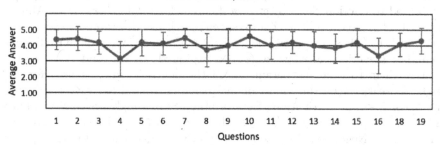

Fig. 2. Average scores and standard deviation for the students' opinion based on a five-level Linkert scale

participating alone will spend more time on the development of the software than a student who is part of a four members team.

Students' Suggestions. From what has emerged from the suggestions, the main lack of our competition had been the absence of a "language agnostic" referee. The choice to have a referee that communicated the states through a Java object seems to have, understandably, made the participants feel forced (or at least encouraged) to use Java as development language.

Another strong desire has been to have results of the concluded matches immediately available, not only at the end of the competition, thus indicating that the competitive component is important for the students.

One last popular request has been about a greater amount of time for developing the project, and for studying and developing better AI techniques which are not taught during the course, for example machine learning algorithms.

Some minor suggestion have been the following: to use a less known game as benchmark, to dedicate one laboratory lesson to the development of an artificial player, to give a special reward for the winner of the competition and to run the competition on a hardware equipped with a modern graphic card, so as to exploit it for, e.g., training deep networks [8].

Besides these helpful suggestions, some students have expressed a deep appreciation toward the competition.

4.2 Evaluation of the Used Techniques

To collect information about the techniques used by the students, two instruments have been used. The first one is a mandatory presentation of the project that each work group made to illustrate its software: the audience comprised the course teachers and the students. The second one is a questionnaire with multiple choices and open questions. As the quality questionnaire, its filling was completely volunteer, therefore available information regards only 24 teams out of 25.

The most frequently chosen programming language is Java, and only one team opted to develop the project in a different language, choosing C. Almost every team has used traditional state-space search as AI technique, except one team which has chosen to apply neuroevolution, in particular the NEAT algorithm [16]. Genetic algorithms were also exploited by a second team, which has used them to tune the parameters of the heuristic function used for the search. As search algorithm, most of the teams have used Iterative Deepening with A* or MiniMax with Alpha-Beta pruning. Surprisingly, seven teams have studied and applied other algorithms which are not covered by the university course, namely Negamax, NegaScout [13] and Best Node Search [15]. Four teams have also exploited part of the problem symmetries and transposition tables to speed-up the search. Many students have chosen to develop the whole software code by themselves; nonetheless, 10 teams relied on libraries such as AIMA and minimax4j[4].

As emerged from the questionnaire and from the presentations, even though most of the teams have implemented techniques which have been taught during the university course, some teams have demonstrated spirit of entrepreneurship: students have autonomously studied and implemented techniques which were new for them.

The software agents which, so far, have obtained the best results, rely on Iterative Deepening, compact and easily accessible representation of the game state and symmetries consideration to reduce spatial search.

4.3   Comparison Between Exam Marks

For the sake of completeness, we have also analyzed how the students have performed in the course exam. We have taken into account the results obtained between June 2015 and July 2017, for a total of 246 exams. We have computed the average mark scored by students and the relative standard deviation, considering only sufficient marks (above 18/30) and only the most recent mark for each student[5], for a total amount of 228 tests. The "30 cum laude" mark has been counted as 31. The average mark of students who have participated to the competition is 28.22, while students who did not participate got an average mark of 27.55. The standard deviation for the former group is 2.76, while the one for the latter group is 3.18. On average, students who have taken part to the initiative have obtained a mark of 0.67 points higher than the other students. Moreover, considering all the exams performed during the same time span, the percentage of failed exams results to be 14% for students who have not taken part to the competition and 5% for students who have.

Apparently, students who took part to the competition witness better results, in terms of final marks, and in terms of less failed tests. Even if this result seems to suggest that the initiative has been effective, there are other aspects to be considered as well. First of all, it is debatable if students advancements can be

---

[4] https://github.com/avianey/minimax4j.
[5] Students are allowed to repeat the test, even in case of sufficient marks.

testified only by the final marks. For example, it might be worthy to look at the number of time that students have repeated the exam and their previous results, the time occurred between the end of the lessons and the exam, and whether the students have personally attended the course lessons or not. Second, it is not possible to determine whether the competition has improved the students' performance or the participants were already the most skilful and motivated students: in the latter case, collected data would simply show that motivated students are more prone to take part to side initiatives such as our challenge.

5   Conclusions and Discussion

On the basis of the results emerged from the questionnaires, we deem this experience successful. Students confirmed the improvement of their knowledge and stated an increased interest toward the course topics and AI in general. The effectiveness of the adopted learning approaches is confirmed as well.

According to [17], and also from what has emerged from the students suggestions, an important lack is related to not making the competition sufficiently independent of the developing language: many students felt "obliged" to use the Java language. The amount of hours dedicated by students to this experience is highly variable and some of them have expressed the need for more time. This could be possible only by extending the competition beyond the course end. This possibility has been taken into account but it has been discarded due to the community environment that the course offers to the students. Often students took advantage of pauses between lessons to discuss about the competition both with professors and members of other teams. We think that this opportunity is a fundamental part of the competition, because it can be interpreted as an informal discussion group, another important element of success suggested by [17]. One last important aspect to underline is that the enthusiasm towards this experience has led many students to develop game-related university projects and master thesis, which may led to further research works, such as genetic algorithms or deep networks applications to the game context [5].

This experience can be extended to learn other AI techniques such as machine learning, natural language processing, constraints solving optimization, planning and scheduling, and computational logic. Also, it would be interesting to investigate other AI platforms developed in academic contexts or industrial settings, and to determine how suitable these platforms would be for creating similar experiences and for improving students learning.

Acknowledgements. We would like to thank all the students who have participated to the competition, and whose names are available on the competition website. Moreover, we are especially grateful to those students who answered our questionnaires. We would like to thank also the reviewers for their helpful and detailed suggestions.

References

1. Allis, L.V., et al.: Searching for Solutions in Games and Artificial Intelligence. Ponsen & Looijen, Wageningen (1994)

2. Bell, R.C.: Board and Table Games from Many Civilizations, vol. 1. Courier Corporation, New York (1979)
3. Carpio Caada, J., Mateo Sanguino, T., Merelo Guervs, J., Rivas Santos, V.: Open classroom: enhancing student achievement on artificial intelligence through an international online competition. J. Comput. Assist. Learn. **31**(1), 14–31 (2015). http://dx.doi.org/10.1111/jcal.12075
4. Dewey, J.: How We Think. DC Heath, Lexington (1910)
5. Galassi, A.: Symbolic versus sub-symbolic approaches: a case study on training Deep Networks to play Nine Men's Morris game. Master's thesis, University of Bologna, Italy. http://amslaurea.unibo.it/12859/
6. Gasser, R.: Solving Nine Men's Morris. Comput. Intell. **12**(1), 24–41 (1996). http://dx.doi.org/10.1111/j.1467-8640.1996.tb00251.x
7. Gévay, G.E., Danner, G.: Calculating ultrastrong and extended solutions for Nine Men's Morris, Morabaraba, and Lasker Morris. IEEE Trans. Comput. Intell. AI Games **8**(3), 256–267 (2016)
8. Goodfellow, I., Bengio, Y., Courville, A.: Deep Learning. MIT Press (2016). http://www.deeplearningbook.org
9. Kaye, A.: Learning together apart. In: Kaye, A.R. (ed.) Collaborative Learning Through Computer Conferencing, vol. 90, pp. 1–24. Springer, Heidelberg (1992)
10. Lave, J., Wenger, E.: Situated Learning: Legitimate Peripheral Participation. Cambridge University Press, Cambridge (1991)
11. Petcu, S.A., Holban, S.: Nine Men's Morris: evaluation functions. In: International Conferencs on Development and Application Systems, pp. 89–92 (2008)
12. Pumilia-Gnarini, P.M.: Handbook of Research on Didactic Strategies and Technologies for Education: Incorporating Advancements: Incorporating Advancements. IGI Global, Hershey (2012)
13. Reinefeld, A.: Spielbaum-Suchverfahren, vol. 200. Springer, Heidelberg (2013)
14. Russell, S.J., Norvig, P.: Artificial Intelligence: A Modern Approach. Prentice-Hall, Inc., Upper Saddle River (2010)
15. Rutko, D.: Fuzzified algorithm for game tree search. In: Second Brazilian Workshop of the Game Theory Society, BWGT (2010)
16. Stanley, K.O., Miikkulainen, R.: Evolving neural networks through augmenting topologies. Evol. Comput. **10**(2), 99–127 (2002). http://dx.doi.org/10.1162/106365602320169811
17. Togelius, J.: How to run a successful game-based AI competition. IEEE Trans. Comput. Intell. AI Games **8**(1), 95–100 (2016)
18. Vygotskij, L.S.: Myslenie i rec Psichologiceskie issledovanija. Movska-Leningrad: Gosudarstvennoe Socialno-Ekonomiceskoe Izdatelstvo (Bari, Laterza, It. tr. Pensiero e linguaggio 1992) (1934)

Natural Language Processing

A Similarity-Based Abstract Argumentation Approach to Extractive Text Summarization

Stefano Ferilli[(✉)], Andrea Pazienza, Sergio Angelastro, and Alessandro Suglia

Dipartimento di Informatica, Università di Bari, Bari, Italy
{stefano.ferilli,andrea.pazienza,sergio.angelastro}@uniba.it,
alessandro.suglia@gmail.com

Abstract. Sentence-based extractive summarization aims at automatically generating shorter versions of texts by extracting from them the minimal set of sentences that are necessary and sufficient to cover their content. Providing effective solutions to this task would allow the users to save time in selecting the most appropriate documents to read for satisfying their information needs or for supporting their decision-making tasks. This paper proposes 2 contributions: (i) it defines a novel approach, based on abstract argumentation, to select the sentences in a text that are to be included in the summary; (ii) it proposes a new strategy for similarity assessment among sentences, adopting a different similarity measure than those traditionally exploited in the literature. The effectiveness of the proposed approach was confirmed by experimental results obtained on the English subset of the benchmark MultiLing2015 dataset.

Keywords: Text summarization · Information extraction · Abstract argumentation

1 Introduction

Text summarization is the process of automatically creating a shorter version of one or more text documents. Basically, text summarization techniques are classified as *extractive* or *abstractive*. Abstractive techniques [1] may produce summaries containing sentences that were not present in the input document(s). On the other hand, extractive techniques [14] work by selecting sentences from the input document(s) according to some criterion. An accurate summarization method must optimize two important properties [21]: *coverage*, expressing how much the method is able to cover a sufficient amount of topics from the original source text, and *diversity*, which refers to the capability of the method of generating non-redundant information in the summary. Graph-based methods for automatic text summarization have provided encouraging results. The graph is set up by associating nodes to sentences in the input document(s), and placing edges whenever a node/sentence refers to another. Edges are weighted, and weights are used to generate the scores of sentences.

© Springer International Publishing AG 2017
F. Esposito et al. (Eds.): AI*IA 2017, LNAI 10640, pp. 87–100, 2017.
https://doi.org/10.1007/978-3-319-70169-1_7

Argumentation is an inferential strategy that aims at selecting reliable items in a set of conflicting claims (the *arguments*). Specifically, the Abstract Argumentation Frameworks introduced by Dung [6] work on graphs in which nodes represent arguments, and edges represent attack (or, sometimes, support) relations among arguments. Several non-monotonic reasoning approaches have been defined, that allow one to understand which subsets of arguments in the graph are mutually compatible, based on the fact that they are able to defend each other from attacks of other disputing arguments. Some of these approach may handle weighted graphs/edges.

Given the apparent connections between these two approaches, in this paper we focus on extractive text summarization, and propose a novel approach based on abstract argumentation to select the sentences in the input text that are to be included in the summary. To this purpose, we considered the degree of similarity between two sentences as an indicator of their being unsuited (or suited) to be both selected to make up the summary. Indeed, in order to cover a larger portion of the original text, different sentences should be selected, while similar sentences are likely to bear much redundancy. The underlying idea is to place an attack relation between pairs of sentences whose similarity is high, in order to enforce the diversity property. *Vice versa*, a support relation is introduced between pairs of sentences with low similarity, in order to enforce the coverage property.

This paper is organized as follows. The next section discusses past works on text summarization, while Sect. 3 briefly recalls the basics of abstract argumentation, with particular reference to the specific approach that will be used in this work. Section 4 introduces our proposals, by designing a general summarization framework which combines natural language processing along with abstract argumentation evaluation techniques to produce a final solution scoring function. Section 5 evaluates the performance of our approach. Finally, Sect. 6 concludes the paper.

2   Related Work on Text Summarization

Extractive Text Summarization methods are usually performed in three steps [18]: (i) creation of an intermediate representation of the input which captures only the key aspects of the text (by dividing the text into paragraphs, sentences, and tokens); (ii) scoring of the sentences based on that representation; and (iii) generation of a summary consisting of several sentences, selected by appropriate combination of the scores computed in the previous step.

The score of sentences should be computed using a measure that is able to express how significant they are to the understanding of the text as a whole. For instance, [10] proposed to score sentences using a new measure that expresses their similarity. Its computation encompasses three linguistic layers: (i) the lexical layer, which includes lexical analysis, stop words removal and stemming; (ii) the syntactic layer, which performs syntactic analysis; and (iii) the semantic layer, that mainly describes the annotations that play semantic role. These three layers handle the two major problems in measuring sentence similarity, i.e., the meaning and word order problems, in order to automatically combine different levels of information in the sentence while assessing similarity.

In this setting, many strategies have been proposed in the literature to determine which sentences in a given text can be considered as representative of its content. *Word scoring* approaches [12] assigns scores to the most important words. On the other hand, *sentence scoring* approaches determine the features of sentences by detecting and by leveraging the presence of cue-phrases [20] and numerical data [9]. Finally, *graph scoring* analyzes the relationships between the sentences that make up the text. The TextRank algorithm [16] extracts important keywords from a text document, where the weight expressing the importance of a word within the entire document is determined using an unweighted graph-based model.

Some efforts spent in combining the various approaches prove that hybrid approaches may lead to better results. Indeed, [9] show that combining scoring techniques leads to an improvement in the performance of both single- and multi-document summarization tasks, as measured by the traditional metrics used in this setting (ROUGE scores—see next). In general, the same techniques used in single document summarization systems are applicable to multi-document ones.

Finally, in order to form a paragraph length summary, one approach is based on *Maximal Marginal Relevance* [2], in which the best combination of important sentences is selected.

3 Abstract Argumentation

Since the approach to extractive text summarization that we will propose in this paper is based on argumentative reasoning, it is appropriate that we first recall here the basics of this inference strategy. As said, Abstract Argumentation is an inferential strategy that aims at selecting reliable items in a set of conflicting claims (the *arguments*). In particular, the focus is just on how relations interact between arguments, whose inner structure and actual content is neglected. These relations may be expressed by a graph in which nodes represent arguments, and edges represent attack or support relations among arguments. One of the most influential computational models of argument proposed in this setting is represented by Dung's Argumentation Frameworks [6], defined as follows.

Definition 1. *An Argumentation Framework (**AF**) is a pair $F = \langle \mathcal{A}, \mathcal{R} \rangle$, where $\mathcal{A}$ is a set of arguments and $\mathcal{R} \subseteq \mathcal{A} \times \mathcal{A}$. Relation $a\mathcal{R}b$ means that a attacks b.*

The precise conditions for arguments acceptance are defined by different semantics. Semantics produce acceptable subsets of the arguments, called *extensions*, that correspond to various positions one may take based on the available arguments.

Definition 2. *Given an AF $F = \langle \mathcal{A}, \mathcal{R} \rangle$, and $S \subseteq \mathcal{A}$:*

- *S is conflict-free if $\nexists a, b \in S$ s.t. $a\mathcal{R}b$;*
- *$a \in \mathcal{A}$ is defended by S if $\forall b \in \mathcal{A}: b\mathcal{R}a \Rightarrow \exists c \in S$ s.t. $c\mathcal{R}b$;*

- S is admissible *if S is conflict-free and S is defended by itself, i.e. $\forall a \in S, \forall b \in \mathcal{A} : b\mathcal{R}a \Rightarrow \exists c \in S$ s.t. $c\mathcal{R}b$;*
- S is a complete *extension iff S is admissible and every argument defended by S is in S;*
- S is a grounded *extension iff S is the $\subseteq$-minimal complete extension;*
- S is a preferred *extension iff S is a $\subseteq$-maximal complete extension;*
- S is a stable *extension iff $\forall a \in \mathcal{A}, a \notin S, \exists b \in S$ s.t. $b\mathcal{R}a$.*

A Bipolar AF (*BAF*) [3] is an extension of Dung's AF in which two kinds of interactions between arguments are possible: the attack and the support relation.

Definition 3. *A **BAF** is a triplet $B = \langle \mathcal{A}, \mathcal{R}_{att}, \mathcal{R}_{sup} \rangle$, where $\mathcal{A}$ is a set of arguments, $\mathcal{R}_{att}$ is a binary relation on $\mathcal{A}$ called attack relation and $\mathcal{R}_{sup}$ is another binary relation on $\mathcal{A}$ called support relation. For two arguments a and b, $a\mathcal{R}_{att}b$ (resp., $a\mathcal{R}_{sup}b$) means that a attacks b (resp., a supports b).*

In BAFs, new kinds of attack emerge from the interaction between the direct attacks and the supports: there is a *supported attack* for an argument b by an argument a iff there is a sequence of supports followed by one attack, while, there is an *indirect attack* for an argument b by an argument a iff there is an attack followed by a sequence of supports. Taking into account sequences of supports and attacks leads to the following definitions applying to sets of arguments [3].

Definition 4. *Let $B = \langle \mathcal{A}, \mathcal{R}_{att}, \mathcal{R}_{sup} \rangle$ be a BAF. A set $S \subseteq \mathcal{A}$ set-attacks an argument $b \in \mathcal{A}$, iff there exists a supported attack or an indirect attack for b from an element of S. A set $S \subseteq \mathcal{A}$ set-supports an argument $b \in \mathcal{A}$, iff there exists a sequence $a_1 \mathcal{R}_{sup} \ldots \mathcal{R}_{sup} a_n$, $n \geq 2$, such that $a_n = b$ and $a_1 \in S$. A set $S \subseteq \mathcal{A}$ defends an argument $a \in \mathcal{A}$, iff for each argument $b \in \mathcal{A}$, if $\{b\}$ set-attacks a, then b is set-attacked by S.*

In the following, we define the semantics for acceptability in BAFs.

Definition 5. *Let $B = \langle \mathcal{A}, \mathcal{R}_{att}, \mathcal{R}_{sup} \rangle$ be a BAF and $S \subseteq \mathcal{A}$. Then, S is:*

- conflict-free, *iff $\nexists a, b \in S$ s.t. $\{a\}$ set-attacks b;*
- safe, *iff $\nexists b \in \mathcal{A}$ s.t. S set-attacks b and either S set-supports b or $a \in S$;*
- a d-admissible *set, iff S is conflict-free and $\forall a \in S, a$ is defended by S;*
- an s-admissible *set, iff S is safe and $\forall a \in S$, a is defended by S;*
- a d-preferred *(resp. s-preferred) extension is a $\subseteq$-maximal d-admissible (resp. s-admissible) subset of $\mathcal{A}$.*

4   Argumentation-Based Text Summarization

We design a general summarization framework, based on the *WordNet* lexical database [17], which is divided in four fundamental phases: *natural language processing pipeline, weighted graph building, semantics evaluation* and *solution scoring function*, each of which will be described in a separate subsection.

Given a document to be summarized, we apply a preprocessing procedure that progressively splits the document into sentences, then splits each sentence into a sequence of tokens, and finally filters out stopwords. After that, we compute the similarity between each sentence that are exploited to generate a weighted graph whose nodes are sentences and whose edges represent the degree of similarity between two sentences. The resulting weighted graph is exploited to generate a suitable graph structure composed by support and attack relations that are used by the adopted argumentation framework to evaluate solutions according to a chosen semantics. Finally, we design a procedure that is able to evaluate the relevance of a given solution which is used in order to determine which is the best solution for the summarization task among the one evaluated by the argumentation framework.

4.1   Natural Language Processing Pipeline

The natural language processing (NLP) pipeline is carried out in order to extract from the input document its basic components which are sentences and tokens. In order to effectively complete it, we apply the NLP techniques provided by the *Stanford CoreNLP* toolkit [15]. In particular, we apply sentence splitting so as to split the input document into n sentences $\langle s_1, s_2, \ldots, s_n \rangle$, and we apply tokenization, which splits each sentence s_i in k tokens $\langle w_1, w_2, \ldots, w_k \rangle$. Then, lemmatization and stopword removal tasks are applied in order to obtain a sequence of k' tokens $\tilde{s}_i = \langle w_1, w_2, \ldots, w_{k'} \rangle$, with $k' \leq k$.

In order to grasp the meaning of each sentence, we use the *Simplified Lesk* algorithm [22] that is able to determine a unique sense $sense(w_j)$ for each token w_j in the sentence s_i, by selecting the one with highest *overlap* (computed as *cosine similarity*) between the vectorial representation of the sense gloss (extracted from WordNet) and s_i (i.e., the token context), respectively $vec(sense(w_j))$ and $vec(s_i)$. Specifically, we exploit a word embedding matrix $\boldsymbol{W} \in \mathbb{R}^{|W| \times d}$ where W is the word vocabulary and d is the word embedding size, to generate a representation for each sentence obtained by composing word vectors associated to its tokens through vectorial operations. Intuitively, the word embedding matrix encodes latent representations associated to each word learned from a corpus of documents. We denote as $W(x)$ the lookup operation over the matrix $\boldsymbol{W}$ used to obtain the word vector $\boldsymbol{x}$ (i.e., a row of $\boldsymbol{W}$) related to the word x. Then, we define vectorial representation of a sequence of tokens $x = \langle x_1, x_2, \ldots, x_m \rangle$ as follows:

$$c = \frac{1}{|W|} \sum_{w \in W} W(w), \qquad vec(x) = \sum_{x_i \in x} \boldsymbol{x}_i - \boldsymbol{c}$$

where $\boldsymbol{c}$ is the centroid of the vector space defined by the word embeddings and $vec(x)$ represents the resulting vectorial representation of dimension d associated to the input sequence x, which is built by removing the common features encoded in the centroid of the vector space and summing only the relevant ones.

4.2   Weighted Graph Building

The weighted graph building procedure is concerned with the definition of a graph structure which is derived from the similarities between sentences. First, we define a graph $G = (V, E)$ where $V = \{s_1, s_2, \ldots, s_n\}$ is the set of sentences of the documents while $E \subset V \times V$ is the set of edges between the sentences in V. We define a weighting function $f_w \colon E \to \mathbb{R}$ which associates to each edge a weight. In this context, the weight is determined by the similarity function sim between two sentences which is computed as follows:

$$sim(s_i, s_j) = \frac{1}{|U(\tilde{s}_i, \tilde{s}_j)|} \sum_{w_p \in U(\tilde{s}_i, \tilde{s}_j)} \max_{w_q \in U(\tilde{s}_i, \tilde{s}_j) \setminus \{w_p\}} \phi(w_p, w_q),$$

where $U(s_i, s_j)$ represents the set of unique words in the sentences $\tilde{s}_i$ and $\tilde{s}_j$ and ϕ is a similarity function between the tokens w_p and w_q. The function ϕ is defined as a linear combination of three different similarity functions which are described as follows:

$$\phi(w_i, w_j) = \mu_1 \cdot sim_{syn}(w_i, w_j) + \mu_2 \cdot sim_{sem}(w_i, w_j) + \mu_3 \cdot sim_{emb}(w_i, w_j)$$

The *syntactic similarity* $sim_{syn}(\cdot)$ is defined as the *Jaccard Index* between the outgoing and incoming syntactic dependencies associated to the token w_i and w_j, respectively. Each dependency relationship is uniquely identified by the long name associated to it by the Stanford dependency parser [5]. With the syntactic similarity we try to understand if the two words in the sentence share, in some sense, linguistic patterns of usage that can be used to assess if they are similar from a grammatical point of view.

The *semantic similarity* $sym_{sem}(\cdot)$ is a function proposed in [19]. This function, using the sense associated to the tokens $sense(w_i)$ and $sense(w_j)$, is able to exploit taxonomic information associated to the synsets defined in *WordNet* in order to evaluate the similarity between the tokens. In particular, it defines a function which blends two similarity functions that mutually smooth each other, reported in the following equation:

$$sym_{sem}(w_i, w_j) = sim_{Fa}(w_i, w_j) * sim_{WP}(w_i, w_j)$$

The former, $sim_{Fa}(\cdot)$, is based on the similarity framework presented in Sect. 3 of [8] in which we consider as features of the items w_i and w_j the hypernyms of the words $synset(w_i)$ and $synset(w_j)$, extracted from the adopted taxonomy. While, the latter, $sim_{WP}(\cdot)$, as presented in Sect. 2.2.3 of [19], considers the single path information where the concepts exploited in the formula are represented by synsets. In particular, it takes into account the depth of both the couple of words synset and their *Least Common Subsumer (LCS)* (informally, the closest common synset), which are extracted from the *WordNet* taxonomy.

The *embedding similarity* $sym_{emb}(\cdot)$ is defined as the *cosine similarity* between the word embeddings $\boldsymbol{w}_i$ and $\boldsymbol{w}_j$ associated to the words w_i and w_j extracted from the matrix $\boldsymbol{W}$. In this way, we are able to exploit word embedding latent representations to compute word similarities in an efficient way.

We define the graph G associated to the input document where nodes are sentences and the edges represent the degree of similarity between them. After that, we design a graph transformation procedure that allows us to define a BAF from the graph G that will be exploited to evaluate specific argumentation semantics. In order to obtain a BAF, we define an heuristic, inspired by the concept of weighted argumentation framework's *inconsistency budget* [7], to derive support and attack relations starting from the relations in the original graph. First of all, we define two different thresholds that are used to filter out some relations and to distinguish between attack or support relations. Specifically, we define the *attack threshold* as $\alpha \in [0,1]$ and we define the *support threshold* as $\beta \in [0,1]$. After that, we normalize the edge weights in $[0,1]$ and we generate a $BAF\ B = \langle \mathcal{A}, \mathcal{R}_{att}, \mathcal{R}_{sup} \rangle$ where $\mathcal{A}$ is the set of sentences of V which are involved in at least one relation of the generated graph B, $\mathcal{R}_{sup} = \{e \in E \mid w(e) \leq \beta\}$ is the set of support relations and $\mathcal{R}_{att} = \{e \in E \mid w(e) \geq \alpha\}$ is the set of attack relations, with the constraint that $\beta < \alpha$. Intuitively, we decide to consider as support relations those that connect sentences which are not similar with each other. In some sense, they may express independent concepts that are worth to be included in the summary in order to guarantee the *coverage* property. On the other hand, we use attack relations to model the fact that two sentences are really similar so they do not convey any additional information to the summary, violating the property of *diversity*.

4.3   Evaluation by Argumentation Semantics

Once the BAF is instantiated, we can exploit semantics to evaluate the acceptability of arguments. What we expect from the arguments evaluation is that:

- *conflict-free* sets will collect the larger subsets of arguments which encompass the main principle of argumentation solutions, namely, the idea that winning arguments should not attack each other. This requirement would reward those sentences which maximize the diversity property. However, for the coverage property, we require that a solution would defend its element, too.
- *d-/s-admissible* sets will collect a large number of arguments. Ideally, these solutions may be appropriate for the task of text summarization. However, when a constraint is required for a summary (i.e., a maximum number of chars), admissible solutions may include too many arguments, getting, hence, a summary which is ideally good but exceeding as number of required chars.
- *complete* extensions will collect sets of arguments which can defend all and only its element from external attacks. They are still admissible and will achieve at most as many solutions as the admissible ones. Anyway, complete semantics may include too small sets.
- *d-/s-preferred* extensions will collect those sets of arguments maximally-included in d-/s-admissible sets. Therefore, preferred semantics should ideally behave better than admissible and complete ones both in terms of quality of the summary and in the number of elements (by chars constraint reasons).

– *stable* extensions will collect those sets of arguments which are able to attack all the remaining arguments not included in the solution. In terms of summary requirements, it will contain the most dissimilar sentences. Since its strong requirement, it turns out that stable semantics may not achieve solutions at all.

Therefore, for our purposes, the d-/s-admissible, d-/s-preferred extension-based semantics and, occasionally, conflict-free sets seem to provide the most suitable sets of arguments as a trade-off between acceptability membership conditions and justification state. It will be the task of the experimental validation confirming or rejecting this hypothesis.

4.4   Evaluation of Solution Relevance

For each semantics among the chosen ones, the argumentation framework is capable to generate a set of solutions. Each solution consists of a set of arguments which are considered acceptable or justified by the specific semantics. In order to generate a summary, we need to select a solution among the generated ones and from it we determine the subset of sentences that is relevant and whose length does not exceed the summary target length defined in the ground-truth data.

Hence, we define an iterative strategy to select the set of *authoritative* arguments that are worth to be included in the summary based on an *authority score* which is derived from the support and attack relations in the BAF graph B from which the solution was generated. We can informally define an *authoritative* argument in a BAF a node that does not receive a lot of attacks and that is supported by a lot of arguments. Indeed, an argument a which satisfy these properties can be considered a relevant part of the document that should be included in the summary. Formally, we define the *authority* score as follows:

$$auth(a) = [1 + \log(sup(a))] * [\log(\frac{|\mathcal{R}_{att}|}{att(a) + 1})],$$

where $sup(a)$ and $att(a)$ represent the number of supports and attacks received by a, respectively, and $\mathcal{R}_{att}$ is the set of attack relations. For the summary generation we define two alternative procedures, the first selects the best subset of arguments from the semantic solutions (AUTH-MMR), whereas the second selects the solution which approximates the target length and which maximizes the intra-cohesion coefficient of the arguments (AUTH).

As concerns the former, we define, inspired by the *Maximal Marginal Relevance* procedure described in [2], an iterative procedure to rank the set of most relevant arguments that will represent the summary of the input document. In particular, the first similarity measure in the original formula is represented by the authority score $auth(a)$, while the latter is represented by the similarity between two arguments. An argument a has an high marginal relevance if it has an high authority score $auth(a)$ and contains minimal similarity to previously selected arguments. In order to satisfy the *diversity* property, we select those arguments which maximize the marginal relevance. The procedure keeps select-ing arguments until the desired summary length is reached. The summary is considered as the solution subset which has the higher average arguments score.

For the latter, we select the semantic solution which has both the minimal characters difference from the target-length and has the higher average argu-ments score. We expect that the solution satisfying this constraints will be, at the same time, the shorter and more precise summary for the document.

5   Evaluation

The effectiveness of the proposed approach was assessed by evaluating its per-formance on the *single-document text summarization* task of the English version of the *MultiLing 2015* dataset [11]. This allowed us to have the ground truth, published after the competition, available for testing purposes. On average, the input texts were made up of about 25542 characters, while the ground truths were made up of about 1857 characters (i.e., about 7% of the source texts). We followed the same experimental protocol as defined in the *MultiLing 2015* challenge in which two variants of the ROUGE (*Recall-Oriented Understudy for Gisting Evaluation*) [13] measure were used to quantitatively evaluate the gener-ated summaries. Formally, ROUGE-N is an N-gram recall between a candidate summary and one or more reference summaries. The two adopted variants are *ROUGE-1* and *ROUGE-2*, which consider the ratio of co-occurring unigrams (i.e., single words) and bi-grams, respectively, in a candidate summary over the reference summaries.

In this respect, it is important to point out that the ground truth in this dataset is obtained by humans using an abstractive approach. This means that: (i) the comparison under these conditions is partly unfair, because there is no exact match between the sentences in the input text and those in the summary; (ii) since the summaries may include words that were not present at all in the input texts, the whole ground truth summary might be impossible to match, even considering the whole input text; (iii) condensing the original content into just 7% opens significant possibilities that the authors of the summary have taken many subjective decisions about what to include in, and what to filter out from, the ground truth, leaving the possibility that different summaries might be as good as theirs, but quite different from theirs.

In the following, we compared our method with the following baselines, taken from the published results of the *MultiLing 2015* competition:

WORST the worst-performing approach of the challenge with ROUGE-1 of 37.17% and ROUGE-2 of 9.93%;

BEST the best-performing approach of the challenge with ROUGE-1 of 50.38% and ROUGE-2 of 15.10%;

ORACLE [4] can be considered as an upper bound on the extractive text summarization performance with ROUGE-1 of 61.91% and ROUGE-2 of 22.42%.

These approaches are set so as to return summaries having the exact length in characters as the ground truth. This is questionable as well, since by truncating a candidate summary to a pre-defined number of character spoils the very aims and motivations of summarization, which is returning a shorter version of the text that still conveys most of the original content and is human-understandable.

5.1   Standard Argumentation-Based Approach

As already specified, by its very nature argumentation semantics return subsets ('extensions') of arguments (sentences) that are mutually consistent ('justified'). This means that, using this approach in its standard setting, (i) one has no control on the number of sentences that are selected to make up the summary, except for choosing different semantics that tend to return larger or smaller extensions; and (ii) the control is at the level of sentences, whereas length comparison to the ground truth in the dataset is made in terms of characters. So, as a first attempt, we wanted to check the results of the approach in its natural setting. For semantics that returned several extensions, in the spirit of summarization, the shortest one was adopted.

To have an immediate idea of the trade-off between the summarization performance and the length of a summary s, we defined a compound indicator:

$$\text{Quality}(s) = \text{ROUGE-1}(s)/\text{length}(s)$$

where the length of the summary, placed at the denominator, penalizes the quality of the solution s.

We computed the different semantics on the argumentation graphs obtained for different threshold settings for α (to determine attacks) and β (to determine supports). Specifically, we considered thresholds for β ranging into $[0.1, 0.8]$, and thresholds for α ranging into $[0.15, 0.9]$, using a 0.05 step for both and ensuring that $\beta < \alpha$ in each setting. Overall, this resulted in several hundreds of argumentation computations for each summarization task.

Due to lack of space, we graphically summarize the results in Fig. 1, where the y axis reports Quality values, and items on the x axis correspond to the average

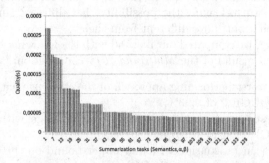

Fig. 1. Quality results for the different argumentation settings on the MultiLing 2015 dataset

performance on all summarization tasks for selected (Semantics,α,β) settings, ordered by decreasing Quality. Specifically, the graphic includes values for the s-admissible, d-admissible, stable and complete semantics only, with values β in $[0.1, 0.8]$ and α in $[0.2, 0.9]$, using a 0.1 step. This resulted in 144 cases, that were selected as representative of the whole behavior.

While in most of the graphic a smooth shape is visible, it is also apparent that 4 'steps' naturally emerged, associated to sudden changes (drops) in the level of quality, as if a phase transition occurred. So, we focused on these steps to select the most relevant settings to investigate in more depth. We ignored the first step, corresponding to summaries shorter than the ground truth. Interestingly, in the second step the length of the summaries jumps from 1352 to 4365 characters, making it impossible for us to find a summary which has comparable length with the ground truth (1857 characters). The detailed outcomes for the second, third, and fourth steps are reported in Table 1. Each step corresponds to two different semantics that returned exactly the same results.

Table 1. Experimental evaluation results for AUTH approach (with natural use of argumentation). Average size of full texts is 25542 characters, average size of the ground truths is 1857 (7% of the full texts)

Step	Semantics	β	α	Length (%)	Quality	Rouge-1		Rouge-2	
						Recall	Precision	Recall	Precision
2	s/d-admissible	0.1	0.4	4365 (17%)	1.13E-04	49.28%	30.32%	15.49%	7.22%
3	Stable, complete	0.1	0.5	8544 (33%)	7.07E-05	60.44%	24.44%	23.98%	7.43%
4	s/d-admissible	0.1	0.5	9826 (38%)	7.33E-05	72.09%	26.65%	27.26%	6.16%

The ROUGE-1 results are comparable to the state-of-the-art at step 2, comparable to Oracle at step 3, and much (>10%) better than Oracle at step 4, but using the 17%, 33% and 38% of the input texts, respectively (compared to 7% of the ground truth). In other words, the argumentation approach requires more than twice as many characters as the ground truth to obtain the same ROUGE-1 results as the state-of-the-art, and 1/3 of the whole text to reach Oracle. By allowing it to use a little more text, but however less than 2/5 of the input text, it is able to catch nearly 3/4 of the content. Considering ROUGE-2, the same comments as above still hold, but in this case the recall value is slightly larger than the reference systems. These results suggest that the proposed Argumentation-based approach is sensible and effective in returning relevant summaries, and is competitive in performance, albeit paying in summary length.

Confirming the hypothesis we made in the previous section, s- and d-preferred semantics are among those that provide relevant results. Moreover, we may note that also the stable and complete semantics may yield interesting results that somehow represent a trade-off corresponding to the performance of ORACLE. Given the considerations about possible unfairness of the ground truth construction, we wanted to carry out also a qualitative evaluation of our summaries, by asking human beings to read them and provide their sensations. Very interestingly, they reported that the proposed summaries have little redundancy, yet provide a sensible account of the original document, also ensuring smooth discourse flow, even if they were obtained by filtering out sentences, since present in the original text, presumably included relevant parts as regards the content and/or the flow of discourse.

5.2 Relevance-Based Approach

While the natural application of the proposed argumentation-based approach leaves to the approach itself the task of determining a proper summary length, we tried to obtain a summary having a given length upon request in order to check what performance level we can reach under the same constraints as the other approaches in the literature. Since all sentences in an argumentation extension are 'equal' as regards their belonging to the extension, we had to introduce an additional post-processing procedure for determining the relevance of each sentence in an extension, and then select the most relevant until the desired length is reached, as explained in the previous sections.

The best results obtained by applying the relevance-based post-processing to the results reported in the previous experiment are the following:

Semantics	β	α	Length	ROUGE-1	ROUGE-2
Conflict-free	0.65	0.80	1966	46.30%	10.58%
s/d-preferred	0.25	0.75	1942	44.12%	10.54%

We note that, while still lower than that of BEST approach, the performance becomes now significantly closer to the state-of-the-art. s-preferred and d-preferred semantics confirm their ability to provide good results, as hypothesized in the previous section. However, the best result overall is obtained by another semantics, namely the conflict-free one. Thresholds α and β are neatly larger than those used in Table 1, which could be expected because larger extensions are needed to have a wider range of options among which selecting the most relevant ones. In this sense, the argumentation step now plays the role of a filter, that returns a preliminary summary to be further reduced by the relevance-based step.

6   Conclusion

This paper proposed 2 contributions to sentence-based automatic text summarization. First, it defined a novel approach, based on abstract argumentation, to select the sentences in a text that are to be included in the summary. Also, it proposed a new strategy for similarity assessment among sentences, and a different similarity measure than those traditionally exploited in the literature.

Experimental results obtained on the English subset of the benchmark MultiLing2015 dataset confirmed the viability and effectiveness of the proposed approach. Allowing longer summaries than in the dataset's ground truth, but still significantly shorter than the original text, very high performance can be reached. While in its basic and natural setting the argumentation-based approach autonomously determines the number of sentences to be included in the summary, which is typically larger than required by the dataset's ground truth, a post-processing procedure was provided to impose the desired length to the summary.

Future work will carry out further investigations on the possibility of improving the performance of the approach, both in its natural setting and in the constrained one. This will include exploring other argumentation frameworks, and defining better strategies for determining the relevance of sentences to be included in the summary.

Acknowledgments. This work was partially funded by the Italian PON 2007-2013 project PON02_00563_3489339 'Puglia@Service'.

References

1. Banerjee, S., Mitra, P., Sugiyama, K.: Multi-document abstractive summarization using ILP based multi-sentence compression. In: IJCAI 2015 (2015)
2. Carbonell, J., Goldstein, J.: The use of MMR, diversity-based reranking for reordering documents and producing summaries. In: ACM SIGIR, pp. 335–336. ACM (1998)
3. Cayrol, C., Lagasquie-Schiex, M.C.: On the acceptability of arguments in bipolar argumentation frameworks. In: Godo, L. (ed.) ECSQARU 2005. LNCS (LNAI), vol. 3571, pp. 378–389. Springer, Heidelberg (2005). doi:10.1007/11518655_33
4. Davis, S.T., et al.: OCCAMS—an optimal combinatorial covering algorithm for multi-document summarization. In: ICDMW, pp. 454–463. IEEE (2012)
5. De Marneffe, M., Manning, C.D.: The Stanford typed dependencies representation. In: Coling 2008, pp. 1–8. ACL (2008)
6. Dung, P.M.: On the acceptability of arguments and its fundamental role in nonmonotonic reasoning, logic programming and n-person games. Artif. Intell. **77**(2), 321–357 (1995)
7. Dunne, P.E., et al.: Weighted argument systems: basic definitions, algorithms, and complexity results. Artif. Intell. **175**(2), 457–486 (2011)
8. Ferilli, S., Biba, M., Di Mauro, N., Basile, T.M.A., Esposito, F.: Plugging taxonomic similarity in first-order logic horn clauses comparison. In: Serra, R., Cucchiara, R. (eds.) AI*IA 2009. LNCS, vol. 5883, pp. 131–140. Springer, Heidelberg (2009). doi:10.1007/978-3-642-10291-2_14
9. Ferreira, R., et al.: Assessing sentence scoring techniques for extractive text summarization. Expert Syst. Appl. **40**(14), 5755–5764 (2013)
10. Ferreira, R., et al.: A new sentence similarity assessment measure based on a three-layer sentence representation. In: DocEng, pp. 25–34. ACM (2014)
11. Giannakopoulos, G., et al.: Multiling 2015: multilingual summarization of single and multi-documents, on-line fora, and call-center conversations. In: SIGDIAL, pp. 270–274 (2015)

12. Gupta, P., et al.: Summarizing text by ranking text units according to shallow linguistic features. In: ICACT, pp. 1620–1625. IEEE (2011)
13. Lin, C.: Rouge: a package for automatic evaluation of summaries. In: ACL-04 Workshop, vol. 8 (2004)
14. Lloret, E., Palomar, M.: Text summarisation in progress: a literature review. Artif. Intell. Rev. **37**(1), 1–41 (2012)
15. Manning, C.D., et al.: The Stanford CoreNLP natural language processing toolkit. In: ACL (System Demonstrations), pp. 55–60 (2014)
16. Mihalcea, R., Tarau, P.: TextRank: bringing order into texts. In: Association for Computational Linguistics (2004)
17. Miller, G.: WordNet: a lexical database for English. Commun. ACM **38**(11), 39–41 (1995)
18. Nenkova, A., McKeown, K.: A survey of text summarization techniques. In: Aggarwal, C., Zhai, C. (eds.) Mining Text Data, pp. 43–76. Springer, Boston (2012)
19. Rotella, F., Leuzzi, F., Ferilli, S.: Learning and exploiting concept networks with ConNeKTion. Appl. Intell. **42**(1), 87–111 (2015)
20. Shardan, R., Kulkarni, U.: Implementation and evaluation of evolutionary connectionist approaches to automated text summarization (2010)
21. Umam, K., et al.: Coverage, diversity, and coherence optimization for multi-document summarization. Jurnal Ilmu Komputer dan Informasi **8**(1), 1–10 (2015)
22. Vasilescu, F., Langlais, P., Lapalme, G.: Evaluating variants of the lesk approach for disambiguating words. In: Lrec (2004)

Named Entity Recognition and Linking in Tweets Based on Linguistic Similarity

Arianna Pipitone, Giuseppe Tirone, and Roberto Pirrone[✉]

Dipartimento dell'Innovazione Industriale e Digitale (DIID),
Università degli Studi di Palermo, Palermo, Italy
{arianna.pipitone,giuseppe.tirone,roberto.pirrone}@unipa.it

Abstract. This work proposes a novel approach in Named Entity rEcognition and Linking (NEEL) in tweets, applying the same strategy already presented for Question Answering (QA) by the same authors. The previous work describes a rule-based and ontology-based system that attempts to retrieve the correct answer to a query from the DBPedia ontology through a similarity measure between the query and the ontology labels. In this paper, a tweet is interpreted as a query for the QA system: both the text and the thread of a tweet are a sequence of statements that have been linked to the ontology. Provided that tweets make extensive use of informal language, the similarity measure and the underlying processes have been devised differently than in the previous approach; also the particular structure of a tweet, that is the presence of mentions, hashtags, and partially structured statements, is taken into consideration for linguistic insights. NEEL is achieved actually as the output of annotating a tweet with the names of the ontological entities retrieved by the system. The strategy is explained in detail along with the architecture and the implementation of the system; also the performance as compared to the systems presented at the #Micropost2016 workshop NEEL Challenge co-located with the World Wide Web conference 2016 (WWW '16) is reported and discussed.

1 Introduction

Named Entity rEcognition and Linking (NEEL) is a sub-task of information extraction that aims at locating and classifying each named entity mention in text into the classes of a knowledge base. The interest for such a task has been growing exponentially with the advent of the Web 2.0 technologies, leading to the Social Semantic Web research field; unlike the Semantic Web that is considered a model for solving the epistemic interoperability issues, the Social Semantic Web makes users free to publish uncontrolled texts without grammatical constraints, spreading them to a multitude of other people. Semantic annotation of social data by linking them into structured knowledge attempts to control such phenomena, making the social data both machine-readable and traceable.

When the social data are tweets, the main problems arise in both the informal language and shortness of the text [17]: the use of a 'loose' language with

© Springer International Publishing AG 2017
F. Esposito et al. (Eds.): AI*IA 2017, LNAI 10640, pp. 101–113, 2017.
https://doi.org/10.1007/978-3-319-70169-1_8

abbreviations, sparsity of contents and not enough precise context in place of a formal one, are serious obstacles for the typical semantic annotation approaches. Moreover, the shorter is the text, the worse are results produced by the context disambiguation, and the annotation can fail. A grammatical evaluation of the informal language may be useful for solving many of these issues but such a grammar must not be a formal and strict one. Hand-crafted grammar-based systems typically produce good results, but at the cost of hard work for manual annotations by experts in Computational Linguistics (CL). Moreover, if the systems perform statistical evaluations, they typically require a large amount of training data too. Semisupervised approaches have been suggested to avoid part of the annotation effort as at [12], but they do not exhibit better performances than the previous ones. We attempted to perform the semantic annotation of tweets applying the strategy we developed in [14]; in such an approach, the answer corresponding to a natural language query is retrieved from the DBPedia ontology. The result is a rule-based QA system that uses a similarity measure based on the linguistic properties of the involved texts (both the query and the support text if provided). The approach was defined *cognitive* according to the procedural semantics view: in this perspective, understanding and producing a sentence are two cognitive processes run on a perceptually grounded model of the world. Such a system does not perform statistical inference and it is not based on any machine learning paradigm, rather it attempts to simulate the cognitive processes that take place in humans when they infer the correct answer. Processes are encoded through the rules and the similarity measure used to link the query to the ontology: as a result, the 'semantic sense' of the query is inferred, and the answer is produced. In the same perspective, we defined the 'web sense' of the tweet by creating hyperlinks between the tweet itself and the linked data source DBPedia. The similarity measure and the cognitive processing rules are properly re-defined for highlighting the particular kind of both the text, that is a tweet with its typical features, and the task. In a few words, the main contribution of this paper is the definition of new aspects in the implementation of the cognitive processes to allow linking a tweet's informal text to DBPedia; such processes consider the particular structure of a tweet (mentions, hashtags, and partially structured statements) and the nature of the NEEL task. The whole approach is based also on linguistic considerations about the informal language.

The rest of the paper is arranged as follows. We first introduce the typical issues of the informal language in Sect. 2, highlighting the problems and the motivations leading traditional approaches to fail. Existing approaches are discussed in Sect. 3. In Sect. 4 we report the background of our work; in particular, we describe the original strategy as it was conceived for the QA system, and the problems posed by the tweets structure. Section 5 reports our approach, that is all the modifications to the original strategy we made for applying it to NEEL in tweets. Comparative evaluations versus the systems participating in the #Micropost2016 workshop NEEL Challenge co-located with the World Wide Web conference 2016 (WWW '16) are reported in Sect. 6. Finally, conclusions and future works are discussed in Sect. 7.

2   The Informal Language and Its Linguistic Issues

The main characteristics of informal language are ill-formed syntax [6] and dynamicity [9]; ill-formedness is related to the presence of abbreviations, unconventional spellings, and unstructured expressions that give to the tweet a noisy lexical nature. Dynamicity regards the fact that informal language changes more frequently than the formal one; there are not strict grammatical rules for describing the informal language, however the sentences expressed in such a language can be understood by a reader or a hearer even if they do not have rigid structures. Moreover, the informal language is characterized by the possibility to add new grammatical units or delete old ones over time: either new structures can emerge during conversation or existing ones can be removed if they are not frequently used. Substantially, social web users contribute to rapid emergence of new grammatical forms, symbols, and unconventional expressions as they own the skills to understand and re-use such novelties. This is one of the reasons for which the traditional Natural Language Processing (NLP) techniques fail when applied to NEEL in tweets. In particular, statistical approaches do not perceive such linguistic changes until huge annotated text corpora are at disposal for the scientific community; manual intervention through explicit annotations of data is needed in this perspective to allow even very good performances for these techniques. Challenges are a way to create such reference corpora, and this is an activity that has to be repeated frequently to address changes in language along with re-training and fine tuning of such systems.

We choose an inherently unsupervised strategy to be sensitive to both dynamicity and ill-formed syntax avoiding manual annotations: even if we make some linguistic considerations about the tweet, they are not based on strict grammatical rules, which also need frequent manual updating to cope with language dynamicity. Rather, the rules we implemented attempt to simulate the cognitive processes that can be involved in understanding the meaning of a tweet, and produce semantic annotation as their outcome.

3   State of the Art

Because of nature of tweets that are noisy and short, the performance of standard NLP software significantly suffers. Derczynski et al. [2] demonstrated that the performance of various state-of-the-art NLP software (e.g., Stanford NER and ANNIE) is typically lower than 50% F_1 for tweets. Many studies, such as [1] and [8] perform "informal language normalization" for disambiguating informal tokens; normalization is achieved defining a set of correspondences with the traditional natural language, that are called the *formal counterparts*. In particular, [11] employs (external) web mining to collect the counterparts of informal tokens. To optimize the labeling process, a large set of tokens are put automatically in correspondence with words by searching for the informal tokens in Google, and selecting the counterparts from the top 32 snippets based on the length of the shared character sequence.

In [4] the authors propose a strategy for entities disambiguation that refines their previous works [5]. They start with an initial extraction-like phase aimed at finding mention candidates, based on segmentation and KB lookup. Next, the disambiguation process is applied to the extracted candidates; this process uses three typical modules (the matcher, the feature extractor, and the Support Vector Machine ranker) and gives extra features to the mention candidates. Finally, another classification extracts mention candidates as either true or false entities, using the features obtained from the disambiguation process. Authors in [16] integrated some typical NLP processes for extracting entities from informal tokens, while in [10] authors attempt to discover a global context of informal sentences from both Wikipedia and Web N-Gram corpus. The sentences are segmented by a dynamic program, and each of these segments is a candidate entity. Finally they rank segments according to their probability of being an entity. In [19] a linguistic analysis is carried out to make prevision on tweets; differently from our work, the authors adopt a statistical approach that estimates trends and distributions into a big collection of tweets.

An important set of systems is referenced at [17], that is the final report of the #Micropost2016 workshop NEEL Challenge co-located with the World Wide Web conference 2016 (WWW '16) we refer to for evaluating our approach. The reader should refer to such a report for a deeper description of the methodology adopted by the cited systems. The aim of our contribution is avoiding statistical analysis, considering that social information has a fast and rapid changing over time, so we attempt to perform an analysis that is not influenced from previous trends and collections.

4   Background of the Proposed Approach

We were inspired to the cognitive model already proposed for QA [14] to overcome the problems posed by informal language, and apply our system to NEEL in tweets. In this section we first introduce briefly the cognitive strategy defined in the previous work, and then we show the typical constraints of NEEL task highlighting the features that require a modification in the base strategy.

4.1   QuASIt: The Cognitive System for Question Answering

QuASIt [14] is a QA system based on a cognitive architecture that attempts to simulate the human cognitive processes for understanding natural language queries, and producing an answer. Such an architecture is shown in Fig. 1: in particular, the DBPedia ontology represents the knowledge of the world owned by the system. Two kinds of processes have been devised: the first is related to the *conceptualization of meaning* that associates a perceived external object (i.e. a word, a visual percept, and so on) to an internal concept. Such a conceptualization associates a meaning to a perceived form; in QuASIt a form is a word of the query, and the internal concepts are the nodes of the ontology. This process is implemented by the Mapping to Meanings module. The second process is related

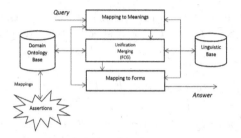

Fig. 1. The QuASIt cognitive architecture

to the *conceptualization of form* and is implemented by the Mapping to Forms module; it associates a syntactic expression to a meaning to be produced, but such a process is out of the scope of this paper, such as the other module of the figure. For detail, please refer to the cited paper. To understand the devised processes we must formally define the ontology of the system.

Formal definition of the domain ontology. Formally, the domain ontology is the tuple $O = \langle C_o, P_o, T_s, L, P_d \rangle$ defined according to the W3C technical report specification reported at https://www.w3.org/TR/owl-ref/, where:

- $C_o = \{cl_i\}$ is the set of type 1 classes that are is syntactically represented as named instances of `owl:Class`;
- P_o is the set of the object properties, so that:

$$P_o = \{o_i \mid o_i = (cl_j, cl_k) \ \ cl_j, cl_k \in C_o\};$$

- $T_s = \{t_i\}$ is the set of literal datatypes;
- $L = \{l_i\}$ is the set of literal strings used in the ontology as values of t_i;
- P_d is the set of the datatype properties, so that:

$$P_d = \{d_i \mid d_i = (cl_j, l_k) \ \ cl_j \in C_o, \ l_k \in L\}.$$

This ontology formal definition does not include individuals, that are the so-called *instances*. The instances are obtained from a set of strategies for mapping assertions of a separated database to the classes of the ontology, that are formalized by the *map* function so that $map : C_o \cup P_o \cup P_d \cup L \rightarrow I$, and $map(oe)$ returns the set I containing the instances for the ontological element oe defined by the assertion mapping.

Modeling the cognitive processes. To access the meanings of the natural language query, the query is first chunked by a POS tagger. A chunk is a set of consecutive tokens with the same POS tag; it is a n-gram of query words having the same syntactic category. The set of operations implementing the comprehension in QuASIt are formalized in what follows.

Let consider the query $Q = \{q_1, q_2, ..., q_n\}$, where q_i is the i-th token. Being T the set of all POS tags, and $t \in T$ a specific tag, the chunks set C is the partition of Q so that:

$$C = \{c_i \mid c_i = \bigcup_l^k q_j, \; pos(q_j) = t_i \; \forall j \in [l \ldots k], l, k \in [1 \ldots n], \; t_i \in T, \; q_j \in Q\}$$

where the function $pos : Q \rightarrow T$ returns the POS tag of a token. Then the F set of chunks grouped in syntactic categories for different tags in T is defined; in particular, we considered $F = F_p \cup F_v \cup F_q$, where F_p contains the chunks with the adverbial tag, F_v contains the verb phrase chunks, and F_q contains the noun phrase chunks. The *topic* of the query is what the user wants to know, and we assumed that it can be referred to a chunk in F_q, that is *each noun in a sentence is a possible candidate to be the topic of the sentence itself regardless it is a proper noun or a common one*; for this reason, it is searched for in the domain ontology to extract the corresponding *assertion subgraph*. Extracting the assertion subgraph corresponds exactly to the process of conceptualization of the perceived words, and it is simply implemented by rough intersections between the stems of the words in F, and the labels of the nodes in the domain ontology. Let be $stem(\cdot)$ the function that returns the stem of the words in its argument, $couple(\cdot)$ the function that returns both elements of a couple, and finally f_i a generic element belonging to either F_q or F_v; the assertion extraction process is modeled by the following functions:

- $a_c : F_q \rightarrow C_o$ that returns the set $a_c(f_i) = \{ cl_k \mid stem(f_i) = stem(i_j), \; i_j = map(cl_k), \; cl_k \in C_o\}$ composed by the ontological classes whose instances label's stems map to the stems of topic words contained in F_q. The set $I = \{i_j\}$ will contain all such instances;
- $a_p : F_v \rightarrow P_o \cup P_d$ returning the set $a_p(f_i) = \{ p_j \mid stem(f_i) = stem(p_j), \; p_j \in P_o \cup P_d, \; couple(p_j) \supset a_c(f_i)\}$ composed by the properties of the classes in $a_c(f_i)$ whose label's stems map to the stems of the verb in F_v.

The result is a sub-ontology $A = \langle C_a, P_a, I \rangle$ where $C_a = \bigcup_{F_q} a_c(f_i)$, $P_a = \bigcup_{F_v} a_p(f_i)$, and I the set of individuals retrieved by a_c that represents what the system understands about the query, and its conceptualization through the concepts identification in the ontology. These processes have been modified suitably for NEEL of entity mentions.

4.2   NEEL in Tweets

A tweet is a post on the social media application Twitter for which we identified four main components in the structure, that are:

1. the *micropost*, that is the message shared by the user. It can not be longer than 140 characters;
2. the *hashtag*, that is each metadata tag with the # prefix, that allows to categorize a tweet's topic(s), and then makes it easier for users to search other tweets about such topic(s);

3. the *tag*, that is the metadata tag with the @ prefix, that allows to associate an entity (other people, locations and so on) already existing in the social platform;

4. the *thread*, that are the set of comments of other people to the main micropost.

According to [17] semantic annotation of tweets consists of two main operations: *mention detection* and *candidate selection*. The former is related to the identification of the entity mention in the tweet, the latter is the operation related to the identification of the link in DBPedia that defines such an entity. We devised some adjustments to the cognitive processes of QuASIt with the aim to model these operations. The proper nature of the NEEL task poses some constraints in the elaboration of a tweet, and if the task is executed by a human, she/he should keep in mind these constraints thus acting inside these boundaries. The NEEL constraints that we used to model our system are:

- a mention of an entity in a tweet is a proper noun or an acronym;
- the complete extent of an entity is the entire string representing the name, without any pre-posed (i.e. the articles, the title such as "Mrs", "Dr", and so on...) or post-posed modifiers. The sub-strings of an extent, if exist, are not considerable as single entity mention; for example, the mention "Micheal Jackson" is a complete extent of a single entity, while the sub-words "Michael" and "Jackson" are not single mentions. These words can be considered as single mentions when they are the only string in the extent;
- an embedded entity must be considered an entity mention, while the broader one not. An embedded entity is encapsulated into a more generic one (the broader one) that is not explicitly mentioned; for example, in the statement "The art director of Harry Potter", the extent "Harry Potter" is an embedded entity that must be annotated, while "The art director person" is the broader entity, and must not be annotated;
- the words in the hashtag ('#') or in the tag ('@') are entities only if they are proper nouns or acronyms.

5   Cognitive Processes for NEEL in Tweets

The key of the proposed strategy was to consider a tweet as a query to be understood by the QuASIt system. As consequence, the *conceptualization of meaning* process has been applied for understanding a tweet, hence to link the tweet to the ontology. New linguistic aspects have been considered due the informal language and the particular structure of tweets, and considering the NEEL task nature. The processes we defined for the NEEL task are:

- chunking activity;
- chunk conceptualization;

These processes implement the NEEL operations previously described; in particular, the chunk conceptualization process is an insight of the conceptualization of meaning in QuASIt for allowing NEEL. As a consequence, the QuASIt architecture was modified as shown in Fig. 2.

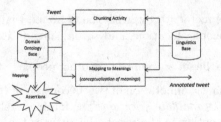

Fig. 2. The cognitive architecture for NEEL in tweets

5.1 Chunking Activity

To perform mention detection in a tweet, chunking is the base cognitive process performed by humans for understanding a not plain text [18]. Humans break down a difficult text into more manageable pieces, and rewrite such "chunks" in their own words. Given the tweet t, we classified its components into two main categories in terms of the linguistic properties of the inherent chunks. The categories are:

1. the M category, where $M = \{m_i \mid m_i$ is a micropost of $t\}$; such category contains the microposts of the tweet, comprising the main micropost that generates a discussion, and the microposts in the thread that are the comments to the main one;
2. the H category, where $H = \{h_i \mid h_i$ is a hashtag or a tag of $t\}$, that contains the hashtags and the tags in t.

Trivially, both hashtags and tags in M require a more deep chunking activity than microposts, for which blank spaces and/or punctuation separate tokens. We implemented chunking for tags and hashtags using a cognitive inspired approach: here the linguistic problem can be stated as obtaining a "meaningful" splitting of a word concatenation where there are no separation characters. The term "meaningful" has to be intended as "finding the words, which make more sense while taking into account morphology", and it will be the key for selecting between multiple chunks. The process has been implemented by means of the A^* semantic tokenizer proposed by some of the authors at [13]. A tree of possible alternatives for chunking a concatenated string is built by means of proper heuristics relying on linguistic considerations that set proper cost functions too. A left-to-right scanning is used to model the reading activity, that was inspired to the Simple View of Reading (SVR) [7]. Input strings are scanned from left to right and candidate words are generated by subsequent character concatenations from the very first character to the entire string. The tree is explored by best-first search, and the path with lower cost links nodes that correspond to the identified tokens. In this approach, differently from the original tokenizer, the source we used for retrieving meaningful words is formed by both DBPedia ontology and Wordnet linguistic source [3]. In fact, the tags and the hashtags can contain proper nouns that are not in Wordnet even if they are referred to in DBPedia, and vice versa. If no sense words are retrieved, the whole string is returned. After chunking the text in H, the microposts in M are chunked too, performing at first a simple tokenization based on blank spaces; due to the presence of informal language, such tokens are chunked again according to the A^* strategy. For completing the chunking activity process, the chunks devised so far must be rewritten using words already owned by the system. In particular, considering the informal language, such an operation implies the substitution of ill-formed syntax words with well-formed ones that are in the sources used by the system, and represent its language knowledge. Such a substitution is performed considering the words that are syntactically nearest to the token; more simply, an automatic correctorbased on Wordnet that is downloadable at https://www.icbld.com/ is applied to the tokens, and a list of similar words is returned. Formally, let be $a\_star(s)$ the function that returns the list of chunks L_c for the string s based on the A^* strategy; $tok(s)$ is the function that returns the list of tokens L_t split using blank spaces for the string s; $icbl(k)$ is the function that returns the list L_w of syntactically similar words to the token k. The chunking activity process is modeled by the following functions:

$$c_a : H \cup M \to L_c, \quad c_a(s) = \begin{cases} a\_star(s) & s \in H \\ a\_star(tok(s)) & s \in M \end{cases}$$

$$icbl : L_c \to L_w, \qquad icbl(k) = \{w_i \mid w_i \text{ is a word syntactically similar to } k\}$$

The output of the chunking activity is the set $C = H \cup M \cup L_w$ composed by all the possible words to be analyzed for mention detection. Next, a POS tagger allows filtering such words to identify only the proper nouns, and hence the *topic* of the tweet; differently from QuASIt, where the topics were the noun phrases contained in the query (both common and proper nouns), in this case the topics are only the proper nouns in the chunk set C according to the NEEL task specifications defined previously. Finally, being w a generic set of words, $pos(w)$ the function that returns the set of POS tags of the words in w according to the chosen tagset specified at https://courses.washington.edu/hypertxt/csar-v02/penntable.html, the mention detection process ends with the definition of the set MD that will contain all candidate mentions:

$$MD = \{m_i \mid m_i = \{c_j, c_{j+1}, ..., c_{j+n_i}\} \subset C, \ pos(m_i) \in \{NP, NPS\}\}.$$

The n_i value represents the extent of the i-th mention, and NP and NPS are the tags associated to the proper noun (rispectively singular and plural).

5.2   Chunk Conceptualization

Once the set MD containing all the possible candidate mentions is built, the chunk conceptualization process attempts to select from DBPedia the entities to link to such mentions. Such a process is based on the conceptualization of meaning defined in QuASIt, particularly in the part related to the extraction of the assertion subgraph. The assertion subgraph corresponds exactly to the conceptualization of a perceived statement because it links the statement itself to the ontology used by the system; its extraction is now implemented for the tweet. The rough intersections between the stems of the mentions in MD, and the stems of the labels in DBPedia is extended here considering a suitable syntactic similarity and not a perfect match. Recalling the definitions for the functions *stem* and *map*, and the formal definition of the ontology in Sect. 4, we define the new function $sim(w_1, w_2) = 0.5 * jaro(w_1, w_2) + 0.5 * lev(w_1, w_2)$ that returns a similarity measure that is a weighted sum of the Jaro-Winkler $jaro(\cdot, \cdot)$ and Levenstein $lev(\cdot, \cdot)$ distances between the words w_1 and w_2 in its argument. The use of a string similarity metric enhances the mapping process taking into account also ill-formed words in informal language that could make the *stem* function return no results, thus resulting in an empty intersection with the stems coming from the labels of DBPedia. In this case, the Jaro-Winkler distance is computed from the original forms of the chunks; the chunks of a mention have to be concatenated by the *concat* function. The chunk conceptualization process is formalized by the function $a_{c_{neel}} : MD \rightarrow C_o$ that returns the set:

$$a_{c_{neel}}(m_i) = \{ cl_k \mid stem(m_i) = stem(i_j) \vee$$
$$sim(concat(m_i), i_j) > \tau, \ i_j = map(cl_k), \ cl_k \in C_o\}$$

composed by the ontological classes such that either the stems of their instance labels is equal to the stems of mentions in MD or the Jaro-Winkler distance between such labels and the form of mentions in MD is above a suitable threshold. The value for τ has been fixed to 0.7 experimentally. The set $I = \{i_j\}$ will contain all such instances.

The candidate selection process is modeled by the $a_{c_{neel}}$ function that returns for each mention in MD the entities in DBPedia which better match to it, according to the criterion specified in the function definition. Finally, the set of nodes C_a and the set of correspondent instances I, where $C_a = \bigcup_{MD} a_{c_{neel}}(m_i)$, and I the set of individuals correspondent to $a_{c_{neel}}$ represent what the system understands about the whole tweet, that is its assertion subgraph.

6   Experiments and Comparative Evaluations

In this section we describe briefly the challenge dataset and the evaluation scores that we referred to for evaluating our approach. Then we show and discuss our results in comparison to the participant systems.

6.1   The Dataset and the Metrics

The dataset proposed for the #Microposts2016 NEEL Challenge extends the ones presented in the previous editions of the challenge with the only change in the DBPedia version that is DBPedia 2015-04. Particular attention was devoted to include both event and non-event tweets. Both Training and Development sets were not used to perform our experiments, because our system uses a symbolic unsupervised approach that can be applied in every context and does not require neither training nor tuning data. The Test set contains 45,164 tokens and 1,022 total entities; it was created by adding tweets collected in December 2015 around the US primary elections and the Star Wars The Force Awakens Premiere.

The challenge evaluations is based on four metrics, but only three of them have to be considered for our case. In fact, a metric was introduced for discriminating in case of tie in evaluation score, that is the *latency* but we have not such kind of problem in our experiments. The three main metrics are:

1. *strong_typed_mention_match (stmm)* that considers the micro average F_1 score on the annotations related to the mention extent and the type identification;
2. *strong_link_match (slm)* that considers the micro average F_1 score on the annotations related to the link for each mention;
3. *mention_ceaf (mc)* that considers the F_1 score for the NIL and not-NIL in the annotations.

The final score is computed considering such metrics, according to the formula: $score = 0.4 * mc + 0.3 * stmm + 0.3 * slm$. The scorer proposed for the TAC KBP 2014 task at https://github.com/wikilinks/neleval/wiki/Evaluation was used to perform the evaluation.

6.2   Results and Discussion

Table 1 reports the results of our system (in bold) compared with the best performances obtained by the participants to the #Micropost2016 workshop NEEL Challenge. The state-of-the-art approach *ADEL* developed by [15] was used as the baseline. The last four columns report the micro average F_1 score on each of the three metrics taken into consideration, along with the the global *score* value. Particularly, the second column refers to the use of a supervised/unsupervised approach in each system. As it is shown, our system ranked second, compared to the challenge participants, and this is a very remarkable result if we consider that our system has a performance very close to *kea* but we make use of an unsupervised strategy, while both *kea* and *ADEL* use a supervised one. Our systems

Table 1. Results

Rank	Approach	Team name	F_1^{mc}	F_1^{stmm}	F_1^{slm}	$Score$
1	sup	kea	0.641	0.473	0.501	0.5486
2	**unsup**	**our**	**0.616**	**0.515**	**0.406**	**0.5227**
3	unsup	insight-centre @ nuig	0.621	0.246	0.202	0.3828
4	sup	mit lincoln laboratory	0.366	0.319	0.396	0.3609
5	sup	ju team	0.467	0.312	0.248	0.3548
6	sup	unimib	0.203	0.267	0.162	0.3353
*	*sup*	*adel*	*0.69*	*0.61*	*0.536*	*0.6198*

performs similarly to *kea* in the *mc* measure, and outperforms it in the *stmm*, while has a decay in the *slm* that can be observed also in *ADEL* and *kea*.

7   Conclusions and Future Works

A novel system for Named Entity rEcognition and Linking (NEEL) has been presented in this paper, that searches for proper nouns in all the components of a tweet, and links them to concepts in the DBPedia ontology. The presented approach relies on QuASIt, the QA system already presented by the authors, and considers a tweet as a query to be understood; our NEEL system modifies suitably the QuASIt strategy for *conceptualization of meaning* to link tokens inside the tweet to DBPedia. At first tweets have to be chunked suitably as regards both tokens in the text and multi-word hashtags or tags. Then chunks are mapped to the instance labels of the classes in DBPedia using a mixed Jaro-Winkler/Levenstein distance. Our system ranked second when compared to the outcomes of the #Micropost2016 workshop NEEL Challenge. Future work will be devoted to deepen the analysis of the whole assertion subgraph extracted by the system to devise more semantic information about the tweet like the mood of each post in a thread as regards the topic of the main tweet.

References

1. Beaufort, R., Roekhaut, S., Cougnon, L.A., Fairon, C.: A hybrid rule/model-based finite-state framework for normalizing SMS messages. In: Hajic, J., Carberry, S., Clark, S. (eds.) ACL, pp. 770–779. The Association for Computer Linguistics (2010). http://dblp.uni-trier.de/db/conf/acl/acl2010.html#BeaufortRCF10
2. Derczynski, L., Maynard, D., Rizzo, G., van Erp, M., Gorrell, G., Troncy, R., Petrak, J., Bontcheva, K.: Analysis of named entity recognition and linking for tweets. Inf. Process. Manag. **51**(2), 32–49 (2015)
3. Fellbaum, C. (ed.): WordNet An Electronic Lexical Database. The MIT Press, Cambridge; London (1998)
4. Habib, M.B., van Keulen, M.: Need4tweet: a twitterbot for tweets named entity extraction and disambiguation. In: Proceedings of the System Demonstrations of the 53rd Annual Meeting of the Association for Computational Linguistics (ACL 2015), Beijing, China. The Association for Computer Linguistics, Beijing, July 2015
5. Habib, M., van Keulen, M.: A generic open world named entity disambiguation approach for tweets. In: 5th International Conference on Knowledge Discovery and Information Retrieval, KDIR 2013. SciTePress, September 2013. http://doc.utwente.nl/86471/
6. Han, B., Baldwin, T.: Lexical normalisation of short text messages: makn sens a #twitter. In: Proceedings of the 49th Annual Meeting of the Association for Computational Linguistics: Human Language Technologies, HLT 2011, vol. 1, pp. 368–378. Association for Computational Linguistics, Stroudsburg (2011). http://dl.acm.org/citation.cfm?id=2002472.2002520
7. Hoover, W.A., Gough, P.B.: The simple view of reading. Read. Writ. **2**(2), 127–160 (1990). doi:10.1007/BF00401799

8. Kaufmann, M., Kalita, J.: Syntactic normalization of Twitter messages. In: International Conference on Natural Language Processing, Kharagpur, India (2010)
9. Kobus, C., Yvon, F., Damnati, G.: Normalizing SMS: are two metaphors better than one? In: Proceedings of the 22nd International Conference on Computational Linguistics, COLING 2008, vol. 1, pp. 441–448. Association for Computational Linguistics, Stroudsburg (2008). http://dl.acm.org/citation.cfm?id=1599081.1599137
10. Li, C., Weng, J., He, Q., Yao, Y., Datta, A., Sun, A., Lee, B.S.: Twiner: named entity recognition in targeted Twitter stream. In: Proceedings of the 35th International ACM SIGIR Conference on Research and Development in Information Retrieval, SIGIR 2012, pp. 721–730. ACM, New York (2012). http://doi.acm.org/10.1145/2348283.2348380
11. Liu, F., Weng, F., Wang, B., Liu, Y.: Insertion, deletion, or substitution?: normalizing text messages without pre-categorization nor supervision (2011)
12. Nothman, J., Ringland, N., Radford, W., Murphy, T., Curran, J.R.: Learning multilingual named entity recognition from Wikipedia. Artif. Intell. **194**, 151–175 (2013). doi:10.1016/j.artint.2012.03.006
13. Pipitone, A., Campisi, M.C., Pirrone, R.: An A* based semantic tokenizer for increasing the performance of semantic applications. In: 2013 IEEE Seventh International Conference on Semantic Computing, Irvine, CA, USA, 16–18 September 2013, pp. 393–394. IEEE Computer Society (2013). https://doi.org/10.1109/ICSC.2013.75
14. Pipitone, A., Tirone, G., Pirrone, R.: QuASIt: a cognitive inspired approach to question answering for the Italian language. In: Adorni, G., Cagnoni, S., Gori, M., Maratea, M. (eds.) AI*IA 2016. LNCS, vol. 10037, pp. 464–476. Springer, Cham (2016). doi:10.1007/978-3-319-49130-1_34
15. Plu, J., Rizzo, G., Troncy, R.: Enhancing entity linking by combining NER models. In: Sack, H., Dietze, S., Tordai, A., Lange, C. (eds.) SemWebEval 2016. CCIS, vol. 641, pp. 17–32. Springer, Cham (2016). doi:10.1007/978-3-319-46565-4_2
16. Ritter, A., Clark, S., Mausam, Etzioni, O.: Named entity recognition in tweets: an experimental study. In: Proceedings of the Conference on Empirical Methods in Natural Language Processing, EMNLP 2011, pp. 1524–1534. Association for Computational Linguistics, Stroudsburg (2011). http://dl.acm.org/citation.cfm?id=2145432.2145595
17. Rizzo, G., van Erp, M., Plu, J., Troncy, R.: Making sense of microposts (#microposts2016) named entity recognition and linking (NEEL) challenge. In: Dadzie, A., Preotiuc-Pietro, D., Radovanovic, D., Basave, A.E.C., Weller, K. (eds.) Proceedings of the 6th Workshop on 'Making Sense of Microposts' co-located with the 25th International World Wide Web Conference (WWW 2016), Montréal, Canada, 11 April 2016. CEUR Workshop Proceedings, vol. 1691, pp. 50–59. CEUR-WS.org (2016). http://ceur-ws.org/Vol-1691/microposts2016_neel-challenge-report/
18. Rupley, W.H., Blair, T.R., Nichols, W.D.: Effective reading instruction for struggling readers: the role of direct/explicit teaching. Read. Writ. Q. **25**(2–3), 125–138 (2009). doi:10.1080/10573560802683523
19. Wang, A., Chen, T., Kan, M.Y.: Re-tweeting from a linguistic perspective. In: Proceedings of the Second Workshop on Language in Social Media, LSM 2012, pp. 46–55. Association for Computational Linguistics, Stroudsburg (2012). http://dl.acm.org/citation.cfm?id=2390374.2390380

Sentiment Spreading: An Epidemic Model for Lexicon-Based Sentiment Analysis on Twitter

Laura Pollacci[1]([⊠]), Alina Sîrbu[1], Fosca Giannotti[2], Dino Pedreschi[1],
Claudio Lucchese[2], and Cristina Ioana Muntean[2]

[1] Department of Computer Science, University of Pisa, Pisa, Italy
`laura.pollacci@di.unipi.it`, {`alina.sirbu,dino.pedreschi`}`@unipi.it`
[2] ISTI-CNR, Pisa, Italy
{`fosca.giannotti,claudio.lucchese,cristina.muntean`}`@isti.cnr.it`

Abstract. While sentiment analysis has received significant attention in the last years, problems still exist when tools need to be applied to microblogging content. This because, typically, the text to be analysed consists of very short messages lacking in structure and semantic context. At the same time, the amount of text produced by online platforms is enormous. So, one needs simple, fast and effective methods in order to be able to efficiently study sentiment in these data. Lexicon-based methods, which use a predefined dictionary of terms tagged with sentiment valences to evaluate sentiment in longer sentences, can be a valid approach. Here we present a method based on epidemic spreading to automatically extend the dictionary used in lexicon-based sentiment analysis, starting from a reduced dictionary and large amounts of Twitter data. The resulting dictionary is shown to contain valences that correlate well with human-annotated sentiment, and to produce tweet sentiment classifications comparable to the original dictionary, with the advantage of being able to tag more tweets than the original. The method is easily extensible to various languages and applicable to large amounts of data.

1 Introduction

Sentiment analysis has been an important research challenge in the last years, especially with the availability of large amounts of user generated content from various on-line platforms. Although several methods have been introduced [14], issues still exist both when it comes to applying and evaluating new methods. In particular, for microblogging data such as Twitter, difficulties arise due to the length and structure of the messages. These are typically very short, providing little semantic context, and do not always abide to grammatical rules, which means preprocessing is not straightforward. Additionally, the size of the data to be processed is very large, so methods need to be powerful and fast.

Many approaches to sentiment analysis on Twitter are lexicon-based. They use a dictionary of words that are either manually or automatically tagged with a sentiment valence to assign sentiment to tweets. These methods have the advantage of being easily translatable to other languages (by translating the small

© Springer International Publishing AG 2017
F. Esposito et al. (Eds.): AI*IA 2017, LNAI 10640, pp. 114–127, 2017.
https://doi.org/10.1007/978-3-319-70169-1_9

dictionary) and they are fast enough to process large amounts of data in a short time, which is an important feature when it comes to big data processing. However, a main disadvantage of this approach is that, since tweets are short, it may happen that no term is found in the dictionary, reducing the amount of tweets that can be classified.

Here we introduce a method to extend the dictionary automatically starting from an existing seed dictionary. The method uses the tweets to be classified themselves to create a network of terms, which are then tagged with sentiment using an epidemics-like process. This method allows us to increase the number of classified tweets by about 45%, while maintaining classification performance similar to a smaller manually-tagged dictionary. Additionally, an important possible application of the method is evaluating language superdiversity [20] in a population, since the resulting dictionary is strongly population-dependent, thus can provide important insight into how language is used by various populations on Twitter. In this work we will concentrate on validating the new dictionary, while the analysis of superdiversity will be approached in future work.

2   Related Work

Over the past decade, there has been a large amount of work on sentiment analysis that focuses on social media content and microblogging platforms, such as Twitter. In [14] the authors provide an exhaustive survey. For Twitter, we can identify several main approaches for sentiment analysis.

Lexicon-Based Approaches. Lexicon based approaches exploit dictionaries of words with positive and negative valence and then calculate the polarity score of a text according to the positive and negative words found in the text. Dictionaries can be created automatically, such as SentiWordNet [7], or manually, such as ANEW (Affective Norms for English Words) [2]. In [6], the overall sentiment score for a text is computed based on the frequency and the valence of each word in the text, using a frequency-weighted average. A similar approach is the VAD method [13], which performs Emotion Detection. In VAD the score for each sentence is calculated by averaging the valences of each word in the sentence. Results achieved for three datasets (Semeval 2013, ISEAR and Fairy Tales) show a Precision score between 0.46 and 0.53, Recall values from 0.40 to 0.42 and F1 score between 0.37 and 0.41. In [8], authors build two discriminatory-word lexicons, one for positive sentiment words, and one for negative sentiment words using twitrratr.com, a website that provides keyword-based sentiment analysis. For each tweet the number of keywords is counted (both positives and negatives). If in the tweet the positive count is higher than the negative count, the tweet is positive, negative vice-versa. If counts are equal, the tweet is tagged as neutral.

This type of lexicon-based approaches present some known problems. As underlined in [13], many words change their meaning in different contexts. However, dictionaries are annotated based on the general mood evoked by a term and not how it changes with context. Second, if words with opposite polarity are found in a sentence, frequently the sentence's average polarity score falls in the neutral state. These issues decrease the overall accuracy obtained with these methods.

Another important aspect is that, when it comes to processing Twitter data, the dictionaries are too restricted and small amounts of Tweets can be actually classified. To tackle this last issue, means to extend the labelled dictionary have been investigated. For instance, Velikovich [19] build a network of words and phrases from a collection of Web documents. For each word, they first build a vector of co-occurrence with the other words. Then they construct a word graph in which each word is a node, and edges are weighted with the cosine similarity over the co-occurrence vectors. Sentiment scores are propagated from seed words into other nodes. The algorithm computes both a positive and a negative polarity for each node in the graph (pol_i^+ and pol_i^-). Positive and negative scores are equal to the sum over the maximum weighted path from every seed word to a specific node. The final polarity score for the word is calculated as $pol_i = pol_i^+ - \beta pol_i^-$, where β is a constant meant to account for the difference in overall mass of positive and negative flow in the graph. The method was also employed by [12] using emoticons as original seeds.

In this work we provide another method to automatically extend the dictionary based directly on the corpus to be classified. Compared to previous approaches, the method simplifies significantly both the graph building stage, and the sentiment propagation stage. In particular, we use the unweighted co-occurrence network and simple propagation based on ideas from contagion models. These simplifications are important in order to be able to process larger amounts of data.

Machine Learning Approaches. A different class of methods use machine learning to perform sentiment classification. In general, better accuracy is obtained by these methods compared to the simple lexicon-based approaches above.

In [15], machine learning is applied to sentiment classification of movie reviews. They test three standard algorithms: Naive Bayes, Support Vector Machines (SVM) and MaxEntropy using a bag-of-words framework. They select a predefined set of n features: 16,165 unigrams that occur at least four times in the data and 16,165 bigrams that occur most often. They analyse two means of constructing the features. The first uses presence features, i.e. boolean features that flag whether a unigram or bigram is present in the text. The second uses the number of times the unigram or bigram appears. Their work shows that best results are achieved exploiting SVMs and unigram presence as features. Accuracy scores ranged from 0.72 from 0.82 and Recall ranged from 50% to 69%. Implementing a two-phase approach, they first separate subjective messages from objective ones, then they classify the former into positive or negative.

In [8], three-class sentiment classification is implemented using Naive Bayes, Multinomial Naive Bayes, and SVM classifiers. Results show that best accuracy is achieved for SVMs, both for presence and frequency features using unigrams+bigrams. Accuracy for unigrams+bigrams is 79% for presence features and 81% for frequency features. Instead, separate unigrams and bigrams achieved accuracy scores that range from 76% to 78.6%. SVMs are shown to outperform other machine learning methods in [9] as well. Here, the training data is obtained through mining of tweets with negative and positive emoticons, while features are based on unigrams, bigrams and parts of speech.

Hybrid Lexicon-Based Machine Learning. Some of the machine learning methods used for sentiment analysis can include features obtained through a lexicon labelled with sentiment valences. However, classification does not rely merely on computing a sentiment score through averaging of valences, but uses more complex calculations.

In [1] syntactical features are combined with real-valued prior polarity or words (e.g. number of negative words) and part of speech tagging. They classify tweets into positive, negative and neutral sentiment classes. Their results show that models that combine prior polarity features with unigrams, and with a new tweet representation based on trees, outperform the unigram baseline. Another recent approach is [12], where adaptive logistic regression is used to classify tweets. Authors show that combining lexicon-based features with standard machine learning approaches improves performance.

In this work we validate our extended dictionary using SVM classifiers and lexicon-based features, since these methods appear to provide best performance in most cases presented above. We achieve accuracy, precision and recall rates similar to other methods. However, our goal is not to introduce a new sentiment analysis method, but to show that our automatically-extended lexicon produces results comparable to those obtained by a high-quality manually-tagged established lexicon.

Social Relations Approaches. Another approach to sentiment analysis on Twitter exploits the social relations between the users and their followers. For instance, [18] show that the use of label propagation within the Twitter follower graph improves the polarity classification. In [11], a sociological approach is proposed, showing that social theories such as Emotional Contagion and Sentiment Consistency could be useful for sentiment analysis. We also propose the use of ideas from contagion models, in particular epidemic spreading and opinion dynamics, to automatically extend the dictionary used for sentiment analysis, although we do not base our spreading process on the follower network, but on an un-weighted co-occurrence graph.

3   Data and Preprocessing

Our analysis is based on two Twitter datasets (one tagged with sentiment classes, one untagged), and lexical resources, i.e. dictionaries of words enriched with sentiment valences.

3.1 Tagged Twitter Dataset

This dataset is composed of 3,718 publicly available tweets and their sentiment classifications, retrieved from three different sources:

The Semeval 2013 Message Polarity Classification Competition (task B)[1]. The original dataset consisted of a 12–20K messages corpus on a range of topics, classified into positive, neutral and negative classes. We retrieved 2,752 such tweets, that were still available on the Twitter platform. These were passed through the language detection algorithm provided by the Python package Langdetect, to ensure they were written in English, leaving us with 2,547 tweets in the final dataset (428 negative, 1,347 neutral and 970 positive).

The Semeval 2014 Message Polarity Classification Competition (task B)[2]. Similar to Semeval 2013, this corpus consisted originally in 10000 tweets, out of which we downloaded 687 English tweets (142 negative, 319 neutral and 226 positive).

Earth Hour 2015 Corpus.[3] This dataset contains 600 tweets annotated with Sentiment information (Positive, Negative, Neutral) where each annotation is triply-annotated through a crowdsourcing campaign. Out of these, 370 tweets were still available for download through the Twitter platform (30 negative, 185 neutral and 80 positive).

We observe that a small proportion of tweets' is tagged with a negative valence, with neutral tweets being most prevalent, in all three datasets. This can be seen as a characteristic of Twitter messages in general. This dataset will be used in the following to evaluate the performance of our extended dictionary, compared to an already established dictionary, in classifying tweet sentiment. For this, we first proceeded to pre-process data and then to normalize and lemmatize the entire dataset obtained, through a general-purpose pipeline of linguistic annotation tools, as explained in Sect. 3.4.

3.2 Untagged Twitter Dataset

This dataset is a subset of that used in [5] and composed of just under one million and seven hundred geolocalised English Twitter messages retrieved for 6 days, from the 14th to the 20th of August 2015. All tweets were linguistically treated following the method described in Sect. 3.4.

This dataset was used in two ways. First, it is at the base of our method for extending the dictionary of terms tagged with sentiment valences. Second, sentiment analysis is performed on it, and the resulting sentiment scores compared between our extended dictionary and a previously established dictionary from the literature.

---

[1] The Semeval 2013 Message Polarity Classification competition (task B), https://www.cs.york.ac.uk/semeval-2013/.

[2] The Semeval 2014 Message Polarity Classification competition (task B), http://alt.qcri.org/semeval2014/.

[3] The Earth Hour 2015 corpus: https://gate.ac.uk/projects/decarbonet/datasets.html.

3.3   Lexical Resources

In order to develop our algorithm and validate results we identified several resources of lemmas annotated with sentiment valences.

The *Affective Norms for English Words* (ANEW) [2] provides a set of normative emotional ratings for 1,034 terms. Using Self-Assessment Manikin (SAM), an affective rating system, emotional ratings in terms of pleasure, arousal, and dominance were collected from human subjects. Pleasure represents positive versus negative emotions. Arousal finds the two extremes of the scale of values in "calm" and "exciting". The dominance dimension determines if the subject feels in control of the situation or not. Each dimension is represented as a number between 0 and 10. For our algorithm, we used the pleasure dimension as a sentiment valence, as evaluated by both male and female subjects.

SentiWordNet [7] is a publicly available lexical resource in which words are associated with three numerical scores ($Obj(s)$, $Pos(s)$ and $Neg(s)$) describing how objective, positive, and negative they are. In order to be able to use these together with the ANEW lexicon, we computed a unique polarity for each word. Following the methods presented in [10], we choose to adopt the difference between the positive and the negative score as an overall sentiment valence, properly scaled to interval $[0, 10]$ like ANEW.

After calculating polarities from SentiWordNet, we observed that the distribution is strongly heterogeneous: neutral words are much more than positives and negatives. Therefore, we decided to balance classes choosing the number (n) of items in the least represented class (negative), and selecting from other classes the n most strongly polarized lemmas, for a total of 16,914 lemmas.

We built an in-house *bad words lexicon*, including 63 common curse and swear English words. We selected the words starting from all the dirty words from Google's "what do you love" project. Each word of the lexicon is tagged with a 0.0 polarity score, hence is considered strongly negative.

3.4   Data Preprocessing and Annotation

The aim of the preprocessing phase of tweets is their grammatical annotation. The first problem we decided to deal with was to obtain cleaned data which can be processed in an effective way by automatic methods. The annotation of linguistic constituents required the development of a dedicated rule-based cleaning procedure. This consisted of removing punctuation, links and usernames, and normalising hashtags and emphasis words.

The output of this cleaning phase is linguistically-standardized tweets that are subsequently treated by a general-purpose pipeline of linguistic annotation tools. Specifically, tweets are lemmatized and tagged with the Part-Of-Speech tagger TreeTagger, described in [16]. In order to reduce the number of noisy words which could be wrongly identified and uselessly increase the data to be processed, we selected, for each tweet, only words belonging to specific grammatical classes: nouns, adjectives, and verbs. This allowed us to obtain only significant words from the sentiment and meaning point of view.

We applied the pre-processing procedure to both the tagged and the untagged tweets above. Hence the two datasets contain cleared standardized English texts composed of only nouns, verbs, and adjectives.

4   Extending the Dictionary

We adopt an epidemics-based approach to extend the dictionary of terms used for lexicon-based sentiment analysis. Our method consists of two stages: building the network and sentiment spreading.

4.1   Building the Network

Starting from the preprocessed Untagged Twitter Dataset (Sect. 3), we build a network of lemmas where each lemma corresponds to one node. Two nodes are connected by an edge if there is at least one tweet where both lemmas appear. Hence, the network is an unweighted co-occurrence graph based on the target tweets to be classified. We use a large amount of tweets to build this network, thus we expect that lemmas with positive valence will be mostly connected to other positive lemmas, while those with negative valences will be connected among themselves. We consider only tweets not containing a negation ("don't", "not", etc.), since with negations it is difficult to understand which lemmas from the negated tweet can be considered connected in the network, and which not.

4.2   Sentiment Spreading

Once the network of lemmas is obtained, we start to add valences to each node in the network. We start from a *seed dictionary*, which is typically reduced in size. In the next section we will show results obtained when the seed is 50% of the ANEW dictionary (the other half is used to validate the results), together with all lemmas in the SentiWordNet and Bad words lexicon. This seed allows us to assign valences to a reduced number of nodes in the network. This is the initial state of our epidemic process.

Starting from the initial state, we follow a discrete time process where at each step sentiment valences spread through the network. At time t, for all nodes i which do not have any valence, the set of neighbouring nodes $N(i)$ is analyzed, and i takes the valence that aggregates the distribution of valences in $N(i)$. The update is synchronous for all untagged nodes that can be tagged at this step. The epidemic procedure continues until no new valences are assigned to the nodes, i.e. when the population reaches a stable state. The process is similar to those seen in continuous opinion dynamics models [17], where agents take into account the aggregated opinion of their entire neighbourhood when forming their own. The difference here is that once a valence is assigned, it is never modified.

To decide the aggregation procedure we took into account several observations. In general, tweets appear to be very heterogeneous, most containing both positive and negative words. Hence a simple averaging of valences would most of the time result in neutral lemmas, although they actually contain meaningful sentiment. So, we decided to use instead the mode of the distribution of valences in the neighbourhood, which is a much more meaningful criterion in these conditions. However, the mode was only considered in special circumstances. We observed that in some cases the distribution of valences in the neighbourhood is very heterogeneous. That means the range of valences is very large, or the entropy of the distribution is very high. In this case, it is unclear what the valence of the new lemma should be, so we chose not to assign one at all. Again, this was inspired by works from opinion dynamics (e.g. the q-voter model [3]), taking into account the concept of social impact: agents are better able to influence their neighbours as a consensual group rather than isolated, hence a heterogeneous group will have no influence on its neighbours. Here, this was implemented as thresholds on the range and entropy on the neighbouring valence distribution: a node will be infected with the aggregated valence of its neighbourhood only if the range and entropy are below these thresholds. In order to avoid outliers, we consider the range to be the difference between the 10th and the 90th percentile. The two thresholds (range and entropy) become two parameters of our model, that need to be tuned to maximise performance.

5   Evaluation of the New Dictionary

In order to evaluate the extended dictionary, we perform two different analyses. First, we concentrate on the valences obtained after our sentiment spreading process. For this we use cross validation on the ANEW dictionary. Specifically, the ANEW dictionary is divided into two halves: one half is used as a seed dictionary during the epidemic process, together with SentiWordNet and the Bad words dictionary; the second half is used as a test dataset, i.e. the valence obtained through our procedure is compared to the original valence in the ANEW dictionary. We use Pearson correlation to quantify the similarity. This gives us an indication on whether our process produces valid sentiment valences.

It is important to note that while a significant correlation between the modelled and real valences is desired, we do not expect to obtain very large such values. This because the correlation depends highly on the corpus, i.e. how language is used by the Twitter users, the topic, etc. We expect that by changing the Twitter population, the correlation changes as well. In fact, we propose the correlation to be a means to quantify superdiversity on Twitter, and we believe this can be very useful in understanding effects of population migration both on the receiving and incoming population. However, in this paper we concentrate only on validating our method for sentiment analysis.

In order to extract optimal values for the entropy and range thresholds, we repeated the spreading procedure ten times for various thresholds. Figure 1 shows the average correlation obtained for each threshold combination. We observe that the range parameter is more important in obtaining higher correlations, with small ranges resulting in better results. The optimal performance is obtained for a range threshold of 3, and entropy threshold of 1.38 (we consider the distribution

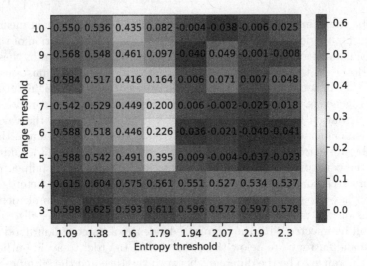

Fig. 1. Average correlation between modelled and real word valence.

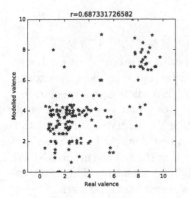

Fig. 2. Modelled and real word valence for a selected run with best parameters.

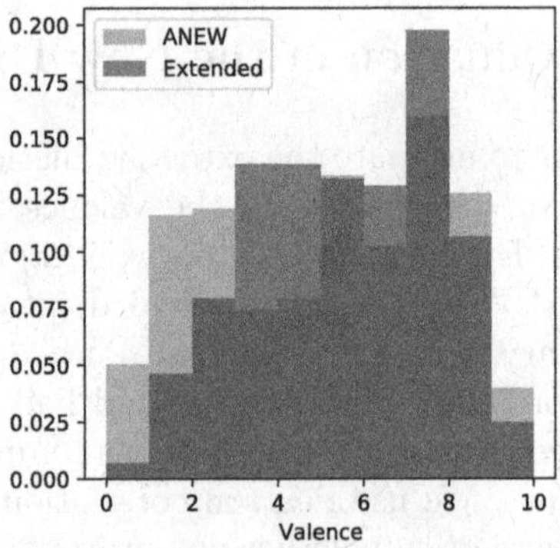

Fig. 3. Histogram of valences for ANEW and extended dictionary.

described by 10 bins of equal size, hence the maximum entropy is approximately 2.3). Figure 2 displays the modelled and real valences on test data for the run with the best correlation with these parameter values. The plot shows clearly that the valences obtained by our method align well with human-tagged data, validating our approach. For further comparison, we also display the distribution of valences in the ANEW dictionary, compared to the extended dictionary obtained through our method (Fig. 3). We observe some differences here. While negative lemmas make a small fraction of the dictionary in both cases, the extended dictionary still contains a larger fraction of neutral and positive lemmas, compared to the ANEW dictionary. This is, however, not a concern, given that we observed this trend for other dictionaries as well (see description of Sentiwordnet in Sect. 3). A second criterion for validation of the extended dictionary is classification performance on the Tagged Twitter Dataset (Sect. 3). We implemented a sentiment classifier based on Support Vector Machines (SVM), that used several features to classify sentiment of tweets into three classes: negative, neutral and positive. The features used include, for each tweet, several statistics over the valence of individual lemmas contained by the tweet: arithmetic and geometric mean, median, standard deviation, minimum and maximum. To these, we added the number of lemmas with a valence over 7 and over 9, to understand the presence of positive terms. Conversely, we also computed the number of lemmas with a valence under 3 and under 1. Finally, we included the total length of the tweet, and a boolean feature flagging the presence of a negation. We only considered tweets for which at least 3 lemmas were found in the dictionary.

The features above can be computed using any dictionary, and SVM performance can vary when changing the dictionary. We compare the performance of our extended dictionary (described in Figs. 2 and 3) with that of ANEW, which is an established dictionary in the literature. We expect no decrease in performance with our extended dictionary.

To validate results, we used a cross-validation approach, where 80% of tagged tweets were used to train the SVM and 20% to test it. The analysis was repeated ten times for each dictionary, with average performance displayed in Fig. 4. Error bars show one standard deviation from the mean. The plot shows that the performance with the extended dictionary is comparable to ANEW, validating our approach. The F1 score increases on the negative class and decreases on the other two. Precision increases on negative and neutral, while recall increases on negative and positive tweets. Hence, our extended dictionary seems to perform slightly better on negative tweets, however it overestimates the positives. Given that negative tweets are a small part of the corpus, accuracy decreases slightly. The performance range across repeated runs always overlaps between the two dictionaries compared.

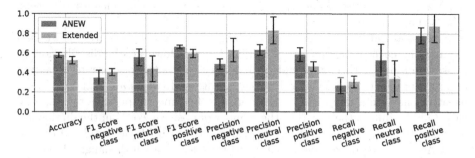

Fig. 4. Performance of SVM classifier using the original ANEW dictionary only and our extended dictionary.

6 Twitter Sentiment Analysis

To further evaluate the goodness of our algorithm, we compare the behaviour of the SVM in classifying the Untagged Twitter Dataset using our epidemic extended sentiment dictionary versus ANEW. Figure 5 shows the number of tweets classified by each dictionary, and then the distribution in the negative, neutral and positive classes. The SVM used was trained with all the Tagged Twitter Dataset, while the extended dictionary used was that analysed in Figs. 2 and 3.

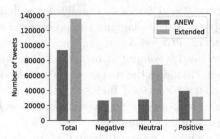

Fig. 5. Applying the SVM to untagged Twitter data using the original ANEW dictionary versus our extended dictionary.

Applying the SVM using ANEW we are able to label 93,447 tweets. As we can see, the number of positive tweets is almost twice that of the neutral and negative tweets. We classify 48,409 tweets as positive, 20,222 as neutral and 24,816 as negative.

Results obtained applying the SVM classifier with the extended dictionary show an increase in the number of labelled tweets compared to ANEW, by about 45%. We are able to classify 135,341 tweets. As opposed to ANEW, the number of positives and negatives tweets is not that unbalanced. We classify 31,278 tweets as positives and, 30,544 as negatives. We also see a significant increase of tweets classified as neutral.

Since the dataset has no polarity labels, we cannot validate the classes obtained by each dictionary for individual tweets. However, the distribution of classes obtained with our extended dictionary seems to be closer to what we observed in the Tagged Twitter Dataset, i.e. neutral tweets are a majority and negative ones are a minority. ANEW tends to find mostly positive tweets, and this could be due to the fact that the number of positive words in the dictionary is higher than other classes. However, this is true also for the extended dictionary. A second reason could be that Twitter users use a youth slang: a large set of unstandardized lemmas which are not included in ANEW lexicon, but which are captured by our extended dictionary.

7   Discussion and Conclusions

A method for enhancing lexicon-based sentiment analysis by extending the base lexicon of terms was presented. The extended dictionary was shown to contain term valences that correlate well with human-labelled lexicons. Furthermore, performance of SVM-based sentiment classification was maintained. At the same time, the number of tweets labelled by the new dictionary grew by about 45%. Our method is particularly suitable for Twitter data, where the short length of the text to be analysed makes classification impossible with a small dictionary, since most tweets do not contain any of the terms for which the sentiment valence is known. Additionally, the procedure to extend the dictionary is very fast (running times of the order of minutes for over 1.5 million tweets), hence can be applied to very large amounts of data.

The results presented here validated our method, however we believe the potential stays in the power of big data. Hence we plan to apply it to much larger amounts of Twitter data in future work. During our experiments, we observed an increase in the amount of tweets tagged by about 45% compared to ANEW, while the extended dictionary was much wider than ANEW. This indicates the fact that some terms in the network remain isolated, so that sentiment valences do not percolate the entire network, hence many tweets remain untagged. This issue is exacerbated by the fact that we also impose thresholds on the neighbourhood from which a node can be 'infected' with sentiment. In these conditions, additional data can improve the percolation power of sentiment valences and further increase performance of our method. A careful analysis of the network structure, and its dependence on the amount of data used, is thus required and will be pursued in the future.

The extended dictionary obtained through our method depends highly on the set of tweets used to build the network of terms. Here we used a random selection of tweets, however one could also select user subpopulations, or various languages. An advantage of our method is that it is easily extendible to other languages, since it is enough to translate the seed dictionary in order to obtain a much larger annotated lexicon. The correlation between modelled and real valences becomes, in this case, a measure to describe the way language is used in a Twitter subpopulation, allowing for comparison for various purposes. One application that we have in mind is evaluating superdiversity due to population migration.

While useful for standard sentiment analysis, as shown here, our method is also suitable for novel and more advanced techniques similar to supervised aggregated sentiment analysis [4]. These techniques concentrate not on classification of individual tweets, but on quantifying the aggregated distribution of sentiment in a collection of tweets. Our extended dictionary could prove to be an important resource to develop new such methods. These would be useful not only to predict election or debate results, which is why they were proposed in the first place, but also to quantify aggregated sentiment in various populations. This could help understand superdiversity better, hence we plan to investigate the link between our proposed superdiversity index and sentiment quantification on Twitter.

Acknowledgment. This work has been funded by the European project SoBigData Research Infrastructure - Big Data and Social Mining Ecosystem under the INFRAIA-H2020 program (grant agreement 654024).

References

1. Agarwal, A., Xie, B., Vovsha, I., Rambow, O., Passonneau, R.: Sentiment analysis of Twitter data. In: Proceedings of the Workshop on Languages in Social Media, pp. 30–38. ACL (2011)
2. Bradley, M.M., Lang, P.J.: Affective norms for English words (ANEW): Instruction manual and affective ratings. Technical report. Citeseer (1999)
3. Castellano, C., Muñoz, M.A., Pastor-Satorras, R.: Nonlinear q-voter model. Phys. Rev. E **80**(4), 041129 (2009)
4. Ceron, A., Curini, L., Iacus, S.: Using social media to fore-cast electoral results: a review of state-of-the-art. Italian J. Appl. Stat. **25**(3), 237–259 (2015)
5. Coletto, M., Esuli, A., Lucchese, C., Muntean, C.I., Nardini, F.M., Perego, R., Renso, C.: Perception of social phenomena through the multidimensional analysis of online social networks. Online Soc. Netw. Media **1**, 14–32 (2017)
6. Dodds, P.S., Danforth, C.M.: Measuring the happiness of large-scale written expression: songs, blogs, and presidents. J. Happiness Stud. **11**(4), 441–456 (2010)
7. Esuli, A., Sebastiani, F.: SentiWordNet: a high-coverage lexical resource for opinion mining. Evaluation 1–26 (2007)
8. Gebremeskel, G.: Sentiment analysis of Twitter posts about news. Ph.D. thesis, Department of Computer Science and Artificial Intelligence, University of Malta (2011)
9. Go, A., Bhayani, R., Huang, L.: Twitter sentiment classification using distant supervision. CS224N Project Report Stanford **1**(12) (2009)
10. Guerini, M., Gatti, L., Turchi, M.: Sentiment analysis: how to derive prior polarities from SentiWordNet. arXiv preprint arXiv:1309.5843 (2013)
11. Hu, X., Tang, L., Tang, J., Liu, H.: Exploiting social relations for sentiment analysis in microblogging. In: Proceedings of the Sixth ACM International Conference on Web Search and Data Mining, pp. 537–546. ACM (2013)
12. Khuc, V.N., Shivade, C., Ramnath, R., Ramanathan, J.: Towards building large-scale distributed systems for Twitter sentiment analysis. In: Proceedings of the 27th Annual ACM Symposium on Applied Computing, pp. 459–464. ACM (2012)
13. Mulcrone, K.: Detecting emotion in text. University of Minnesota-Morris CS Senior Seminar Paper (2012)
14. Pang, B., Lee, L.: Opinion mining and sentiment analysis. Found. Trends® Inf. Retrieval **2**(1–2), 1–135 (2008)
15. Pang, B., Lee, L., Vaithyanathan, S.: Thumbs up?: sentiment classification using machine learning techniques. In: Proceedings of the ACL-02 Conference on Empirical Methods in Natural Language Processing, vol. 10, pp. 79–86. ACL (2002)
16. Schmid, H.: Part-of-speech tagging with neural networks. In: Proceedings of the 15th Conference on Computational Linguistics, vol. 1, pp. 172–176. ACL (1994)

17. Sîrbu, A., Loreto, V., Servedio, V.D., Tria, F.: Opinion dynamics: models, extensions and external effects. In: Loreto, V., et al. (eds.) Participatory Sensing, Opinions and Collective Awareness. UCS, pp. 363–401. Springer, Heidelberg (2017). doi:10.1007/978-3-319-25658-0_17

18. Speriosu, M., Sudan, N., Upadhyay, S., Baldridge, J.: Twitter polarity classification with label propagation over lexical links and the follower graph. In: Proceedings of the First Workshop on Unsupervised Learning in NLP, pp. 53–63. ACL (2011)

19. Velikovich, L., Blair-Goldensohn, S., Hannan, K., McDonald, R.: The viability of web-derived polarity lexicons. In: HLT-NAACL, pp. 777–785 (2010)

20. Vertovec, S.: The emergence of super-diversity in Britain. Centre of Migration, Policy and Society, University of Oxford (2006)

Semantic Measures for Keywords Extraction

Davide Colla, Enrico Mensa, and Daniele P. Radicioni[✉]

Dipartimento di Informatica, Università di Torino, Turin, Italy
davide.colla@edu.unito.it, {mensa,radicion}@di.unito.it

Abstract. In this paper we introduce a minimalist hypothesis for keywords extraction: keywords can be extracted from text documents by considering concepts underlying document terms. Furthermore, central concepts are individuated as the concepts that are more related to title concepts. Namely, we propose five metrics, that are diverse in essence, to compute the centrality of concepts in the document body with respect to those in the title. We finally report about an experimentation over a popular data set of human annotated news articles; the results confirm the soundness of our hypothesis.

Keywords: Keywords extraction · Natural language semantics · Conceptual similarity · Word similarity · Lexical resources

1 Introduction

Keywords extraction is a principal task in the analysis of text documents: keywords represent in compact fashion the main topics of document contents, and they are fundamental in a plethora of tasks including information extraction, selection and retrieval. Keywords extraction is a challenging task: it involves analyzing and characterizing documents semantic content—which is a relevant open research problem—, and it has also many applications, in diverse fields such as feature extraction, document filtering and clustering. Furthermore, keywords are customarily used in compiling minimal, dense summaries and in the broader and neighboring field of automatic summarization; they are used to browse document collections, they are beneficial in refining search engine queries and in building contextual advertisements. Attempts to individuate salient textual elements (be them words, phrases or whole sentences) exist that date back to several decades ago [2]. However, despite their relevance and their usefulness for many purposes, explicit keywords are absent from most documents. Providing documents with this meta-information about their content is a costly and time-consuming activity that still requires professionals to manually provide documents with keywords, either chosen from a given thesaurus/taxonomy or based on their own evaluation.

Keyword extraction has been traditionally performed based on lexical information, by adopting support corpora, or controlled vocabularies, moreover, the extraction step has been performed mostly based on statistical methods or on

© Springer International Publishing AG 2017
F. Esposito et al. (Eds.): AI*IA 2017, LNAI 10640, pp. 128–140, 2017.
https://doi.org/10.1007/978-3-319-70169-1_10

machine learning techniques. The analysis is frequently performed at the terms level, having terms relations represented as graphs [11,19].

Our approach differs from those in literature in several aspects: first, we aim at finding salient *concepts* rather than counting *term* frequencies/occurrences. Also, we define concepts relevance as a *relational* feature: our hypothesis is that concepts in a document are relevant in so far as they are semantically connected to the concepts that are present in the title. We define the notion of *centrality*, that can be computed to estimate how tightly the concepts in the body are connected to the title concepts. To compute the conceptual centrality, we propose some novel metrics and some metrics that to the best of our knowledge have never been used before for keywords extraction.

Our approach has the following strengths: it is simple (it basically tests in different manners how conceptual similarity is suitable for keyword extraction); it scales to evolving document collections; and it does not require training the construction of neither *ad hoc corpora* nor controlled vocabularies/thesauri.

The paper is organized as follows: after a brief survey on related work (Sect. 2), we introduce our approach (Sect. 3), by providing full details on the five metrics being proposed (Sect. 3.2). We then report about the experimentation, discuss the obtained results (Sect. 4), and close by elaborating on future work (Sect. 5).

2   Related Work

Several works have been carried out that share some traits with our system. Most approaches to keyword extraction involve three main phases, that are aimed at identifying candidate keywords, at ranking them, and finally at selecting the top ranked ones.

The Rule Discovery System (RDS) uses syntactic information (namely, some given POS patterns such as ADJ-NOUN, NOUN-NOUN, *etc.*) and collects information both internal to the document and collection-based [5]. Ensemble techniques are adopted herein: different classifiers are learned and then combined with a voting mechanism to predict the class associated to a given keyword. In this setting, the keyword extraction task is converted into a binary categorization task, where candidate terms are classified either as keywords or as non-keywords. The RDS is grounded on a pool of features such as term frequency, collection frequency, relative position of the first occurrence, and POS tag. It has been subsequently improved with further filtering of the NP chunks (to eliminate determiners) and with a different choice (more general) of the corpus upon which to compute frequencies.

The authors of TextRank [11] propose an unsupervised graph-based algorithm for both keyword and sentence extraction that leverages a graph representation of the document. Graph nodes contain information on document terms (the algorithm allows for POS-based filtering, and the authors report the best results for nouns and adjectives). The edges are built based on the co-occurrence relation, that accounts for the distance intervening between terms: two vertices are connected if they co-occur within a window of fixed length (2–10 terms). Edges represent an estimation of the cohesion between the terms in the document. In our approach, we use a quite similar measure, the main difference is that we do not collect information about the cohesion between terms but between concepts. Also, the relatedness we measure involves each concept in the document body, and the concepts in the document title.

The co-occurrence of document terms in a graph-based representation is central also in [17], where the relevance of terms is computed on the base of word frequency, word degree, and ratio of degree to frequency. Degree is a measure devised to favor words that occur frequently and in longer candidate keywords. The authors extract one-third keywords w.r.t. the number of words in the graph, as it had been earlier done by [11].

The work [4] proposes the notion of semantic similarity to extract keywords: in this setting, the author exploits a dynamic programming technique for computing Word Sense Disambiguation (WSD). In particular, by referring to the WordNet sense inventory, the maximal similarity between terms is computed, based on the assumption that semantic similarity is an estimator of the strength of the relationship between words. Our work shares some traits with [4]: we also refer to the conceptual level, but we adopt a much broader sense inventory (the vectors in NASARI [1]), and we compute some similarity measures not between each pair of terms in the document, but between terms in the body and in the title.

SemanticRank introduces a method which can be applied to both individual terms and text segments [19]; it relies on the *omiotis* measure, which allows employing the same approach to both keywords extraction and automatic summarization. To compute the semantic relatedness, the SemanticRank algorithm makes use of the WordNet sense inventory paired with a measure based on Wikipedia. The semantic relatedness between two terms is computed by accounting for the path length, for the types of involved edges, and for the depth of the intermediate nodes in the WordNet hierarchy. This measure is then refined through another graph-based formula, that implements one simple and sound intuition: two terms are more related when the number of articles linking to their corresponding Wikipedia pages is higher than the number of articles linking to either of them [19].

3   Semantic Metrics for Keyword Extraction

One major assumption underlying this work is that keywords extraction should be based on the semantic content of documents rather than on the statistics describing terms frequency or terms co-occurrence. As regards as this feature, our approach is close to several of those surveyed above. One difference, in these respects, is in the sense inventory that we use: most previous attempts rely on the WordNet sense inventory, and on similarity measures deriving from those proposed by [15]. We experiment over a much broader sense inventory, namely that of BabelNet [13], and on its vectorial counterpart, NASARI [1].

However, we also hypothesize that only investigating the connections intervening between terms (or concepts) inside the body of a document is not sufficient to individuate its keywords. This is why among the many possible cues that have been proposed in literature, we single out the role of title, and test different measures to investigate in how far the concepts that are expressed in the title may be relevant to extract keywords: to these ends, text documents are represented as a ⟨title,body⟩ pair.

Furthermore, we focus on documents rather than on documents collections, since they are useful for dealing with collections that change over time, such as news articles directories. Additionally, document-oriented methods "scale to vast collections and can be applied in many contexts to enrich IR systems and analysis tools" [17].

The keywords extraction process has two main phases, the *semantic preprocessing* and the proper *keywords extraction*. The first phase is aimed at individuating the concepts involved in the document, while the latter one is designed to rank them according to some metrics and to select the highest scoring ones.

3.1 Semantic Preprocessing

In this first phase we perform the disambiguation of the document title and body, that is presently carried out through the Babelfy service.[1] The semantic preprocessing allows to filter out stop words (only verbs, nouns and adjectives are retained), permits individuating concepts that are especially frequent in the document being processed (synonyms are rewritten through a single Babel synset ID), and also makes it possible to compare the semantic content conveyed by the title and by the body of the document.

3.2 Keywords Extraction

In the keywords extraction phase, the following steps are performed:

- Matching between body and title concepts, to select the concepts in the body that are most *relevant* to those in the title;
- Keywords are selected as the highest ranked concepts.

Many efforts have been invested to define heuristics to individuate relevant places where typically the more informative terms can be found, for example in the close field of automatic summarization. In this setting, some features have been individuated—since the pioneering work by [2]—as chief factors in conveying document semantic content. Such main features are: *(i)* term frequency, *(ii)* the elements shared between title and body, *(iii)* structural information on the position of such elements within the text, *(iv)* some specific linguistic cues (basically depending on the kind of documents being considered), such as 'In sum', 'For all these factors', *etc.*. However, interestingly enough, it was early found by [2] that term frequency was less relevant than the other mentioned features. Among

---

[1] http://babelfy.org.

these, we focus on investigating the semantic links between concepts in the title and in the body of documents. In particular, we start from the main assumption

"that an author conceives the title as circumscribing the subject matter of the document. Also, when the author partitions the body of the document into major sections he summarizes it by choosing appropriate headings. The hypothesis that words of headings are positively relevant was statistically accepted at the 99% of significance" [2, p. 272].

We acknowledge that this assumption only fits documents with title, and does not allow handling some kinds of documents (e.g., novels and narrative in general) where headings may have no title. However, most documents we are interested in (such as scientific articles, news feeds, newspapers articles, goods descriptions, *etc.*) are typically characterized by having titles. Ultimately, we explore simple features obtained by shifting features *(i)* and *(ii)* to a semantic space.

Our control strategy relies on computing the centrality of each concept in the body of documents with respect to the concepts mentioned in its title. The general approach consists in averaging centrality contributions associated to each (body) concept w.r.t. concepts in the title; keywords are then selected by retaining the highest scoring ones.

In detail, the system starts from the lists $T = \{y_1, y_2, \ldots, y_L\}$ such that $y \in$ title and $B = \{x_1, x_2, \ldots, x_M\}$ such that $x \in$ body, that contain the Babel synset IDs in the title and in the body, of length L and M, respectively. We then compute the centrality c of the concepts corresponding to the terms x in the body as a function of their semantic relatedness[2] to those in the title:

$$c(x) = \frac{1}{|T|} \sum_{y_i \in T} \mathrm{semrel}(x, y_i). \tag{1}$$

We devised five metrics that implement the semrel function by exploiting different resources and techniques. Namely, we propose the following metrics: NASARI, NASARIE, UCI, UMASS and TTCS$^{\mathcal{E}}$, that can be arranged into two classes of metrics: those based on NASARI conceptual representations, and those based on coherence measures.

Regardless of the employed metrics, for each document we select as the best keywords those with maximum centrality, that is:

$$Keywords = \operatorname*{argmax}_{x \in B} c(x).$$

Using NASARI vectors to compute semantic relatedness. As our first measure, we exploit the semantic vectors of NASARI, that are the vectorial counterpart of BabelNet synsets. Concepts herein (corresponding to a merge of

---

[2] There is a subtle though neat difference between semantic relatedness and similarity: consider, e.g., that 'eraser' and 'pencil' are related but not similar, whilst 'pencil' and 'pen' are similar.

WordNet synsets with Wikipedia pages) are described through vector representations, whose features are synset IDs themselves. Each such feature is provided
with a weight, computed through the metrics of lexical specificity [1]. In the
following we will denote the concept identifier by y or x, and the corresponding
vector by $\vec{y}$ or $\vec{x}$.

The semantic relatedness between a concept $x \in B$ and the concept $y \in T$ is
computed by considering $\rho_x^{\vec{y}}$, that is the *rank* of x in the vector representation
for y. More specifically, given two arbitrary elements x and y_i, we compute their
relatedness as

$$\text{semrel}(x, y_i) = \left(1 - \frac{\rho_x^{\vec{y_i}}}{length(\vec{y_i})}\right).$$

The rationale underlying this formula is that x is more relevant to concept y_i
if x has smaller rank (and heavier weight), that is it is found among the first
concepts associated to y_i in $\vec{y_i}$. For example, if we inspect[3] the NASARI vector
for the concept door, we find—in decreasing relevance order—that the third term
associated to door is window, the tenth wall, the twelfth is lock, and around the
hundredth position interior door: the above formula emphasizes the contribution
of heavier features, having lower rank.

The centrality of the concept x with respect to each concept $y_i \in T$ can be
determined as

$$\text{semrel}(x, y_i) = \begin{cases} 1 & \text{if } \rho_x^{\vec{y_i}} = 1; \\ 0 & \text{if } x \notin \vec{y_i}; \\ \left(1 - \frac{\rho_x^{\vec{y_i}}}{length(\vec{y_i})}\right) & \text{otherwise.} \end{cases}$$

Specifically, in case the concept x is found to have rank 1 for the concept y_i
its relevance is supposed to be maximal to the meaning of y_i (it is likely the same
term or a close term which is part of the same synset); conversely, in case it is not
found in the vector associated to y (thus obtaining $\rho_x^{\vec{y_i}} = 0$), the relatedness (x, y_i)
will not contribute anything to the overall centrality of x to the concepts in T.

Using NASARI embed vectors to compute semantic relatedness. We
also explored the NASARI Embed version (NASARIE in the following), that
contains embedded vector representations of 300 dimensions; the computation
of the centrality can be computed in this case by resorting to standard cosine
similarity, thus

$$\text{semrel}(x, y_i) = cosSim(\vec{x}, \vec{y_i}).$$

Using UCI coherence measure to compute semantic relatedness. Moreover, we propose two metrics, the UCI measure [14] and the UMass measure [12]
that—originally conceived for evaluating Latent Dirichlet Allocation—, have

---

[3] For the sake of clarity in this example we consider the *lexical* rather than the *unified*
vector, i.e. having terms in place of conceptual IDs that are actually used by the
system.

been used in the automated semantic evaluation of different latent topic models [18].[4]

Because both the UCI and the UMASS measures natively handle terms rather than concepts, after the semantic preprocessing phase, we need to translate back concepts into terms. However, by exploiting BabelNet, we map all synonyms for a given concept onto a single shared lexicalization, that is chosen as the most common term according to BabelNet counts. This strategy allows reconciling different terms underlying the same sense, thus preserving some semantic trait.

The UCI metrics [14] computes the cohesion between two terms w_1 and w_2 through their pointwise mutual information, that is

$$score(w_1, w_2, \epsilon) = \log \frac{p(w_1, w_2, \epsilon)}{p(w_1)p(w_2)},$$

where the probabilities are estimated by counting word co-occurrence frequencies in a sliding window over an external corpus, such as Wikipedia, Google or MEDLINE,[5] and the ϵ correction is used to ensure that the function always returns real numbers (presently ϵ is set to 1). In our setting, we are interested in computing the cohesion score between the terms in the body and the terms in the title, so that for each concept $x \in B$ lexicalized as w_x and $y_i \in T$ lexicalized as w_{y_i} we compute

$$\text{semrel}(x, y_i) = score(w_x, w_{y_i}, 1).$$

Using UMass coherence measure to compute semantic relatedness. This metrics define a coherence score based on the co-occurrence of the terms w_1 and w_2 as (adapted from [18])

$$score(w_1, w_2, \epsilon) = \log \frac{D(w_1, w_2) + \epsilon}{D(w_2)},$$

where $D(w_1, w_2)$ and $D(w_2)$ count the number of documents containing both w_1 and w_2, and only w_2, respectively. The adopted formula follows the rationale illustrated for the UCI metrics:

$$\text{semrel}(x, y_i) = score(w_x, w_{y_i}, 1),$$

where the concept $x \in B$ is lexicalized as w_x, and $y_i \in T$ is lexicalized as w_{y_i}.

Using the TTCS$^{\mathcal{E}}$ to compute semantic similarity. The last metrics we used in our experimentation relies on a recent lexical resource, the TTCS$^{\mathcal{E}}$, that consists of a vector-based semantic representation. The TTCS$^{\mathcal{E}}$ is compliant with the Conceptual Spaces, a geometric framework for common-sense knowledge representation and reasoning, and contains a novel mixture of common-sense and encyclopedic knowledge [7,10].[6]

---

[4] In order to compute such measures we used the Palmetto library [16].

[5] Specifically, in the Palmetto implementation, the pointwise mutual information (PMI) and word co-occurrence counts were computed by using Wikipedia as reference corpus [16].

[6] The TTCS$^{\mathcal{E}}$ resource is available for download at the URL http://ttcs.di.unito.it.

Concept representation and similarity computation with the TTCS$^\mathcal{E}$. Let D be the set of N dimensions. Such dimensions are relations that report common-sense information like, e.g., IsA, AtLocation, UsedFor, PartOf, MadeOf, HasA, CapableOf, *etc.*. Each concept c_i in the linguistic resource is defined as a vector $\vec{c}_i = [s_1^i, .., s_N^i]$, where each s_h^i constitutes the set of concepts filling a dimension. Each s can contain an arbitrary number of values, or be empty. The TTCS$^\mathcal{E}$ can be used to compute the conceptual similarity between concept pairs: specifically, the Symmetrical Tversky's Ratio Model (STRM) has been adopted to compute conceptual similarity [9].

The similarity computed through the TTCS$^\mathcal{E}$ is quite different from popular semantic distance measures, that either employ distances between WordNet nodes, or rely on information content measures [15]. One main assumption underlying this approach is that two concepts are similar insofar as they share values on the same dimension, such as when they are both used for the same ends, they share the same components, *etc.*: in this view, e.g., pencil is deemed more similar to pen than to eraser in that both of them are UsedFor writing or drawing.

In the present setting, the TTCS$^\mathcal{E}$ is employed to compute the conceptual similarity between concepts in the title and those in the documents body according to the formula

$$semrel(x, y_i) = STRM(\vec{x}, \vec{y_i}),$$

where $\vec{x}$ and $\vec{y_i}$ represent the TTCS$^\mathcal{E}$ vectors for the concepts $x \in B$ and $y_i \in T$, respectively.

4   Evaluation

In the last few years several sets of keywords-annotated documents have been collected, annotated and made available, that allow assessing algorithms and their underlying assumptions on scientific articles, news documents, Broadcast News and Tweets (see, for example, [8]).

Dataset. We experimented on the Crowd500 dataset [8], which has been extensively used for testing. The dataset contains overall 500 documents (450 for training and 50 for testing purposes), arranged into 10 classes: Art and Culture, Business, Crime, Fashion, Health, US politics, World politics, Science, Sport, Technology. Documents herein have been annotated by several annotators recruited through the Amazon's Mechanical Turk service. Each keyphrase is provided with a score equal to the number of annotators who selected it as a keyphrase.

Participants. In the following, for the sake of self-containedness, we report the experimental results obtained by [6], where the authors performed a systematic assessment of an array of keyword extractors and online semantic annotators. In particular, we report the results obtained by 2 keyword extractors that participated in the "SemEval-2010 Task 5: Automatic Keyphrase Extraction from Scientific Articles" (namely, KP-Miner [3] and Maui [20]), and 5 semantic annotators (AlchemyAPI, Zemanta, OpenCalais, TagMe, and TextRazor[7]). With regards to Alchemy, both the keyword extraction (Alch Key) and concept tagging (Alch Con) services were considered. More details can be found in [6].

Experimental setting. We adopted the same setting as in [6], where two experiments have been carried out: in the first one the authors restricted to considering the top 15 keywords for each document in the dataset, while in the second one they considered all annotated keywords. Given the diversity of the metrics employed, some of them typically return a centrality score for each concept in the document (NASARIE, UCI, UMASS), while the other ones (NASARI and TTCS) are only able to express a centrality score for some of the concepts in the document. For this reason, we defined the number of keywords returned by each metrics by considering as minimum the number of keywords having positive centrality score, and as maximum the average of keywords provided for each document in the training set (this figure amounts to 48 keywords per document). Also, since all metrics assessed were used at a conceptual level, our output is mostly composed by individual keywords rather than by keyphrases: accordingly, in the evaluation of the results, we disregarded all keyphrases and focused on the keywords in the gold standard.

Results. The results obtained by testing on the Crowd500 dataset are illustrated in Table 1. Specifically, in Table 1(a) we present the results obtained by comparing the keywords extracted to the top 15 keywords in the Crowd500 dataset, while the results obtained by considering all of the gold standard keywords are provided in Table 1(a). Regarding the first experiment, over the top 15 keywords, we note that in 3 out of 5 of the considered metrics (namely, NASARIE, UCI and UMASS), the F_1 score is higher than those reported in the paper by [6]. Also in the second experiment NASARIE, UCI and UMASS obtained highest F_1 score, whilst the results of NASARI and $TTCS^{\mathcal{E}}$ are featured by the highest precision.

Discussion. Given the simplicity of the hypothesis being tested (that is: the title-body conceptual coherence is sufficient to individuate the keywords), the adopted metrics performed surprisingly well, and seem to confirm that our hypothesis is sound. We notice that in computing the results over the 15 top ranked keywords (Table 1(a)), the precision of all our measures is quite low, on average half of that obtained by KP-Miner, Maui and TagMe. In any case, this datum would make our metrics inapplicable in a real setting. Although the precision over all keywords (Table 1(b)) is in line with the other systems (except for KP-Miner, that has an advantage of around 10% on our score), the low precision over the first 15 keywords (that are the more relevant ones) shows that the ranking component in the extraction phase must be improved.

---

[7] Available at the URLs http://www.alchemyapi.com/api/keyword-extraction/, http://developer.zemanta.com/, http://www.opencalais.com/, http://TagMe.di.unipi.it/ and http://www.textrazor.com/, respectively.

Table 1. Results obtained on the test set of the Crowd500 dataset: for each system Precision (P), Recall (R) and F1 Score (F) are reported.

participant	k	P(%)	R(%)	F(%)	participant	k	P(%)	R(%)	F(%)
Alch Con	15	16.71	2.81	4.82	Alch Con	all	16.71	2.81	4.82
Alch Key	15	21.63	6.32	9.78	Alch Key	all	12.40	16.71	18.24
Calais_Soc	15	6.67	0.09	0.17	Calais_Soc	all	13.69	2.60	4.29
KP-Miner	15	**41.33**	8.05	13.48	KP-Miner	all	40.19	14.46	21.27
Maui	15	35.87	9.78	15.37	Maui	all	27.46	20.30	23.34
TagMe	15	34.53	11.21	16.93	TagMe	all	21.02	35.89	26.51
TxtRaz Top	15	15.78	5.02	7.62	TxtRaz Top	all	6.28	11.52	8.13
Zem Key	15	29.75	5.15	8.78	Zem Key	all	29.75	5.15	8.78
NASARI	15	24.89	10.40	14.67	NASARI	all	39.83	10.86	17.06
NASARIE	15	15.62	35.47	21.69	NASARIE	all	27.72	36.16	31.38
UCI	15	16.06	**44.40**	**23.59**	UCI	all	29.68	**46.28**	**36.17**
UMASS	15	15.49	42.53	22.71	UMASS	all	26.76	43.08	33.02
TTCS$^{\mathcal{E}}$	15	29.08	8.13	12.71	TTCS$^{\mathcal{E}}$	all	**50.36**	8.49	14.54

(a) Results on the top 15 keywords in the gold standard.   (b) Results on all keywords.

On the other side, one weakness of our experimentation (which is, admittedly, a preliminary one) is due to the fact that our results do not actually include keyphrases but only keywords, and thus they cannot be directly compared to those of the other systems. We started devising a module for the recognition of Named Entities (which is to date an open problem) to be integrated into the described system. However, even though we were forced to disregard keyphrases, at a closer inspection of the data, in some cases the annotated keyphrases seem to be rather inaccurate: for example, it is frequent to find locutions such as 'video below', 'although people', 'SeaWorld and', 'size allows' and many others.

Finally, by referring to Table 1(b) we note that the traditional trade-off between precision and recall seems to be intertwined with the degree of semantics adopted. In fact, the metrics based on the TTCS$^{\mathcal{E}}$—which is semantically more sophisticated than the other metrics and represents concepts as entities related to other concepts—obtained over 50% precision, whilst the UMASS metrics, which basically counts terms occurrence in documents, obtained 26.76% precision. A full account of the precision over the 10 domains is provided in Table 2: consistently with previous observations and findings, metrics with highest results have higher standard deviation: this fact is trivially explained by the fact that metrics that perform poorly get low scores on most of the domains, which tend to increase their stability [6].

Moreover, in Table 3 we present the number of keywords available on average over the 10 domains, and the actual number of keywords extracted through the considered metrics. These figures have been obtained in the experiment considering all keywords. By comparing the number of keywords returned by TTCS$^{\mathcal{E}}$

Table 2. Analysis of the precision scores by domain (all-keywords experimentation).

Domain	NASARI	NASARIE	UCI	UMASS	TTCS$^{\mathcal{E}}$
Tech	33.92	35.56	31.25	25.00	**60.00**
Sports	**34.05**	18.10	24.99	23.70	28.33
Business	40.29	30.76	27.08	27.50	**50.00**
US politics	38.71	30.63	34.17	32.92	**66.67**
Art and culture	**32.50**	21.95	23.75	22.08	20.00
Science	41.90	26.21	24.58	23.75	**59.58**
Health	33.81	20.39	27.08	22.92	**46.67**
World politics	**68.00**	41.95	46.44	46.44	34.00
Crime	45.12	27.92	27.08	21.25	**60.00**
Fashion	30.04	23.75	30.44	22.08	**78.33**
Median	39.83	27.72	29.68	26.76	50.36
Average	36.38	27.07	27.08	23.73	54.79
STDEV	10.96	7.30	6.73	7.72	18.28

Table 3. Comparison between the average number of keywords actually returned by each metrics, and (first column) the average number of keywords available in the test set.

Domain	DATASET	NASARI	NASARIE	UCI	UMASS	TTCS$^{\mathcal{E}}$
Tech	45	14	43	48	48	2
Sports	26	12	43	45	45	11
Business	37	10	45	48	48	2
US politics	19	5	27	38	38	1
Art and culture	21	5	39	48	48	1
Science	40	20	47	48	48	12
Health	33	14	44	48	48	3
World politics	18	3	20	34	34	9
Crime	37	5	48	48	48	11
Fashion	55	12	48	48	48	11

and NASARI, we observe that even in cases when the TTCS$^{\mathcal{E}}$ returns 'many' keywords, its precision still scores high: this is the case, for example, of the domains Sports, Science, Crime and Fashion.

5   Conclusions

In this paper we have explored a novel hypothesis for keyword extraction. It has been designed by starting from the observation that keywords need to be individuated by accessing the conceptual level behind document *lexica*. Building on this tenet, our system performs word sense disambiguation before executing the extraction step. Some of the proposed metrics natively handle concepts (NASARI, NASARIE and $\text{TTCS}^{\mathcal{E}}$), while other metrics (UCI and UMASS) require terms, as their statistics are computed at the lexical level.

We have investigated a simple though effective hypothesis: the title provides fundamental (and perhaps sufficient) cues to extract keywords. Different from the literature where basically pools of criteria are investigated at once, we have then proposed five metrics to assess the coherence between documents title and body.

The experimentation showed that our hypotheses are reasonable. Although much work is still needed to improve the quality of the resources we use (in particular for the $\text{TTCS}^{\mathcal{E}}$), we obtained results that—as regards as the F_1 score—are competitive with state of the art systems, and show a good performance especially when considering the precision score, which is relevant also for practical uses.

Acknowledgements. We desire to thank Simone Donetti and the Technical Staff of the Computer Science Department of the University of Turin, for their support in the setup and administration of the computer system used in the experimentation.

The authors are also grateful to the anonymous reviewers for their valuable comments and suggestions.

References

1. Camacho-Collados, J., Pilehvar, M.T., Navigli, R.: NASARI: a novel approach to a semantically-aware representation of items. In: Proceedings of NAACL, pp. 567–577 (2015)
2. Edmundson, H.P.: New methods in automatic extracting. J. ACM **16**(2), 264–285 (1969)
3. El-Beltagy, S.R., Rafea, A.: KP-Miner: a keyphrase extraction system for English and Arabic documents. Inf. Syst. **34**(1), 132–144 (2009)
4. Haggag, M.H.: Keyword extraction using semantic analysis. Int. J. Comput. Appl. **61**(1), 1–6 (2013)
5. Hulth, A.: Improved automatic keyword extraction given more linguistic knowledge. In: Proceedings of EMNLP 2003, pp. 216–223 (2003)
6. Jean-Louis, L., Zouaq, A., Gagnon, M., Ensan, F.: An assessment of online semantic annotators for the keyword extraction task. In: Pham, D.-N., Park, S.-B. (eds.) PRICAI 2014. LNCS (LNAI), vol. 8862, pp. 548–560. Springer, Cham (2014). doi:10.1007/978-3-319-13560-1_44
7. Lieto, A., Mensa, E., Radicioni, D.P.: A resource-driven approach for anchoring linguistic resources to conceptual spaces. In: Adorni, G., Cagnoni, S., Gori, M., Maratea, M. (eds.) AI*IA 2016. LNCS (LNAI), vol. 10037, pp. 435–449. Springer, Cham (2016). doi:10.1007/978-3-319-49130-1_32
8. Marujo, L., Gershman, A., Carbonell, J.G., Frederking, R.E., Neto, J.P.: Supervised topical key phrase extraction of news stories using crowdsourcing and co-reference normalization. In: Proceedings of LREC, pp. 399–403. ELRA (2012)

9. Mensa, E., Radicioni, D.P., Lieto, A.: MERALI at SemEval-2017 task 2 subtask 1: a cognitively inspired approach. In: Proceedings of SemEval-2017, pp. 236–240. ACL (2017). http://www.aclweb.org/anthology/S17-2038

10. Mensa, E., Radicioni, D.P., Lieto, A.: TTCS$^{\mathcal{E}}$: a vectorial resource for computing conceptual similarity. In: EACL 2017 Workshop on Sense, Concept and Entity Representations and their Applications, pp. 96–101. ACL (2017). http://www.aclweb.org/anthology/W17-1912

11. Mihalcea, R., Tarau, P.: Textrank: Bringing Order into Texts. Association for Computational Linguistics (2004)

12. Mimno, D.M., Wallach, H.M., Talley, E.M., Leenders, M., McCallum, A.: Optimizing semantic coherence in topic models. In: EMNLP, pp. 262–272. ACL (2011)

13. Navigli, R., Ponzetto, S.P.: BabelNet: the automatic construction, evaluation and application of a wide-coverage multilingual semantic network. Artif. Intell. **193**, 217–250 (2012)

14. Newman, D., Noh, Y., Talley, E., Karimi, S., Baldwin, T.: Evaluating topic models for digital libraries. In: Proceedings of the ACM/IEEE JCDL2010. ACM (2010)

15. Pedersen, T., Patwardhan, S., Michelizzi, J.: Wordnet: similarity: measuring the relatedness of concepts. In: HLT-NAACL, pp. 38–41. ACL (2004)

16. Röder, M., Both, A., Hinneburg, A.: Exploring the space of topic coherence measures. In: Proceedings of WSDM 2015, pp. 399–408. ACM (2015)

17. Rose, S., Engel, D., Cramer, N., Cowley, W.: Automatic keyword extraction from individual documents. In: Text Mining, pp. 1–20 (2010)

18. Stevens, K., Kegelmeyer, P., Andrzejewski, D., Buttler, D.: Exploring topic coherence over many models and many topics. In: Proceedings of EMNLP-CoNLL, pp. 952–961. ACL (2012)

19. Tsatsaronis, G., Varlamis, I., Nørvåg, K.: Semanticrank: ranking keywords and sentences using semantic graphs. In: Proceedings of the 23rd International Conference on Computational Linguistics, pp. 1074–1082. ACL (2010)

20. Witten, I.H., Paynter, G.W., Frank, E., Gutwin, C., Nevill-Manning, C.G.: Kea: practical automatic keyphrase extraction. In: Proceedings of JCDL, pp. 254–255. ACM (1999)

Evaluating Industrial and Research Sentiment Analysis Engines on Multiple Sources

Emanuele Di Rosa[1]([✉]) and Alberto Durante[2]

[1] Head of Artificial Intelligence at Finsa s.p.a., Genoa, Italy
emanuele.dirosa@finsa.it
[2] Research Scientist at Finsa s.p.a., Genoa, Italy
alberto.durante@finsa.it

Abstract. Sentiment Analysis has a fundamental role in analyzing users opinions in all kinds of textual sources. Computing accurately sentiment expressed in huge amount of textual data is a key task largely required by the market, and nowadays industrial engines make available ready-to-use APIs for sentiment analysis-related tasks. However, building sentiment engines showing high accuracy on structurally different textual sources (e.g. reviews, tweets, blogs, etc.) is not a trivial task. Papers about cross-source evaluation lack of a comparison with industrial engines, which are instead specifically designed for dealing with multiple sources.

In this paper, we compare the results of research and industrial engines on an extensive experimental evaluation, considering the document-level polarity detection task performed on different textual sources: tweets, apps reviews and general products reviews, in both English and Italian. The experimental evaluation results help the reader to quantify the performance gap between industrial and research sentiment engines when both are tested on heterogeneous textual sources and on different languages (English/Italian). Finally, we present the results of our multi-source solution X2Check. Considering an overall cross-source average F-score on all of the results, X2Check shows a performance that is 9.1% and 5.1% higher than Google CNL, respectively on Italian and English benchmarks. Compared to the research engines, X2Check shows a F-score that is always higher than tools not specifically trained on the test set under evaluation; it is lower at most of 3.4% in Italian and 11.6% on English benchmarks, compared to the best research tools specifically trained on the target source.

Keywords: Sentiment analysis · Natural language processing · Machine learning · Experimental evaluation · Industrial and research tools comparison · Cross-domain sentiment classification

1 Introduction

Sentiment Analysis (SA) has a fundamental role in modern natural language processing systems analyzing users' opinions in all kinds of textual sources. More

© Springer International Publishing AG 2017
F. Esposito et al. (Eds.): AI*IA 2017, LNAI 10640, pp. 141–155, 2017.
https://doi.org/10.1007/978-3-319-70169-1_11

specifically, automatically performing polarity detection in user reviews, tweets, facebook posts, blogs, chats, etc., can lead to a large amount of applications. Accurately computing sentiment expressed in a huge amount of textual data is a key task largely required by the market, since sentiment mis-classifications risk to be an obstacle in the adoption of sentiment-based applications and decrease the perceived quality of the final users. Nowadays, industrial tools make available ready-to-use APIs for sentiment analysis-related tasks. However, building sentiment engines showing high accuracy on different topics domains and, even more difficult –and important for the market–, on structurally different textual source (e.g. reviews, tweets, blogs, etc.) is not a trivial task. Each textual data source may have specific features that are not carefully managed by general purpose cross-domain engines: tweets are structurally different than products reviews, news, facebook posts, or apps reviews. Textual content expressing user opinion is most of the times conditioned by the communication channel used, which may have implicit or explicit communication rules. Textual sources may differ in length, level of formality (some of them are sometimes considered to be almost *grammar free*), more keen to contain slang words, irony or even being characterized by a high level of *objectivity*, i.e. not containing opinions at all. Apps reviews, tweets and Amazon products reviews are great representative examples of different ways in which users express their own opinion. In fact, apps reviews evaluate the app itself or the service offered through the app and they are often quite short. Amazon products reviews are usually long, structured, more formal and mainly just related to a product. Tweets are short, related to possibly any kind of topic, containing slang words and often irony.

Academic research advances in sentiment analysis in recent years are valuable, and research engines are usually trained and fine-tuned to work well on specific tasks (e.g. polarity, subjectivity or irony detection), on specific sources (e.g. tweets, product reviews, or blogs), on specific languages or topic domains (e.g. politics); international challenges are organized every year, asking researchers to train/tune their engines to work well on such specific tasks, since the main goal is to find the best approach or algorithm to face a specific task. This approach however is a bit far away from the market and the needs of industrial engines: production tools needed by industry are asked to show a high average cross-source/domain performance. Commercial engines cannot be designed or fine-tuned on just a very specific setting, defined by a source and a sub-domain (e.g. political tweets in a specific time range) like in many experimental evaluations or competitions. Such tools have to be built to meet the needs of general purpose applications and show an overall high accuracy on heterogeneous sources and cross-domains.

Cross-domain sentiment analysis techniques have already been largely studied. Their development is due to the fact that sentiment classifiers trained in one domain may not perform well in another domain. In fact, sentiment expressions used in different domains may lead to different sentiment classifications. For example, we found apps reviews about games containing expressions like *"this game is my drug"* or *"it's an addictive great game"*, used by the young users in positive meaning, confirmed by other sentences in the review and by the overall rating. The terms *drug* and *addictive* used in other contexts have a negative meaning. Thus, a sentiment classifier trained in one domain usually cannot be applied to another domain directly [15]. In order to tackle this problem, sentiment domain adaptation has been widely studied like in [4,5,11,14,21,22]. In some cases, performance of sentiment domain adaptations is even worse than the one reached without any adaptation; this is usually known as negative transfer [14].

The problem faced by cross-domain sentiment classification may be even more difficult when considering multiple sources, i.e. when a sentiment classifier trained or designed mainly to deal with a specific text source (e.g. tweets), is then asked to analyze another source (e.g. reviews). In [12] the concept of cross-domain adaptation for sentiment classification is extended to multiple sources, and the authors study cross-source classifiers for the same topic. For example, they study SA classifiers trained on reviews and blogs and tested on tweets for the same topic. Many other papers have been published about cross-source sentiment analysis, and we mention here [8,9,22], since all of them evaluate their approaches on online reviews and tweets.

In particular, in [9], authors show that more robust classifiers can be trained by using a smaller number of in-domain instances augmented with instances from a related domain, rather than using purely in-domain instances. They recommend that using a training data set composed of both tweets and reviews, when training a sentiment classifier for use in predicting both tweet and review sentiment. A similar results is found by [22], where authors show that by fusing the sentiment information extracted from multiple sources can effectively improve the performance of sentiment classification and reduce the dependence on labeled data. Both approaches focus on building just one single sentiment classifier with wider domain knowledge, to avoid to train a domain-specific sentiment classifier for each target source/domain, since labeled data in target domain may be insufficient, and time-consuming to annotate enough samples.

All of the mentioned research work agrees that the best performance results in a multiple-source setting are obtained when a specific model for each source is built. Moreover, all of them lack of a comparison with industrial engines, which are instead specifically designed for production settings, and structurally dealing with cross-domain and multiple sources sentiment analysis.

In this paper, we focus on the market need for having the best possible performance in all of the sources, domains and languages, while delivering just one commercial API able to overall perform well in all of the settings. We compare the results of research and industrial engines on an extensive experimental evaluation, mainly considering the document-level polarity detection task performed on different textual sources: tweets, apps reviews and general products reviews, in both English and Italian. Moreover, we take into account and compare both research and industrial engines, by including in our evaluation relevant engine APIs available in the market and state-of-the-art research tools. Finally, we show the results of our X2Check solution, in which we use a meta-model acting as a model selector, and estimating which is the best specialized model to consider to analyze the input message.

The paper innovative contribution lies in:

1. An overall experimental comparison between industrial engines (Google CNL and X2Check) and state-of-the-art research tools that competed in the last international competitions.
2. For each source under evaluation (tweets, apps reviews and general product reviews), the quantification of the performance gap between industrial and research tools when they are specifically trained on the target source versus their not fine-tuned version on the target source.
3. A multi-language evaluation in which test sets are considered in both English and Italian.
4. Two new testsets for document-level polarity detection, each containing 10 thousand apps reviews in Italian and English, made available to the research community.
5. An approach in which, given the input source, a metamodel estimates which classification model is better to use, then the chosen model is used to extract sentiment.

Considering an overall average cross-source F-score on all of the results, X2Check shows a performance that is overall 9.1% and 5.1% higher than Google CNL, respectively for Italian and English benchmarks. Compared to the research engines, X2Check shows a F-score that is always higher than tools not specifically trained on the test set under evaluation; it is lower at most of 3.4% in Italian and 11.6% on English benchmarks, compared to research tools specifically trained on the target source.

This paper is structured as follows. After the introduction, we briefly introduce the systems included in our evaluation, and explain the reasons why they have been selected. Then, we present the experimental evaluation on tweets, apps reviews and Amazon product reviews; finally, we present the paper conclusions.

2   Systems Under Evaluation

2.1   Industrial Engines: Google CNL and Finsa X2Check

We consider industrial tools with a pre-trained ready-to-use model that is possible to call from API (Google CNL and X2Check), and X2Check cross-source adaptations to the specific target source. Industrial engines are shown in all of the experimental results, since their comparison with research engines constitutes one the main paper contributions.

About the industrial engines selection, unfortunately, most of the commercial engines for SA do not allow to use their APIs to perform an experimental comparative analysis and publish the results. In our opinion, this is a lack of transparency for the final user/buyer: in fact, the goal of SA tools is to measure user opinion, and being aware of its accuracy on the specific source/domain of interest is a valuable information in order to decide its adoption. This is especially important in sentiment analysis since, as we recalled, engines may in general show a significant different performance depending on the target source. We checked to possibly include in our evaluation sentiment engines as IBM Watson, Semantria by Lexalytics, Expert System Cogito API, to mention the ones from big companies. Considering well known sentiment engines at international level, performing research about sentiment analysis at their labs, we did not read, in their terms of use, legal obstacles to run Google CNL and Finsa X2Check for an experimental evaluation.

Google CNL. Google CNL is an API made available for natural language processing tasks which is delivered at global scale. Here, we focus on the evaluation of the pre-trained and ready-to-use sentiment model that is offered to the public for general sources and domains. No additional training is allowed on top of the pre-trained *general purpose* model. In particular, we use in this paper the versions made available for English and Italian in May-June 2017. Unfortunately, we could not find any documentation, even at high level, about the techniques used by Google or the training set used. We can just expect that, given their huge resources, they could have been using all of the available public sources for training, even potentially, all of the apps reviews from their Google Play Store. We cite here the last available papers published on their webpage about sentiment analysis: [10,17,18].

X2Check, App2Check, Tweet2Check, Amazon2Check. X2Check is an industrial engine implementing supervised learning techniques that allowed us to create predictive models for sentiment quantification. Training of predictive models is performed by considering a huge variety of *domains* and different textual *sources* like reviews, tweets, etc. It provides, as answer to a sentence in Italian or English, a quantification of the sentiment polarity scored from 1 to 5, according to the most recent trend shown in the last sentiment evaluation SemEval [13], where tracks considering quantification have been introduced. Thus, we consider the following quantification: as "positive", sentences with score 4 (positive) or 5 (very positive); as "negative", sentences with score 1 (very negative) or 2 (negative); as "neutral", sentences with score 3. In order to compute the final answer, X2Check applies a set of algorithms which take into account natural language processing techniques, allowing e.g. to also automatically perform topic/named entity extraction. It is not possible to give more details on the engine due to non-disclosure restrictions.

In the following, we call App2Check, Tweet2Check and Amazon2Check, the versions of our industrial engine when it is specifically trained and *fine-tuned* respectively on apps reviews, tweets and Amazon products reviews. X2Check is the general purpose API that we offer (with free trial for research purposes), that is composed by a meta-model that understands which is the best predictive model to use according to the provided input text. All of the specialized versions of our engine (App2Check, Tweet2Check, etc.) are associated with a user-friendly web application for customer experience analytics, and whose features are out of the scope of this paper.

2.2 Systems and Benchmarks from Evalita SentiPolc 2016

Evalita SentiPolc [3] is the main international evaluation for sentiment polarity classification on benchmarks in Italian. Thus, we decided to include here the results from the last available evaluation (2016) for the *polarity* task.

iFeel research platform allows to run multiple sentiment engines on the specified sentences (see Sect. 2.4). Tools included in iFeel are quite general purpose and, for this reason, in order to ensure in our evaluation the fairest comparison with our tools about tweet analysis in Italian language, we decided to also take into account research tools that have been specifically built to manage and analyze tweets in Italian. To this aim, we considered all of the tools that participated in the last international competition called SentiPolc2016. These tools are basically machine learning-based tools using mainly supervised learning techniques, including different kinds of features; most of them considered features obtained observing the typical tweets structure, and some of the best ranking tools considered also semantic features (e.g. UNIBA). Thanks to that, a fair comparison with our Tweet2Chéck is made available. We do not go deeper in the description of these tools since it is fully discussed here [3].

2.3 Systems and Benchmarks from SemEval 2017

We decided to include in our evaluation a comparison of the results obtained in [16], which is the main international challenge about SA, and the industrial engines that we take into account here. Systems that participated to SemEval 2017 are 41 engines that participated to *Task 4 - Subtask A*, implementing the state-of-the-art techniques for sentiment analysis, mainly machine learning-based, and that have been fine-tuned and trained on the specific target source, constituted by tweets.

2.4 iFeel Platform

iFeel is a research web platform [1, 2] allowing to run multiple sentiment analysis tools on the specified list of sentences. It allows to run tools natively supporting English or first translate sentences from other languages into English, and then run 19 tools on the English translated sentences. Since it has been experimentally shown in [2] that language specific methods do not have a significant advantage over a simple machine translation approach before sentiment evaluation, and since most of the research tools do not have a publicly available Italian version, the results of the tools ran by iFeel are used for both Italian and English. However, for the comparison oriented to research tools not specifically trained on the target source, we also considered the only research tool we found which natively processes Italian, Sentistrenght [19] (SentiStrengthIta in the following), and it is our reference tool with no translation before sentiment evaluation. Tools included in iFeel are (in alphabetical order): AFINN, Emolex, Emoticon Distance Supervised, Emoticons, Happiness Index, NRC Hashtag, Opinion Finder, Opinion Lexicon, Panas-t, SANN, SASA, Senticnet, Sentiment140, SentiStrength, SentiWordNet, SO-CAL, Stanford Deep Learning, Umigon, Vader.

Such tools are included in our evaluation to show a comparison of research tools *not* specifically trained on the target source versus industrial tools.

2.5   Benchmarks from ESWC Semantic Sentiment Analysis 2016

We propose here to compare research and industrial tools performance also on general product reviews. To his aim, we included as testset in our evaluation, a portion of the training set proposed at the ESWC challenge on Semantic Sentiment Analysis 2016 (SSA 2016) [7]. We chose a balanced subset with randomly selected instances, to reduce the prediction time of all of the systems.

3   Experimental Evaluation

In our experimental evaluation, we proceed by first taking into account the results on tweets from the main competitions in Italian and English, and we show how industrial engines *–with no specific training on the target source–* (X2Check and Google CNL) perform compared to the most recent research approaches. In this setting, we are aware that the industrial generic APIs cannot perform well compared to the specifically trained and fine-tuned engines from the competitions, and our goal is to quantify their performance gap and generalization power. Moreover, we evaluate on a cross-source basis our industrial tool to understand how the specialized version App2Check, trained on apps reviews, performs on tweets.

Tables 4, 5, and 6 show columns macro-F1 (MF1), accuracy (Acc), F1 on each class (resp. F1($-$) for negative, F1(x) for neutral – if present–, and F1($+$) for positive), and are sorted by macro F1, considered as our scoring system for the tools. In Table 1, the SentiPolC organizers used a different metric and evaluated separately results obtained for positive and negative classes: Pos/Neg and F1($+$)/F1($-$) are different measures, and F-score is the average of Pos and Neg (see [3] for more details). About results from SemEval 2017 in Table 2, organizers chose the averaged recall (column *AvgR*) as scoring system. Here, column *AvgF1-PN* indicates the average F1 on the positive and negative classes. Some of the tables are shortened, full tables can be found in [3,6] or [16].

All of the reported experiments are repeatable: *(i)* Apps reviews and Amazon product reviews benchmarks that we used are available online[1]; *(ii)* about industrial engines, a free access to X2Check API and its adaptations will be guaranteed to this aim, and Google CNL is available online as well.

---

[1] https://app2check.com/performance.

3.1 Evaluation on Tweets

In Table 1, we show the performance obtained by Tweet2Check (in its last, slightly improved version), and X2Check, on the testset of SentiPolc 2016, composed by two thousand tweets in Italian. In this challenge, two kinds of submission were allowed: a *constrained run*, allowing to use only the provided training set as labeled resource; an *unconstrained run*, which let the participants use any resource available to perform well in the specific task. Being a challenge on Italian, all of the engines were built with explicit support of Italian language without translations.

Table 1. Comparison on 2000 tweets in Italian from Evalita Sentipolc 2016

	System	Const/unc	Pos	Neg	F
1	SwissCheese	c	0.6529	**0.7128**	**0.6828**
2	UniPI	c	**0.6850**	0.6426	0.6638
3	Unitor	u	0.6354	0.6885	0.662
4	**Tweet2Check**	u	0.6696	0.6442	0.6569
5	ItaliaNLP	c	0.6265	0.6743	0.6504
6	X2Check	u	0.6629	0.6442	0.6491
7	IRADABE	c	0.6426	0.648	0.6453
8	UniBO	c	0.6708	0.6026	0.6367
9	IntIntUniba	c	0.6189	0.6372	0.6281
10	CoLingLab	c	0.5619	0.6579	0.6099
11	INGEOTEC	u	0.5944	0.6205	0.6075
12	ADAPT	c	0.5632	0.6461	0.6046
13	App2Check	u	0.5466	0.6250	0.5857
14	samskara	c	0.5198	0.6168	0.5683
15	Google CNL_05-2017	u	0.5426	0.5530	0.5478
16	*Baseline*		*0.4518*	*0.3808*	*0.4163*

X2Check ranks sixth in this tables, reaching a F-score of 0.6491, just 3.4% (0.0337) lower than the winner SwissCheese. X2Check is lower than just 1.3% (0.0129) from Unitor, which is the best engine for the unconstrained run, even if it is specifically fine-tuned to work on tweets in this domain. Since the difference between Tweet2Check and X2Check is less than 0.008, the use of the meta-model showed here a performance very close to the one of the model specific for the target source. Google CNL reached a MF1 10.1% lower than X2Check and 0.0379 lower than App2Check, which is trained on another source. The meta-model of X2Check correctly recognized as tweet the 91.4% of the testset, choosing the best model for this source.

In Table 2, Tweet2Check is not fine-tuned on this domain, even if it is an engine specifically trained on tweets. Again, thanks to the accuracy reached by its meta-model (95.7% on this testset), the performance of X2Check is really close to Tweet2Check (almost the same) and it ranks higher than 9 specifically-trained research tools, with a macro-averaged recall of just 0.118 lower than the best tool. X2Check is still higher than Google CNL, but here the difference between them is just 0.013 in AvgR, and 4.7% in AvgF1-PN. It is interesting to see that App2Check is still 5 positions higher than the last tool, even if trained on reviews.

Table 2. Results from SemEval-2017 Task 4, subtask A.

	System	AvgR	AvgF1-PN	Acc
1	DataStories	**0.681**	0.677	0.651
	BB_twtr	**0.681**	**0.685**	0.658
3	LIA	0.676	0.674	0.661
4	Senti17	0.674	0.665	0.652
5	NNEMBs	0.669	0.658	**0.664**
...	...	...	...	...
28	ej-za-2017	0.571	0.539	0.582
	LSIS	0.571	0.561	0.521
30	Tweet2Check	0.566	0.565	0.526
31	X2Check	0.563	0.561	0.523
32	XJSA	0.556	0.519	0.575
33	Neverland-THU	0.555	0.507	0.597
34	MI& T-Lab	0.551	0.522	0.561
35	Google CNL_06-2017	0.550	0.514	0.567
36	diegoref	0.546	0.527	0.540
37	App2Check	0.541	0.508	0.545
38	xiwu	0.479	0.365	0.547
39	SSN_MLRG1	0.431	0.344	0.439
40	YNU-1510	0.340	0.201	0.387
41	WarwickDCS	0.335	0.221	0.382
	Avid	0.335	0.163	0.206

In Table 3, we show a further step of evaluation on tweets, considering 1000 randomly selected tweets in English from [2,13]. In this case, tweets have been randomly selected (with test set equally split on positive/negative) because iFeel introduced a limitation of 1000 runs while performing our evaluation. This test set does not contain the neutral class. Here we show a comparison with research tools that are not trained/tuned on the selected domain, and not necessarily optimized to work on the tweet source. For example, Standford Deep Learning is trained on movies reviews, and other research engines on tweets but on different domains.

Considering the industrial tools, surprisingly X2Check here is the best engine: it seems that when the model selector chose a model different than Tweet2-Check, in 12.8% of the tweets, the specific models called managed to classify tweets better than Tweet2Check. In Table 3, Google CNL ranks considerably lower than X2Check, at a distance of 20,7% of MF1.

Table 3. Comparison on 1000 tweets in English

	Tool	Acc	MF1	F1(−)	F1(+)
1	X2Check	**0.867**	**0.873**	**0.869**	**0.877**
2	Tweet2Check	0.858	0.863	0.860	0.865
3	AFINN	0.709	0.772	0.796	0.748
4	Sentistrength	0.668	0.751	0.763	0.740
5	App2Check	0.692	0.716	0.730	0.702
6	Senticnet	0.660	0.684	0.642	0.725
7	Umigon	0.588	0.680	0.692	0.667
8	Vader	0.542	0.671	0.653	0.690
9	Google CNL_05-2017	0.524	0.666	0.604	0.728
10	Sentiment140	0.644	0.649	0.706	0.592
11	SentiWordNet	0.614	0.637	0.616	0.658
12	Op. Lexicon	0.508	0.625	0.653	0.598
13	SOCAL	0.509	0.621	0.655	0.588
14	NRC Hashtag	0.596	0.591	0.678	0.505
15	H. Index	0.448	0.539	0.459	0.618
16	Stanford DL	0.452	0.520	0.614	0.427
17	Emolex	0.458	0.511	0.614	0.407
...	...	...	...	...	...

3.2   Evaluation on Apps Reviews

We analyze now the results on apps reviews. Apps reviews benchmark set is constituted by *Test set Apps*, made of 10 thousands comments from the following 10 different very popular apps (one thousand comments per app).

- *Test set Apps-ita*: Angry Birds, Banco Posta, Facebook, Fruit Ninja, Gmail, Mobile Banking Unicredit, My Vodafone, PayPal, Twitter, Whatsapp. It has been already used in [6].
- *Test set Apps-eng*: Candy Crush Soda Saga, Chase Mobile, Clash Of Clans, Facebook Messenger, Gmail, Instagram, My Verizon, PayPal, Snapchat and Wells Fargo.

Each comment has a score, called app rating, associated by the user to the app.

In Table 4 we can see that App2Check, implementing a specific model, outperforms the research tools with about a 19.8% of better accuracy from the first research tool in the table (SentiWordnet), and shows also a 45% of better accuracy respect to SentiStrenght for Italian. X2Check shows also here a performance very close to App2Check, since the metamodel chooses App2Check the 89.3% of the times. Google CNL shows a MF1 that is about 8% lower than X2Check. In Table 5, Google CNL shows a 2.9% higher accuracy than X2Check, and the latter is higher than App2Check: the metamodel chose it the 92.6% of the times. Since the maximum engines accuracy measured on app benchmarks in English is 66.2%, we further investigated the reason why this occurs, especially in relationship with the much higher accuracy measured in the case of benchmarks in Italian. It turns out that, the average length of apps reviews in Italian is 74.4 characters, while the length is almost double on apps reviews in English (139.5). By manually inspecting apps reviews, it seems that long reviews are usually more likely to have a *mixed* sentiment, since the user explains in their reviews both positive, neutral and negative aspects of the product under evaluation. In such cases, calculating a document-level (overall) sentiment score is probably less meaningful or useful for the analysis point of view. Even the app rating value

Table 4. Comparison on 10.000 apps reviews in Italian wrt app rating.

	Tool	Acc	MF1	F1($-$)	F1(x)	F1($+$)
1	App2Check	**0.857**	**0.733**	**0.827**	**0.456**	**0.917**
2	X2Check	0.843	0.714	0.814	0.420	0.908
3	Google CNL_05-2017	0.791	0.634	0.799	0.217	0.888
4	SentiWordNet	0.659	0.479	0.604	0.062	0.771
5	AFINN	0.603	0.475	0.492	0.166	0.767
6	SentiStrength	0.597	0.475	0.463	0.193	0.768
7	Stanford DL	0.540	0.456	0.565	0.135	0.668
8	Op. Lexicon	0.553	0.449	0.451	0.175	0.722
9	Sentiment140	0.587	0.441	0.574	0.067	0.682
10	Umigon	0.501	0.428	0.478	0.146	0.662
11	SO-CAL	0.493	0.418	0.458	0.138	0.656
12	NRC Hashtag	0.529	0.412	0.536	0.083	0.617
13	Senticnet	0.631	0.409	0.366	0.091	0.769
14	Vader	0.462	0.385	0.295	0.197	0.663
15	Emolex	0.455	0.383	0.385	0.141	0.623
16	SASA	0.488	0.377	0.296	0.164	0.671
17	SentiStr. Ita	0.396	0.340	0.320	0.139	0.562
...	...	...	...	...	...	...

Table 5. Comparison on 10.000 apps reviews in English wrt app rating.

	Tool	Acc	MF1	F1(−)	F1(x)	F1(+)
1	Google CNL_05-2017	**0.662**	**0.629**	**0.717**	**0.376**	**0.793**
2	X2Check	0.633	0.539	0.698	0.193	0.726
3	App2Check	0.631	0.524	0.708	0.149	0.714
4	Umigon	0.511	0.488	0.527	0.294	0.644
5	Stanford DL	0.514	0.475	0.607	0.242	0.574
6	AFINN	0.499	0.455	0.460	0.273	0.634
7	Op. Lexicon	0.481	0.450	0.434	0.285	0.632
8	SentiStrength	0.475	0.450	0.429	0.301	0.620
9	SO-CAL	0.447	0.424	0.465	0.250	0.557
10	Sentiment140	0.537	0.420	0.643	0.092	0.525
11	NRC Hashtag	0.518	0.405	0.634	0.092	0.489
12	Vader	0.421	0.405	0.268	0.343	0.604
13	SentiWordNet	0.508	0.403	0.529	0.080	0.600
14	Emolex	0.407	0.393	0.379	0.276	0.523
15	SASA	0.402	0.380	0.348	0.264	0.527
16	H. Index	0.377	0.344	0.222	0.283	0.527
17	Senticnet	0.441	0.335	0.327	0.107	0.571
...	...	...	...	...	...	...

itself, used as a reference, can have a low usefulness in cases of mixed sentiment in the review. Thus, if sentiment engines show a significant gap in accuracy compared to the reference rating, it may indicate that we are facing reviews with a mixed sentiment or that, for example, that the user gives an overall positive product evaluation through the app rating, and then writes only about negative aspects to improve. We think that app rating can be anyway a good reference to use for experimental evaluations with a high number of reviews, since it is provided by a third party –the product/service evaluator–, and considering that anyway group of humans agree in around the 80% of cases [20] about sentiment classification. In the case of mixed sentiment, in particular, we recommend a focus on sentence-level and entity-level sentiment analysis. In order to give an example, the review *"I like this game but after the iOS update I get a crash when the app starts. Please do something!!"* contains a mixed sentiment even if the overall rating given by this specific user is positive: positive in the first part (*"I like this game"*) and negative in the second and third parts (*"after the iOS update I get a crash when the app starts"* and *"Please do something!!"*). App2Check manages to split the first part from the second and third part and assigns a positive sentiment to the entity *"game"* (called topic) and negative to the remaining entities involved. We do not further investigate these aspects, since sentence-level and entity-level sentiment analysis are out of the scope of this paper.

3.3 Experimental Evaluation on Generic Product Reviews

In Table 6, we show the results on amazon product reviews. Amazon2Check is the model optimized for such benchmark, and is the best engine here. X2Check approximates very well its performance, since the metamodel chooses Amazon2-Check the 97.5% of the times. X2Check is 4.1% better than Google CNL. As a reference, we ran here also SentiStrenght and StandfordDL, which score more than 20% lower than X2Check.

Table 6. Comparison on Amazon products reviews in English - internal evaluation.

	Tool	M-F1	Acc	F1($-$)	F1($+$)
1	**Amazon2Check**	**0.865**	**0.864**	**0.869**	**0.860**
2	X2Check	0.862	0.862	0.868	0.856
3	Google CNL_05-2017	0.821	0.827	0.853	0.790
4	App2Check	0.729	0.736	0.772	0.685
5	SentiStrength	0.630	0.552	0.568	0.692
6	StanfordDL	0.602	0.604	0.705	0.498

4 Conclusion

In this paper we focused on the industrial perspective of building and evaluating sentiment engines that have to show a high average performance on heterogeneous sources (tweets, product reviews, etc.), domains (politics, banking, games, etc.), and languages. We recalled that research engines are usually built to deal with a specific setting, and that papers that take into account the topic of multiple source/domain adaptation techniques, and making evaluations on heterogeneous sources, lack of a comparison with industrial engines that are, instead, specifically designed to deal with this case. We presented an extensive experimental comparison between industrial engines and state-of-the-art research tools that also competed in the last international competitions. We discussed the fact that many industrial engines do not allow in their terms of use to make a comparative analysis, and that this is a strong limitation especially in sentiment analysis, since it is well known that performance can change significantly depending on the target source under evaluation. For this reason, we took into account in our evaluation only Google CNL and X2Check as industrial engines. Systems have been evaluated on tweets, apps reviews and general product reviews, on Italian and English. Two new testsets for document-level polarity detection, each containing 10 thousand apps reviews in Italian and English, are used for the evaluation and made available to the research community. Our new general purpose industrial API, called X2Check, has been included in the evaluation; given the input source, it uses a metamodel estimating which classification model is more suitable for the specific input. Considering an overall cross-source average

F-score on all of the results, which is our main goal, X2Check shows a performance that is overall 9.1% and 5.1% higher than Google CNL, respectively for
Italian and English benchmarks. Compared to the research engines, X2Check
shows a macro-f1 score that is always higher than tools not specifically trained
on the source set under evaluation (reaching 23% on general product reviews); it
is lower at most of 3.4% in Italian and 11.6% on English benchmarks, compared
to best research tools specifically trained on the target source.

References

1. Araújo, M., Gonçalves, P., Cha, M., Benevenuto, F.: iFeel: a system that compares and combines sentiment analysis methods. In: Proceedings of WWW 2014
   Companion, pp. 75–78 (2014)
2. Araújo, M., dos Reis, J.C., Pereira, A.M., Benevenuto, F.: An evaluation of machine
   translation for multilingual sentence-level sentiment analysis. In: Proceedings of the
   31st Annual ACM Symposium on Applied Computing, Pisa, Italy, 4–8 April 2016,
   pp. 1140–1145 (2016)
3. Barbieri, F., Basile, V., Croce, D., Nissim, M., Novielli, N., Patti, V.: Overview of
   the evalita 2016 sentiment polarity classification task. In: Proceedings of CLiC-it
   2016 & EVALITA 2016 (2016)
4. Blitzer, J., Dredze, M., Pereira, F.: Biographies, bollywood, boom-boxes and
   blenders: domain adaptation for sentiment classification. In: Proceedings of ACL
   2007 (2007)
5. Bollegala, D., Mu, T., Goulermas, J.Y.: Cross-domain sentiment classification using
   sentiment sensitive embeddings. IEEE Trans. Knowl. Data Eng. 28(2), 398–410
   (2016)
6. Di Rosa, E., Durante, A.: App2check: a machine learning-based system for sentiment analysis of app reviews in Italian language. In: Proceedings of the International Workshop on Social Media World Sensors (Sideways)- Held in conjunction
   with LREC 2016, pp. 8–11 (2016)
7. Dragoni, M., Recupero, D.R.: Challenge on fine-grained sentiment analysis within
   ESWC2016. In: Sack, H., Dietze, S., Tordai, A., Lange, C. (eds.) Semantic Web
   Challenges - Third SemWebEval Challenge at ESWC 2016, vol. 641, pp. 79–94.
   Springer, Heidelberg (2016)
8. Heredia, B., Khoshgoftaar, T.M., Prusa, J.D., Crawford, M.: Cross-domain sentiment analysis: an empirical investigation. In: Proceedings of IRI 2016, pp. 160–165
   (2016)
9. Heredia, B., Khoshgoftaar, T.M., Prusa, J.D., Crawford, M.: Integrating multiple
   data sources to enhance sentiment prediction. In: Proceedings of IEEE CIC 2016,
   pp. 285–291 (2016)
10. Li, F., Wang, S., Liu, S., Zhang, M.: SUIT: a supervised user-item based topic
    model for sentiment analysis. In: Proceedings of AAAI 2014, pp. 1636–1642 (2014)
11. Liu, B.: Sentiment Analysis and Opinion Mining. Morgan & Claypool Publishers,
    San Rafael (2012)
12. Mejova, Y., Srinivasan, P.: Crossing media streams with sentiment: domain adap-
    tation in blogs, reviews and Twitter. In: Proceedings of ICWSM 2012 (2012)
13. Nakov, P., Ritter, A., Sara, R., Sebastiani, F., Stoyanov, V.: Semeval-2016 task 4:
    sentiment analysis in Twitter. In: Proceedings of SemEval 2016. Association for
    Computational Linguistics (2016)

14. Pan, S.J., Ni, X., Sun, J., Yang, Q., Chen, Z.: Cross-domain sentiment classification via spectral feature alignment. In: Proceedings of WWW 2010, pp. 751–760 (2010)
15. Pang, B., Lee, L.: Opinion mining and sentiment analysis. Found. Trends Inf. Retr. **2**(1–2), 1–135 (2008)
16. Rosenthal, S., Farra, N., Nakov, P.: SemEval-2017 task 4: sentiment analysis in Twitter. In: Proceedings of SemEval 2017. Association for Computational Linguistics (2017)
17. Täckström, O., McDonald, R.: Discovering fine-grained sentiment with latent variable structured prediction models. In: Clough, P., Foley, C., Gurrin, C., Jones, G.J.F., Kraaij, W., Lee, H., Mudoch, V. (eds.) ECIR 2011. LNCS, vol. 6611, pp. 368–374. Springer, Heidelberg (2011). doi:10.1007/978-3-642-20161-5_37
18. Täckström, O., McDonald, R.T.: Semi-supervised latent variable models for sentence-level sentiment analysis. In: Proceedings of HLT 2011, pp. 569–574 (2011)
19. Thelwall, M., Buckley, K., Paltoglou, G., Cai, D., Kappas, A.: Sentiment strength detection in short informal text. JASIST **61**(12), 2544–2558 (2010)
20. Wilson, T., Wiebe, J., Hoffmann, P.: Recognizing contextual polarity: an exploration of features for phrase-level sentiment analysis. Comput. Linguist. **35**(3), 399–433 (2009)
21. Wu, F., Huang, Y.: Sentiment domain adaptation with multiple sources. In: Proceedings of ACL 2016 (2016)
22. Wu, F., Huang, Y., Yuan, Z.: Domain-specific sentiment classification via fusing sentiment knowledge from multiple sources. Inf. Fusion **35**, 26–37 (2017)

Knowledge Representation and Reasoning

Service Composition in Stochastic Settings

Ronen I. Brafman[1], Giuseppe De Giacomo[2(✉)], Massimo Mecella[2],
and Sebastian Sardina[3]

[1] Ben-Gurion University, Beer-Sheva, Israel
brafman@cs.bgu.ac.il
[2] Sapienza University of Rome, Rome, Italy
{degiacomo,mecella}@dis.uniroma1.it
[3] RMIT University, Melbourne, Australia
sebastian.sardina@rmit.edu.au

Abstract. With the growth of the Internet-of-Things and online Web services, more services with more capabilities are available to us. The ability to generate new, more useful services from existing ones has been the focus of much research for over a decade. The goal is, given a specification of the behavior of the target service, to build a controller, known as an orchestrator, that uses existing services to satisfy the requirements of the target service. The model of services and requirements used in most work is that of a finite state machine. This implies that the specification can either be satisfied or not, with no middle ground. This is a major drawback, since often an exact solution cannot be obtained. In this paper we study a simple stochastic model for service composition: we annotate the target service with probabilities describing the likelihood of requesting each action in a state, and rewards for being able to execute actions. We show how to solve the resulting problem by solving a certain Markov Decision Process (MDP) derived from the service and requirement specifications. The solution to this MDP induces an orchestrator that coincides with the exact solution if a composition exists. Otherwise it provides an approximate solution that maximizes the expected sum of values of user requests that can be serviced. The model studied although simple shades light on composition in stochastic settings and indeed we discuss several possible extensions.

1 Introduction

With the growth of the Internet-of-Things (IoT) and online Web services, more and more services with more and more capabilities are available to us. By combining the functionalities offered by multiple services, we can provide much added value. A classic example is the ability to offer a complete vacation by combining Web services that offer (functionalities for buying) flights, ground transportation, accommodations, and event tickets. But as more physical devices are controlled through the Web via services, this can also be used to orchestrate the behavior of various kitchen devices, home entertainment systems, and home security services [1,2].

© Springer International Publishing AG 2017
F. Esposito et al. (Eds.): AI*IA 2017, LNAI 10640, pp. 159–171, 2017.
https://doi.org/10.1007/978-3-319-70169-1_12

The problem of service composition has been considered in the literature for over a decade, starting from seminal manual approaches, e.g., [3–5], which mainly focussed on modeling issues as well as on automated discovery of services described making use of rich ontologies, to automatic ones based on planning, e.g., [6,7] or on KR techniques, e.g., [8], or on automated synthesis [9–11]. The reader interested in a survey of approaches can refer to [1,12,13]. Here we concentrate on the approach known in literature as the "Roman model" whose original paper [9] was awarded the most influential SOC paper of the decade prize at ICSOC 2013. Actually, for sake of simplicity, in our mathematical treatment we will consider the Roman model in its most pristine form. Though we will describe several extension in the discussion section.

In the Roman model, composition is as follows: each available (i.e., to be used in the composition, therefore referred to as *component*) service is modeled as a finite state machines (FSM), in which at each state, the service offers a certain set of actions, where each action changes the state of the service in some way. The designer is interested in generating a new service (referred to as *composite*, or *target*) from the set of existing services. The required service (the *requirement*) is specified using a FSM, too. The computational problem is to see whether the requirement can be satisfied by properly orchestrating the work of the component services. That is, by building a scheduler (called the *orchestrator*) that will use actions provided by existing services to implement action request of the requirement. Thus, a new service is synthesized using existing services.

Unfortunately, it is not always possible to synthesize a service that fully conforms with the requirement specification. Furthermore, a deterministic model (adopted in many approaches) is inappropriate for most services. Many services have various failure modes and different potential transitions for the same action. This can be addressed by allowing for non-determinism, but satisfying the requirement in this case can be even harder. This zero-one situation, where we can either synthesize a perfect solution or fail, should be improved. Rather than returning no answer, we need a notion of the "best-possible" solution, and the main contribution of this paper is to provide a solution to this problem.

In this paper we discuss and elaborate upon a probabilistic model for the service composition problem, first presented in [14]. In this model, an optimal solution can be found by solving an appropriate probabilistic planning problem (a Markov decision process – MDP) derived from the services and requirement specifications. Specifically, it is natural to make the requirement probabilistic, associating a probability with each action choice in each state. This probability captures how likely the user is to request the action in that state. Such information can be, initially, supplied by the designer, but can also be learned in the course of service operation in order to adapt the composition to user behavior. Next, a reward is associated with the requirement behavior. This reward can be defined in different ways depending on the designer's objectives. For example, we can associate a reward with different states that represent achieving certain milestones, so that solutions that make sure that the service is able to reach these milestones will be preferred. Or, we can associate a reward with actions at a state, modeling how important it is to provide the user with this option at this state. Thus, if certain actions represent crucial aspects of the service, they will be associated with high rewards, whereas actions that have added value, but are less important, can be associated with lower rewards.

We observe that rewards can be related to Quality-of-Service (QoS), which is often considered crucial in modeling Web services [15,16]. Rewards on some states represent situations that the designer wants to enforce in order to guarantee QoS, while rewards on actions represent non-functional QoS requirements. As we discuss later on, one can use complex reward specifications in the form of transducers, or formulas in expressive logics such as LTL_f and LDL_f – linear-time temporal logic and dynamic logic on finite traces [17].

Given a set of available services and a probabilistic requirement specification, we formulate a new MDP that aggregates this information – it is very similar in spirit to the product automata used to solve the non-stochastic case – such that an optimal policy for this MDP generates an orchestrator that maximizes the expected sum of rewards. In some sense, the orchestrator will ensure that target transitions of highest value are provided for the longest possible time.

This model can also accommodate various useful extensions. For example, we can associate a cost with existing service actions or service states – e.g., energy use in the case of smart homes or service cost in the case of travel services. If these costs are commensurable with the value of services offered by the synthesized service, we still obtain a standard MDP. Otherwise, we obtain a multi-objective MDP (if we want to optimize both aspects) or a constrained MDP (if we have an energy or travel budget). Both models have been studied in literature and solution algorithms for them exist. In the last section, we discuss a number of such useful extensions.

Before continuing, we observe that our probabilistic extension to service composition is orthogonal to that proposed in [18], where available services are probabilistic, but the target specification (expressed as ω-regular languages, there) is not and the orchestrator is required to satisfy the target specification with probability 1.

The paper is structured as follows: Sect. 2 introduce our model of services, whereas Sect. 3 presents the model for the requirement and the solution of the proposed problem. In Sect. 5 we conlcude with a discussion some extensions of the basic framework.[1]

2   The Non-stochastic Model

We adopt the Roman model for *service composition* [1], in its most pristine form [9], which we describe below. A *service* is defined as a tuple $S = (\Sigma, \sigma_0, F, A, \delta)$, where:

– Σ is the finite set of service's *states*;

---

[1] A preliminary version of this paper has been presented at the ICAPS 2017 Workshop on Generalized Planning. (The workshop does not have published proceedings.).

- $\sigma_0 \in \Sigma$ is the *initial state*;
- $F \subseteq \Sigma$ is the set of service's *final* states;
- A is the finite set of service's *actions*;
- $\delta \subseteq \Sigma \times A \mapsto \Sigma$ is the service's *transition (partial) function*, i.e., *actions are deterministic*.

We interchange notations $s' \in \delta(\sigma, a)$ and $\sigma \xrightarrow{a} \sigma'$ in δ, possibly keeping implicit δ when no ambiguity arises. Finally, we write $A(\sigma)$ to denote $\{a \in A : \delta(\sigma, a)$ is defined$\}$ – the set of actions available at s.

In the Roman model, we focus on the interface that services expose, which capture a *conversational* model of the service, i.e., one that represents the sequences of requests a service can serve, as the interaction with a client goes on. More specifically, from a given state, a service can serve only requests for actions that "label" an outgoing transition. Such actions, although atomic from the client perspective, correspond, in general to complex activities that may include, e.g., conversations with software modules or interactions with external users. Upon execution of the requested action, the service moves to a successor state, i.e., a state reachable from the current one via a transition labeled with the executed action.

A *history h* of a service S is a, possibly infinite, sequence alternating states and actions (necessarily ending with a state)

$$\sigma^0 \cdot a_1 \cdot \sigma^1 \cdot a_2 \cdots \cdot a_n \cdot \sigma^n \cdots$$

s.t. $\sigma^0 = \sigma_0$ and $\sigma^i \xrightarrow{a_{i+1}} \sigma^{i+1}$, for all $i \geq 0$. That is, a possible progression of the states of the service, annotated by an appropriate action. Note that the above implies that $a_i \in A(\sigma_{i-1})$.

We assume we have a finite set of available services $S_i = (\Sigma_i, \sigma_{i0}, F_i, A, \delta_i)$, over the same set of actions A. The set of all such services is referred to as the *service community*, denoted as $\mathcal{S} = \{S_1, \ldots, S_n\}$.

Given $\mathcal{S}$, [1] defines a *target* service as a further service $T = (\Sigma_t, \sigma_{t0}, F_t, A, \delta_t)$, again over the actions A. The target service provides a formal characterization of a desired service that may not be available in the community. We denote the set of possible target service histories by H_t.

Informally, the target represents a business process that one would like to offer to clients, where each state represents a decision point. At each state, the client is provided with a set of options to choose among, each corresponding to an action available in the state. Notice that typically the target service is not available. Further, the only entities able to execute actions, i.e., activities, are the available services. Thus, one cannot build the target service by simply combining the actions of the target service, but has to resort to the available services, which impose constraints on the execution of actions, depending on the conversations they can actually carry out.

The goal of service composition is to combine the available services in an appropriate way so as to mimic, from a client point of view, the behavior of the target service. This can be done by interposing an *orchestrator* between the available services and the client. The orchestrator delegates the current action requested by the client to some available service, waits for the service to fulfill it, then notifies the client, receives a new request, delegates it again, waits, and so on. In order to do this correctly, one not only needs to find a service that is able to execute the current action, but also has to choose the service so that *all possible future requests* compliant with the target service can be fulfilled.

To formally define the computational problem and its solution, we require some preliminary notions: The *system service* of $\mathcal{S}$ is the service $Z = (\Sigma_z, \sigma_{z_0}, F_z, A_z, \delta_z)$, s.t.:

- $\Sigma_z = \Sigma_1 \times \cdots \times \Sigma_n$;
- $\sigma_{z0} = (\sigma_{10}, \dots, \sigma_{n0})$;
- $F_z = \{(\sigma_1, \dots, \sigma_n) \mid \sigma_i \in F_i, 1 \leq i \leq n\}$
- $A_z = A \times \{1, \dots, n\}$ is the set of pairs (a, i) formed by a shared action a and the index i of the service that executes it;
- $\sigma \xrightarrow{(a,i)} \sigma'$ iff, for $\sigma = (\sigma_1, \dots, \sigma_n)$ and $\sigma' = (\sigma'_1, \dots, \sigma'_n)$, it is the case that $\sigma_i \xrightarrow{a} \sigma'_i$ in δ_i, and $\sigma_j = \sigma'_j$, for $j \neq i$.

Intuitively, Z is the service stemming from the product of the asynchronous execution of the services in $\mathcal{S}$. This is a virtual entity, i.e., without any actual counterpart, that offers a formal account of the evolution of the available services, when the community is seen as a whole. Note that in the transitions of Z, the service executing the corresponding action, is explicitly mentioned. Also $(a, i) \in A(\sigma_z)$ indicates that a can be executed by service i in the current state. We denote the set of system service histories by H_z.

An *orchestrator* for a community $\mathcal{S}$ is a partial function[2]:

$$\gamma : \Sigma_z \times A \mapsto \{1, \dots, n\}.$$

Intuitively, γ is a decision maker able to keep track of the way the services in $\mathcal{S}$ have evolved up to a certain point, and that, in response to an incoming action request, returns the index of a service.

Notice that, in general, γ is not guaranteed to return a service able to execute the requested action, nor that delegating the action to the returned service guarantees that all possible future requests can be served. Obviously, only the orchestrator that guarantees such features can be actually used to realize the desired service, as formalized below.

The dynamics of the system is deterministic given the actions selected by the user. Hence, together with the orchestrator choice, it determines a system history. That is, an orchestrator defines a partial function from target-service histories to system histories, based on the (partial) mapping from system state and action to a service and the (partial) mapping from system state, action, and service, to the next system state. We denote this mapping by τ. More formally,

---

[2] In the original orchestrator definition γ is a function of the entire history instead of the system service's current state only. It can be shown that if an orchestrator of the previous form exist then one of the current form exists [9,11]. So we adopt this simpler notion.

$\tau : H_t \mapsto H_z$ is defined inductively as follows: $\tau(\sigma_{t0}) = \sigma_{z0}$. Let $\tau(h_t) = h_z$, and let s_t, s_z denote the last states, respectively, in h_t, h_z. Then, τ is also defined on $h_t \cdot a \cdot s'_t$ provided: $a \in A(s_t)$ and $s'_t = \delta_t(s_t, a)$, and that γ is defined on (s_z, a), and $(a, \gamma(s_z, a)) \in A(s_z)$. That is, provided the orchestrator function is defined on s_z and a, assigning some value i, and δ_z is well defined on (s_z, i), we have $\tau(h_t \cdot a \cdot s'_t) = h_z \cdot a \cdot \delta_z(s_z, (a, i))$. Otherwise, $\tau(h_t \cdot a \cdot s'_t)$ is undefined.

If $\tau(h_t)$ is well defined, we say that target history h_t is *realizable* by the orchestrator.

The orchestrator γ is said to *realize* a target service Z if it realizes all histories of Z. In this case, γ is also called a *composition* of Z (on $\mathcal{S}$).

The problem of service composition in known to be EXPTIME-complete, in fact exponential on the number of the available services [9, 19] and techniques based on model checking, simulation, and LTL synthesis are available [1]. Also, several variants have been studied, including the case of nondeteministic (i.e., partially controllable but fully observable) available services [11].

3   The Valued Requirement Model

The main limitation of the composition approach outlined above is that if a composition does not exists, no notion of a "good" or "approximate" solution exists. An interesting notion of unique supremal composition has been introduced in [20]. But this notion puts the burden on the client executing the target to foresee in advance what requests it will ask in the future, and this may be too limiting in various contexts. Furthermore, in actual applications, requests are not usually of uniform importance. Some parts of the target service may be good to have, but not essential, while other parts may be central to its functionality. And typically, different requests are not equally likely. These considerations are not captured by the above model and its solution concepts. Hence, we propose a modified model that takes these considerations into account, thus obtaining a richer, finer grained, formulation of the objective that allows us to define appealing notions of "optimal" compositions.

To model the value and likelihood of request, we augment the target service model with two additional elements. P_t will be a distribution over the actions given the state. $P_t(s, a)$ is the likelihood that a user will request a in target state s. Technically, $P_t(s)$ returns a distribution over the actions, or the empty set, when s is a terminal state on which no actions are possible. R_t is the reward function, associating a non-negative reward with the ability to provide the action requested by a user. $R_t(s, a)$ is the value we associate with being able to provide action a in state s. Formally, a target service is $T = (\Sigma_t, \sigma_{t0}, F_t, A, \delta_t, P_t, R_t)$, where $\Sigma_t, \sigma_{t0}, F_t, A, \delta_t$ are defined as before, $P_t : \Sigma_t \to \pi(A) \cup \emptyset$ is the action distribution function, and $R_t : \Sigma_t \times A \to \mathbb{R}$ is the reward function. We assume rewards are non-negative.

One can specialize this definition in various ways: R_t can depend on Σ_t only, if for example, we assume that the reward is given for reaching a final state, or some particular "normal" finite states, capturing the fact that the service has completed appropriately. R_t could simply assign an identical positive value to every pair (σ, a) such that $a \in A(\sigma)$. This essentially implies that what we care about is the ability to service as many actions as possible in a state.

The definitions of an orchestrator, a target history, a realizable target history, and a realizable target do not change. But we can now define additional notions. First, P_t induces a probability density function over the set of all infinite target histories, which we will denote by P_∞. (This follows by the Ionescu Tulcea extension theorem.) Second, R_t can be used to associate a value with every infinite history. The standard definition of the value of a history h_t, which we adopt here, is that of the sum of discounted rewards: $v(\sigma_0, a_1, \sigma_1, \cdots) = \sum_{i=0}^{\infty} \lambda^i R_t(\sigma_i, a_{i+1})$, where $0 < \lambda < 1$ is the discount factor. The discount factor can be viewed as measuring the factor by which the value of rewards is reduced as time progresses, capturing the intuition that the same reward now is better than in the future.[3,4]

Given the above, we can define the expected value of an orchestrator γ to be:

$$v(\gamma) = E_{h_t \sim P_\infty}(v(h_t) \cdot real(\gamma, h_t))$$

where $real(\gamma, h_t)$ is 1 if h_t is realizable in γ, and 0 otherwise. That is, $v(\gamma)$ is the expected value of histories realizable in γ. Finally, we define an *optimal* orchestrator to be $\gamma = \arg\max_{\text{orchestrator } \gamma'} v(\gamma')$. The following is reassuring:

Theorem 1. *If the target is realizable and every target history has strictly positive value then γ realizes the target iff it is an optimal orchestrator.*

That is, if it is possible to realize the target requirement, then any orchestrator realizing it is optimal, and any orchestrator that does not realize some history, is non-optimal. The former stems from the fact that if the set of histories realizable using orchestrator γ contains the set realizable using orchestrator γ', then $v(\gamma) \geq v(\gamma')$. The latter stems from the fact that if, in addition, the set of histories realizable by γ but not by γ' has positive probability, then $v(\gamma) > v(\gamma')$. Now, if h is not realizable by γ', there exists a point in h where γ' does not assign the required action to a service that can supply it. Thus, any history that extends the corresponding prefix of h is not realisable, and the set of such histories has non-zero probability. Since we assume all histories have positive value, we obtain the desired result.

The importance of this new model is that we now have a clear notion of an optimal orchestrator that works even when the target service is not fully realizable, and this notion is clearly an extension of the standard notion, coinciding with it when the service is realizable by some orchestrator. An optimal controller is simply one that is able to handle more (in expectation) valued histories.

---

[3] It can also be viewed as quantifying the probability $(1 - \lambda)$ that the process will terminate at some state.

[4] An alternative notion, for which similar results can be obtained is that of average reward, defined, e.g., as $\liminf_{m \to \infty} \frac{1}{m} \sum_{i=0}^{m} R_t(\sigma_i, a_{i+1})$, which requires more mathematical sophistication to handle.

4   Computing an Optimal Orchestrator

We now explain how to solve the above model by formulating an appropriate MDP. An MDP is a four-tuple $M' = (S', A', Tr', R')$, where S' is a finite set of states, A' a finite set of actions, $Tr' : S' \times A' \to \pi(S')$ is the transition function, and $R : S' \times A' \to \mathbb{R}$ is the reward function. The two latter terms were defined above in the context of the valued composition model.

The composition MDP is a function of the system service and the target service as follows $M(Z,T) = (S_M, A_M, Tr_M, R_M)$, where (i) $S_M = \Sigma_Z \times \Sigma_T \times A \cup s_{M0}$ (ii) $A_M = \{a_{M0}, 1, \ldots, n\}$ (iii) $Tr_M(s_{M0}, a_{M0}, (\sigma_{z0}, \sigma_{t0}, a)) = P_t(\sigma_{t0}, a)$ (iv) $Tr_M((\sigma_z, \sigma_t, a), i, (\sigma'_z, \sigma'_t, a')) = P_t(\sigma'_t, a')$ if $\sigma_z \xrightarrow{(a,i)} \sigma'_z$ and $\sigma_t \xrightarrow{a} \sigma'_t$, and 0 otherwise. (v) $R((\sigma_z, \sigma_t, a), i) = R_t(\sigma_s, a)$ if $(a, i) \in A(\sigma_z)$ and 0 otherwise.

That is, the set of states is the product of the states of the system service, the states of the target service, and the set of actions. Intuitively, the state (σ_z, σ_t, a) denotes the fact that the system state is currently σ_z, the target state is currently σ_t and the requested action is a. In addition, there is a distinguished initial state s_{M0}. The actions correspond to selecting the service that will provide the current requested actions, together with a special initializing action, a_{M0}. A transition in state s_{M0} is defined only for action a_{M0}. From this state, we can get to state $(\sigma_{z0}, \sigma_{t0}, a)$ with probability that is equal to the probability that action a would be requested from the target service at its initial state. The state $(\sigma_{z0}, \sigma_{t0}, a)$ represents the situation that the system and target service are in their initial state, and that a is requested of the target service. In general, the defintion of $Tr((\sigma_z, \sigma_t, a), i, (\sigma'_z, \sigma'_t, a'))$ captures the fact that if service S_i provides action a in system and target states σ_z and σ_t, then the next system state is determined by (a, i) and the previous system state, and the next target state is determined by a and the previous target state. The probability associated with this transition is the probability that action a' will be requested in the new target state. Finally, the reward function associates a positive reward with states in which the assigned service S_i is able to perform the requested action a, and the value of this reward is the value of doing actions a at the target state.

Theorem 2. *Let ρ be an optimal policy for $M(Z,T)$. Then, the orchestrator γ such that $\gamma((\sigma_z, \sigma_t), a) = \rho(\sigma_z, \sigma_t, a)$ is an optimal orchestrator.*

Above we assume that an optimal policy for the MDP is one maximizing expected discounted sum of rewards with discount factor λ. The result follows from the fact that there is a one-to-one correspondence between orchestrators and policies for $M(Z,T)$, via the relationship: $\gamma((\sigma_z, \sigma_t), a) = \rho(\sigma_z, \sigma_t, a)$, and the fact that the value of policy ρ so defined equals $v(\gamma)$.

5   Extensions

With the basic setting introduced, here we can now discuss several possible extensions.

Stochastic available services. For the sake of simplicity, we have assumed so far that the component and target services are deterministic. Extending our model to capture stochastic services, where the service transitions are probabilistic too, is quite easy, see [14]. One needs to simply alter the relevant transition functions. The precise definition of realizability now becomes slightly more cumbersome to write, but the underlying intuitions are the same. The MDP construction, too, need only be modified slightly to take into account the stochastic transitions of the system state and target state.

Handling exceptions. Our current model does not explicitly capture a critical aspect of many real-world scenarios, exception handling [21]: if the target/composite service terminates before a terminal state has been reached, work done so far has to be undone. This work is distributed across different services. For example, if while booking a vacation, we book a flight but cannot book a hotel, we must cancel the flight reservation, which can be costly. If we also booked a car by now, the cost would be higher. We can augment the MDP defined earlier to take these costs into account by adding a negative reward to states (s_z, s_t, a) and service choice i such that i cannot supply action a in its current state. The size of the reward can depend on the states of the various services, as reflected in s_z, which reflects the work that needs to be undone in each of the existing services.

Separate rewards specifications. In the setting considered here, we have coupled the rewards with the likelihood of the client making certain action requests into the target service to be realized. In fact it may be convenient to keep the two specification separated, and use the target service only to specify the likelihood of action request, in line with what happens in the deterministic case. Rewards in this case could be expressed dynamically on the history of actions executed so far by the target, through a transducer.

More precisely a *transducer* $R = (\Sigma, \Delta, S, s_0, f, g)$ is a deterministic transition system with inputs and outputs, where Σ is the input alphabet, Δ is the output alphabet, S is the set of states, s_0 the initial state, $f : S \times \Sigma \longrightarrow S$ is the transition function (which takes a state and an input symbol and returns the successor state) and $g : S \times \Sigma \longrightarrow \Delta$ is the output function (which returns the output of the transition).

In our case the input alphabet would be the set of actions A, the output alphabet the possible rewards expressed as reals $\mathbb{R}$. In this way the output function $g : S \times A \longrightarrow \mathbb{R}$, would correspond the *reward function*. The point is that now the rewards do not depend on the state of the target, but on the sequence of actions executed so far. Interestingly if we take the synchronous product of the target T (without rewards, but with stochastic transitions) and of R (which is deterministic but outputs rewards), we get a target of the form specified in Sect. 3, though this time computed from the two separated specifications, and we can apply the MDP construction presented here (or its extension with stochastic available services discussed previously).

Non-Markovian rewards. In line with the above point, it has long been observed [22,23] that many performance criteria call for more sophisticated reward functions that do not depend on the last state only.

For example, in Robotics [24], we may want to reward a robot for picking up a cup only if it was requested to do so earlier, where the pick-up command may have been given a number of steps earlier. Similarly, we may want to reward an agent for behavior that is conditional on some past fact – for example, if the person was identified as a child earlier, we must provide her with food rich in protein, and if he is older, in food low in sodium. Or we may want to reward the robot for following some rules, such as executing an even number of steps back and forth, so as to end up in the starting position.

All these proposal share the idea of specifying rewards on (partial traces or histories) through some variant of linear-time temporal logic over finite traces LTL_f. The research on variants of LTL_f has become very lively lately with promising results [17,25–28]. A key point is that formulas in these logics can be "translated" into standard deterministic finite state automata DFAs that recognize exactly the traces that fulfill the formula. Such DFAs can be combined with probabilistic transition systems to generate suitable MDPs to be used for generating optimal solutions. This can be done also in our context. Essentially we replace (or enhance) the target specification with a declarative set of logical constraints. Then we compute the synchronous product with a target transition system that us the likelihood of action choice, hence getting a target specification as that of Sect. 3, analogously to the case of the transducer above. This can be solved by the techniques presented earlier.

High-level programs as target services. Often certain non-Markovian specifications can be expressed more naturally by using procedural constraints [25,29,30]. In particular, we can introduce a sort of propositional variant of GOLOG [31]:

$$\delta ::= A \mid \varphi? \mid \delta_1 + \delta_2 \mid \delta_1; \delta_2 \mid \delta^* \mid$$
$$\textbf{if } \phi \textbf{ then } \delta_1 \textbf{ else } \delta_2 \mid \textbf{while } \phi \textbf{ do } \delta$$

Hence, we can assign rewards to traces that correspond to successful computations of such programs.

For example in a smart environment such as that in [32] we could have a reward associated to completing the following program:

```
while(true) do
    if(cold ∧ windowOpen)) then
        closeWindow;
        turnOnFirePlace + turnOnHeating
```

which says that, all along, if it is cold and the window is open, then immediately close the window and either turn on the fire place or the heating system (no other actions can interleave this sequence).

Note that **if** and **while** can be seen as abbreviations for regular expression [33], namely:

$$\textbf{if } \phi \textbf{ then } \delta_1 \textbf{ else } \delta_2 \doteq (\phi?; \delta_1) + (\neg\phi?; \delta_2)$$
$$\textbf{while } \phi \textbf{ do } \delta \doteq (\phi?; \delta)^*; \neg\phi?$$

Hence these programs can also be translated into *regular expressions* and hence in DFA to be used as above.

Interestingly, we can combine procedural and declarative temporal constraints by adopting a variant of LTL_f, called linear-time dynamic logic on finite traces, or LDL_f, as specification language [17]. For example we may write

$$[true^*]\langle \textbf{while}(\, cold \wedge heatingOn)) \textbf{ do}$$
$$(\neg turnOffHeating^*; heat)\rangle$$

which says that at every point in time, while it is cold and the heating is on then heat, possibly allowing other action except turning off heating. Again we are able to transform these formulas into DFAs and proceed as discussed above.

Finally these ideas are related to so called agent planning programs [34], where the target is specified as a network of declarative goals. Such programs can also be extended to the stochastic setting presented here.

Learning. Although we focus on this paper on model specification and model-based solution techniques, we point out that for Web services, statistics gathering is very simple, and in fact, is carried out routinely nowadays. Consequently, it is not difficult to learn the stochastic transition function of existing services online, and use it to specify the probabilistic elements of the model.

6   Conclusion

In the service composition problem, we attempt to satisfy a specification of a new service using existing services. This allows users and businesses to define new, complicated services with added value on top of an existing set of services. By improving the Roman model of service composition to include request likelihood and values, we were able to not only provide a more faithful formal model of the problem, but also to address the long-standing problem of defining optimal orchestrators when no orchestrator can realize all possible desirable behaviors. Thanks to the correspondence established between orchestrators and policies of a suitably defined MDP, we can also show how such orchestrators can be easily computed. Moreover the setting proposed can be extended in several directions of great theoretical and practical interest.

References

1. De Giacomo, G., Mecella, M., Patrizi, F.: Automated service composition based on behaviors: the Roman model. In: Bouguettaya, A., Sheng, Q., Daniel, F. (eds.) Web Services Foundations, pp. 189–214. Springer, New York (2014). doi:10.1007/ 978-1-4614-7518-7_8

2. Bronsted, J., Hansen, K.M., Ingstrup, M.: Service composition issues in pervasive computing. IEEE Pervasive Comput. **9**(1), 62–70 (2010)

3. Medjahed, B., Bouguettaya, A., Elmagarmid, A.: Composing web services on the semantic web. Very Larg. Data Base J. **12**(4), 333–351 (2003)

4. Yang, J., Papazoglou, M.: Service components for managing the life-cycle of service compositions. Inf. Syst. **29**(2), 97–125 (2004)

5. Cardoso, J., Sheth, A.: Introduction to semantic web services and web process composition. In: Cardoso, J., Sheth, A. (eds.) SWSWPC 2004. LNCS, vol. 3387, pp. 1–13. Springer, Heidelberg (2005). doi:10.1007/978-3-540-30581-1_1

6. Wu, D., Parsia, B., Sirin, E., Hendler, J., Nau, D.: Automating DAML-S web services composition using SHOP2. In: Fensel, D., Sycara, K., Mylopoulos, J. (eds.) ISWC 2003. LNCS, vol. 2870, pp. 195–210. Springer, Heidelberg (2003). doi:10.1007/978-3-540-39718-2_13

7. Pistore, M., Marconi, A., Bertoli, P., Traverso, P.: Automated composition of web services by planning at the knowledge level. In: IJCAI (2005)

8. McIlraith, S., Son, T.: Adapting golog for composition of semantic web services. In: KR (2002)

9. Berardi, D., Calvanese, D., De Giacomo, G., Lenzerini, M., Mecella, M.: Automatic composition of E-services that export their behavior. In: Orlowska, M.E., Weerawarana, S., Papazoglou, M.P., Yang, J. (eds.) ICSOC 2003. LNCS, vol. 2910, pp. 43–58. Springer, Heidelberg (2003). doi:10.1007/978-3-540-24593-3_4

10. Hu, Y., De Giacomo, G.: A generic technique for synthesizing bounded finite-state controllers. In: ICAPS (2013)

11. De Giacomo, G., Patrizi, F., Sardiña, S.: Automatic behavior composition synthesis. Artif. Intell. **196**, 106–142 (2013)

12. Hull, R.: Artifact-centric business process models: brief survey of research results and challenges. In: Meersman, R., Tari, Z. (eds.) OTM 2008. LNCS, vol. 5332, pp. 1152–1163. Springer, Heidelberg (2008). doi:10.1007/978-3-540-88873-4_17

13. Su, J.: Semantic web services: composition and analysis. IEEE Data Eng. Bull. 31(3) (2008)

14. Yadav, N., Sardiña, S.: Decision theoretic behavior composition. In: AAMAS (2011)

15. Menasce, D.: QoS issues in web services. IEEE Internet Comput. **6**(6), 72–75 (2002)

16. Zeng, L., Benatallah, B., Ngu, A., Dumas, M., Kalagnanam, J., Chang, H.: QoS-aware middleware for web services composition. IEEE Trans. Softw. Eng. **30**(5), 311–327 (2004)

17. De Giacomo, G., Vardi, M.Y.: Linear temporal logic and linear dynamic logic on finite traces. In: IJCAI (2013)

18. Nain, S., Lustig, Y., Vardi, M.Y.: Synthesis from probabilistic components. Log. Methods Comput. Sci. 10(2) (2014)

19. Muscholl, A., Walukiewicz, I.: A lower bound on web services composition. Log. Methods Comput. Sci. 4(2) (2008)

20. Yadav, N., Felli, P., De Giacomo, G., Sardiña, S.: Supremal realizability of behaviors with uncontrollable exogenous events. In: IJCAI, pp. 1176–1182 (2013)

21. Pistore, M., Barbon, F., Bertoli, P., Shaparau, D., Traverso, P.: Planning and monitoring web service composition. In: Bussler, C., Fensel, D. (eds.) AIMSA 2004. LNCS, vol. 3192, pp. 106–115. Springer, Heidelberg (2004). doi:10.1007/978-3-540-30106-6_11

22. Bacchus, F., Boutilier, C., Grove, A.J.: Rewarding behaviors. In: AAAI (1996)

23. Thiébaux, S., Gretton, C., Slaney, J.K., Price, D., Kabanza, F.: Decision-theoretic planning with non-Markovian rewards. J. Artif. Intell. Res. **25**, 17–74 (2006)
24. Lacerda, B., Parker, D., Hawes, N.: Optimal policy generation for partially satisfiable co-safe LTL specifications. In: IJCAI (2015)
25. De Giacomo, G., Vardi, M.Y.: Synthesis for LTL and LDL on finite traces. In: IJCAI (2015)
26. De Giacomo, G., Vardi, M.Y.: LTL$_f$ and LDL$_f$ synthesis under partial observability. In: IJCAI (2016)
27. Torres, J., Baier, J.A.: Polynomial-time reformulations of LTL temporally extended goals into final-state goals. In: IJCAI (2015)
28. Camacho, A., Triantafillou, E., Muise, C., Baier, J.A., McIlraith, S.: Nondeterministic planning with temporally extended goals: LTL over finite and infinite traces. In: AAAI (2017)
29. Fritz, C., McIlraith, S.A.: Monitoring plan optimality during execution. In: ICAPS (2007)
30. Baier, J.A., Fritz, C., Bienvenu, M., McIlraith, S.A.: Beyond classical planning: procedural control knowledge and preferences in state-of-the-art planners. In: AAAI (2008)
31. Levesque, H.J., Reiter, R., Lesperance, Y., Lin, F., Scherl, R.: GOLOG: a logic programming language for dynamic domains. J. Log. Program. **31**, 59–83 (1997)
32. De Giacomo, G., Di Ciccio, C., Felli, P., Hu, Y., Mecella, M.: Goal-based composition of stateful services for smart homes. In: OTM (2012)
33. Fischer, M.J., Ladner, R.E.: Propositional dynamic logic of regular programs. J. Comput. Syst. Sci. **18**, 194–211 (1979)
34. De Giacomo, G., Gerevini, A.E., Patrizi, F., Saetti, A., Sardiña, S.: Agent planning programs. Artif. Intell. **231**, 64–106 (2016)

External Computations and Interoperability
in the New DLV Grounder

Francesco Calimeri[1,2(✉)], Davide Fuscà[1], Simona Perri[1], and Jessica Zangari[1]

[1] Department of Mathematics and Computer Science,
University of Calabria, Rende, Italy
{calimeri,fusca,perri,zangari}@mat.unical.it
[2] DLVSystem Srl, Rende, Italy
calimeri@dlvsystem.com

Abstract. In this paper we focus on some of the most recent advancements in $\mathcal{I}$-DLV, the new intelligent grounder of DLV; the system has been endowed with means aimed at easing the interoperability and integration with external systems and accommodating external source of computation and value invention within ASP programs. In particular, we describe here the support for external computations via explicit calls to Python scripts, and tools for the interoperability with both relational and graph databases.

Keywords: Knowledge representation and reasoning · Answer Set Programming · DLV · Artificial Intelligence · Deductive database systems · Grounding · Instantiation

1 Introduction

Answer Set Programming (ASP) [3,17] is a declarative programming paradigm proposed in the area of non-monotonic reasoning and logic programming. ASP applications include product configuration, decision support systems for space shuttle flight controllers, large-scale biological network repairs, data-integration and scheduling systems (cfr. [11]). In ASP, computational problems are encoded by logic programs whose answer sets, corresponding to solutions, are computed by an ASP system [22]. State-of-the-art ASP systems combine two modules, the grounder and the solver [19]; the first module takes as input a program Π and instantiates it by producing a program Π' semantically equivalent to Π, but not containing variables. Then, the second module computes answer sets of Π' by adapting and extending SAT solving techniques [21].

DLV [20] has been one of the first solid and reliable ASP system; its project dates back a few years after the first definition of answer set semantics [16,17], and encompassed system development and continuous enhancements. It is widely used in academy, and it is still employed in many relevant industrial applications, significantly contributing in spreading the use of ASP in real-world scenarios.

$\mathcal{I}$-DLV, the new instantiator of DLV, has been recently introduced in [7]; it features good performance and stability, being competitive both as an ASP

© Springer International Publishing AG 2017
F. Esposito et al. (Eds.): AI*IA 2017, LNAI 10640, pp. 172–185, 2017.
https://doi.org/10.1007/978-3-319-70169-1_13

grounder and as a deductive database system. Furthermore, the flexible nature of $\mathcal{I}$-DLV allows to widely experiment with ASP and its applications, and to better tailor ASP-based solutions to real-world applications. Since its first release, in order to further ease the use in such practical contexts, $\mathcal{I}$-DLV has been extended in several ways. In this paper we focus on a set of mechanisms and tools introduced in $\mathcal{I}$-DLV with the aim of easing the interoperability and integration with external systems and accommodating external source of computation and value invention within ASP programs. In particular, $\mathcal{I}$-DLV now supports calls to Python scripts via *external atoms*, and connection with relational and graph databases via explicit *directives* for importing/exporting data.

The present work is structured as follows. In Sect. 2 we introduce Answer Set Programming by formally describing syntax and semantics, and in Sect. 3, we provide the reader with a brief overview of $\mathcal{I}$-DLV. Hence, we illustrate the novel features: while Sect. 4 presents syntax and semantics of external atoms, Sect. 5 formally describes importing/exporting directives; both sections contain a few examples showing how typical KRR tasks can benefit from these features. In Sect. 6 we report the results of some experimental activities aiming at assessing the performance of $\mathcal{I}$-DLV while making use of its novel features. Eventually, in Sect. 7 we draw our conclusions and discuss ongoing work.

2   Answer Set Programming

A significant amount of work has been carried out for extending the basic language of ASP, and the community recently agreed on a standard input language for ASP systems: ASP-Core-2 [6], the official language of the ASP Competition series [8,15]. For the sake of simplicity, we focus next on the basic aspects of the language; for a complete reference to the ASP-Core-2 standard, and further details about advanced ASP features, we refer the reader to [6] and the vast literature. In this section, we briefly recall syntax and semantics.

Syntax and Semantics. A *term* is either a *simple term* or a *functional term*. A *simple term* is either a constant or a variable. If $t_1 \ldots t_n$ are terms and f is a function symbol of arity n, then $f(t_1, \ldots, t_n)$ is a *functional term*. If $t_1, \ldots, t_k$ are terms and p is a *predicate symbol* of arity k, then $p(t_1, \ldots, t_k)$ is an *atom*. A *literal* l is of the form a or $not\ a$, where a is an atom; in the former case l is *positive*, otherwise *negative*. A *rule* r is of the form $\alpha_1 | \cdots | \alpha_k :- \beta_1, \ldots, \beta_n,$ $not\ \beta_{n+1}, \ldots, not\ \beta_m.$ where $m \geq 0$, $k \geq 0$; $\alpha_1, \ldots, \alpha_k$ and $\beta_1, \ldots, \beta_m$ are atoms. We define $H(r) = \{\alpha_1, \ldots, \alpha_k\}$ (the *head* of r) and $B(r) = B^+(r) \cup B^-(r)$ (the *body* of r), where $B^+(r) = \{\beta_1, \ldots, \beta_n\}$ (the *positive body*) and $B^-(r) = \{not\ \beta_{n+1}, \ldots, not\ \beta_m\}$ (the *negative body*). If $H(r) = \emptyset$ then r is a *(strong) constraint*; if $B(r) = \emptyset$ and $|H(r)| = 1$ then r is a *fact*. A rule r is safe if each variable of r has an occurrence in $B^+(r)$[1]. An ASP program is a finite set P

---

[1] We remark that this definition of safety is specific for rules featuring only classical literals. For a complete definition we refer the reader to [6].

of safe rules. A program (a rule, a literal) is said to be *ground* if it contains no variables. A predicate is defined by a rule if the predicate occurs in the head of the rule. A predicate defined only by facts is an *EDB*predicate, the remaining predicates are *IDB*predicates. The set of all facts in P is denoted by $Facts(P)$; the set of instances of all *EDB* predicates in P is denoted by $EDB(P)$.

Given a program P, the *Herbrand universe* of P, denoted by U_P, consists of all ground terms that can be built combining constants and function symbols appearing in P. The *Herbrand base* of P, denoted by B_P, is the set of all ground atoms obtainable from the atoms of P by replacing variables with elements from U_P. A *substitution* for a rule $r \in P$ is a mapping from the set of variables of r to the set U_P of ground terms. A *ground instance* of a rule r is obtained applying a substitution to r. The *full instantiationGround(P)*of P is defined as the set of all ground instances of its rules over U_P. An *interpretation* I for P is a subset of B_P. A positive literal a (resp., a negative literal *not a*) is true w.r.t. I if $a \in I$ (resp., $a \notin I$); it is false otherwise. Given a ground rule r, we say that r is satisfied w.r.t. I if some atom appearing in $H(r)$ is true w.r.t. I or some literal appearing in $B(r)$ is false w.r.t. I. Given a ground program P, we say that I is a *model* of P, iff all rules in *Ground(P)*are satisfied w.r.t. I. A model M is *minimal* if there is no model N for P such that $N \subset M$. The *Gelfond-Lifschitz reduct* [17] of P, w.r.t. an interpretation I, is the positive ground program P^I obtained from *Ground(P)* by: (i) deleting all rules having a negative literal false w.r.t. I; (ii) deleting all negative literals from the remaining rules. $I \subseteq B_P$ is an *answer set* for a program P iff I is a minimal model for P^I. The set of all answer sets for P is denoted by $AS(P)$.

3 $\mathcal{I}$-DLV Overview

The $\mathcal{I}$-DLV [7] system, that fully supports the ASP-Core-2 [6] language standard, relies on a set of theoretical results and techniques proved to be effective in the old DLV grounder [12]. In particular, it follows a bottom-up evaluation strategy based on a semi-naïve approach [23]; this latter has been extended with a number of optimization techniques that have been explicitly designed in the context of ASP instantiation along with a number of additional techniques and features purposely designed for $\mathcal{I}$-DLV. A more accurate description of the system and the underlying techniques is out of the scope of this paper, and hence we refer the interested reader to [7]; we briefly discuss some design choices, instead, in order to better understand the flexible and customizable nature of the system.

The long-lasting experience over the DLV grounder proved that a monolithic set of optimizations, most of which were activated or deactivated at the same time, does not pay in general. For such reason, even though $\mathcal{I}$-DLV comes with a general-purpose default configuration, it has been conceived to provide the user with a fine-grained control over the whole computational process; $\mathcal{I}$-DLV allows to enable, disable, and customize every single strategy, so that the behaviour of the system can be tailored to very different application scenarios. Notably, $\mathcal{I}$-DLV provide the users with the capability of controlling and driving the internal grounding process at a more fine-grained level with respect to what one might do via command-line options; in particular, it introduces annotations within the ASP code, which consist in meta-data statements allowing to "annotate" the ASP programs in a Java-like fashion. While embedded in comments, they can express explicit steering instructions both at global and rule level. It is worth noting that $\mathcal{I}$-DLV is part of a greater project aiming at developing a full, efficient ASP system [1] featuring *wasp* [2] as a solver. In this context, annotations can also be used for customizing heuristics and extending solving capabilities.

For a comprehensive list of customizations and options, along with further details, we refer the reader to [7] and to the online documentation [9].

4   External Computations

The availability of external sources of computation has been already recognized as desirable feature of ASP systems in the literature; indeed, all major ASP systems are endowed with such capabilities to different extents: we mention here the support for Python computation by *clingo* [13] and the hex programs supported by *dlvhex* [10]. Notably, some forms of external computation and value invention were supported also by the ASP system DLV [4,5].

External computation in $\mathcal{I}$-DLV is achieved by means of *external atoms*, whose extension is not defined by the semantics within the logic program, but rather is specified by means of external defined Python programs. They are inspired by the ones supported in *dlvhex* [10], although there are some differences; for instance, while relational inputs are not permitted in $\mathcal{I}$-DLV, in *dlvhex* external atoms can have as input parameters also predicates; this implies that $\mathcal{I}$-DLV external atoms can be completely evaluated at the grounding stage, while in *dlvhex* an external atom, in general, might need to wait the solving phase in order to be evaluated, depending on the interpretation at hand. If, on the one hand, these look like a limitation, on the other hand they greatly simplify the evaluation strategy, leading also to improvements of overall performance.

In the following we describe syntax and semantics of the constructs, then illustrating their use by a few examples.

Syntax and Semantics. An external atom is of the form $\&p(t_0, \ldots, t_n; u_0, \ldots, u_m)$, where $n + m \geq 0$, $\&p$ is an *external predicate*, $t_0, \ldots, t_n$ are intended as *input terms*, and are separated from the *output terms* $u_0, \ldots, u_m$ by a semicolon (";"). In the following, we denote an external atom by $\&p(In;Out)$, where In and Out represent input and output terms, respectively.

An external literal is either *not e* or *e*, where *e* is an external atom, and the symbol *not* represents default negation. An external literal is safe if all input terms are safe, according to the safety definition in ASP-Core-2 standard [6]. External literals can appear only in the rule bodies, and each instance of an external predicate must appear with the same number of input and output terms throughout the whole program.

Given an external atom $\&p(In;Out)$ and a substitution σ, a ground instance of such external atom is obtained by applying σ to variables appearing in In and

Out, obtaining $\sigma(\&p(In; Out)) = \&p(In_g; Out_g)$. The truth value of a ground external atom is given by the value $f_{\&p}(In_g, Out_g)$ of a decidable $n+m$-ary two-valued oracle function, where n and m are the lengths of In_g and Out_g, respectively. A negative ground external literal *not e* is *true/false* if e is *false/true*.

Intuitively, output terms are computed on the basis of the input ones, according to a semantics which is provided externally (i.e., from the outside of the logic program) by means of the definition of oracle functions. Currently, $\mathcal{I}$-DLV supports oracle definitions via Python scripts. Basically, for each external predicate $\&p$ featuring n/m input/output terms, the user must define a Python function whose name is p, and featuring n/m input/output parameters. The function has to be compliant with Python[2] version 3.

Example 1. As an example, let us consider the following rule, that makes use of an external predicate with two input and one output terms:

$$sum(X,Y,Z) :- number(X), number(Y), X \leq Y, \&compute\_sum(X,Y;Z).$$

A program containing this rule must come along with the proper definition of *compute_sum* within a Python function, as, for instance, the one reported next.

```
def compute_sum(X,Y):
    return X+Y
```

According to the given definition, as they are completely evaluated by $\mathcal{I}$-DLV as true or false, external predicates do not appear in the produced instantiation. Furthermore, for each value returned by a Python function defining an external predicate, a proper conversion is necessary from its Python type to an ASP-Core-2 term type. By default, on the Python side the following types are permitted: *numeric, boolean* or *string*[3]. These types are mapped to terms accordingly to the following default policy: an integer returned value is mapped to a corresponding *numeric constant*, while all other values are tentatively associated to a *symbolic constant*, if the form is compatible to the ASP-Core-2 syntax; values are associated to a *string constant* in case of failure. Nevertheless, $\mathcal{I}$-DLV allows the user to customize the mapping policy of a particular external predicate by means of a directive of the form: `#external_predicate_conversion(&p,type:T`$_1$`,...,T`$_N$`).`, that specifies the sequence of conversion types for an external predicate $\&p$ featuring n output terms. A conversion type can be: (1) `@U_INT` (the value is converted to an unsigned integer); (2) `@UT_INT` (the value is truncated to an unsigned integer); (3) `@T_INT` (the value is truncated to an integer); (4) `@UR_INT` (the value is rounded to an unsigned integer); (5) `@R_INT` (the value is rounded to an integer); (6) `@CONST` (the value is converted to a string without quotes); (7) `@Q_CONST` (the value is converted to a string with quotes). In cases $(1-5)$, the value is mapped to a *numeric term*, in case (6) to a *symbolic constant*, while in case (7)

---

[2] https://docs.python.org/3.

[3] https://docs.python.org/3/library/stdtypes.html.

to a *string constant*. Directives can be specified at any point within an ASP program, and have a global effect: once a conversion directive for an external predicate has been included, say &*p*, it is applied each time the predicate is found. For instance, if the following directive is added to the piece of program in Example 1: `#external_predicate_conversion(&compute_sum,type:Q_CONST).`, then for each external call, the output variable Z is bounded to the value returned by the Python function interpreted as a quoted string. Further details about options and conversion types are available at [9].

External atoms can be both functional and relational, i.e., they can return a single tuple or a set of tuples, as output. In Example 1, &*compute_sum* is *functional*: the associated Python function returns a single value for each combination of the input values. In general, a functional external atom with $m > 0$ output terms must return a *sequence*[4] containing m values. If $m = 1$, the output can be either as sequence containing a single value, or just a value, as in the example; if $m = 0$, the associated Python function must be boolean. A relational external atom with $m > 0$ is defined by a Python function that returns a sequence of m-sequences, where each inner sequence is composed by m values.

Example 2. The following rule uses a relational external atom:

$$prime\_factor(X, Z) \; :- \; number(X), \&compute\_prime\_factors(X; Z).$$

Intuitively, given a number X, the rule computes prime factors of X, demanding this task to a relational external atom, that receives as input the number X, and returns as output its factors. The semantics has to be provided via a Python function called *compute_prime_factors* returning a sequence of numbers each one representing a different factor of X.

We remark that, currently, input and output terms can be either *constants* or *variables*; the support for other kinds of term is subject of ongoing works.

KRR with External Computations. Interfacing ASP with external tools represents an important additional power for modelling KRR tasks. Let us consider, as a running example, the problem of automatically assigning a score to students after an assessment test: given a list of students, a list of topics, and a set of questions regarding the given topics along with corresponding student answers, we want to determine the score of each student. In particular, let us suppose that each student is represented by a fact of the form $student(id)$, where id is a unique identifier code, and topics are expressed by facts of type $topic(to)$, where to is a string representing the topic name, such as "Computer_Science". Each question can be expressed by a fact of the form $question(id, to, tx, ca)$ where id is a unique identifier number, to is the topic covered, tx is the text containing also the possible answers, and ca is the only option which is the correct answer. Each student's answer is modelled by a fact of the form $answer(sid, qid, ans)$ where ans represents the answer given by student sid to the question qid.

---

[4] https://docs.Python.org/3/library/stdtypes.html#sequence-types-list-tuple-range.

In addition, let us suppose that the score is computed as the sum of the single scores obtained by answering the questions on each topic, and that some topics can have a higher relevance with respect to others; for instance, the score obtained in Mathematics might be more important than the one in English. Interestingly, the score could be computed differently each time the assessment test takes place; for instance, English might be the most relevant topic, in a different session. Moreover, the number of wrong answers may also be considered while computing the score, for instance in case of negative marking.

Given these requirements, the following program encodes our problem:

s_1 : $correctAnswers(St, To, N)$:– $topic(To), student(St),$
        $N = \#count\{QID : question(QID, To, Tx, Ca),$
        $answer(St, QID, Ca)\}.$

s_2 : $wrongAnswers(St, To, N)$: $-topic(To), student(St),$
        $N = \#count\{QID : question(QID, To, Tx, Ca),$
        $answer(St, QID, Ans), Ans! = Ca\}.$

s_3 : $topicScore(St, To, Sc)$:– $correctAnswers(St, To, Cn),$
        $wrongAnswers(St, To, Wn),$
        $\&assignScore(To, Cn, Wn; Sc).$

s_4 :   `#external_predicate_conversion(predicate=&assignScore,type=R_INT).`

s_5 : $testScore(St, Sc)$:– $student(St), Sc = \#sum\{Sc : topicScore(St, To, Sc)\}.$

Intuitively, rule s_1 and rule s_2 count the number of correct and wrong answers for each student on each topic, respectively. Rule s_3 determines the score on each topic for each student; to this end, an external atom is in charge of assigning the score. Interestingly, each time relevances of the topics need to change, it is enough to change the Python function defining its semantics. For instance, supposing that among the concerned topics Mathematics and Computer Science have the highest importance, and that for each wrong answer the value 0.5 is subtracted from the score, a possible implementation for the Python function defining the score computation could be:

```
def assignScore(topic, numCorrectAns, numWrongAns):
    if(topic=="ComputerScience" or topic=="Mathematics"):
        return numCorrectAns*2−numWrongAns*0.5
    return numCorrectAns−numWrongAns*0.5
```

Statement s_4 is a directive stating that values returned by the Python function have be rounded to ASP-Core-2 integers, while rule s_5 computes the final score by summing up the scores on each topic. Notably, rules s_1, s_2 and s_5 make use of aggregate literals [6] in order to perform some aggregation operations.

5   Interoperability

As discussed in the previous sections, $\mathcal{I}$-DLV has been intended to ease the interoperability of ASP with external sources of knowledge. To further comply with this aim, its input language, still fully supporting ASP-Core-2, has been enriched with explicit directives for connecting with relational and graph databases.

Relational Databases. $\mathcal{I}$-DLV inherits from DLV directives for *importing/exporting* data from/to relational DBs. An import directive is of the form:

```
#import_sql(db_name, "user", "pwd", "query", pred_name [, type_conv]).
```

where the first three parameters are straightforward, `query` is an *SQL* statement that defines the imported table (must be double quoted), `pred_name` indicates the predicate whose extension will be enriched with the result of the query, and `type_conv` is an optional parameter for specifying how DBMS data types have to be mapped to ASP-Core-2 terms: it provides a conversion for each column imported by the database. The `type_conv` parameter is a string with the same syntax described in Sect. 4. An export directive is of the form:

```
#export_sql(db_name, "user", "pwd", pred_name,
    pred_arity, table_name, "REPLACE where SQL-Condition").
```

first three params are self-explanatory; `pred_name`/`pred_arity` indicate name/arity of the predicate whose extension will be exported into the external `table_name` table, and ``REPLACE where SQL-Condition`` indicates the tuples to be deleted from the relational table before the export actually takes place.

The adopted syntax mimic the old DLV one; slight differences are due to the fact that $\mathcal{I}$-DLV complies with the ASP-Core-2 syntax. In particular, ASP-Core-2 features negative numbers, thus requiring more conversion types, and allows a predicate name to be associated with predicates with different arities, thus requiring that in an `export` directive the predicate has to be uniquely specified by indicating both the predicate name and arity.

Graph Databases. While connections with relational DBs is, to some extent, inherited by DLV, interoperability with graph databases is a novel feature of $\mathcal{I}$-DLV. In particular, data can be imported via SPARQL queries, both from *Local* DBs in RDF/XML files and *remote* SPARQL *EndPoints*, of the form:

```
#import_local_sparql("rdf_file","query",predname,predarity,[,typeConv]).
#import_remote_sparql("endpnt_url","query",predname,predarity,[,typeConv]).
```

where `query` is a SPARQL statement defining data to be imported and `typeConv` is optional and specifies the conversion for mapping RDF data types to ASP-Core-2 terms. For the local import, `rdf_file` can be either a local or remote URL pointing to an RDF/XML file: in this latter case, the file is downloaded and treated as a local RDF/XML file; in any case, the graph is built in memory. On the other hand, for the remote import, the `endpnt_url` refers to a remote endpoint and building the graph is up to the remote server; this second option might be convenient in case of large datasets.

Concerning implementation, for a fast prototyping, we started with a solution based on external atoms. For instance, for each remote SPARQL import directive, an auxiliary rule of the following form is added to the input program: $predname(X_0, ..., X_N) :\!-\&sparqlEndPoint(\text{``}endpnt\_url\text{''}, \text{``}query\text{''}; X_0, ..., X_N)$.

The head atom has `predname` as name, and contains `predarity` variables. The body contains an external atom *&sparqlEndPoint* in charge of performing the remote query. Intuitively, when grounding the rule, the extension of the specified predicate will be filled in with information extracted by the query.

The approach relying on external atoms for implementing graph-databases connection directives perfectly reaches the goal; in addition, it shows how external atoms give the user a powerful mean for significantly extending the grounder capabilities. Nevertheless, there are some reasons in favour of a "native" support for interoperability with graph databases. First of all, it is easy to imagine that native support should enjoy much better performance, as we discuss in later on; furthermore, in many scenarios (as it is often the case in the deductive database settings) the use of external atoms is not crucial, whilst accessing standard knowledge sources is vital: in such cases, taking care of the burden of the external Python runtime machinery does not look useful. Hence, the idea is to incorporate into the system the directives that are most likely to be used "per se", and let external atoms address cases that need extended functionalities.

KRR with Database Directives. We show the use of the features introduced above, by means of the running example of Sect. 4.

Let us suppose that general data, such as questions and topics, are permanently stored on a relational database, while test-related data, such as students and their answers, are gathered into an RDF/XML file which is specifically referred to the test itself. Then, questions can be retrivied from the relational DB by means of the following directive:

```
#import_sql(relDB, "user", "pwd", "SELECT * FROM question",
    question, type:U_INT,Q_CONST,Q_CONST,Q_CONST).
```

where `relDB` is the name of the database, `"user"` and `"pwd"` are the data for the user authentication, `"SELECT * FROM question"` is an SQL query that constructs the table to import, `question` is the predicate name used for building the new facts, and the first field (the question identifier) is imported as an integer, while the remaining ones as quoted strings. Topics can be retrieved similarly. Moreover, answers of students can be retrieved with the following directive:

```
#import_local_sparql("answers.rdf",
    "PREFIX rdf: <http://www.w3.org/1999/02/22-rdf-syntax-ns#>
    PREFIX my: <http://sample/rdf#>
    SELECT ?St, ?Qe, ?Ans
    WHERE {?X rdf:type my:test. ?X my:student ?St.
    ?X my:question ?Qe. ?X my:answer ?Ans.}",
    answer, 3, type:U_INT,U_INT,Q_CONST).
```

where `"answers.rdf"` is the XML file containing the answers, and the subsequent quoted string is the SPARQL query filling the relation `answer/3` in with two integers and a quoted string. Students can be imported in a similar way. Interestingly, if the XML file is hosted on a remote server, #import_local_sparql directives allow the users to get rid of implementing the import mechanism.

6   Experimental Evaluation

In the following, we report the results of an experimental activity carried out in order to assess performance of the herein discussed $\mathcal{I}$-DLV features.

Experiments on external computations have been performed on a NUMA machine equipped with two 2.8 GHz AMD Opteron 6320 processors and 128 GiB of main memory, running Linux Ubuntu 14.04.5 kernel v. 4.4.0-45-*generic*; binaries were generated with the *GNU* C++ compiler v. 4.9. As for memory and time limits, we allotted 15 GiB and 600 s for each system, per each run.

About interoperability mechanisms, experiments have been performed on machine equipped with an Intel Core i7-4770 processor and 16 GiB of main memory, running Linux Ubuntu 14.04.5 *kernel* v. 3.13.0-107-*generic*; binaries were generated with the *GNU* C++ compiler v. 4.9. As for memory and time limits, we allotted 15 GiB and 600 s for each system, per each single run.

External Atoms. We compared $\mathcal{I}$-DLV with other currently available systems supporting similar mechanisms for dealing with external sources of computations via Python: the ASP grounder *gringo* [14] and the *dlvhex* [10] system. In particular, we considered the latest available releases at the time of writing: *clingo* 5.2.0 executed with the --mode=gringo and *dlvhex* 2.5.0 executed with the default provided ASP solver that combines *gringo* 4.5.4 and *clasp* 3.1.4, respectively.

In order to assess efficiency of the systems in integrating external computations we considered different kinds of benchmarks. We first considered a set of problems, focused on the spatial representation and reasoning domain, originally appeared in [24]. In this setting, two scenarios have been taken into account. The first scenario requires the determination of relations among randomly-generated circular objects in a 2-*D* space. For each pair of circles one is interested in knowing which of the following relations hold: having some contacts, being disconnected, being externally connected, overlapping or partially overlapping, one being part of the other, one being proper part of the other, one being tangential proper part of the other, one being non-tangential proper part of the other. For each possible relation, an ASP encoding that makes use of an external Python script checks if it holds. The encodings have been paired with instances of increasing sizes containing random generated circles, from 10 to 190. In the second scenario we re-adapted the encodings of *Growth*, *Move* and *Attachment* problems introduced in [24], that solves some geometrical problems over triples of circular objects in a 2D space. Again, instances of increasing size have been given to the tested systems: in this case, we generated triples of circles, from 7 to 70.

Notably, ASP-Core-2 only supports integer numbers; hence, the encodings have been re-adapted in order to result independent from the way data are expressed. Each object is associated with an identifier, and information about coordinates and dimensions are stored in a csv file; thus, from the ASP side, objects are managed via their ids, and computations involving real numbers are handled externally via the same Python scripts that, in turn, are invoked by the external mechanisms typical of each tested system. Hence, the encodings reported in [24] have been carefully translated into ASP-Core-2 encodings. In this respect, it is worth noticing that in [24] two versions for Attachment problem are reported: in our setting, due to the described translation, they coincide.

Since the benchmarks introduced above involve non-disjunctive stratified encodings and only numeric (integer) constants as ground terms, we considered three further domains: the reachability problem, where edges are retrieved via Python scripts; concatenation of two randomly-generated strings with arbitrary lengths varying from 1000 to 3000 chars; generation of first k prime numbers, with k ranging from 0 to 100000.

Results, reported in Table 1, show satisfactory performance for $\mathcal{I}$-DLV, both in comparison with *gringo*, which solves approximately the same number of instances but spending larger times, and with *dlvhex*, which, yet offering a more complete support for external source of knowledge, suffers from its architecture that makes use of an ASP solver as a black box.

Interoperability. We analyzed the effective gain on performance obtainable with a native support of SQL/SPARQL local import directives against the same directives implemented via Python scripts (see Sect. 5). In particular, we compared two different importing approaches: (1) a version exploiting explicit

Table 1. External atoms: experiment results (TO/MO stands for Time/Memory Out).

Problem	# inst.	DLVHEX		GRINGO		I-DLV	
		#solved	Time	#solved	Time	#solved	Time
Attachment	10	0	TO	10	149.55	10	45.50
Growth	10	0	TO/MO	9	164.21	10	67.20
Move	10	0	TO/MO	9	163.89	10	68.08
Contact	10	6	93.05	10	11.21	10	4.94
Disconnect	10	8	127.72	10	10.85	10	4.86
Discrete	10	8	127.44	10	10.85	10	4.96
Equal	10	8	101.07	10	10.95	10	4.93
Externally connect	10	8	100.43	10	10.79	10	4.68
Nontangential proper part	10	7	107.14	10	10.89	10	4.88
Overlap	10	6	92.80	10	11.11	10	4.94
Part of	10	8	126.56	10	11.00	10	4.93
Partially overlap	10	8	126.37	10	11.00	10	4.83
Proper part	10	6	93.34	10	11.21	10	4.99
Tangential proper part	10	7	106.54	10	10.90	10	4.72
String concatenation	5	0	TO/MO	5	64.73	5	52.09
Prime numbers	10	1	93.34	10	21.94	10	13.26
Reachability	10	0	TO/MO	10	36.71	10	37.18
Solved instances		81/165		163/165		165/165	
Total running time		59341		8362		3109	

directives natively implemented in C++, (2) a version where the import mechanism is performed externally. The benchmarks are divided into two categories:

- Importing data from a Relational Database, by means of SQL statements.
- SPARQL imports from a local RDF/XML file.

For the first set of benchmarks, a DB containing a randomly generated table has been created: such table contains 1000000 tuples and features three columns, one of integer type and two of alphanumeric type. Several encodings have then been tested, each one importing a different number of tuples from the aforementioned table, ranging from 100000 to 1000000. In both cases, each SQL column is mapped, respectively, to a numeric term, a symbolic constant and a string constant (we refer the reader to ASP-Core-2 term types [6]).

For the second set of benchmarks, we generated OWL ontologies via the Data Generator(UBA) by means of the Lehigh benchmark LUBM [18], referred to a University context; each university has a number of departments ranging from 15 to 22, and the encodings import graduate and undergraduate students from a different number of universities, ranging from 1 to 5.

Table 2. Interoperability: experimental results.

Problem	I-DLV-C++	I-DLV-Python
sql-100K	0.55	1.63
sql-200K	0.98	3.06
sql-300K	1.49	4.58
sql-400K	2.07	6.19
sql-500K	2.47	7.61
sql-600K	2.99	9.20
sql-700K	3.51	10.64
sql-800K	4.17	11.94
sql-900K	4.69	13.24
sql-1M	5.02	15.19
sparql-lubm -1	7.86	13.92
sparql-lubm-2	16.62	29.49
sparql-lubm-3	25.03	44.39
sparql-lubm-4	31.74	56.86
sparql-lubm-5	38.08	66.85

Results, reported in Table 2, show that the native approach clearly outperforms the other by 66% when dealing with SQL directives, and by 43% when dealing with SPARQL local import directives. Intuitively, an internal management of import/export mechanism can be performed directly interfacing C++ and SQL/SPARQL, while with external atoms Python acts as a mediator causing an overhead which is not always negligible, as our tests evidenced.

7 Conclusion and Ongoing Work

$\mathcal{I}$-DLV is a project under active development; besides improvements of the presented features, both in functionalities and performance, further enhancements are planned, related to language extensions, customizability means, performance, and a tight integration with the ASP solver *wasp* [2] in the new full-fledged ASP system DLV2 [1]. More in detail, more native directives for interoperating with external data will be added; the $\mathcal{I}$-DLV language will be extended with constructs for explicitly managing complex terms such as lists; the set of annotations for a fine-grained control of the grounding process will be enlarged; a new set of annotations for integrating and tuning *wasp* will be added; in addition, we are studying a proper way of manipulating the produced ground program in order to better fit with the computational mechanisms carried out by the solver.

References

1. Alviano, M., et al.: The ASP system DLV2. In: Balduccini, M., Janhunen, T. (eds.) LPNMR 2017. LNCS, vol. 10377, pp. 215–221. Springer, Cham (2017). doi:10.1007/978-3-319-61660-5_19

2. Alviano, M., Dodaro, C., Leone, N., Ricca, F.: Advances in WASP. In: Calimeri, F., Ianni, G., Truszczynski, M. (eds.) LPNMR 2015. LNCS, vol. 9345, pp. 40–54. Springer, Cham (2015). doi:10.1007/978-3-319-23264-5_5

3. Brewka, G., Eiter, T., Truszczynski, M.: Answer set programming at a glance. Commun. ACM **54**(12), 92–103 (2011)

4. Calimeri, F., Cozza, S., Ianni, G.: External sources of knowledge and value invention in logic programming. Ann. Math. Artif. Intell. **50**(3–4), 333–361 (2007)

5. Calimeri, F., Cozza, S., Ianni, G., Leone, N.: An ASP system with functions, lists, and sets. In: Erdem, E., Lin, F., Schaub, T. (eds.) LPNMR 2009. LNCS, vol. 5753, pp. 483–489. Springer, Heidelberg (2009). doi:10.1007/978-3-642-04238-6_46

6. Calimeri, F., Faber, W., Gebser, M., Ianni, G., Kaminski, R., Krennwallner, T., Leone, N., Ricca, F., Schaub, T.: Asp-core-2: input language format. Technical Report, ASP Standardization Working Group (2012)

7. Calimeri, F., Fuscà, D., Perri, S., Zangari, J.: I-DLV: the new intelligent grounder of DLV. Intelligenza Artificiale **11**(1), 5–20 (2017)

8. Calimeri, F., Gebser, M., Maratea, M., Ricca, F.: Design and results of the fifth answer set programming competition. Artif. Intell. **231**, 151–181 (2016)

9. Calimeri, F., Perri, S., Fuscà, D., Zangari, J.: $\mathcal{I}$-DLV homepage (since 2016). https://github.com/DeMaCS-UNICAL/I-DLV/wiki

10. Eiter, T., Fink, M., Ianni, G., Krennwallner, T., Redl, C., Schüller, P.: A model building framework for answer set programming with external computations. TPLP **16**(4), 418–464 (2016)

11. Erdem, E., Gelfond, M., Leone, N.: Applications of answer set programming. AI Mag. **37**(3), 53–68 (2016)

12. Faber, W., Leone, N., Perri, S.: The intelligent grounder of DLV. In: Erdem, E., Lee, J., Lierler, Y., Pearce, D. (eds.) Correct Reasoning. LNCS, vol. 7265, pp. 247–264. Springer, Heidelberg (2012). doi:10.1007/978-3-642-30743-0_17

13. Gebser, M., Kaminski, R., Kaufmann, B., Ostrowski, M., Schaub, T., Wanko, P.: Theory solving made easy with clingo 5. In: ICLP TCs, pp. 2:1–2:15 (2016)

14. Gebser, M., Kaminski, R., König, A., Schaub, T.: Advances in *gringo* series 3. In: Delgrande, J.P., Faber, W. (eds.) LPNMR 2011. LNCS, vol. 6645, pp. 345–351. Springer, Heidelberg (2011). doi:10.1007/978-3-642-20895-9_39
15. Gebser, M., Maratea, M., Ricca, F.: What's hot in the answer set programming competition. In: AAAI 2016, pp. 4327–4329. AAAI Press (2016)
16. Gelfond, M., Lifschitz, V.: The Stable Model Semantics for Logic Programming. In: ICLP 1988, pp. 1070–1080. MIT Press, Cambridge (1988)
17. Gelfond, M., Lifschitz, V.: Classical negation in logic programs and disjunctive databases. New Gener. Comput. **9**(3/4), 365–385 (1991)
18. Guo, Y., Pan, Z., Heflin, J.: LUBM: a benchmark for OWL knowledge base systems. Web Semant.: Sci. Serv. Agents World Wide Web **3**(2), 158–182 (2005)
19. Kaufmann, B., Leone, N., Perri, S., Schaub, T.: Grounding and solving in answer set programming. AI Mag. **37**(3), 25–32 (2016)
20. Leone, N., Pfeifer, G., Faber, W., Eiter, T., Gottlob, G., Perri, S., Scarcello, F.: The DLV system for knowledge representation and reasoning. ACM Trans. Comput. Log. (TOCL) **7**(3), 499–562 (2006)
21. Lierler, Y., Maratea, M., Ricca, F.: Systems, engineering environments, and competitions. AI Mag. **37**(3), 45–52 (2016)
22. Lifschitz, V.: Answer set planning. In: ICLP, pp. 23–37. MIT Press (1999)
23. Ullman, J.D.: Principles of Database and Knowledge-Base Systems, vol. 1. Computer Science Press, New York (1988)
24. Walega, P.A., Schultz, C.P.L., Bhatt, M.: Non-monotonic spatial reasoning with answer set programming modulo theories. CoRR abs/1606.07860 (2016). http://arxiv.org/abs/1606.07860

Deciding Refinement Relation in Belief-Intention Databases

Zhanhao Xiao[1,2]($\boxtimes$), Andreas Herzig[1,3], Laurent Perrussel[1],
and Dongmo Zhang[2]

[1] IRIT, University of Toulouse, Toulouse, France
`zhanhao.xiao@ut-capitole.fr`
[2] SCEM, Western Sydney University, Penrith, Australia
[3] IRIT, CNRS, Toulouse, France

Abstract. Bratman's Belief-Desire-Intention (BDI) theory is seminal in
the literature on BDI agents. His BDI theory is taken into account to
extend Shoham's database perspective on beliefs and intentions. In the
extended framework, an intentions is considered as a high-level action,
which cannot be executed directly, with a duration. They have to be
progressively refined until executable basic actions are obtained. Higher-
and lower-level actions are linked by the means-end relation, alias instrumentality relation. In this paper, we investigate the complexity of the
decision problems for satisfiability, consequence, refinement and instrumentality in the database. Moreover, we translate these problems into
the satisfiability and validity problems in propositional linear temporal
logic (PLTL). With such translations, we can utilize the efficient automated theorem provers for PLTL to solve the problem of deciding the
refinement relation between an intention and an intention set, as well as
the instrumentality relation.

1 Introduction

Bratman's Belief-Desire-Intention (BDI) theory [4,5] is at the basis of the huge
literature on BDI agents. According to his theory, intentions are high-level plans
to which the agent is committed and they play a fundamental role in autonomous
agents. Typically such high-level plans cannot be executed directly: they have
to be *refined* as time goes by, resulting in more and more elaborate plans. A
means-end relation, which is called *instrumentality*, should link the higher-level
intention, which is refined, and the lower-level intentions which are inserted
because of the refinement. At the end of the refinement process, there are only
basic actions: actions the agent can perform intentionally. For example, my high-
level plan to submit a paper to a conference is refined into writing a paper and
uploading it to the paper submission management system; further down the line,
the second intention is refined into logging into the system entering information
about the paper and uploading the PDF file.

While operations of refinement is of fundamental importance and should be
central in BDI agents, as more extensively discussed in [11], the literature on BDI

© Springer International Publishing AG 2017
F. Esposito et al. (Eds.): AI*IA 2017, LNAI 10640, pp. 186–199, 2017.
https://doi.org/10.1007/978-3-319-70169-1_14

theories only contains very few such a concept [2,14]. The operation of refinement is notably absent from Cohen&Levesque's logic [8] which is one of the most influential BDI logics and Shoham's belief-intention database framework [16]. Compared with Cohen and Levesque's logic, Shoham's database framework is a much simpler account that is based on a database of time-indexed basic actions and beliefs. Compared with the heavily implementation-driven BDI agents, the belief-intention database is more logical and more suitable for revising beliefs and intentions. In [13], Herzig *et al.* followed Shoham's database perspective and extended his belief-intention database framework to formalize such a refinement relation between intentions. In the extended framework, beliefs and intentions are organized in a so-called belief-intention database: a belief is a propositional formula indexed by time points and an intention is considered as a high-level action, which cannot be executed directly, with a duration. To capture the change of the environments or actions of other agents, environment actions, alias events, are introduced in belief-intention databases.

As intention refinement plays an important role in BDI theories, the problem of deciding the refinement relation between an intention set and an intention is pivotal. The contributions of this paper are summarized as follows. First, we investigate the complexity of the decision problems for satisfiability, consequence, refinement and instrumentality in belief-intention databases. We show that the satisfiability and consequence problems in the belief-intention database are both PSPACE-complete and further show that the problems of deciding refinement and instrumentality are also PSPACE-complete by reducing them to the satisfiability and consequence problems.

Second, we translate the satisfiability and consequence problems in belief-intention databases into the satisfiability and validity problems in propositional linear temporal logic (PLTL). Then we can translate the problems of deciding refinement and instrumentality into PLTL. In the last decades, PLTL has obtained a lot of attention from the researchers, both theocratically and practically. Taking advantage of the automated tools of PLTL[1], we can solve the decision problems for satisfiability, consequence, refinement and instrumentality of belief-intention databases by translating into the satisfiability and validity problems in PLTL.

Our paper is organized as follows. Section 2 recalls notions of belief-intention databases. Section 3 shows the complexity results. Section 4 gives the translation to PLTL. Section 5 concludes the paper.

2   Belief-Intention Databases

In this section we recall the main definitions of belief-intention databases initially proposed in [13].

---

[1] Several theorem provers for PLTL can be found on
http://users.cecs.anu.edu.au/~rpg/PLTLProvers/ (accessed on 2 Sep. 2017).

2.1   Coherent Dynamic Theory

Let $\mathsf{Evt}_0 = \{e, f, \ldots\}$ be a set of basic events and $\mathsf{Act}_0 = \{a, b, \ldots\}$ a set of basic actions. Basic events and basic actions take one time unit. Basic actions can be directly executed by the planning agent. The set Act_0 is contained in the set of all actions $\mathsf{Act} = \{\alpha, \beta, \ldots\}$ which also contains non-basic, high-level actions. The set of propositional variables is $\mathbb{P} = \{p, q, \ldots\}$. The language of boolean formulas built on $\mathbb{P}$ is denoted by $\mathscr{L}_{\mathbb{P}}$.

We suppose that the sets $\mathbb{P}$, Evt_0, and Act are all finite. The behavior of actions and events is described by dynamic theories.

Definition 1 (Dynamic theory). *A dynamic theory is a tuple $\mathcal{T} = \langle \mathsf{pre}, \mathsf{post} \rangle$ with $\mathsf{pre}, \mathsf{post} : \mathsf{Act} \cup \mathsf{Evt}_0 \longrightarrow \mathscr{L}_{\mathbb{P}}$. The effects of basic actions and events are conjunctions of literals, given by $\mathsf{eff}^+, \mathsf{eff}^- : \mathsf{Act}_0 \cup \mathsf{Evt}_0 \longrightarrow 2^{\mathbb{P}}$ where for every $x \in \mathsf{Act}_0 \cup \mathsf{Evt}_0$, $\models \mathsf{post}(x) \leftrightarrow \left(\bigwedge_{p \in \mathsf{eff}^+(x)} p \right) \wedge \left(\bigwedge_{p \in \mathsf{eff}^-(x)} \neg p \right)$ and $\mathsf{eff}^+(x) \cap \mathsf{eff}^-(x) = \emptyset$.*

So basic actions and events are STRIPS-like. The functions $\mathsf{pre}, \mathsf{post}, \mathsf{eff}^+$ and eff^- are extended to sets, e.g. $\mathsf{pre}(X) = \bigwedge_{x \in X} \mathsf{pre}(x)$ for $X \subseteq \mathsf{Act}_0 \cup \mathsf{Evt}_0$.

We use $|S|$ to denote the cardinality of a set S. We use $len(\varphi)$ to denote the length of a formula φ which is the number of symbols used to write down φ except for parentheses. The length of a dynamic theory $\mathcal{T}$, denoted by $len(\mathcal{T})$, is the sum of the length of all pre- and postcondition formulas in $\mathcal{T}$.

Definition 2. *A dynamic theory $\mathcal{T}$ is coherent if and only if for every basic action $a \in \mathsf{Act}_0$ and event set $E \subseteq \mathsf{Evt}_0$, if $\mathsf{pre}(\{a\} \cup E)$ is consistent then $\mathsf{post}(\{a\} \cup E)$ is consistent.*

Proposition 1. *A dynamic theory $\mathcal{T}$ is coherent iff the following formula, denoted by $Coh(\mathcal{T})$, is valid:*

$$\bigwedge_{\substack{e \in \mathsf{Evt}_0, x \in \mathsf{Act}_0 \cup \mathsf{Evt}_0, \\ (\mathsf{eff}^+(e) \cap \mathsf{eff}^-(x)) \cup (\mathsf{eff}^-(e) \cap \mathsf{eff}^+(x)) \neq \emptyset}} (\mathsf{pre}(e) \wedge \mathsf{pre}(x) \rightarrow \bot). \tag{1}$$

Proof. "$\Rightarrow$": Suppose dynamic theory $\mathcal{T}$ is coherent and $\mathsf{post}(\{a\} \cup E)$ is inconsistent. Because all basic actions and events have a consistent postcondition in form of a conjunction of literals, only a pair of an action or event $x \in \{a\} \cup E$ and an event $e \in E$ such that one has a positive effect on propositional variable p and the other has a negative effect on p, would make $\mathsf{post}(\{x, e\})$ inconsistent and further $\mathsf{post}(\{a\} \cup E)$ inconsistent. definition of coherence their jointly precondition $\mathsf{pre}(\{x, e\})$ is inconsistent. Thus $Coh(\mathcal{T})$ is valid.

"$\Leftarrow$": Suppose $Coh(\mathcal{T})$ is valid and there exists some action a and event set E such that $\mathsf{pre}(\{a\} \cup E)$ is consistent while $\mathsf{post}(\{a\} \cup E)$ is inconsistent. As $\mathsf{post}(a)$ and $\mathsf{post}(E)$ can be rewritten into a conjunction of literals, there is a pair of p and $\neg p$ occurring in $\mathsf{post}(\{a\} \cup E)$. Then there are $x, y \in \{a\} \cup E$ such that $x \neq y$ and $p \in \mathsf{eff}^+(x) \cap \mathsf{eff}^-(y)$. Being a conjunct of $Coh(\mathcal{T})$, $\mathsf{pre}(x) \wedge \mathsf{pre}(y) \rightarrow \bot$ is true, which entails $\mathsf{pre}(a) \wedge \mathsf{pre}(E) \rightarrow \bot$, contradicting that $\mathsf{pre}(\{a\} \cup E)$ is consistent.

Theorem 1 (Complexity of Coherence). *Given any dynamic theory $\mathcal{T}$, to decide whether $\mathcal{T}$ is coherent is co-NP-complete.*

Proof. As the length of the formula $Coh(\mathcal{T})$ is bounded by $O(|\mathsf{Act_0} \cup \mathsf{Evt_0}|^2 \times len(\mathcal{T}))$, the problem of deciding coherence is in co-NP.

To establish hardness, let $\mathsf{Act_0} = \{a\}$, $\mathsf{Evt_0} = \{e\}$ with $\mathrm{pre}(a) = \mathrm{pre}(e) = \varphi$, $\mathrm{post}(a) = p$ and $\mathrm{post}(e) = \neg p$. As $\mathrm{post}(a) \wedge \mathrm{post}(e)$ is inconsistent, φ is inconsistent iff $\mathcal{T}$ is coherent. It follows that deciding coherence is co-NP-hard.

Therefore, to decide whether $\mathcal{T}$ is coherent is co-NP-complete.

2.2 Belief-Intention Databases

An agent's belief-intention database contains her intentions plus her beliefs about initial state and event occurrences which may be incomplete.

Occurrence of an event $e \in \mathsf{Evt_0}$ at time point t is noted (t, e). The non-occurrence of events is also considered: let $\overline{\mathsf{Evt_0}} = \{\bar{e} : e \in \mathsf{Evt_0}\}$ be the set of event complements. Non-occurrence of e is noted $(t, \bar{e})$. An intention is a triple $i = (t, \alpha, d) \in \mathbb{N}^0 \times \mathsf{Act} \times \mathbb{N}$ with $t < d$. It means that the agent wants to perform α in the time interval $[t, d]$: action α should start after t and end before d. When $\alpha \in \mathsf{Act_0}$ then i is a *basic intention*.

Definition 3. *A database is a finite set*

$$\Delta \subseteq (\mathbb{N}^0 \times \mathcal{L}_{\mathbb{P}}) \cup (\mathbb{N}^0 \times \mathsf{Evt_0}) \cup (\mathbb{N}^0 \times \overline{\mathsf{Evt_0}}) \cup (\mathbb{N}^0 \times \mathsf{Act} \times \mathbb{N}).$$

Given an intention $i = (t, \alpha, d)$, we define $\mathrm{end}(i) = d$. For a database Δ, we let $\mathrm{end}(\Delta)$ be the greatest time point occurring in Δ. When $\Delta = \emptyset$, $\mathrm{end}(\Delta) = 0$. This is well defined because databases are finite.

2.3 Semantics

The semantics of dynamic theories and databases is in terms of *paths*. A path defines for each time point which propositional variables are true, which basic actions the agent will perform, and which events will occur.

Definition 4. *A $\mathcal{T}$-path is a triple $\pi = \langle V, H, D \rangle$ with $V : \mathbb{N}^0 \longrightarrow 2^{\mathbb{P}}$, $H : \mathbb{N}^0 \to 2^{\mathsf{Evt_0}}$, and $D : \mathbb{N}^0 \to \mathsf{Act_0}$.*

So a path π associates to every time point t a valuation $V(t)$ (alias a state), a set of events $H(t)$ happening at t, and a basic action $D(t)$ performed at t.

Definition 5. *A model of $\mathcal{T}$, or $\mathcal{T}$-model, is a path $\pi = \langle V, H, D \rangle$ such that for every time point $t \in \mathbb{N}^0$,*

$$\mathrm{eff}^+(H(t) \cup \{D(t)\}) \cap \mathrm{eff}^-(H(t) \cup \{D(t)\}) = \emptyset \tag{2}$$

$$and \quad V(t{+}1) = \big(V(t) \cup \mathrm{eff}^+(H(t) \cup \{D(t)\})\big) \setminus \mathrm{eff}^-\big(H(t) \cup \{D(t)\}\big)$$

$$H(t) = \{e \in \mathsf{Evt_0} \mid V(t) \models \mathrm{pre}(e)\}$$

$$D(t) \in \{a \in \mathsf{Act_0} \mid V(t) \models \mathrm{pre}(a)\}$$

So in a $\mathcal{T}$-model: (1) the state at $t+1$ is determined by the state at t and the basic action and events occurring at t; (2) event e occurs *iff* $\mathrm{pre}(e)$ is true; (3) basic action a occurs *implies* that $\mathrm{pre}(a)$ is true. Next we show the satisfaction relation $\Vdash_\mathcal{T}$ between a path and an intention or a database.

Definition 6. *Intention $i = (t,\alpha,d)$ is satisfied at a path $\pi = \langle V, H, D\rangle$, noted $\pi \Vdash_\mathcal{T} i$, if there exist t', d' such that $t \leq t' < d' \leq d$, $V(t') \models \mathrm{pre}(\alpha)$, $V(d') \models \mathrm{post}(\alpha)$, and $\alpha \in \mathsf{Act}_0$ implies $D(t') = \alpha$.*

So π satisfies (t,α,d) if α is executable at some point after t and can end before the deadline at a point where the postcondition of α is true. Moreover, when α is basic then it conforms to the 'do'-function D of π.

Definition 7. *A $\mathcal{T}$-model $\pi = \langle V, H, D\rangle$ is a $\mathcal{T}$-model of Δ, noted $\pi \Vdash_\mathcal{T} \Delta$, if*

- *for every $(t,\varphi) \in \Delta$: $V(t) \models \varphi$;*
- *for every $(t,e) \in \Delta$: $e \in H(t)$;*
- *for every $(t,\bar{e}) \in \Delta$: $e \notin H(t)$;*
- *for every $i \in \Delta$: $\pi \Vdash_\mathcal{T} i$.*

When $\pi \Vdash_\mathcal{T} \Delta$, the agent's beliefs about the state and the (non-)occurrence of events are correct w.r.t. π, and all intentions in Δ are satisfied on π. A database Δ is $\mathcal{T}$-*satisfiable* when Δ has a $\mathcal{T}$-model.

Δ is a $\mathcal{T}$-*consequence* of Δ', noted $\Delta' \models_\mathcal{T} \Delta$, if every $\mathcal{T}$-model of Δ' is also a $\mathcal{T}$-model of Δ. When Δ is a singleton $\{i\}$ we write $\Delta' \models_\mathcal{T} i$ instead of $\Delta' \models_\mathcal{T} \{i\}$.

2.4   Refinement and Instrumentality

Refinement consists in adding new intentions to the database while staying consistent. Intuitively, to refine an intention i means to add a minimal set of new intentions J to the database which, together with other intentions but i, suffice to entail i. Moreover, the deadlines of the means are before that of the end.

Definition 8. *Intention i is refined by intention set J in Δ, noted $\Delta \models_\mathcal{T} i \lhd J$, iff*

1. *there is no $j \in J$ such that $\Delta \models_\mathcal{T} j$;*
2. *$\Delta \cup J$ has a $\mathcal{T}$-model;*
3. *$(\Delta \cup J) \setminus \{i\} \models_\mathcal{T} i$;*
4. *$(\Delta \cup J') \setminus \{i\} \not\models_\mathcal{T} i$ for every $J' \subset J$;*
5. *$\mathrm{end}(j) \leq \mathrm{end}(i)$ for every $j \in J$.*

A higher-level intention and the lower-level intentions refining it should stand in an instrumentality relation: the lower-levels contribute to the higher-levels.

Definition 9. *For a $\mathcal{T}$-satisfiable database Δ, let intention $i \in \mathcal{I}(\Delta)$ and intention set $J \subseteq \mathcal{I}(\Delta)$. Then J is instrumental for i in Δ, noted $\Delta \models_\mathcal{T} J \rhd i$, iff*

1. $\Delta \setminus J \not\models_\mathcal{T} i$;
2. $(\Delta \setminus J) \cup \{j\} \models_\mathcal{T} i$ for every $j \in J$;
3. $\mathsf{end}(j) \leq \mathsf{end}(i)$ for every $j \in J$.

When $\Delta \models_\mathcal{T} J > i$ then J is a minimal set of intentions satisfying the counterfactual "if J was not in Δ then i would no longer be guaranteed by Δ" and all intentions of J terminate before or together with i. Note that when $\Delta \models_\mathcal{T} J > i$ then J cannot be empty (because we require $i \in J$).

Instrumentality is connected with intention refinement: when $\Delta \models_\mathcal{T} i \triangleleft J$ then every element of J is instrumental for i in the refined database. Formally, $\Delta \cup J \models_\mathcal{T} \{i, j\} > i$ for every $j \in J$.

3 Complexity

In this section, we show the complexity results of the decision problems for satisfiability, consequence, refinement and instrumentality in belief-intention databases.

3.1 Complexity of Satisfiability

The coherence condition guarantees that there is no conflict on the effect of the action and the events occurring simultaneously at every time points, entailing the constraint formula (2) in the definition of $\mathcal{T}$-model (Definition 5). That is, if dynamic theory $\mathcal{T}$ is coherent, then the empty database is $\mathcal{T}$-satisfiable. Given a coherent dynamic theory, it is not necessary to check whether the infinite path is a $\mathcal{T}$-model of a database and we only need to check the former part bounded by the greatest time point occurring in the database.

We define the restriction of natural number set $\mathbb{N}$ by a natural number δ as a set of sequential natural numbers $[0, \ldots, \delta]$, denoted by $\mathbb{N}_\delta$. We define the restriction of a function $f : \mathbb{N} \longrightarrow S$ such that the domain is natural number set to a natural number δ as $f|_\delta = \{(n, s) \mid n \in \mathbb{N}_\delta\}$.

Then we introduce the notion of bounded paths.

Definition 10. For a path $\pi = \langle V, H, D \rangle$ and a natural number δ we call the tuple $\overline{\pi} = \langle V|_{\delta+1}, H|_\delta, D|_\delta, \delta \rangle$ a bounded path of π and call δ the bound of $\overline{\pi}$.

Then we define bounded models by bounded paths.

Definition 11 (Bounded $\mathcal{T}$-model). Given a coherent dynamic theory $\mathcal{T}$, a $\mathcal{T}$-model π and a database Δ such that $\pi \Vdash_\mathcal{T} \Delta$, we call the bounded path $\overline{\pi}$ of π a bounded model of Δ, noted $\overline{\pi} \Vdash_\mathcal{T} \Delta$, if the bound of $\overline{\pi}$ is greater than $\mathsf{end}(\Delta)$.

The coherence condition of the dynamic theory allows us to decide if a database has a model by checking a finite path, stated as follows.

Proposition 2. Given a coherent dynamic theory $\mathcal{T}$, a database Δ is $\mathcal{T}$-satisfiable iff Δ has a bounded model.

Proof. "⇒": Straightforward.

"⇐": When the dynamic theory T is coherent, for every time point t, the sets $\texttt{eff}^+(H(t) \cup \{D(t)\})$ and $\texttt{eff}^-(H(t) \cup \{D(t)\})$ are totally disjoint. So, there is no state in which the performed action has an effect conflicting with the effect of the events which are happening. Thus, we can construct an infinite T-model starting from the bounded model according to the definition of T-models.

The lower bound of the complexity of the satisfiability problem comes from the reduction to a plan-existence problem. A plan-existence problem with bounded horizon is a tuple $\mathcal{P} = \langle \mathcal{I}, \mathcal{G}, T_{\mathsf{Act}_0}, \delta \rangle$ where δ is a natural number, $\mathcal{I}$ is a subset of propositional variable set $\mathbb{P}$ and $\mathcal{G}$ is a conflict-free conjunction of literals and T_{Act_0} is a dynamic theory only for basic actions. The plan-existence problem is to decide whether there exists a sequence of basic actions, called plan, with a length less than δ from a initial state $\mathcal{I}$ to a goal state satisfying $\mathcal{G}$. The plan-existence problem is PSPACE-complete [7].

Theorem 2. *Given a coherent dynamic theory T, the T-satisfiability problem of a belief-intention database is PSPACE-complete.*

Proof. First, we prove the problem is in PSPACE. Suppose the number of intentions in Δ is m. Consider a memory space with the size of $|\mathbb{P}| + 2m$. When the $|\mathbb{P}|$ cells can denote a state, the $2m$ cells can indicate the satisfaction of pre- and postcondition of the action in the corresponding intentions.

Guess a path $\overline{\pi} = \langle V, H, D, \mathsf{end}(\Delta) \rangle$, we can change the $|\mathbb{P}|$ cells according to the valuation of each time point defined by $\overline{\pi}$. Because the basic actions and events are finite, it can be checked whether $\overline{\pi}$ is a T-model in polynomial time. The $2m$ cells are initially set to 0 and with time point changing, we change the $2m$ cells according to the satisfaction of intentions. To be specific, consider an intention $i = (t, \alpha, d)$, from time point t if $\mathsf{pre}(\alpha)$ is satisfied then the cell corresponding to the precondition of i is set to 1. Then in the following time points once $\mathsf{post}(\alpha)$ is satisfied the cell corresponding to postcondition of i is set to 1. Unless this cell is 1 at time point d, we stop and conclude that the path guessed does not satisfy i and further does not satisfy Δ. Therefore, we can check whether the path is a T-model of Δ in polynomial time, because every effect, pre- and postcondition is defined as a propositional formula which can be checked to be satisfied by the state in polynomial time. As only finite sets of basic actions, events, and propositional variables can be nondeterministically chosen, deciding whether the path guessed is a T-model of Δ is in NPSPACE. Because NPSPACE = PSPACE, the T-satisfiability problem is in PSPACE.

Next we prove the problem is PSPACE-hard by reducing the plan-existence problem with bounded horizon. For a plan-existence problem $\mathcal{P} = \langle \mathcal{I}, \mathcal{G}, T_{\mathsf{Act}_0}, \delta \rangle$, we construct a dynamic theory T by extending T_{Act_0} with a high-level action $\mathsf{Goal} \in \mathsf{Act} \setminus \mathsf{Act}_0$ such that $\mathsf{pre}(\mathsf{Goal}) = \top$ and $\mathsf{post}(\mathsf{Goal}) = \mathcal{G}$. We also suppose the event set Evt_0 is empty, entailing that T is coherent. Suppose $\varphi_{\mathcal{I}} = \bigwedge_{p \in \mathcal{I}} p \land \bigwedge_{q \in \mathbb{P} \setminus \mathcal{I}} \neg q$. Then the database $\Delta = \{(0, \varphi_{\mathcal{I}}), (0, \mathsf{Goal}, \delta)\}$ has a T-model iff there exists a plan in $\mathcal{P}$. So the T-satisfiability problem is PSPACE-hard.

Hence the T-satisfiability problem is PSPACE-complete.

3.2   Complexity of Consequence

Next we will show the complexity of the consequence problem in belief-intention databases which is also PSPACE-complete.

Theorem 3. *Given a coherent dynamic theory $\mathcal{T}$, the $\mathcal{T}$-consequence problem deciding whether $\Delta' \models_{\mathcal{T}} \Delta$ is PSPACE-complete.*

Proof. For the lower bound, consider the special case of the consequence problem that $\Delta' \models_{\mathcal{T}} \bot$ which means Δ' is $\mathcal{T}$-unsatisfiable. Because the $\mathcal{T}$-satisfiable problem is PSPACE-complete by Theorem 2, the problem deciding whether Δ' is $\mathcal{T}$-unsatisfiable is co-PSPACE-complete. As co-PSPACE = PSPACE, the $\mathcal{T}$-consequence problem PSPACE-hard.

For the upper bound, suppose the number of intentions in Δ and Δ' is m and m' respectively. As $\mathcal{T}$ is coherent, we can consider the complementary problem deciding whether there exists a path which $\mathcal{T}$-satisfies Δ' but not Δ. Consider a memory space with a size of $|\mathbb{P}| + 2(m + m')$ where the $|\mathbb{P}|$ cells denote a state and the $2(m + m')$ cells indicate the satisfaction of pre- and postcondition of the actions w.r.t. intentions in Δ and Δ'.

Suppose $k = \mathsf{max}(\mathsf{end}(\Delta), \mathsf{end}(\Delta')$. Guess a path $\overline{\pi} = \langle V, H, D, k \rangle$, we can change the $|\mathbb{P}|$ cells according to the valuation of each time point defined by $\overline{\pi}$. Because the basic actions and events are finite, it can be check if $\overline{\pi}$ is a $\mathcal{T}$-model in polynomial time. The $2(m + m')$ cells are initially set to 0 and with time point changing, we change the $2(m + m')$ cells according to the satisfaction of intentions. Consider an intention $i = (t, \alpha, d)$, in the time points after t if $\mathsf{pre}(\alpha)$ is satisfied then the cell corresponding to the precondition of i is set to 1. Then in the following time points once $\mathsf{post}(\alpha)$ is satisfied the cell corresponding to the postcondition of i is set to 1. Unless this cell is 1 at time point d, we stop and conclude that the path guessed satisfies neither i nor the database containing i. Therefore, it can be checked whether the path is a $\mathcal{T}$-model of Δ or Δ' in polynomial time, because every effect, pre- and postcondition is defined as a propositional formula which can be decided to be satisfied by the state in polynomial time. As only finite sets of basic actions, events, and propositional variables can be nondeterministically chosen, deciding whether the path guessed is a $\mathcal{T}$-model of Δ' but not Δ is in NPSPACE. Because NPSPACE = PSPACE, the $\mathcal{T}$-consequence problem is in PSPACE.

Hence, the $\mathcal{T}$-consequence problem is PSPACE-complete.

3.3   Complexity of Refinement and Instrumentality

From the definition of refinement and instrumentality, we know that the satisfiability and consequence problems are subproblems of deciding refinement and instrumentality. So, the problems deciding refinement and instrumentality are both PSPACE-hard. Next we show that these two problems are PSPACE-complete by translating them into several satisfiability and consequence problems.

Theorem 4. *Given a coherent dynamic theory $\mathcal{T}$ and a belief-intention database Δ, to check whether an intention $i \in \Delta$ is refinable to an intention set J in Δ is PSPACE-complete.*

Proof. Condition 1, 2 and 4 are $\mathcal{T}$-satisfiability problems and Condition 3 is a $\mathcal{T}$-consequence problem and it is easy to check Condition 5 in polynomial time. As the refinement checking problem can be reduced to several $\mathcal{T}$-satisfiability problems and a $\mathcal{T}$-consequence problem which are all in PSPACE, the decision problem of deciding refinement is also in PSPACE. As the $\mathcal{T}$-satisfiability problem is its subproblem, deciding refinement is PSPACE-complete.

Theorem 5. *Given a coherent dynamic theory $\mathcal{T}$ and a belief-intention database Δ, to decide whether an intention set is instrumental for an intention in Δ is PSPACE-complete.*

Proof. (1) Condition 1 is a $\mathcal{T}$-satisfiability problem; (2) Condition 2 is a set of $\mathcal{T}$-consequence problems with a number of $|J|$; (3) it is easy to check condition 3 in polynomial time. As the instrumentality checking problem can be reduced polynomially to a $\mathcal{T}$-satisfiability problem and a $\mathcal{T}$-consequence problem which are both in PSPACE, the decision problem of deciding instrumentality is also in PSPACE. As the $\mathcal{T}$-satisfiability problem is its subproblem, deciding instrumentality is PSPACE-complete.

4   Translating to PLTL

Linear temporal logics are widely used to describe infinite behaviors of discrete systems. In the last decades, different model checking techniques for PLTL have been developed, such as approaches based on binary decision diagrams (BDD-based) [6] and based on propositional satisfiability problems (SAT-based) [3]. Besides, by translating to Büchi automata, kinds of satisfiability and validity checkers for PLTL have been developed, such as LTL3BA [1] and SPOT [9]. Furthermore, the tableau-based decision procedure for the satisfiability problem of PLTL has been studied [15,17].

In this section we translate the satisfiability and consequence problems in belief-intention databases into the satisfiability and validity problems of PLTL. As the problems of deciding refinement and instrumentality are based on the satisfiability and consequence problems, we can further translate them into PLTL. The translations are not in polynomial time,[2] but nevertheless we believe that the translations are of assistance to solve the decision problems of databases by taking advantage of theorem provers of PLTL.

Following the notations in [10], we define PLTL on a countably infinite set $\mathbb{P}_L$ of propositional variables, classical propositional connectives and restrict it on the unique temporal operator $\mathbf{X}$ (next). Propositional connectives $\neg, \wedge, \vee, \rightarrow, \leftrightarrow$

---

[2] For the database, time points are encoded in a binary way while they are considered as decimal in the size of the resulted PLTL formula. Therefore, the size of the resulted formula is not polynomial with respect to the size of the database.

in PLTL formulas are defined in the standard way with abbreviating $\mathbf{X}^n$ as n continuous operator $\mathbf{X}$ where $\mathbf{X}^0$ is nothing.

Next, we introduce the semantics of PLTL which is based on a linear-time structure. A linear-time structure is a pair of $M = (S, \varepsilon)$ where S is a set of states and $\varepsilon : S \rightarrow 2_L^{\mathbb{P}}$ is a function mapping each state s_i to a set of propositional variables which hold in s_i. Let M be a linear-time structure, $i \in \mathbb{N}^0$ a position, and φ, ψ are PLTL formulas. We define the satisfiable relation $\models$ as follows:

$$M, i \models p \text{ iff } p \in \varepsilon(s_i), \text{ where } p \in \mathbb{P}_L$$
$$M, i \models \neg\varphi \text{ iff } M, i \not\models \varphi$$
$$M, i \models \varphi \wedge \psi \text{ iff } M, i \models \varphi \text{ and } M, i \models \psi$$
$$M, i \models \mathbf{X}\varphi \text{ iff } M, i+1 \models \varphi$$

If there exists a linear-time structure M such that $M, 0 \models \varphi$, we say φ is satisfiable. If for all linear-time structure M we have $M, 0 \models \varphi$, we say φ is valid.

We first start by defining some auxiliary propositional variables. For every event e we introduce an auxiliary propositional variable h_e, defining the set $\mathbb{P}_h = \{h_e | e \in \mathsf{Evt}_0\}$ and for every basic action a we introduce an auxiliary propositional variable do_a, defining the set $\mathbb{P}_d = \{do_a | a \in \mathsf{Act}_0\}$. Moreover, we introduce a set $\mathbb{P}_c$ auxiliary propositional variables $pre_\alpha, post_\alpha, pre_e$ and $post_e$ for every action and event to denote their pre- and postcondition.

Definition 12. *Given a coherent dynamic theory $\mathcal{T}$, we define a conjunction of formulas $\mathsf{Tr}(\mathcal{T})$ as:*

$$\bigwedge_{a \in \mathsf{Act}_0} (do_a \rightarrow \mathbf{pre}_a) \wedge \bigwedge_{e \in \mathsf{Evt}_0} (h_e \leftrightarrow \mathbf{pre}_e) \tag{3}$$

$$\wedge \bigvee_{a \in \mathsf{Act}_0} do_a \wedge \bigwedge_{a,b \in \mathsf{Act}_0, a \neq b} \neg(do_a \wedge do_b) \tag{4}$$

$$\wedge \bigwedge_{p \in \mathbb{P}} (\mathbf{X}p \leftrightarrow \bigvee_{\substack{e \in \mathsf{Evt}_0 \\ p \in \mathsf{eff}^+(e)}} h_e \vee \bigvee_{\substack{a \in \mathsf{Act}_0 \\ p \in \mathsf{eff}^+(a)}} do_a \vee (p \wedge \bigwedge_{\substack{e \in \mathsf{Evt}_0 \\ p \in \mathsf{eff}^-(e)}} \neg h_e \wedge \bigwedge_{\substack{a \in \mathsf{Act}_0 \\ p \in \mathsf{eff}^-(a)}} \neg do_a)) \tag{5}$$

$$\wedge \bigwedge_{\alpha \in \mathsf{Act}} ((pre_\alpha \leftrightarrow \mathbf{pre}(\alpha)) \wedge (post_\alpha \leftrightarrow \mathbf{post}(\alpha))) \tag{6}$$

$$\wedge \bigwedge_{e \in \mathsf{Evt}_0} ((pre_e \leftrightarrow \mathbf{pre}(e)) \wedge (post_e \leftrightarrow \mathbf{post}(e))) \tag{7}$$

Intuitively, formula (3) means that basic action a is executable if its precondition is satisfied and that events are reactive: when their precondition is satisfied they will happen. Formula (4) says that exactly one basic action is allowed at one time point. Formula (5) means propositional variable p is true in the next state if and only if either it is "activated" or both it is already currently true and there is no action or event making it false. Formulas (6) and (7) link the formulas of pre- and postcondition of actions and events with propositional variables. Finally, $\mathsf{Tr}(\mathcal{T})$ captures the definition and progression of valuations in one time point. Then we define $\mathsf{Tr}(n, \mathcal{T})$ as $\mathsf{Tr}(\mathcal{T}) \wedge \mathbf{X}\mathsf{Tr}(\mathcal{T}) \wedge \ldots \wedge \mathbf{X}^n \mathsf{Tr}(\mathcal{T})$ to capture the first n time points of a $\mathcal{T}$-model.

Definition 13. *We translate a database Δ into a conjunction of formulas $\mathsf{Tr}(\Delta)$ as:*

$$\bigwedge_{(t,\varphi) \in \Delta} \mathbf{X}^t \varphi \wedge \bigwedge_{(t,e) \in \Delta} \mathbf{X}^t h_e \wedge \bigwedge_{(t,\bar{e}) \in \Delta} \mathbf{X}^t \neg h_e \tag{8}$$

$$\wedge \bigwedge_{\substack{\alpha \notin \mathsf{Act}_0 \\ (t,\alpha,d) \in \Delta}} \bigvee_{t \leq t' < d' \leq d} (\mathbf{X}^{t'} pre_\alpha \wedge \mathbf{X}^{d'} post_\alpha) \tag{9}$$

$$\wedge \bigwedge_{\substack{a \in \mathsf{Act}_0 \\ (t,a,d) \in \Delta}} \bigvee_{t \leq t' < d} \mathbf{X}^{t'} do_a \tag{10}$$

The above definition actually formalizes the satisfaction of database in a path. For a coherent dynamic theory, we only consider the fragment of $\mathcal{T}$-model from time point 0 to $\mathrm{end}(\Delta)$. The following proposition shows the satisfiability problem of database is connected to the satisfiability problem of PLTL.

Proposition 3. *Given a coherent dynamic theory $\mathcal{T}$, a database Δ is $\mathcal{T}$-satisfiable iff $\mathsf{Tr}(\mathrm{end}(\Delta), \mathcal{T}) \wedge \mathsf{Tr}(\Delta)$ is satisfiable.*

Proof. Let $M = (S, \varepsilon)$ be a linear-time structure where $S = \{s_0, s_1, \ldots\}$ and $\varepsilon : S \to 2^{\mathbb{P}_L}$ such that $\mathbb{P}_L = \mathbb{P} \cup \mathbb{P}_d \cup \mathbb{P}_h \cup \mathbb{P}_c$.

" $\Rightarrow$ " : Suppose there exists a $\mathcal{T}$-model $\pi = \langle V, H, D \rangle$ of Δ. Let us build a linear-time structure M as follows: for every time point t, (i) $\varepsilon(s_t) \cap \mathbb{P} = V(t)$; (ii) $\varepsilon(s_t) \cap \mathbb{P}_h = \{h_e | e \in H(t)\}$; (iii) if $D(t) = a$ then $\varepsilon(s_t) \cap \mathbb{P}_d = do_a$; (iv) $\varepsilon(s_t) \cap \mathbb{P}_c = \{pre_x, post_y | V(t) \models \mathsf{pre}(x), V(t) \models \mathsf{post}(y), x, y \in \mathsf{Act} \cup \mathsf{Evt}_0\}$.

Now we first prove $M, 0 \models \mathsf{Tr}(\mathrm{end}(\Delta), \mathcal{T})$. According to the definition of $\mathcal{T}$-model, we immediately have $M, t \models (3) \wedge (4) \wedge (6) \wedge (7)$ for each time point t. For every propositional variable p, $M, t+1 \models p$ iff either there is a basic action or event to make it true or $M, t \models p$ and there is no action or event to make it false. Thus, for every time point t, we obtain $M, t \models \mathsf{Tr}(\mathcal{T})$ and then $M, 0 \models \mathsf{Tr}(\mathrm{end}(\Delta), \mathcal{T})$. Next we prove $M, 0 \models \mathsf{Tr}(\Delta)$. For every $(t, \varphi) \in \Delta$, we obtain $M, t \models \varphi$. For every $(t, e) \in \mathcal{E}(\Delta)$, $M, 0 \models \mathbf{X}^t h_e$ because $e \in H(t)$ and $h_e \in \varepsilon(s_t)$. The case of $(t, \bar{e})$ is similar. By the definition of satisfying an intention (Definition 6), if $\pi \Vdash_\tau i$ we have $M, 0 \models (9) \wedge (10)$. So we have $M, 0 \models \mathsf{Tr}(\Delta)$.

Thus, we conclude that $M, 0 \models \mathsf{Tr}(\mathrm{end}(\Delta), \mathcal{T}) \wedge \mathsf{Tr}(\Delta)$.

" $\Leftarrow$ " : Suppose there exists a linear-time structure M such that $M, 0 \models$ $\mathsf{Tr}(\mathsf{end}(\Delta), \mathcal{T}) \wedge \mathsf{Tr}(\Delta)$. Now we build a path $\pi = \langle V, H, D \rangle$ as follows: for every time points $t \leq \mathsf{end}(\Delta)$, (i)$V(t) = \varepsilon(s_t) \cap \mathbb{P}$; (ii)$H(t) = \{e | h_e \in \varepsilon(s_t) \cap \mathbb{P}_h\}$; (iii)$D(t) = a$ if $do_a \in \varepsilon(s_t)$. For those time points $t > \mathsf{end}(\Delta)$, we can construct π according to Definition 5, because $\mathcal{T}$ is coherent.

Next we show π is a $\mathcal{T}$-model. For every time point $t \leq \mathsf{end}(\Delta)$, due to (4), there must be an action a such that $M, t \models do_a$. So $M, t \models \mathbf{pre}(a)$ then we have $V(t) \models \mathbf{pre}(a)$ and $D(t) = a$. Because $M, t \models h_e$ iff $M, t \models \mathbf{pre}(e)$, we have $H(t) = \{e | V(t) \models \mathbf{pre}(e)\}$. For propositional variable p, it is in $V(t+1)$ iff either at time point t, there exists an action or event making it true or both $p \in V(t)$ and there is no action or event making it false. The constraint formula (2) of $\mathcal{T}$-models is satisfied because $\mathcal{T}$ is coherent. So, we have π is a $\mathcal{T}$-model.

As Definition 7, it is easy to prove $\pi \Vdash_{\mathcal{T}} \Delta$ for $M, 0 \models \mathsf{Tr}(\Delta)$.

The next proposition states the equivalence between the consequence problem in belief-intention databases and the validity problem in PLTL.

Proposition 4. *Given a coherent dynamic theory $\mathcal{T}$, Δ' is a $\mathcal{T}$-consequence of Δ iff $\mathsf{Tr}(k, \mathcal{T}) \rightarrow (\mathsf{Tr}(\Delta) \rightarrow \mathsf{Tr}(\Delta'))$ is valid where k is the greater number between $\mathsf{end}(\Delta)$ and $\mathsf{end}(\Delta')$.*

Proof. "$\Rightarrow$": for all $\mathcal{T}$-models of Δ, we have $\mathsf{Tr}(\mathsf{end}(\Delta), \mathcal{T}) \wedge \mathsf{Tr}(\Delta)$. Then if these models are also models of Δ', then $(\mathsf{Tr}(\mathsf{end}(\Delta), \mathcal{T}) \wedge \mathsf{Tr}(\Delta)) \rightarrow (\mathsf{Tr}(\mathsf{end}(\Delta'), \mathcal{T}) \wedge \mathsf{Tr}(\Delta'))$. Because $\mathcal{T}$-model is infinite on time, either $\mathsf{end}(\Delta) \geq \mathsf{end}(\Delta')$ or not, $\mathsf{Tr}(k, \mathcal{T})$ must be satisfied. Thus, we have $\mathsf{Tr}((k, \mathcal{T}) \rightarrow (\mathsf{Tr}(\Delta) \rightarrow \mathsf{Tr}(\Delta'))$.

"$\Leftarrow$": from the proof of Proposition 3, if $\mathsf{Tr}(k, \mathcal{T})$ is satisfied we can construct a $\mathcal{T}$-model π. Further if $\mathsf{Tr}(\Delta)$ is satisfied then $\pi \Vdash_{\mathcal{T}} \Delta$. Thus, if $\mathsf{Tr}(\Delta) \rightarrow \mathsf{Tr}(\Delta')$, then we have $\Delta \models_{\mathcal{T}} \Delta'$.

As shown in the proof of Theorems 4 and 5, the problems of deciding refinement and instrumentality are based on the satisfiability and consequence problems. By Propositions 3 and 4, we can further translate these two decision problems into the satisfiability and validity problems of PLTL.

5   Conclusion

In this paper, we investigate the complexity of the decision problems for satisfiability, consequence, refinement and instrumentality in belief-intention databases and prove these problems are all PSPACE-complete. Moreover, we translate the satisfiability and consequence problems, and further, the problems of deciding refinement and instrumentality, in belief-intention databases into the satisfiability and validity problems of PLTL. With such reductions, the state of the art in the automated tools of PLTL contributes to develop an implementation for refining high-level intentions in the belief-intention databases.

Intention refinement is closed to Hierarchical Task Network (HTN) planning where higher-level actions are refined step-by-step into lower-level actions. In

HTN planning, refinement is defined in an explicit way while in the database the refinement is given in a derived way. The former requires the user to think throughout all possible refinement ways for all actions, which is a big challenge. Considering refinement in a derived way helps us to complete the refinement ways by discovering the implicit refinement relation between actions. Postulates of the soundness and completeness for refining actions were proposed in [12] and we believe, they provide rational postulates for improving the HTN domains.

Acknowledgments.. The work was supported by Chinese Scholarship Council and the project ANR-11-LABX-0040-CIMI within ANR-11-IDEX-0002-02.

References

1. Babiak, T., Křetínský, M., Řehák, V., Strejček, J.: LTL to Büchi automata translation: fast and more deterministic. In: Flanagan, C., König, B. (eds.) TACAS 2012. LNCS, vol. 7214, pp. 95–109. Springer, Heidelberg (2012). doi:10.1007/978-3-642-28756-5_8
2. Baral, C., Gelfond, M.: Reasoning about intended actions. In: Proceedings of the 20th National Conference on Artificial Intelligence (AAAI), Menlo Park, CA, vol. 20, pp. 689–694. AAAI Press, MIT Press, Cambridge 1999 (2005)
3. Biere, A., Cimatti, A., Clarke, E.M., Fujita, M., Zhu, Y.: Symbolic model checking using SAT procedures instead of BDDs. In: Proceedings of the 36th annual ACM/IEEE Design Automation Conference, pp. 317–320. ACM (1999)
4. Bratman, M.E.: Intention, Plans, and Practical Reason. Harvard University Press, Cambridge (1987). (reedited 1999 with CSLI Publications)
5. Bratman, M.E., Israel, D.J., Pollack, M.E.: Plans and resource-bounded practical reasoning. J. Comput. Intell. **4**, 349–355 (1988)
6. Burch, J.R., Clarke, E.M., McMillan, K.L., Dill, D.L., Hwang, L.J.: Symbolic model checking: 10^{20} states and beyond. Inf. Comput. **98**(2), 142–170 (1992)
7. Bylander, T.: The computational complexity of propositional STRIPS planning. Artif. Intell. **69**(1), 165–204 (1994)
8. Cohen, P.R., Levesque, H.J.: Intention is choice with commitment. J. Artif. Intell. **42**(2), 213–261 (1990)
9. Duret-Lutz, A., Poitrenaud, D.: Spot: an extensible model checking library using transition-based generalized büchi automata. In: Proceedings of the IEEE Computer Society's 12th Annual International Symposium on Modeling, Analysis, and Simulation of Computer and Telecommunications Systems (MASCOTS 2004), pp. 76–83. IEEE (2004)
10. Emerson, E.A.: Temporal and modal logic. Handb. Theor. Comput. Sci. Volume B: Formal Models Sematics (B) **995**(1072), 5 (1990)
11. Herzig, A., Lorini, E., Perrussel, L., Xiao, Z.: BDI logics for BDI architectures: old problems, new perspectives. KI - Künstliche Intelligenz **31**(1), 73–83 (2017)
12. Herzig, A., Perrussel, L., Xiao, Z.: On hierarchical task networks. In: Michael, L., Kakas, A. (eds.) JELIA 2016. LNCS (LNAI), vol. 10021, pp. 551–557. Springer, Cham (2016). doi:10.1007/978-3-319-48758-8_38
13. Herzig, A., Perrussel, L., Xiao, Z., Zhang, D.: Refinement of intentions. In: Michael, L., Kakas, A. (eds.) JELIA 2016. LNCS (LNAI), vol. 10021, pp. 558–563. Springer, Cham (2016). doi:10.1007/978-3-319-48758-8_39

14. Sardina, S., de Silva, L., Padgham, L.: Hierarchical planning in BDI agent programming languages: a formal approach. In: Proceedings of the 5th International Conference on Autonomous Agents and Multiagent Systems (AAMAS), pp. 1001–1008 (2006)
15. Shilov, N.V.: Designing tableau-like axiomatization for propositional linear temporal logic at home of arthur prior. Bull. Novosibirsk Comput. Cent. Ser.: Comput. Sci. 23, 113–136 (2005)
16. Shoham, Y.: Logical theories of intention and the database perspective. J. Philos. Logic 38(6), 633–647 (2009)
17. Wolper, P.: The tableau method for temporal logic: an overview. Logique et Analyse 28(110–111), 119–136 (1985)

lp2cpp: A Tool For Compiling Stratified Logic Programs

Bernardo Cuteri[✉], Alessandro Francesco De Rosis, and Francesco Ricca

DeMaCS, Università della Calabria, Rende, CS, Italy
{cuteri,ricca}@mat.unical.it, alessandrof.derosis@gmail.com

Abstract. The evaluation of logic programs is traditionally implemented in monolithic systems that are general-purpose in the sense that
they are able to process an entire class of programs. In this paper, we
follow a different approach; we present a compilation procedure that is
able to generate a problem-specific executable implementation of a given
(non-ground) logic program. Our implementation follows a bottom-up
evaluation strategy. Moreover, we implemented such procedure into a
C++ tool and we present an experimental analysis that shows the performance benefits that can be obtained by a compilation-based approach.

Keywords: Compilation · Logic programming · Stratified programs ·
Deductive databases

1 Introduction

Logic programming has proven to be very successful at tackling many computational problems in AI, and this fact lies in the inherent properties of logic languages and also in the implementation of efficient systems [7]. Yet, many modern
applications might involve very large inputs requiring very efficient techniques
to be processed.

The evaluation of logic programs is traditionally performed by systems that
are *general-purpose* in the sense that they are able to process an entire class of
programs. In this paper, we follow a different approach; we consider a compilation strategy for the evaluation of a well-known class of logic programs. The
target language of this work is Datalog with stratified negation [5,19]: a simple,
yet flexible logic language for deductive databases. This language is sufficiently
expressive to model many practical problems, and it recently found new applications in a variety of classical and emerging domains such as ontologies [3], data
integration, information extraction, networking, program analysis, security, and
cloud computing (cf. [9]). Moreover, it is a kernel sub-language of Answer Set
Programming (ASP) [2], which is a very expressive language for Knowledge Representation and Reasoning. Notably, core modules of ASP systems are based on
algorithms for evaluating stratified Datalog programs [10], and, basically, any
monolithic ASP system is also an efficient engine for this class of programs.

F. Esposito et al. (Eds.): AI*IA 2017, LNAI 10640, pp. 200–212, 2017.
https://doi.org/10.1007/978-3-319-70169-1_15

A common way of solving a problem in logic programming includes the modeling of the problem in terms of two parts, the first contains rules and the second only facts. Whereas rules allow the declarative specification of the problem, facts can be used to model problem instances. It is custom in the logic programming community to refer to the rules of a program as the *intensional part* (or *encoding*), while the set of facts is referred to as the *extensional part* (or *instance*). Basically, the same uniform encoding is used several times with different instances. A general-purpose system (often needlessly) processes the same encoding every time a new instance is processed. By compiling the encoding in a specialized procedure, one can wire it inside the evaluation procedure so that one does not have to process it every time. Moreover, specialized evaluation strategies on a per-rule basis can be determined at compilation time, possibly increasing the evaluation performance.

In this paper we present *lp2cpp* a compiler for stratified Datalog programs. In our prototype implementation, both the compiler and its output (the compiled logic programs) are written in C++. Figure 1 shows a high-level architecture of Datalog compilation and evaluation as designed in our system. The compiler takes as input a stratified program and generates a C++ procedure which is then compiled into an executable implementation that follows a bottom-up evaluation strategy. The compiled program can then be run on any instance of the input problem to retrieve solutions.

To assess the performance of *lp2cpp*, we have compared our implementation against existing general-purpose systems capable of handling stratified logic programs obtaining encouraging results. The experimental analysis has been carried out on benchmarks from OpenRuleBench [13], which is a well-known suite for logic programming engines.

The rest of the paper is structured as follows: in Sect. 2 we overview the Datalog language; in Sect. 3 we describe our compilation strategy and we present an example of compilation; in Sect. 4 we present and discuss some experimental results; in Sect. 5 we present some related works; finally, in Sect. 6 we draw the conclusion and present future works.

2   Preliminaries

In the following, we overview the language supported by *lp2cpp*, namely Datalog with stratified negation. We refrain from reporting a formal definition of the language (the interested reader is referred to [5,19] for a formal account), rather we provide an informal description of the syntax of the language and focus on the concepts that are mentioned in this paper for describing the compilation procedure implemented in *lp2cpp*.

A Datalog program with stratified negation Π is a set of rules of the form

$$\mathtt{a_0}(X_0) :\!-a_1(X_1),\ldots,a_m(X_m), not\ a_{m+1}(X_{m+1}),\ldots not\ a_n(X_n)$$

where $a_i(X_i)$ are atoms, and X_i denotes a tuple of terms, which are either constants of variables. According to a traditional convention dating back to Prolog,

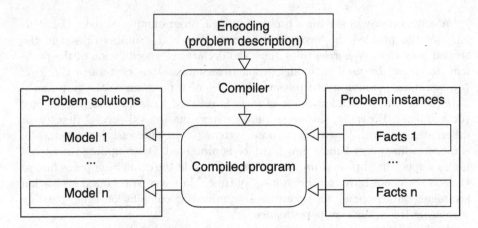

Fig. 1. The *lp2cpp* architecture.

constants are denoted by strings starting by lowercase letter, whereas strings starting by uppercase letter denote variables. A literal is either an atom (positive literal) or an atom preceded by the negation symbol (negative literal). An atom, a literal or a rule is ground if no variable occurs in it. Atom $a_0(X_0)$ is called the head of the rule, whereas the conjunction of atoms denoted by $a_1(X_1), \ldots a_m(X_m)$ is called the positive body and the conjunction of negated atoms (or negative literals) $not\ a_{m+1}(X_{m+1}), \ldots not\ a_n(X_n)$ is called the negative body. A rule can be seen as an implication where the body implies the head. If a variable appears in the head of a rule or in a negative literal, it must then appear also in some positive literal of the same rule (safety), and recursive definitions involving negation are not allowed (stratification).[1] As an example, the following program models the well-known Reachability problem:

```
reaches(X,Y) :- edge(X,Y).
reaches(X,Y) :- edge(X,Z), reaches(Z,Y).
```

Here facts of the form edge(i,j) for each arc (i,j) are used to model the input graph. Intuitively, the first rule says that node X is reached by node Y if there is an edge between the two, and the second rule recursively defines the property by stating that the reachability property is transitive.

The above program is positive (no negated literal occurs). The presence of negation in recursive definitions can be problematic [5,19], and for this reason it is syntactically forbidden by the stratification condition.

In order to describe the stratification condition more formally, we recall the concept of *dependency graph* [5,19]. Given a program Π the dependency graph $DG = <V, E>$ of Π has a vertex $p \in V$ for each predicate p that appears in some head of Π, and a (direct) edge of the form $(b, h) \in E$ whenever b occurs in the body and h in the head of a rule of Π. Edges are labeled as negative if

---

[1] Safety and stratification are standard properties of Datalog programs cfr. [19].

the body literal is negated. A program is said to be *stratified* if there is no cycle with a negative edge in its dependency graph.

As an example, the above program augmented by rule:

```
noReach(Y) :- vertex(Y), not reaches(2,Y).
```

is stratified, since no cycle of its dependency graph contains negative edges.

The dependency graph is also useful for defining evaluation algorithms. First, we observe that it can be partitioned into strongly connected components (SCC)s. An SCC is a maximal subset of the vertices, such that every vertex is reachable from every other vertex. We say that a rule $r \in P$ defines a predicate p if p appears in the head of r. For each strongly connected component C of DG, the set of rules defining all the predicates in C is called the module of C. The dependency graph yields a topological order $[C_1], ..., [C_n]$ over the SCCs: for each pair (C_i, C_j) with $i < j$, there is no path in the dependency graph from C_j to C_i. Program modules corresponding to components can be evaluated by following a topological order [5,19]. If two predicates do not belong to the same SCC it means that they do not depend on each other, thus their defining rules can be evaluated separately (possibly increasing evaluation performance). Since, by definition, stratified programs admit no negative edge inside any SCC (i.e. no loop can contain a negative edge), an evaluation performed according to a topological order ensures a sound computation of programs with negation.

3   Compilation of Stratified Logic Programs

In this section, we first provide a high-level description of the compilation procedure adopted by *lp2cpp*, then we illustrate how it works by commenting on an example of compilation.

3.1   Compilation Procedure Description

Given a stratified Datalog program Π, Algorithm 1 describes the compilation of Π. The algorithm takes in input Π and generates imperative code implementing the evaluation of Π on an input set of facts. The first step of the algorithm consists in the computation of a topologically ordered list of the strongly connected component of the *dependecy graph* (DG) of the input program Π (line 2); then our compilation procedure generates the declaration of data structures (lines 4–16).

Two types of data structures are used: *predicate sets* and *auxiliary maps*. Predicate sets are used to store ground atoms that will be part of the output, grouped by predicate. The operations associated with predicate sets are insertion, iteration and containment check. Since predicate sets correspond to mathematical sets of ground atoms, insertion avoids duplicates. Auxiliary maps are key-value maps, where keys are tuples and values are sets of tuples. In the following, we denote a ground atom of p as the n-tuple $\langle a_1, a_2, ..., a_n \rangle$ where n is

Algorithm 1. Compilation procedure

Input: DatalogProgram Π

1: *//Computation of strongly connected components*
2: $SCCs \leftarrow ComputeSCCs(\Pi)$
3:
4: *//Predicate Sets declarations*
5: **for all** $p \in Predicates(\Pi)$ **do**
6:     $write("PredicateSet" + p.name)$
7: **end for**
8:
9: *//Auxiliary Maps declarations*
10: $AuxMapsVariables \leftarrow \emptyset$
11: **for all** $rule \in \Pi$ **do**
12:     $AuxMapsVariables \leftarrow AuxMapsVariables \cup getAuxMapsVariables(rule)$
13: **end for**
14: **for all** $v \in AuxMapsVariables$ **do**
15:     $write("AuxiliaryMap" + v)$
16: **end for**
17:
18: $WriteFactsReadingProcedure()$
19:
20: *//Evaluation of Π by component*
21: **for all** $C \in SCCs$ **do**
22:     **for all** $rule \in rules(C)$ **do**
23:         **for all** $start \in starters(rule)$ **do**
24:             $WriteEvaluationProcedure(rule, start)$
25:         **end for**
26:     **end for**
27: **end for**
28:
29: **for all** $p \in Predicates(\Pi)$ **do**
30:     $write(p.name + ".print()")$
31: **end for**

the arity of p and $a_1, a_2, ..., a_n$ are ground terms (i.e. constants). Given a predicate p of arity n and a subset $S \subseteq \{1, ..., n\}$ of cardinality m; an auxiliary map implements a mapping that maps an m-tuple *key* to the subset of tuples in p that *matches key*. In particular, given a *key*, which is an m-tuple $\langle k_{s_1}, k_{s_2}, ..., k_{s_m} \rangle$, the auxiliary map for p on S maps *key* into a set of n-tuples V, where V is the subset of tuples in p such that, for each v in V and for each i in S $v_{s_i} = k_{s_i}$.

We introduced auxiliary maps since rules are evaluated as nested-joins [19] of the body literals appearing in them, and we would like to perform join operations efficiently. For example, assume to have the following ground atoms:

$$p(5, 2, 3), p(2, 3, 4), p(1, 3, 5), p(5, 2, 6)$$

and assume to have the following rule to evaluate:

$$h(X, Y) : -b(X, W, Z), p(W, Z, Y)$$

Then we need to perform a join operation between p and b. In particular, we might be interested in retrieving all instances of p that joins a given ground tuple of b. For this purpose we can use an auxiliary map on p where the subset S is $\{1, 2\}$, that is the set consisting of the positions (or indices) of p terms that also appear (join) in b (i.e. the positions of variables W and Z). For example, if we have a ground atom $b(3, 5, 2)$ such atom joins with $p(5, 2, 3)$ and $p(5, 2, 6)$. Indeed $\{p(5, 2, 3), p(5, 2, 6)\}$ is the subset of tuples in p that is retrieved by an auxiliary map when $key = \langle 5, 2 \rangle$. Note that auxiliary maps retrieve an empty set $\emptyset$ when a key tuple maps to no atoms.

Going back to the algorithm description, let Q_p be the set of predicates appearing in Π, we write in the output in the declaration of data structures the declaration of a predicate set ρ for every predicate p in Q_p (lines 4–7). Then, for each rule r in Π the auxiliary maps needed for the evaluation of r are detected, added to a set to avoid duplicates, and printed (lines 9–16).

In order to determine what auxiliary maps are needed, we have to fix a join order for our rules. Essentially, we follow the same order in which literals appears in rules bodies, beside that we push negative literals to the end of the rules. Negative literals are pushed at the end of the join so to be sure that all variables involved in a negative literal are bound (i.e. they have assumed a value) and we handle negative literals by performing a containment check operation on the corresponding working set. Containement checks are also done for positive literals when all variables are bound. In all other cases, we always use auxiliary maps. The auxiliary maps are always maintained up-to-date with respect to its predicate set, i.e. every time we insert a new ground atom of a given predicate p in its predicate set, we then insert the same tuple into every auxiliary map of p.

At this point, we can continue the explanation of the compilation procedure described in Algorithm 1. So far we computed SCCs and we declared data structures in terms of predicate sets and auxiliary maps. After that, the compiler prints a procedure which is able to read input facts and load predicate sets and auxiliary maps with them (line 18).

After facts reading, we are ready to print the evaluation of rules in Π. As explained above, the computation follows a topological order of the SCCS of the dependency graph of Π. For each component C in $SCCs$ we loop over the rules in the module of C (i.e. the rules whose head belongs to C) (lines 21–22). Then we print the statements performing the evaluation of each rule of a module (24), and this is done for each starter predicate of a rule. Intuitively, the join operation starts from a starter predicate whose definition is given in terms of the one of exit and recursive rule. A rule r in a component C is an exit rule if and only if all predicates that appear in the body of r belong to a component that precedes C. This means that the body predicates are already computed when the rule is processed. Otherwise r is said to be recursive (i.e. there is some body predicate in the body of r that belongs to C). The first predicate is the starter for an exit rule, whereas all recursive predicates are starters for recursive rules. Thus, the evaluation procedure of a rule iterates over all atoms in the predicate set of the starter and implements a nested join starting from it. For example, consider the rule:

$$h(X, Z) : -b1(X, Y), not\ b2(Z), b3(Z, Y)$$

and assume it is an exit rule. To evaluate it, we use the following order:

$$b1(X, Y), b3(Z, Y), not\ b2(Z)$$

Thus, the compiled program will iterate over the ground atoms in the predicate set of $b1$, and for each ground atom, performs the join with $b3$ using an auxiliary map with key $\langle Y \rangle$ and finally it checks if the tuple $\langle Z \rangle$ is contained in the predicate set of $b2$. Note that, in the above example, to make the notation more readable, we used variable names instead of their positions. If everything succeeds (i.e. the auxiliary map returns a nonempty set and $\langle Z \rangle$ is not contained in the predicate set of $b2$), we can infer the head and add it into the predicate set of h. The evaluation of recursive rules adds an external loop that continues until no new atoms of the predicates in C are generated.

Finally, the code needed to print the result is added to the output (lines 29–31).

3.2   An Example of Compilation

In this section we provide an example of compilation. Consider once more the program Π^{GR} that models the Reachability problem with an extra rule to derive all vertices that do not reach vertex 2:

```
(1) reaches(X,Y) :- edge(X,Y).
(2) reaches(X,Y) :- edge(X,Z), reaches(Z,Y).
(3) noReach(Y) :- vertex(Y), not reaches(2,Y).
```

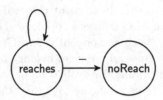

Fig. 2. Dependency graph for reachability with negation.

The dependency graph for the Reachability program is shown in Fig. 2. The example produces an acyclic graph, thus every Strongly Connected Component is composed by a single node in the graph. The dependency graph analysis basically ensures that rule (3) is evaluated after rule (1) and (2).

The core part of the compilation process applied to Π^{GR} is presented in Algorithm 2. The algorithm starts with the declaration of predicate sets: *edge,*

Algorithm 2. Reachability compiled program

1: *//Predicate Sets declarations*
2: *PredicateSet vertex*
3: *PredicateSet edge*
4: *PredicateSet reaches*
5: *PredicateSet noreaches*
6:
7: *//Auxiliary maps declarations*
8: *AuxiliaryMap edge_1*
9:
10: *...Facts reading procedure...*
11:
12: *//Evaluation of rule(1)*
13: **for all** *tuple* ∈ *edge* **do**
14:     *head* ← ⟨*tuple*[0], *tuple*[1]⟩
15:     *reaches.add(head)*
16: **end for**
17:
18: *//Evaluation of rule(2)*
19: *current_index_tuple_reaches* ← 0
20: **while** *current_index_tuple_reaches* ≠ *reaches.size()* **do**
21:     **while** *current_index_tuple_reaches* ≠ *reaches.size()* **do**
22:         *tuple* ← *reaches.at(current_index_tuple_reaches)*
23:         **for all** *X* ∈ *edge_1.at(tuple*[0]) **do**
24:             *head* ← ⟨*X*, *tuple*[1]⟩
25:             *reaches.push_back(head)*
26:         **end for**
27:         *current_index_tuple_reaches* ← *current_index_tuple_reaches* + 1
28:     **end while**
29: **end while**
30:
31: *//Evaluation of rule(3)*
32: **for all** *tuple* ∈ *vertex* **do**
33:     **if not** *reaches.contains*(⟨2, *tuple*[0]⟩) **then**
34:         *head* ← ⟨*tuple*[0]⟩
35:         *noreaches.add(head)*
36:     **end if**
37: **end for**
38:
39: *//Print model*
40: *vertex*.print()
41: *edge*.print()
42: *reaches*.print()
43: *noreaches*.print()

---

reaches, *vertex*, and *noReach*. After that, we have the declaration of auxiliary maps. In the example, one auxiliary map is needed, i.e. the map for predicate *edge* on its second term, because of the rule (2).

At line 10, we omit the facts reading procedure because of space, but it basically reads all facts and loads predicate sets and auxiliary maps accordingly. Now the evaluation starts. Remember that the evaluation follows a topological order of the input program and the order is computed at compilation time. The first rule to be evaluated is the rule (1). Thus, for each tuple in *edge* a ground atom of *reaches* is inferred and added to its predicate set.

Note that, in our procedure, $\langle t_1, t_2, \ldots, t_n \rangle$ denotes a ground atom of arity n, while $t[i]$ denotes the random access to tuple t at index i. We adopt a 0-start indexing notation.

Rule (1) is an exit rule and the evaluation follows the description provided in the previous section. Instead, rule (2) is a recursive rule. It is the only recursive rule of the example and it has a single recursive predicate (i.e. *reaches*), thus we would not need an external loop (line 20), but we reported it anyway to strictly follow the description provided in the previous section. At line 21 we iterate over all ground atoms in *reaches* and then we retrieve joining *edge* tuples from an auxiliary map whose keys are the values of the second terms of *edge* atoms. If the join succedes (i.e. the auxiliary map returns a non-empty set of joining *edge* tuples), we can derive ground atoms for *reaches*, which is in the head of rule (2). Note that we perform iteration and insertion at the same time so we had to implement predicate sets in such a way that these two operations can be performed simultaneously.

The last part of the evaluation, from line 32 to line 37, handles rule (3), which belongs to the second component of the program in the topological order given by the SCCs analysis. Rule (3) is an exit rule. This rule is evaluated by iterating over all vertices of the graph and checking whether that vertex is reachable from node 2, which is a containment check into the predicate set *reaches*.

Finally, the model of the program is given by the union of all predicate sets. Thus we output all tuples in each predicate set.

4   Experimental Analysis

To assess the potential of our tool, we performed an experimental analysis where we compared our system against existing general-purpose systems that can evaluate stratified logic programs by using bottom-up strategies, namely: *Clingo* [8], *DLV* [12] and *I-DLV* [4]. *Clingo* and *DLV* are two well-known ASP solvers, while *I-DLV* is a recently-introduced grounder. Even though the target language of such systems is *ASP* they can also be considered as rather efficient implementations for stratified logic programs.

The experimental analysis has been carried out on benchmarks from Open-RuleBench [13], which is a well-known suite for rule engines. We run all experiments on a Debian Linux server (64bit kernel), equipped with 2.30 GHz Intel Xeon E5-4610 v2 Processors and 128 GB RAM. Time and memory for each run are limited to 10 min CPU-time and 4 GB, respectively.

Results are summarized in Table 1 and in Fig. 3. In particular, Table 1 reports both the number of instances solved and the sum of the execution times for each

Table 1. Average execution times in seconds and number of solved instances grouped by solvers and domains, best performance outlined in bold face.

Benchmark	Inst.	lp2cpp		Clingo		DLV		I-DLV	
		Time	Sol.	Time	Sol.	Time	Sol.	Time	Sol.
LargeJoins	20	**319**	**18**	677	15	578	16	637	15
Recursion	20	**337**	**19**	510	18	458	19	356	19
Stratified negation	5	**72**	**5**	195	5	237	5	76	5
Totals	45	**300**	**42**	545	38	484	40	444	39

compared tool. The totals are reported in the bottom of the table, whereas the performance obtained in each class of Datalog programs from OpenRuleBench with different features is reported in a separate row. By looking at the table, we observe that our tool solves more instances than any alternative on the overall, and is the fastest on average on all benchmark sets. For completeness, we report that compilation required 2.6 s on average, considering all benchmarks, but one. The exceptional benchmark is the wine problem, which has an encoding of almost 1000 rules and takes 12 min to compile. This performance is acceptable given that compilation is intended as a one-time process in our approach. An aggregate view of the results is reported in Fig. 3 by means of a cactus plot. Cactus plots are customarily used to report the overall performance of tools in competitions. A point (x, y) belongs to a line in the plot whenever the corresponding method solved x instances in less than y seconds. Figure 3 confirms that *lp2cpp* performs well on the overall both in terms of speed and number of instances.

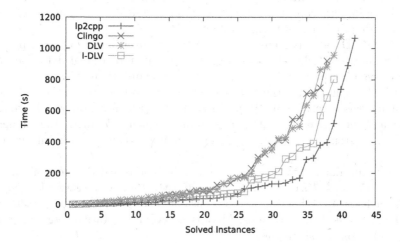

Fig. 3. Overall performance: cactus plot of the execution times.

5   Related Works

Actually, the idea of compiling declarative programs is not new and some implemented systems adopt compilation, which is also called program synthesis in the literature since an intermediate language is used before a compilation in a binary executable.

In the logic programming context, the *LDL* language is an early attempt of combining logic programming with relational databases and the evaluation implemented in the *LDL* system follows a compilation-based approach [1,5,11]. Anyway, *LDL++*, which is the successor of *LDL*, departed from the compilation-based approach.

In [14], Liu and Stoller describe a method for transforming Datalog programs into efficient specialized SETL programs. They focus on guaranteed worst-case time and space complexities and present some specific data-structures for the evaluation. Anyway, they do not come up with an available system and they also impose several restrictions on the input language, for example, they consider rules with at most two literals in the body and do not support stratified negation.

In [6] we presented a prototypical implementation of our compiler inspired to the translation of Liu and Stoller. Initial results were promising for some domains, but then we departed from the original implementation by moving to a new data structure design and we restructured and simplified the evaluation procedure. A clear difference w.r.t. the current work is evident when comparing the reachability example (see Sect. 3) with the same example presented in [6].

Soufflé [15] is a Datalog engine devoted to program analysis. It adopts a staged compilation framework for compiling Datalog programs in C++. Unlike our system, it uses intermediate representations before generating the C++ code and adopts a typed variant of Datalog for program analysis. Soufflé input language is not directly compatible with the one of OpenRuleBench and we refrained from including it in the experimental analysis.

In [16,17] Datalog is translated into SQL. Translation to SQL can produce complex queries and huge amounts of data. Current relational database management systems may struggle at handling such translations [15].

DLV^{DB}[18] integrates the facilities of logic programming with the high memory capabilities of relational DBMS. In DLV^{DB} rules are transformed into SQL queries and the evaluation follows a bottom-up schema. It allows the storage of data on persistent memory, while datalog engines typically work only in main memory.

In our experimental we compared our system against existing general-purpose systems: *Clingo* [8], *DLV* [12] and *I-DLV* [4]. Even though the target language of such systems is *ASP* they can also be considered as rather efficient implementations for stratified logic programs. All of them evaluate stratified logic programs by using bottom-up strategies.

6   Conclusions and Future Works

In this paper, we presented a new compiler for stratified Datalog programs.[2] The prototype takes as input a stratified Datalog program and generates a specialized implementation for that program. Experimental results are very encouraging. Ongoing work concerns the improvement of data structures generated by our compiler and the inclusion of other known optimization techniques used by ASP grounders [10]. As for future works, we aim at applying compilation-based techniques to the instantiation of ASP programs. Indeed the problem of instantiating ASP programs can be seen as an extension of Datalog programs evaluation.

References

1. Arni, F., Ong, K., Tsur, S., Wang, H., Zaniolo, C.: The deductive database system LDL++. TPLP **3**(1), 61–94 (2003)
2. Brewka, G., Eiter, T., Truszczynski, M.: Answer set programming at a glance. Commun. ACM **54**(12), 92–103 (2011)
3. Calì, A., Gottlob, G., Lukasiewicz, T., Pieris, A.: Datalog+/-: a family of languages for ontology querying. In: de Moor, O., Gottlob, G., Furche, T., Sellers, A. (eds.) Datalog 2.0 2010. LNCS, vol. 6702, pp. 351–368. Springer, Heidelberg (2011). doi:10.1007/978-3-642-24206-9_20
4. Calimeri, F., Fuscà, D., Perri, S., Zangari, J.: $\mathcal{I}$-DLV: the new intelligent grounder of DLV. In: Adorni, G., Cagnoni, S., Gori, M., Maratea, M. (eds.) AI*IA 2016. LNCS, vol. 10037, pp. 192–207. Springer, Cham (2016). doi:10.1007/978-3-319-49130-1_15
5. Ceri, S., Gottlob, G., Tanca, L.: Logic Programming and Databases. Springer, Heidelberg (1990). doi:10.1007/978-3-642-83952-8
6. Cuteri, B., Ricca, F.: A compiler for stratified datalog programs: preliminary results. In: 25th Italian Symposium on Advanced Database Systems, SEBD 2017, Squillace, Catanzaro, Italy, 25–29 June 2017. (2017, to appear)
7. Erdem, E., Gelfond, M., Leone, N.: Applications of answer set programming. AI Mag. **37**(3), 53–68 (2016)
8. Gebser, M., Kaminski, R., Kaufmann, B., Ostrowski, M., Schaub, T., Wanko, P.: Theory solving made easy with clingo 5. In: ICLP 2016 TCs. pp. 2:1–2:15 (2016)
9. Huang, S.S., Green, T.J., Loo, B.T.: Datalog and emerging applications: an interactive tutorial. In: Proceedings of SIGMOD 2011, pp. 1213–1216. ACM (2011)
10. Kaufmann, B., Leone, N., Perri, S., Schaub, T.: Grounding and solving in answer set programming. AI Mag. **37**(3), 25–32 (2016)
11. Kifer, M., Lozinskii, E.L.: On compile-time query optimization in deductive databases by means of static filtering. ACM TDS **15**(3), 385–426 (1990)
12. Leone, N., Pfeifer, G., Faber, W., Eiter, T., Gottlob, G., Perri, S., Scarcello, F.: The DLV system for knowledge representation and reasoning. ACM TOCL **7**(3), 499–562 (2006)
13. Liang, S., Fodor, P., Wan, H., Kifer, M.: Openrulebench: an analysis of the performance of rule engines. In: Proceedings of WWW 2009, pp. 601–610. ACM (2009)
14. Liu, Y.A., Stoller, S.D.: From datalog rules to efficient programs with time and space guarantees. ACM Trans. Program. Lang. Syst. **31**(6), 21:1–21:38 (2009)

---

[2] The tool can be downloaded from http://goo.gl/XhZXWh.

15. Scholz, B., Jordan, H., Subotić, P., Westmann, T.: On fast large-scale program analysis in datalog. In: Proceedings of the 25th International Conference on Compiler Construction, pp. 196–206. ACM (2016)

16. Scholz, B., Vorobyov, K., Krishnan, P., Westmann, T.: A datalog source-to-source translator for static program analysis: an experience report. In: 2015 24th Australasian Software Engineering Conference (ASWEC), pp. 28–37. IEEE (2015)

17. Sereni, D., Avgustinov, P., de Moor, O.: Adding magic to an optimising datalog compiler. In: Proceedings of the 2008 ACM SIGMOD International Conference on Management of Data, pp. 553–566. ACM (2008)

18. Terracina, G., Leone, N., Lio, V., Panetta, C.: Experimenting with recursive queries in database and logic programming systems. Theory Pract. Logic Program. 8(2), 129–165 (2008)

19. Ullman, J.D.: Principles of Database and Knowledge-Base Systems. Computer Science Press, New York (1988)

Knowledge Engineering, Ontologies and the Semantic Web

Business Processes and Their Participants: An Ontological Perspective

Greta Adamo[1,3(✉)], Stefano Borgo[2], Chiara Di Francescomarino[1], Chiara Ghidini[1], Nicola Guarino[2], and Emilio M. Sanfilippo[2]

[1] FBK-IRST, Via Sommarive 18, 38050 Trento, Italy
{adamo,dfmchiara,ghidini}@fbk.eu
[2] ISTC-CNR Laboratory for Applied Ontology, Trento, Italy
{stefano.borgo,nicola.guarino}@cnr.it, sanfilippo@loa.istc.cnr.it
[3] DIBRIS, University of Genova, via Dodecaneso 35, 16146 Genoa, Italy

Abstract. Business process modelling (BPM) notations, such as BPMN, UML-Activity Diagram (UML-AD), EPC and CMMN describe processes using a graphical representation of process-relevant entities and their interplay. Despite the wide literature on the comparison between different modelling languages, the BPM community still lacks an ontological characterisation of process elements, among which process participants, that is, the main entities involved in a business process. Purpose of this paper is to start filling this gap by providing an ontological analysis of business processes from the standpoint of process participants. In particular, by discussing participants common to languages such as BPMN, EPC, UML-AD, and CMMN we characterize them on the basis of their ontological properties.

1 Introduction

Business process modelling (BPM) notations describe processes using a graphical representation of process-relevant entities and their interplay. Examples include well known imperative languages such as BPMN, UML-Activity Diagram (UML-AD) and EPC together with declarative notations such as CMMN[1]. Despite the wide literature on both the investigation of execution semantics and the comparison between the graphical elements of different languages [9,11,13,22], the BPM community still lacks an ontological characterisation of process elements. While some efforts have been devoted to an ontological characterisation of specific modelling languages (see e.g., [18] for an investigation of the ontological commitments of activities and events in BPMN), this characterisation concerns only the behavioural component and neglects important structural entities which can

---

[1] Traditional process modelling notations rely on an imperative paradigm which aims at producing models that describe all allowed flows: every flow that is not specified in the model is implicitly disallowed. Recent declarative process modelling notations instead allow the production of more flexible models obtained by describing constraints on the allowed activity flows: all flows are allowed provided that they do not violate the specified constraints.

© Springer International Publishing AG 2017
F. Esposito et al. (Eds.): AI*IA 2017, LNAI 10640, pp. 215–228, 2017.
https://doi.org/10.1007/978-3-319-70169-1_16

be modelled using the languages above, that is, process participants. As a result, process participants, such as actors or (data) objects, are exposed to a dichotomy: on the one hand they are among the main entities in a business process (diagram) and a fundamental component of an informative process model; on the other hand they are emblematically neglected when explaining or illustrating the very notion of process. In fact, for instance, what is the identity of a data object, i.e., whether different actors deal with the same or different data objects, or what is the status of a data object throughout the process execution, remain unclear.

The purpose of the paper is to provide an analysis of business processes from the standpoint of process participants. We first provide an illustration of different constructs used by imperative and declarative modelling notations (Sect. 2), and identify the ones that refer to process participants (Sect. 3). Then, by discussing the process participants common to the different notations, we dig into their ontological properties (Sect. 4). The analysis, and the subsequent characterisation of process participants within the different languages, provided in Sect. 5, is a first step toward the illustration of how an ontological analysis enlarged to process participants can support the interpretation of business process diagrams, the comparison between modelling notations, and the illustration of the different perspectives that BPM languages implicitly take on business processes.

2   Background

We briefly illustrate here the business process modelling languages taken into account throughout the paper. In order to aim for a general analysis and avoid possible biases due to the imperative/declarative nature of the modelling paradigms, we have selected three among the most popular languages that follow the imperative paradigm (BPMN, UML-AD, and EPC) and a notation that follows the declarative approach (CMMN). To support our brief description we make use of process diagrams illustrating a self explanatory scenario of a customer buying a flight ticket from a travel agency. Besides illustrating the scenario, the diagrams are "annotated" with speech balloons indicating the type of entity denoted by the graphical constructs.

BPMN. The BPMN[2] (Business Processing Modeling Notation) is a standard language, proposed by the Object Management Group (OMG) to design business processes. BPMN defines a Business Process Diagram (BPD) which includes a set of graphical elements divided in: (i) flow objects; (ii) data; (iii) connecting objects; (iv) swimlanes and (v) artefacts. The flow objects define the behaviour of a business process, as the one reported in Fig. 1. They are divided in *events*, *activities* and *gateways*. Events represent something that "happens" during the process and are divided in *start*, *intermediate* and *end* events. An activity is a generic term of work to be performed. An activity can be atomic (*task*) or compound (*sub-process*). A gateway determines the forking, merging and joining of

---

[2] http://www.omg.org/spec/BPMN/2.0/.

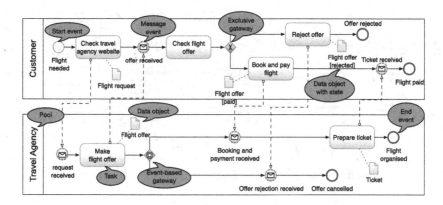

Fig. 1. A business process diagram in the BPMN language.

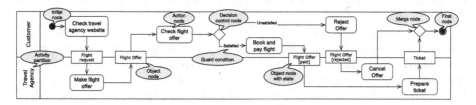

Fig. 2. A business process diagram in the UML AD language.

paths. In BPMN 2.0 information is represented through data, which include: *data objects*, *data inputs*, *data output* and *data stores*. The various flow objects are linked to each other through *connecting objects* which are not further discussed here. *Swimlanes* represent organisation units through pools and lanes, and they are usually used to answer the "who" question. BPMN provides further elements, called *artefacts*, to describe the context (or information) of the process. Artefacts are divided into groups and text annotations. Groups are useful to graphically cluster elements belonging to the same category; text annotations are used to specify additional textual information that can be valuable to the user of the diagram.

UML-ADs. UML Activity Diagrams[3] (ADs) are one of the diagram families of the OMG standardised language UML. Purpose of the activity diagrams, such as the one depicted in Fig. 2, is to describe the control and the data flow as a sequence of activity nodes connected by activity edges.

In detail, two main types of activity nodes are responsible of describing the control flow, i.e., the *action nodes* and the *control nodes*. While the former represent atomic steps within an activity, the latter allow for controlling the execution flow by means of the typical AND, OR and XOR logical operations. Two additional control flow nodes are used to depict the initial and final nodes. The

---

[3] http://www.omg.org/spec/UML/.

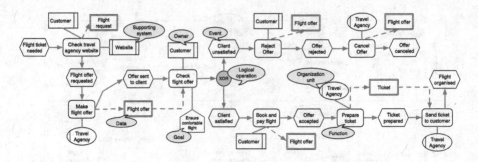

Fig. 3. A business process diagram in the EPC language.

intuitive semantics of AD can be explained in terms of *control flow tokens* flowing through the activity diagram, starting from the initial node and ending in the final node.

As for the data flow description, object nodes and object flows are, instead, the main ADs elements. Indeed, the object nodes represent objects at a given point of the flow and, as such, they can also have an associated *state*. Object flows are instead used for connecting the object nodes to the actions. In order to also capture the object flow semantics, besides the control flow tokens, object tokens are also introduced. They are similar to control flow tokens but also carry a reference to an object.

Furthermore, ADs provide a mechanism for grouping together activity nodes which have characteristics in common (*activity partitions*) mainly used as a means for defining organisational units. Finally, the notation allows for specifying activity pre- and post-conditions, for instance annotating activity edges with guards.

EPCs. Event-driven process chains (EPCs) are a workflow modelling language developed in the early 1990s as part of the Architecture of Integrated Information Systems (ARIS) framework [19].

In detail, three types of nodes are responsible of describing the control flow: the *function nodes*, the *event nodes* and the *logical operators nodes*[4] (see Fig. 3). While function nodes represent atomic activities and can thus be considered the active part of a control flow, event nodes represent the states in which the process happens to be, and can therefore be considered the passive part of the control flow. Functions and event alternate, capturing the intuition that states lead to activities (in a sort of pre-condition fashion), and activities generate states (in a sort of port-condition fashion). Finally, the XOR, AND and OR logical operators allow for controlling the execution flow.

Functions within the control flow can be connected to objects belonging to the other views of an ARIS model, namely the organisational, data, function

---

[4] The list of symbols of EPCs can vary, depending on the specific system implementation. The analysis and diagrams contained in this paper refer to the description provided in [20].

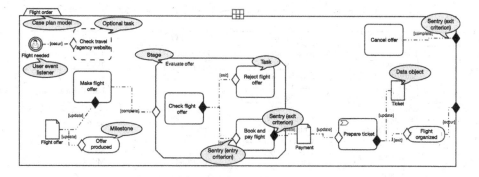

Fig. 4. A business process diagram in the CMMN language.

and product service views. While the number of objects differs from version to version, the core elements usually comprise: (i) input and output *data, material, services or resource objects* required or produced by a function; (ii) *owners* who are responsible for a specific function; (iii) *organisation units* (e.g., a department) responsible for a specific function; and (iv) *supporting systems* (e.g., a database) upon which the function acts. Depending on the version of the language, *goals*, denoted by house shaped pentagons, can be also connected to specific functions.

CMMN. The Case Management Model And Notation[5] (CMMN) language is a OMG standard notation for the declarative representation of process models. The main entity of CMMN is the *case*, which is described by a case diagram.

Differently from the previous languages, CMMN aims at capturing variable and flexible cases, following a declarative approach (see Fig. 4). Thus, rather than describing all the allowed flows of a process from start to end, it models cases as composed of process segments (*stages*) and *tasks*.

A case plan model, which is the component of CMMN devoted to the specification of the behaviour, contains: (possibly discretionary) *tasks, stages, milestones, event listeners, connectors*, and *sentries*. A task is a unit of work. Stages are plan fragments which can be composite or atomic. A milestone represents an accomplishment which occurs during the process of a case. Events can be related to: a case file (created, deleted, modified, and so on); tasks, stages and milestones (started, cancelled, finished, and so on); event listeners (timer and user event listener). Connectors are used to link different plan items. Finally sentries represent the entry and exit criteria for path items and can be used to direct the control flow using the AND and OR logical operators.

3   A Brief Comparison of Business Process Languages

We present here a short categorisation and comparative summary of the main elements of BPMN, UML-AD, EPC and CMMN. Modelling elements are grouped

---

[5] http://www.omg.org/spec/CMMN/1.1/.

Table 1. A comparison among modelling languages

		BPMN	UML-AD	EPC	CMMN
BEV	Func	Task Subprocess	Action node Activity	Function Process path	Task Stage
	Event	Start/End Intermediate Send/receive	Start/End node Accept event action Send signal action	–	Timer User Event Listener
	Flow	Gateway Sequence Flow Message Flow	Control node Control Flow Object Flow	Logical operators Control Flow Info Flow	Connector Sentry
	State	Guard on gateway	Guard on control node Pre- Post-condition on activity	Event Start/End event	Sentry Milestone
DT		Data input, data output, data store	Object node	Taxonomy of (I/O) data object	Case file item
ORG		Pool, Lane	Activity Partition	Organization Activity Owner	–

into the three basic categories of process modelling languages, namely the *behavioural* (BEV) category related to the control flow, the *data* (DT) category related to the data flow, and the *organisational* (ORG) category related to the "who question". Being the behavioural section the most articulated, we further describe it in terms of *Functional* (the executable pro-active actions), *Event* (what happens), *Flow* (how elements are connected and routed), and *State* (of the world) categories. The result of this grouping is summarised in Table 1.

First, we can observe that all the imperative languages, namely BPMN, EPC, and UML-AD, provide distinctive elements to indicate the start and the end of a process. CMMN, instead, is focused on the representation of flexible workflows and therefore does not force a specific start and a specific end, but only exiting conditions. Not surprisingly all four languages have graphical symbols for atomic activities. Similarly, subprocesses and generic groups of activities are foreseen in all languages but EPCs. Other common elements are routing nodes, connectors, and data objects. Routing nodes route the control flow using the typical XOR, OR and AND logical constructors. While CMMN does not have explicit graphical symbols for gateways, its specification indicates how to use sentries and connectors to represent them. Connectors are instead typically used to connect the various graphical elements indicating the flow of the process. BPMN and EPCs augment connectors with special symbols to denote connections different from the control flow, namely, the connection between actors (data) and an activity, or the messages exchanged between different activities. Also, the granularity and level of detail of data objects can vary, with EPCs particularly rich in defining a taxonomy of data objects to be used while modelling. Alternative (OR, XOR) routing nodes can incorporate guards, that is conditions that specify which branch to follow, in all the languages but EPCs (where this role can be taken by states). "Actors" and organisational entities who "own"/"perform" parts of a process are another rather common element, only absent in CMMN case plan model.[6]

---

[6] CMMN allows to associate organisational entities to cases during the run-time phase.

4   Process Participants: An Ontological Analysis

Roughly speaking, the agreement across the literature [13] about what a business process is boils down to this: given a goal, a process is a set of actions that, together, contribute to achieving that goal. Although in the literature one finds that the type and the token levels are often mixed,[7] the previous definition is about process types: the goal is a description of a desired state, e.g., that a certain product is assembled or an ordered item is shipped, whereas the actions are event types like sending a message or identifying a customer. The way actions contribute to the achievement of the goal is not commonly made explicit in notations like those considered in the previous sections,[8] but there is an implicit assumption that the process clarifies at least the sequence of actions to be performed, or the possible alternative sequences. The interpretation of the precedence relation in the sequence is however left open, and one can read it in terms of temporal, causal or dependence constraints, perhaps depending on context.

The above generality is common in application domains where large communities have to agree on a common language that mediates among different perspectives and interests. One consequence is that it is unclear what the identity and unity conditions for a process are, that is, when two process definitions actually define the same process, or when an action should be seen as part of a process. Although here we concentrate on process modelling, these problems are pretty general and affect also process mining tasks: in absence of unity and identity principles, it is hard to decide which actions should be registered in a single process log.

The strategy we propose to ground the unity and identity of business processes relies on their *participants*. The intuition is that if two processes have different participants, they are different processes. Also, we assume that if two actions have some participants in common, then—under suitable constraints—they may belong to the same process.

Consider, for example, a process type *pty* composed of two different actions act_1 and act_2 such that act_1 precedes act_2. Let us say that act_1 is *create form* and act_2 is *send form*. Even ignoring whether act_1 and act_2 belong to the same process type, or whether there is a precedence constraint between them, we may reconstruct this information by knowing that the two actions involve the same form, and that no form can be sent before it was created. Generalising from the example, the changes of (or in) a process participant may provide information to identify processes, establish the correct relations between actions and decide when different actions are part of the same process.

---

[7] 'Token' is hereby synonym of a process *occurrence* (an instance of a process type). While a process token occurs at a specific time, a process type is an abstract entity with no specific temporal location (see the distinction between **Activity** (type) and **ActivityOccurrence** (token) in the *Process Specification Language* (PSL) [7]).

[8] As a matter of fact, a language like BPMN does not force modellers to explicitly represent what changes in the (local) world are expected after an activity is performed.

To investigate business processes from this viewpoint, we firstly need to clarify what is an action and what are its participants. Recall that in the BPM literature actions (at the token level) refer to intentional transformations from some initial state (of the local world at stake) to some other state. Their participants are the entities that take part in the transformations. In the terminology of [2], action tokens are *events*,[9] while their participants are *objects*. As we shall see, the very same action may involve several types of objects as participants: physical objects (e.g., a knife used to cut a piece of bread); information objects (e.g., personal data involved in submitting a request); agents and/or organisations playing certain roles (e.g., an administrative employee receiving a form). Turning back to the four modelling languages described in Sects. 2 and 3, examples of participants are the entities denoted by means of the constructs classified under the data (DT) and the organisational (ORG) categories in Table 1.

From a general perspective, participants can be physical or non-physical: both exist in time, but only the former are located in the physical space. A person is an example of physical participant, whereas an *information object* such as the content of a person's ID (not its physical support) is a non-physical participant.

Information objects (a.k.a. *data objects*) are rather common in business processes and, as seen in the previous sections, modelling notations include different constructs for them. In applied ontology, only a few systems [1,12,14,21] have attempted a formal treatment of information objects. These ontologies agree in distinguishing between information objects and their physical carriers like paper sheets or computer files; also, the same information object may be encoded in multiple carriers while retaining its identity. For example, John's and Mary's copies of the *Divine Comedy* are two different carriers of the same information object. Generalising, we consider an information participant as a non-physical participant that is somehow 'manipulated' during a process. Additionally, we consider information participants as *dependent* entities that, in order to participate in a process, have to be encoded in at least one carrier. Note also that all the actions performed within a particular process occurrences are ultimately physical actions involving physical participants, so that information objects are actually *indirect* participants, which participate to the process by means of *information-bearing objects* containing their physical encodings.

Regarding physical participants, we may distinguish between material and immaterial entities. Material participants do have some physical body (e.g., a human body or a metallic frame), differently from immaterial objects like holes, which in some cases may still be considered as participants (e.g., in a process including a pin to be inserted in a hole). Holes belong to the broader class of *features*, which are dependent entities like information objects.

Another crucial distinction in BPM is between *agentive* and *non-agentive* participants. The former are indirectly represented in BPMN, whose pools and lanes refer to participants that are committed to and are responsible for the execution of the depicted process. Notoriously, the definition of agency is largely debated in AI. For our purposes, we take the view that an agent is an entity with

---

[9] 'Event' is the most general term used in [2] for entities occurring in time.

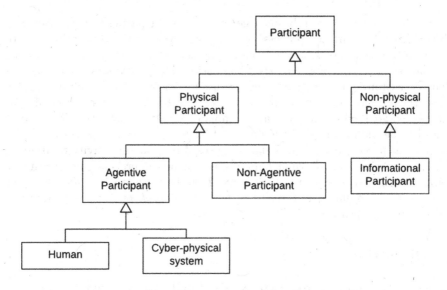

Fig. 5. Taxonomy of participants

sensors, actuators and the capability to act on itself or on the environment [17]. Human beings and organisations, such as those denoted with 'customer' and 'travel agency' in Fig. 2, are clearly agents. In a manufacturing domain, a lathe machine is an agent when, e.g., it has sensors by which it acquires data from the objects to be manufactured and acts upon them by elaborating these data through some software. So, in general, a cyber-physical system is an agent, while a traditional mechanical late is not an agent.

A minimal UML taxonomy of process participants based on some of the distinctions discussed so far is reported in Fig. 5. Notice that the agentive/non-agentive dichotomy only applies to physical participants, since we assume that non-physical lack the capability of interacting with the environment. Note also that some of the distinctions discussed above are orthogonal to those shown in the figure, so that they have not been reported explicitly. In particular, we assume that all agentive participants are material, while non-agentive participants may be either material or immaterial. Moreover, all physical participants may (or may not) be information-bearers.

Apart from the classification above, all participants can play *roles*. Non-agentive participants may be distinguished according to whether they undergo a change during an action. If so, they are called the *patients* of the action; otherwise, they may play the role of *instruments* or *resources*.

From an ontological perspective, roles correspond to properties that objects only contingently satisfy within the process context, like being used as a resource during a drilling process. In this sense, one object can loose or acquire a role while remaining the same entity. We assume that roles can be ascribed to any type of participant represented in Fig. 5, including information objects.

Finally, note that we rely on a general notion of participant covering any object that takes part in a process. One may however restrict this notion only to "relevant" objects. For instance, considering the flight purchase process of the previous sections, one may not want to consider as participants the computers that the customer and the travel agency use to perform their activities. In this sense, the relevant participants of a process are those that are directly related to the desired goal, which are typically common to multiple activities. This seems indeed to be the idea behind the notion of *business artifacts* [3], which may be intended as process participants that are passed by from an activity to another, somehow keeping track of what happens as long as the process goes on. In this spirit, the flight offer shown in Figs. 1 and 2 can be understood as a data object that can undergo different states (e.g., *requested, payed, rejected*) depending on how the process evolves.

5   Discussion

In this section, starting from the analysis of participants previously presented and looking at the diagrams in Figs. 1, 2, 3 and 4, we provide some insights on the modelling notations and the perspectives they take on the processes, focusing on the data and organisational constructs of Table 1.

The participants relevant in the flight purchase example are the customer, the travel agency and different information objects. The process thus includes different types of participants, material and immaterial ones.

By looking at the diagrams, we observe that no actors appear in CMMN and neither BPMN nor UML-AD specify whether 'customer' explicitly refers to a single individual (e.g., John) or to an organisation. In both cases, this individual is playing the *role* of a participant, who desires to book a flight ticket. This consideration reveals, besides the fact that CMMN lacks graphical constructs for specifying actors, the underspecification of both BPMN and UML-AD with respect to our analysis, since pools and activity partitions can't distinguish between different types of participants, nor between the participants themselves and the roles they play. Differently, the distinction between single actors and organisations can be explicitly conveyed in EPC, although the difference between participants and their roles is blurred.

In Figs. 1, 2 and 3, *Check travel agency website* results in a *Flight request* which is sent to the agency. On the basis of our analysis, such request is an *information-bearing object*, since what the customer sends to the agency is a (copy of a) physical object encoding an information object. The distinction between information objects and their physical support is not explicitly addressed by the languages we considered. On the one hand, it seems clear that when different agents share a data object, a certain file (support) is exchanged. On the other hand, it is implicitly assumed that the file displays some information.

According to the diagrams, when an instance of *Make flight offer* is accomplished, the new information object *Flight offer* is generated and sent to the customer. We may wonder whether the customer and the agency handle the same flight offer. None of the graphical notations provide a means to address this issue.

When the flight offer is received by the customer, she checks the offer and decides either to reject, or to accept it and hence to proceed with the booking of the flight. This means that the offer—under the control of the customer—undergoes some update along with the execution of the tasks; e.g., it acquires new properties, namely, that of *having been accepted* or *rejected*. As we can see from the diagrams, indeed, the *Reject offer* and *Book and pay flight* tasks create further information objects, which can be understood as updates of the offer. At the same time, however, the flight offer handled by the agency remains "frozen", since it is updated with the customer's information only when the customer shares it with the agency. More precisely, during the time interval from the *Check flight order* to either *Reject offer* or *Book and pay flight*, the customer's offer and the agency's offer share some part in common but the former has more information than the latter. Once either the event *Booking and payment received* or *Offer rejection received* happens, the two information objects are again the same.The agency indeed receives the customer's order and updates its information with the customer's information.

Here we observe that BPMN (and in part UML-AD) offers the possibility to model the status of the data objects, e.g., the *Flight offer* being *paid* or *refused*. On the contrary, in EPC and CMMN this cannot be explicitly modelled, although it can be inferred by looking at the changes of the world. From a more general perspective, BPMN and EPC separate the data from the control flow (they have explicit different graphical notations for the two flows). Differently, in UML-AD and CMMN, data objects are represented in a unique flow with activities and control flow elements, so that the process execution cannot proceed unless the data object is processed/available. In this sense, data object participants play a fundamental role within the overall process, and it becomes necessary to properly identify which data objects the process manipulates.

To conclude, the analysis of participants needs to be extended to shed some light on the ontological characterisation of activity sequences, as well as to identify the different modelling approaches in the languages at hand. Once we recognise the changes that participants undergo in the context of a process, indeed, we can better understand how activities are related (e.g., via precedence constraints) in order for those changes to take place. This latter topic however deserves more attention and is left for future work.

6   Related Work

A number of works in the literature focused on the analysis and comparison of process languages and notations [11,22], as well as on the definition of a shared reference metamodel [9,13] for process description at an informal level. Several works at the intersection between knowledge engineering and business process modelling (e.g., [10,23]) focus on formal techniques aimed at verifying the consistency of process models, as well as their smooth execution.

Focussing on *ontology-based* business process modelling, which is the context of our paper, disparate ontologies have been proposed to semantically enrich process models. Among these, some ontologies axiomatise the properties that graphical elements satisfy according to modelling notations. In [16], for example, the authors present an OWL-based representation of BPMN that is used for reasoning on the consistency of the process models [5] and for the management of exceptional flows [6]. In a more general setting, De Nicola and colleagues [4] propose an upper-level ontology for business processes. In both these works, however, the authors do not attempt a clarification of the modelling notations on the basis of some reference ontology.Some initial works towards the analysis of BPMN based on foundational ontologies are presented in [8,15,18]. These however focus only on some modelling elements, i.e., activities and events, while leaving aside the analysis of participants, which is the focus of the presented work.

7   Conclusions and Future Work

In this work we focused on an ontology-based analysis of the properties characterising the process participants common to the main process modelling languages and notations. In the future we plan to extend such a preliminary analysis in order to deepen the investigation on the ontological commitments of process participants by further inspecting the different perspectives that BPM languages implicitly take on business processes, as well as providing modellers with guidelines to make an appropriate choice when selecting among different notations.

By observing Figs. 1, 2, 3 and 4 and Table 1, we can notice that differences exist also on the behavioural component. As an example, a key difference among the languages we considered concerns the representation of the (state of the) world in response to a process execution. Figure 3 emphasises this as one of the focuses of EPCs. UML-AD and CMMN lie in the middle by exploiting data objects and sentries for describing how the world is changed because of the process execution. For instance, in Fig. 4 the *Flight Offer* is the postcondition of the *Make flight offer*. BPMN, instead, only provides (optional) constructs for representing the state of data objects. From an ontological perspective, we would say that, differently from BPMN, EPC drives the modeller to explicitly represent the world's states affected by the designed process, while UML-AD and CMMN guide the modeller to implicitly represent the world's states through data objects and sentries. A further example concerns the relation between activities, and more in general the way the activities contribute to the achievement of the goal. For instance, assume that in a slight variation of the example of Sect. 2, the travel agency splits the activity *Make flight offer* in two subsequent steps *Send flight offer to customer* and *Archive offer* which, for purely organisational reasons, must be executed in this order. This would be a pure temporal relation between the activities in this specific setting. Instead the activity of *Paying for a flight* causes the *Preparation of the ticket*. Nonetheless these relations would be denoted by means of the same connector symbol. From an ontological perspective, we would say that all the languages we considered here do not guide the modeller to represent different types of precedence relations. Recognising the changes that participants undergo in the context of a process, and connecting them to the way activities are related, is another topic that deserves specific attention and is left for future work.

Acknowledgments. This research has been partially carried out within the Euregio IPN12 KAOS, which is funded by the "European Region Tyrol-South Tyrol-Trentino" (EGTC) under the first call for basic research projects.

References

1. Bekiari, C., Doerr, M., Le Boeuf, P., Riva, P.: FRBR object-oriented definition and mapping from FRBRER, FRAD and FRSAD (version 2.4). International Working Group on FRBR and CIDOC CRM Harmonisation (2015)

2. Borgo, S., Masolo, C.: Foundational choices in DOLCE. In: Staab, S., Studer, R. (eds.) Handbook on Ontologies. IHIS, pp. 361–381. Springer, Heidelberg (2009). doi:10.1007/978-3-540-92673-3_16

3. Cohn, D., Hull, R.: Business artifacts: a data-centric approach to modeling business operations and processes. IEEE Data Eng. Bull. **32**(3), 3–9 (2009)

4. De Nicola, A., Lezoche, M., Missikoff, M.: An ontological approach to business process modeling. In: 2007 3th Indian International Conference on Artificial Intelligence (2007). ISBN 978-0-9727412-2-4

5. Di Francescomarino, C., Ghidini, C., Rospocher, M., Serafini, L., Tonella, P.: Semantically-aided business process modeling. In: Bernstein, A., Karger, D.R., Heath, T., Feigenbaum, L., Maynard, D., Motta, E., Thirunarayan, K. (eds.) ISWC 2009. LNCS, vol. 5823, pp. 114–129. Springer, Heidelberg (2009). doi:10.1007/978-3-642-04930-9_8

6. Ghidini, C., Di Francescomarino, C., Rospocher, M., Tonella, P., Serafini, L.: Semantics-based aspect-oriented management of exceptional flows in business processes. IEEE Trans. Syst. Man Cyber. Part **42**(1), 25–37 (2012)

7. Grüninger, M.: Using the PSL ontology. In: Staab, S., Studer, R. (eds.) Handbook on Ontologies. IHIS, pp. 423–443. Springer, Heidelberg (2009). doi:10.1007/978-3-540-92673-3_19

8. Guizzardi, G., Wagner, G.: Can BPMN be used for making simulation models? In: Barjis, J., Eldabi, T., Gupta, A. (eds.) EOMAS 2011. LNBIP, vol. 88, pp. 100–115. Springer, Heidelberg (2011). doi:10.1007/978-3-642-24175-8_8

9. Heidari, F., Loucopoulos, P., Brazier, F.M.T., Barjis, J.: A meta-meta-model for seven business process modeling languages. In: IEEE 15th Conference on Business Informatics, CBI 2013, pp. 216–221. IEEE Computer Society (2013)

10. Lam, V.S.W.: Formal analysis of BPMN models: a NUSMV-based approach. Int. J. Softw. Eng. Knowl. Eng. **20**(7), 987–1023 (2010)

11. List, B., Korherr, B.: An evaluation of conceptual business process modelling languages. In: Proceedings of the 2006 ACM Symposium on Applied Computing, pp. 1532–1539. SAC 2006. ACM, New York (2006)

12. Masolo, C., Vieu, L., Bottazzi, E., Catenacci, C., Ferrario, R., Gangemi, A., Guarino, N.: Social roles and their descriptions. In: Dubois, D., Welty, C., Williams, M. (eds.) Principles of Knowledge Representation and Reasoning, pp. 267–277. AAAI Press, Palo Alto (2004)

13. Mili, H., Tremblay, G., Jaoude, G.B., Lefebvre, E., Elabed, L., Boussaidi, G.E.: Business process modeling languages: sorting through the alphabet soup. ACM Comput. Surv. **43**(1), 4:1–4:56 (2010)

14. Mizoguchi, R.: Yamato: yet another more advanced top-level ontology. In: Proceedings of the Sixth Australasian Ontology Workshop, pp. 1–16 (2010)

15. Recker, J., Indulska, M., Rosemann, M., Green, P.: Do process modelling techniques get better? A comparative ontological analysis of BPMN. Australasian Chapter of the Association for Information Systems (2005)

16. Rospocher, M.; Ghidini, C., Serafini, L.: An ontology for the business process modelling notation. In: Garbacz, P., Kutz, O. (eds.) Proceedings of the 8th International Conference on Formal Ontology in Information Systems (FOIS 2014). Frontiers in Artificial Intelligence and Applications, vol. 267, pp. 133–146. IOS Press, Amsterdam (2014)

17. Russell, S., Norvig, P.: Intelligence Artificial: A Modern Approach. Prentice-Hall, Egnlewood Cliffs (1995)

18. Sanfilippo, E.M., Borgo, S., Masolo, C.: Events and activities: is there an ontology behind BPMN?. In: Garbacz, P., Kutz, O. (eds.) Proceedings of the 8th International Conference on Formal Ontology in Information Systems (FOIS 2014). Frontiers in Artificial Intelligence and Applications, vol. 267, pp. 147–156. IOS Press, Amsterdam (2014)

19. Scheer, A.: ARIS - vom Geschaftsprozess zum Anwendungssystem. Springer, Berlin (2002). (4, durchges. aufl. edn.)

20. Scheer, A.W., Thomas, O., Adam, O.: Process modeling using event-driven process chains. In: Dumas, M., van der Aalst, W.M.P., ter Hofstede, A.H.M (eds.) Process-Aware Information Systems: Bridging People and Software Through Process Technology, pp. 119–146. Wiley, October 2005

21. Smith, B., Ceusters, W.: Aboutness: towards foundations for the information artifact ontology. In: Proceedings of the International Conference on Biomedical Ontology (ICBO) 2015 (2015)

22. Söderström, E., Andersson, B., Johannesson, P., Perjons, E., Wangler, B.: Towards a framework for comparing process modelling languages. In: Pidduck, A.B., Ozsu, M.T., Mylopoulos, J., Woo, C.C. (eds.) CAiSE 2002. LNCS, vol. 2348, pp. 600–611. Springer, Heidelberg (2002). doi:10.1007/3-540-47961-9_41

23. Wong, P., Gibbons, J.: Formalisations and applications of BPMN. Sci. Comput. Program. **76**(8), 633–650 (2011)

Feeding a Hybrid Recommendation Framework with Linked Open Data and Graph-Based Features

Cataldo Musto$^{(\boxtimes)}$, Pasquale Lops, Marco de Gemmis, and Giovanni Semeraro

Department of Computer Science, University of Bari Aldo Moro, Bari, Italy
{cataldo.musto,pasquale.lops,marco.degemmis,giovanni.semeraro}@uniba.it

Abstract. In this article we propose a *hybrid recommendation framework* based on classification algorithms such as Random Forests and Naive Bayes, which are fed with several heterogeneous groups of features. We split our features into two classes: *classic features*, as popularity-based, collaborative and content-based ones, and *extended features* gathered from the LOD cloud, as basic ones (i.e. *genre* of a movie or the *writer* of a book) and graph-based features calculated on the ground of the different topological characteristics of the *tripartite* representation connecting users, items and properties in the LOD cloud.

In the experimental session we evaluate the effectiveness of our framework on varying of different groups of features, and results show that both LOD-based and graph-based features positively affect the overall performance of the algorithm, especially in *highly sparse* recommendation scenarios. Our approach also outperforms several state-of-the-art recommendation techniques, thus confirming the insights behind this research.

Keywords: Recommender systems · Machine learning · Linked open data

1 Introduction

According to recent statistics[1], 150 billions of RDF triples and almost 10,000 linked datasets are now available in the so-called LOD cloud: such RDF triples interconnect in a semantics-aware fashion the information covering many topical domains, such as geographical locations, people, books, films, music, and so on. The *nucleus* of such data is commonly represented by DBpedia [1], the RDF mapping of Wikipedia. This huge availability of semantics-aware machine-readable data attracted researchers and practitioners in the area of Content-based Recommender Systems (RS) [5], willing to investigate how such information can be exploited to improve the effectiveness of existing algorithms or to tackle several problems RSs typically suffer from.

In this article we investigate the impact of such *exogenous knowledge* on the performance of a *hybrid* recommendation framework based on classification

---

[1] http://stats.lod2.eu/.

© Springer International Publishing AG 2017
F. Esposito et al. (Eds.): AI*IA 2017, LNAI 10640, pp. 229–242, 2017.
https://doi.org/10.1007/978-3-319-70169-1_17

techniques as Random Forests and Naive Bayes. In this work we followed the hybridization strategy which is typically referred to as *feature combination* [2], that is to say, we represented the items by means of different heterogeneous groups of features and we used this unique representation to feed the classifiers with training examples. Such a model is then exploited to classify new and unseen items as *relevant* or not relevant for the *target user*.

The features we used are roughly classified in two groups: *classic features* and *extended* ones. The features that are typically used in hybrid item representations, as unstructured *content-based* features, *collaborative* features and simple *popularity-based* ones, fall in the first group. Next, we extended the representation by introducing data points gathered from the LOD cloud, as *basic* structured features (as the *genre* of a movie or the *writer* of a book) and *graph-based features*, calculated by mining the different topological characteristics of the *tripartite* graph-based representation that connects users, items and properties in the LOD cloud.

In the experimental session we evaluated the effectiveness of our framework on varying of these sets of features, and results provided several interesting insights, since it emerged that the overall accuracy significantly benefits from the introduction of LOD-based and graph-based features. Moreover, the results we obtained also overcame several state-of-the-art recommendation techniques.

To sum up, the contributions of the paper follow:

- We developed a hybrid recommendation framework based on classification techniques, and we designed several sets of features to feed the framework;
- We investigated to what extent the injection of the knowledge coming from the LOD cloud influences the performance of the recommendation framework;
- We identified the subsets of features that maximize the performance of the algorithm for each experimental setting.

The rest of the paper is organized as follows: Sect. 2 analyzes related literature. The description of the different features we adopted in our recommendation framework is provided in Sect. 3, while the details of the experimental evaluation we carried out are described in Sect. 4. Finally, Sect. 5 sketches conclusions and future work.

2   Related Work

The idea of *casting* the recommendation task to a classification one dates back to the late 90s, when Pazzani et al. [16] proposed a news recommender system that adopted a Naive Bayes classifier to learn user profiles. Next, the use of such techniques has been largely investigated, especially for content-based recommendation algorithms [6]. In this case several work gave evidence of the good performance of classification algorithms in a wide set of domains, as movies [8] and artwork suggestion [7,17].

The use of features directly extracted from the LOD cloud is one of the distinguishing aspects of this work, since in most of the current literature, properties gathered from `DBpedia` are only exploited to define semantics-aware similarity measures [14]. However, differently from these work we used these features to feed a comprehensive model of user interests. Next, several work tried to assess about the effectiveness of LOD-based features on the overall accuracy of a recommender system, as Musto et al. [9]. These work confirmed that LOD can significantly improve the performance of RSs. Recently, some work [10,11] also investigated the problem of automatically selecting the best subset of LOD-based features to feed a recommendation algorithms. In this case, results showed that feature selection can be helpful to select the most promising properties and can lead to further improvement of the accuracy of the recommendations.

Finally, the predictive power of graph-based features for recommendation task was investigated. As an example, Tiroshi et al. [18] showed that graph-based topology measures as *node centrality, PageRank* and so on can significantly improve the prediction accuracy of a RS. In this case, a distinguishing aspect of our work is that we calculate the measures by also calculating the metrics on the *tripartite* user-item-properties graph (instead of the simple *user-item* graph), thus including also the information coming from the LOD cloud.

Differently from the current work, that often used features directly extracted from the LOD cloud (as the genre of a movie or the writer of a book), we designed a more comprehensive *hybrid recommendation model* merging several different features in a unique representation. A similar attempt towards the definition of a hybrid recommendation model based on feature combination is presented in [15], where the authors present some preliminary results of a music recommender system merging graph-based features with textual data and collaborative features.

To sum up, the goal of this work is to take the best out of the current research in the area of LOD-enabled RSs: our idea was to define a comprehensive *hybrid* representation model merging heterogeneous features with the novel data points gathered from the LOD cloud. To the best of our knowledge, an in-depth and extensive analysis of the impact of both LOD-based and graph-based features on many classification algorithms is a poorly investigated research direction.

3   Methodology

In this section we provide the details of our methodology, by introducing the groups of features we used to feed the classification algorithms and by describing our recommendation framework.

3.1   Description of the Features

Popularity features. This set of features includes basic popularity-based information about the items, such as the *number of ratings* received by the item, the number of *positive* ratings received by the item and the *ratio* between positive ratings and the overall number of ratings.

This (tiny) group of features may seem trivial and not useful, but this kind of data is typically very informative for a recommendation task, since it gives information about how popular is a certain item among the users and how positive is their general opinion about it.

Collaborative features. This class of features models the information encoded in the *user-item matrix* which is typically exploited in collaborative filtering (CF) algorithms Differently from classical CF algorithms, that use the *whole* matrix to calculate the *neighbors* of the target user and to predict the items the user may be interested in, in our approach we are only interested in extracting the *column vector* modeling the ratings received by an item in order to include them in our *hybrid* item representation. Accordingly, the number of *collaborative features* we encoded for each item corresponds to the number of the *rows* of the matrix, that is to say, to the number of the *users* in the dataset.

The choice of including this set of features in our hybrid representation is quite straightforward, since CF algorithms and matrix factorization techniques tend to obtain very good performance especially when the *sparsity* of the original matrix is not high.

Content-based features. Textual content is another interesting source that can be exploited to provide items with useful and descriptive features. As an example, the *plot* of a movie contains several distinctive characteristics of the item, which can be extracted from such data.

However, *textual descriptions* are typically *noisy*, thus it is necessary to properly process such data by adopting Natural Language Processing (NLP) techniques before including them in our items representation. In our pipeline the content was first tokenized, then stop-words were removed and the entities occurring in the text were identified. Next, the remaining tokens were stemmed. In this case, the amount of features added to the model corresponds to the size of the *vocabulary*, that is to say, to the number of different tokens occurring in the description of *all the items* in the dataset.

Basic LOD-based features. The first group of *extended features* includes structured basic properties gathered from the LOD cloud, as the *genre* of a *movie* or the author of a book. To gather LOD-based features we preliminarily carried out a mapping procedure to obtain the corresponding URI for each item in the dataset. The goal of the mapping procedure is to identify, for each available item, the corresponding element in the LOD cloud the item refers to. As an example, we associate the movie *The Matrix* with its corresponding URI in the LOD cloud[2]. It is worth to emphasize that the mapping is a necessary and mandatory step to get an *entry point* to the LOD cloud.

---

[2] http://dbpedia.org/resource/The_Matrix.

Next, for each domain, we defined a subset of relevant properties by exploiting the outcomes of our previous research [10,11] and finally we used SPARQL to extract such data.

As we did for content-based features, we built a *vocabulary* of LOD-based properties and we provided each item with these new features. The score of each feature was set to 1 if the item is described through that RDF property, 0 otherwise. Table 1 reports some of the properties describing *The Matrix* gathered from the LOD cloud. In this case, each feature is represented through the couple $< property, value >$, since each entity can have different roles in the same movie (and in different ones, as well).

Table 1. Partial representation of the vector modeling the LOD-based features extracted from DBpedia for the movie *The Matrix*

Property - value	The Matrix
dbo:director - dbr:The_Wachowski	1
dbo:director - dbr:Mel_Gibson	0
dbo:composer - dbr:Ennio_Morricone	0
dct:subject - dbc:Dystopian_films	1
dct:subject - dbc:American_Horror_movies	0
...	...
dbo:producer - dbr:Joel_Silver	1

Graph-based features. The second group of extended features is built on the ground of the graph-based representation obtained by connecting the users to the items they liked and, in turn, the items to the properties gathered from DBPEDIA (see Fig. 1). We refer to these features as *tripartite* ones.

Given such representations, we decided to mine this graph and to calculate some measures describing its *topological characteristics*. Specifically, in our item representation we encoded five graph-based features calculated on the tripartite user-item graph, that is to say: *Degree Centrality*, *Average Neighbor Degree*, *PageRank* score, *Node Redundancy* and *Cluster Coefficient*. As mentioned in the related work, most of these measures have already been successfully used in literature for recommendation tasks.

3.2 Recommendation Framework

In this work we *cast* the recommendation task to a classification one, that is to say, we used the vectors representing the items the user liked as *positive examples* and those he did not like as *negative examples*. Next, we trained the classifiers and we exploited them to classify all the items the user did not consumed yet as *interesting* or not *interesting* for her.

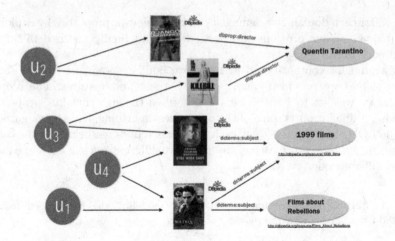

Fig. 1. A toy example of a tripartite graph, modeling users, items and properties gathered from the LOD.

To sum up, given a target user u, a training set $TR(u)$ (the items the user previously rated), and a group of features F, our classifier is fed with the examples $i_F \in TR(u)$ and we use the classification model to predict the most interesting items for the target user. Specifically, items in the test set are ranked according to the *confidence* of the prediction returned by the classification algorithm and the *top-K* items are returned to the target user. In the experimental session the overall effectiveness of our recommendation framework has been evaluated by varying different sets of features and by using two different classification algorithms, namely *Random Forests* and *Naïve Bayes*.

4   Experimental Evaluation

Our experiments were designed on the ground of four different research questions: which *group of classic features* maximizes the predictive accuracy? (*Experiment 1*). How do *LOD-based features* impact on the overall performance of the recommendations? (*Experiment 2*). How do *graph-based features* impact on the overall performance of the recommendations? (*Experiment 3*). How does our best-performing configuration perform with respect to *state-of-the-art techniques*? (*Experiment 4*).

Experimental protocol. Experiments were carried out on two state-of-the-art datasets, i.e. MovieLens-1M[3], and DBBOOK. The first one is a widespread dataset for movie recommendation, the second was used in the ESWC 2014 Recommender Systems challenge[4] and focuses on book recommendation, Some statistics about the datasets are reported in Table 2.

---

[3] http://grouplens.org/datasets/movielens/1m/.
[4] http://challenges.2014.eswc-conferences.org/index.php/RecSys.

Table 2. Statistics of the datasets

	MovieLens-1M	DBbook
Users	6,040	6,181
Items	3,883	6,733
Ratings	1,000,209	72,372
Sparsity	96.42%	99.85%
Positive ratings	57.51%	45.86%
Avg. rat./user ± stdev	165.59 ± 192.74	11.70 ± 5.85
Avg. rat./item ± stdev	269.88 ± 384.04	10.74 ± 27.14

Experiments were performed by adopting different protocols. We used a 80%-20% training-test split for MovieLens-1M. For DBbook we used the training-test split that provided with the data.

Different protocols were also adopted to build user profiles. In MovieLens-1M, user preferences are expressed on a 5-point discrete scale, thus we decided to consider as *positive* only those ratings equal to 4 and 5. On the other side, the DBbook dataset is already available as *binarized*, thus no further processing was needed. As classification algorithms we used the implementations of *Random Forest* and *Naive Bayes* made available in the Weka Toolkit[5].

Popularity features were extracted by simply processing the original data and by counting the ratings received by each item. As regards *collaborative features*, we replaced missing values with a special character and we used a binary representation to encode positive and negative ratings. Next, to generate *content-based features* we used the methods implemented in the Apache Lucene[6] library for tokenization, language detection and stop-words removal. Textual descriptions were all gathered from the Wikipedia pages of the items. Finally, tokens were stemmed by exploiting the Snowball library[7].

As previously explained, each item was mapped to a DBpedia entry in order to gather the features from the LOD cloud. To this end, we exploited some mappings already available in literature. In our setting, 3,300 MovieLens-1M entries and 6,600 items (98.02%) from DBbook (85% of the items) were successfully mapped. The items for which a DBpedia entry was not found were represented by using the basic groups of features alone. Finally, *graph-based features* were calculated by exploiting the Jung framework[8], a Java library to manage graph-based data. As previously explained, for each item node we calculated *Degree Centrality*, *Average Neighbor Degree*, *PageRank* score, *Node Redundancy* and *Cluster Coefficient* for tripartite graph.

---

[5] http://www.cs.waikato.ac.nz/ml/weka/.
[6] https://lucene.apache.org/.
[7] http://snowball.tartarus.org/.
[8] http://jung.sourceforge.net/.

Table 3 we recap the number of features encoded by each group. *Popularity* and *graph-based features* do not differ among the datasets since they do not depend on data, while the number of *collaborative features* corresponds to the number of users in the dataset. Finally, the *vocabulary* used to encode content-based and LOD-based data makes the number of features much higher than the other groups. Clearly, when the recommendation framework is fed with different groups of features (e.g. Collaborative and Content-based, at the same time), the features encoded in each training example are the merge of the features encoded by each single group.

Table 3. Features encoded for each group

Feature group	ML1M	DBbook
Popularity	3	3
Collaborative	6,040	6,181
Content-based	53,332	100,935
LOD-based	19,991	17,589
Tripartite graph-based	5	5

The performance of each configuration of our recommendation framework was evaluated in terms of *F1@5*, calculated through the Rival toolkit[9]. Statistical significance was assessed by exploiting Wilcoxon and Friedman tests.

4.1   Discussion of the Results

Experiment 1. Results of Experiment 1 are reported in Table 4. From now on we will refer to Random Forests and Naive Bayes as RF and NB, respectively. As we reported in the tables, we also used some abbreviations to refer to the name of the configurations. On `MovieLens-1M` data, the best F1@5 is obtained by merging *popularity-based* and *collaborative* features. As shown in Table 4, such configuration overcomes all the others. All the improvements are also statistically significant ($p < 0.05$), with the exception of the comparison between *popular + collaborative* and the *collaborative* features alone, on both RF and NB. This means that the *collaborative* group of features is highly significant on this dataset, and the simple *popularity-based* information can further improve the performance of the framework. This is an expected behavior, which is probably due to the low sparsity of `MovieLens-1M` dataset.

As regards `DBbook`, the characteristics of the dataset (it is negatively unbalanced) and the high sparsity make the simple *popularity-based* features very informative. As shown in Table 4, if we limit the analysis to single groups of basic features, *popularity-based ones* obtain the best results on RF. However,

---

[9] http://rival.recommenders.net/.

Table 4. Results of Experiment 1. Best-performing configuration for each algorithm is highlighted in **bold**

	MovieLens-1M		DBbook	
	RF	*NB*	*RF*	*NB*
Popular (P)	0.5338	0.5458	0.5610	0.5575
Collaborative (C)	0.5618	**0.5486**	0.5421	0.5610
Content-based (T)	0.4913	0.4913	0.5532	0.5465
P + C	**0.5635**	0.5483	**0.5627**	**0.5615**
P + T	0.5051	0.4965	0.5567	0.5467
C + T	0.5187	0.5180	0.5549	0.5464
P + C + T	0.5246	0.5189	0.5583	0.5468

the overall best combination is obtained again by merging *popular* and *collaborative* features, as for `MovieLens-1M`, by using RF as classification algorithm;

To sum up, the outcomes of this first experiment confirmed the goodness of *collaborative* features and showed that *content-based* features are too noisy to be used alone in a recommendation framework, for most of the scenarios. Moreover, also *non-personalized features* are very important to improve the effectiveness of single features by just introducing simple popularity-based data points.

Experiment 2. In the second experiment we tried to extend the representations by introducing structured features gathered from the LOD cloud. Results are reported in Tables 5 and 6. By analyzing the behavior of LOD features on `MovieLens-1M` data (Table 5). The only configuration that benefits of such injection is the one exploiting *content-based features*: if we consider only *content-based* and *popular+content-based* representations, the introduction of the features gathered from the LOD cloud produces a improvement with both RF and NB.

This behavior can be probably due to the low sparsity of the dataset, which makes superfluous most of the features except *collaborative* ones. However, even if these experimental settings showed that the adoption of LOD features has to be carefully evaluated, the overall best configuration actually *includes LOD features*, since the configuration merging popular, collaborative and LOD features obtained the higher F1@5 and significantly overcame ($p < 0.05$) the other representations.

The results emerging from `DBbook` data are reported in Table 6. An interesting outcome emerging from this experiment is that when data are sparse, as for `DBbook`, *LOD-based* data points represent a good alternative also to *collaborative* features. Indeed, even if *Popular + Collaborative* resulted as the best representation in Experiment 1, in this experiment *Popular + LOD* obtained the best overall F1@5. This means that, when the rating patterns are noisy, LOD features can be used to enrich the representation with new and relevant information.

Table 5. Results of Experiment 2 on `MovieLens-1M` data. Improvements over the baseline are reported in bold. The best configuration is emphasized with (*)

F1@5	RF		NB	
	No-LOD	LOD	*No-LOD*	LOD
Popular (P)	*0.5338*	0.5312	*0.5458*	0.5320
Collaborative (C)	*0.5618*	0.5609	*0.5486*	0.5450
Content-based (T)	*0.4913*	**0.4943**	*0.4913*	**0.4932**
P + C	*0.5635*	**0.5642 (*)**	*0.5483*	0.5451
P + T	*0.5051*	**0.5079**	*0.4965*	**0.4974**
C + T	*0.5187*	**0.5188**	*0.5180*	0.5169
P + C + T	*0.5246*	0.5246	*0.5189*	0.5174

Table 6. Results of Experiment 2 on `DBbook` data. Improvements over the baseline are reported in bold. The overall best configuration is emphasized with (*)

F1@5	RF		NB	
	No-LOD	LOD	*No-LOD*	LOD
Popular (P)	*0.5610*	**0.5659 (*)**	*0.5576*	**0.5577**
Collaborative (C)	*0.5421*	**0.5560**	*0.5610*	0.5564
Content-based (T)	*0.5532*	**0.5551**	*0.5465*	**0.5494**
P+C	*0.5627*	**0.5630**	*0.5615*	0.5580
P+T	*0.5567*	**0.5569**	*0.5467*	**0.5497**
C+T	*0.5549*	**0.5553**	*0.5464*	**0.5491**
P+C+T	*0.5583*	0.5560	*0.5468*	**0.5497**

To sum up, we can conclude this experiment by stating that our framework can generally benefit from the information coming from the LOD cloud, especially when RF is used as recommendation algorithm. Indeed, in all the datasets we considered, the best-performing configuration always encodes LOD-based features. Finally, a clear connection between the sparsity of the dataset and the exploitation of such features emerged: the more the sparsity, the more the need for features that are merged to (and in some cases, as for DBbook, even replace) *collaborative* data points.

Experiment 3. In Experiment 3 we evaluated the impact of graph-based features on our recommendation framework. Specifically, for each dataset we considered as *baseline* the best-performing configuration emerged from Experiment 1 and Experiment 2, and we extended the representation by introducing *tripartite* features.

By considering `MovieLens-1M` dataset, whose results are reported in Table 7, also the use of such features has to be carefully evaluated, since they rarely improve the predictive accuracy of the baseline configuration. This is a quite surprising result, since, none of the configurations exploiting *graph-based features* improve the baseline, and this is in contradiction with most of the related literature which showed the positive impact of topological information for recommendation tasks.

On the other side, a positive impact emerged when *graph-based* features are merged with *LOD-based* ones. Indeed, if we consider as baseline the best configuration emerged from Experiment 2, both RF and NB are able to improve F1@5 with a statistically significant improvement ($p < 0.05$) when *tripartite graph-based features* are exploited. Overall, the best configuration for `MovieLens-1M` data is that based on RF exploiting both *LOD-based* and *tripartite graph-based*. Similar outcomes emerge if we take into account the results on `DBbook` data.

Table 7. Results of Experiment 3. Improvements over the baselines are reported in **bold**. Best-performing configuration for each algorithm is emphasized with (*). The term *baseline* and *baseline + LOD* refer to the best configurations emerged from Experiment 1 and Experiment 2, respectively.

	MovieLens-1M		DBbook	
	RF	NB	RF	NB
Baseline	*0.5635*	*0.5486*	*0.5627*	*0.5615*
Baseline + Trip.	0.5621	0.5483	0.5607	0.5542
Baseline + LOD	*0.5642*	*0.5451*	*0.5659*	*0.5580*
Baseline + LOD + Trip.	**0.5678(*)**	**0.5481**	**0.5667(*)**	**0.5589**

Similar outcomes emerge if we take into account the results on `DBbook` data.

These results further confirmed the outcomes behind this research, since they showed that the injection of exogenous data points gathered from the LOD cloud (in the form of both *semantics content-based features* and *topological tripartite* ones) can increase the predictive accuracy of our recommendation framework, leading to an interesting improvement over the baselines.

Experiment 4. In the last experiment we compared the effectiveness of our hybrid recommendation methodology with several state of the art recommendation algorithms. First, we compared our methodology to some state-of-the-art baselines, i.e. User-to-User (U2U-KNN), Item-to-Item Collaborative Filtering (I2I-KNN), the Bayesian Personalized Ranking (BPRMF) which uses Matrix Factorization as the learning model with Bayesian Personalized Ranking (BPR) optimization criterion and an implementation of PageRank with Priors. Moreover, we also compared our methodology to other *LOD-aware recommendation* *techniques.* Specifically, we used the features gathered from the LOD as side information for BPRMF, as proposed by Gantner et al. [4], next we also extended PageRank with Priors (PPR) with LOD-based features as we investigated in our previous research [10]. PPR was run by using default settings (80% of the weight distributed to the items the user liked).

For U2U-KNN and I2I-KNN, experiments were carried out by setting the neighborhood size to 50, 80 and 100 and by using cosine similarity as similarity measure, while BPRMF was run by setting the factor parameter equal to 10, 20, 50, 100 and adopting 0.05 as learning rate. For brevity, we only report the results obtained by the best-performing configurations (80 neighbors for U2U-KNN and I2I-KNN, 100 factors for BPRMF, 50 factors for BPRMF with side information). For U2U-KNN, I2I-KNN and BPRMF we exploited the implementations already available in MyMediaLite[10], while the methods implemented in the Jung framework[11] were used to run PPR.

Table 8. Results of Experiment 4. The best-performing algorithm is highlighted in **bold**. The term *LOD-RecSys* refers to the overall best-performing configuration emerged for each dataset from the previous experiments.

Algorithm	*F1@5*	
	MovieLens-1M	DBbook
LOD-RecSys	**0.5678**	**0.5667**
U2U-KNN	0.4270	0.5193
I2I-KNN	0.4320	0.5111
BPRMF	0.5218	0.5290
BPRMF + LOD	0.5215	0.5304
PPR	0.5397	0.5502
PPR + LOD	0.5400	0.5540

As shown in Table 8, our hybrid recommendation framework always overcomes all the baselines on MovieLens-1M and DBbook data. All the increases are statistically significant. It is worth to note that our approach obtains better results when compared to both classic baselines as well as to other LOD-aware techniques as BPRMF+LOD and PPR+LOD.

5   Conclusions and Future Work

In this article we presented a hybrid recommendation framework based on the combination of different groups of features. The distinguishing aspect of this work is the usage of extra groups of features gathered from the LOD cloud, as

---

[10] http://www.mymedialite.net/.
[11] http://jung.sourceforge.net/.

basic structured features and *extended graph-based ones* built on the ground of the tripartite graph connecting users, items and properties.

The main outcome of the experiments is that the combined use of LOD-based and graph-based features led to the best overall results we obtained with our framework. Furthermore, we noted a the connection between the *sparsity* of the dataset and the choice of the features to be included in the model: the more the sparsity, the more the benefit of injecting the exogenous knowledge coming from the *Linked Open Data.*

As future work we will try to evaluate different groups of features: as an example, we can replace content-based features with a more compact version based on word embedding [12], distributional semantics techniques [13] or more complex representation languages [3]. Similarly, we can extend our set of graph-based features by introducing other topological measures.

References

1. Auer, S., Bizer, C., Kobilarov, G., Lehmann, J., Cyganiak, R., Ives, Z.: DBpedia: a nucleus for a web of open data. In: Aberer, K., et al. (eds.) ASWC/ISWC - 2007. LNCS, vol. 4825, pp. 722–735. Springer, Heidelberg (2007). doi:10.1007/978-3-540-76298-0_52

2. Burke, R.: Hybrid recommender systems: survey and experiments. User Model. User-Adap. Inter. **12**(4), 331–370 (2002)

3. Esposito, F., Malerba, D., Semeraro, G.: Flexible matching for noisy structural descriptions. In: IJCAI, pp. 658–664 (1991)

4. Gantner, Z., Drumond, L., Freudenthaler, C., Rendle, S., Schmidt-Thieme, L.: Learning attribute-to-feature mappings for cold-start recommendations. In: ICDM 2010, pp. 176–185. IEEE Computer Society (2010)

5. de Gemmis, M., Lops, P., Musto, C., Narducci, F., Semeraro, G.: Semantics-aware content-based recommender systems. In: Ricci, F., Rokach, L., Shapira, B. (eds.) Recommender Systems Handbook, pp. 119–159. Springer, Boston, MA (2015). doi:10.1007/978-1-4899-7637-6_4

6. Lops, P., de Gemmis, M., Semeraro, G.: Content-based recommender systems: state of the art and trends. In: Ricci, F., Rokach, L., Shapira, B., Kantor, P. (eds.) Recommender Systems Handbook, pp. 73–105. Springer, Boston (2011). doi:10.1007/978-0-387-85820-3_3

7. Lops, P., de Gemmis, M., Semeraro, G., Musto, C., Narducci, F., Bux, M.: A semantic content-based recommender system integrating folksonomies for personalized access. In: Castellano, G., Jain, L.C., Fanelli, A.M. (eds.) Web Personalization in Intelligent Environments. Studies in Computational Intelligence, vol. 229, pp. 27–47. Springer, Heidelberg (2009). doi:10.1007/978-3-642-02794-9_2

8. Mak, H., Koprinska, I., Poon, J.: Intimate: a web-based movie recommender using text categorization. In: WI 2003, pp. 602–605. IEEE (2003)

9. Musto, C., Basile, P., Lops, P., de Gemmis, M., Semeraro, G.: Linked open data-enabled strategies for top-n recommendations. In: CEUR Workshop Proceedings CBRecSys 2014, vol. 1245, pp. 49–56 (2014). ceur-ws.org

10. Musto, C., Basile, P., Lops, P., de Gemmis, M., Semeraro, G.: Introducing linked open data in graph-based recommender systems. Inf. Process. Manag. **53**(2), 405–435 (2017)

11. Musto, C., Lops, P., Basile, P., de Gemmis, M., Semeraro, G.: Semantics-aware graph-based recommender systems exploiting linked open data. In: Proceedings of UMAP 2016, pp. 229–237. ACM (2016). http://doi.acm.org/10.1145/2930238.2930249

12. Musto, C., Semeraro, G., de Gemmis, M., Lops, P.: Learning word embeddings from wikipedia for content-based recommender systems. In: Ferro, N., Crestani, F., Moens, M.-F., Mothe, J., Silvestri, F., Di Nunzio, G.M., Hauff, C., Silvello, G. (eds.) ECIR 2016. LNCS, vol. 9626, pp. 729–734. Springer, Cham (2016). doi:10.1007/978-3-319-30671-1_60

13. Musto, C., Semeraro, G., Lops, P., de Gemmis, M.: Random indexing and negative user preferences for enhancing content-based recommender systems. In: Huemer, C., Setzer, T. (eds.) EC-Web 2011. LNBIP, vol. 85, pp. 270–281. Springer, Heidelberg (2011). doi:10.1007/978-3-642-23014-1_23

14. Musto, C., Semeraro, G., Lops, P., de Gemmis, M., Narducci, F.: Leveraging social media sources to generate personalized music playlists. In: Huemer, C., Lops, P. (eds.) EC-Web 2012. LNBIP, vol. 123, pp. 112–123. Springer, Heidelberg (2012). doi:10.1007/978-3-642-32273-0_10

15. Ostuni, V., Di Noia, T., Di Sciascio, E., Oramas, S., Serra, X.: A semantic hybrid approach for sound recommendation. In: WWW 2015, pp. 85–86. ACM (2015)

16. Pazzani, M., Muramatsu, J., Billsus, D.: Syskill & webert: identifying interesting web sites. In: AAAI/IAAI, vol. 1, pp. 54–61 (1996)

17. Semeraro, G., Lops, P., de Gemmis, M., Musto, C., Narducci, F.: A folksonomy-based recommender system for personalized access to digital artworks. J. Comput. Cult. Herit. (JOCCH) 5(3), 11 (2012)

18. Tiroshi, A., Berkovsky, S., Kâafar, M.A., Vallet, D., Chen, T., Kuflik, T.: Improving business rating predictions using graph based features. In: IUI 2014, pp. 17–26 (2014)

Reasoning over RDF Knowledge Bases:
Where We Are

Simona Colucci[1]([⊠]), Francesco M. Donini[2], and Eugenio Di Sciascio[1]

[1] DEI, Politecnico di Bari, Bari, Italy
simona.colucci@poliba.it
[2] DISUCOM, Università della Tuscia, Viterbo, Italy

Abstract. This paper aims at investigating the state of realization of
the Semantic Web initiative, through the analysis of some applications
taking background knowledge from RDF datasets. In particular, it shows
the design and the implementation of an extended experiment, which
demonstrates that input datasets are often used only as data structures, without taking into account the logical formalization of properties
involved in such RDF models.

1 Motivation

After more than 15 years since the launch of the Semantic Web (SW) [1] initiative, the way of conceiving knowledge modeling has radically changed, by
going through heterogeneous phases. In the envisioned SW architecture, graphically synthesized in the well-known SW layer-cake, the data interchange layer
is detached from the ontology level and different modeling languages enable
them. In particular, Resource Description Framework (RDF) [7] is the language
implementing the data interchange layer; as for the ontology level, languages of
different expressiveness have been defined to cover different modeling needs. Such
languages may provide a relatively low expressiveness, like the schema language
associated to RDF, RDF Schema (RDFS) [3], or may present a modeling potential comparable to really expressive languages for knowledge representation, like
the Web Ontology Language (OWL), today at its second version, OWL-2 [13].

Currently, the so-called Web of Data [12] offers a huge amount of data, modeled in RDF according to vocabularies defined in different ontology languages.
Independently on the expressiveness of such languages, RDF data come with
their own—although simple—semantics.

Nevertheless, most SW applications seem to completely disregard the implicit
informative content embedded in RDF data sources, exploiting them just as
rough *data structures*—in particular, directed graphs.

In order to support this claim, we here design an extended experiment aimed
at testing the compliance to the SW initiative of applications using RDF data
sources as background knowledge. The experiment can be used to discriminate
SW applications on the basis of their ability to interpret some predicates defined
in RDFS-semantics [7] and to manage *blank nodes* as special RDF resources.

© Springer International Publishing AG 2017
F. Esposito et al. (Eds.): AI*IA 2017, LNAI 10640, pp. 243–255, 2017.
https://doi.org/10.1007/978-3-319-70169-1_18

We devised the designed experiments in one representative SW application managing RDF datasets as data source. Results show that: (i) in most cases, the application behaves differently when working with datasets which are logically equivalent—according to RDFS semantics—although expressed in syntactically different ways; (ii) blank nodes are not given special handling. This experiment demonstrates that the application does not consider the semantics of properties involved in the input datasets and does not follow the intuition about blank nodes.

Such a result raises important questions about the state of realization of the SW initiative: was not RDF conceived for data interchange? Was not the *meaning* of data part of the envisioned interoperability? Is really a flat transformation from RDF models to feature sets what the SW creators expected from released applications?

In this paper we start from the experimental results to discuss issues still open in the development of RDF applications fully realizing the SW initiative.

The rest of the paper is organized as follows: in the next section, we explain the rationale of the experiments we devised. Then, we show the execution of the experiments in Sect. 3. In Sect. 4 results and main lesson learned from the experiments are synthesized, before concluding the paper with Sect. 5.

2   Rationale of the Experiments

We explain here our strategy for devising experiments that can discriminate whether some application based on SW data exploits just the syntax of data, or instead its semantics.

2.1   RDFS Semantics

Experiment 1. The first experiment is based on the RDFS predicate `rdfs:subClassOf`. According to RDFS semantics, such a predicate should be interpreted as transitive, meeting the intuition conveyed by its bare name. Consider the following RDF data patterns:

x `rdfs:subClassOf` u.	x `rdfs:subClassOf` u.
u `rdfs:subClassOf` z.	u `rdfs:subClassOf` z.
x `rdfs:subClassOf` z.	

where x, u, z are generic IRIs.

Two data sources D_1, D_2, where D_1 contains the left-hand pattern, and D_2 the right-hand pattern, must be completely equivalent with respect to RDFS semantics (see Rule *rdfs1* in the definition of the semantics of RDFS [7]). So, for instance, if a SW application computes a similarity measure $s(x, y)$ between x and another IRI y, the similarity $s(x, y)$ computed using triples in D_1 should be the same as the one computed using triples in D_2. If this experiment yields a "no" answer, the SW application is using just the *syntactic* form of triples—like a database—not their semantics. While this might be fine for the results of the application at hand, one should be clear about the *sensitivity* of such an application to apparently redundant triples. The intuition about how "semantic" is a SW application here may be misleading, since syntactic differences that may be judged irrelevant may be in fact not so.

Experiment 2. The second experiment is based on the RDFS predicate `rdfs:domain`. Consider the following RDF data patterns:

$x\ r\ u.$	$x\ r\ u.$
r `rdfs:domain` $z.$	r `rdfs:domain` $z.$
x `rdf:type` $z.$	

where x, r, u, z stand for some IRIs.

Consider, again, two data sources D_1, D_2, defined to include the left-hand and the right-hand pattern above, respectively. According to RDFS semantics, the third triple in D_1 is trivially redundant w.r.t. to the content in D_2 (see Rule *rdfs2* in the RDFS semantics [7]). Also in this case, a SW application computing, for instance, a similarity measure $s(x, y)$ between x and y should return the same value when either D_1 or D_2 are used as data sources. Any different behavior of the application would reveal that triples are only syntactically parsed.

Experiment 3. The third experiment is based on the RDFS predicate `rdfs:range`. Consider the following RDF data patterns:

$x\ r\ u.$	$x\ r\ u.$
r `rdfs:range` $z.$	r `rdfs:range` $z.$
u `rdf:type` $z.$	

where x, r, u, z stand for generic IRIs. The same arguments as for Experiment 2 apply if two data sources D_1, D_2 are defined to include the left-hand and the right-hand pattern above, respectively. Again, D_1 and D_2 are logically equivalent according to RDFS semantics (see Rule *rdfs3* in the document defining RDFS semantics [7]), and any application claiming to be SW-oriented should return identical results when either D_1 or D_2 are used as data sources. Also in this experiment, the reader may think to an application computing the similarity between two IRIs, for the sake of example.

Observe that the same experiments could be conducted if instead of a similarity measure, the application performs a clusterization of IRIs. In this case, the test must ascertain whether the IRI x is put in the same cluster or in a different cluster, depending on which of the two patterns above x is involved in.

2.2   The Status of Blank Nodes

The second type of experiment analyzes if the SW application follows the intuition about *blank nodes*. In the original semantics of RDF, blank nodes are existential variables, whose scope is the entire RDF file they occur in. As such, they may stand for any IRI or literal, even one not occurring already in the file. We stress that blank nodes appear in the syntax and semantics of simple RDF, and that RDFS in this case inherits them from the simpler language. Hence this experiment can be set up even if one does not adopt RDFS semantics.

Experiment 4. Consider the three RDF data patterns below:

x	r	ex:a.	x	r	_:b1.	x	r	ex:a.
y	r	ex:c.	y	r	_:b2.	y	r	ex:a.

where, following Hayes and Patel-Schneider [7], blank nodes are prefixed by an empty namespace "_"as in _:b, and x, y, r denote generic IRIs. In the first pattern, IRIs x and y are linked through r to different, known, IRIs ex:a, ex:c. In the second pattern, they are linked to two blank nodes, that might coincide in one interpretation, while they might not in another. In the third pattern, both x and y are linked to the same IRI ex:a. Now let D_1, D_2, D_3 be three data sources which are the same but for the fact that, for some IRI x, D_1 contains the first pattern, while D_2 contains the second one, and D_3 the third.

Suppose now that a SW application estimates the similarity of x and y. Clearly, *ceteris paribus*, in D_1 IRIs x and y are less similar than in D_3, in which they share the same predicate-object pair. The situation for D_2 is an intermediate one: in fact, *both* the first and the third pattern can be instantiations of this one—among may others. Denoting by $s_1(x, y)$ the similarity the SW application computes when D_1 is given as data source, and by $s_2(x, y)$ and $s_3(x, y)$ those computed for D_2 and D_3, respectively, $s_2(x, y)$ should be an intermediate value between $s_1(x, y)$ and $s_3(x, y)$—that is, one should obtain $s_1(x, y) \leq s_2(x, y) \leq s_3(x, y)$.

We observed instead that many SW applications treat each blank node as a new IRI, different from every other one. This is what is logically called *skolemization*. While skolemization yields a data source which—considered as a formula—is roughly equivalent to the original one for what regards *entailment* [7, Sect. 6], the picture is much different here. In fact, SW applications compute values and do other operations on the data—such as clusterization—as if RDF triples specified a *model*, not a formula (which represents a *set* of models). Performing a skolemization and then use the result for computations amounts to treating the second pattern above as if it were the first—or, treating D_1 and D_2 to be in the same situation. Again, the so-called "RDF graph" is treated in this case as a *real* graph—a data structure—bypassing its logical meaning.

When a SW application treats blank nodes by skolemizing them, the result of the experiment shows that always $s_1(x, y) = s_2(x, y) < s_3(x, y)$. Again, while this may be acceptable for the SW application at hand, one should clarify that blank nodes appearing in the data source are always treated as new, distinguished, IRIs. This treatment may be counterintuitive especially when the blank node stands for one in a short, limited list of possible values—say, when $r = $ foaf:gender, its object is intuitively either foaf:male or foaf:female—while Skolem constants add more values to the initial list, with no real meaning, but for the fact that they are values different from any other one.

In data analysis research community, the problem of correctly interpreting unbounded information is acknowledged and a florid research field is specifically devoted to the prediction of (so-called) missing values [2,11], which are the analogous of blank nodes in RDF data sources. In our opinion, solutions predicting missing values (the value of blank nodes, in our case) by estimating the expected value of the variable they quantify [10] are not adequate to SW settings. In fact, this could prematurely make discrete features that should be kept general for further inference purpose.

3   Deployment of the Experiments

We here show how the experiments designed in Sect. 2 may serve as a test checking if an application working on RDF data sources may be considered compliant with the SW requirements.

As use case, we choose a very popular SW application: the Linked Open Data extension (LODExtension) [9] of the Machine Learning tool RapidMiner [8]. The RapidMiner LODExtension enables several learning tasks on example sets automatically extracted by mining data sources in RDF.

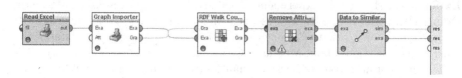

Fig. 1. Rapidminer workflow of performed experiments

All performed experiments follow the RapidMiner workflow shown in Fig. 1, aimed at computing the similarity of RDF resources through the operations described below:

1. **Read Excel.** This operator loads data from Microsoft Excel spreadsheets; in this workflow, the spreadsheet includes a column with the IRIs of resources to compare.
2. **Graph Importer.** This operator generates an RDF graph for all input instances, either from SPARQL endpoint or local file, with user-specified graph depth. In our experiment, an RDF dataset is queried to import specific RDF graphs, whose root and depth are user-specified.
3. **RDF Walk Count Kernel.** This kernel method counts the different walks in the subgraphs (up to the provided graph depth) around the instance nodes. The method implements the algorithm by de Vries *et al.* [5]. In this workflow, it is applied on the RDF graph imported in Step 2 for generating features describing the resources of interest according to the knowledge in the dataset; in particular, RDF Walk Count Kernel counts the different walks in the subgraphs (up to the provided graph depth) around the root. The operator returns a so-called "ExampleSet": a set of kernel-generated features describing the resources of interest. The generation process may be set to make use of inference on explicit knowledge.

4. **Remove attributes.** This is an auxiliary operator which cuts columns from example sets. In this workflow, it is used to remove the IRI of the root from the set generated at Step 4, because it is not object of comparison.
5. **Data to similarity.** This operator measures the similarity of each example of a given ExampleSet with every other example of the same ExampleSet. A similarity measure may be chosen by the user among available ones.

We now detail the execution of four experiments following the rationale in Sect. 2. For all of them, the "inference" option is set "on" in Step 4 and the similarity measure chosen at Step 5 is the one denoted as "Euclidean Distance" in RapidMiner[1] (based on the well-know measure of the same name [6]).

The first three experiments aim at testing the sensitivity of the workflow in Fig. 1 to knowledge-irrelevant changes in the RDF input dataset. In particular, we show the similarity values returned by the selected SW application when two logically-equivalent RDF models are given as input. For each experiment, we describe the two input datasets—from now on D_1 and D_2—below:

Experiment 1. In this experiment, D_1 and D_2 describe resources Mandarin Orange (IRI http://dbpedia.org/resource/Mandarin_orange) and Tangerine (IRI http://dbpedia.org/resource/Tangerine). In particular, D_1 and D_2 syntactically differ in the assertions about Mandarin Orange (Resource 2), although being logically equivalent according to RDFS-semantics (see predicate `rdfs:subClassOf`). In fact, D_1 is depicted in Fig. 2 and matches the left-hand pattern provided in the the description of Experiment 1 in Sect. 2.1, while D_2, depicted in Fig. 3, matches the right-hand one.

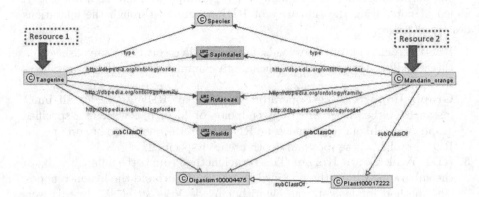

Fig. 2. D_1: an RDF dataset about Mandarin Orange and Tangerine. The graph matches the left-hand data pattern given in Experiment 1 in Sect. 2.1, by binding x to Resource 2

---

[1] Intuitively, distance is meant to be inversely proportional to similarity.

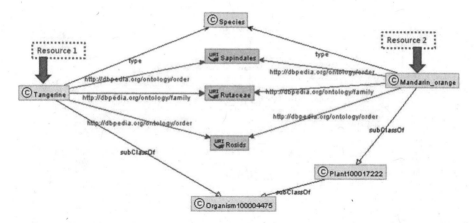

Fig. 3. D_2: a dataset logically equivalent to the one in Fig. 2. The graph matches the right-hand data pattern given in Experiment 1 in Sect. 2.1, by binding x to Resource 2.

Experiment 2. This experiment uses two datasets about Mandarin Orange (IRI http://dbpedia.org/resource/Mandarin_orange) and Coffea (IRI http://dbpedia.org/resource/Coffea). Coherently with the rationale provided in Sect. 2.1, D_1 and D_2 are syntactically different but logically equivalent according to RDF-S semantics (see predicate `rdfs:domain`). In Fig. 4 (respectively Fig. 5), it is shown D_1 (respectively D_2), that matches the left-hand (respectively, right-hand) pattern given in the description of Experiment 2 in Sect. 2.1.

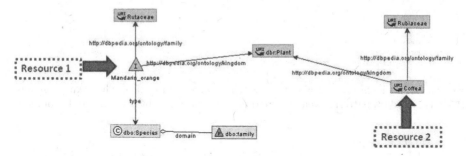

Fig. 4. D_1: an RDF dataset about Mandarin Orange and Coffea. The graph matches the left-hand data pattern given in Experiment 2 in Sect. 2.1, by binding x to Resource 1

Experiment 3. This experiment uses two other datasets about Mandarin Orange (IRI http://dbpedia.org/resource/Mandarin_orange) and Coffea (IRI http://dbpedia.org/resource/Coffea) involving predicate `rdfs:range`. According to the rationale of Experiment 3 explained in Sect. 2.1, the two datasets are logically equivalent, even though syntactically D_1 (Fig. 6) matches the left-hand graph pattern in the experiment description, while D_2 (Fig. 7) matches the right-hand one.

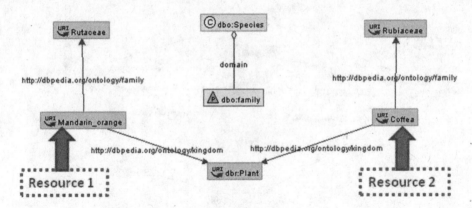

Fig. 5. D_2: a dataset logically equivalent to the one in Fig. 4. The graph matches the right-hand data pattern given in Experiment 2 in Sect. 2.1, by binding x to Resource 1

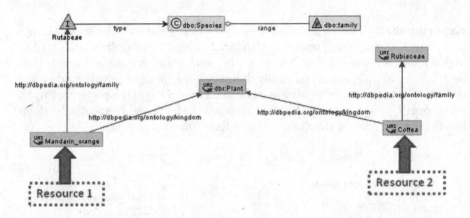

Fig. 6. D_1: an RDF dataset about Mandarin Orange and Coffea. The graph matches the left-hand data pattern given in Experiment 3 in Sect. 2.1, by binding x to Resource 1

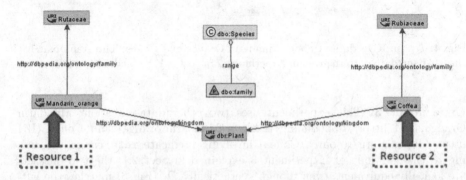

Fig. 7. D_2: A dataset logically equivalent to the one in Fig. 6. The graph matches the right-hand data pattern given in Experiment 3 in Sect. 2.1, by binding x to Resource 1

The three experiments share the goal to test that:

$$dist_1(x, y) = dist_2(x, y) \tag{1}$$

where for $i = 1, 2$, $dist_i(x, y)$ denotes the Euclidean Distance between x and y, when they are defined in D_i.

Experiment 4. This experiment aims at testing if the workflow for computing similarity gives anonymous resources special handling or considers them exactly as any other resource. The experiment follows the rationale described in Sect. 2.2 and uses the dataset in Fig. 8.

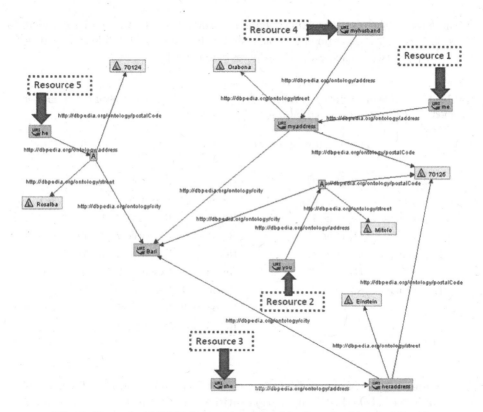

Fig. 8. Example of RDF dataset involving blank nodes (denoted by A).

In particular, we show below how to retrieve in Fig. 8 three graph patterns given in the description of Experiment 3 in Sect. 2.2:

- by binding x to Resource 1 and y to Resource 3, the graph in Fig. 8 matches the first graph pattern (on the left of the table);
- by binding x to Resource 2 and y to Resource 5, the graph in Fig. 8 matches the second graph pattern (on the center of the table);

- by binding x to Resource 1 and y to Resource 4, the graph in Fig. 8 matches the third graph pattern (on the right of the table);

According to the rationale provided in Sect. 2.2, the experiment goal is verifying that:

$$dist(Resource1, Resource3) \geq dist(Resource1, Resource3) \geq dist(Resource1, Resource4) \quad (2)$$

where $dist(x, y)$ denotes the Euclidean Distance between x and y (recall Footnote 3).

4   Results and Discussion

We here report the results of experiments performance w.r.t. the settings detailed in Sect. 3. For each experiment, Table 1 shows the values of Euclidean Distance $(dist_i(x, y))$ between each pair of resources x and y (defined in D_i).

Table 1. Euclidean Distance $(dist_i(x, y))$ between each pair of resources x and y (defined in D_i), to be compared in designed experiments.

	Input data source: D_i	Binding		$dist_i(x, y)$
		x	y	
Experiment 1	D_1 (Fig. 2)	Resource 2	Resource 1	4
	D_2 (Fig. 3)	Resource 2	Resource 1	4
Experiment 2	D_1 (Fig. 4)	Resource 1	Resource 2	4, 472
	D_2 (Fig. 5)	Resource 1	Resource 2	2, 449
Experiment 3	D_1 (Fig. 6)	Resource 1	Resource 2	3, 162
	D_2 (Fig. 7)	Resource 1	Resource 2	2, 449
Experiment 4	Figure 8	Resource 1	Resource 3	4, 243
		Resource 2	Resource 5	4, 243
		Resource 1	Resource 4	0

Experiment 1–3. We recall from Sect. 3 that Experiment 1–3 are focused on checking if the selected SW application satisfies the goal in Eq. 1. This reverts to check if, for each experiment, the values of $dist_i(x, y)$ coincide in the rows related to data sources D_1 and D_2. The reader may verify that this happens only for Experiment 1, while the test fails for Experiment 2 and 3.

In other words, the analyzed SW application takes into account the transitivity of predicate rdfs:subClassOf by applying inference rules on knowledge extracted from input data sources. On the contrary, it seems not to apply the entailment patterns about rdfs:domain and rdfs:range in the process of generating features from the input data sources. In fact, in both Experiment 2 and 3, the application does not notice that $D_1 \equiv D_2$ according to RDF-S-semantics.

The reason for such a dichotomy lays in the kernel method applied in Step 3 of the process workflow. The Walk Count Kernel operator generates features by visiting paths in the input RDF-graph rooted in the resource to describe. But this operator does not take into account one important peculiarity of RDF-grahs: the fact that the set of labels of nodes and arcs may overlap in RDF, causing some paths to be connected through the predicate and not through the object of an RDF statement (as an example, the right-hand patterns given for Experiment 2 and 3 in Sect. 2.1 are connected through r and not through u). A definition of such paths in terms of RDF-paths may be found in previous work [4].

We believe that a SW application should be able to manage such paths when mining knowledge from data sources in order to be compliant with RFDS-semantics. This would avoid the production of completely misleading results, like the ones of Experiment 2 and 3 given in Table 1. In fact, by comparing Row 3 and Row 4 (alternatively, Row 5 and 6), the reader may notice that Resource 1 and Resource 2 are considered more distant from each other if (in dataset D_1) Resource 1 is further described by the statement:

http://dbpedia.org/resource/Mandarin_orange
http://www.w3.org/1999/02/22-rdf-syntax-ns#type
http://dbpedia.org/ontology/Species

which is completely redundant with respect to the content of D_2 according to RDFS-semantics.

Experiment 4. The results of Experiment 4 are formalized in the last three rows of Table 1. We recall that the experiment goal, formalized in Eq. 2, is checking if there is any special handling for blank nodes w.r.t. IRIs in the computation of similarity. This reverts to check: (i) if the application considers Resource 1 and 3 (which are linked to different *IRIs* through the predicate http://dbpedia.org/ ontology/address) more distant from each other than Resource 2 and 5 (which, instead, are linked to different *blank nodes* through the predicate http://dbpedia. org/ontology/address); (ii) if both the distances above are bigger than the distance between Resource 1 and 4 (which are linked to *the same IRI* through the predicate http://dbpedia.org/ontology/address).

The reader may notice that the application satisfies only the second part (item ii) of the goal: it computes a distance equal to 0 between Resource 1 and 4, as one may expect. On the contrary, it fails to address the first part of the goal: Resource 1 and 3 are considered as distant from each other as Resource 2 and 5, showing that blank nodes are treated the same as any other IRI.

We believe that a SW application (even only compliant with simple-entailemnt regime) should give the proper treatment to blank nodes, in order to avoid undesirable loss of information which are evident even in our simple example data source. By looking at Fig. 8, the reader may notice that all resources are connected to an address, which is in turn connected to the resource http://dbpedia.org/resource/Bari through the property http://dbpedia.org/ontology/city.

The Walk Count Kernel operator generates one feature for each path rooted in the five resources. In particular, by mining the model of Resource 2 (analogously, 5) it generates (among the others) a feature stating that the resource is connected to *some address* in the city of Bari. In our opinion, such a feature should be matched by all the other resources, but the application considers it exclusive of Resource 2 (analogously, 5). This happens because the application gives to *some address* a symbolic name (a Skolem constant), which by definition is different by any other IRI (in thi case, address) it manages.

5 Conclusion

We designed a set of experiments which can be used to discriminate applications involving RDF data sources on the basis of their compliance to the SW initiative. In particular, three experiments focus on the compliance to RDFS-semantics, and check if an application correctly interprets the predicates `rdfs:subClassOf`, `rdfs:domain` and `rdfs:range`. The fourth experiment is focused on the management of blank nodes and aims at discriminating applications on the basis of the handling they give to such–special–resources.

In order to show how the set of experiments may be performed, we chose as test application a RapidMiner process computing the Euclidean distance between two IRIs. The workflow embeds operators from the LODExtension of RapidMiner, which is meant to support classical data mining tasks with information extracted from RDF data sources (also by applying inference techniques). Results show that the chosen application fails three of the tests induced by the four experiments: it is not able to manage predicates `rdfs:domain` and `rdfs:range` and blank nodes. Knowledge deriving by transitivity of predicate `rdfs:subClassOf` is instead correctly inferred. In other words, the application may not be considered fully compliant to the SW initiative.

Our future work will be devoted to run the designed experiments in a broader set of applications traditionally considered as SW-oriented. Results of such an extended experiment would reveal the current state of realization of the SW initiative.

References

1. Berners-Lee, T., Hendler, J., Lassila, O.: The semantic web. Sci. Am. **248**(4), 34–43 (2001)
2. Bischof, S., Martin, C., Polleres, A., Schneider, P.: Collecting, integrating, enriching and republishing open city data as linked data. In: Arenas, M., et al. (eds.) ISWC 2015. LNCS, vol. 9367, pp. 57–75. Springer, Cham (2015). doi:10.1007/978-3-319-25010-6_4
3. Brickley, D., Guha, R.: RDF Schema 1.1. W3C Recommendation (2014). https://www.w3.org/TR/rdf-schema/
4. Colucci, S., Donini, F., Giannini, S., Di Sciascio, E.: Defining and computing Least Common Subsumers in RDF. Web Semant.: Sci. Serv. Agents World Wide Web **39**, 62–80 (2016). doi:10.1016/j.websem.2016.02.001

5. De Vries, G.K.D., De Rooij, S.: A fast and simple graph kernel for RDF. In: Proceedings of the 2013 International Conference on Data Mining on Linked Data, DMoLD 2013, vol. 1082, pp. 23–34. CEUR-WS.org, Aachen (2013). http://dl.acm.org/citation.cfm?id=3053776.3053781

6. Deza, M.M., Deza, E.: Encyclopedia of Distances (2009)

7. Hayes, P., Patel-Schneider, P.F.: RDF semantics, W3C recommendation (2014). http://www.w3.org/TR/2014/REC-rdf11-mt-20140225/

8. Hofmann, M., Klinkenberg, R. (eds.): RapidMiner: Data Mining Use Cases and Business Analytics Applications. Chapman & Hall/CRC Data Mining and Knowledge Discovery Series. CRC Press, Boca Raton (2013)

9. Paulheim, H., Fümkranz, J.: Unsupervised generation of data mining features from linked open data. In: Proceedings of the 2nd International Conference on Web Intelligence, Mining and Semantics, p. 31. ACM (2012)

10. Perez-Rey, D., Anguita, A., Crespo, J.: OntoDataClean: ontology-based integration and preprocessing of distributed data. In: Maglaveras, N., Chouvarda, I., Koutkias, V., Brause, R. (eds.) ISBMDA 2006. LNCS, vol. 4345, pp. 262–272. Springer, Heidelberg (2006). doi:10.1007/11946465_24

11. Qi, Z., Wang, H., Meng, F., Li, J., Gao, H.: Capture missing values with inference on knowledge base. In: Bao, Z., Trajcevski, G., Chang, L., Hua, W. (eds.) DASFAA 2017. LNCS, vol. 10179, pp. 185–194. Springer, Cham (2017). doi:10.1007/978-3-319-55705-2_14

12. Shadbolt, N., Hall, W., Berners-Lee, T.: The semantic web revisited. IEEE Intell. Syst. 21(3), 96–101 (2006)

13. W3C OWL Working Group: OWL 2 Web Ontology Language Document Overview, 2nd edn. W3C Recommendation (2012). https://www.w3.org/TR/owl2-overview/

Between CONTACT and SUPPORT: Introducing a Logic for Image Schemas and Directed Movement

Maria M. Hedblom[1,2(✉)], Oliver Kutz[1], Till Mossakowski[2], and Fabian Neuhaus[2]

[1] Free University of Bozen-Bolzano, Bozen-Bolzano, Italy
mhedblom@unibz.it

[2] Otto-von-Guericke University Magdeburg, Magdeburg, Germany

Abstract. Cognitive linguistics introduced image schemas as a missing link between embodied experiences and high-level conceptualisation in language and metaphorical thinking. They are described as the abstract spatio-temporal relationships that function as conceptual building blocks for everyday concepts and events. Although there is increasing interest in the area of cognitively motivated artificial intelligence, where image schemas are suggested to be a core piece in the puzzle to model human-level conceptualisation and reasoning, so far rather few formal logical approaches can be found in the literature, in particular regarding attention to the dynamic aspects of image schemas. A fundamental problem here is that the typical mainstream approaches in contemporary KR do not map well to various scenarios found in image schema modelling. In this paper, we introduce a spatio-temporal logic for 'directed movement of objects', with the aim to model formally image schematic events such as BLOCKAGE, CAUSED_MOVEMENT and 'bouncing'.

1 Introduction

Embodied cognition states that all cognition occurs as a consequence of the body's sensorimotor experiences with its environment [24]. Within this framework the theory of image schemas was introduced as a link between embodied experiences and mental representations [11,16]. As natural language understanding remains one of the major obstacles in the advancement of artificial intelligence, there has been an increased interest in utilising image schemas as a stepping stone towards simulating human cognition through formal representations.

Image schemas may be described as spatio-temporal relationships between objects and their environment [15]. In developmental psychology, they are thought to develop as infants are repeatedly exposed to certain spatial relationships [20]. In cognitive linguistics, image schemas are primarily studied as conceptual skeletons that underlie metaphors, analogical reasoning and abstract concepts [8].

However, research on image schemas raises many challenges. As image schemas are abstract mental patterns, there exists currently no complete and

© Springer International Publishing AG 2017
F. Esposito et al. (Eds.): AI*IA 2017, LNAI 10640, pp. 256–268, 2017.
https://doi.org/10.1007/978-3-319-70169-1_19

agreed upon list of image schemas. Despite this lack of common ground in the research field, some commonly investigated image schemas are CONTAINMENT, SUPPORT and SOURCE_PATH_GOAL.[1]

Regarding identification, classification and formalisation of image schemas, there are three main considerations to be taken into account. The first is that image schemas are rarely clear-cut notions in themselves, but rather appear as networks of closely associated relationships [10]. The second, related issue, is that while image schemas are, by definition, the most generic conceptual building blocks, they also function as building blocks for each other. For example, when investigating established image schemas such as BLOCKAGE or CAUSED_MOVEMENT, these more complicated image schemas can be dissected into simpler image schemas such as SOURCE_PATH_GOAL and CONTACT. A third, unfortunately often neglected, aspect of image schemas is their dynamic nature. Not only are they spatially complex, but they are also temporally complex, and they involve force dynamics.

In this paper we try to address these issues by applying methods from *qualitative spatial reasoning* (QSR) [19]. QSR is an area of AI that studies spatio-temporal reasoning that approximates human common-sense understanding of space. Research in QSR is, typically, about a given set of spatial relations (e.g., Left, Right, FrontOf, Behind, Above, Below), their logical dependencies, and how they may be used to describe complex spatial arrangements.

The main hypothesis of this paper is the following: image schemas may be represented in a language that combines features from several existing QSR theories. This representation enables the analysis of dependencies and connections between image schemas and it enables us to take into account the temporal dimension of image schemas. Therefore, this paper introduces a novel logic, called ISL^M, for image schemas combining the Region Connection Calculus (RCC-8), Qualitative Trajectory Calculus (QTC), Cardinal Directions (CD) and Linear Temporal Logic (LTL).

To illustrate the modelling capabilities of ISL^M, we introduce a static Two-Object image schema family involving CONTACT and SUPPORT. Considering the addition of movement and temporal change, we then show how ISL^M can express more complex and dynamic image-schematic scenarios: BLOCKAGE, the ceasing of MOVEMENT_OF_OBJECT; CAUSED_MOVEMENT, the beginning of MOVEMENT_OF_OBJECT through an impact with another object; and 'bouncing', the event in which an object encountering BLOCKAGE reverses in the opposite trajectory.

2   A Logic for Directed Movement ISL^M

In general, the rich models of time investigated in more cognitively-driven studies on how humans understand time in poetry, everyday cognition, language in general, and communication can not be mapped easily to existing temporal

---

[1] We write established image schemas in small caps.

logic approaches [3,5]. The limitations of off-the-shelf calculi also extends to the spatial domain, and to standard spatio-temporal combined logics, see e.g. [13]. The well known Region Connection Calculus (RCC) has been used extensively in qualitative spatial reasoning [4]. However, cognitive studies have supported the claim that humans do not typically make, or accept, some of the distinctions inherent in the RCC calculus [12]. A simpler calculus (usually called RCC-5), can be obtained by removing the distinction between e.g., 'proper part' and 'tangential proper part', however collapsing the logic to pure mereology [17]. At the other end of the spectrum is the work of [1], who attempted to model the image schema of containment from the linguistic perspective. To map the pertinent distinctions made in natural language concerning variations of containment (such as 'surround', 'enclose'), they needed to *extend axiomatically* the RCC theory to capture the identified eight different kinds of containers.

2.1   The Spatial Dimension – Topology of Regions

Before we can move on to the modelling scenarios sketched in the introduction, we need to introduce the logical framework in some detail. First, following the work that has been laid out by amongst others [1,7], the Region Connection Calculus (RCC) is used as a method to represent basic topological spatial relationships. Here we are using the RCC-8 relation [21]. The reason is that a mere mereology would not suffice for modelling image schemas as we need a means to express that two objects touch each other (EC).[2]

2.2   The Spatial Dimension – Cardinal Directions

Directions can be absolute or relative. Usually, left and right denote relative directions [23], which however are conceptually and computationally much more complicated than (absolute) cardinal directions [18] like North or West. We here assume a naive egocentric view (i.e. with a fixed observer that is not part of the model), from which directions like left/right, front/behind and above/below can be recognised as cardinal directions. This leads to six binary predicates on objects: *Left*, *Right*, *FrontOf*, *Behind*, *Above* and *Below*. Note that these relations are unions of base relations in a three-dimensional cardinal direction calculus as in [18], and the latter can be recovered from these relations by taking suitable intersections and complements (for example, it is possible that none of the above six relations hold, which happens to be the case if two regions are equal or largely overlap).

2.3   The Movement Dimension

In order to take the dynamic aspects of the image schemas into account, the Qualitative Trajectory Calculus (QTC) [26] is used to represent how two objects

---

[2] For this paper, we only use EC and DC (disconnected). However, when looking at image schemas such as CONTAINMENT additional members of these qualitative relations are needed. Moreover, proximity spaces and point-free Whiteheadian systems based on 'connection' [25] will be considered as alternatives in future work.

relate in terms of movement. In its variant QTC_{B1D}, the trajectories of objects are described in relation to one another. While [26] use nine different relations[3], these are composed of two independent parts, with three possibilities for each part. We here simplify the calculus by only considering these three possibilities: if object O_1 moves towards O_2's position, this is represented as $O_1 \rightsquigarrow O_2$, if O_1 moves away from O_2's position, this is represented as $O_1 \hookleftarrow O_2$, while O_1 being at rest with respect to O_2's position is expressed as $O_1 \mid\circ O_2$. This way of writing the relative movement of two objects is intuitive and expressive. The calculus of [26] can be recovered by taking intersections of these relations, combining the description of the movement of O_1 with respect to O_2's position with the description of the movement of O_2 with respect to O_1's position. For example, $O_1 \rightsquigarrow O_2 \wedge O_2 \hookleftarrow O_1$ is denoted as $O_{1-} + O_2$ in [26].

With QTC, we can speak about relative movement for a given time point. What is missing is the ability to speak about the future.

2.4 The Temporal Dimension

We use the simple linear temporal logic LTL [14,22], but interpreted over the reals instead of over the naturals. The syntax is as follows:

$$\varphi ::= p \mid \top \mid \neg\varphi \mid \varphi \wedge \varphi \mid \varphi U \varphi$$

$\varphi U \psi$ reads as "φ holds, until ψ holds". As is standard in temporal logic, we can define the following derived operators:

- $F\varphi$ (at some time in the future, φ) is defined as $\top U\varphi$,
- $G\varphi$ (at all times in the future, φ) is defined as $\neg F\neg\varphi$.

We moreover use $\rightarrow$ for material implication, $\leftrightarrow$ for biimplication, and $\veebar$ for exclusive disjunction.

2.5 The Combined Logic ISL^M

Syntax of ISL^M: The syntax of ISL^M is defined over the combined languages of RCC-8, QTC_{B1D}, cardinal direction (CD), and linear temporal logic (LTL) over the reals, with 3D Euclidan space assumed for the spatial domain. Note that we need LTL over real-time in order to interpret QTC relations, the semantics of which assume continuous time. ISL^M therefore stands for 'Image Schema Logic' and $M = \langle RCC\text{-}8, QTC_{B1D}, CD, LTL, \text{3D-Euclid} \rangle$. The combination of the spatial and temporal modalities follows the temporalisation strategy of [6].

Signatures (vocabularies). A signature $\Sigma = (R_r, R_f)$ consist of a set R_r of rigid and a set R_f of flexible object names. In the context of modelling image schemas, though not playing a central role in the present paper, this will be useful to handle the modelling of objects that do not change their position nor

---

[3] The reason for using nine relations is the wish to obtain a partition of the space of all relations between two objects, as is usually done in qualitative spatial reasoning.

their extension during a period of time (like a house) vs. objects that essentially have to change (like a moving ball or a balloon being inflated).

Σ-**Sentences** are LTL temporal formulas (see Sect. 2.4) built over (ground) atomic formulas taken from the union of RCC-8 statements (see Sect. 2.1), 3D cardinal directions (see Sect. 2.2) and QTC_{B1D} (see Sect. 2.3), plus the forces predicate. Atomic formulas apply predicates to object names $O_1, O_2, \ldots \in R_r \cup R_f$.[4]

Example 1. Here are a few examples of well-formed sentences that can be written in this language (and might be considered true in specific scenarios). Note, however, that none of them are valid (i.e. true in all models), but can be valid in scenarios where the geometry of objects and possible movements are further restricted in the description of the semantics, or can alternatively be used to prescribe admissible models.

- *FrontOf*$(a, b) \wedge \mathbf{F}\neg$*FrontOf*$(a, b) \longrightarrow \mathbf{F}(a \rightsquigarrow b \vee a \hookleftarrow b \vee b \rightsquigarrow a \vee b \hookleftarrow a)$ 'If a is in front of b, but ceases to do so in the future, then sometime in the future, either a or b must move with respect to the other object's original position';
- *Above*$(a, b) \wedge \mathbf{G} a \mid\circ b \longrightarrow \mathbf{G}$*Above*$(a, b)$ 'If a is above b and never moves relative to b, it will be always above b'. Note that this sentence is not valid: consider e.g. that a circles around b with constant distance. However, it holds if for example a and b always stay on the same line (that is, their relative movement is 1D only);
- $DC(a, b) \wedge \mathbf{G} a \hookleftarrow b \longrightarrow \mathbf{G}DC(a, b)$ 'If a is disconnected to b and always moves away from it, it will always stay disconnected to b'. This is actually a validity.

Semantics of ISL^M: We interpret the combined logic ISL^M spatially over regions in $\mathbb{R}^3$ and temporally over the real line. Note that we need continuous time in order to interpret QTC properly.[5] An interpretation (model) $M = (\text{-}|_M\text{-}, forces_M)$ consists of

- a function

$$\text{-}|_M\text{-} : (R_r \cup R_f) \times \mathbb{R} \to \mathcal{P}(\mathbb{R}^3)$$

such that $r|_M t$ is the region covered by object r at time t, and $r|_M t$ does not depend on t for $r \in R_r$, and
- a relation

$$forces_M(t) \subseteq (R_r \cup R_f) \times (R_r \cup R_f)$$

such that $forces_M(t)(r, s)$ if object r imposes force on object s at time t.

Given a formula φ and a time point $t \in \mathbb{R}$, we define its satisfaction $M, t \models \varphi$ as follows. If φ is an atomic formula, we define

---

[4] Introducing variables and (controlled, cognitively-motivated) quantification over objects is left for a future extension of the logic.

[5] Studying alternatives to this choice is part of future work.

- If R is an RCC-8 relation, $M, t \models R(r, s)$ holds if $r|_M t$ is in relation R with $s|_M t$, following the RCC-8 semantics in [21].
- if R is a cardinal direction relation, then
  - $M, t \models \mathit{Left}(r, s)$ holds if $\inf\{x \mid (x, y, z) \in r|_M t\} \geq \sup\{x \mid (x, y, z) \in s|_M t\}$.
    $M, t \models \mathit{Right}(r, s)$ holds if $M, t \models \mathit{Left}(s, r)$ holds.
  - $M, t \models \mathit{FrontOf}(r, s)$ holds if $\inf\{y \mid (x, y, z) \in r|_M t\} \geq \sup\{y \mid (x, y, z) \in s|_M t\}$.
    $M, t \models \mathit{Behind}(r, s)$ holds if $M, t \models \mathit{FrontOf}(s, r)$ holds.
  - $M, t \models \mathit{Above}(r, s)$ holds if $\inf\{z \mid (x, y, z) \in r|_M t\} \geq \sup\{z \mid (x, y, z) \in s|_M t\}$.
    $M, t \models \mathit{Below}(r, s)$ holds if $M, t \models \mathit{Above}(s, r)$ holds.
- $M, t \models \mathsf{forces}(r, s)$ holds if $\mathit{forces}_M(t)(r, s)$.
- QTC_{B1D} formulas are interpreted as in [26], but over regions as moving objects. Therefore, we define distance between regions as follows, based on the usual Euclidean distance d:

$$d(Y, Z) = \inf\{d(y, z) \mid y \in Y, z \in Z\}$$

Then, given region names r and s, exactly one of three cases occurs:
  - $M, t \models r \rightsquigarrow s$ iff r is moving towards s's position, that is, if
    $$\exists t_1 (t_1 < t \wedge \forall t^- (t_1 < t^- < t \rightarrow d(r|_M t^-, s|_M t) > d(r|_M t, s|_M t))) \wedge$$
    $$\exists t_2 (t < t_2 \wedge \forall t^+ (t < t^+ < t_2 \rightarrow d(r|_M t, s|_M t) > d(r|_M t^+, s|_M t)))$$
  - $M, t \models r \leftarrowtail s$ iff r is moving away from s's position, that is, if
    $$\exists t_1 (t_1 < t \wedge \forall t^- (t_1 < t^- < t \rightarrow d(r|_M t^-, s|_M t) < d(r|_M t, s|_M t))) \wedge$$
    $$\exists t_2 (t < t_2 \wedge \forall t^+ (t < t^+ < t_2 \rightarrow d(r|_M t, s|_M t) < r(k|_M t^+, s|_M t)))$$
  - $M, t \models r \mid \circ\; s$ iff r is of stable distance with respect to s, that is, in all other cases. Note that stable distance does not imply absence of relative movement. For example, consider that r moves around s but keeps the distance stable (e.g. a satellite moves around the earth). It could even be that r is inside s and moves there (and the distance is constantly 0).

Satisfaction of complex formulas is inherited from LTL:

- for atomic p, $M, t \models p$ has been defined above
- $M, t \models \neg\varphi$ iff not $M, t \models \varphi$
- $M, t \models \varphi \wedge \psi$ iff $M, t \models \varphi$ and $M, t \models \psi$
- $M, t \models \varphi U \psi$ iff for some $u > t$, $M, u \models \psi$ and $M, v \models \varphi$ for all $v \in [t, u)$.

Finally, φ holds in M, denoted $M \models \varphi$, if for all $t \in \mathbb{R}$, $M, t \models \varphi$.

A notable feature of this semantics is that the timepoint where relative movement starts or stops does itself not belong to the set of timepoints where relative movement occurs. As a consequence, relative movement implies disconnectedness, that is

$$(r \rightsquigarrow s \vee r \leftarrowtail s) \rightarrow DC(r, s)$$

is a validity. If two objects are e.g. externally connected (EC), their distance is 0, and therefore, they cannot move away from or towards to each other. Suppose that the distance of two objects is 0 at time 1, and relative movement starts at time 1. Then the two objects will be EC and stable (unmoved) at time 1, but will be DC and in relative movement for the interval $(1, 1 + \varepsilon]$ for some $\varepsilon > 0$.

3   VERTICALITY, ATTRACTION and the Static 'Two-Object' Family

Before moving on to image schemas that encompass two objects in spatial contact with each other, here referred to as a subset of the 'Two-Object family', we need to introduce two other important image schemas: the VERTICALITY schema and the ATTRACTION schema. This is important as we need image schematic components from these to successfully build the Two-Object family.

VERTICALITY is believed to be one of the earliest image schemas to be learned based on the human body's vertical axis and the perceived effect gravity has on objects [11]. In its static form, VERTICALITY represents orientation and relational notions of above and below.

Likewise, image schemas such as ATTRACTION and conceptual structures that encompass physical forces are experienced and conceptualised in the first six months [20]. Objects fall to the ground, not because of VERTICALITY in itself, but because of the "ATTRACTION objects have to the ground"[6]. ATTRACTION is part of the force group of image schemas [11], and while it is more complicated than simple 'force towards/from', we ascertain that for the purpose of extracting conceptual primitives of force relations, ATTRACTION provides a good starting point.

THE TWO-OBJECT FAMILY: **an excerpt from the extended image schema family of relationships between two objects**

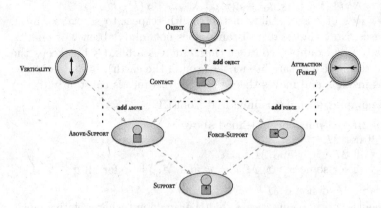

Fig. 1. How CONTACT can be hierarchically connected to SUPPORT through addition of spatial primitives from VERTICALITY and ATTRACTION.

Figure 1 illustrates how some of the image schemas involving two objects can be formally developed. In the most general form, CONTACT represents the object relation in which two objects are physically touching. This is strongly related

---

[6] Children naturally do not understand gravity, yet they learn to predict that objects are 'forced' downwards.

to the notion of SUPPORT. However, it is unlikely that infants understand the forces acting in an image schema like SUPPORT. Therefore, in many scenarios it might be sufficient to speak of SUPPORT in terms of CONTACT with 'above' orientation. By merging the image schema CONTACT with the static form of VERTICALITY ('above') we get an Above-SUPPORT image schema.

If instead of VERTICALITY, force is added to CONTACT, another weaker SUPPORT can be distinguished, Force-SUPPORT. Here the important aspect is that the supporting object offers physical support, which does not have to be vertical. For instance, a plank that 'leans against a wall' also captures a form of SUPPORT. The most specific and traditional form of SUPPORT is constructed when both Above-SUPPORT and Force-SUPPORT are combined.[7]

In the next section we will demonstrate how the CONTACT and SUPPORT notions as presented in the Two-Object family can be formally represented.

3.1 Formalising the Static Image Schemas Contact and Support

As discussed above, CONTACT is the most general image schema in which two objects have a (physical) connection to each other. For CONTACT, the object relationship is without any force dynamics neither does it contain any topological or orientational requirements.

CONTACT is one of the simplest image schemas to conceptualise and consequently also to formally represent using our logic. For our purposes, CONTACT is formalised as two regions, here represented by object names O_1 and O_2, touching, which is represented in RCC-8 as $\text{CONTACT}(O_1, O_2) \leftrightarrow EC(O_1, O_2)$.

SUPPORT requires a more involved formalisation given that ATTRACTION or 'force' and/or VERTICALITY and 'above'-ness are involved to keep one object in contact with another object. Therefore, we first need a formal representation of both 'above' and 'force'. VERTICALITY in terms of above (and below) orientation is expressed with the following predicate $Above(x, y)$ where x is above y, and $forces(x, y)$ demonstrate how x puts physical force on y (see Sect. 2.5 for details). Given this, we can formalise the two weaker SUPPORT versions, Above-SUPPORT and Force-SUPPORT, and when these are merged the union correspond to universal and more complete version of SUPPORT (see Fig. 1).

$$Above\text{-}\text{SUPPORT}(O_1, O_2) \leftrightarrow EC(O_1, O_2) \wedge Above(O_1, O_2)$$
$$Force\text{-}\text{SUPPORT}(O_1, O_2) \leftrightarrow EC(O_1, O_2) \wedge \mathsf{forces}(O_1, O_2)$$
$$\text{SUPPORT}(O_1, O_2) \leftrightarrow EC(O_1, O_2) \wedge Above(O_1, O_2) \wedge \mathsf{forces}(O_1, O_2)$$

In the next section we proceed to use these formalisations to demonstrate some more intricate examples by formalising the dynamic image schematic events BLOCKAGE, CAUSED_MOVEMENT and bouncing.

---

[7] The authors acknowledge that additional CONTACT and SUPPORT relationships may exist that have not been considered in this paper.

4   The Dynamic Image Schemas BLOCKAGE, CAUSED_MOVEMENT and Bouncing

Before we move on to dynamic image schema combinations, we need to introduce the image schemas for movement. The SOURCE_PATH_GOAL schema can be dissected into a range of different simpler (and more complex) forms of movements (see [9] for an overview). In our logic we simplify movement by using the QTC primitives.

4.1   Formalisations of the Narratives Behind BLOCKAGE, CAUSED_MOVEMENT and Bouncing

Following the arguments presented in [2] where complex image schemas and simple events emerge as consequences of combinations of simpler image schemas, we now proceed to demonstrate how using the logic presented above yields a formal rendering of BLOCKAGE, CAUSED_MOVEMENT and 'bouncing'.

(a) O_1 On PATH Toward O_2 (b) O_1 BLOCKED by O_2 (c) O_1 in CONTACT with O_2

Fig. 2. Illustrations of the three time intervals of BLOCKAGE.

BLOCKAGE. The simplest form of blocked movement is the scenario in which the movement of an object simply ceases to exist. While BLOCKAGE is considered an image schema in its own right, it is also possible to describe blockage using a series of simple image-schematic events: MOVEMENT_OF_OBJECT[8], CONTACT and force followed by the lack of MOVEMENT_OF_OBJECT, see Fig. 2. Formalised, it reads:

$$\text{On\_PATH\_Toward}(O_1, O_2) = (O_1 \rightsquigarrow O_2 \land DC(O_1, O_2))$$
$$((a)\ O_1 \text{ on PATH toward } O_2)$$

$$\text{Blocked\_By}(O_1, O_2) = (O_1 \mid\circ O_2 \land O_2 \mid\circ O_1 \land \textit{Force-}\text{SUPPORT}(O_1, O_2))$$
$$((b)\ O_1 \text{ BLOCKED by } O_2)$$

$$\text{In\_CONTACT}(O_1, O_2) = (O_1 \mid\circ O_2 \land O_2 \mid\circ O_1 \land EC(O_2, O_1))$$
$$((c)\ O_1 \text{ in CONTACT with } O_2)$$

The temporal scenario of 'blocked movement' is temporally captured as follows:

$$\text{On\_PATH\_Toward}(O_1, O_2) \land$$
$$\mathbf{F}\big(\text{Blocked\_By}(O_1, O_2) \land \mathbf{G}(\text{In\_CONTACT}(O_1, O_2))\big)$$

---

[8] Alternatively, it is possible to make it more specific by determining also the path that the object is moving on, namely through MOVEMENT_ALONG_PATH.

Here, the nested future time operator guarantees that these events happen in the correct temporal order.

As these first steps until contact happens between two objects reoccur for all the subsequent scenarios, we will make repeated use of these defined predicates of On_PATH_Toward(O_1, O_2) and BLOCKed_By(O_1, O_2). One interesting thing to note here is that formalised and in combination with motion, BLOCKAGE works much like Force-SUPPORT. Compare the definition for SUPPORT and the definition for BLOCKed_By. The only difference is the addition of a temporal aspect through the lack of movement. This is an interesting observation, as our experience is affected by the physical world, meaning that gravitational pull could be viewed as a sort of 'downward' movement and that all SUPPORT is simply BLOCKAGE of that movement.

CAUSED_MOVEMENT. There are more scenarios that can result from BLOCK-AGE than the static relation of CONTACT between the moving object and the blocking object, presented above. One of the first more 'complex' image schemas that appear in the literature is CAUSED_MOVEMENT. Namely the spatio-temporal relationship that results from one object colliding with another and causing that object to move.

Simplified, the image schema comes in three different forms. First, in the scenario in which the hitting object comes to rest while the hit object continues onward (e.g. as in a well executed billiards chock) referred to as "Pure_CM". Second, in which both objects continue in disjoint forward movement, "Pursuit_CM". There is also a third scenario in which the objects continue forward movement together, "Joint_CM". However, as CAUSED_MOVEMENT focus on the second object, this third form is currently ignored as it implies 'pushing' and agency of the first object, a modality not yet present in the logic.

Formalised, it reads:

$$\text{On\_PATH\_Toward}(O_1, O_2) \qquad\qquad (O_1 \text{ on PATH toward } O_2)$$
$$\text{BLOCKed\_By}(O_1, O_2) \qquad\qquad (O_1 \text{ BLOCKed by } O_2)$$

CAUSED_MOVEMENT alternative ending one, Pure_CM (see Fig. 3a) followed by alternative ending two Pursuit_CM in which both objects move forward (see Fig. 3b):

$$\text{Pure\_CM}(O_1, O_2) = O_2 \hookleftarrow O_1 \wedge O_1 \mathbin{|\!\circ} O_2 \wedge DC(O_1, O_2)$$
$$\text{Pursuit\_CM}(O_1, O_2) = O_1 \rightsquigarrow O_2 \wedge O_2 \hookleftarrow O_1 \wedge DC(O_1, O_2)$$

$$((a) \ O_2 \text{ moves away from } O_1, \ O_1 \text{ is at rest in respect of } O_2)$$
$$((b) \ O_1 \text{ moves towards } O_2 \text{ which moves away from } O_1)$$

In temporal representation, the full scenario of CAUSED_MOVEMENT looks as follows:

$$\text{On\_PATH\_Toward}(O_1, O_2) \wedge$$
$$\mathbf{F}\big(\text{BLOCKed\_By}(O_1, O_2) \wedge \mathbf{F}(\text{Pure\_CM}(O_1, O_2) \mathbin{\underline{\vee}} \text{Joint\_CM}(O_1, O_2)) \big)$$

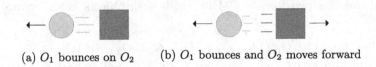

(a) O_2 move away from O_1 (b) O_1, O_2 move forward

Fig. 3. Illustrations of the two formalised alternative endings of CAUSED_MOVEMENT.

Bouncing. Another natural scenario that happens as one object hits another, is 'bouncing'. In comparison to CAUSED_MOVEMENT the object of interest here is not the object that is hit but rather the object that is doing the hitting.

The formalisations below correspond to the picture in Fig. 4a.

$$\text{On\_PATH\_Toward}(O_1, O_2) \hspace{3cm} ((a)\ O_1 \text{ on PATH toward } O_2)$$
$$\text{BLOCKed\_By}(O_1, O_2) \hspace{3cm} ((b)\ O_1 \text{ BLOCKed by } O_2)$$
$$\text{Bouncing}(O_1, O_2) = O_1 \leftharpoonup O_2 \wedge O_2 \mid\!\circ O_1 \wedge DC(O_1, O_2)$$
$$((c)\ O_1 \text{ on PATH from } O_2 \text{ which is at rest in respect of } O_1)$$

In full temporal representation the scenario looks as follows:

$$\text{On\_PATH\_Toward}(O_1, O_2) \wedge \mathbf{F}\big(\ \text{BLOCKed\_By}(O_1, O_2) \wedge \mathbf{F}(Bouncing(O_1, O_2))\big)$$

Combination of CAUSED_MOVEMENT and Bouncing. Another, quite natural scenario is the combination of *bouncing* with CAUSED_MOVEMENT. In this scenario the hitting object O_1 bounces on O_2 while at the same time the impact pushes the blocking object away (see Fig. 4b). Formalised, it reads:

$$\text{On\_PATH\_Toward}(O_1, O_2) \hspace{3cm} ((a)\ O_1 \text{ on PATH toward } O_2)$$
$$\text{BLOCKed\_By}(O_1, O_2) \hspace{3cm} ((b)\ O_1 \text{ BLOCKed by } O_2)$$
$$\text{Bouncing\_CM}(O_1, O_2) = O_1 \leftharpoonup O_2 \wedge O_2 \leftharpoonup O_1 \wedge DC(O_1, O_2)$$
$$((c)\ O_1 \text{ and } O_2 \text{ are on PATHs away from each other})$$

(a) O_1 bounces on O_2 (b) O_1 bounces and O_2 moves forward

Fig. 4. Illustrations of the results of bouncing respectively the result of the combination of CAUSED_MOVEMENT and bouncing.

5 Conclusion and Future Work

Developing a formal theory of image schemas is essential for several areas of cognitively motivated AI, such as computational conceptual blending [10], and can also be used, as done in this paper, to better analyse formally distinctions motivated by empirical research.

The paper has presented a novel way to formally represent image schemas in a language that combines features from several existing QSR theories. The representation illuminates the internal structure of image schemas. One result is that there are families of image schemas that contain closely related image schemas (e.g., the different kinds of SUPPORT). Further, some image schemas are part of others (e.g., Force-SUPPORT is part of BLOCKAGE). The formalism also allows us to represent the different stages of an image schema and, thus, represent its temporal dimension.

The formalisation builds on a combination of Linear Temporal Logic (LTL) [14], Qualitative Trajectory Calculus [26], Cardinal Directions, and the RCC-8 relations [21] that previously were used to formally approach image schemas. The combination approach following [6] allows for controlled interaction between the dimensions, and a decidability and complexity analysis is part of future work.

The modelling approach is illustrated with the 'Two Object' family, capturing some static relationships between two objects, as well as using it to narratively express the dynamic image schemas and simple events 'BLOCKAGE', 'CAUSED-MOVEMENT' and 'bouncing', originally introduced in [2].

Future work includes to use the logic to model concrete scenarios, and to illustrate how it supports common sense reasoning based on image schemas and e.g. the logical prediction of future events such as BLOCKAGE, as well as extend the logic with other modalities, for instance, the notion of agency.

References

1. Bennett, B., Cialone, C.: Corpus guided sense cluster analysis: a methodology for ontology development (with examples from the spatial domain). In: 8th International Conference on Formal Ontology in Information Systems (FOIS). Frontiers in Artificial Intelligence and Applications, vol. 267, pp. 213–226. IOS Press (2014)
2. Besold, T.R., Hedblom, M.M., Kutz, O.: A narrative in three acts: using combinations of image schemas to model events. BICA **19**, 10–20 (2017)
3. Boroditsky, L.: Metaphoric structuring: understanding time through spatial metaphors. Cognition **75**(1), 1–28 (2000)
4. Cohn, A.G., Bennett, B., Gooday, J., Gotts, N.: RCC: a calculus for region based qualitative spatial reasoning. GeoInformatica **1**, 275–316 (1997)
5. Coulson, S., Cánovas, C.P.: Understanding timelines: conceptual metaphor and conceptual integration. Cogn. Semiot. **5**(1–2), 198–219 (2014)
6. Finger, M., Gabbay, D.M.: Adding a temporal dimension to a logic system. J. Log. Lang. Inform. **1**, 203–233 (1993)
7. Galton, A.: The formalities of affordance. In: Bhatt, M., Guesgen, H., Hazarika, S. (eds.) Proceedinds of Workshop Spatio-Temporal Dynamics, pp. 1–6 (2010)
8. Hampe, B., Grady, J.E.: From Perception to Meaning: Image Schemas in Cognitive Linguistics, vol. 29. Walter de Gruyter, Berlin (2005)
9. Hedblom, M.M., Kutz, O., Neuhaus, F.: Choosing the right path: image schema theory as a foundation for concept invention. JAGI **6**(1), 22–54 (2015)

10. Hedblom, M.M., Kutz, O., Neuhaus, F.: Image schemas in computational conceptual blending. Cogn. Syst. Res. **39**, 42–57 (2016)
11. Johnson, M.: The Body in the Mind: The Bodily Basis of Meaning, Imagination, and Reason. The University of Chicago Press, Chicago (1987)
12. Knauff, M., Rauh, R., Renz, J.: A cognitive assessment of topological spatial relations: results from an empirical investigation. In: Hirtle, S.C., Frank, A.U. (eds.) COSIT 1997. LNCS, vol. 1329, pp. 193–206. Springer, Heidelberg (1997). doi:10.1007/3-540-63623-4_51
13. Kontchakov, R., Kurucz, A., Wolter, F., Zakharyaschev, M.: Spatial logic + temporal logic=? In: Aiello, M., Pratt-Hartmann, I., Van Benthem, J. (eds.) Handbook of Spatial Logics, pp. 497–564. Springer, Dordrecht (2007). doi:10.1007/978-1-4020-5587-4_9
14. Kröger, F., Merz, S.: Temporal Logic and State Systems. (Texts in Theoretical Computer Science. An EATCS Series). Springer, Heidelberg (2008). doi:10.1007/978-3-540-68635-4
15. Kuhn, W.: An image-schematic account of spatial categories. In: Winter, S., Duckham, M., Kulik, L., Kuipers, B. (eds.) COSIT 2007. LNCS, vol. 4736, pp. 152–168. Springer, Heidelberg (2007). doi:10.1007/978-3-540-74788-8_10
16. Lakoff, G.: Women, Fire, and Dangerous Things. What Categories Reveal about the Mind. The University of Chicago Press, Chicago (1987)
17. Lehmann, F., Cohn, A.G.: The EGG/YOLK reliability hierarchy: semantic data integration using sorts with prototypes. In: Proceedings of Conference on Information Knowledge Management, pp. 272–279. ACM Press (1994)
18. Ligozat, G.: Reasoning about cardinal directions. J. Vis. Lang. Comput. **9**(1), 23–44 (1998)
19. Ligozat, G.: Qualitative Spatial and Temporal Reasoning. Wiley, New York (2011)
20. Mandler, J.M.: The Foundations of Mind: Origins of Conceptual Thought: Origins of Conceptual Though. Oxford University Press, New York (2004)
21. Randell, D.A., Cui, Z., Cohn, A.G.: A spatial logic based on regions and connection. In: Proceedings of 3rd International Conference on Knowledge Representation and Reasoning (KR-1992) (1992)
22. Reynolds, M.: The complexity of temporal logic over the reals. Ann. Pure Appl. Log. **161**(8), 1063–1096 (2010)
23. Scivos, A., Nebel, B.: The finest of its class: the natural point-based ternary calculus $\mathcal{LR}$ for qualitative spatial reasoning. In: Freksa, C., Knauff, M., Krieg-Brückner, B., Nebel, B., Barkowsky, T. (eds.) Spatial Cognition 2004. LNCS, vol. 3343, pp. 283–303. Springer, Heidelberg (2005). doi:10.1007/978-3-540-32255-9_17
24. Shapiro, L.: Embodied Cogn. New problems of philosophy, Routledge, London and New York (2011)
25. Vakarelov, D., Düntsch, I., Bennett, B.: A note on proximity spaces and connection based mereology. In: Proceedings of International Conference on Formal Ontology in Information Systems (FOIS), pp. 139–150 (2001)
26. Weghe, N.V.D., Cohn, A.G., Tré, G.D., Maeyer, P.D.: A qualitative trajectory calculus as a basis for representing moving objects in geographical information systems. Control Cybern. **35**(1), 97–119 (2006)

Document Layout Analysis for Semantic Information Extraction

Weronika T. Adrian[1,2(✉)], Nicola Leone[1], Marco Manna[1], and Cinzia Marte[1]

[1] Department of Mathematics and Computer Science, University of Calabria,
87036 Rende, Italy
{w.adrian,leone,manna,marte}@mat.unical.it
[2] AGH University of Science and Technology, Krakow, Poland

Abstract. Using machines to automatically extract relevant information from unstructured and semi-structured sources has practical significance in todays life and business. In this context, although understanding the meaning of words is important, the process of identifying self-consistent geometric and logical regions of interest—blocks, cells, columns and tables, as well as paragraphs, titles and captions, only to mention a few—is of paramount importance too. This complex process goes under the name of document layout analysis. In this work, we discuss newly designed techniques to solve this problem effectively, by combining both syntactic and semantic document aspects. These techniques described here are at the basis of KnowRex, a comprehensive system for ontology-driven Information Extraction.

Keywords: Document Layout Analysis · Information Extraction · Table recognition · Answer Set Programming · Ontologies · Knowledge representation

1 Introduction

Nowadays, it is increasingly needed to acquire, analyze and process complex documents digitally. To this end, multiple areas of Artificial Intelligence study the problem under different viewpoints and propose complementary approaches and techniques. In particular, (semantic) *Information Extraction* [6,14] faces new challenges related to processing large volumes of data, which are often "heterogeneous" in the sense that analyzed documents contain complex objects such as diagrams, images, and tables besides plain text. For humans, the visual presentation of data is often helpful for conveying and understanding information. Conversely, for a machine, it may be an additional challenge to correctly process document contents presented through a variety of page layout.

The analysis of documents with heterogeneous information normally starts with the so-called *semantic annotation* [22], which basically maps words or phrases to preconceived ontological concepts. This way, the meaning of such portions of text is self-consistent, and unambiguous also for machines. However,

© Springer International Publishing AG 2017
F. Esposito et al. (Eds.): AI*IA 2017, LNAI 10640, pp. 269–281, 2017.
https://doi.org/10.1007/978-3-319-70169-1_20

the spatial "context" in which certain strings of text appear in a document often adds an extra value to the overall process of interpreting the given document [4]. To get and exploit this kind of information, one should analyze layout and structure of the document.

The field of *Document Layout Analysis* (DLA) [20, 28] is concerned with geometrical and logical labeling of document content. Existing techniques approach the problem on different levels: from pixels, through words, sentences, lines, up to two-dimensional blocks. The solutions usually focus on specific applications and domains, such as academic papers [25] medical reports [26] or other collections of complex documents [3, 4, 24]. The complexity of the task of document analysis stems from the fact that strictly geometrical features (alignment of words, lines, columns) and logical intentions (arrangement of sections, headings etc.) are often interconnected. However, most of the existing tools fail to fully address this interconnections, operating only within one of the two dimensions. Ideally, one should try to maximally exploit the geometric information intrinsically owned by an arbitrary document to identify the basic self-consistent blocks of text, and then enhance the analysis by taking into account semantic information recognized inside these blocks to fully understand the actual layout.

In this paper, we address the problem of document layout analysis for semantic information extraction. Specifically, we propose to combine geometrical, structural and semantic analysis, to obtain more precise representation of complex documents. We use Answer Set Programming [7], table recognition [29] and semantic annotation to implement the technique. This syntactic-semantic approach is used in a successful ontology-driven IE framework called *KnowRex* [1] that is able to automatically process arbitrary collections of complex documents sharing the domain of data and a common layout. The contributions of this work can be summarized as follow:

- We propose a novel method for *document layout analysis* based on geometric analysis of the regions within the document and logical understanding of its headings i.e. parts of text that semantically indicate placement of other data.
- We present an ASP-based design and implementation of the geometrical analysis of complex documents in PDF format.
- We propose a method for analysis of tabular structures with use of semantic annotation of domain-specific headings.

2   Information Extraction

The goal of Information Extraction is to obtain structured information from unstructured or semi-structured documents. The problem originally defined in 1970s in the *Natural Language Processing* (NLP) community over time evolved into an area with different sub-tasks, such as: *entity recognition, relation extraction* or *co-reference resolution*. Methods for solving these problems predominantly use variants of *text analysis*. By parsing and analyzing text and annotating it with lexical, grammatical and semantic information, the IE systems are able to comprehend the meaning of words, phrases and sentences. Recent proposals of ontology-based IE solutions [2,15] allow to manipulate collections of documents on a higher level of abstraction partially independently from the input files encoding and their low-level characteristics.

Currently Information Extraction "in the context of emerging novel kinds of large-scale corpora assumes new dimensions and reinvents itself" [23]. Dealing with the new types of document collections and the ever-increasing volumes of data poses new challenges for the IE systems. To address them, it is often necessary to analyze the input data by taking into consideration different aspects of the collection. When a human extract information from a set of somehow "similar" documents (be it with respect to their layout, structure or content) they intuitively use the common properties to locate and extract relevant information. We can understand, for instance, that some portions of text, which repeat from one document to another, serve only as special "labels" or headings that point to relevant information (e.g. specific sections in scientific papers indicate the kind of content located within them). Sometimes the structure of a document itself conveys some meaning and gives useful hints for locating desired information. For instance, a two-column layout may in fact "semantically" be a table, if in the one column there are names of "attributes" and in the others – the values of them. This is why the results of *document layout analysis* has been recently taken into consideration for the improvement of IE techniques [10,11,27]. Examples from different domains shows the benefits of combining visual, logical and semantic analysis. While there exist numerous solutions for text and documents tagged with some kind of markup language, extracting information from complex files such as PDF, where textual and graphical elements can be organized in different layouts, poses additional challenges [12,18]. PDF format in general does not guarantee a machine-readable representation of layout and structure. Instead, they must often be "recovered".

KnowRex [1] is a framework that allows to develop systems for *Semantic Information Extraction* (i.e. based on the meaning of data). The ontology-driven approach of KnowRex means that an ontology is both a reference model for the input documents, and for a "target schema" defined by user. KnowRex extracts information from collections of PDF documents that share some specific features, related to their content, structure or layout. When one considers such collections, they can informally capture the "template" which is a description of these similarities. Based on it, one can define a conceptualization of the documents in a more formal way – with an ontology that captures the sort of data contained within the documents and, to some extend, the way it is organized. KnowRex uses several techniques to extract information from the documents and populate the ontology with instances ; in particular: (i) a *two-dimensional processor* for recognizing structural elements of documents, (ii) one- and two-dimensional *tokenizers* for identifying basic elements of text, (iii) *semantic annotators* that label single words or phrases with categories, (iv) *semantic descriptors* that allow to build objects using the results of structural and semantic analysis, (v) *logical rules* to formulate mappings between representations.

Development of a new project with KnowRex consists in adapting the system to work on specific data to obtain desired results. In particular, the user extends the basic ontology with domain-specific features and "explains" to the system how to extract particular objects using available tools or creating their own *semantic descriptors*. With a few logical rules, the user defines mapping from the extracted objects to the target schema. The process of extracting information works on a different level of abstraction: layout and structure recognition, semantic annotation of text, object identification and extraction. The first stage, that influences the rest of the process, is the document layout analysis.

3   Document Layout Analysis

Document Structure and Layout Analysis [20] is a problem of decomposing a document image into its component regions and understanding their functional roles and relationships. In particular, the is concerned with the of the document, while aims to assign and labels to the recognized regions. The input of DLA is a document image. The main steps are: pre-processing (to minimize noise and correct the skew angle), page segmentation and region classification. The output is the set of regions. This basic setting can be extended e.g., the output can be a more involved, labels can be attached also to the parts of regions etc.

3.1   Classical Approaches

In literature, there exist two main approaches to document layout analysis: *bottom-up* (or aggregating) methods and *top-down* (or divisive) methods. Below we present the main characteristics of both approaches and introduce representative algorithms (for more detailed surveys see [9, 13]).

Aggregating Methods. This is a "traditional" approach, that analyzes iteratively a document, starting to link together base elements specified in detail a priori (e.g. pixels, words or text lines) to form larger subsystems, which then in turn are linked, until a complete top-level system is formed. The advantage of this kind of methods is that no hypothesis is required about the overall structure of the document. On the other hand, an iterative segmentation and clustering can require a lot of time which is the main disadvantage. One of the earliest attempts within this approach was RLSA proposed by Wong *et al.* [28]. The method works on a pixel sequence and aims to merge characters into words and words into text lines, by "smearing" the text to join single characters into bigger "blobs". This method required the image to be skew-corrected and the spacing be known and uniform within the image. An approach by Kieniger [16] starts from bigger objects, namely words. The algorithm considers an arbitrary word as a starting point and recursively expands the block formed from this word, adding the horizontally overlapping words from the previous and next lines. While many algorithms assume a Manhattan layout of the documents, the Docstrum algorithm by Gorman [21] is a bottom-up page segmentation technique based on nearest-neighborhood clustering of connected components exacted from the document image that can be applied to document page with non-Manhattan layout and arbitrary skew angle. Another bottom-up approach that works on non-Manhattan layout is the Voronoi-diagram based segmentation algorithm by Kise *et al.* [17]. The method initially extracts sample points from the boundaries of the connected components and then, after noise has been removed, generate Voronoi diagram using them. Finally, superfluous Voronoi edges are deleted. Unfortunately, these last two techniques do not perform well when the document page contains spacing variations due to different styles and font size. Since the spacing among characters and lines is estimated from the document image, spacing variations result in split errors.

Divisive Methods. In this more recent approach, a document is iteratively "cut" into columns and blocks, based on various geometric information and white spaces. The main advantage over the bottom-up techniques is the velocity of the approach, as it analyzes the overall structure of the document, removing the need to combine the characters, ranging from hundreds to thousands on a single page. In [5], the authors, describe a top-down technique that first analyzes white spaces to isolate blocks and than uses "projection profiles" to find lines. The page must have a Manhattan layout. More recent "X-Y cut" segmentation algorithm [19] is a tree-based top-down technique that represents a document by means of a rooted tree. The idea of the algorithm is to recursively split the document into two or more rectangular zones which represent the nodes of the tree. All the leaf nodes together represent the final segmentation.

It is possible to combine the two approaches into a hybrid one that uses a combination of top-down and bottom-up strategies, see for instance [8].

3.2   A Step Further

The set of regions obtained with classical algorithms represents the segmentation of a document. Despite the differences of the algorithms, their output reflects the geometrical layout of the analyzed pages. However, this is not optimally suited for our purpose, that is the Information Extraction based on the results of the layout analysis. In fact, for building extraction rules that exploit the spatial relations between pieces of text, we would like to "normalize" the purely geometrical results to obtain a "regular" layout representation: a set of regions that do not overlap and together fill the whole document (one could imagine a flat grid in which some cells are merged).

To this end, we base our method on a refinement of the classical aggregating algorithms (see Sect. 4) and combine it with table recognition and semantic annotation (see Sect. 5). More specifically, first we perform a bottom-up geometrical analysis, and then we analyze subsets of regions that together "look like" a table, and compare the text within them with a predefined "heading ontology". Thanks to this, we get to understand if some pieces of text logically follow others, even if their coordinates do not match perfectly. Based on this, we align or merge some regions, and we obtain a more meaningful two-dimensional representation of the analyzed document.

4   Words, Lines and Blocks Identification

In this section, we describe the process of identifying "self-consistent" blocks of text from a PDF document. Intuitively, the term self-consistent may refer to a paragraph, a column, a cell of table or even a title. Due to the variety of different document layouts, it is difficult to provide a universal notion of a block. In what follows, inspired by the pioneer work of Gorman [21] and a seminal paper by Kieninger [16], we propose a novel approach that seems to unify most of the previous techniques.

4.1   Geometric Approach

Form a physical point of view, any PDF document stores in a proprietary format the positional information of each "atomic" word (as well as any other kind of object, such as lines or images) occurring in it. From a logical viewpoint, each such a *word* can be characterized basically as a tuple

$$w = \langle id, val, x_1, y_1, x_2, y_2, \kappa \rangle,$$

where: (i) its first element id is a positive integer that unequivocally identifies w in the document, and that implicitly induces some total ordering among all the words in the document; (ii) the element val is a string of characters excluding every whitespace, and representing the actual content value of this word; (iii) the pair (x_1, y_1) represents the Cartesian coordinates of the top-left corner of w; (iv) the pair (x_2, y_2) represents the Cartesian coordinates of the bottom-right corner of w; and (v) the number κ is a parameter—depending on the actual size and style of the characters of w—that provides an upper-bound on the width that a standard whitespace wollowing w should have. Further on, we assume a notation for referring to particular elements of a tuple as $id(w)$, $val(w)$ etc.

As an example, consider the following pair of words selected from some PDF: $w_1 = (14, \text{"dummy"}, 75, 65, 125, 50, 8)$ and $w_2 = (15, \text{"string"}, 130, 65, 170, 50, 8)$. By analyzing these two words, one can realize that they should be visually rendered in the same "text line". In fact, the value of y_1 is 65 in both words, as well as the value of y_2 being equal to 50 both in w_1 and w_2. (In practice, to conclude that w_1 and w_2 belong to the same line, it suffices to verify that at least one of these two conditions about y_1 or y_2 is satisfied.) Moreover, one can also observe that the right-hand side of w_1 stops at $x_2 = 125$, while the left-hand side of w_2 starts at $x_1 = 130$. But since $130 - 125 = 5 < 8 = \kappa$, one can also conclude that w_2 follows w_1 not only from a visual point of view but also from a semantic viewpoint since they are sufficiently close to each other to be assumed as part of the same sentence.

Let us formally define some of the notions introduced above. Consider words $w = \langle id, val, x_1, y_1, x_2, y_2, \kappa \rangle$, and $w' = \langle id', val', x_1', y_1', x_2', y_2', \kappa' \rangle$. We say that w' *follows* w if $x_2 < x_1'$ and if at least one of the following conditions is satisfied:

1. $y'_2 \leq y_1 \leq y'_1$, and $x'_1 - x_2 \leq \kappa$; or
2. $y'_2 \leq y_2 \leq y'_1$, and $x'_1 - x_2 \leq \kappa$; or
3. $y_2 < y'_2 < y'_1 < y_1$, and $x'_1 - x_2 \leq \kappa$.

Note that these three conditions also capture cases that have not been addressed in the previous example. For instance, if we consider the words $w = (35, \text{"Adrian"}, 100, 30, 160, 10, 10)$ and $w' = (36, \text{"1, 2"}, 163, 35, 178, 25, 5)$ representing the sequence $\texttt{Adrian}^{1,2}$ of characters, the fact that w' (logically) follows w can be inferred by condition (1) as above.

To identify self-consistent blocks of text, our first step exploits the relation *follows* to aggregates words in line of text. Informally, we partition the original set of words (that represent the document) so that each element of this partition contains only words connected by the above relation. More formally, we consider a set $W = \{w_1, \ldots, w_n\}$ of words representing some PDF document. Then, we define the *document graph* $G(W)$ associated to W as the pair $\langle W, A \rangle$, where W are the nodes, and $A \subseteq W \times W$ are arcs such that $(w, w') \in A$ if, and only if, w' follows w. With this notion in place, a *line block* is formally defined as any maximal connected component of $G(W)$. (By definition, a word that is not followed by and does not follows any other word is trivially a line block.) For example, consider the set $\overline{W} = \{w_1, \ldots, w_5\}$ representing the string of text:

Document Layout Analysis: First approach

Naturally, we assume $val(w_1) = \text{"Document"}, \ldots, val(w_5) = \text{"approach"}$. Regarding $G(\overline{W}) = \langle \overline{W}, A \rangle$ we have that $A = \{(w_1, w_2), (w_2, w_3), (w_4, w_5)\}$. Observe that the pair (w_3, w_4) is not an arc of $G(\overline{W})$. In fact, w_4 does not follows w_3 due to their high distance. Hence, inside this portion we identify two different line blocks, one for w_1, w_2, and w_3, and the other for w_4 and w_5.

We have so far described the "horizontal clustering" of words, used to construct line blocks. Observe that from a logical viewpoint, also a line block can be characterized basically as a tuple $LB = \langle id, x_L, y_T, x_R, y_B \rangle$, where: (*i*) *id* is a positive integer that represent the $id(w)$ of the first word contained in the line block; (*ii*) the pair (x_L, y_T) represents the coordinates of the top-left corner of LB, where $x_L = min\{x_1(w_i) : w_i$ is a word in the LB$\}$ and $y_T = max\{y_1(w_i) : w_i$ is a word in the LB$\}$; (*iii*) the pair (x_R, y_B) represents the coordinates of the bottom-right corner of LB, where $x_R = max\{x_2(w_i) : w_i$ is a word in the LB$\}$ and $y_B = min\{y_2(w_i) : w_i$ is a word in the LB$\}$.

By applying vertically the same principle at the basis of our horizontal clustering (identifying line blocks from words), we are able to obtain *blocks* of text, by grouping line blocks. Similarly to what has been done in [16], the idea to construct a text block is to "draw a virtual stripe" over the bounding box (rectangle designated by the coordinates of the LB described above) of the line block in exam. This stripe has the width of the bounding box itself and reaches vertically to the directly adjacent line blocks. All block lines that overlap with that stripe will be bounded to the same text block. Hence, consider two line blocks $LB_{Down} = \langle id, x_L, y_T, x_R, y_B \rangle$ and $LB'_{Up} = \langle id', x'_L, y'_T, x'_R, y'_B \rangle$. We say that LB_{Down} and LB'_{Up} are *linked lines* if $y_T < y'_B$ and if at least one of the following conditions is satisfied: (1) $x'_L \leq x_L \leq x'_R$, (2) $x'_L \leq x_R \leq x'_R$, or (3) $x_L < x'_L < x'_R < x_R$. To reduce the number of comparisons, we set a limit B up to which comparisons between lines are made, i.e. we require that the line space $y'_B - y_T < B$. For example, consider the part of text

```
Department of Mathematics and Computer Science,
   University of Calabria, 87036 Rende, Italy
```

represented by $LB'_{Up} = \langle 6, 30, 165, 480, 145 \rangle$, and $LB_{Down} = \langle 12, 50, 138, 440, 118 \rangle$. We can deduce that these lines are linked because condition (1) is satisfied.

We can summarize the principal algorithm's steps as follow: (1) cluster horizontally the words into line blocks, (2) build the bounding boxes of the line blocks, (3) cluster vertically line blocks into text blocks, and (4) build the bounding boxes of the text blocks.

4.2 Logic-Based Enconding

As explained in Sect. 4.1, our input consists of a set of words, each of which can now be represent by a logic fact of the form `word(id, val, x1, y1, x2, y2, k)`. To identify pairs of words connected by the relation *follows* defined in the previous section, we use a logic rule for each of the three conditions. Due to space limits, we now report only the first one:

```
follows(IdL, IdR) :- word(IdL, ValL, X1L, Y1L, X2L, Y2L, K1),
                     word(IdR, ValR, X1R, Y1R, X2R, Y2R, K2),
                     Y2R<=Y1L, Y1L<=Y1R, X2L<X1R, Delta=X1R-X2L, Delta<=K1.
```

where `IdL` and `IdR` refer to the left and the right word, respectively. To to identify "isolated words" we use the rules:

```
follows_AUX(IdL) :- follows(IdL, IdR).
follows_AUX(IdR) :- follows(IdL, IdR).
isolateWord(Id)  :- word(Id, _, X1, Y1, X2, Y2, K), not follows_AUX(Id).
```

To identify the first element of a text line, we use a concept of an "ancestor" which is inferred from the *follows* relation, and then keep it in `inLine` predicate:

```
ancestorOf(IdA,IdB) :- follows(IdA, IdB), IdA < IdB.
ancestorOf(IdA,IdC) :- ancestorOf(IdA, IdB), follows(IdB, IdC), IdA < IdC.
child(Id) :- ancestorOf(_,Id).
inLine(IdA, IdA) :- ancestorOf(IdA, IdB), not child(IdA).
inLine(IdA, IdB) :- ancestorOf(IdA, IdB), not child(IdA).
inLine(Id, Id) :- isolateWord(Id).
```

Afterwards, we calculate the bounding box of the text line:

```
blockLine(IDln,X1,Y1,X2B,Y2B):-word(IDln,_, X1, Y1, X2, Y2, _),
                       word(IdB, _, X1B, Y1B, X2B, Y2B,_),
                       inLine(IDln, IdB), not overcome(IDln, X2B).
blockLine(IDln,X1,Y1,X2,Y2):-word(IDln, _, X1, Y1, X2, Y2, _),
                     isolateWord(IDln).
```

using `inLine` and `not overcome` to find, respectively, the minimum and maximum abscissa among the words that compose the text line.

Applying the same principle as for words that follow one another, we build rules that encode conditions for the linked lines. With these rules, we find line blocks linked to each other and then find the first line block of the text block. The rules for lines are analogous to the ones applied to words.

Finally, we find the bounding box of the entire text block. To do this we consider all the lines that are in the same block (determined by a logic rule named `inBlock`) and calculate respectively, the minimum abscissa and the maximum ordinate between all the block line to find the coordinate of the top-left corner, and the maximum abscissa and the minimum ordinate to find the bottom-right corner of the text block. The rules used for the top-left corner are:

```
abscissaTL(IDblk, X1):-inBlock(IDblk,IDln), blockLine(IDln,X1,Y1,X2,Y2),
                    not existsLowerThanTL(IDblk,X1).
ordinateTL(IDblk, Y1):-inBlock(IDblk,IDln), blockLine(IDln,X1,Y1,X2,Y2),
                    not overcomeTL(IDblk,Y1).
angleTopLeft(IDblk,X1,Y1):-abscissaTL(IDblk,X1), ordinateTL(IDblk,Y1).
```

After the segmentation of a document into a set of self-consistent blocks, we perform an additional step. Roughly, we identify some "virtual section breaks" that vertically split groups of blocks (see Fig. 1). In the depicted example, we recognize four sections. The first section is composed by two blocks far away from each other, while the second one contains two blocks very close to each other, misaligned with respect to the blocks of the first section. In this case, we conclude that we have two distinct sections. Then we have the third section, where we find several aligned blocks that could form a table (with headings up and several columns below). Finally, in the last section the number of blocks in the same line decreases to a two-column structure, except for the first block of this section that seems to be some heading.

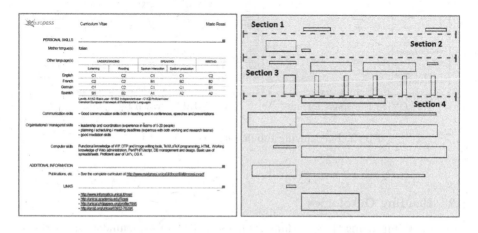

Fig. 1. Self-consistent text blocks from a PDF document.

5   Headings and Content Recognition

In this section, we proceed to the second step of our DLA, namely the structure recognition technique that combine table recognition and semantic annotation of predefined domain-specific headings. The results of the preceding geometrical analysis serve as input to this phase, improving the accuracy of the results and contributing to obtaining a meaningful grid representation of a document.

5.1   Table Recognition with Quablo

Quablo (http://quablo.eu) is a tool for managing PDF files and in particular for identifying and extracting tabular data from them. Among the tools available on market, Quablo stands out with its advanced configuration possibilities and flexible modular architecture. Within the KnowRex project, we have worked out an algorithm that operates on top of Quablo, by "injecting" some semantic analysis into the tool's generic algorithm.

The basic algorithm of Quablo works in two modes: the tool can either recognize a table or *draw* one within a requested area. The first task seems more natural and it is well suited for the documents containing real tables. The second, however, opens up possibilities for a non-standard use. More precisely, asking Quablo to draw a table in a region that do not contain an explicit table, but we believe has a tabular structure, can help structure the content within it. For example, in a multi-column layout, where values in one column determine the ones in other columns (e.g., in two-column layout, text in the right refer to those on the left), or in a layout of subsequent section names and content, the information can be grouped as if it was stored in a table (see Fig. 2).

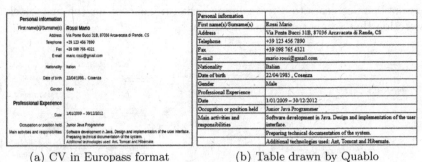

(a) CV in Europass format   (b) Table drawn by Quablo

Fig. 2. Recognizing tabular structures in a PDF file.

5.2   Heading Ontologies

The idea of improving the two-dimensional structure of a document with a set of domain knowledge, consists in interleaving the layout analysis with the semantic annotation of content. Recognizing a domain concept in a particular place can improve the structure of the recognized table, repair some imperfections and, by merging or aligning cells, improve the representation of the document. The domain-specific knowledge is codified in a simple *heading ontology*. For each heading, a user define a concept (a sub-class of a general 'category marker' class) and associate to it a set of strings and regular expressions e.g.:

```
<entity name="eu_cv_name_label">
    <value type="regexp"> Cognome\(i\)\s*/\s*Nome\(i\) </value>
    <value type="regexp"> First name\(s\)\s*/\s*Surname\(s\) </value>
</entity>
```

In KnowRex this is realized via a graphical interface, where user defines classes of headings and write extraction patterns for each of them. This dictionary is used to improve the two-dimensional representation of the tabular regions.

5.3   Grid Construction

The behavior of the algorithm that searches for the labels within a tabular structure depends on the documents characteristics. In particular, the orientation of the virtual table is set (horizontal or vertical), and the column (or row) in which domain labels are expected to appear is fixed. Then the algorithm proceeds as follows: for the selected "heading" column (resp., row), it tries to match the content with the heading ontology entries. As headings may span across several rows (resp., columns), the algorithm tries to take into account the combined content of the analyzed and following rows (resp., columns) up to a fixed threshold. If a match is found, the cells are merged and the content is annotated with the recognized heading. The algorithm then proceeds to calculate the vertical (resp., horizontal) span of the area related to the recognized label. Having this value, in the other columns (resp., rows) it merges appropriate number of rows (resp., columns) into one cell and by doing this it aligns the values, potentially spanned across rows (resp., columns) to the particular heading. Thus, we obtain more meaningful representation of the content of the tabular structure (see Fig. 3).

(a) Raw tabular structure 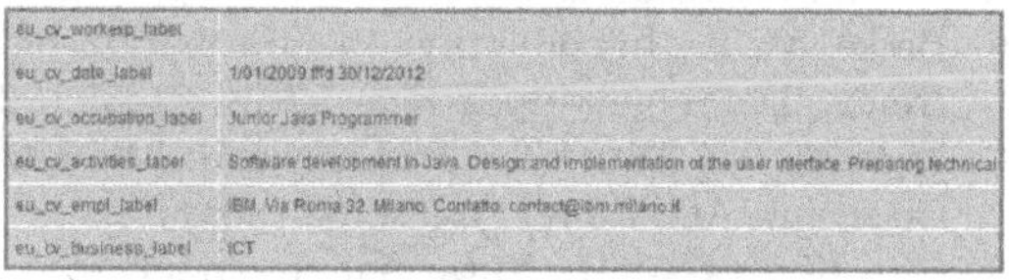   (b) Annotated grid representation

Fig. 3. Constructing a two-dimensional representation of a document

The obtained grid representation is a base for further IE steps. In particular, it allow to formulate extraction rules that take into account the spatial context of text portions e.g., *after label X, there is the object Y that I need*, but at the same time are not "wired" to physical encoding of particular file, because the actual layout has been "normalized" into a grid during the layout analysis process.

6   Discussion and Conclusion

We have presented a syntactic-semantic approach to document layout analysis that combines geometrical analysis, table recognition and semantic annotation. Our approach shares similarities with Kieniger, Docstrum and Voronoi algorithms. All the methods consider the proximity of the elements to merge the parts of the text, even if the parameters to evaluate the distance among the object are obtained in different way. Unlike RLSA algorithm that starts from pixels, or Docstrum and Voronoi that start from connected components, we assume that a document consists of words and we start from them. We have applied our approach successfully in KnowRex system for Information Extraction from PDF documents. Currently, our technique works only for words, ignoring images. For future work, we plan to extend the analysis, such that it also takes into account graphical objects, and, moreover, we would like to refine the computed parameters, because we believe that it is possible to obtain a better segmentation.

References

1. Adrian, W.T., Leone, N., Manna, M.: Semantic views of homogeneous unstructured data. In: ten Cate, B., Mileo, A. (eds.) RR 2015. LNCS, vol. 9209, pp. 19–29. Springer, Cham (2015). doi:10.1007/978-3-319-22002-4_3
2. Anantharangachar, R., Ramani, S., Rajagopalan, S.: Ontology guided information extraction from unstructured text. CoRR abs/1302.1335 (2013)
3. Antonacopoulos, A., Clausner, C., Papadopoulos, C., Pletschacher, S.: Historical document layout analysis competition. In: Proceedings of ICDAR 2011, pp. 1516–1520. IEEE (2011)
4. Apostolova, E., Tomuro, N.: Combining visual and textual features for information extraction from online flyers. In: Proceedings of EMNLP, pp. 1924–1929 (2014)
5. Baird, H.S., Jones, S.E., Fortune, S.J.: Image segmentation by shape-directed covers. In: Proceedings of ICPR, vol. 1, pp. 820–825. IEEE (1990)
6. Balke, W.T.: Introduction to information extraction: basic notions and current trends. Datenbank-Spektrum 12(2), 81–88 (2012)
7. Brewka, G., Eiter, T., Truszczynski, M.: Answer set programming at a glance. Commun. ACM 54(12), 92–103 (2011)
8. Cao, H., Prasad, R., Natarajan, P., MacRostie, E.: Robust page segmentation based on smearing and error correction unifying top-down and bottom-up approaches. In: Proceedings of ICDAR 2007, vol. 1, pp. 392–396. IEEE (2007)
9. Cattoni, R., Coianiz, T., Messelodi, S., Modena, C.: Geometric layout analysis techniques for document image understanding: a review. In: IRST, Trento, Italy (1998)
10. Corbelli, A., Baraldi, L., Grana, C., Cucchiara, R.: Historical document digitization through layout analysis and deep content classification. In: Proceedings of ICPR 2016, pp. 4077–4082. IEEE (2016)

11. Della Penna, G., Orefice, S.: Supporting information extraction from visual documents. J. Comput. Commun. **4**(06), 36 (2016)
12. Flesca, S., Masciari, E., Tagarelli, A.: A fuzzy logic approach to wrapping pdf documents. IEEE Trans. Knowl. Data Eng. **23**(12), 1826–1841 (2011)
13. Jain, A.K., Yu, B.: Document representation and its application to page decomposition. IEEE Trans. Pattern Anal. Mach. Intell. **20**(3), 294–308 (1998)
14. Jiang, J.: Information extraction from text. In: Aggarwal, C., Zhai, C. (eds.) Mining Text Data, pp. 11–41. Springer, Boston (2012). doi:10.1007/978-1-4614-3223-4_2
15. Karkaletsis, V., Fragkou, P., Petasis, G., Iosif, E.: Ontology based information extraction from text. In: Paliouras, G., Spyropoulos, C.D., Tsatsaronis, G. (eds.) Knowledge-Driven Multimedia Information Extraction and Ontology Evolution. LNCS, vol. 6050, pp. 89–109. Springer, Heidelberg (2011). doi:10.1007/978-3-642-20795-2_4
16. Kieninger, T.G.: Table structure recognition based on robust block segmentation. In: Photonics West 1998 Electronic Imaging, pp. 22–32. International Society for Optics and Photonics (1998)
17. Kise, K., Sato, A., Iwata, M.: Segmentation of page images using the area voronoi diagram. Comput. Vis. Image Underst. **70**(3), 370–382 (1998)
18. Lipinski, M., Yao, K., Breitinger, C., Beel, J., Gipp, B.: Evaluation of header metadata extraction approaches and tools for scientific PDF documents. In: Proceedings of JCDL 2013, pp. 385–386. ACM, New York (2013)
19. Nagy, G., Seth, S., Viswanathan, M.: A prototype document image analysis system for technical journals. Computer **25**(7), 10–22 (1992)
20. Namboodiri, A.M., Jain, A.K.: Document structure and layout analysis. In: Chaudhuri, B.B. (ed.) Digital Document Processing, pp. 29–48. Springer, London (2007). doi:10.1007/978-1-84628-726-8_2
21. O'Gorman, L.: The document spectrum for page layout analysis. IEEE Trans. Pattern Anal. Mach. Intell. **15**(11), 1162–1173 (1993)
22. Oren, E., Möller, K., Scerri, S., Handschuh, S., Sintek, M.: What are semantic annotations. Relatório técnico. DERI Galway **9**, 62 (2006)
23. Piskorski, J., Yangarber, R.: Information extraction: past, present and future. In: Poibeau, T., Saggion, H., Piskorski, J., Yangarber, R. (eds.) Multi-source, Multilingual Information Extraction and Summarization, pp. 23–49. Springer, Heidelberg (2013). doi:10.1007/978-3-642-28569-1_2
24. Simon, A., Pret, J.C., Johnson, A.P.: A fast algorithm for bottom-up document layout analysis. IEEE Trans. Pattern Anal. Mach. Intell. **19**(3), 273–277 (1997)
25. Singh, M., Barua, B., Palod, P., Garg, M., Satapathy, S., Bushi, S., Ayush, K., Rohith, K.S., Gamidi, T., Goyal, P., et al.: OCR++: a robust framework for information extraction from scholarly articles. arXiv preprint arXiv:1609.06423 (2016)
26. Toepfer, M., Corovic, H., Fette, G., Klügl, P., Störk, S., Puppe, F.: Fine-grained information extraction from German transthoracic echocardiography reports. BMC Med. Inform. Decis. Mak. **15**(1), 91 (2015)
27. Vasilopoulos, N., Kavallieratou, E.: Unified layout analysis and text localization framework. J. Electron. Imaging **26**(1), 013009 (2017)
28. Wong, K.Y., Casey, R.G., Wahl, F.M.: Document analysis system. IBM J. Res. Dev. **26**(6), 647–656 (1982)
29. Zanibbi, R., Blostein, D., Cordy, J.R.: A survey of table recognition. Doc. Anal. Recogn. **7**(1), 1–16 (2004)

A Criminal Domain Ontology for Modelling Legal Norms

Mirna El Ghosh[1(✉)], Habib Abdulrab[1], Hala Naja[2], and Mohamad Khalil[3]

[1] LITIS, INSA, Rouen, France
{mirna.elghosh, habib.abdulrab}@insa-rouen.fr
[2] Faculty of Sciences, Lebanese University, Tripoli, Lebanon
hala.naja70@gmail.com
[3] Faculty of Engineering, CRSI Research Center, Lebanese University,
Tripoli, Lebanon
mohamad.khalil@ul.edu.lb

Abstract. This work discusses an ontological model for legal norms of the criminal domain. An ontology-based modelling approach is proposed for this purpose. The approach tends to build a criminal domain ontology and then formalize the legal rules based on it. A middle-out approach is applied for building the criminal domain ontology based on ontology reuse and modularization processes. This approach tends to simplify the complexity and difficulty of ontology building process by reusing foundational and legal core ontologies.

Keywords: Criminal domain ontology · Modelling legal norms · Ontology reuse · Ontology modularization · Logic rules

1 Introduction

In the legal domain, the purpose of building ontologies is to describe the facts of legal cases at a comfortable level of abstraction and the "law" of the domain application which consists of "norms" and "concepts" [1]. Legal ontologies are defined as social constructs that can be used to express shared meaning within a community of practice [2]. It is commonly known that the legal domain is dominated by the use of natural language. Generally, legal norms are expressed in natural language textual sources, such as legislations and codes, which make them ambiguous since an expression can have multiple meanings. This problem causes some difficulties in interpreting them [3]. The general rule is that any document of this domain is always embedded in a context of norms. Thus, understanding concepts of a legal norm is important to understanding other legal norms [4]. The aim of this paper is to describe a well-founded ontological model for modelling the legal norms of the criminal domain aiming to capture a clear, concise and unambiguous view of the domain. The domain application of this work is the Lebanese criminal system. Thus the available sources are the legal norms of the Lebanese criminal code. The proposed ontological model is composed of four independent modules for modelling the legal sources. For this purpose, a middle-out

© Springer International Publishing AG 2017
F. Esposito et al. (Eds.): AI*IA 2017, LNAI 10640, pp. 282–294, 2017.
https://doi.org/10.1007/978-3-319-70169-1_21

approach is proposed to build the modules by applying two different strategies: *top-down* and *bottom-up*.

2 Legal Norms

Generally, norms are defined as an abstract mandatory command concerning rights or duties [5]. According to [6], this definition is very general and extends well over the notion of norms in the legal reasoning. According to some studies, such as [7], a legal norm is a rule of conduct of people that may contain a rule on the application of a sanction in the case of its violation. This definition is limited to the regulatory form of a legal norm. Meanwhile, other studies such as [8] classified legal norms into three main types:

- Determinative: define concepts or constitute activities that cannot exist without such rules.
- Technical: state that something has to be done in order for something else to be attained.
- Regulative: regulate actions by making them obligatory, permitted, or prohibited [9].

In the domain application of this work, which is the Lebanese criminal code, the legal norms are represented in unstructured natural language texts distributed on 770 articles. Two main types of norms are identified: determinative, known also as terminological, and regulative, known also as normative. The determinative rules consist in definitions of some of the concepts of the criminal domain that are used to describe the criminal facts. For instance, the concept *perpetrator* is defined in article 212 as: *"The perpetrator of an offence is anyone who brings into being the constituent elements of an offence or who contributes directly to its commission"*. Meanwhile, the normative rules connect the legal consequences to descriptions of certain facts and situations, such as in article 217: *"Anyone who induces or seeks to induce another person to commit an offence shall be deemed to be an instigator"*.

3 Modelling of Legal Norms

The modelling of legal norms consists of legal interpretation of text's meaning in order to transform the norms in logical rules for legal reasoning. It is commonly known that legislative documents are semi-structured and hierarchically structured in nature. In this context, the structure consists of normative parts rather than simply textual documents which facilitates the understanding of legal concepts and thus the interpretation of text [10, 11]. In the legal domain, three conceptual layers are distinguished: norms, textual provisions and rules [12]. The legal norms usually are expressed in written using legal text. The textual provisions are the instantiation of the norms in one possible textual representation (sentence, article, and paragraph). The legal rules, in their regulatory sense [6], are interpretation of the textual provisions formalized using logical rules [12]. Generally, the legal norms have basically the following structure [13, 14]:

$$\text{If } A1, \ldots, A1 \text{ then } B;$$

where "A1, ..., A2" are the conditions of the norm, "B" is the legal effect and "if... then" is a normative conditional. This view highlights an immediate link between the concepts of the norms and the rules [6]. This link relies mainly on legal ontologies since they are used for *filling the gap* between document representation, expressed in natural language, and norms modelling using logical formalisms [15]. However, according to [16], the scholars in the domain of AI & Law, have focused only on the rules modelling and on the foundational logical theory, and apart the isomorphism principles [17] and neglected the ontology aspects. Actually, there is a theoretical and important debate in the AI & Law community on the interpretation of the legal textual provisions and on formalizing of the rules using logical formalisms [16]. Based on these perspectives, an ontology-based modelling methodology is proposed that relies mainly on a well-founded legal domain ontology and thus filling the gap between texts and norms modelling.

3.1   Ontology-Based Modelling Methodology

As aforementioned, the domain application of this study is the Lebanese criminal Law and the legal texts and the specific provisions within them that are relevant to the legal norms of the Lebanese criminal code are provided as input. Generally, different formalisms are used in the literature to represent the legal norms such as formal logic, rules and ontologies [18–20]. Inspired by what found in the literature, and based on the need to explain the relations between the normative context of the textual provisions and the legal norms, an ontology-based modelling methodology is proposed to represent the legal norms of the criminal domain and is composed of two main tasks (see Fig. 1):

- Modelling the content of the legal norms that reflect the criminal domain. This task results in an ontological model, which is the criminal domain ontology, aiming to provide a well-founded representation of concepts and semantic relationships among them in the context of the norms of the criminal domain.
- Modelling the procedural aspect of the legal norms using logical formalisms in order to obtain list of formalized rules. In this task, following the isomorphism principle stated by [21, 22] for connecting legal textual provisions with formalized rules is preliminary. The result of this task is list of logic rules formalized using rule language based on the criminal domain ontology.

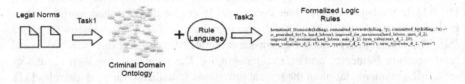

Fig. 1. Ontology-based methodology for modelling legal norms.

4   Building a Criminal Domain Ontology

Ontologies are considered by definition as descriptive models of a domain with respect to the knowledge sources and the type of use [23]. In the current work, the knowledge sources are the legal norms documents represented by a set of normative contexts identified by the articles. The target ontology is intended to be used for supporting reasoning purposes. Thus, a conceptualization process is needed for modelling the criminal domain in the context of the legal norms provided as input texts. In this regard, an issue must be recognized is that there is no agreement on the basic conceptualization aspects of the legal domain in general. Thus, the same domain can be conceptualized in different ways. What is needed is rather for the ontologies to be sufficiently clearly stated [24]. It is commonly known that building ontologies from scratch is not an easy task due to the complexity, difficulty and time-consuming of the process. Moreover, the development of the criminal domain ontology for modelling the legal norms can be considered as a specialization of a general ontology for law [23]. For this reason, starting the modelling activity from theoretical assumptions and semantic resources already developed by the scientific community in the field of legal ontologies can lead to a well-founded ontological model. Additionally, the literature suggests that legal ontologies may be distinguished by the levels of abstraction of the ideas they represent [25], with the key distinction being between core and domain levels. The core level ontology is a model of general concepts common for all legal domains [26]. Accordingly, research in this field should not concentrate on creating a single ontology of the legal domain but on the creation of a library that contains several dedicated ontologies at different abstraction levels and supports their mapping to create a composite ontology [27]. Based on these perspectives, a modular middle-out approach has been proposed to simplify the ontology building process as well as to obtain a composite well-founded ontology [28]. We will discuss this approach in the following sections.

5   Middle-Out Approach for Building the Criminal Domain Ontology

A middle-out approach has been proposed to build the criminal domain ontology for modelling legal norms (see Fig. 2).

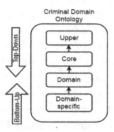

Fig. 2. Middle-out approach for building criminal domain ontology.

The approach is composed of two complementary strategies *top-down* and *bottom-up* aiming to modularize the ontology into four independent modules which are themselves ontologies: *upper, core, domain* and *domain-specific*. The *upper* and *core* modules are built by applying the *top-down* strategy that is considered as a conceptual modelling process performed by reusing partially existent foundational ontology (UFO) [29] and legal core ontology (LKIF-Core) [30]. Meanwhile, the bottom-up strategy starts from textual analysis and conceptual representation of the intended meaning of the legal norms as an ontology learning process for building the *domain* and *domain-specific* modules (for more details about this part refer to [31]). Furthermore, the four modules are integrated together using mapping strategies to compose the global ontology. Thus, it is noticed the usage of two processes: ontology reuse and ontology modularization. The ontology reuse process, which is now one of the important research issues in the ontology field [32], is recommended as a key factor to develop cost effective and high quality ontologies. Actually, ontology reuse reduces the cost and the time required for building ontologies from scratch [33–35]. Moreover, by reusing validated ontology components, the quality of the newly implemented ontologies is increased. Concerning the ontology modularization process, it is considered as a major topic in the field of formal ontology developments and a way to facilitate and simplify the ontology engineering process [36]. Additionally, ontology modularization has several benefits where modular representations are easier to understand, reason with, extend and reuse [37]. Therefore, using these representations tends to reduce the complexity of designing and to facilitate the ontology reasoning, development, and integration.

5.1 Top-Down Strategy

The *top-down* strategy represents a conceptual modelling process based on reusing partially existent validated ontologies for building the *upper* and *core* modules. The *upper* module consists of abstract concepts and relations which are effectively independent of any specific domain. For a well-founded building of this module, a partial reuse of existent foundational, or top-level, ontologies can help. The foundational ontologies are theoretically well-founded domain independent systems of categories that have been successfully used to improve the quality of conceptual models and semantic interoperability [38]. In addition to this, partial reuse of foundational ontologies can facilitate and speed up the ontology development process by preventing to reinvent the wheel concerning basic categories [39]. In this work, the unified foundational ontology UFO is selected for this purpose [40]. UFO permits the building of an ontology by reusing some generic concepts such as *category, kind, subkind, relator, role* and *role mixin* where the ontologist does not need to rebuild these concepts. UFO is divided into three layered sets: (1) UFO-A, ontology of objects, defines terms related to endurants such as *universal, relator, role, intrinsic moment;* (2) UFO-B, ontology of events, defines terms related to perdurants such as *event, state, atomic event, complex event;* (3) UFO-C defines terms related to intentional and social entities including linguistic aspects such as *social agent, social object, social role* and *normative description* [41]. In the current work, UFO-B and UFO-C are needed to ground the criminal domain ontology since they define some basic concepts for the criminal domain such as *Agent, Intentional_Moment, Action, Event,* and *Normative_Description.* In order to make possible the activity of conceptual modeling via UFO, the conceptual modeling language OntoUML [42] is used. OntoUML uses the ontological constraints of UFO as modeling primitives and is specified above the UML 2.0 meta-model [43].

Reusing Concepts from UFO-C. UFO-C, ontology of endurants, defines two main entities *Agents* and *Objects* [44]. *Agents* can be physical (e.g. *Person*) or social (e.g. *Organization*). *Objects* are also categorized in physical (e.g. book) and social objects (e.g. normative description). *Normative_Description* defines one or more rules/norms recognized by at least one *Social_Agent.* Regulations and constitutions are examples of normative description. Therefore, reusing these concepts, the *upper* module is developed (see Fig. 3).

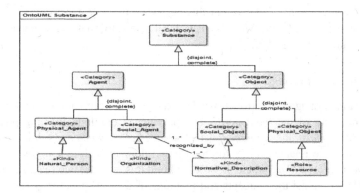

Fig. 3. Fragment of the *upper* module in ONTOUML.

Reusing Concepts from UFO-B. The ontology of perdurants UFO-B defines *Event,* which is a basic concept in the criminal domain (e.g. a crime is an event), as a main category [44]. In UFO-B, events can be atomic or complex depending on their mereological structure [45]. Complex events are aggregations of at least two events that can themselves be atomic or complex. In UFO-B, an event can be an *Action* or *Participation.* Actions are performed by agents and considered as intentional events caused by intentions [44]. Participation can be for agents and objects.

Concerning the *core* module, it consists of concepts and relations that are common across the domains of law and can provide the basis for specialization into domain and domain-specific concepts. In order to build this module, the legal core ontology LKIF-Core [30] have been reused since it contains essential legal concepts such as *Medium, Document, Legal_Source, Legal_Document,* and *Code.* Actually, list of basic concepts of LKIF-Core are represented using the generic concepts of UFO (see Fig. 4).

Therefore, for knowledge representation and reasoning capabilities in the semantic web, there is a need to transform the conceptual models of the *upper* and *core* module represented in OntoUML language to a computational ontology language such as the

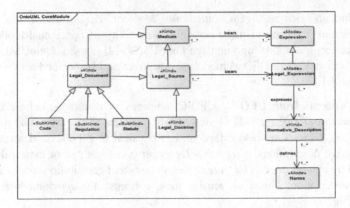

Fig. 4. Fragment of the *core* module in ONTOUML.

Ontology Web Language (OWL). For this purpose, OLED features defined automatic transformations of the OntoUML models to OWL files [46] that can be managed using ontology editors such as Protégé.

5.2 Bottom-Up Strategy

The *bottom-up* strategy starts from textual analysis and conceptual representation of the intended meaning of the legal norms by applying an ontology learning process for building the *domain* and *domain-specific* modules. The *domain* module consists of categories that are related mainly to the criminal domain such as *Criminal_Act*, *Penalty*, *Misdemeanor*, *Violation*, etc. In order to build this module, two main strategies are applied: (1) specialize the concepts and relations of the core module (*Creation*, *Public_Act*, *Act_Of_Law*, and *Reaction* are specialized in domain concepts such as: *Criminal_Act*, *Punishments* and *Defence*); (2) extract semi-automatically the knowledge from textual resources (the English version of the Lebanese criminal code, for more details refer to [31]). Examples of extracted domain concepts: *Felony*_Penalty, *Death_Penalty* and *Fixed_Term_Penalty* (see Fig. 5). In the other hand, the *domain-specific* module consists of instances for the concepts and relations of the domain module. These instances are specific for the Lebanese criminal domain.

Fig. 5. Excerpt of the *domain* module in Protégé.

5.3   Modules Integration

After building the ontology modules (*upper*, *core*, *domain* and *domain-specific*), there is a need for an integration process to combine them for composing the global ontology CriMOnto. Thus, it is essential to consider heterogeneity resolution and related ontology matching or mapping strategies to be an internal part of ontology integration [47]. In this context, list of semantic mappings will be created among concepts of the different modules. For ontology mappings, several studies, such as [48, 49], have proposed a number of specialized semantics. Meanwhile, for other studies, such as [50], ontology mappings are represented as OWL axioms of the form *SubClassOf*, *EquivalentClass* and *DisjointClass* [51]. In CriMOnto, the modules are located on vertical conceptual levels from general (*upper* module) to specific (*domain-specific* module). For this reason, the mappings will be based mainly on a parent-child, or subsumption, hierarchical relationship [52] and established manually as structural axiom of the form *subClassOf* (see Fig. 6). Thus, the hierarchical relationship is established among the concepts of modules. For this purpose, a linguistic-based matcher, such as WordNet, is used to deal with ontology mapping for calculating the similarity values between concepts [53]. Then a domain expert, knowledgeable about the semantics of legal concepts, validates the proposed mappings.

Fig. 6. Example of hierarchical mapping.

6   Logic Rules

In the legal domain, a norm is represented by an *obligation rule* that denotes that the conclusion of the rule will be treated as an obligation [54]. Thus, representing legal contents though *obligation rules* comports with the widespread idea that legal norms typically have the conditional form:

IF *condition* (operative facts)THEN *conclusion* (legal effect).

Indeed, obligation rules provide the most widespread and successful representational model for legal knowledge where the concepts of the legal norms are linked to the rules [55]. For representing them, a modelling process is needed, as well as a rule language. According to the proposed ontology-based methodology, the modelling process is based on the criminal domain ontology. For this purpose, the rule language has to be compatible with the OWL syntax. In the literature, there is a variety of languages for modelling rules such as: RuleML, SWRL, KIF, etc. In this study, SWRL is selected because of its simplicity and compatibility with the OWL syntax. An additional reason is that the legal norms of the Lebanese criminal code can almost be expressed in first-order logic. SWRL (Semantic Web Rule Language) is probably the most popular formalism in Web community for expressing knowledge in the form of rules. It is the only approach that gathers ontology and rules in product development [56] where users are permitted to write rules that can be expressed in terms of OWL concepts and that can reason about OWL individuals. In SWRL, rules are of the form of an implication between an antecedent (body) conjunction and a consequent (head) conjunction in the following form [57]:

$$a_1 \wedge a_2 \wedge \ldots \wedge a_n \rightarrow b_1 \wedge b_2 \wedge \ldots \wedge b_m;$$

where description logic expressions can occur on both sides, "$\wedge$" is an operator for the logical AND, "$\rightarrow$" is an operator for drawing the conclusion and a_i and b_i are OWL atoms such as, among others, concepts, object properties, data properties, sameAs, and differentFrom. In Table 1, some examples of SWRL rules are presented.

Table 1. Excerpt of the Lebanese criminal norms expressed in SWRL logic rules.

Legal norms	Logic rules expressed in SWRL
Article 547: "Anyone who intentionally kills another person shall be punishable by hard labour for a term of between 15 and 20 years"	Intentional_Homicide(killing), committed_towards(killing, ?y), committed_by(killing, ?x) → is_punished_by(?x, hard_labour), imposed_for_maximum(hard_labour, max_d_2), imposed_for_minimum (hard_labour, min_d_2), term_value (max_d_2, 20), term_value(min_d_2, 15), term_type(max_d_2, "years"), term_type (min_d_2, "years")
Article 213: "An accomplice to an offence shall be liable to the penalty prescribed by law for the offence"	Accomplice(?x), commit(?x, ?y), is_punishable_by(?y, ?z) → is_liable_to_punished_by(?x, ?z)

7   Related Work

In the literature, some legal ontologies have modeled legal norms such as DOLCE +CLO [58], OWL Ontology of Fundamental Legal Concepts [59] and LKIF-Core [60]. Moreover, some recent works such as [12, 23, 61] have described an ontology-based models of legal norms. In [23], the authors differ between ontology of procedural norms and ontology of procedures. Concerning the ontology of norms, they started from theoretical assumptions and semantic resources already developed such as the Core Legal Ontology[1]. Meanwhile, for the ontology of procedures, the process is understood as a sequence of patterns including classes of agents and normative

---

[1] The Core Legal Ontology (CLO) was developed on top of DOLCE [http://www.loacnr.it/ontologies/DLP.owl].

definitions of events and behaviors. In [12], the authors have used three main concepts: the translation of textual provisions into XML using Akoma Ntoso, developing the corresponding rules in LegalRuleML, and an ontology for modelling and defining macro-concepts specific for the legal domain is developed and expressed in LKIF-Core. Finally, in [61], the authors described a formal model of legal norms, using their elements and elements of legal relations they regulate, intended for semiautomatic drafting of legislation. What differs our work is the usage of two essentials processes: reuse and modularization. These processes simplify the ontology building process as well as permit the development of domain ontologies by integrating heterogeneous sources, such as textual documents and pre-existent validated ontologies.

8 Conclusion

In this paper, an ontological model of legal norms for the criminal domain is discussed and the ontological modelling process is outlined. For this purpose, an ontology-based modelling methodology is proposed in order to fill the gap between document representation in natural language and rules modelling using logical formalisms. The methodology is composed of two main phases: modelling the content of the legal norms that reflect the criminal domain in order to obtain a criminal domain ontology and then modelling the procedural aspect of the legal norms using logical formalisms in order to obtain list of formalized rules. In fact, the proposed methodology tends to simplify the modelling process of the legal norms and leads to a well-founded ontological model. Furthermore, the resulted criminal domain ontology and the list of rules will be integrated and used for building a rule-based reasoning model that performs rule-guided legal reasoning for decision support purposes.

References

1. McCarty, L.T.: Intelligent legal information systems: problems and prospects. Rutgers Comput. Technol. Law J. 9(2), 265–294 (1983)
2. Valente, A., Breuker, J.: Ontologies: the missing link between legal theory and AI & Law. In: Proceedings of Jurix 1994, pp. 138–149 (1994)
3. Van Gog, R., van Engers, T.M.: Modelling legislation using natural language. In: 2001 IEEE Systems Proceedings, Man and Cybernetics Conference, USA (2001)
4. Machado, A.L., de Oliveira, J.M.P.: A legal ontology of relationships for civil law system. In: 1st Joint Workshop ONTO.COM/ODISE Proceedings on Ontologies in Conceptual Modeling and Information Systems Engineering (2014)
5. Kelsen, H.: Pure Theory of Law. The Lawbook Exchange, LTD, Clark (2005)
6. Gordon, T.F., Governatori, G., Rotolo, A.: Rules and norms: requirements for rule interchange languages in the legal domain. In: Governatori, G., Hall, J., Paschke, A. (eds.) RuleML 2009. LNCS, vol. 5858, pp. 282–296. Springer, Heidelberg (2009). doi:10.1007/978-3-642-04985-9_26
7. Gostojic, S., Milosavljevic, B.: Ontological model of legal norms for creating and using legal acts. IPSI BgD J. 9(1), 19–25 (2013)
8. Von Wright, G.H.: Norm and Action. Routledge, London (1963)

9. Biagioli, C.: Towards a legal rules functional micro-ontology. In: 1st International Workshop Proceedings on Legal Ontologies, University of Melbourne, Law School, Australia (1997)
10. Heflin, J., Hendler, J.: Semantic interoperability on the web. In: Extreme Markup Languages 2000, p. 16 (2000)
11. Ouksel, A.M., Sheth, A.: Semantic interoperability in global information systems. ACM SIGMOD Rec. **28**, 5–12 (1999)
12. Palmirani, M., Ognibene, T, Cervone, L.: Legal rules, text and ontologies over time. In: Proceedings of RuleML@ECAI 2012 (2012)
13. Davis, R., King, J.: The origin of rule-based systems in AI. In: Buchanan, B.G., Shortlie, E. H. (eds.) Rule Based Expert Systems-The MYCIN Experiments of the Stanford Heuristic Programming Project, pp. 20–52. Addison-Wesley, Reading (1984)
14. Kelsen, H.: General Theory Of Norms. Clarendon, Oxford (1991)
15. Palmirani, M., Contissa, G., Rubino, R.: Fill the Gap in the Legal Knowledge Modelling. In: RuleML 2009 roceedings, pp. 305–314 (2009)
16. Boella, G., Governatori, G., Rotolo, A., van der Torre, L.: Lex Minus Dixit Quam Voluit, Lex Magis Dixit Quam Voluit: a formal study on legal compliance and interpretation. In: Casanovas, P., Pagallo, U., Sartor, G., Ajani, G. (eds.) AICOL -2009. LNCS, vol. 6237, pp. 162–183. Springer, Heidelberg (2010). doi:10.1007/978-3-642-16524-5_11
17. Bench-Capon, T., Coenen, F.: Isomorphism and legal knowledge based systems. Artif. Intell. Law **1**(1), 65–86 (1992)
18. Biagioli, C., Grossi, D.: Formal aspects of legislative meta-drafting. In: Francesconi, E., Sartor, G., Tiscornia, D. (eds.) Proceedings of 2008 Conference on Legal Knowledge and Information Systems: JURIX 2008: 21st Annual Conference, 192–201. IOS Press, Amsterdam (2008)
19. Sartor, G.: A formal model of legal argumentation. Ratio Juris **7**(2), 177–211 (1994)
20. Gordon, T.: The Legal Knowledge Interchange Format (LKIF). University of Amsterdam, Amsterdam (2008)
21. Bench-Capon, T.J.M., Gordon, T.F.: Isomorphism and argumentation. In: ICAIL 2009 Proceedings, pp. 11–20 (2009)
22. Karpf, J.: Quality assurance of legal expert systems. Jurimatics no. 8, Copenhagen Business School (1989)
23. Cherubini, M., Tiscornia, D.: An ontology-based model of procedural norms and regulated procedures. In: eGov International Conference Proceedings (2008)
24. Bench-Capon, T., Visser, R.S.: Ontologies in legal information systems; the need for explicit specifications of domain conceptualisations. In: 6th International Conference on Artificial Intelligence and Law Proceedings, pp. 132–141 (1995)
25. Breuker, J., Casanovas, P., Klein, M.C., Francesconi, E.: The flood, the channels and the dykes: managing legal information in a globalized and digital world. In: Law, Ontologies and the Semantic Web - Channelling the Legal Information Flood. IOS Press (2009)
26. Valente, A.: Legal knowledge engineering: a modelling approach. Ph.D. thesis, University of Amsterdam, Amsterdam (1995)
27. Piovesan, L., Molino, G., Terenziani, P.: An ontological knowledge and multiple abstraction level decision support system in healthcare. Decis. Anal. **1**(1), 8 (2014)
28. El Ghosh, M., Naja, H., Abdulrab, H., Khalil, M.: Towards a middle-out approach for building legal domain reference ontology. Int. J. Knowl. Eng. **2**(3), 109–114 (2016)
29. Guizzardi, G.: Ontological Foundations for Structural Conceptual Model. Universal Press, Veenendaal (2005)

30. Hoekstra, R., Breuker, J., Di Bello, M., Boer, A.: The LKIF core ontology of basic legal concepts. In: Casanovas, P., Biasiotti, M.A., Francesconi, E., Sagri, M.T. (eds.) 2nd Workshop on Legal Ontologies and Artificial Intelligence Techniques, CEUR Workshop Proceedings, pp. 43–63 (2007)

31. El Ghosh, M., Naja, H., Abdulrab, H., Khalil, M.: Ontology learning process as a bottom-up strategy for building domain-specific ontology from legal texts. In: 9th International Conference on Agents and Artificial Intelligence proceedings, ICAART, vol. 2, pp. 473–480 (2017)

32. Pinto, H., Martins, J.: Ontology integration: how to perform the process. In: International Joint Conference on Artificial Intelligence Proceedings, pp. 71–80 (2001)

33. Bontas, E.P., Mochol, M., Tolksdorf, R.: Case studies on ontology reuse. In: IKNOW 2005 International Conference on Knowledge Management Proceedings, vol. 74 (2005)

34. Caldarola, E.G., Picariello, A., Rinaldim A.M.: An approach to ontology integration for ontology reuse in knowledge based digital ecosystems. In: 7th International Conference on Management of Computational and Collective intElligence in Digital EcoSystems Proceedings, pp. 1–8. ACM (2015)

35. Modoni, G., Caldarola, E., Terkaj, W., Sacco, M.: The knowledge reuse in an industrial scenario: a case study. In: eKNOW 2015, 7th International Conference on Information, Process, and Knowledge Management, pp. 66–71 (2015)

36. Hois, J., Bhatt, M., Kutz, O.: Modular ontologies for architectural design. In: FOMI-2009, Proceedings of Frontiers in Artificial Intelligence and Applications, Vicenza, Italy, vol. 198. IOS Press (2009)

37. Grau, B.C., Horrocks, I., Kazakov, Y., Sattler, U.: A logical framework for modularity of ontologies. In: IJCAI 2007 Proceedings, pp. 298–303. AAAI Press (2007)

38. Guizzardi, G.: The role of foundational ontology for conceptual modeling and domain ontology representation. In: 7th International Baltic Conference on Databases and Information Systems Proceedings, pp. 17–25 (2006)

39. Keet, M.: The use of foundational ontologies in ontology development: an empirical assessment. In: 8th Extended Semantic Web Conference Proceedings, Greece, vol. 6643, pp. 321–335 (2011)

40. Guizzardi, G., Wagner, G.: Using UFO as a foundation for general conceptual modeling languages. In: Poli, R., Healy, M., Kameas, A. (eds.) Theory and Application of Ontologies. Springer, Dordrecht (2010). doi:10.1007/978-90-481-8847-5_8

41. Guizzardi, G., Wagner, G.: Towards ontological foundations for agent modelling concepts using the unified foundational ontology (UFO). Agent-Oriented Inf. Syst. II(3508), 110–124 (2005)

42. Guizzardi, G.: Ontological foundations for structural conceptual models. Ph.D. Thesis. Telematica Instituut, Enschede, The Netherlands (2005)

43. Guerson, J., Sales, T.P., Guizzardi, G., Almeida, J.P.A.: OntoUML lightweight editor: a model-based environment to build, evaluate and implement reference ontologies. In: IEEE 19th International Enterprise Distributed Object Computing Workshop (EDOCW), pp. 144–147. IEEE (2015)

44. Guizzardi, G., Falbo, R.A., Guizzardi, R.S.S.: Grounding software domain ontologies in the unified foundational ontology (UFO): the case of the ODE software process ontology. In: IberoAmerican Workshop on Requirements Engineering and Software Environments Proceedings, pp. 244–251 (2008)

45. Guizzardi, G., Wagner, G., Falbo, A., Guizzardi, R.S.S., Almeida, J.P.A.: Towards ontological foundations for the conceptual modeling of events. In: 32th International Conference Proceedings, ER 2013, pp. 327–341 (2013)

46. Barcelos, P.P.F., dos Santos, V.A., Silva, F.B., Monteiro, M.E., Garcia, A.S.: An automated transformation from OntoUML to OWL and SWRL. In: ONTOBRAS 2013, CEUR Workshop Proceedings, vol. 1041, pp. 130–141 (2013)
47. Caldarola, E.G., Picariello, A., Rinaldi, A.M.: An approach to ontology integration for ontology reuse in knowledge based digital ecosystems. In: 7th International Conference on Management of Computational and Collective intElligence in Digital EcoSystems Proceedings, pp. 1–8. ACM (2015)
48. Euzenat, J.: Semantic precision and recall for ontology alignment evaluation. In: IJCAI Proceedings, pp. 348–353 (2007)
49. Borgida, A., Serafini, L.: Distributed description logics: assimilating information from peer sources. J. Data Semant. **1**, 153–184 (2003)
50. Jimenez-Ruiz, E., Cuenca-Grau, B., Horrocks, I., Berlanga, R.: Ontology integration using mappings: towards getting the right logical consequences. Technical report, Universitat Jaume, University of Oxford (2008)
51. Cuenca Grau, B., Horrocks, I., Motik, B., Parsia, B., Patel-Schneider, P., Sattler, U.: OWL 2: the next step for OWL. J. Web Semant. **6**(4), 309–322 (2008)
52. Wang, Y., Liu, W., Bell, D.: A concept hierarchy based ontology mapping approach. In: KSEM, pp. 101–113 (2010)
53. Miller, G.A.: WordNet: a lexical database for english. Commun. ACM **38**, 39–41 (1995)
54. Governatori, G., Rotolo, A.: Logic of violations: a Gentzen system for reasoning with contrary-to-duty obligations. Australas. J. Log. **4**, 193–215 (2006)
55. Sartor, G., Legal concepts: an inferential approach. In: European University Institute, Working Papers Law No. 2008/03 (2008). http://papers.ssrn.com/sol3/papers.cfm?abstract_id=1093627[10.01.2009]
56. Fiorentini, X., Sudarsan, R., Suh, H., Lee, J., Sriram, R.: An analysis of description logic augmented with domain rules for the development of product models. J. Comput. Inf. Sci. Eng. **10**, 1–13 (2010)
57. Antoniou, G., Damasio, C.V., Grosof, B., Horrocks, I., Kifer, M., Maluszynski, J., Patel-Schneider, P.F.: Combining rules and ontologies - a survey. Deliverables I3-D3, REWERSE, http://rewerse.net/deliverables/m12/i3-d3.pdf. Accessed Mar 2005
58. Valente, A., Breuker, J., Brouwer, B.: Legal modeling and automated reasoning with ON-LINE. Int. J. Hum.-Comput. Stud. **51**(6), 1079–1125 (1999)
59. Rubino, R., Rotolo, A., Sartor, G.: An OWL ontology of fundamental legal concepts. In: van Engers, T. (ed.) 2006 19th Annual Conference on Legal Knowledge and Information Systems proceedings, JURIX 2006, pp. 101–110. IOS Press, Amsterdam (2006)
60. Breuker, J., Hoekstra, R., Boer, A., Van den Berg, K., Sartor, G., Rubino, R., Wyner, A., Bench-Capon, T. Palmirani, M.: Deliverable 1.4: OWL ontology of basic legal concepts (LKIF-Core). University of Amsterdam, Amsterdam, The Netherlands (2007)
61. Gostojić, S., Milosavljević, B., Konjović, Z.: Ontological model of legal norms for creating and using legislation. Comput. Sci. Inf. Syst. **10**(1), 151–171 (2013)

Semantic Models for the Geological Mapping Process

Vincenzo Lombardo[1,2](✉), Fabrizio Piana[2,3], Dario Mimmo[3,4], Enrico Mensa[1], and Daniele P. Radicioni[1]

[1] Dipartimento di Informatica, Università di Torino, Torino, Italy
vincenzo.lombardo@unito.it
[2] Consiglio Nazionale delle Ricerche, Istituto di Geoscienze e Georisorse, Torino, Italy
[3] Gi-RES srl, Torino, Italy
[4] Dipartimento di Scienze della Terra, Università di Torino, Torino, Italy
http://www.di.unito.it/~vincenzo

Abstract. The geologic mapping process requires the organization of data according to the general knowledge about the objects in the map, namely the geologic units, and to the objectives of a graphic representation of such objects in a map, following some established model of geotectonic evolution. Semantics can greatly help such a process in providing a terminological base to name and classify the objects of the map and supporting the application of reasoning mechanisms for the derivation of novel properties and relations about the objects of the map.

The OntoGeonous initiative has built a terminological base of geological knowledge in a machine-readable format, following the Semantic Web tenets and the Linked Data paradigm, with the construction of an appropriate data base schema that can be then filled with the objects of the map. The paper will present the conceptual model of the geologic system and how the elements of the cartographic database are classified from general definitions. Also, the paper addresses the setup of web-based services that respond to queries concerning the properties of the map elements that are not explicitly asserted in the underlying data base, but are inferred through a reasoning process.

Keywords: Ontology · Geomapping · OntoGeonous · Geologic knowledge

1 Introduction

Modern geological maps, which are supported by large geo-databases and are implemented through interactive representations on WebGIS services, need explicit geological assumptions for their design and compilation. This task has been supported by the use of controlled vocabularies, such as those belonging to GeoSciML (GeoScience Markup Language), published by the IUGS CGI

© Springer International Publishing AG 2017
F. Esposito et al. (Eds.): AI*IA 2017, LNAI 10640, pp. 295–306, 2017.
https://doi.org/10.1007/978-3-319-70169-1_22

Commission[1] and the INSPIRE "Data Specification on Geology" directives[2]. Recently, there has been an interest toward the semantic models, in order to provide a formal and interoperable representation of the geologic knowledge. The effective encoding of geologic knowledge through the formal languages of the semantic web technologies can improve the consistency of the represented knowledge and benefit from the inferential system that automatically produces novel knowledge [3]. The semantic approaches are fundamental for the integration and harmonization of geological information and services across cultural (e.g. different scientific disciplines) and/or physical barriers (e.g. administrative boundaries). A semantic approach to data representation (referring to existing ontologies and vocabularies) was used as an essential tool for providing data interoperability, as recently done at a transnational scale by [6,13]. Initiatives such as GeoSciML and INSPIRE, as well as the recent terminological shepherding of the Geoscience Terminology Working Group (GTWG), have been promoting information exchange of the geologic knowledge, providing the authoritative standard for geological knowledge encoding. The interconnection between the geologic knowledge in its various forms (such as geologic events, units, morphologies, etc.) and the several knowledge sources (such as lithological materials, geochronologic units, etc.) can be addressed through the recourse to the Linked Data paradigm [4,10].

The OntoGeonous initiative has built a terminological base of geological knowledge in a machine-readable format, following the Semantic Web tenets and the Linked Data paradigm [14,15,21]. The major knowledge sources are GeoSciML schemata and vocabularies and INSPIRE directives. The Linked Data paradigm has been exploited by linking the already existing machine-readable encoding for some specific domains, such as the lithology domain and the geochronologic time scale. Finally, for the upper level knowledge, shared across several geologic domains, OntoGeonous resorted to NASA SWEET ontology. The OntoGeonous initiative has also produced a wiki that explains how the geologic knowledge has been encoded from shared geoscience vocabularies[3]. In particular, the sections dedicated to axiomatization support the construction of an appropriate data base schema that are filled with the elements of a map.

This paper describes how the semantic encoding of the geologic knowledge in an ontological format has contributed to the realization of the Piemonte Geological Map[4] [21] and how semantic services have been built to answer prototypical questions posed by the geologists. In the next two sections, we review the related work on semantics for geological knowledge and sum up the OntoGeonous initiative. Then, we describe how the ontological knowledge has served the task

---

[1] Commission for the Management and Application of Geoscience Information (CGI) of the International Union of Geological Sciences (IUGS).

[2] An operative simplification of GeoSciML, published by INSPIRE Thematic Working Group Geology of the European Commission.

[3] https://www.di.unito.it/wikigeo/.

[4] http://arpapiemonte.maps.arcgis.com/apps/webappviewer/index.html?id=fff17326 6afa4f6fa206be53a77f6321.

of constraining the map legend and implementing the classification criteria of the map elements. Finally, we present the web-based application schema and the first prototype designed to answer basic questions that require the reasoning services, overcoming the limitations of the underlying data base.

2   Related Work

Semantics-informed interpretation of datasets in the context of geomapping tasks has been addressed in three types of literature works: the technical infrastructures for semantics-informed applications, the ontological encoding of specialized domains, and the creation of controlled vocabularies (such as GeoScienceML and INSPIRE).

The technical infrastructures are very numerous in the geomatic literature. They are generally complementary approaches to OntoGeonous: where they introduce technical systems for realizing services, OntoGeonous introduces actual knowledge to support those services, also including consistency checking and automatic classification, which currently lack. Geon[5] is a cyber-infrastructure for the integration of 3D- and 4D-data, where formal ontologies (SWEET, among others) are used to coordinate and integrate conceptual schemas of heterogeneous geological maps (cf. [18]). OpenEarth Framework and OpenTopography, both developed from Geon, are a semantics-based toolsuite for integration and visualization of multi-dimensional data [17], and a high-resolution topographic data application[6]. AuScope[7] is an integrated Australian national framework [26] that allows real time access to data, information and knowledge, stored in distributed repositories. For querying geological maps, AuScope uses vocabulary-based services which overcome differences in geoscience terms due to language, synonyms and local variations. SETI (Semantics Enabled Thematic data Integration) [7] is a system that enables the retrieval of information from thematic data archives via semantic search (including the development of ontologies for the classification schemata and the integration of several applications). Finally, Ma's ontology mentioned above is the subject of the pilot interactive multimedia project developed by [19], which provided an animated visualization of this ontology and interaction functions over the ontology, the animation and an online geologic map, in synchronization with the RDF-based Geologic Time Scale ontology.

Approaches aimed at the ontological encoding of specialized domains are Virtual Solar-Terrestrial Observatory (VSTO) and Space Physics Archive Search and Extract (SPASE). VSTO[8] is a semantic data framework based on an ontology of the domains of solar physics, space physics and solar-terrestrial physics [8].

---

[5] http://www.geongrid.org/.

[6] http://www.opentopography.org/.

[7] https://www.researchgate.net/publication/234183449_AuScope's_use_of_Standards_to_Deliver_Earth_Resource_Data.

[8] https://www.vsto.org.

As in the case of OntoGeonous, VSTO also refers to the functional decomposition of SWEET, reusing, e.g., the notions of earth and sun realms, respectively. The SPASE consortium[9] is an international group of space physics researchers, Virtual Observatory developers and data providers who have created a comprehensive space physics data model, converted into an OWL ontology, consisting of terminology, definitions, and protocols for the documentation of a data product [20]. These approaches employ ontological encoding of specialized domains; as such, ontologies are a commodity for terminology and documentation rather than an effective machine-interpretable knowledge.

Finally, there are a number of approaches that make the effort of relying on authoritative resources (such as GeoScienceML), without introducing ad hoc knowledge specifications. All these approaches currently make a very basic use of ontological encoding: OntoGeonous improves such methods by providing a comprehensive approach to the formal encoding of the geologic knowledge, aimed at subsequent automatization of application algorithms. Examples of these approaches are OneGeology[10], an international initiative of the geological surveys in the world. Its goal is to create a worldwide geological map by harmonizing data from different providers, using GeoSciML standard, TaxonConcept[11] [12], which stores Open Nomenclature synonymy lists in the field of taxonomic classification of fossil species, The United States Geoscience Information Network[12] a federated information-sharing framework that uses GeoSciML as data transfer standard [24].

The OntoGeonous approach, described in this paper, integrates the knowledge sources in a machine-readable format and applies the encoded knowledge to the geomapping task, also proposing a software architecture for its exploitation.

3   Conceptual Modeling for Geologic Knowledge: The OntoGeonous Initiative

The geologic mapping process, which produces the map, requires the organization of data according to the general knowledge about the objects in the map, namely the geologic units, and to the objectives of a graphic representation of such objects in a map, following some established model of geotectonic evolution. Semantics can greatly help such a process in two concerns: on the one hand, it provides a terminological base to name and classify the objects of the map; on the other, the machine-readable encoding of the geologic knowledge base supports the application of reasoning mechanisms and the derivation of novel properties and relations about the objects of the map [14,15].

OntoGeonous is an initiative of the University of Turin and the Institute of Geosciences and Georesources of the Italian National Research Council (CNR-IGG) for the construction of a terminological knowledge base that is, on the

---

[9] http://www.spase-group.org/.
[10] http://portal.onegeology.org/OnegeologyGlobal/.
[11] http://taxonconcept.stratigraphy.net/.
[12] http://usgin.org/.

one hand, specific enough to classify the instances of a specific geodatabase, concerning the entries of the Geological Map of Piedmont and, on the other hand, general enough to connect all the knowledge required for the classification of the instances. OntoGeonous has produced a merged set of computational ontologies that has been realized through the OWL encoding of the statements reported in authoritative resources (see Fig. 1). In particular,

- GeoScience Markup Language (GeoSciML)[13] a standard data interchange format supporting structures for geologic and earth science information, expressed in a number of UML schemata (classes, features, attributes, associations) and statements in natural language, for the major core geological concepts;
- INSPIRE (Infrastructure for Spatial Information in the European Community)[14], a EU Commission directive of the Thematic Working Group Geology, aiming at creating a European Union spatial data infrastructure which will enable the sharing of environmental information among public sector organizations; INSPIRE encoding is based on a simplification of GeoSciML (GeoSciML+INSPIRE cookbook, addressing the major vocabularies) and is expressed through natural language statements;
- SWEET (Semantic Web for Earth and Environmental Terminology)[15], developed by NASA-Jet Propulsion Laboratory since 2002, a set of ontologies in OWL format that represent a knowledge base for environmental and Earth system science terms [2,23], considered for major upper, generic concepts;
- vocabularies of specific subdomains of geologic knowledge that are relevant for the geomapping task, developed by the IUGS/CGI IWG Concept Definition Task Group[16]: for example, we have imported the lithology domain vocabulary named Simple Lithology[17], and the ICS Geological Time Scale Ontology [18] as a subtaxonomy of the Geochronologic Unit class of SWEET Representation. There were many cross-reference issues to address during the encoding: for example, the Geochronologic Unit class of OntoGeonous referes to SWEET GeologicTimeUnit class (actually the hierarchical path Representation – NumericalEntity – Interval – Duration – GeologicTimeUnit).

The core of the geologic knowledge is a taxonomy rooted by Geologic Feature, which encompasses all the geologic core knowledge, related to (1) MappedFeature, i.e. the spatial extent of the geologic feature on the map, (2) GeoChronologicUnit, root of the ICS GTS taxonomy, (3) CGIVocabularyTerm (an OntoGeonous taxonomy for CGI vocabularies), which provide specific concepts for the several subdomains, such as the ones for the earth materials, and to the

---

[13] Version 4.0 (2015), http://www.geosciml.org.
[14] D2.8.II.4 INSPIRE Data Specification on Geology – Technical Guidelines v. 3.0. (10.12.2013) (http://inspire.jrc.ec.europa.eu/documents/Data_Specifications/ INSPIRE_DataSpecification_GE_v3.0.pdf).
[15] https://sweet.jpl.nasa.gov/.
[16] http://resource.geosciml.org/vocabulary/cgi/201211/.
[17] http://resource.geosciml.org/vocabulary/cgi/201211/simplelithology.rdf.

abstract descriptions in GeoSciML, which encode attributes, such as, the unit thickness. GeologicFeature is subdivided into four sub-taxonomies, namely Geomorphologic Feature (the landforms), GeologicUnit (the bodies of some material), GeologicStructure (configurations or patterns in which the geologic units are arranged), GeologicEvent (relevant events in geology).

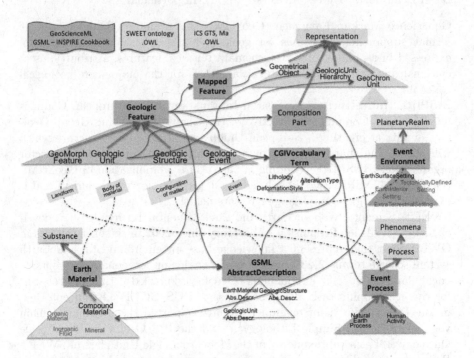

Fig. 1. The major taxonomies of OntoGeonous and their connections.

4   Application of Semantic Knowledge to a Cartographic Project

The Piemonte Geological Map [21] is grounded on a regional-scale Geodatabase consisting of some hundreds of Geologic Units that have several thousands instances in the Map [22]. Each Geologic Unit in the map is bounded by some Geologic Structures. The structure of the Geodatabase is grounded on the hierarchy of the Geologic Units, their characteristics (description) and their lithology (Simple Lithology encoded classes). The relations between the GeoDB contents (raws and columns describing the properties of the Mapped Features) and the general knowledge (concepts) stored in OntoGeonous are illustrated in Fig. 2 through a specific example, where links between the two knowledge sources are evidenced by arrowed lines. A specific geologic unit (Baldissero Formation) is a Lithostratigraphic unit made up of two parts (CP1 and CP2 represented by lithotypes) belonging to a higher rank geologic unit, the Synthem (i.e. the BTP3 Synthem) (as reported in the GeoDB). This Geologic Unit has also relations with a more general and conceptual knowledge framework, here represented by the Earth Material class (a Taxonomic Class of the GeoSciML Data Model) and the Simple Lithology controlled vocabulary (resources of the IUGS CGI Interoperability Working Group). These two knowledge sources are ideally linked with the GeoDB by arrowed lines, namely the Lithology and Geol_Unit3 columns of the GeoDB table.

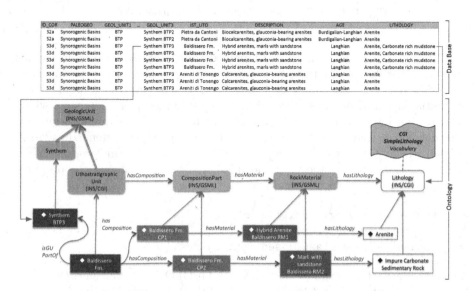

Fig. 2. A specific Geologic Unit (Baldissero Formation) is classified as a Lithostratigraphic unit made up of lower rank geologic units (compositional parts CP1 and CP2) represented by lithotypes belonging to a higher rank geologic unit, the BTP3 Synthem. This Geologic Unit has relations with a more general knowledge (represented in the Earth Material class, see Fig. 2) and is described by the CGI Simple Lithology vocabulary, as reported in the Geodatabase column Lithology.

In Fig. 3, we illustrate an application schema that can be deployed into several subtasks: the knowledge base OntoGeonous (an .owl file, possibly interconnected with other knowledge sources in the web, upper middle) resides in a server that hosts a service which is able to respond to queries posed about the encoded knowledge. The server runs on a physical machine equipped with four 2.30 GHz Intel(R) Xeon(R) CPUs and 65 GB RAM, executing a Scientific Linux 7.3 (Nitrogen) operating system. The described architecture is implemented as a

Java program using the Jena framework;[18] inference is performed based on the HermiT reasoner[19], which is accessed through the OWL API interface[20].

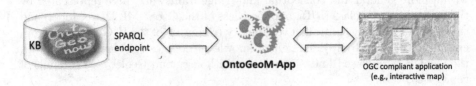

Fig. 3. The application schema for OntoGeonous server.

The specific application, generally named OntoGeoM-App in the figure, for implementing its specific task, poses queries to the knowledge base. We have currently implemented a prototype interface for querying the content of the instantiated knowledge base through a human-friendly query language, which works as an interface to semantic server that handles class expression queries. The query interface consists of a triple, addressing a subject (intended as "Find all entities XXX such that ..."), a property (intended as "... this property YYY valued as ..."), and an object (intended as "... ZZZ, the value of the property YYY"). Figure 4 reports the results for the query

```
''subject = geologic unit''
''property = made of material''
''object = some classic sedimentary rock''
```

expressed in natural language as "Find any GEOLOGIC UNIT such that ... is composed of some part that consists of some lithological material that is ... some classic sedimentary rock." and translated into the class expression query

```
GeologicUnit and
  (hasComposition some
    (CompositionPart and
      (hasMaterial some
        (EarthMaterial and
          (hasLithology some ClasticSedimentaryRock)))))
```

Several applications can be developed on this skeleton. For example, if we want to build a more detailed geological map (the current one is at 1:250K scale), we need an application that can fill automatically a number of entries in the data base by performing some effective reasoning on the knowledge base (after queries posed in the SPARQL language); or, for example, if we want to support

---

[18] Available at the URL https://jena.apache.org.

[19] http://www.hermit-reasoner.com.

[20] http://owlapi.sourceforge.net.

the cartographer with a draft map coloring based on some features of the units that are included in the knowledge base, such as the geochronologic reference and/or their lithology, the application can implement a map coloring algorithm informed by the semantic knowledge queried through the SPARQL endpoint.

Fig. 4. The interface of the web app to query the map knowledge.

5   Lessons Learned and Conclusions

This paper has presented a machine-readable encoding of geologic knowledge, in the paradigm of the Semantic Web and the Linked Data, and its application to an actual geomapping task, namely the definition and the legend compilation of a cartographic map of the geologic units in a regional area. We have also seen how applications and web services can be developed from the encoded knowledge, accessible through a semantic server. In the rest of this section (and paper), we report on the lesson learned from the encoding of the geologic knowledge and its application of the geomapping process.

In general, the ontological encoding has supported the investigation on the epistemological nature of the relations existing between the different orders of Geological units. In particular, the ontological encoding has moved the terminological problem from the intuitive conception of relations to motivated and coherent sets of instances, assuring the re-traceability of the knowledge path (steps) followed during the implementation of the synthetic geological model, as required by the geomapping task. For example, the reasoner has classified the Lithostratigraphic class under the Lithologic class, so the ontology has induced a taxonomic relation upon the flat vocabulary of geologic unit terms.

The clear explicitation and formal encoding of the intended meaning of the concepts strongly constrain the definition and even the accuracy of the spatial location of the mapped features [25]. This improves the applicability of the knowledge "stored" in the geodatabase across several domains (e.g. geology, geo-physics, geo-engineering, geo-environmental sciences, etc.), overcoming problems due to the use of different taxonomies. The analysis of the meaning of the geo-logical knowledge chunks, as well as their disambiguation through the encoding into axioms, can cause the deprecation of some concepts. For instance, concept "Tectonostratigraphic Unit", largely used in the geological literature although with slightly different meanings, was deprecated. Indeed, concept "Tectonostrati-graphic Unit" is a powerful tool that geologists often use to compare/distinguish portions of a sedimentary domain that originated in partially different paleo-environments and were later separated by tectonic contacts. Since each Tectonos-tratigraphic Unit can only be defined by comparison with its adjoining units (now distant bodies), it cannot be defined in an absolute, unambiguous way, and, then, not expressed by axioms. Anyway, all together the axioms defined for the Lithos-tratigraphic, Lithotectonic and Geologic Event concepts, respectively, give the necessary and sufficient conditions to formally (and fully) encode the knowledge that is inherent to the Tectonostratigraphic Unit concept. As a consequence, the Tectonostratigraphic Unit concept was deprecated in OntoGeonous (in a way that is consistent with CGI vocabularies and INSPIRE codelists, which actually do not report such a term).

OntoGeonous has been the product of the interaction between geologists and computer scientists, who exchanged many ideas during the encoding process. From a methodological perspective, of a paramount importance has been the initial attempt of the geologist to address the construction of the terminological knowledge. This practice has brought the geologist the awareness of the diffi-culty of the terminological vocabulary conception; then, later, when driven by the axiomatic encoding process, led by the computer scientist, the geologist can contribute effectively to the axiom building and address effectively the view-point of the task at hand, namely the geomapping process. During the ontology development, an effective tool for discussion of the axiomatic encoding ongoing was the implementation of a wiki[21]. For each concept definition, we created a page and the most debated issues opened discussion pages with links to the most relevant sources. Now, the wiki is released as a resource for further investigation as well as a human readable version of the knowledge (cf. [11] on the importance of wiki's for knowledge creation). It reports the motivations that have driven the encoding choices, which can be susceptible of novel updates.

The formal encoding of the geological knowledge opens new perspectives for the analysis and representation of the geological systems. These often have a very complex internal setting and a large range of physical properties, acquired in distinct geochronological steps (punctuated by geologic events), but rarely fully explicitly described [1,5,9,16]. In fact, once that the major concepts employed in the implementation of a geological map data base are defined, with their mean-ing explicitly expressed through a computational ontology, the resulting formal conceptual model of the geologic system can hold across different technical and scientific communities. Furthermore, this would allow for a semi-automatic or

---

[21] https://www.di.unito.it/wikigeo/.

automatic classification of the cartographic database, where a significant number of properties (attributes) of the recorded instances could be deduced (inferred) through computational reasoning.

Acknowledgements. We, the authors acknowledge a grant (direct beneficiary Dario Mimmo) for the Lagrange Project - CRT Foundation/ISI Foundation. We also thank Rossana Damiano, Claudio Mattutino, Simone Donetti, and the Technical Staff of the Computer Science Department of the University of Turin gave us support in the setup of the wiki and the semantic server. We thank ARPA Piemonte for the collaboration on the implementation of the application interface with the semantic server (http://webgis.arpa.piemonte.it/Geoviewer2D).

References

1. Balestro, G., Piana, F.: The representation of geological knowledge and uncertainty in databases of GIS geological maps. Boll. Soc. Geol. Ital. (Ital. J. Geosci.) **126**(3), 487–495 (2007)
2. Barahmand, S., Taheyrian, M., Al-Ashri, S.: Upadhyay: a survey on SWEET ontologies and their applications. Technical report, University of Southern California (2010). http://www-scf.usc.edu/taheriya/reports/csci586-report.pdf
3. Berners-Lee, T., Hendler, J., Lassila, O.: The semantic web. Sci. Am. Mag. **284**, 28–37 (2001)
4. Bizer, C., Heath, T., Berners-Lee, T.: Linked data - the story so far. Int. J. Semant. Web Inf. Syst. **5**(3), 1–22 (2009)
5. Brodaric, B., Gahegan, M., Harrap, R.: The art and science of mapping: computing geological categories from field data. Comput. Geosci. **30**(7), 719–740 (2004)
6. Cipolloni, C., Pantaloni, M.: La standardizzazione dei dati geologici. mem. descr. carta geol. d'it. In: La Cartografia del Servizio Geologico d'Italia, vol. 100, pp. 260–263 (2016)
7. Durbha, S., King, R., Shah, V., Younan, N.: A framework for semantic reconciliation of disparate earth observation thematic data. Comput. Geosci. **35**, 761–773 (2009)
8. Fox, P., McGuinness, D.L., Cinquini, L., West, P., Garcia, J., Benedict, J.L., Middleton, D.: Ontology-supported scientific data frameworks: the virtual solar-terrestrial observatory experience. Comput. Geosci. **35**, 724–738 (2009)
9. Frodeman, R.: Geological reasoning: geology as an interpretive and historical science. Geol. Soc. Am. Bull. **107**(8), 960–968 (1995)
10. Heath, T., Bizer, C.: Linked data: evolving the web into a global data space. Synth. Lect. Semant. Web: Theory Technol. **1**, 1–136 (2011)
11. Howard, A.S., Hatton, B., Reitsma, F., Lawrie, K.I.: Developing a geoscience knowledge framework for a national geological survey organisation. Comput. Geosci. **35**, 820–835 (2009)
12. Huber, R., Klump, J.: Charting taxonomic knowledge through ontologies and ranking algorithms. Comput. Geosci. **35**, 862–868 (2009)
13. Laxton, J.L.: Geological map fusion: Onegeology-Europe and inspire. Geol. Soc. Lond. Spec. Publ. **408** (2016). http://sp.lyellcollection.org/content/early/2016/09/27/SP408.16.abstract

14. Lombardo, V., Piana, F., Fioraso, G., Irace, A., Mimmo, D., Mosca, P., Tallone, S., Barale, L., Morelli, M., Giardino, M.: The classification scheme of the piemonte geological map and the ontogeonous initiative. Rendiconti Online Società Geologica Italiana. **39**, 117–120 (2016)

15. Lombardo, V., Piana, F., Mimmo, D.: Semantics-informed geological maps: conceptual modeling, knowledge encoding, workflow, and application. Comput. Geosci. (2017, resubmitted)

16. Loudon, T.V.: Geoscience after IT: part J human requirements that shape the evolving geoscience information system. Comput. Geosci. **26**(3A), A87–A97 (2000)

17. Ludäscher, B., Lin, K., Brodaric, B., Baru, C.: GEON: toward a cyberinfrastructure for the geosciences–a prototype for geological map interoperability via domain ontologies. In: Soller, D. (ed.) Digital Mapping Techniques, 2003–Workshop Proceedings, pp. 223–229. Millersville, PA, USA (2003)

18. Ma, X.: Ontology spectrum for geological data interoperability. Ph.D. thesis, University of Twente (2011)

19. Ma, X., Carranza, E., Wu, C., der Meer, F.V.: Ontology-aided annotation, visualization and generalization of geological time scale information from online geological map services. Comput. Geosci. **40**, 107–119 (2012)

20. Narock, T., Szabo, A., Merka, J.: Using semantics to extend the space physics data environment. Comput. Geosci. **35**, 791–797 (2009)

21. Piana, F., Fioraso, G., Irace, A., Mosca, P., d'Atri, A., Barale, L., Falletti, P., Monegato, G., Morelli, M., Tallone, S., Vigna, G.B.: Geology of piemonte region (NW Italy, Alps-apennines interference zone). J. Maps **13**(2) (2017). https://doi.org/10.1080/17445647.2017.1316218

22. Piana, F., Lombardo, V., Mimmo, D., Mulazzano, E., Barale, L., D'Atri, A., Irace, A., Morelli, M., Mosca, P., Tallone, S.: The geodatabase of the piemonte geological map: conceptual design for knowledge encoding. Rendiconti Online Società Geologica Italiana **42**, 85–89 (2017)

23. Raskin, R., Pan, M.: Semantic web for earth and environmental terminology. Comput. Geosci. **31**(9), 1119-1125 (2005). SWEET – http://ceur-ws.org/vol-83/sia_7.pdf

24. Richard, S., Allison, L.: Capitalizing on global demands for open data access and interoperability - the USGIN story. In: EGU2016-9540, Geophysical Research Abstracts, vol. 18, EGU General Assembly (2016). http://meetingorganizer.copernicus.org/EGU2016/EGU2016-9540.pdf

25. Soller, D.R., Lindquist, T., Matti, J.: Field description of the scientific and locational accuracy of geological features. In: Soller, D.R. (ed.) DMT 2002 - USGS Open-File Report, 02-370, pp. 33–40. USGS (2002)

26. Woodcock, R., Simons, B., Duclaux, G., Cox, S.: Auscope's use of standards to deliver earth resource data. In: Geophysical Research Abstracts 12, EGU General Assembly. p. 1556 (2010)

Machine Learning

Sampling Training Data for Accurate Hyperspectral Image Classification via Tree-Based Spatial Clustering

Annalisa Appice[1,2]([✉]), Sonja Pravilovic[3], Donato Malerba[1,2],
and Antonietta Lanza[1]

[1] Dipartimento di Informatica, Università Degli Studi di Bari Aldo Moro,
via Orabona, 4, 70126 Bari, Italy
{annalisa.appice,donato.malerba,antonietta.lanza}@uniba.it
[2] Consorzio Interuniversitario Nazionale per l'Informatica - CINI, Bari, Italy
[3] Faculty of Information Technology, Mediterranean University Vaka Djurovica,
81000 Podgorica, Montenegro
sonja.pravilovic@unimediteran.net

Abstract. The classification of hyperspectral images is a challenging task due to the high dimensionality of the task (i.e. large amount of pixels described over a high number of spectral channels) coupled with the small number of labeled examples typically available for learning. In the last decades, Support Vector Machines (SVMs) have gained in popularity in the field of the hyperspectral image classification as they address large attribute spaces and produce solutions from sparsely labeled data. However, they require "representative" training samples of the unknown class distribution to be accurate. In general, these samples are manually selected by expert visual inspection or field survey. This paper describes a learning schema, where the most suitable pixels to train the classifier are automatically selected via a spectral-spatial clustering phase. This reduces the expert effort required for sampling training pixels. Experimental results highlight that the proposed solution allows us to achieve a classification accuracy that outperforms the accuracy of both random and baseline sampling schemes.

1 Introduction

Hyperspectral remote sensing is one of the most important additions to remote sensing technology. Nowadays it allows the acquisition of data simultaneously in hundreds of spectral bands with narrow bandwidths. This high spectral resolution increases the possibility of more accurate classification of materials of interest in the spectral domain [5].

From a methodological point of view, the automatic classification of hyperspectral data is not a trivial task. It is made complex by the high cost of true sample labeling coupled with the high number of spectral attributes. The human-supervised effort needed to collect only few labeled imagery pixels, properly distributed among the classes, makes the definition of the proper training set for

© Springer International Publishing AG 2017
F. Esposito et al. (Eds.): AI*IA 2017, LNAI 10640, pp. 309–320, 2017.
https://doi.org/10.1007/978-3-319-70169-1_23

learning an imagery classifier still an open challenge [1,15]. In addition, the low number of collected ground truth labels, compared to the high number of spectral variables (also known as Hughes's phenomenon [11]), is not always sufficient for a reliable estimate of the classifier parameters.

In the last decades, Support Vector Machines (SVMs) have been widely investigated in the context of hyperspectral image classification, in order to deal with Hughes's phenomenon. In fact, they are robust classifiers in presence of large variable spaces, which produce accurate solutions also from sparsely labeled data [8,12]. In alternative, dimensionality reduction techniques (e.g. Principal Component Analysis) have been adopted, in order to mitigate this phenomenon [8,17]. However, in all these studies, pixels to train a classifier (i.e. training pixels) are still picked randomly over the remotely sensed data. Consequently, selected samples can lie in uninteresting areas and then some classes can be missed. Instead, from the classifier point of view, the most representative samples should be *smartly* identified and labeled by the expert, in order to construct training sets, where all classes are appropriately represented. At the same time, the expert action is expected to be minimized in the labeling of the training samples.

Even the most recent studies, that investigate active learning for the hyperspectral image classification (e.g. [13,14]), start learning from an initial pool of randomly selected, training samples. To the best of our knowledge, the problem of automatically and smartly selecting optimal training samples for learning an accurate classifier has nowadays attracted some attention in the remotely sensed imaging literature. Rajadell et al. [16] have authored a seminal study in this field. They have introduced the idea of adopting a clustering scheme, in order to sample the representative pixels, that should be manually labeled from the expert and used to learn the classifier. A clustering model has been constructed on the spectral signature of a remotely sensed image. This model has been used as a means to identify the imagery pixels that potentially belong to the same (unknown) object. Under the hypothesis that the clustering model is accurate (i.e. every cluster actually groups pixels belonging to the same (unknown) object), training pixels have been selected throughout clusters. The empirical study in [16] has proved that this spectral clustering phase has contributed to properly distribute training sample among the various thematic objects hidden in the remotely sensed data. Appice and Guccione [1] have recently advanced on this idea by leveraging the power of the expected spatial correlation of the spectral signature, in order to improve the clustering accuracy and, consequently, the ability of selecting properly distributed, suitable training pixels. In particular, they have accommodated the spatial autocorrelation of the spectral variables into the clustering process performed via Partioning Around Medoids. They have proved that new accuracy can be gained when using spectral-spatial information to detect objects over the remotely sensed data. In their proposal, the clusters are detected in a completely unsupervised manner, while the training pixels are sampled throughout the discovered clusters only after that the clustering phase is completed. Finally, the number of clusters to be discovered is required as a user-defined parameter.

This study achieves a new milestone by carrying on this research direction. It still proposes sampling examples for labeling through a spectral-spatial clustering phase, but the pixel sampling and labeling process is embedded in the clustering process instead of waiting for the clustering to be completed. In addition, the number of clusters is automatically determined during the clustering process. Procedurally, pixels are repeatedly partitioned along a tree-based cluster model so that the top node (cluster) of the tree contains the entire sample of the imagery pixels. The tree is grown by repeatedly considering any leaf node in the current tree and partitioning the cluster associated with the considered node into smaller sub-clusters. New nodes are added to the tree, in order to represent these sub-clusters. During tree construction, as a new node is built, a number of pixels is sampled throughout the cluster associated with it and labeled by the expert. Therefore, labels fed during the clustering process are immediately available to drive the clustering itself according to a semisupervised-like policy. In particular, sub-clusters are built by trying to reduce both the variance of the spatial autocorrelation of the spectral variables and the variance of the acquired labels simultaneously.

The paper is organized as follows. The next Section introduces some basic concepts, while Sect. 3 illustrates the proposed semi-supervised learning scheme. Section 4 describes the empirical study. Finally, in Sect. 5 some conclusions are drawn and future work is outlined.

2   Basic Concepts

Introductory concepts of this study include hyperspectral data and local indicators of spatial autocorrelation.

2.1   Hyperspectral Data

Let $\mathcal{D}$ be a *hyperspectral imagery dataset*, that is, a set of pixels (examples). Every pixel represents a region of around a few square meters of the Earth's surface (i.e. the pixel region is a function of the sensor's spatial resolution). It is associated with the spatial coordinates XY, as well as with the m-dimensional vector of spectral attributes $\mathbf{S} = S_1, S_2, \ldots, S_m$. Every spectral attribute S_i is a numeric attribute that expresses how much radiation is reflected, on average, across the pixel region, at the i-th band of the considered spectral profile. Pixels of $\mathcal{D}$ are labeled according to an unknown target function, whose values belong to a finite set of classes $C = \{C_1, C_2, \ldots, C_k\}$. Every class C_i represents a distinct theme (i.e. type of Earth's morphology). In general, pixels are equally distributed in space over a regular grid, so that a hyperspectral dataset can be represented by a matrix. A *spatial neighborhood* is a set of pixels q (task-relevant pixels) surrounding p (target pixel) in the matrix. In the imagery analysis literature, spatial neighborhoods frequently have a square shape [15], although alternative shapes like a circle or a cross can be also considered. Formally, let R be a positive, integer-valued radius, the *square-shaped* spatial neighborhood $\mathcal{N}(p, R)$ of pixel p is the set of imagery pixels $q(x + I, y + J)$, so that $-R \leq I, J \leq +R$.

2.2   Local Indicators of Spatial Autocorrelation

Local indicators look for "local patterns" of spatial dependence within the study region (see [4] for a survey). They return one value for each sampled location of a variable; this value expresses the degree to which that location is part of a spatial cluster. Widely speaking, a local indicator of spatial autocorrelation allows us to discover deviations from global patterns of spatial association, as well as hot spots like local clusters or local outliers. Several local indicators of spatial autocorrelation are formulated in the literature. In particular, the standardized Getis and Ord local GI* [10] is a local indicator of spatial autocorrelation, which has gained wide acceptance in the literature coupled with the cluster analysis [2,10]. It is computed as follows:

$$gi^*(Z, i) = \frac{1}{\sqrt{\frac{S^2}{n-1}\left(n \sum_{j=1, j \neq i}^{n} \lambda(i,j)^2 - \Lambda(i)^2\right)}} \left(\sum_{j=1, j \neq i}^{n} \lambda(i,j)z(j) - \bar{z}\,\Lambda(i)\right),$$

(1)

where Z is a measured variable, $\lambda(i, j)$ is a spatial (Gaussian or bi-square) weight between the locations of i and j, $\Lambda(i) = \sum_{j=1, j \neq i}^{n} \lambda(i, j)$ and $S^2 = \dfrac{\sum_{j=1}^{n} (z(j) - \bar{z})^2}{n}$.

We note that the weighting schema $(\lambda(i, j))$ is used to account for the influence of pixels falling into a squared neighborhood (namely neighbors) when computing the local indicator gi^*. A popular choice we adopt in this study defines $\lambda(i, j)$ as a relation inversely proportional to the spatial distance $d(i, j)$, such that the nearer the neighbor, the stronger its influence. Specifically, in this study, $\lambda(i, j) = \frac{1}{d(i,j)}$ if j falls in the considered squared neighborhood of i, $\lambda(i, j) = 0$ otherwise. A positive value for $gi^*(Z, i)$ indicates clusters of high values around i, while a negative value for $gi^*(Z, i)$ indicates clusters of low values around i.

3   Spectra-Spatial Tree-Based Sampler

This Section is devoted to the description of a spectral-spatial top-down induction algorithm named S^3CuT (Spectral-Spatial Sampler through Clustering Tree learning). This algorithm exploits the spectral and spatial information embedded into an hyperspectral image, in order to grow a tree that describes hierarchically-defined clusters of the spatial-close, spectral-similar input imagery pixels. It leverages the expertise of an oracle, in order to label a budget of pixels, which are sampled along the tree induction.

The cluster tree is built by resorting to an iterative algorithm (lines 1–12, main procedure, Algorithm 1) that takes as its input: (1) the unlabeled hyperspectral image $\mathcal{D}$ spanned on the spatial coordinate space XY and the spectral attribute space $\mathbf{S}$, (2) the number of pixels p and (3) the budget B. Procedurally, the iterative algorithm partitions pixels of image $\mathcal{D}$ into hierarchically-defined clusters. To this purpose, it starts with a node grouping all pixels into a single cluster. A clustering step corresponds to considering a leaf node in the current tree and partitioning the cluster of pixels associated with it into two disjoint subclusters. Two child nodes are associated with the constructed sub-clusters in the tree (line 9, main procedure, Algorithm 1). As a new node (i.e. cluster) is constructed in the tree, a sample of p pixels falling within this node is randomly sampled; the oracle (expert) is queried, in order to label these sampled pixels (lines 7–8, main procedure, Algorithm 1). The clustering step (and consequently the tree growth) is iterated over the current set of leaf nodes until a budget B of pixels has be sampled and labeled (stopping condition, line 5, main procedure Algorithm 1). During the iterative clustering process, leaf nodes are visited level-by-level in the tree (lines 2–4, 6, 10–11, main procedure, Algorithm 1).[1] We note that, according to this level-wise induction of the cluster tree, pixels are sampled and labeled as any leaf is visited for the tree growth. This allows us to construct a labeled sample set with pixels, which are distributed proportionally to actual density and shape of the clustered imagery areas.

The clustering phase is done by maximizing the (inter-cluster) variance reduction (lines 1, 5, 6, clustering procedure, Algorithm 1) of both the local indicators of the property of spatial autocorrelation on the spectral attributes $(\mathrm{var}(n, gi^*(\mathbf{S})))$ and the labels acquired from the oracle $(\mathrm{var}(\mathrm{labeled}(n), C))$. In particular, the main loop (lines 3–10, clustering procedure, Algorithm 1) looks for the best spectral attribute-value test c that can be associated with the internal node.

A candidate test c is in the form $S \leq \alpha$ for a spectral attribute $S \in \mathbf{S}$. Possible values of α are found by sorting the distinct values of S in the cluster of pixels, which are associated with the current node, then considering a threshold between each pair of adjacent bins of the equally-sized discretization of the ordered values of S. Thus, if the discretization has d distinct bins for S, at most $d-1$ thresholds are considered (by default, number of bins $d = 20$). The algorithm evaluates the split test c according to the split heuristic $\Delta\mathrm{var}_c$, defined in Formula 2 and computed in lines 1,5,6, procedure clustering Algorithm 1.

$$\Delta\mathrm{var}_c = \underbrace{(\mathrm{var}(n, gi^*(\mathbf{S})) + \mathrm{var}(\mathrm{labeled}(n), C))}_{\textit{line 1, procedure clustering, Algorithm 1}} -$$
$$\underbrace{(var(n_L, n_R, \mathbf{S}) + var(\mathrm{labeled}(n_L), \mathrm{labeled}(n_R), C))}_{\textit{line 5, procedure clustering, Algorithm 1}}, \tag{2}$$

---

[1] A queue structure is used to collect the leaf nodes visited to construct the tree level-wise (lines 2–6, 10–11, main procedure, Algorithm 1).

Algorithm 1. Spectral-Spatial Sampler through Clustering (Tree learning S^3CuT).

– *Main routine*$(D, \mathbf{S}, XY, p, B) \mapsto \mathcal{L}$

Require: $(\mathcal{D}, \mathbf{S}, XY)$ {hyperspectral image $\mathcal{D}$ spanned on both spectral space $\mathbf{S}$, spatial coordinate space XY and (initially unknown) class C}
Require: p {number of pixel sampled per node/cluster}
Require: B {budget (i.e. total number of sampled pixels)}
Ensure: $\mathcal{L}$ {labeled set}
1: $gi^*(\mathbf{S}) \leftarrow gi^*(\mathcal{D}, \mathbf{S})$;
2: $queue \leftarrow new$ Queue ();
3: $root \leftarrow new$ node$(\mathcal{D})$;
4: inqueue$(queue, root)$;
5: **while** (not empty$(queue)$ and $B > 0$) **do**
6:    $n \leftarrow$ dequeue$(queue)$;
7:    $\mathcal{L} \leftarrow \mathcal{L} \cup$oracle$(n, p)$;
8:    $B \leftarrow B - p$;
9:    $(n_L, n_R) \leftarrow$clustering(n);
10:    inqueue$(queue, n_L)$;
11:    inqueue$(queue, n_R)$;
12: **end while**

– *clustering*$(n) \mapsto (n_{L,R})$

1: var $\leftarrow$ var$(n, gi^*(\mathbf{S}))$ + var(labeled$(n), C$);
2: $(c^*, \Delta^*\text{var}) \leftarrow (null, 0)$;
3: **for** (each possible Boolean test c according to values of $\mathbf{S}$) **do**
4:    $(n_L, n_R) \leftarrow$splitting (n, c); {clustering induced by c on n}
5:    var$_c \leftarrow var(n_L, n_R, \mathbf{S})$ + var(labeled(n_L), labeled$(n_R), C$);
6:    Δvar$_c \leftarrow$ var $-$ var$_c$;
7:    **if** (Δvar $\geq \Delta^*$var) **then**
8:        $(c^*, \Delta^*\text{var}) \leftarrow (c, \Delta\text{var})$;
9:    **end if**
10: **end for**
11: $(n_L, n_R) \leftarrow$splitting (n, c^*);

---

where $var(n_L, n_R, \mathbf{S}) = \frac{|n_L|\text{var}(n_L, gi^*(\mathbf{S})) + |n_R|\text{var}(n_R, gi^*(\mathbf{S}))}{|n_L| + |n_R|}$ and var(labeled(n_L),

labeled$(n_R), C) = \frac{|\text{labeled}(n_L)|\text{var}(\text{labeled}(n_L), C) + |\text{labeled}(n_R)|\text{var}(\text{labeled}(n_R), C)}{|\text{labeled}(n_L)| + |\text{labeled}(n_R)|}$.

Specifically, $|\cdot|$ denotes the cardinality of a set and labeled$(\cdot)$ denotes the subset of labels acquired in a set. This formula is the variance reduction of local indicators of the property of spatial autocorrelation on the spectral attributes $(gi^*(\mathbf{S}))$ combined with the variance reduction of the acquired labels (C). We consider the standardized Getis and Ord local gi^* (see Formula 1, Sect. 2.2 for details). This indicator is chosen for its ability to distinguish high-valued areas from low-valued areas in the row. This spatial clustering power of an autocorrelation measure is attractive here, since it allows the integration of the spatial autocorrelation into the spectral information during the clustering phase. The local autocorrelations are considered for each spectral attribute $S \in \mathbf{S}$. To deal with multiple spectral attributes, the multi-variate analysis is achieved by computing the reduction of the sums of variances of the indicators of local autocorrelation over the set of spectral attributes, where each attribute contributes equally to the overall Δvar value. We use sums since they are common ways to combine statistics in multivariate analysis [2,3]. Formally, let n a node, the variance on the local indicators of the spectral signature $(gi^*(\mathbf{S}))$ of the cluster of pixels associated with n is computed follows:

$$\text{var}(n, gi^*(\mathbf{S})) = \frac{\sum\limits_{gi^*(S) \in gi^*(\mathbf{S})} \text{var}(n, gi^*(S))}{|gi^*(\mathbf{S})|}, \tag{3}$$

where $gi^*(S)$ is the local indicator computed on the spectral attribute $S \in \mathbf{S}$.

4   Empirical Study

The presented algorithm is evaluated by considering two benchmark hyperspectral images, namely Indian Pines and Pavia University (http://www.grss-ieee.org/community/technical-committees/data-fusion/). These data sets are selected for the following reasons: (1) They have a high spatial resolution. (2) They contain rich spectral information (100–200 bands) and a high number of classes (9–16 classes). (3) They correspond to different scenarios. (4) Ground truths are available for these data. Additionally, they are considered standard benchmark data in hyperspectral image classification (e.g. [15]).

The empirical study is performed to investigate the accuracy of the classifier learned by considering a training set smartly constructed via a spectra-spatial clustering phase. Before we proceed to present the empirical results (see Subsect. 4.3), we provide a description of the datasets used (see Subsect. 4.1), as well as of the experimental set-up performed (methodology, metrics and parameters described in Subsect. 4.2).

4.1   Hyperspectral Data

AVIRIS Indian Pines was obtained by the Airborne Visible Infrared Imaging Spectrometer (AVIRIS) sensor over the Indian Pines region in Northwestern Indiana in 1992. The image contains 220 spectral bands, but 20 spectral bands have been removed due to the noise and water absorption phenomena. The spatial resolution is 20 m and the spatial size is of 145 × 145 pixels, which are classified into 16 mutually exclusive classes (see Fig. 1(a)). This data set represents a very challenging land-cover classification scenario, in which the primary crops of the area (mainly corn and soybeans) were very early in their growth cycle, with only about 5% canopy cover [15]. Discriminating among the major crops under these circumstances can be a very difficult task. This scenario is also made more complex by the imbalanced number of available labeled pixels per class.

ROSIS Pavia University was obtained by the Reflective Optics System Imaging Spectrometer (ROSIS) sensor during a flight campaign over the Engineering School at the University of Pavia, in 2003. Water absorption bands were removed, and the original 115 bands were reduced to 103 bands. It has a spatial resolution of 1.3 m. The image has a spatial size of 610 × 340 pixels, which are classified into 9 classes (see Fig. 1(b)).

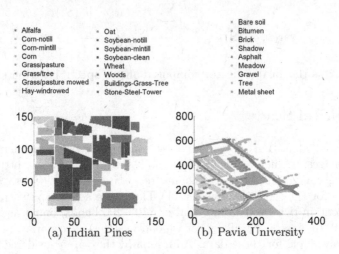

Fig. 1. The AVIRIS data of Indian Pines and the ROSIS data of Pavia University: ground truth labels.

4.2   Experimental Set-Up

For each hyperspectral image, we consider budget B and evaluate the training sets constructed by: (1) sampling B training pixels via the spectral-spatial cluster tree-based sampler described in this study (S^3CuT); (2) sampling B training pixels via the spectral-spatial sampler described in [1] (GOPAM); (3) sampling B training pixels via a random sampler throughout the entire image (Random).

We construct training sets with B equal to 1%, 5% and 10% of the entire imagery pixel set. Additionally, we set-up p (number of pixels sampled and labeled per node) equal to 1 for S^3CuT, k (number of clusters discovered by PAM) equal to the number of ground truth classes for GOPAM (as described in [1]) and the pixel neighborhood radius R equal to 5 during the calculation of Getis and Ord indicator for both for S^3CuT and GOPAM. For each data set, for each sampler, we construct 10 training set trials. For each trial, the inductive Support Vector Machine (SVM) [7] is learned from the trial training set and used to label the entire image. This choice of inducing SVMs for the classification phase is motivated by several studies reported in the literature (e.g. [6,9,15]), which show that inductive SVMs are applied to hyperspectral image classification with great success, outperforming several other inductive classifiers. As the hyperspectral classification problem is a multi-class problem, we learn multi-class SVMs with the "one-against-all" strategy. SVMs are learned with the Gaussian kernel rule, while parameters are optimally selected according to a grid-search method and a three-fold cross validation of the labeled set.

The classification performance is evaluated in terms of accuracy of the subsequent classifiers. The accuracy of a classifier is measured in terms of overall accuracy (OA) and average accuracy (AA) computed on the classified images. The metrics are averaged on the various trials. For both accuracy metrics (OA and AA), the higher the metric, the more accurate the classifier. In particular, these metrics are defined in terms of elements x_{ij} of the confusion matrix associated to the classified pixels. Each element x_{ij} denotes the number of pixels with ground truth c_j, which are labeled with class c_i. C is the number of distinct classes in the image. Let us consider $x_i = \sum_i x_{ii}$, (i.e. the sum over the principal diagonal),

$$x_{+j} = \sum_i x_{ij} \text{ (i.e. the sum over all rows for column } j) \text{ and } N = \sum_i \sum_j x_{ij}. \text{ (i.e.}$$

the number of pixels). Then, $OA = \frac{x_i}{N}$ and $AA = \frac{1}{C} \sum_i \frac{x_{ii}}{X_{+i}}$.

Table 1. Accuracy analysis: Mean $\pm$ Standard Deviation of Overall Accuracy (OA) and Average Accuracy (AA) of SVMs induced from training set trials constructed by S³CuT varying budget B among 1%, 5% and 10% of the pixel number.

		1%	5%	10%
Indian Pines	OA	.5472 ± .1074	.7555 ± .0050	.8814 ± .0018
	AA	.4408 ± .2854	.7330 ± .0503	.8337 ± .0221
Pavia University	OA	.8569 ± .0196	.9206 ± .0023	.9442 ± .0087
	AA	.7532 ± .0583	.9012 ± .0665	.9109 ± .0011

Table 2. Computation time analysis: Mean $\pm$ Standard Deviation of Computation time (in seconds) spent to sample training sets and induce SVMs from training set trials constructed by S³CuT varying budget B among 1%, 5% and 10% of the pixel number.

		1%	5%	10%
Indian Pines	Sampling and labeling	107.02 ± 195.16	182.69 ± 47.37	220.11 ± 659.14
	SVM	10.00 ± 9.44	57.82 ± 274.24	146.92 ± 41.06
Pavia University	Sampling and labeling	134.55 ± 121.03	179.83 ± 220.67	206.03 ± 154.30
	SVM	13.07 ± 14.11	371.59 ± 173.86	2321.93 ± 3256.90

4.3   Results and Discussion

We start this study by analyzing the sensitivity of the performance of S^3CuT to budget B (as 1%, 5% and 10% of imagery data). Accuracy results and computation times (in seconds) are reported in Tables 1 and 2. The results achieved confirm the expectation. They show that the larger the training set size, the more accurate the classification accuracy (see Table 1). However, the higher accuracy is at the expenses of the higher computation time spent to construct the training set, as well as to induce the SVM (see Table 2). On the other hand, the larger the training size, the lower the standard deviation of the accuracy computed on various trials (both OA and AA). This final result suggests that the induced classifier is less sensitive to the samples, which are actually labeled throughout the clusters constructed along the cluster tree, if we enlarge the budget with the labeled pixels.

We proceed the discussion by comparing the accuracy of S^3CuT to that of its baseline competitors, namely GOPAM and Random. Accuracy results are compared in Figs. 2(a) and (b). They confirm the efficacy of the idea of feeding a training set by accounting for spatio-spectral cluster information. In fact, the two spectral-spatial samplers, namely S^3CuT and GOPAM, outperform the baseline Random, that neglects clustering and spatial autocorrelation. Furthermore, this study confirms that the tree-based strategy performed by S^3CuT gains in accuracy compared to the flat strategy performed by GOPAM by empirically proving the advantage of acquiring labels during the clustering phase, instead of doing so once the clustering phase is completed.

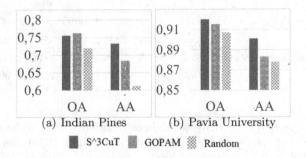

Fig. 2. Comparative analysis: Mean of Overall Accuracy (OA) and Average Accuracy (AA) of SVMs induced from training sets constructed by S^3CuT, GOPAM and Random with budget B equal to the 5% of the pixel number.

5   Conclusion

This paper addresses the challenging problem of smartly sampling the optimal representative training pixels of an hyperspectral image. Sampled pixels are manually labeled by the expert and processed via an inductive learning process, in order to automatically derive accurate classifications of unlabeled pixels in the image. We describe a top-down induction algorithm that accounts for the property of spatial autocorrelation of the spectral data, in order to sample the representative training data. In the presented algorithm, labels are acquired during a spectral-spatial hierarchical clustering process, hence a few labels are available during the clustering refinements. Consequently, clusters are built by trying to reduce both the variance of the spatial autocorrelation of the spectral variables and the variance of the acquired labels, simultaneously. The empirical study involves benchmark data. It proves that considering spectral-spatial information, as well as embedding labeling in the clustering phase allow us to define a sampling methodology that outperforms both the traditional random sampling methodology, as well as the existing spectral spatial sampling strategies. As a direction for further work, it would be interesting to investigate the use an adaptive procedure to automatically fit the number of pixels sampled per cluster based on properties like cluster size or cluster variance. Additionally, although the presented method is specifically designed for imagery data, we are interested in investigating how it can be generalized to other high-dimensional data (e.g. geo-localized time-series). Finally, we intend to explore the use of some big-data technologies (e.g. MapReduce) in the design of the proposed algorithm, in order to be able to evaluate the performances when large volume of hyperspectral data are processed via specific parallel processing architectures.

Acknowledgments. Sonja Pravilovic's research was supported by the Ministry of Science of Montenegro, Higher Education and Research for Innovation and Competitiveness (INVO/HERIC). She received the national scholarship for excellence (1/10/2016-1/10/2017) funded by the proceeds of a loan from the International Bank for Reconstruction and Development. Authors thank Francesco Dammacco for his support in developing the algorithm presented and anonymous reviewers for useful suggestions provided to improve this paper. This work is carried out in partial fulfillment of the research objectives of the European project "MAESTRA - Learning from Massive, Incompletely annotated, and Structured Data (Grant number ICT-2013-612944)" funded by the European Commission, as well as the ATENEO 2012 project "Mining Complex Patterns" and the ATENEO 2014 project "Mining of network data" funded by University of Bari Aldo Moro.

References

1. Appice, A., Guccione, P.: Exploiting spatial correlation of spectral signature for training data selection in hyperspectral image classification. In: Calders, T., Ceci, M., Malerba, D. (eds.) DS 2016. LNCS, vol. 9956, pp. 295–309. Springer, Cham (2016). doi:10.1007/978-3-319-46307-0_19
2. Appice, A., Malerba, D.: Leveraging the power of local spatial autocorrelation in geophysical interpolative clustering. Data Min. Knowl. Disc. **28**(5–6), 1266–1313 (2014)
3. Appice, A., Džeroski, S.: Stepwise induction of multi-target model trees. In: Kok, J.N., Koronacki, J., Mantaras, R.L., Matwin, S., Mladenič, D., Skowron, A. (eds.) ECML 2007. LNCS, vol. 4701, pp. 502–509. Springer, Heidelberg (2007). doi:10.1007/978-3-540-74958-5_46

4. Boots, B.: Local measures of spatial association. Ecoscience **9**(2), 168–176 (2002)
5. Camps-Valls, G., Tuia, D., Bruzzone, L., Benediktsson, J.A.: Advances in hyper-spectral image classification: earth monitoring with statistical learning methods. IEEE Sig. Process. Mag. **31**(1), 45–54 (2014)
6. Chen, C., Li, W., Su, H., Liu, K.: Spectral-spatial classification of hyperspectral image based on kernel extreme learning machine. Remote Sens. **6**(6), 5795–5814 (2014)
7. Cortes, C., Vapnik, V.: Support-vector networks. Mach. Learn. **20**(3), 273–297 (1995)
8. Dong, P., Liu, J.: Hyperspectral image classification using support vector machines with an efficient principal component analysis scheme. In: Wang, Y., Li, T. (eds.) ISKE 2011. AISC, vol. 122, pp. 131–140. Springer, Heidelberg (2012). doi:10.1007/978-3-642-25664-6_17
9. Fauvel, M., Tarabalka, Y., Benediktsson, J., Chanussot, J., Tilton, J.: Advances in spectral-spatial classification of hyperspectral images. Proc. IEEE **101**(3), 652–675 (2013)
10. Getis, A., Ord, J.K.: The analysis of spatial association by use of distance statistics. Geogr. Anal. **24**(3), 189–206 (1992)
11. Hughes, G.: On the mean accuracy of statistical pattern recognizers. IEEE Trans. Inf. Theory **14**(1), 55–63 (1968)
12. Melgani, F., Bruzzone, L.: Classification of hyperspectral remote sensing images with support vector machines. IEEE Trans. Geosci. Remote Sens. **42**(8), 1778–1790 (2004)
13. Pasolli, E., Melgani, F., Tuia, D., Pacifici, F., Emery, W.J.: SVM active learning approach for image classification using spatial information. IEEE Trans. Geosci. Remote Sens. **52**(4), 2217–2233 (2014)
14. Pasolli, E., Yang, H.L., Crawford, M.M.: Active-metric learning for classification of remotely sensed hyperspectral images. IEEE Trans. Geosci. Remote Sens. **54**(4), 1925–1939 (2016)
15. Plaza, A., Benediktsson, J.A., Boardman, J.W., Brazile, J., Bruzzone, L., Camps-Valls, G., Chanussot, J., Fauvel, M., Gamba, P., Gualtieri, A., Marconcini, M., Tilton, J.C., Trianni, G.: Recent advances in techniques for hyperspectral image processing. Remote Sens. Environ. **113**(Suppl. 1), S110–S122 (2009)
16. Rajadell, O., Garcia-Sevilla, P., Dinh, V.C., Duin, R.P.W.: Semi-supervised hyper-spectral pixel classification using interactive labeling. In: 2011 3rd Workshop on Hyperspectral Image and Signal Processing: Evolution in Remote Sensing (WHIS-PERS), pp. 1–4 (2011)
17. Stearns, S.D., Wilson, B.E., Peterson, J.R.: Dimensionality reduction by optimal band selection for pixel classification of hyperspectral imagery. vol. 2028, pp. 118–127 (1993)

Do You Feel Blue? Detection of Negative Feeling from Social Media

Marco Polignano[✉], Marco de Gemmis, Fedelucio Narducci,
and Giovanni Semeraro

Department of Computer Science, University of Bari "Aldo Moro",
via Edoardo Orabona 4, Bari, Italy
{marco.polignano,marco.degemmis,fedelucio.narducci,
giovanni.semeraro}@uniba.it

Abstract. The blue feeling is the sensation which affects people when
they feel down, depressed, sad and more generally when they are in a
bad feeling state. In some cases, it is a recurring situation in their everyday life and it can be the first symptom of more complex psychological
diseases such as depression. In the last decade, as consequence of the
quick increase of detected cases of depression in children and teenagers,
it has become very important to find strategies for a timely detection
of this pathology. In this work, we describe a model that can support
the detection task, by identifying some warning scenarios of blue feeling.
The proposed architecture is composed by modules focused on different
aspects that characterize the scenario: changes in heart rate, reduction
of sleep, reduction of activities performed, increases of use of negative
phrases and words. In particular, in this paper, we describe the approach adopted to analyze users posts on social media networks (SMNs)
by using natural language processing techniques. The proposed approach
is evaluated through an experimental session over a dataset of Facebook
posts. The results show good performance in the detection of negative
feeling.

Keywords: Natural Language Processing · Emotion · Text annotation ·
Word embedding · Social media · User modeling

1 Introduction

The detection of psychological pathologies, including depression, is an articulate
task that involves experts in psychology, doctors, and tutors of the subject, who
should monitor the patient constantly for observing symptoms of the pathology. This process cannot be substituted by an automated process, but it can
be supported by systems able to detect scenarios in which relevant symptoms
are shown. The Diagnostic and Statistical Manual Volume IV (DSM-IV) [18] is
usually used as a guide to recognizing psychological pathologies and provides a
complete list of symptoms for the clinical detection of depression:

© Springer International Publishing AG 2017
F. Esposito et al. (Eds.): AI*IA 2017, LNAI 10640, pp. 321–333, 2017.
https://doi.org/10.1007/978-3-319-70169-1_24

- difficulties to sleep and to feel relaxed. More than the 90% of the depressed subjects are affected by sleep disorders and problems with the quality of sleep [7,27];
- changes in heart rate. The subject is affected by unusual patterns of heart rate variability. Corney detected increases in resting heart rates [3,23];
- reduction of activities performed. Subject affected by depression are associated with a reduction of the activities performed during the day. In particular, Haley [10] had found a strong correlation with an increase of daytime reclining;
- increase of negative sentences and words used. Depressed individuals use significantly more negative emotional words [22]. The same behavior is shown by depressed persons when using Social Networks, as described by Moreno [20].

We have defined a model (Fig. 1), based on the above-mentioned symptoms, which is able to detect possible situations of risk (according to literature) and to provide a timely notification of "warning situations" to the tutor of the subject monitored (parents, teachers, etc.). Four main phases are defined: Data Collection, Data Analysis, Detection, Alerting phase. The user is constantly monitored by using data collected from her smartphone, computer and wearable smartwatch. Moreover, information about her Heart Rate Variability (HRV) and sleep time can be used for detecting situations of risk that can be difficult to detect without specific instruments. Each module has functions for collecting, analyzing and managing a specific data, while rules for detecting warning situation of blue feeling are defined according to DSM-IV [18].

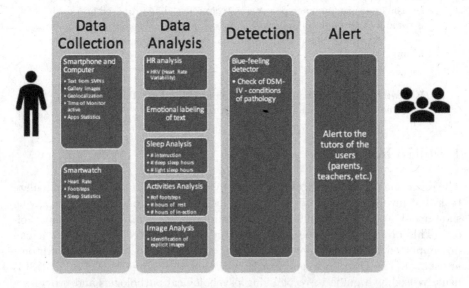

Fig. 1. Detection model of "waring scenario" for possible cases of blue feeling

One of the core components of the architecture is the module for text analysis, whose aim is to associate the text with an emotional label such as *happiness* or *sadness*. The main contribution of this paper is the description of the techniques adopted to perform this task. Furthermore, we show the results obtained by an in-vitro experimental evaluation performed on messages collected from social media networks (SMNs).

2 Related Work

Information which comes from SMNs has been already used in literature as a source of information for detecting many user's tendencies [21] but also physiological pathologies such as depression [20,22]. These studies have demonstrated how the information that comes from demographic data as age and relationship status, Facebook statistics such as the number of friends, and words used in sentences, are relevant aspects to be considered for the detection of physiological diseases. In order to use these findings in our architecture (Fig. 1), a module of text analysis has been defined. It automatically builds a lexicon, associated with Ekman's emotions: happiness, anger, sadness, fear, disgust, surprise [6], and it uses this information to annotate SMNs textual messages (i.e. posts on pages, status updates) with the corresponding emotional label. In literature, both lexicon-based and machine learning-based approached are used to perform sentiment detection from text [1,2,4].

Lexicon-based models use word lexicons for counting the number of words in the phrases associated with each emotion. Most of them are manually annotated and contain specific words defined in a standard vocabulary [11,16]. This approach exposes a problem correlated with the validity of the association between word and emotion because it does not take into account that the same word might express different emotions according to the context in which it is used. Moreover, the words contained in a standard thesaurus can be totally different from the lexicon used in the "everyday" spoken language. It is obvious that words such as 'omg', 'hahaha', and emoticons like provide relevant information about the emotion felt by the user, but they are not detectable using standard lexicons [5]. In the field of emotion classification, different machine learning approaches to the problem have been proposed, some based on supervised learning strategies, others based on unsupervised [1] techniques. The main limitation of learning approaches is that they need a large amount of data, thus a complex process of collection and annotation of sentences taken from the reference domain is required. Moreover, in order to have an accurate training set, the annotation process is often performed manually, thus it is a time-consuming process. In this work, an approach for constructing a *dynamic* lexicon for labeling messages from SMNs is proposed. The approach can be used to produce a lexicon for lexicon-based classification strategies, as well as for the automatic annotation of datasets for machine learning approaches.

3   Emotional Labeling of Text

The approach used for text labeling is based on the idea that it is possible to automatically annotate user's post on SMNs using *emoticons*, i.e. symbols which express the emotion and sentiment felt by users. They can be considered as a good source to assign a sentence with an emotional label [5, 26]. Following this idea, an emoticon-based labeling approach for textual sentences has been proposed. In this study, we decided to adopt the model defined by Ekman [6] based on six emotions: happiness, anger, sadness, fear, disgust, surprise. The labeling of SMNs messages with emoticons is used for creating training data to be used by a categorization algorithm to classify messages which do not contain emoticons. The process of emotional labeling of text collected from SMNs requires an accurate preprocessing step because messages do not follow standard grammar rules and usually contain links, hashtags, repeated words or words with repeated characters [13] ("cooooool!!!!"). Preprocessing operations are: cleaning, stop-word elimination, tokenization and the transformation of words into numerical vectors.

3.1   Emoticon-Based Text Annotation for Training Set

The creation of a dataset to be used by machine learning algorithms is a task which usually involves human annotators. The presence of noisy data is a critical aspect to be considered when a classifier is trained. In the SMNs scenario, sentences are very ambiguous and it is difficult also for the human annotator to associate them with an explicit emotional label. A relevant aspect to consider is, on the contrary, the large quantity of smiles available in these messages. They can be associated mostly with a unique emotion and they resume the sentiment of the entire sentence. As consequence of this observation, the emoticons inside the text have been used as discriminant features for labeling textual sentences. Each smile has been associated with a main emotional sense with a very simple strategy. We identify the most common emotions[1,2] recently included in UNICODE standard version 9 and we manually classify them (considering also their main writing variations), as reported in Fig. 2.

Each sentence has been analyzed and tokenized using TweetNLP[3] in order to replace characters repetitions, words repetition and to extract an ASCII emoticon as a single n-gram. Moreover, links and other noisy elements such as hashtags have been removed. Each token has been compared with the list of emoticons previously defined and, when a match has been found, the sentence until that point has been classified with the corresponding emotion. Sentences whose length was lower than 3 n-grams were removed.

---

[1] http://cool-smileys.com/text-emoticons.

[2] https://it.wikipedia.org/wiki/Emoticon.

[3] http://www.cs.cmu.edu/~ark/TweetNLP/.

Emotion	Smiles
Joy	:-D :'-) =^) 8-D ^ω^ =o) :') =-3 =-)) =-> ^_^ xD =-] x-D =-} 8) =c) (°o°) :) =-) :3 :> :^) :D (^^) :o) =-D :-3 ='-) :] B^D (^_^) :-> (≥∇≤) (^0^) :} :-)) :-] =) =3 => =D :-} =] ^^ 8-) =') :c) =} :-) >;) >:P >=-) 0=) :-P :-b 3=-) =Þ >=) d: d= 0=-3 }:-) }:) >=P 3:) :-Þ 0=-) X-P 0;^) 3:-) }=) >:-) XP 3=) 0=-3 0=-) 0:-3 :P =-P 0:) :b =-b 0:-) #-) }=-) =P 0=) 0:) =b 0:-3 0:-) :P =-Þ
Sadness	:-< (ToT) (T_T) (;_; >:[:-[QQ :-c :'-(>=(('_') >=[(T∇T) (~_~) :'(;n; =-|| </3 ;-; :$:(=-(;_; T.T :< =-< ;; ='-(:[=-[:c (~o~) =-c =$ =((;_:) =< =@ (;0;) (;_;) =[=c (/_;) (:_;) ='(={ Q_Q :-(Q.Q
Anger	(:-& >:-) >:-(X(:@ :Z :-@ :t :z :{ :-Z :-t : -{ :-|| b (>:(>:) X-(
Disgust	>:\ :-X :-| >=/ >=\ (=_=) :# =-# :& :/ =-& =-. =-/ :L :S :X (-_-) =-X :\ :| =# =& =-| =/ =S =X =\ =l =| :-# :-& :-. >:/ :-/
Fear	(>_<)> D8 D: D; D= D:< >.< DX %) D-': %-) (´Д`) (>_<) (°◇°)
Surprise	Oo >:O :-O OO θo O-O O_O >=O 8-O =-θ °o° o-o :θ :O :-θ =-O =θ oθ =O

Fig. 2. Smiles classified for expressed emotion

3.2 Generation of a Lexicon for the Application Domain

The datasets which can be generated using the emoticon-based annotation strategy, as described in Sect. 3.1, are dynamic domain-dependent resources which can be used for extracting information about emotional lexicon. Differently from standard emotional lexicons such as WordNet-Affect [25] or NRC Word-Emotion Association Lexicon [19], which contain a fixed number of manually annotated words, a lexicon extracted from this kind of datasets perfectly fits with the writing style of the domain of reference. The sentences annotated by the approach described in Sect. 3.1, are divided into six independent lists, one for each Ekman emotion. The sentences within each list are tokenized using TweetNLP and the frequency list of each token is calculated. The frequencies are normalized over the maximum frequency detected in the list and the tokens are ranked according to the values obtained. Only the tokens whose frequency is higher than 1% of the number of total sentences are considered relevant, but this is a parameter that can be changed in order to avoid longer or shorter word lists, and can be optimized according to the number of sentences available. Finally, words falling in more than one list are removed, in order to keep only the distinctive words for each class. The weighted list of words is used as a lexicon of keywords which fully represent each emotional class.

3.3 Creation of a Distributional Space for Words

Textual sentences must be translated into a vector representation. We use a word embedding continuous vector representation able to capture both syntactic and semantic information about a word. Several methods have been proposed in order to create word embeddings that follow the Distributional Hypothesis [12]. In our work we use two models, commonly called *word2vec*: continuous bag-of-words and skip-gram, introduced by [17], which can generate for each n-gram a 300 features numeric representation (Fig. 3). These models learn a vector representation for each word by using a neural network language model that can be trained efficiently on billions of words. Word2vec allows to learn complex semantic relationships using simple vector operators, such as: vec($king$) − vec(man) + vec($woman$) ≈ vec($queen$). However, our method is general and other approaches for building word embeddings can be used [9].

	word character varying	f1 double precision	f2 double precision	f3 double precision	f4 double precision	f5 double precision	... double precision
1	great	-0.149268314242363	0.310838729143143	-0.302873075008392	0.087163075847104	-0.10051418095271	-0.100627370178699
2	happy	0.0278087388724089	-0.146649792790413	0.096267856657505	0.0221009831875563	-0.0233133174479008	0.0888253301382065
3	cool	-0.0296492539346218	0.10115023702383	-0.182394281029701	0.146255329251289	0.00244281836785376	0.0700735077261925

Fig. 3. Example of word2vec representation for the words: great, happy and cool

3.4   Building the Classifier

The approach proposed in this work is based on the similarity score between the word2vec centroid of each emotional class and the word2vec numeric vector associated with the sentence to be classified.

Learning Phase - The learning phase consists in computing the word2vec centroid of each emotional class. The six lists of words generated by the approach described in Sect. 3.2 are the sources used as input lexicon. Given a class (e.g. *happiness*), each word is this list is associated with a word2vec vector in the distributional space of word created (Sect. 3.3). The lexicon is subdivided in six meta-documents, one for each emotion considered, which contains all the words in the lexicon annotated with the considered emotion. Each meta-document is transformed in one word2vec centroid by averaging the vectors associated with each word belonging to the meta-document. Moreover, for removing the dependency of each word from the centroid of the whole distributional space, we subtract it from each word vector. The average is weighed with the relative frequency associated with each word (computed as in Sect. 3.2).

The centroid of word2vec vector for each emotional class C_j is computed as follows:

$$AVG\{(\vec{vec}(word2vec_i) - \vec{vec}(centr\_distr\_space)) * f_i\} \tag{1}$$

with $i \in C_j$, the specific word in the list associated with the emotional class C_j.

Classification Phase - The part of the dataset which has not been used for the learning and lexicon generation process is used as test set. The lexicon-based approach performs the Tanimoto Similarity [15] between the numerical vector of the considered text and the numerical vectors of each class. The label of the corresponding highest score will be provided as output.

4   Experimental Evaluation

The proposed approach for emotional labeling of text documents is evaluated from different perspectives. We focused on three research questions:

- **RQ1:** Is it possible to improve the classification accuracy of the algorithm used by adopting a lexicon generated from a dataset automatically annotated using emoticons?
- **RQ2:** Does the proposed classification approach outperform classical approaches of text classification for emotions?
- **RQ3:** Is the proposed classification approach able to detect negative sentences with a good accuracy?

Measures. We used the classical measures of performances adopted for classifiers: *Precision* (*P*, Eq. 2), *Recall* (*R*, Eq. 3) and *F1 measure* (*F1*, Eq. 4).

$$Precision = \frac{tp}{tp + fp} \tag{2}$$

$$Recall = \frac{tp}{tp + fn} \tag{3}$$

$$F1\ Measure = \frac{2PR}{P + R} \tag{4}$$

where tp is the number of true positive, fp is the number of false positive, fn is the number of false negative. *F1* measures the overall performance of the systems.

Statistical significance is reported using a paired one-tailed t-test with 95% confidence (i.e. with p-value $\leq$ 0.05) over the distribution of F1 values. The results highlighted in bold show the best performance obtained on that particular data set.

Datasets. The datasets used for the experiments are *Semeval-2007* dataset[4] [24] and *myPersonality*[5] [14]. The *Semeval-2007* dataset was used for the task "Affective Text" of the 4th International Workshop on Semantic Evaluations, the evaluation campaign for computational semantic analysis systems. The dataset is annotated with the Six Ekman emotions [6] and contains 1000 journal titles as training set and other 250 titles as test set, all manually annotated by six annotators. Each annotation is a value ranging from 0 to 100 for each one of the six emotions. We consider a phrase annotated with a specific emotion only if the corresponding value falls in the interval [50,100].

The *myPersonality* dataset contains information about 4 millions Facebook users and 22 millions posts over their timeline. Data have been collected through

---

[4] http://web.archive.org/web/20080820044702/http://www.cs.unt.edu/~rada/affectivetext.

[5] http://mypersonality.org/.

a Facebook application that infers personality traits of users by means of a Big Five questionnaire [8]. During the interaction, the application collects also other information such as activities on Facebook, demographic data and status updates[6]. In our experiment, we considered only data related to status update messages. Each message has the *'id'* of the user, the timestamp and the published text. We annotated it by using the "emoticon" strategy described in Sect. 3.1. Details of datasets are given in Table 1.

Table 1. Datasets

Emotion	MyPersonality	SemEval2007 test-set	SemEval2007 training-set
Joy	1, 717, 832	75	358
Sadness	396, 268	61	201
Fear	53, 934	33	155
Anger	21, 187	23	67
Disgust	162, 987	20	35
Surprise	69, 672	38	184

Lexicons. In the experimental session we used two lexicons:

- *NRC Word-Emotion Association Lexicon*, a large English lexicon in which each word is linked to one or more emotions among the eight available (anger, fear, anticipation, trust, surprise, sadness, joy, and disgust). It contains 14,182 unigrams and 25,000 n-grams manually annotated by crowd-sourcing;
- *WordNet-Affect*, a well-known extension of English Wordnet which links each synset with many affective information, including emotions. The emotional information is organized hierarchically among four main categories: positive, negative, ambiguous, and neutral. Among them, we can find the six Ekman's Emotions plus others, such as love, anxiety, apathy, etc.

4.1   Experimental Session

Experiment 1. The aim of this experiment is to provide an answer for **RQ1**. The evaluation compares different configurations of the method for building the distributional space for words, described in Sect. 3.3. We keep the strategy for building the space and change only the lexicons used to calculate the centroid which represents the specific class. In particular, we tested NRC Word-Emotion Association Lexicon (NRC) and WordNet-Affect (WN-A) as baseline lexicons against our dynamic lexicon (DYN-TH) generated as described in Sect. 3.1 from 15,000 sentences randomly chosen, for each emotional class, from the *myPersonality* dataset (90.000 sentences in total). The test sets used are SemEval2007

---

[6] http://mypersonality.org/wiki/doku.php?id=list_of_variables_available.

test set plus 1,000 sentences, randomly chosen, for each emotional class, from myPersonality (6,000 sentences in total). Obviously sentences previously used for generating the lexicon are withdrawn. The results for SemEval-2007 are available in Table 2, while those for *myPersonality* are reported in Table 3.

Table 2. Results obtained on SemEval-2007 dataset by varying the lexicon used. The Overall F1-Score is obtained by averaging the scores for each class

	F1-Score on SemEval-2007						
	Anger	*Disgust*	*Fear*	*Joy*	*Sadness*	*Surprise*	*Overall*
NRC	**41.6**	30.0	30.0	**49.2**	16.9	16.8	30.8
WN-A	40.0	17.6	27.8	37.5	17.6	27.6	9.51
DYN-TH	28.6	**31.1**	**35.8**	44.3	**39.1**	**26.1**	**34.1**

Table 3. Results obtained on 6,000 sentences from *myPersonality* by varying the lexicon. The Overall F1-Score is obtained by averaging the scores of each class

	myPersonality F1-Score						
	Anger	*Disgust*	*Fear*	*Joy*	*Sadness*	*Surprise*	*Overall*
NRC	5.45	17.13	20.96	26.74	20.41	26.62	19.55
WN-A	9.35	25.32	25.04	11.67	2.46	28.38	17.04
DYN-TH	**36.06**	**34.11**	**31.60**	**36.08**	**38.22**	**36.24**	**35.49**

Experiment 2. The second experiment aims to compare our text categorization approach with state of the art machine learning algorithms. In particular, we used the Naive Bayes classification algorithm and Neural Networks Multilayer Perceptron (MLP) trained on 15,000 sentences, randomly chosen, for each emotional class, from *myPersonality*. The test sets are the same as Experiment 1 (SemEval-2007 test set; 6000 sentences from *myPersonality*). The Neural Networks Multi-layer Perceptron classifier is configured with a stochastic gradient descendant optimization algorithm and 100 epochs of learning.

4.2   Discussion of Results

The results in Tables 2 and 4 report the results of both experiments on *SemEval-2007*. Highest values are reported in bold. Our DYN-TH strategy overcome the others in almost all the runs. Results reported in Table 3 show that the use of standard lexicons produces lower results compared to DYN-TH, as a consequence of the limited the number of words that they can manage. Real-world sentences contain a wide lexicon which strongly depends on the writing style of the user. It is common to find slang words, acronyms, symbols, tags and words that cannot be included in a static manually annotated lexicon. On the contrary, the use of a lexicon built by exploiting a dataset of dynamically annotated

Table 4. Results obtained on SemEval-2007 dataset by varying the classification algorithms. The overall F1-Score is obtained by averaging the scores of each class

SemEval-2007 F1-Score							
	Anger	Disgust	Fear	Joy	Sadness	Surprise	Overall
SemEval-07 systems							
SWAT [24]	7.06	0.0	18.27	14.91	17.44	11.78	11.57
UA [24]	16.03	0.0	20.06	4.21	1.76	15.00	9.51
UPAR7 [24]	3.02	0.0	4.72	11.87	17.44	15.00	8.67
Baseline							
NaiveBayes	10.9	2.1	3.4	42.8	18.9	22.7	30.9
MLP	14.5	3.7	19.3	20.2	17.1	24.7	20.0
Dynamic lexicon							
DYN-TH	**28.6**	**31.1**	**35.8**	**44.3**	**39.1**	**26.1**	**34.1**

Table 5. Results obtained on 6,000 sentences from *myPersonality* dataset by varying the classification algorithms. The overall F1-Score is obtained by averaging the scores of each class

myPersonality F1-Score							
	Anger	Disgust	Fear	Joy	Sadness	Surprise	Overall
Baseline							
MLP	20.0	12.7	24.5	28.4	26.7	34.1	24.4
NaiveBayes	28.7	17.9	24.8	30.6	35.2	34.3	28.6
Dynamic lexicon							
DYN-TH	**36.06**	**34.11**	**31.60**	**36.08**	**38.22**	**36.24**	**35.49**

sentences allows to manage a larger set of specific tokens, even if they are not correctly written. In particular, as shown in Table 2, DYN-TH outperformed all the other approaches. There is a statistically significance difference with other approaches for $p < 0.02$. These results allow us to provide a positive answer to **RQ1**. The comparison among the proposed DYN-TH classification strategy and other learning approaches (Neural Networks Multi-layer Perceptron and a Naive Bayes classifier) is in favour DYN-TH, as shown by values reported in Table 4 and Table 5.

In particular, the results in Table 5 confirm that there is statistically difference for $p < 0.05$. As consequence of this analysis, we confirm the hypothesis of **RQ2**. In order to quantify the performance of DYN-TH for the detection of negative sentences, the results of F1-measure obtained for the classes sadness, fear, anger, and disgust have been averaged. The values obtained for DYN-TH is **35.00** against **26.65** for MLP and **20.98** for Naive Bayes. The differences among the results are statistically significant for $p < 0.05$ and demonstrate the effectiveness of our approach for detecting negative sentences. This allow us to answer positively to **RQ3**. In general, the observed results show the validity of the approach, but at the same time they reveal also the difficulty of performing a clear classification in spontaneous contexts. When the user is left free to write without any strict syntactical rules, approaches based on strict lexicons are easy to fail. Also strategies based on machine learning are not able to create effective classification rules. For this reason, we suggest that the approach proposed can provide effective results in the specific application domain investigated.

5 Conclusions and Future Work

The proposed work introduced a framework for detecting psychological diseases and blue feeling, by computing a continuous monitoring of the user from heterogeneous sources. The proposed model is based on Diagnostic and Statistical Manual Volume IV (DSM-IV) whose thresholds are taken from the standard literature about the problem. One of the most important modules designed is the text emotional annotator. It takes as input a textual sentence and provides the most probable emotional label for it. The module uses a word2vec representation of textual content and uses the Tanimoto similarity score to select the appropriate emotional class to be assigned to the text. It uses a lexicon generated from a dataset automatically annotated using emoticons. The proposed approach overcomes both Naive Bayes and Neural Networks Multi-layer Perceptron algorithms for the classification task.

Furthermore, the effectiveness of the generated lexicon is shown by the results obtained from the comparison with other lexicons such as WordNet-Affect and NRC Word-Emotion Association Lexicon. Finally, we demonstrated the effectiveness of the approach for detecting negative emotions in a real world context. In order to improve the classification performance of the proposed approach, in the future work we will focus on strategies of hybrid classifiers that use both lexicon-based and machine learning approaches.

Acknowledgment. This research has been supported by "Microsoft Azure for Research program 2016–2017", which provides the access to all the Azure technologies for computing the data described in this work.

References

1. Alm, C.O., Roth, D., Sproat, R.: Emotions from text: machine learning for text-based emotion prediction. In: Proceedings of Conference on Human Language Technology and Empirical Methods in Natural Language Processing, pp. 579–586. Association for Computational Linguistics (2005)
2. Binali, H., Wu, C., Potdar, V.: Computational approaches for emotion detection in text. In: 2010 4th IEEE International Conference on Digital Ecosystems and Technologies (DEST), pp. 172–177. IEEE (2010)
3. Carney, R.M., Freedland, K.E.: Depression and heart rate variability in patients with coronary heart disease. Clevel. Clin. J. Med. **76**(Suppl 2), S13 (2009)

4. Danisman, T., Alpkocak, A.: Feeler: Emotion classification of text using vector space model. In: AISB 2008 Convention Communication, Interaction and Social Intelligence, vol. 1, p. 53 (2008)
5. Dresner, E., Herring, S.C.: Functions of the nonverbal in CMC: emoticons and illocutionary force. Commun. theory **20**(3), 249–268 (2010)
6. Ekman, P., Oster, H.: Facial expressions of emotion. Annu. Rev. Psychol. **30**(1), 527–554 (1979)
7. Franzen, P.L., Buysse, D.J.: Sleep disturbances and depression: risk relationships for subsequent depression and therapeutic implications. Dialogues Clin. Neurosci. **10**(4), 473 (2008)
8. Goldberg, L.R., Johnson, J.A., Eber, H.W., Hogan, R., Ashton, M.C., Cloninger, C.R., Gough, H.G.: The international personality item pool and the future of public-domain personality measures. J. Res. Pers. **40**(1), 84–96 (2006)
9. Goldberg, Y.: A primer on neural network models for natural language processing. CoRR abs/1510.00726 (2015). http://arxiv.org/abs/1510.00726
10. Haley, W.E., Turner, J.A., Romano, J.M.: Depression in chronic pain patients: relation to pain, activity, and sex differences. Pain **23**(4), 337–343 (1985)
11. Hancock, J.T., Landrigan, C., Silver, C.: Expressing emotion in text-based communication. In: Proceedings of SIGCHI Conference on Human Factors in Computing Systems, pp. 929–932. ACM (2007)
12. Harris, Z.: Distributional structure. Word **10**(23), 146–162 (1954)
13. Kalman, Y.M., Gergle, D.: Letter repetitions in computer-mediated communication: a unique link between spoken and online language. Comput. Hum. Behav. **34**, 187–193 (2014)
14. Kosinski, M., Matz, S.C., Gosling, S.D., Popov, V., Stillwell, D.: Facebook as a research tool for the social sciences: opportunities, challenges, ethical considerations, and practical guidelines. Am. Psychol. **70**(6), 543 (2015)
15. Lipkus, A.H.: A proof of the triangle inequality for the tanimoto distance. J. Math. Chem. **26**(1), 263–265 (1999)
16. Ma, C., Prendinger, H., Ishizuka, M.: Emotion estimation and reasoning based on affective textual interaction. Affect. Comput. Intell. Interact. 622–628 (2005)
17. Mikolov, T., Chen, K., Corrado, G., Dean, J.: Efficient estimation of word representations in vector space. arXiv preprint arXiv:1301.3781 (2013)
18. Millon, T., Davis, R.O.: Disorders of Personality: DSM-IV and Beyond. Wiley, New York (1996)
19. Mohammad, S.M., Turney, P.D.: Emotions evoked by common words and phrases: using mechanical turk to create an emotion lexicon. In: Proceedings of NAACL HLT 2010 Workshop on Computational Approaches to Analysis and Generation of Emotion in Text, pp. 26–34. Association for Computational Linguistics (2010)
20. Moreno, M.A., Jelenchick, L.A., Egan, K.G., Cox, E., Young, H., Gannon, K.E., Becker, T.: Feeling bad on facebook: depression disclosures by college students on a social networking site. Depress. Anxiety **28**(6), 447–455 (2011)
21. Polignano, M., Basile, P., Rossiello, G., de Gemmis, M., Semeraro, G.: Learning inclination to empathy from social media footprints. In: Proceedings of 25th Conference on User Modeling, Adaptation and Personalization, pp. 383–384. ACM (2017)
22. Rude, S., Gortner, E.M., Pennebaker, J.: Language use of depressed and depression-vulnerable college students. Cogn. Emot. **18**(8), 1121–1133 (2004)
23. Sheps, D.S., Rozanski, A.: From feeling blue to clinical depression: exploring the pathogenicity of depressive symptoms and their management in cardiac practice (2005)

24. Strapparava, C., Mihalcea, R.: Semeval-2007 task 14: affective text. In: Proceedings of 4th International Workshop on Semantic Evaluations, pp. 70–74. Association for Computational Linguistics (2007)

25. Strapparava, C., Valitutti, A., et al.: Wordnet affect: an affective extension of WordNet. LREC. **4**, 1083–1086 (2004)

26. Suttles, J., Ide, N.: Distant supervision for emotion classification with discrete binary values. In: Gelbukh, A. (ed.) CICLing 2013. LNCS, vol. 7817, pp. 121–136. Springer, Heidelberg (2013). doi:10.1007/978-3-642-37256-8_11

27. Thase, M.E.: Depression, sleep, and antidepressants. J. Clin. Psychiatr. **59**, 55–65 (1997)

Alternative Variable Splitting Methods to Learn Sum-Product Networks

Nicola Di Mauro, Floriana Esposito, Fabrizio G. Ventola[✉],
and Antonio Vergari

Department of Computer Science, University of Bari "Aldo Moro", Bari, Italy
{nicola.dimauro,floriana.esposito,fabrizio.ventola,
antonio.vergari}@uniba.it

Abstract. Sum-Product Networks (SPNs) are recent deep probabilistic models providing exact and tractable inference. SPNs have been successfully employed as density estimators in several application domains. However, learning an SPN from high dimensional data still poses a challenge in terms of time complexity. This is due to the high cost of determining independencies among random variables (RVs) and sub-populations among samples, two operations that are repeated several times. Even one of the simplest greedy structure learner, LearnSPN, scales quadratically in the number of the variables to determine RVs independencies. In this work we investigate approximate but fast procedures to determine independencies among RVs whose complexity scales in sub-quadratic time. We propose two procedures: a random subspace approach and one that adopts entropy as a criterion to split RVs in linear time. Experimental results prove that LearnSPN equipped by our splitting procedures is able to reduce learning and/or inference times while preserving comparable inference accuracy.

Keywords: Machine learning · Deep learning · Structure learning · Probabilistic models · Density estimation · Sum-Product Networks

1 Introduction

Density estimation is the unsupervised task of learning an estimator of a joint probability distribution over a set of random variables (RVs) that are assumed to have generated some observed data. If such a model provides a good estimate of the real distribution, it can be effectively used to perform *inference*, i.e., computing the probability of the queries about some RVs. Density estimation represents one of the central and most general task in machine learning, indeed, many machine learning tasks, e.g. classification and regression can be reframed as performing inference on a probability distribution. While on the one hand one wants to build a highly *expressive and accurate* estimator, on the other hand one may want to be able to *efficiently learn* it from data and to perform *tractable and exact* inference on it as well. Trading off these three performances is one of the current challenges in density estimation, and in practice it is rare to be able to optimize

© Springer International Publishing AG 2017
F. Esposito et al. (Eds.): AI*IA 2017, LNAI 10640, pp. 334–346, 2017.
https://doi.org/10.1007/978-3-319-70169-1_25

all of them. Probabilistic graphical models (PGMs), like Bayesian networks or Markov networks, are able to accurately model highly complex probability distributions, but performing inference and learning on them requires routines that, even if approximate, may scale exponentially in the worst case [22]. Recently introduced tractable probabilistic models (TPMs), allow tractable inference at the expense of a stricter representation bias. TPMs like Arithmetic Circuits [4], Sum-Product Networks (SPNs) [18], and Cutset Networks [7,20] provide a good compromise between expressiveness and tractability by compiling complex distributions in compact data structures. Nevertheless, the cost of learning them to model high dimensional probability distribution is still an issue.

In this paper, we focus on SPNs, and we investigate approximate learning routines to improve both learning and inference complexity, trying to preserve the model expressiveness. SPNs represent a probability distribution as a series of sum and product nodes, arranged in a deep architecture. Under certain structural conditions, SPNs guarantee several kinds of probabilistic queries to be computed exactly and in time linear to the network size. Their success in several application domains like computer vision [18,25], speech recognition [17], natural language processing [3] and for representation learning [23] increased the interest around algorithms able to learn both their structure and parameters [5,9,15,24]. One of the first principled top-down learning schemes, and yet still a state-of-the-art structure learner, is LearnSPN [9]. One of the factors behind its popularity is its simplicity. LearnSPN greedily and recursively decomposes the observed data by either splitting RVs after they have been found independent, or by clustering samples together according to some metric. While several variations of LearnSPN have been proposed in the literature by adapting the splitting RVs and clustering routines, their high complexity constitutes the main bottleneck. Our attention is on the first procedure, splitting RVs into independent groups, whose general complexity, in the worst case, is quadratic in the number of the RVs.

In this paper, we make the following contributions: (i) we advance two alternative procedures to approximate the variable splitting method in LearnSPN while performing it in sub-quadratic time, and (ii) we empirically evaluate their effectiveness in trading-off inference accuracy in favour of inference or learning times. We propose a random subspace approach in which we reduce the number of independence tests to be computed. Additionally, we investigate an even more approximated entropy-based criterion that scales linearly in the number of RVs. A comparison to the original version of LearnSPN on several standard benchmark datasets reveals that the former approach effectively trades off the model likelihood in favour of faster learning times and smaller networks, hence faster inference. On the other hand, the latter approach, surprisingly, leads the construction of more complex networks, hence favouring the model expressiveness.

2   Sum-Product Networks

An SPN S is a rooted DAG, encoding an unnormalized probability distribution over a set of RVs $\boldsymbol{X} = \{X_1, \ldots, X_n\}$, where internal nodes can be either *weighted* sum or product nodes (graphically denoted resp. as $\bigoplus$ and $\bigotimes$), and leaves are univariate distributions defined on a RV $X_i \in \boldsymbol{X}$. Each node $i \in S$ has a *scope* $\boldsymbol{X}_{\psi_i}$ defined as the set of RVs appearing as its descendant leaves. The sub-network S_i, rooted at node i, encodes the unnormalized distribution over its scope. Each edge (i, j) emanating from a sum node i to one of its children j has a non-negative *weight* w_{ij}. The set of all sum node weights corresponds to the *network parameters*. Sum nodes can be viewed as mixtures over probability distributions whose coefficients are the children weights, while product nodes identify factorizations over independent distributions. Examples of SPNs are depicted in Fig. 1. In the following we consider $\boldsymbol{X}$ to be discrete valued RVs.

For a given state $\boldsymbol{x}$ of the RVs $\boldsymbol{X}$, we will indicate $S(\boldsymbol{x})$ the unnormalized probability of $\boldsymbol{x}$ according to the SPN S, that is the root node value when the network is evaluated after $\boldsymbol{X} = \boldsymbol{x}$ is observed. An SPN is defined *decomposable* if the scopes of the children of each product node are disjoint. It is defined *complete* when the scopes of the children of each sum node are the same. These properties together imply *validity* [18], i.e., the ability of exactly computing the probability of each possible complete or partial evidence configuration. When the weights of each sum node i in a valid network S sum to one, i.e., $\sum_j w_{ij} = 1$, and distribution at leaves are normalized, then S computes an exact normalized probability for each possible state [16,18]. W.l.o.g., we assume the SPNs we are considering to be valid and normalized.

In order to compute $S(\boldsymbol{x})$ it is necessary to evaluate the network through a *bottom-up* step. When evaluating a leaf node i, whose scope $\boldsymbol{X}_{\psi_i}$ is $\{X_k\}_{k=1}^{|\boldsymbol{X}_{\psi_i}|}$, $S_i(x)$ corresponds to the probability of the state x for X_k: $S_i(x) = P(X_k = x)$. The value of a product node corresponds to the product of its children values: $S_i(\boldsymbol{x}_{\psi_i}) = \prod_{i \to j \in S} S_j(\boldsymbol{x}_{\psi_j})$; while, for a sum node its value corresponds to the weighted sum of its children values: $S_i(\boldsymbol{x}_{\psi_i}) = \sum_{i \to j \in S} w_{ij} S_j(\boldsymbol{x}_{\psi_j})$.

It is possible to demonstrate that all the marginal probabilities, the partition function and even approximate MPE queries and states can be computed in time linear in the *size* of the network, i.e., its number of edges [9,16]. Hence, tractable inference is achieved when the number of edges is at most polynomial in the number of RVs. Moreover, *the less the number of edges in a network, the faster the inference*. While the size of the network implies its inference efficiency, its *depth*, defined as the longest path from the root to a leaf node in networks with strictly interleaving layers of nodes of the same kind[1], determines its *expressiveness efficiency* [14]. This kind of efficiency relates to the ability of a network to capture more complex distributions than other networks having the same or larger size [24]. Lastly, also the number of parameters of a network, i.e., the number of sum node weights, also called *model capacity*, influences its expressiveness with respect to a weight learning algorithm. While we are not looking at weight learning per se in this work, it is worth noting that the larger a model capacity, the higher the representation space searchable by optimizing the network weights.

---

[1] Note that it is always possible to transform an SPN with adjacent nodes of the same type into an equivalent one with alternating types [24].

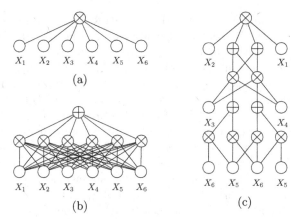

Fig. 1. Examples of SPNs: a naive factorization over 6 random variables (a), a shallow mixture standing for a point-wise kernel density estimation (b) and a deeper architecture (c) over the same scope (weights are omitted for simplicity).

Up to now, however, the research community has put more effort in designing structure learning algorithms and comparing learned SPNs w.r.t. their *inference accuracy*, i.e., the closeness of the probability distribution estimated by the network to the one that generated the data. For density estimators in general, this is usually done in the terms of the average test set log-likelihood [11]. In this work, following [24], we argue that both the network structure quality metrics and its log-likelihood shall be taken into account to better evaluate the inherent trade-off of density estimators between learning and inference tractability and their expressiveness and accuracy.

2.1 Structure Learning

As already stated, we focus our attention to a particular structure learning algorithm for SPNs, LearnSPN [9]. LearnSPN provides a simple, greedy and yet surprisingly effective learning schema that is able to infer both the structure and the parameters of an SPN from the data. Note that, while our approximate approaches are inspired directly by LearnSPN, they can be effectively adapted to other algorithmic variations aiming to learn SPNs, e.g., the ones proposed in [1,21,24]. Furthermore, they can also be adapted to other learning scenarios, in which one has to split RVs into sets of (approximately) independent RVs [8], e.g., eliciting the independencies among RVs for classical PGMs.

LearnSPN performs a greedy top-down structure search in the space of *tree-shaped* SPNs, i.e., networks in which each node has at most one parent. The network structure is built one node at a time by leveraging the probabilistic semantics of an SPN: sum nodes stand for mixtures over sub-populations in the data, while products represent factorizations over independent components. A high level outline is sketched in Algorithm 1. LearnSPN proceeds by recursively partitioning the training data provided as a matrix consisting of a set $\mathcal{D}$ of rows as i.i.d instances, over $\boldsymbol{X}$, the set of columns, i.e., the RVs. For each call on a submatrix, the algorithm first tries to split the submatrix by columns. This is done by splitting the current set of RVs into different groups such that the RVs in a group are statistically dependent while the groups are independent, i.e., the joint distribution factorizes over the groups. We denote this procedure as *Greedy Variable Splitting* (GVS). If the GVS procedure fails, that is all RVs are somewhat dependent and it is not meaningful to split them, then LearnSPN switches to split rows. If this is the case, when GVS is designed to find two split components, we assume the second one to be empty. LearnSPN then tries to aggregate similar submatrix rows (procedure clusterInstances) into a number of clusters. In the original work of [9], the hard online EM algorithm is employed to determine an adaptive number of clusters, l, assuming RVs X_j independent given the row clusters C_i, formally: $P(\boldsymbol{X}) = \sum_i P(C_i) \prod_j P(X_j|C_i)$. To control the cluster number, an exponential prior on clusterings in the form of $e^{-\lambda l|\boldsymbol{X}|}$ is used, with λ as a tuning parameter.

Every time a column split succeeds the algorithm adds a product node to the network whose children correspond to partitioned submatrixes. Analogously, after a row clustering step it adds a sum node where children weights represent the proportions of instances falling into the computed clusters (line 13). To avoid a naive factorization of the whole data matrix the algorithm heuristically forces a row clustering at the first step.

Termination happens in two cases: when the current submatrix contains only one column (line 3) or when the number of its rows falls under a certain threshold μ (line 5). In the former, a leaf node, standing for a univariate distribution, is introduced by a maximum likelihood estimation from the submatrix applying a Laplace smoothing parameter α. In the latter, the submatrix RVs are modeled with a naive factorization, i.e., they are considered to be independent and a product node is put over a set of univariate leaf nodes. As noted in [24], the two splitting procedures depend on each other: the quality of row clusterings is likely to be enhanced by column splits correctly identifying dependent variables and vice versa. As a consequence, while we are proposing to substitute only the GVS procedure, the effects of the introduced approximation will affect also the row clustering step. We will evaluate this effect globally by measuring both the structure quality of the networks learned with our proposed approaches and their likelihood accuracy, in a series of empirical experiments in Sect. 4.

3   Variable Splitting

We now describe in detail the *Greedy Variable Splitting* (GVS) procedure applied by LearnSPN to discover groups of dependent RVs, in order to introduce later our variants. To exactly determine a partitioning of independent RVs, one could recur to Queyranne's algorithm to retrieve two subsets with minimum empirical mutual information (MI), but this will scale in a cubic time w.r.t. the number of RVs considered [19]. Instead, as the name suggests, GVS proceeds in a greedy

---

Algorithm 1. LearnSPN($\mathcal{D}$, $\boldsymbol{X}$, α, μ, ρ)

1: **Input:** a set of row instances $\mathcal{D}$ over a set of RVs $\boldsymbol{X}$; α: Laplace smoothing parameter; μ: minimum number of instances to split; ρ: statistical independence threshold
2: **Output:** an SPN S encoding a pdf over $\boldsymbol{X}$ learned from $\mathcal{D}$
3: **if** $|\boldsymbol{X}| = 1$ **then**
4:     $S \leftarrow$ univariateDistribution($\mathcal{D}, \boldsymbol{X}, \alpha$)
5: **else if** $|\mathcal{D}| < \mu$ **then**
6:     $S \leftarrow$ naiveFactorization($\mathcal{D}, \boldsymbol{X}, \alpha$)
7: **else**
8:     $\{\boldsymbol{X}_{d_1}, \boldsymbol{X}_{d_2}\} \leftarrow$ GVS($\mathcal{D}, \boldsymbol{X}, \rho$)
9:     **if** $|\boldsymbol{X}_{d_2}| > 0$ **then**
10:         $S \leftarrow \prod_{j=1}^{2}$ LearnSPN($\mathcal{D}, \boldsymbol{X}_{d_j}, \alpha, \mu, \rho$)
11:     **else**
12:         $\{\mathcal{D}_i\}_{i=1}^{R} \leftarrow$ clusterInstances($\mathcal{D}, \boldsymbol{X}$)
13:         $S \leftarrow \sum_{i=1}^{R} \frac{|\mathcal{D}_i|}{|\mathcal{D}|}$ LearnSPN($\mathcal{D}_i, \boldsymbol{X}, \alpha, \mu, \rho$)
14: **return** S

---

way, lowering the time complexity to be quadratic (see Algorithm 2). By picking a RV at random (line 3), GVS tries to discover connected components in a graph of dependencies by introducing one edge among two RVs if they are dependent. While pairwise MI could be used to test the independence among the two considered RVs, a more sophisticated statistical test, a G-Test, is applied in the original formulation of GVS. In both cases, two RVs are assumed to be dependent if the statistical test result falls under a used defined threshold ρ. At the first iteration if the algorithm does not find any dependency it returns the first considered node as assuming that it is independent from all the other RVs. The opposite case is when the algorithm finds a connected component comprising all the RVs currently considered by LearnSPN. To understand the worst case time complexity of GVS consider the following case. At most, the algorithm needs to perform $(n^2 + n)/2$ G-tests with $n = |\boldsymbol{X}|$ by looking at all possible pairwise cases (lines 5–12). If we assume the complexity of performing a G-Test to be linear in the number of samples ($m = |\mathcal{D}|$), then the worst case complexity of GVS is $O(n^2 m)$. As a last remark, consider that the alternative splitting procedures presented in other SPN learning algorithms, e.g. [15,21], even if employing different pairwise statistical independence tests, still require a quadratic number of comparisons, in the worst case.

3.1 Stochastic Variable Splitting

The intuition behind our first proposed alternative method for splitting variables is the same behind random *subspace techniques* that have been successfully employed for building ensembles for predictive tasks [2] but also for density estimation [6]. We name this method *Random Greedy Variable Splitting* (RGVS) and we sketch it in Algorithm 3. RGVS randomly selects a subset of $\boldsymbol{X}$ of length k and then applies GVS only on this subset. Since we are not applying it in an

---

Algorithm 2. GVS($\mathcal{D}$, $\boldsymbol{X}$, ρ)

1: **Input:** set of samples $\mathcal{D}$ over RVs $\boldsymbol{X}$; ρ: a statistical independence threshold
2: **Output:** a split of two groups of dependent variables $\{\boldsymbol{X}_{d_1}, \boldsymbol{X}_{d_2}\}$,
3: $\boldsymbol{X}_{d_2} \leftarrow \boldsymbol{X}$, $X_0 \leftarrow$ drawVariableAtRandom($\boldsymbol{X}$)
4: $\boldsymbol{X} \leftarrow \boldsymbol{X} \setminus \{X_0\}$, $\boldsymbol{P} \leftarrow \{X_0\}$, $\boldsymbol{X}_{d_1} \leftarrow \{X_0\}$, $\boldsymbol{R} \leftarrow \emptyset$
5: **repeat**
6:     $X_p \leftarrow$ pop($\boldsymbol{P}$) $\triangleright$ $\boldsymbol{P} \leftarrow \boldsymbol{P} \setminus \{X_p\}$
7:     **for each** $X_k \in \boldsymbol{X}$ **do**
8:         **if** GTest($\mathcal{D}, X_p, X_k$) $< \rho$ **then**
9:             $\boldsymbol{R} \leftarrow \boldsymbol{R} \cup \{X_k\}$, $\boldsymbol{X}_{d_1} \leftarrow \boldsymbol{X}_{d_1} \cup \{X_k\}$, $\boldsymbol{P} \leftarrow \boldsymbol{P} \cup \{X_k\}$
10:     **for each** $X_j \in \boldsymbol{R}$ **do**
11:         $\boldsymbol{X} \leftarrow \boldsymbol{X} \setminus \{X_j\}$
12: **until** $|\boldsymbol{P}| > 0 \wedge |\boldsymbol{X}| > 0$
13: **return** $\{\boldsymbol{X}_{d_1}, \boldsymbol{X}_{d_2} \setminus \boldsymbol{X}_{d_1}\}$

---

ensemble scenario, but to learn a single model, we do expect this model inference accuracy to drop since the independencies discovered by RGVS can only be a subset of those discovered by GVS in a single call. Nevertheless, how much the accuracy degrades depends to the ability of RGVS to recover the missed dependencies in one call in the following calls that LearnSPN performs on the same RVs. At the same time, we aim to reduce the learning times as well as the inference times, by obtaining smaller networks.

If GVS fails on the set of k RVs $\boldsymbol{R}$, then even RGVS will fail assuming dependent the remaining variables in $\boldsymbol{S} = \boldsymbol{X} \setminus \boldsymbol{R}$ (lines 9–10). Otherwise, if the second component returned from GVS is not empty then RGVS will make another stochastic decision about where to put the remaining variables in $\boldsymbol{S}$ (lines 12–15). Consequently, the worst case complexity of RGVS depends on the choice of the parameter k. If k is chosen to be $\sqrt{n}$, then[2] we end up scaling GVS as if it was linear, since $O((\sqrt{n})^2 m) = O(nm)$. Otherwise, depending on a choice of $k < n$ the complexity of a single call varies but remains sub-quadratic. However, note that determining the resulting complexity of a whole run of LearnSPN equipped with RGVS instead of GVS is not immediate. Consider, for example the case in which k is chosen as a small fraction of the RVs in $\boldsymbol{X}$, then, it might happen that LearnSPN calls the splitting routines a larger number of times since in each call the only a few or no RVs are considered independent from the rest. The result is that the network built may be larger, hence the learning time increased, w.r.t. a network learned with a larger k. In Sect. 5 we empirically evaluate the sensitivity of RGVS to the choice of k w.r.t. the model inference accuracy and its learning time.

---

[2] We set k to be at least 2 when $n = |\boldsymbol{X}| < 4$.

Algorithm 3. RGVS($\mathcal{D}, \boldsymbol{X}, \rho$)

1: **Input:** set of samples $\mathcal{D}$ over RVs $\boldsymbol{X}$; ρ: a statistical independence threshold
2: **Output:** a split of two groups of dependent variables $\{\boldsymbol{X}_{d_1}, \boldsymbol{X}_{d_2}\}$
3: $\boldsymbol{X}_{d_1} \leftarrow \emptyset, \boldsymbol{X}_{d_2} \leftarrow \emptyset, n \leftarrow |\boldsymbol{X}|, k \leftarrow max(\lfloor \sqrt{n} \rfloor, 2)$
4: **if** $k = n$ **then**
5:     **return** GVS($\mathcal{D}, \boldsymbol{X}, \rho$)
6: $\boldsymbol{R} \leftarrow$ randomSubspace($\boldsymbol{X}, k$)
7: $\boldsymbol{S} \leftarrow \boldsymbol{X} \setminus \boldsymbol{R}$
8: $\{\boldsymbol{X}_{d_1}, \boldsymbol{X}_{d_2}\} \leftarrow$ GVS($\mathcal{D}, \boldsymbol{R}, \rho$)
9: **if** $\boldsymbol{X}_{d_2} = \emptyset$ **then**
10:     **return** $\{\boldsymbol{X}_{d_1} \cup \boldsymbol{S}, \emptyset\}$
11: $r \leftarrow$ Bernoulli(0.5)
12: **if** $r = 0$ **then**
13:     **return** $\{\boldsymbol{X}_{d_1} \cup \boldsymbol{S}, \boldsymbol{X}_{d_2}\}$
14: **else**
15:     **return** $\{\boldsymbol{X}_{d_1}, \boldsymbol{X}_{d_2} \cup \boldsymbol{S}\}$

3.2 Entropy-Based Variable Splitting

The second proposed variable splitting method is based on the concept of entropy as taken in information theory[3] and it is called *Entropy-Based Variable Splitting* (EBVS). Its pseudocode is listed in Algorithm 4. EBVS performs a linear scan of the RVs in $\boldsymbol{X}$, grouping in one split those RVs whose entropy value falls under a user defined threshold η. The rationale behind this idea is that a RV with exactly zero entropy is independent from all other RVs in $\boldsymbol{X}$. To understand why this is true, consider computing MI between RV X and any RV $X_* \in \boldsymbol{X}$, denoted as $\mathsf{MI}(X; X_*)$ then we have that $\mathsf{MI}(X; X_*) = H(X) - H(X|X_*)$ where $H(\cdot)$ denotes marginal entropy and $H(X|X_*)$ conditional entropy respectively [13]. But since $H(X) = 0$ by hypothesis and it must hold that $H(X) \geq H(X|X_*)$, then it turns out that $\mathsf{MI}(X; X_*) = 0$, hence X must be independent to all other RVs in X. Since the empirical estimator for the entropy is rarely zero on real data, we apply thresholding to increase the method robustness and regularization. Moreover, we may apply Laplacian smoothing to compute the probabilities involved in the entropy computation[4].

While η can be heuristically determined by the user by performing cross-validation, having a global threshold can impose a too strict inductive bias. Therefore, we introduce another method variant, called EBVS-AE, where AE stands for "Adaptive Entropy", in which η is adaptively computed based on the size of the current submatrix processed by LearnSPN. EBVS-AE determines each

---

[3] For a discrete RV X, having values in $\mathcal{X}$, we consider its discrete entropy as $H(X) = -\sum_{x \in \mathcal{X}} p(x) \log(p(x))$.
[4] For convenience, and to avoid the addition of a new hyperparameter, the Laplacian smoothing parameter value will be the same of the hyperparameter α of LearnSPN, used to smooth the univariate distributions at leaves. Note that now η substitutes the hyperparameter ρ which is not needed anymore.

time the actual value of η proportionally to the number of samples $|\mathcal{D}|$ processed w.r.t. the number of samples in the whole dataset. Both EBVS and EBVS-AE involve the computation of the entropy for each RV in $\boldsymbol{X}$, hence their complexity is $O(nm)$. We empirically determine in the next Section whether both EBVS and EBVS-AE provide good approximations to the variable splitting method of LearnSPN. It is reasonable to expect the structures learned by these methods to be quite different from those learned by GVS and RGVS, since the procedure to test for statistical independence relies on a single RV metric for the former and for pairwise metrics for the latter.

Algorithm 4. EBVS($\mathcal{D}$, $\boldsymbol{X}$, η, α)

1: **Input:** set of samples $\mathcal{D}$ over RVs $\boldsymbol{X}$; η: a threshold for entropies, α: Laplacian smoothing parameter
2: **Output:** a split of two groups of dependent variables $\{\boldsymbol{X}_{d_1}, \boldsymbol{X}_{d_2}\}$
3: $\boldsymbol{X}_{d_1} \leftarrow \emptyset, \boldsymbol{X}_{d_2} \leftarrow \emptyset$
4: **for each** $X_i \in \boldsymbol{X}$ **do**
5:     **if** computeEntropy($\mathcal{D}, X_i, \alpha$) $< \eta$ **then**
6:         $\boldsymbol{X}_{d_1} \leftarrow \boldsymbol{X}_{d_1} \cup \{X_i\}$
7:     **else**
8:         $\boldsymbol{X}_{d_2} \leftarrow \boldsymbol{X}_{d_2} \cup \{X_i\}$
9: **if** $|\boldsymbol{X}_{d_1}| = 0$ **then**
10:     **return** $\{\boldsymbol{X}_{d_2}, \boldsymbol{X}_{d_1}\}$
11: **else**
12:     **return** $\{\boldsymbol{X}_{d_1}, \boldsymbol{X}_{d_2}\}$

---

4   Experiments

We empirically evaluate RGVS, EBVS and EBVS-AE as alternative methods for variable splitting by plugging them in LearnSPN-b [24], a simplified variant of LearnSPN. We implemented them in Python[5], in the freely available version of LearnSPN-b [24] and we refer to GVS in the following as the original version of LearnSPN-b employing Algorithm 2. LearnSPN-b only performs binary splits even for the row clustering step while learning an SPN. By doing this, it slows down the greedy search process avoiding too complex structural choices at early stages, therefore implementing a form of the "simplicity bias". With this experimentation we aim to answer the following research questions: **(Q1)** how does RGVS compare to GVS in terms of inference and learning time and model accuracy? **(Q2)** how does EBVS compare to GVS in terms of inference and learning time and model accuracy? **(Q3)** is EBVS-AE able to learn more accurate and compact networks in a faster way than EBVS?

To answer the aforementioned questions, we evaluated the proposed methods on 9 datasets that have been employed as standard benchmarks to compare

---

[5] Code is available at https://github.com/fabriziov/alt-vs-spyn.

Table 1. Times (in seconds) taken to learn the best models on each dataset and average test log-likelihoods for EBVS, EBVS-AE, RGVS and GVS.

	Learning time				Log-likelihood			
	EBVS	EBVS-AE	RGVS	GVS	EBVS	EBVS-AE	RGVS	GVS
NLTCS	98	31	4	8	-6.051	-6.046	-6.329	-6.040
Plants	255	179	24	70	-12.890	-12.853	-16.633	-12.880
Audio	130	108	25	59	-40.763	-40.632	-41.983	-40.697
Jester	73	67	16	41	-53.897	-53.528	-54.881	-53.919
Netflix	131	123	48	89	-58.234	-58.021	-59.752	-58.4360
Accidents	623	96	18	34	-35.336	-35.635	-39.370	-29.002
Retail	105	97	11	22	-11.245	-11.198	-11.290	-10.969
Pumsb-star	256	245	18	34	-29.235	-29.485	-41.969	-23.282
DNA	17	18	3	9	-97.876	-97.764	-99.123	-81.931

Table 2. Structural quality metrics (the number of edges, layers and network parameters) for the best validation models for EBVS, EBVS-AE, RGVS and GVS.

	# edges				# layers				# params			
	EBVS	EBVS-AE	RGVS	GVS	EBVS	EBVS-AE	RGVS	GVS	EBVS	EBVS-AE	RGVS	GVS
NLTCS	8185	3969	316	1129	23	9	9	17	1190	331	58	271
Plants	42318	67821	2770	15129	27	17	15	27	2304	1863	415	2635
Audio	36499	43243	2581	17811	21	11	11	25	550	477	308	2736
Jester	26263	27609	1862	12460	17	5	13	25	308	276	270	2071
Netflix	42033	44512	5097	30417	21	11	15	31	503	465	737	4351
Accidents	98218	33377	1529	11861	33	15	15	27	4315	436	240	2656
Retail	10096	6973	368	1010	41	37	7	19	446	258	31	175
Pumsb-star	32776	137092	1478	12821	29	19	13	27	1941	1885	216	2679
DNA	8694	8694	475	3384	7	7	9	13	52	52	38	938

TPMs, being introduced in [10,12]. They comprise binary data coming from tasks such as frequent item mining, recommendation and classification.

For each method, we select the best parameter configurations based on the average validation log-likelihood scores, then evaluate such models on the test sets. We performed an exhaustive grid search for $\rho \in \{5, 10, 15, 20\}$, $\mu \in \{10, 50, 100, 500\}$ and $\alpha \in \{0.1, 0.2, 1, 2\}$, leaving all other parameters to the default values.

Experiments have been run on an 8-core AMD Opteron 63XX @ 2.3 GHz with 16 GB of RAM and Ubuntu 14.04.4 LTS, kernel 3.13.0-45.

4.1 (Q1) Evaluating RGVS

Regarding RGVS, as expected, making the variable splitting method partially random fosters the learning speed of the models. Table 1 reports the global learning times for the best validation networks. From it is visible how LearnSPN-b equipped with RGVS takes less time to grow a full structure than GVS, requiring

Table 3. Learning times in seconds and average test log-likelihoods for the best validation models for RGVS, varying the proportion of RVs involved in GVS.

	Learning time					Log-likelihood				
	10%	30%	50%	70%	90%	10%	30%	50%	70%	90%
NLTCS	9.35	3.65	3.54	3.40	3.73	−6.196	−6.356	−6.576	−6.562	−6.337
Plants	45.18	21.25	18.84	21.09	26.49	−16.808	−17.786	−17.186	−16.292	−15.223
Audio	43.72	24.93	24.32	26.03	27.20	−41.866	−42.146	−42.206	−42.076	−41.702
Jester	34.33	17.85	18.77	21.51	30.95	−54.806	−54.984	−54.949	−54.866	−54.341
Netflix	67.51	54.72	51.29	49.53	72.75	−60.043	−59.832	−59.464	−59.559	−59.082
Accidents	38.43	18.10	19.55	20.80	30.40	−39.415	−39.871	−40.006	−38.759	−36.677
Retail	24.18	9.06	11.59	15.73	20.51	−11.382	−11.368	−11.358	−11.344	−11.142
Pumsb-star	24.60	21.60	18.83	19.99	29.50	−43.240	−45.732	−42.171	−37.525	−32.310
DNA	7.55	2.06	2.58	2.98	3.89	−99.453	−99.458	−98.920	−98.269	−95.968

in some cases less than half the time. Table 2 reports the structure quality of the learned networks in terms of their number of edges (size), number of layers (depth) and parameters (model capacity). See Sect. 2 for how these values influence both inference and learning. It is evident how RGVS is able to learn very compact models, speeding up inference times. However, this is done trading-off accuracy. In Table 1 average test log-likelihoods are reported for all methods on all datasets. There, accuracy degrades on all datasets, being comparable to other methods on some datasets such as Retail and Jester, but also degrading significantly on Pumsb-star and DNA.

Additionally, to better understand the behavior of RGVS, we evaluate how changing the proportion of RVs involved in a G-test affects accuracy and learning times. We assess this by determining k as the varying proportion of the RVs actually involved in the statistical test, making it range in the 10%, 30%, 50%, 70%, 90% of all of them, for the best configurations found on the validation sets. From Table 3, one can see that generally, when the proportion of involved RVs in the G-test is between 30% and 70%, we obtain faster learning times and less accurate models. The reason behind this is that when this proportion is either small or close to 100%, LearnSPN-b just makes much more calls to the RGVS, evaluating fewer RVs every time. Concluding, we can answer **Q1** by stating that RGVS is able to learn more compact models in less time than GVS, yet compromising on inference accuracy.

4.2 (Q2) Evaluating EBVS

From our results, EBVS learns much less compact networks w.r.t. GVS. Concerning learning times, while it speeds up the building procedure for a single node, the overall time required by the algorithm to grow a whole network increases (Table 1). This is due to the fact that it calls the row clustering procedure less frequently than GVS since it learns networks with more nodes but with fewer parameters (Table 2). Thus, it moves into the search space faster but it favours larger networks than GVS. On the accuracy side, instead, one can see that EBVS has comparable results w.r.t GVS and performs better than RGVS (Table 1). To answer the research question **Q2** we can state that EBVS does not learn more compact networks than GVS but it learns more accurate networks than RGVS. Still, since the increased size of the learned models, their learning time increased.

4.3   (Q3) Evaluating **EBVS-AE**

In the previous Section we questioned the introduction of an adaptive thresholding method for the entropy-based splitting procedure. Results confirm our intuition over the employed datasets. For EBVS-AE, both likelihood and structure characteristics improve if compared to EBVS, as showed in Tables 2 and 1. Concerning accuracy, EBVS-AE on 5 out of 9 considered datasets achieves comparable or better results than our baseline GVS (Table 1). Given that, we can answer **Q3** by stating that EBVS-AE, in general, tends to learn more accurate and compact networks than EBVS, needing less time, and as such shall be preferred over it.

5   Conclusions

Learning an SPN from high dimensional data still poses a challenge in terms of time complexity. The simplest greedy structure learner, LearnSPN, scales quadratically in the number of the variables to determine RVs independencies. Here we propose more approximate but faster procedures to determine independencies among RVs whose complexity scales in sub-quadratic time. We investigate two approaches: a random subspace one and another one that adopts entropy as a criterion to split RVs in linear time. Experimental results prove that there is no free lunch: LearnSPN equipped by the former learns networks that save on learning and inference time, providing less accurate inference; while with the latter procedure, it is able to produce networks that are still accurate estimators but require more time when learning and evaluating due to their size. Future works will investigate how to distill a method being overall optimal.

References

1. Adel, T., Balduzzi, D., Ghodsi, A.: Learning the structure of sum-product networks via an SVD-based algorithm. In: UAI (2015)
2. Breiman, L.: Random forests. Mach. Learn. **45**(1), 5–32 (2001)
3. Cheng, W., Kok, S., Pham, H.V., Chieu, H.L., Chai, K.M.A.: Language modeling with sum-product networks. In: INTERSPEECH 2014, pp. 2098–2102 (2014)
4. Darwiche, A.: A differential approach to inference in Bayesian networks. JACM **50**(3), 280–305 (2003)
5. Dennis, A., Ventura, D.: Learning the architecture of sum-product networks using clustering on variables. In: NIPS 25, pp. 2033–2041 (2012)
6. Di Mauro, N., Vergari, A., Basile, T.M.A.: Learning Bayesian random cutset forests. In: Esposito, F., Pivert, O., Hacid, M.-S., Raś, Z.W., Ferilli, S. (eds.) ISMIS 2015. LNCS (LNAI), vol. 9384, pp. 122–132. Springer, Cham (2015). doi:10.1007/978-3-319-25252-0_13

7. Di Mauro, N., Vergari, A., Esposito, F.: Learning accurate cutset networks by exploiting decomposability. In: Gavanelli, M., Lamma, E., Riguzzi, F. (eds.) AI*IA 2015. LNCS, vol. 9336, pp. 221–232. Springer, Cham (2015). doi:10.1007/978-3-319-24309-2_17

8. Friesen, A., Domingos, P.: The sum-product theorem: a foundation for learning tractable models. In: ICML, pp. 1909–1918 (2016)

9. Gens, R., Domingos, P.: Learning the structure of sum-product networks. In: ICML, pp. 873–880 (2013)

10. Haaren, J.V., Davis, J.: Markov network structure learning: a randomized feature generation approach. In: AAAI. AAAI Press (2012)

11. Koller, D., Friedman, N.: Probabilistic Graphical Models: Principles and Techniques. MIT Press, Cambridge (2009)

12. Lowd, D., Davis, J.: Learning Markov network structure with decision trees. In: ICDM, pp. 334–343. IEEE Computer Society Press (2010)

13. MacKay, D.J.C.: Information Theory, Inference & Learning Algorithms. Cambridge University Press, New York (2002)

14. Martens, J., Medabalimi, V.: On the Expressive Efficiency of Sum Product Networks. CoRR abs/1411.7717 (2014)

15. Molina, A., Natarajan, S., Kersting, K.: Poisson sum-product networks: a deep architecture for tractable multivariate poisson distributions. In: AAAI (2017)

16. Peharz, R.: Foundations of sum-product networks for probabilistic modeling. Ph.D. thesis, Graz University of Technology, SPSC (2015)

17. Peharz, R., Kapeller, G., Mowlaee, P., Pernkopf, F.: Modeling speech with sum-product networks: application to bandwidth extension. In: ICASSP (2014)

18. Poon, H., Domingos, P.: Sum-product networks: a new deep architecture. In: UAI 2011 (2011)

19. Queyranne, M.: Minimizing symmetric submodular functions. Math. Program. 82(1–2), 3–12 (1998)

20. Rahman, T., Kothalkar, P., Gogate, V.: Cutset networks: a simple, tractable, and scalable approach for improving the accuracy of chow-liu trees. In: Calders, T., Esposito, F., Hüllermeier, E., Meo, R. (eds.) ECML PKDD 2014. LNCS, vol. 8725, pp. 630–645. Springer, Heidelberg (2014). doi:10.1007/978-3-662-44851-9_40

21. Rooshenas, A., Lowd, D.: Learning sum-product networks with direct and indirect variable interactions. In: ICML (2014)

22. Roth, D.: On the hardness of approximate reasoning. Artif. Intell. 82(12), 273–302 (1996)

23. Vergari, A., Di Mauro, N., Esposito, F.: Visualizing and understanding sum-product networks. CoRR abs/1608.08266 (2016)

24. Vergari, A., Di Mauro, N., Esposito, F.: Simplifying, regularizing and strengthening sum-product network structure learning. In: Appice, A., Rodrigues, P.P., Santos Costa, V., Gama, J., Jorge, A., Soares, C. (eds.) ECML PKDD 2015. LNCS (LNAI), vol. 9285, pp. 343–358. Springer, Cham (2015). doi:10.1007/978-3-319-23525-7_21

25. Yuan, Z., Wang, H., Wang, L., Lu, T., Palaiahnakote, S., Tan, C.L.: Modeling spatial layout for scene image understanding via a novel multiscale sum-product network. Expert Syst. Appl. 63, 231–240 (2016)

Deepsquatting: Learning-Based Typosquatting Detection at Deeper Domain Levels

Paolo Piredda[2], Davide Ariu[1,2], Battista Biggio[1,2(✉)], Igino Corona[1,2], Luca Piras[1,2], Giorgio Giacinto[1,2], and Fabio Roli[1,2]

[1] Pluribus One, Cagliari, Italy
[2] Department of Electrical and Electronic Engineering, University of Cagliari, Piazza d'Armi, 09123 Cagliari, Italy
{paolo.piredda,davide.ariu,battista.biggio,igino.corona,luca.piras, giacinto,roli}@diee.unica.it

Abstract. Typosquatting consists of registering Internet domain names that closely resemble legitimate, reputable, and well-known ones (e.g., Farebook instead of Facebook). This cyber-attack aims to distribute malware or to phish the victims users (i.e., stealing their credentials) by mimicking the aspect of the legitimate webpage of the targeted organisation. The majority of the detection approaches proposed so far generate possible typo-variants of a legitimate domain, creating thus blacklists which can be used to prevent users from accessing typo-squatted domains. Only few studies have addressed the problem of Typosquatting detection by leveraging a passive Domain Name System (DNS) traffic analysis. In this work, we follow this approach, and additionally exploit machine learning to learn a similarity measure between domain names capable of detecting typo-squatted ones from the analyzed DNS traffic. We validate our approach on a large-scale dataset consisting of 4 months of traffic collected from a major Italian Internet Service Provider.

1 Introduction

The Domain Name System (DNS) is a crucial component of the Internet infrastructure. By means of the DNS, Internet nodes can be reliably identified and located by translating (resolving) a *string* (*i.e.*, a domain name), into an *integer* (*i.e.*, an IP address), through an hierarchical and distributed database. The DNS infrastructure effectively adds a layer of abstraction that allows for high-availability and agility of Internet services, while making them reachable through *human-friendly* domain names. Unfortunately, such DNS properties are also abused by miscreants for a myriad of Internet scams. Typosquatting is one among those subtle, widespread DNS scams mentioned before. In this attack, cybercriminals register (typo) domain names that closely resemble legitimate, reputable, and well-known ones (*e.g.*, `farebook.com` vs `facebook.com`). The main aim of miscreants is to harvest and monetize Internet traffic originally destined to the mimicked (legitimate) services [1], by exploiting their online *popularity* as well as *user mistakes*. Incoming traffic may be due to users who accidentally mistype browser URLs [10], destination emails [3], even HTML code [14], or

F. Esposito et al. (Eds.): AI*IA 2017, LNAI 10640, pp. 347–358, 2017.
https://doi.org/10.1007/978-3-319-70169-1_26

who unluckily *click* on "legitimate-looking", malicious (*e.g.*, phishing) links [13]. An important point exploited by miscreants when building malicious links is the *gap* between user perception of domain names and the actual domain name resolution process. Domain names are usually composed by words which are expected to be read *from left to right*, *e.g.*, in languages derived from *latin* or *greek*. Conversely, domain names are actually resolved from *right to left*. Thus, in DNS entries like `facebook.com.xyz.fakedomain.it` the user-perceived domain name may be `facebook.com`, whereas the most important part is the *effective* second level domain name (2LD), *i.e.*, `fakedomain.it`, which is the domain name that has been actually registered by miscreants. Under such a single 2LD, miscreants may *freely* setup an *arbitrary* large number of domains with lower level, where `facebook.com.xyz.fakedomain.it` is just an instance. From an attacker perspective, this also makes typosquatting attacks very cheap.

Defensive registration is the main countermeasure used by large Internet providers, banks, financial operators, and in general by all the players which are heavily targeted by typosquatting and phishing attacks. Nevertheless, such measure can mitigate only the case of typosquatting occurring at the 2LD (`farebook.com` vs. `facebook.com`) while it remains totally ineffective against typosquatting attacks where the squatting occurs at lower levels. Additionally, given the large number of domain name variations that may take place, defensive registration may be very *expensive*, and *incomplete* by definition, since it may cover only typo-variations that defenders are able to foresee. From a defender perspective, a more effective and cheaper approach against typosquatting may be to detect registered typo-domains and act against them if necessary. This is where past research work focused, the most. All the proposed approaches for typosquatting detection have in common two distinguishing features. First, they focus on detecting 2LD typosquatting, through either generative models [5–12] using legitimate 2LDs as seed, or string similarity measures and time correlation in live traffic [13]. Second, the considered typo-variants where mainly obtained with the substitution (*e.g.*, `faceb0ok`), addition (*e.g.*, `faceboook`), or cancellation (*e.g.*, `facebok`) of one character. This means that typosquatting introducing more of one of these operations would go undetected (*e.g.*, `faceboook`).

In this work, we overcome the aforementioned limits. We present a novel detection approach capable of detecting typosquatting at the 2LD, but also at lower levels. In addition, we do not leverage any generative model, but we detect typo-variations of known domain names observed in the wild in large-scale networks, at the Internet Service Provider (ISP) level, as they are requested by real (victim) users. Finally, our approach is more general than state-of-the-art methods, as it is based on n-grams, and it can thus detect typo-variations with much more than one substitution, addition or cancellation.

2   Background

DNS Basics. As shown in Fig. 1, when a user wants to resolve a domain name (1) (*aiia2017.di.uniba.it* in the example) the resolver (e.g. the DNS server of

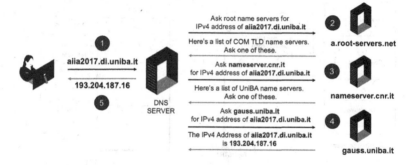

Fig. 1. An example of resolution of an internet domain name.

the Internet Service Provider) makes first a request to the root name servers (**2**), in order to obtain the list of the servers authoritatives for that **T**op-**L**evel **D**omain (.*it* in the example). Then, the resolver makes a request (**3**) to the root servers delegated for the .*it* TLD in order to get the list of nameserver(s) authoritative(s) for the *uniba* Second-Level Domain. Finally, such authoritative nameserver is queried (**4**) to obtain the IP address of *aiia2017.di.uniba.it*. The resolver finally passes such address to the user (**5**) which is then able to reach the website.

Previous work on typosquatting. Typosquatting is also known as cyber-squatting. According to the United States federal law known as the Anticyber-squatting Consumer Protection Act (ACPA, year 1999) [2], Cybersquatting is

> "*the registration, trafficking in, or use of a domain name that is identical to, confusingly similar to [...] a service mark of another that is distinctive at the time of registration of the domain name [...] with the bad-faith intent to profit from the goodwill of another's mark.*"

As shown in Fig. 2, typosquatting may be motivated by many different reasons, including (a) phishing scam advertisement/malware attacks; (b) collection of email messages erroneously sent to the typo domains; (c) monetization of traffic through affiliate marketing links/parked domain advertisements; (d) selling the typo domains to target brand competitors or the legitimate brand itself [1,3]. Please note that legitimate brands may also defend themselves against cyber-squatting by proactively registering, or acquiring control of, typo domains.

Points (c) and (d) were the main aim of a large-scale attack studied by Edelman [4] in 2003, while tracing back domain names registered by a unique individual. Such study highlighted more than 8,000 typo domains, most of them leading victim users (including children) to sexually-explicit websites.

Subsequent work focused on the detection of typo variations of popular domain names, according to a set of *generative* models. Such models typically receive a legitimate domain name as *seed* and then generate a set of candidate typo domain names. Each domain name in such set is investigated through *active* approaches, *e.g.*, resolving it and retrieving web content [5–12].

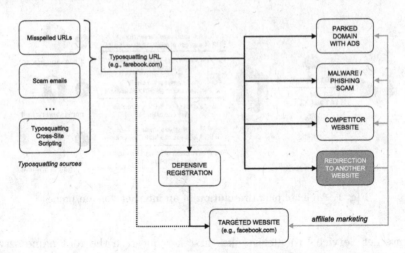

Fig. 2. Main sources of typosquatting, including defensive registrations.

Differently from the aforementioned approach, Khan *et al.* [13] propose a *passive* approach for detecting typosquatting domain names, by passively looking for domain resolutions and HTTP traffic within a live network (University Campus). The main assumption is that target (legitimate) domain names typically appear *close in time* with their typo versions, since users may correct their errors, *e.g.*, correct the typed URL. Under such assumption, typosquatting domain names as well as their legitimate counterparts are clustered together using time-based metrics and a Damerau-Levenshtein edit distance of *one*.

Typosquatting can be also exploited to acquire control of and exfiltrate data from websites relying on third-party (external) JavaScript libraries, thanks to typographical errors in the implementation of web pages. Nikiforakis *et al.* [14] named this threat as Typosquatting Cross-site Scripting (TXSS). The impact of this threat may be very significant as demonstrated by the authors registering several typo domains against popular domain names serving third-party JavaScript libraries (*e.g.*, `googlesyndicatio.com` vs `googlesyndication.com`).

Contributions of this work. Similarly to the work by Khan *et al.* [13], we employ a passive approach to the detection of typosquatting domain names. However, to the best of our knowledge, this is the first typosquatting detection approach that operates at the ISP level. We perform an extensive evaluation that involves traffic about hundreds of thousands of real users. Additionally, we do not rely on any assumption about temporal correlation between legitimate domains and their typo variations. Finally, our similarity measure can operate in realtime (in the sense of detecting malicious domains as they start being observed in DNS traffic, with the purpose of subsequent blacklisting) and it is more general, as it is based on *n-grams* and considers *multiple levels* of the domain name (not only the 2LD). This approach allows us to detect many typo domains in the wild that would be very difficult (if not impossible) to detect with generative approaches, and that involve manipulation at levels lower than the effective 2LD. In this study, we focus our detection on typo variations of two very popular domain names. By using n-grams as machine-learning features, we were able to get useful insights into the strategies currently employed by miscreants in the typosquatting landscape.

3   Typosquatting Domain Detection

The underlying idea used in this work is to use n-gram-based representations to detect typosquatting domains. We adapted this idea from [15], where n-gram-based representations were used to detect misspelled nouns in databases. The rationale behind our idea is that such representations may enable detecting typosquatting domains that are not necessarily within small edit distances from the targeted domain name, $i.e.$, they enable the detection of a wider set of potential *typosquatting patterns*.

Let us consider a simple example to clarify this concept. Consider the 2LD name `google` and its bi-gram representation, using also a special character to denote the beginning (#) and the end of the string ($):

$$\#\texttt{google\$} \rightarrow \texttt{\#g go oo og gl le´ e\$}. \tag{1}$$

Now, consider the typosquatting domain `goooooogle.com`, for which the bi-gram representation of the 2LD is `#g go oo oo ... oo og gl le e$`. By computing the intersection of this bi-grams with the previous ones obtained for `google`, one finds that all the seven bi-grams present in `google` are also present in the typosquatting domain. In practice, by assigning a binary feature to each bi-gram of the targeted domain (`google` in our running example), we can construct a numerical feature vector, suitable to train a machine-learning algorithm. In our case, the feature vector associated to `goooooogle.com` consists of seven 1s, and it is thus likely that it will be classified correctly. To yield a more complete n-gram-based representation, we also consider tri-grams and non-consecutive bi-grams ($i.e.$, skip-grams) skipping one character.

Another relevant difference with state-of-the-art approaches is that we aim to detect whether typosquatting also occurs at lower domain levels than the 2LD. To this end, we consider the aforementioned n-gram-based representations and look for *typosquatting patterns* at lower domain levels, by concatenating such patterns to form a unique feature set. In particular, it is worth remarking two aspects. First, we ignore the TLD, since for most of popular, legitimate websites ($e.g.$, google and facebook), registrations are existing at each national level. Second, to keep the number of features fixed and compact, we concatenate features extracted from the 2LD, 3LD and 4LD. Then, we consider an additional set of n-grams to identify potential typosquatting at lower level domains, from the 5LD up to the 10LD. This set is simply the set of n-grams corresponding to the level (among the 5LD, 6LD, ..., 10LD) in which most of the n-grams match those of the targeted domain ($i.e.$, the sum of the corresponding features is maximum). For example, consider the domain

$$\underbrace{\texttt{google-974}}_{\text{3LD}}.\underbrace{\texttt{zone-one}}_{\text{2LD}}.\underbrace{\texttt{com}}_{\text{TLD}} \tag{2}$$

which has three domain levels. In this case, our feature representation is obtained by concatenating the n-grams of the targeted domain $\texttt{google}$ found at each level:

$$\underbrace{}_{[0...0]}\underbrace{}_{[0...0]}\underbrace{\texttt{google-974}}_{[1...10]}.\underbrace{\texttt{zone-one}}_{[0...0]}.\texttt{com}, \tag{3}$$

namely, $[0\ldots0, 1\ldots10, 0\ldots0]$, where we have fourteen 0 at the beginning (since there is neither match at the 5LD and below, nor at the 4LD), six 1 and one 0 at the 3LD (since $\texttt{google}$ is completely matched except for the termination character), and then we have further seven 0 at the 2LD.

4   Experimental Analysis

We report here an experimental analysis to evaluate the soundness of the proposed approach. In particular, the goal of our experiments is to understand whether a learning algorithm trained on the aforementioned n-gram representation can detect typo-squatting at the 2LD and also at lower domain levels, overcoming the limits of the existing typo-squatting detection techniques [5, 7].

We conduct our experiments using real DNS data collected from an Italian ISP. We focus on detecting typo-squatting against two popular web services, *i.e.*, Google and Facebook. To this end, we built two datasets (one per service) as described below.

Data and ground-truth labels. We first extracted all domain names requested and successfully resolved (along with the corresponding server IP addresses) by the users of the considered ISP between August 1, 2016 and November 30, 2016. Then, to establish the ground-truth labels reliably, *i.e.*, to label each domain as typo-squatting or not, we adopted the following strategy. We started by considering all domain names for which the 2LD is in the Alexa Top 50 as legitimate. Malicious typo-squatting domains were identified by first extracting all domain names whose 2LD has a Damerau-Levenshtein distance equal to 1 from the string *google* (for the Google dataset) and *facebook* (for the Facebook dataset). This includes all domains that one would find using the state-of-the-art generative approaches proposed in [5, 7] along with other domains for which the Damerau-Levenshtein distance is 1 but that are not encompassed by the aforementioned generative approaches. To find suspicious typo-squatting attempts beyond the 2LD, we used the approach in [15], originally proposed to find misspellings in databases. This technique detects words (from a given list) that are potential typing errors of a source word ($\texttt{google}$ or $\texttt{facebook}$ in our case). In particular, we used a simplified version that simply counts how many bigrams the source word has in common with each other word in the list (using special characters to denote the beginning and the end of each word, and considering the order of each gram, as described in the previous section). Once this measure of *overlap* between each word and the source word was computed, as in [15], a simple clustering procedure was used to separate potential typos from words that are clearly not typos of the source word. In our case, we considered as a word the content of each domain level (note that a single domain can consist of more words, *e.g.*, "abc.dot.gooogle.bizz.com" consists of four different words, excluding the TLD ".com", where only `gooogle` is effectively a typo of `google`). The list of potential word typos was then matched against the domain list (at each level) to find all suspicious typo-squatting domain names. However, recall that finding a domain name which is relatively close to the name of a legitimate domain is not enough to declare it as a typo-squatting attempt. As mentioned in previous work [10], roughly half of these suspicious domain names is in fact legitimate (think, *e.g.*, to *defensive registrations*). We thus checked whether the resolved IPs corresponding to the suspicious domains identified as potential typo-squatting host effectively some malicious activity or scam. To this end, we used the API service provided by VirusTotal,[1] and labeled a suspicious domain as malicious only if the resolved IP is known to be at least in a public blacklist. To reduce the probability of labeling errors, we collected such labels in January 2017, some months after our DNS traffic was observed. Eventually, we labeled a domain as typo-squatting only if (*i*) it was identified as similar to `google` or `facebook` (both in terms of Damerau-Levenshtein distance and of the clustering approach discussed in [15]), and if (*ii*) the resolved IP address of the corresponding server was known to be malicious from publicly-available blacklisting services, using the interface provided by VirusTotal (as mentioned before).

However, these services often label legitimate domains as malicious, since they simply report whether a server has been contacted by malware, and malware typically contact also legitimate services for different reasons (*e.g.*, to mislead reverse-engineering analyses, check connectivity, *etc.*). We thus further refine the ground-truth labels with a thorough manual analysis. In particular, we found that most of the domains associated to blacklisting services are labeled as malicious, as they have been probably contacted by malware. This may happen simply when a malware sample checks whether a domain is already known to be malicious or not, to avoid connecting to it. In this way, the operations performed by the malware sample may remain undetected. For example, the DNS query `facebook.com.sbl-xbl.spamhaus.org` checks whether `facebook.com.sbl` has been blacklisted by Spamhaus. If not, the malware sample can contact it incurring a lower risk of detection. These kinds of queries are definitely not typosquatting attempts but rather legitimate queries to blacklisting services. We therefore change their label to legitimate, even if they may be easily misclassified as potential typosquatting domains by our algorithm.

Classifiers. We trained different state-of-the-art learning algorithms on the n-gram-based feature representation proposed in previous section (separately on each dataset, *i.e.*, for each monitored domain). In particular, we considered Support Vector Machines (SVMs) with linear and Radial Basis Function (RBF) kernels, and Random Forests (RFs). We tuned their parameters using a 5-fold cross-validation procedure on the training data, in order to minimize the

---

[1] https://www.virustotal.com/it/documentation/public-api/#getting-ip-reports.

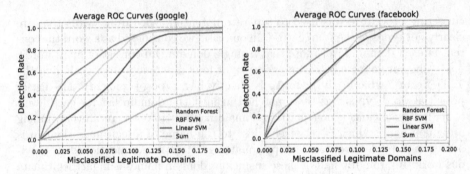

Fig. 3. Average ROC curves exhibited by the considered learning algorithms on `google` (*left*) and `facebook` (*right*) datasets.

classification error. For the RF classifiers, we optimized the number of base decision-tree classifiers $k \in \{10, 15, 20, \dots, 100\}$; for the linear SVM, we optimized the regularization parameter $C \in \{10^{-2}, \dots, 10^3\}$ and for the RBF SVM we additionally tuned the kernel parameter $\gamma \in \{10^{-3}, \dots, 10^3\}$. We also considered a baseline algorithm that corresponds to the sum of the n-gram feature values (denoted with "Sum" for short).

Performance Evaluation. Performance was evaluated in terms of Receiver Operating Characteristic (ROC) curves, averaged on 5 random training-test splits, using 80% of the data for training (and 20% for testing) in each split.

Experimental Results. Results are reported in Fig. 3, for both `google` and `facebook` datasets. First, note that Sum is outperformed by all learning algorithms used in our experiments. This witnesses that using machine learning in this case is really helpful to find some specific *registration patterns* corresponding to malicious typosquatting domains, *i.e.*, the only presence of some specific n-grams in the domain name is not sufficient to classify it as a potential typosquatting domain. Another interesting observation is that Random Forests outperform significantly the SVM-based classifiers. This may be due to the fact that they leverage bagging and the random subspace method to build a classifier ensemble of decision trees, which typically improves the performance over baseline, monolithic learning algorithms.

In Table 1 we additionally report the detection rates of the RF classifier (which performed best) for typosquatting occuring at different domain levels and at different edit distances. This shows that our approach is capable of detecting typosquatting attempts beyond the state-of-the-art techniques proposed so far.

Besides the aforementioned considerations, the reported results clearly show that the proposed method is not ready to be deployed on a large scale, *e.g.*, to monitor the DNS traffic of an ISP, due to a rather high false positive rate (*i.e.*, fraction of misclassified legitimate domains). Nevertheless, the reason is simply that the structure of the domain name does not suffice to correctly identify a typosquatting domain hosting malicious or suspicious activities. To confirm this issue, we report some examples of misclassified domains by our algorithm

Table 1. Detection rates of the Random Forest (RF) classifier for typosquatting at different domain levels (from 2LD to 7LD, 8LD+ denotes the grouping of 8LD, 9LD and 10LD) and Damerau-Levenshtein (DL) distances, for the `google` and `facebook` data. In both cases, the operating point of the RF is set to achieve a 2.5% false positive rate, which roughly corresponds to a detection rate of 50%, as also shown in Fig. 3.

google	DL = 0			DL = 1			DL >1			Overall (DL ≥ 0)		
	True	Detected		True	Detected		True	Detected		True	Detected	
2LD	0	0		576	458	79.5%	412	328	79.6%	988	786	79.6%
3LD	305	162	53.1%	17	5	29.4%	97	63	64.9%	419	230	54.9%
4LD	483	50	10.4%	13	10	76.9%	193	43	22.3%	689	103	14.9%
5LD	161	27	16.8%	0	0		54	31	57.4%	215	58	27.0%
6LD	55	24	43.6%	1	0	0.0%	34	16	47.1%	90	40	44.4%
7LD	17	11	64.7%	0	0		4	1	25.0%	21	12	57.1%
8LD+	8	4	50.0%	0	0		11	7	63.6%	19	11	57.9%
Total										2441	1240	50.8%

facebook	DL = 0			DL = 1			DL > 1			Overall (DL ≥ 0)		
	True	Detected		True	Detected		True	Detected		True	Detected	
2LD	0	0		387	314	81.1%	928	134	14.4%	1315	448	34.1%
3LD	347	26	7.5%	16	14	87.5%	334	282	84.4%	697	322	46.2%
4LD	216	69	31.9%	2	0	0.0%	352	342	97.2%	570	411	72.1%
5LD	83	31	37.3%	0	0		7	2	28.6%	90	33	36.7%
6LD	22	0	0.0%	0	0		0	0		22	0	0.0%
7LD	1	1	100.0%	0	0		89	89	100.0%	90	90	100.0%
8LD+	11	5	45.5%	0	0		0	0		11	5	45.5%
Total										2795	1309	46.8%

Fig. 4. Screenshot of the typosquatting domain `www.gyoogle.net` (*left*), and of the defensive registration at `www.faceboo.com` (*right*).

in Table 2 and Fig. 4. By a deeper inspection of the misclassified legitimate domains, we have discovered that, in practice, some may host malicious activities or even malware although VirusTotal labeled them as legitimate (*e.g.*, this happens for `googllee.co.uk`, while the suspicious `6ooogoogle.ru` is inactive).

Table 2. Some examples of domain names correctly-classified as typosquatting by our algorithm (using the RF classifier) along with some misclassified legitimate ones. Defensive registrations and misclassified queries to blacklisting services are highlighted with (*) and (**), respectively.

google	
Correctly detected	Misclassified legitimate domains
google.com-prize4you.com	www.goolge.de (*)
google.com–support.info	news.gogle.it (*)
google.com-updater.xyz	googlehouse.com
google.com-62.org	googllee.co.uk
google.itoogle.it	www.sxgoogle.net
www.gyoogle.net	www.googlel.com
google.com-1prize4you.com	6ooogoogle.ru

facebook	
Correctly detected	Misclassified legitimate domains
facebook.com-winner.me	www.tai-facebook.xyz
ww25.facebook.comfacebook.com	facebook-jaegermeister.syzygy.de
facebook.com-feed.top	facebook.feargames.it
facebook.com-iii.org	facebook.fantatornei.com
facebook.com-prize4you.com	faceboock.ddns.net (**)
facffebook.com	faceslapbook.blogspot.com
www.faceboo.com (*)	facebook.fantatornei.com

Note also that defensive registrations are not always correctly labeled by Virus-Total. This witnesses that the false positive rate may be even lower than the one effectively reported in our experiments (due to the fact that our ground-truth labeling source is not very reliable). Furthermore, it should be clear from the reported set of examples that categorizing a malicious typosquatting domain by only looking at the structure of its name is an ill-posed problem; e.g., finding "google" at the beginning of a domain name beyond the 2LD is a typosquatting pattern recognized correctly by our algorithm in most of the cases. For this reason, to reduce the false positive rate, more characteristics should be taken into account, as done in previous work aimed to detect malicious domains from DNS traffic [16–18]. Despite this, our analysis shows that characterizing the domain name using n-grams and machine learning may improve the detection of typosquatting domains over the state of the art, i.e., beyond the 2LD and small Damerau-Levenshtein distance values. We thus believe that our approach may be particularly useful to improve the aforementioned existing systems aimed to detect malicious domains while passively monitoring the DNS traffic [16–18], especially since typosquatting makes sense only if the domain name retains some degree of similarity with respect to the targeted website; in other words, this is a constraint for the attack to successfully mislead most of the unexperienced Internet users. To summarize, using n-gram-based representations and machine learning as advocated in this work can be thus deemed an interesting research direction to improve systems that detect malicious domains from DNS traffic.

5   Conclusions and Future Work

In this work, we proposed a passive DNS analysis approach to the detection of typosquatted Internet domain names. The proposed approach provides an advancement with respect to the solutions proposed so far in the literature as it enables the detection of a typosquatting patterns beyond the 2LD and for values of the Damerau-Levenshtein distance higher than 1, which is the kind of typosquatting usually consideres also by preventive registration mechanisms. The main limitation of our approach is currently represented by the false positive rate, which may be reduced using whitelisting; however, we strongly believe that our work may be useful to improve previous work for the detection of malicious domains from DNS traffic [16–18]. Our research work on this area is currently ongoing, and future enhancements will include both the analysis of the contents hosted by the detected domains, as well as the analysis of features extracted at domain registration time and DNS features especially to correctly categorize defensive registrations.

References

1. Spaulding, J., Upadhyaya, S.J., Mohaisen, A.: The landscape of domain name typosquatting: techniques and countermeasures. In: The 11th International Conference on Availability, Reliability and Security. Volume abs/1603.02767 (2016)
2. Senate, U.: The anticybersquatting consumer protection act, 5 August 1999
3. Zetter, K.: Researchers' typosquatting stole 20 GB of e-mail from fortune 500, August 2011. Wired.com
4. Edelman, B.: Large-scale registration of domains with typographical errors. Technical report, Berkman Center for Internet & Society - Harvard Law School (2003)
5. Wang, Y.M., Beck, D., Wang, J., Verbowski, C., Daniels, B.: Strider typo-patrol: discovery and analysis of systematic typo-squatting. In: Proceedings of the 2nd Conference on Steps to Reducing Unwanted Traffic on the Internet, SRUTI 2006, vol. 2, p. 5. USENIX Association, Berkeley (2006)
6. Holgers, T., Watson, D.E., Gribble, S.D.: Cutting through the confusion: a measurement study of homograph attacks. In: Proceedings of the Annual Conference on USENIX 2006 Annual Technical Conference, ATEC 2006, p. 24. USENIX Association, Berkeley (2006)
7. Banerjee, A., Barman, D., Faloutsos, M., Bhuyan, L.N.: Cyber-fraud is one typo away. In: IEEE INFOCOM 2008 - The 27th Conference on Computer Communications, April 2008
8. Moore, T., Edelman, B.: Measuring the perpetrators and funders of typosquatting. In: Sion, R. (ed.) FC 2010. LNCS, vol. 6052, pp. 175–191. Springer, Heidelberg (2010). doi:10.1007/978-3-642-14577-3_15

9. Nikiforakis, N., Acker, S.V., Meert, W., Desmet, L., Piessens, F., Joosen, W.: Bitsquatting: exploiting bit-flips for fun, or profit? In: 22nd International World Wide Web Conference, WWW 2013, Rio de Janeiro, Brazil, 13–17 May 2013, pp. 989–998 (2013)

10. Szurdi, J., Kocso, B., Cseh, G., Spring, J., Felegyhazi, M., Kanich, C.: The long "taile" of typosquatting domain names. In: Proceedings of the 23rd USENIX Conference on Security Symposium, SEC 2014, pp. 191–206. USENIX Association, Berkeley (2014)

11. Nikiforakis, N., Balduzzi, M., Desmet, L., Piessens, F., Joosen, W.: Soundsquatting: uncovering the use of homophones in domain squatting. In: Chow, S.S.M., Camenisch, J., Hui, L.C.K., Yiu, S.M. (eds.) ISC 2014. LNCS, vol. 8783, pp. 291–308. Springer, Cham (2014). doi:10.1007/978-3-319-13257-0_17

12. Agten, P., Joosen, W., Piessens, F., Nikiforakis, N.: Seven months' worth of mistakes: a longitudinal study of typosquatting abuse. In: 22nd Annual Network and Distributed System Security Symposium, NDSS 2015, San Diego, California, USA, 8–11 February 2015 (2015)

13. Khan, M.T., Huo, X., Li, Z., Kanich, C.: Every second counts: quantifying the negative externalities of cybercrime via typosquatting. In: 2015 IEEE Symposium on Security and Privacy, pp. 135–150, May 2015

14. Nikiforakis, N., Invernizzi, L., Kapravelos, A., Van Acker, S., Joosen, W., Kruegel, C., Piessens, F., Vigna, G.: You are what you include: large-scale evaluation of remote Javascript inclusions. In: Proceedings of the 2012 ACM Conference on Computer and Communications Security, CCS 2012, pp. 736–747. ACM, New York (2012)

15. Mazeika, A., Böhlen, M.H.: Cleansing databases of misspelled proper nouns. In: Proceedings of the First International VLDB Workshop on Clean Databases, CleanDB 2006, Seoul, Korea, 11 September 2006 (Co-located with VLDB 2006) (2006)

16. Perdisci, R., Corona, I., Giacinto, G.: Early detection of malicious Flux networks via large-scale passive DNS traffic analysis. IEEE Trans. Dependable Secure Comput. 9(5), 714–726 (2012)

17. Bilge, L., Sen, S., Balzarotti, D., Kirda, E., Kruegel, C.: Exposure: a passive DNS analysis service to detect and report malicious domains. ACM Trans. Inf. Syst. Secur. 16(4), 14:1–14:28 (2014)

18. Hao, S., Kantchelian, A., Miller, B., Paxson, V., Feamster, N.: Predator: proactive recognition and elimination of domain abuse at time-of-registration. In: Proceedings of the 2016 ACM SIGSAC Conference on Computer and Communications Security, CCS 2016, pp. 1568–1579. ACM, New York (2016)

On the Impact of Linguistic Information in Kernel-Based Deep Architectures

Danilo Croce[(✉)], Simone Filice, and Roberto Basili

Department of Enterprise Engineering, University of Roma, Tor Vergata, Rome, Italy
{croce,filice,basili}@info.uniroma2.it

Abstract. Kernel methods enable the direct usage of structured representations of textual data during language learning and inference tasks. On the other side, deep neural networks are effective in learning non-linear decision functions. Recent works demonstrated that expressive kernels and deep neural networks can be combined in a Kernel-based Deep Architecture (KDA), a common framework that allows to explicitly model structured information into a neural network. This combination achieves state-of-the-art accuracy in different semantic inference tasks. This paper investigates the impact of linguistic information on the performance reachable by a KDA by studying the benefits that different kernels can bring to the inference quality. We believe that the expressiveness of data representations will play a key role in the wide spread adoption of neural networks in AI problem solving. We experimentally evaluated the adoption of different kernels (each characterized by a growing expressive power) in a Question Classification task. Results suggest the importance of rich kernel functions in optimizing the accuracy of a KDA.

1 Introduction

Kernel-based methods and Deep Learning are two of the most popular approaches in Computational Natural Language Learning. Although these models are rather different and characterized by distinct strong and weak aspects, they both achieved state-of-the-art accuracies in several Natural Language Processing tasks (NLP).

In many of these tasks, learning processes require to more or less explicitly account for trees or graphs, which capture and formalize syntactic and semantic information expressed in texts. An advantage of kernel-based methods is their capability of exploiting structured information induced from examples, e.g., from sequences or trees. Sequence [1] or tree kernels [2] are of particular interest as they operate over structures reflecting linguistic evidences, such as syntactic information encoded in syntactic parse trees (e.g., discussed in [3]). A kernel function allows applying learning algorithms (such as Support Vector Machine, [4]) over discrete structures: these are *implicitly* projected into high-dimensional geometrical spaces where the learning algorithms can be applied. It is worth

© Springer International Publishing AG 2017
F. Esposito et al. (Eds.): AI*IA 2017, LNAI 10640, pp. 359–371, 2017.
https://doi.org/10.1007/978-3-319-70169-1_27

stressing that the projection is never made explicit as it is surrogated by the kernel function itself (the so-called Kernel Trick, [5]).

Deep Learning methods generally require input instances to be *explicitly* modeled via vectors or tensors, and their application on structure data is made possible only by using ad-hoc architectures, (e.g., [6–8]). Even if these methods obtain outstanding results, their design and architecture are typically tailored to specific tasks, and fail to easily adapt to a different problem. More in general, training complex neural networks is difficult as no common design practice is established against complex data structures. For example, in [9] a careful analysis of neural word embedding models is carried out and the role of the hyper-parameter estimation is outlined. Different neural architectures result in the same performances, whenever optimal hyper-parameter tuning is applied. In this latter case, no significant difference is observed across different architectures, thus confirming that the choice between different neural architectures is a complex and mostly empirical task.

A possible solution for enabling Structured Learning within Neural Networks has been recently proposed in [10], where authors demonstrated that expressive kernels and deep neural networks can be integrated in the so-called *Kernel-based Deep Architecture* (KDA). KDA is a common framework that allows modeling structured information through kernels while learning non-linear decision functions in a neural fashion. In a nutshell, a KDA adopts a dimensionality reduction method, called Nyström, to find the projection function able to approximate any kernel function and convert any structure (here linguistic structures such as trees) into dense linear embeddings. These can be used as the input of a Deep Feed-forward Neural Network that exploits such embeddings to learn non-linear classification functions. In [10], the KDA, combined with expressive kernel functions, allows achieving state-of-the-art accuracy in different semantic inference tasks. At the same time, the adoption of the Nyström method is also beneficial in terms of computational complexity (see [11]): the KDA drastically improves the efficiency and scalability of pure kernel-based methods, such as Support Vector Machines. This is important in many real world applications of NLP and Information Retrieval, such as in answer re-ranking in question answering, where kernel methods are very effective but, at the same time, computationally heavy [12,13].

The major hypothesis underlying KDAs is the ability of the Nyström reconstruction to capture the semantics of the input linguistic data expressed in the kernel feature space to guide the inductive inference. In this work we want to study this property. Are increasingly expressive representations able to achieve better generalization in different semantic tasks? Is the improvement in performance invariant with respect to one given KDA? Is the kernel representation correlated with the accuracy reachable by a given KDA? We think that different kernel functions, even operating on the same training set (but possibly different data structures, e.g., trees) achieve different levels of linguistic generalization.

Notice that the expressiveness of the representation language will play a key role in the application of neural networks to AI problems, as they will increase readability and compliance analysis of the resulting AI agents. As a consequence, it is worth investigating the contribution of different kernel functions, characterized by increasing levels of linguistic expressiveness as they are correspondingly more readable. We evaluated experimentally our hypothesis by studying the application of different kernels to a Question Classification task. Our results confirm the beneficial role of more expressive kernel functions whose linguistic evidences allow to achieve state-of-the-art results within the KDA.

In the rest of the paper, Sect. 2 surveys some of the investigated kernels. In Sect. 3, the Nyström methodology and KDA are described. Section 4 reports the experimental evaluations. Finally, Sect. 5 derives the conclusions.

2   Kernel-Based Semantic Inference

In almost all NLP tasks, explicit models of complex syntactic and semantic structures are required, as in Paraphrase Detection: deciding whether two sentences are valid paraphrases involves learning grammatical rewriting rules, such as semantics preserving mappings among sub-trees. Also in Question Answering, the syntactic information about input questions is crucial [14]. While manual feature engineering is always possible, kernel methods on structured representations of data objects, e.g., sentences, have been largely applied. Since [2], sentences can be modeled through their corresponding parse tree, and Tree Kernels (TKs) compute similarity metrics directly operating over such trees. These kernels correspond to dot products in the (implicit) feature space made of all possible tree fragments [2,15]. Notice that the number of tree fragments in a tree bank is combinatorial with the number of tree nodes and gives rise to billions of features, i.e., dimensions. In this high-dimensional space, kernel-based algorithms, such as SVMs, can implicitly learn robust prediction models [5], resulting in state-of-the-art approaches in several NLP tasks, e.g., Semantic Role Labeling [3], Question Classification [16] or Paraphrase Identification [17]. As the feature space generated by the structural kernels depends on the input structures, different tree representations can be adopted to reflect more or less expressive syntactic/semantic feature spaces.

Tree kernels operate on trees having labeled nodes and unlabeled edges, therefore, they can naturally exploit constituency trees (e.g., [2]). On the contrary, the graphs produced by dependency grammars, need a proper conversion in order to be adopted into tree kernels. For instance, an expressive tree representation of dependency graphs is the Grammatical Relation Centered Tree (GRCT). As illustrated in Fig. 1, PoS-Tags and grammatical relations correspond to nodes, dominating their associated lexemes.

Types of Tree Kernels. Tree kernels are a particular type of convolution kernels that differ in the way they compute similarity between two trees by detecting the tree substructures they share. Different tree kernels can be defined by varying the type of substructures considered during the kernel operation. The *Partial Tree Kernel* (PTK) [18] considers as valid substructures the so-called *partial trees*. i.e., a node and its (possibly partial) dominated subtrees. In its

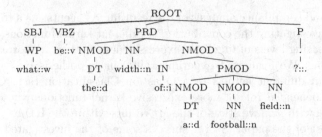

Fig. 1. Grammatical Relation Centered Tree (GRCT) of *"What is the width of a football field?"*.

evaluation, the PTK treats all node labels as mere symbols: the substructures belonging to the compared trees must have exactly the same node labels in order to contribute to the overall PTK evaluation. This requirement is too strict as different but semantically related lexical nodes (e.g., synonyms) do not provide any contribution to the similarity score. The *Smoothed Partial Tree Kernel* (SPTK) described in [16] overcomes this limitation: it extends the PTK formulation by introducing a similarity function between lexical nodes in GRCT representations, i.e., the cosine similarity between word vector representations for the node labels, based on word embeddings (e.g., [19,20]). In this work, we also use a further extension of the SPTK, called *Compositionally Smoothed Partial Tree Kernel* (CSPTK) (as in [21]). In CSPTK, the lexical information provided by the sentence words is propagated along the non-terminal nodes representing head-modifier dependencies. Figure 2 shows a compositionally-labeled tree, where the similarity function at the nodes can model lexical composition, i.e., capturing contextual information. For example, in the sentence, *"What instrument does Hendrix play?"*, the role of the word *instrument* can be fully captured only if its composition with the verb *play* is considered. The CSPTK applies a composition function between nodes: while several algebraic functions can be adopted to compose two word vectors representing the underlying head/modifier pair, here we refer to a simple additive function that assigns to each (h, m) pair the linear combination of the involved vectors, i.e., $(\boldsymbol{h}, \boldsymbol{m}) = A\boldsymbol{h} + B\boldsymbol{m}$: although simple and efficient, it actually produces very effective CSPTK functions.

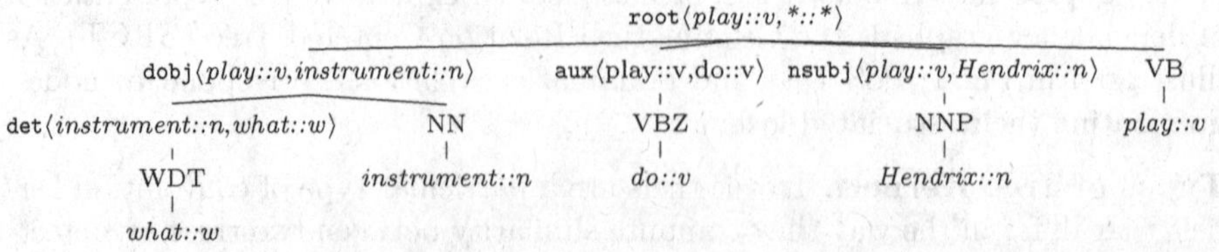

root⟨*play::v, *::**⟩

dobj⟨*play::v,instrument::n*⟩   aux⟨*play::v,do::v*⟩ nsubj⟨*play::v,Hendrix::n*⟩ VB

det⟨*instrument::n,what::w*⟩   NN   VBZ   NNP   *play::v*

WDT   *instrument::n*   *do::v*   *Hendrix::n*

what::w

Fig. 2. Compositional Grammatical Relation Centered Tree (CGRCT) of *"What instrument does Hendrix play?"*.

Complexity. The training phase of an optimal maximum margin algorithm (such as SVM) requires a number of kernel operations that is more than linear (almost $\mathcal{O}(n^2)$) with respect to the number of training examples n, as in [22]. Also the classification phase depends on the size of the input dataset and to the intrinsic complexity of the targeted task: classifying a new instance requires to evaluate the kernel function with respect to each support vector. For complex tasks, the number of selected support vectors tends to be very large, and using the resulting model can be impractical. This cost is also problematic as single kernel operations can be very expensive: the cost of evaluating the PTK on a single tree pair is almost linear in the number of nodes in the input trees, as shown in [18]. When lexical semantics is considered, as in SPTKs and CSPTKs, it is more than linear in the number of nodes, as measured in [16].

3   Deep Learning in Kernel Spaces

In this section, we will first describe the Nyström method for generating low dimensional embeddings that approximate high dimensional kernel spaces. Then we will review the Kernel-based Deep Architecture discussed in [10], that efficiently combines kernel methods and Deep Learning by using a Nyström layer into a multi-layer perceptron.

3.1   Linearizing Kernel Representations: The Nyström Method

Given an input training dataset D, a kernel $K(o_i, o_j)$ is a similarity function over $\mathcal{D}^2$ that corresponds to a dot product in the implicit kernel space, i.e., $K(o_i, o_j) = \Phi(o_i) \cdot \Phi(o_j)$. The advantage of kernels is that the projection function $\Phi(o) = \boldsymbol{x} \in \mathbb{R}^n$ is never explicitly computed [5]. In fact, this operation may be prohibitive when the dimensionality n of the underlying kernel space is extremely large, as for Tree Kernels [2]. Kernel functions are used by learning algorithms, such as SVM, to operate only implicitly on instances in the kernel space, by never accessing their explicit definition.

Imagine we apply the projection function Φ over all examples from $\mathcal{D}$ to derive representations $\boldsymbol{x}$ being the rows of the matrix X. The Gram matrix can be computed as $G = XX^\top$, with each single element corresponding to $G_{ij} = \Phi(o_i)\Phi(o_j) = K(o_i, o_j)$. The aim of the Nyström method is to derive a new low-dimensional embedding $\tilde{x}$ in a l-dimensional space, with $l \ll n$ so that $\tilde{G} = \tilde{X}\tilde{X}^\top$ and $\tilde{G} \approx G$. $\tilde{G}$ is an approximation of G that is obtained by using a subset of l columns of the matrix, i.e., a subselection $L \subset \mathcal{D}$ of the available examples, called *landmarks*. Suppose we randomly sample l columns of G, and let $C \in \mathbb{R}^{|D| \times l}$ be the matrix of these sampled columns. Then, we can rearrange the columns and rows of G and define $X = [X_1 \ X_2]$ such that:

$$G = XX^\top = \begin{bmatrix} W & X_1^\top X_2 \\ X_2^\top X_1 & X_2^\top X_2 \end{bmatrix}$$

$$\text{and } C = \begin{bmatrix} W \\ X_2^\top X_1 \end{bmatrix} \tag{1}$$

where $W = X_1^\top X_1$, i.e., the subset of G that only considers landmarks. The Nyström approximation can be defined as:

$$G \approx \tilde{G} = CW^\dagger C^\top \tag{2}$$

where $W^\dagger$ denotes the Moore-Penrose inverse of W. The Singular Value Decomposition (SVD) is used to obtain $W^\dagger$ as it follows. First, W is decomposed so that $W = USV^\top$, where U and V are both orthogonal matrices, and S is a diagonal matrix containing the (non-zero) singular values of W on its diagonal. Since W is symmetric and positive definite $W = USU^\top$. Then $W^\dagger = US^{-1}U^\top = US^{-\frac{1}{2}}S^{-\frac{1}{2}}U^\top$ and the Eq. 2 can be rewritten as

$$G \approx \tilde{G} = CUS^{-\frac{1}{2}}S^{-\frac{1}{2}}U^\top C^\top$$
$$= (CUS^{-\frac{1}{2}})(CUS^{-\frac{1}{2}})^\top = \tilde{X}\tilde{X}^\top \tag{3}$$

Given an input example $o \in \mathcal{D}$, a new low-dimensional representation $\tilde{x}$ can be thus determined by considering the corresponding item of C as

$$\tilde{x} = \Theta(o) = cUS^{-\frac{1}{2}} \tag{4}$$

where c is the vector whose dimensions contain the evaluations of the kernel function between o and each landmark $o_j \in L$. Therefore, the method produces l-dimensional vectors.

Complexity. If k is the average number of basic operations required during a single kernel computation, the overall cost of a single projection is $\mathcal{O}(kl + l^2)$, where the first term corresponds to the cost of generating the vector c, while the second term is needed for the matrix multiplications in Eq. 4. Typically, the number of landmarks l ranges from hundreds to few thousands and, for complex kernels (such as Tree Kernels) the projection cost can be reduced to $\mathcal{O}(kl)$. Several policies have been defined to determine the best selection of landmarks to reduce the Gram Matrix approximation error. In this work the uniform sampling without replacement is adopted, as suggested by [23], where this policy has been theoretically and empirically shown to achieve results comparable with other (more complex) selection policies.

3.2   A Kernel-Based Deep Architecture

The above introduced Nyström representation $\tilde{x}$ of any input example o is linear and can be adopted to feed a neural network architecture. We assume a labeled dataset $\mathcal{L} = \{(o, y) \mid o \in \mathcal{D}, y \in Y\}$ being available, where o refers to a generic instance and y is its associated class. In this section, we discuss the Kernel-based Deep Architecture (KDA) presented in [10]. It is a Multi-Layer Perceptron (MLP) architecture, with a specific Nyström layer based on the Nyström embeddings of Eq. 4. KDA has an *input layer*, a *Nyström layer*, a possibly empty sequence of non-linear *hidden layers* and a final *classification layer*, which produces the output.

The *input* layer corresponds to the input vector c, i.e., the row of the C matrix associated to an example o. Notice that, for adopting the KDA, the values of the matrix C should be all available. In the training stage, these values are typically computed once and accessed several times using a caching mechanism. During the classification stage, the c vector corresponding to an example o is directly computed by l kernel computations between o and each one of the l landmarks.

The input layer is mapped to the *Nyström* layer, through the projection in Eq. 4. Notice that the embedding provides also the proper weights, defined by $US^{-\frac{1}{2}}$, so that the mapping can be expressed through the Nyström matrix $H_{Ny} = US^{-\frac{1}{2}}$: it corresponds to a pre-trained stage derived through SVD, as discussed in Sect. 3.1. Equation 4 provides a static definition for H_{Ny} whose weights can be left invariant during the neural network training. However, the values of H_{Ny} can be made available for the standard back-propagation adjustments applied for training[1]. Formally, the low-dimensional embedding of an input example o, is $\tilde{x} = c\,H_{Ny} = c\,US^{-\frac{1}{2}}$.

The resulting outcome $\tilde{x}$ is the input to one or more non-linear *hidden* layers. Each t-th hidden layer is realized through a matrix $H_t \in \mathbb{R}^{h_{t-1} \times h_t}$ and a bias vector $b_t \in \mathbb{R}^{1 \times h_t}$, whereas h_t denotes the desired hidden layer dimensionality. Clearly, given that $H_{Ny} \in \mathbb{R}^{l \times l}$, $h_0 = l$. The first hidden layer in fact receives in input $\tilde{x} = cH_{Ny}$, that corresponds to $t = 0$ layer input $x_0 = \tilde{x}$ and its computation is formally expressed by $x_1 = f(x_0 H_1 + b_1)$, where f is a non-linear activation function. The generic t-th layer is modeled as:

$$x_t = f(x_{t-1}H_t + b_t) \tag{5}$$

The final layer of KDA is the *classification layer*, realized through the output matrix H_O and the output bias vector b_O. Their dimensionality depends on the dimensionality of the last hidden layer (called O_{-1}) and the number $|Y|$ of different classes, i.e., $H_O \in \mathbb{R}^{h_{O-1} \times |Y|}$ and $b_O \in \mathbb{R}^{1 \times |Y|}$, respectively. In particular, this layer computes a linear classification function with a softmax operator, so that $\hat{y} = softmax(x_{O_{-1}} H_O + b_O)$.

In order to avoid over-fitting, two different regularization schemes are applied. First, the dropout is applied to the input x_t of each hidden layer $(t \geq 1)$ and to the input $x_{O_{-1}}$ of the final classifier. Second, a L_2 regularization is applied to the norm of each layer[2] H_t and H_O.

Finally, the KDA is trained by optimizing a loss function made of the sum of two factors: first, the cross-entropy function between the gold classes and the predicted ones; second the L_2 regularization, whose importance is regulated by a meta-parameter λ. The final loss function is thus

$$L(y, \hat{y}) = \sum_{(o,y) \in \mathcal{L}} y \, log(\hat{y}) + \lambda \sum_{H \in \{H_t\} \cup \{H_O\}} ||H||^2$$

---

[1] In our preliminary experiments, adjustments to the H_{Ny} matrix have been tested, but it was not beneficial.

[2] The input layer and the Nyström layer are not modified during the learning process, and they are not regularized.

where $\hat{y}$ are the softmax values computed by the network and y are the true one-hot encoding values associated with the example from the labeled training dataset $\mathcal{L}$.

4   Empirical Investigation

To study the impact of different kernels in the investigated KDA architecture, we perform several experiments on the Question Classification task by varying the KDA model in terms of number of landmarks and kernel functions.

Task and Data Description. Question Classification (QC) is the task of mapping a question into a closed set of answer types in a Question Answering system. We used the UIUC dataset [24], including a training and test set of $5,452$ and 500 questions, respectively, organized in 6 classes (like ENTITY or HUMAN). In this task, TKs resulted very effective, as shown in [14].

Experimental Setting. We implemented the Nyström projector using KeLP [3] [25]. The neural network has been implemented in Tensorflow[4], with 2 hidden layers whose dimensionality corresponds to the number of involved Nyström landmarks. The *rectified linear unit* is the non-linear activation function in each layer. The dropout has been applied in each hidden layer and in the final classification layer. The values of the dropout parameter and the λ parameter of the L_2-regularization have been selected from a set of values via grid-search. The Adam optimizer with a learning rate of 0.001 has been applied to minimize the loss function, with a multi-epoch (500) training, each fed with batches of size 256. We adopted an early stop strategy, where we selected the best model according to the performance over the development set. Every performance measure is obtained against a specific sampling of the Nyström landmarks. Hereafter, we report the averaged results of 5 of these samplings.

The input vectors for the KDA are modeled using the Nyström method (with different kernels) based on a number of landmarks ranging from 100 to 1000. We tried different kernels with increasing expressiveness:

- BOWK: a liner kernel applied over bag-of-words vectors having lemmas as dimensions. It provides a pure lexical similarity.
- PTK: the partial tree kernel over the GRCT representations. It provides a lexical and syntactic similarity.
- SPTK: the smoothed partial tree kernel over the GRCT representations. It improves the reasoning of the PTK by including the semantic information derived by word embeddings.
- CSPTK: the compositionally smoothed partial tree kernel over the GRCT representations. It adds the semantic compositionality to the SPTK.

---

[3] http://www.kelp-ml.org/.
[4] https://www.tensorflow.org/.

The lexical vectors used in the SPTK and CSPTK are generated using the Word2vec tool with a Skip-gram model. The tree kernels have default parameters (i.e., $\mu = \lambda = 0.4$).

Results. Figure 3 shows the impact of different kernels in the proposed KDA model. Curves are computed by changing the number of landmarks in the Nyström formulation.

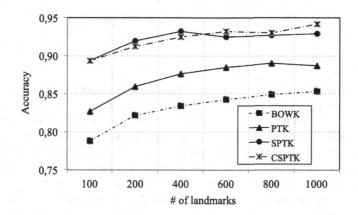

Fig. 3. Accuracy measure curves w.r.t. the number of landmarks.

The increasing complexity of the investigated kernels directly reflects on the accuracy achieved by the KDA. The BOWK is the simplest kernel and obtain poor results: it needs 800 landmarks to reach 85% of accuracy.

The contribution of the syntactic information provided by tree kernels is straightforward. The PTK achieves about 90% of accuracy starting from 600 landmarks.

This results are significantly improved by SPTK and CSPTK when the semantic information of the word embeddings is employed: even when only 100 landmarks are used, the KDA using these kernels can obtain 90% of accuracy and overcomes 94% with more landmarks. Table 1 shows that KDA with CSPTK also improves the accuracy achieved by the state-of-the-art Convolutional Neural Network (CNN) described in [26].

These results demonstrate that (*i*) it is possible to improve the KDA results by simply adopting more expressive kernel functions; (*ii*) the accuracy vs complexity tradeoff of the KDA can be easily controlled by varying the number of landmarks.

Computational Savings. Regarding the saving that can be achieved by the KDA, we compared this solution with a traditional SVM formulation (such as the one provided by [22]) fed with the investigated kernels. The resulting model includes 3,933 support vectors for the BOWK (87% of accuracy) 3,925 for the PTK (91% of accuracy), 3,659 for the SPTK (94% of accuracy) and 3,873 for the

Table 1. Results of the KDA on the QC task with different kernels and number of landmarks.

Model	Kernel	#Landmarks					
		100	200	400	600	800	1000
KDA	BOWK	78.8%	82.2%	83.4%	84.2%	84.9%	85.3%
	PTK	82.7%	86.0%	87.7%	88.5%	89.0%	88.7%
	SPTK	89.4%	92.0%	93.2%	92.5%	92.7%	93.0%
	CSPTK	88.5%	92.2%	93.7%	**94.3%**	94.3%	94.2%
CNN	-				93.6%		

CSPTK (95% of accuracy). In a traditional kernel-based method, the number of support vectors corresponds to the number of kernel operations required to classify each new input test instance (here questions). This cost is reduced in a KDA as it requires only to evaluate the kernel function between the test instance and each landmark in the Nyström projection function. In Table 2 computational saving are shown in terms of the percentage of avoided kernel computations with respect to the application of the traditional SVM to each test instance. As discussed in [10] the percentage of avoided kernel computation is impressive, as it is reduced for each kernel from about 97% (for 100 landmarks) to about 74% (for 1,000) landmarks.

Table 2. Saving of the KDA on the QC task with different kernels and number of landmarks with respect to a traditional kernel-based classification.

Kernel	#Landmarks					
	100	200	400	600	800	1000
BOWK	97.5%	94.9%	89.8%	84.7%	79.7%	74.6%
PTK	97.5%	94.9%	89.8%	84.7%	79.6%	74.5%
SPTK	97.3%	94.5%	89.1%	83.6%	78.1%	72.7%
CSPTK	97.4%	94.8%	89.7%	84.5%	79.3%	74.2%

5   Conclusions

In this work, the Kernel-based Deep Architecture recently proposed in [10] is studied along the aspects related to linguistic expressiveness of the involved kernels. KDA corresponds to a methodology aiming at embedding structured linguistic information within a NN, according to mathematically rich semantic similarity models, based on a kernel function. KDA is general as it can be applied to any kernel: its application to structured data, such as trees, is particularly interesting in NLP as it allows to map trees into dense vectors according to the Nyström methodology. As the NN can be effectively applied to capture non-linearities over these representations, a KDA is overall capable of improving generalization at the reasonable complexity bounded by the Nyström parameter (i.e., the number of landmarks).

The impact of the Nyström linear approximation applied to feed a general well-known neural network architecture, i.e., a multilayer perceptron has been already shown in [10]. No specific manual feature engineering nor any ad-hoc network architectures are shown necessary to achieve high accuracy level and impressive computational gains. This architecture is largely applicable, and it was shown successful in achieving state-of-the-art performances in three different NLP tasks [10].

In this work, we investigated if expressive representations due to semantic kernel functions of increasing complexity are correlated with better performances in semantic tasks. This allows to demonstrate that neural learning within the kernel space can be effectively carried by the KDA formulation.

The experimental outcomes have been produced in a Question Classification task, over a well known data set for which state-of-the-art performances were achieved through the use of SVMs based on compositional semantic tree kernels (i.e., the CSPTK discussed in [21]). All results confirm that increasingly expressive kernel functions, even operating on the same training set, are able to improve the performances of a KDA, based on the same NN architecture. This proves that different levels of linguistic generalization are consistently expressed by kernels, so that the corresponding Nyström reconstruction is an expressive, efficient and scalable linear representation for complex semantic phenomena. This paves the way for a variety of application to linguistic inference tasks whereas structured kernels as tree kernels can be systematically adopted to trigger neural learning, without resorting to task-specific architectures.

More experimentation is certainly useful to validate the KDA property across diverse natural languages and tasks. In particular, the adoption of tree (or graph) kernels over hybrid information networks (mixing knowledge and lexical graphs) and the use of a KDA for injecting (knowledge) constraints within a neural network learning process is a relevant target for short term research.

References

1. Cancedda, N., Gaussier, É., Goutte, C., Renders, J.M.: Word-sequence kernels. J. Mach. Learn. Res. **3**, 1059–1082 (2003)
2. Collins, M., Duffy, N.: Convolution kernels for natural language. In: Proceedings of Neural Information Processing Systems (NIPS 2001), pp. 625–632 (2001)
3. Moschitti, A., Pighin, D., Basili, R.: Tree kernels for semantic role labeling. Comput. Linguist. **34**(2), 193–224 (2008)
4. Vapnik, V.N.: Statistical Learning Theory. Wiley, Hoboken (1998)
5. Shawe-Taylor, J., Cristianini, N.: Kernel Methods for Pattern Analysis. Cambridge University Press, New York (2004)

6. Socher, R., Perelygin, A., Wu, J., Chuang, J., Manning, C.D., Ng, A., Potts, C.: Recursive deep models for semantic compositionality over a sentiment treebank. In: Proceedings of EMNLP 2013 (2013)

7. Hochreiter, S., Schmidhuber, J.: Long short-term memory. Neural Comput. **9**(8), 1735–1780 (1997)

8. LeCun, Y., Bottou, L., Bengio, Y., Haffner, P.: Gradient-based learning applied to document recognition. Proc. IEEE **86**(11), 2278–2324 (1998)

9. Levy, O., Goldberg, Y., Dagan, I.: Improving distributional similarity with lessons learned from word embeddings. Trans. Assoc. Comput. Linguist. **3**, 211–225 (2015). https://transacl.org/ojs/index.php/tacl/article/view/570

10. Croce, D., Filice, S., Castellucci, G., Basili, R.: Deep learning in semantic kernel spaces. In: Proceedings of the 55th Annual Meeting of the Association for Computational Linguistics, pp. 345–354 (2017). http://aclanthology.coli.uni-saarland.de/pdf/P/P17/pp.17-1032.pdf

11. Croce, D., Basili, R.: Large-scale kernel-based language learning through the ensemble Nyström methods. In: Ferro, N., Crestani, F., Moens, M.-F., Mothe, J., Silvestri, F., Di Nunzio, G.M., Hauff, C., Silvello, G. (eds.) ECIR 2016. LNCS, vol. 9626, pp. 100–112. Springer, Cham (2016). doi:10.1007/978-3-319-30671-1_8

12. Severyn, A., Nicosia, M., Moschitti, A.: Building structures from classifiers for passage reranking. In: CIKM 2013, pp. 969–978. ACM, New York (2013)

13. Filice, S., Croce, D., Moschitti, A., Basili, R.: KeLP at SemEval-2016 task 3: learning semantic relations between questions and comments. In: Proceedings of SemEval 2016, June 2016

14. Zhang, D., Lee, W.S.: Question classification using support vector machines. In: Proceedings of the 26th Annual International ACM SIGIR Conference on Research and Development in information retrieval, pp. 26–32. ACM Press (2003)

15. Haussler, D.: Convolution kernels on discrete structures. Technical report UCS-CRL-99-10. University of California, Santa Cruz (1999)

16. Croce, D., Moschitti, A., Basili, R.: Structured lexical similarity via convolution kernels on dependency trees. In: Proceedings of EMNLP 2011, pp. 1034–1046 (2011)

17. Filice, S., Da San Martino, G., Moschitti, A.: Structural representations for learning relations between pairs of texts. In: Proceedings of ACL 2015, Beijing, China, pp. 1003–1013. http://www.aclweb.org/anthology/pp.15-1097

18. Moschitti, A.: Efficient convolution kernels for dependency and constituent syntactic trees. In: Fürnkranz, J., Scheffer, T., Spiliopoulou, M. (eds.) ECML 2006. LNCS (LNAI), vol. 4212, pp. 318–329. Springer, Heidelberg (2006). doi:10.1007/11871842_32

19. Mikolov, T., Chen, K., Corrado, G., Dean, J.: Efficient estimation of word representations in vector space. CoRR abs/1301.3781 (2013)

20. Sahlgren, M.: The word-space model. Ph.D. thesis, Stockholm University (2006)

21. Annesi, P., Croce, D., Basili, R.: Semantic compositionality in tree kernels. In: Proceedings of CIKM 2014. ACM (2014)

22. Chang, C.C., Lin, C.J.: LIBSVM: a library for support vector machines. ACM Trans. Intell. Syst. Technol. **2**(3), 27:1–27:27 (2011)

23. Kumar, S., Mohri, M., Talwalkar, A.: Sampling methods for the Nyström method. J. Mach. Learn. Res. **13**, 981–1006 (2012)

24. Li, X., Roth, D.: Learning question classifiers: the role of semantic information. Nat. Lang. Eng. **12**(3), 229–249 (2006)

25. Filice, S., Castellucci, G., Croce, D., Basili, R.: KeLP: a kernel-based learning platform for natural language processing. In: Proceedings of ACL-IJCNLP 2015 System Demonstrations, Beijing, China, pp. 19–24, July 2015. http://www.aclweb.org/anthology/pp.15-4004

26. Kim, Y.: Convolutional neural networks for sentence classification. In: Proceedings EMNLP 2014, Doha, Qatar, pp. 1746–1751, October 2014

Converse-Et-Impera: Exploiting Deep Learning and Hierarchical Reinforcement Learning for Conversational Recommender Systems

Claudio Greco, Alessandro Suglia, Pierpaolo Basile[✉], and Giovanni Semeraro

Department of Computer Science, University of Bari Aldo Moro, Bari, Italy
claudiogaetanogreco@gmail.com, alessandro.suglia@gmail.com,
{pierpaolo.basile,giovanni.semeraro}@uniba.it

Abstract. In this paper, we propose a framework based on *Hierarchical Reinforcement Learning* for dialogue management in a *Conversational Recommender System* scenario. The framework splits the dialogue into more manageable tasks whose achievement corresponds to goals of the dialogue with the user. The framework consists of a meta-controller, which receives the user utterance and understands which goal should pursue, and a controller, which exploits a goal-specific representation to generate an answer composed by a sequence of tokens. The modules are trained using a two-stage strategy based on a preliminary *Supervised Learning* stage and a successive *Reinforcement Learning* stage.

1 Introduction

During their lives, humans need to solve tasks of varying complexity which require to satisfy different types of information needs, ranging from simple questions about common facts (whose answers can be found in encyclopedias) to more sophisticated ones in which they need to know what movie to watch during a romantic evening or what is the recipe for a good lasagne. These tasks can be solved by an intelligent agent able to answer questions formulated in a proper way, eventually considering user context and preferences.

Conversational Recommender Systems (CRS) assist online users in their information-seeking and decision making tasks by supporting an interactive process [17] which could be goal oriented. The goal to reach consists in starting general and, through a series of interaction cycles, narrowing down the user interests until the desired item is obtained [24].

Generally speaking, a dialogue can be defined as a sequence of turns, each one consisting of an action performed by a speaker or by a hearer. A CRS can be considered a goal-driven dialogue system whose main goal, due to its complexity, can be solved effectively by dividing it in simpler goals. Indeed, a dialogue with this kind of system can include different phases, such as chatting, answering questions about specific facts and providing suggestions enriched by explanations, with the aim of satisfying the user information needs during the whole dialogue. The *Hierarchical Reinforcement Learning (HRL)* literature has

© Springer International Publishing AG 2017
F. Esposito et al. (Eds.): AI*IA 2017, LNAI 10640, pp. 372–386, 2017.
https://doi.org/10.1007/978-3-319-70169-1_28

been consistently shown that, given the right decomposition, problems can be learned and solved more efficiently, that is to say in less time and with less resources [19]. The most popular HRL framework, called the *Options* framework [29], explicitly uses subgoals to build temporal abstractions, which allow faster learning and planning. An option can be conceptualized as a sort of macro-action which includes a list of starting conditions, a policy and a termination condition.

In this work we present a CRS called *Converse-Et-Impera (CEI)* which leverages ideas presented in [12] to design a framework able to manage the different phases of a dialogue. The main contributions of our paper are the following:

1. a framework based on HRL in which each CRS goal is modeled as a *goal-specific representation module* which learns a useful representation for the given goal;
2. an *answer generation module* leveraging the learned *goal-specific representations* and the user preferences to generate appropriate answers.

2 Methodology

A dialogue can be considered as a temporal process because the assessment of how "good" an action is depends on the options and opportunities available while the dialogue progresses further. For this reason, action choice requires foresight and long-term planning to complete a satisfying dialogue for the user. We employ the mathematical framework of *Markov Decision Processes (MDP)* [2] represented by states $s \in S$, actions $a \in A$ and a transition function $T : (s, a) \rightarrow s$. An agent operating in this framework receives a state s from the environment and can take an action a, which results in a new state s'. We define the reward function as $F : S \rightarrow \mathbb{R}$. The objective of the agent is to maximize F over long periods of time.

Our work takes inspiration from [12] to design a framework able to manage the different phases of a goal-driven dialogue by learning a stochastic policy π_g which defines a probability distribution over the agent goals $g \in G$ given a state $s \in S$. The agent goals can be considered as high-level actions, thus they can be consistently modeled by the *Options Framework* [29]. In fact, the completion of a goal g can be achieved by a temporally extended course of actions, starting from a given timestep t and ending after some number of steps k. A module of the framework called *meta-controller* is responsible of selecting a goal g_t in a given state s_t. Moreover, an additional module called *controller* selects an action a_t given the state s_t and the current goal g_t following a goal-specific policy π_{ga}, which defines a probability distribution over the actions that the agent is able to execute to satisfy the goal g_t. Given the two modules, an *external critic* evaluates the reward signal f_t which the environment generates for the *meta-controller*, while an *internal critic* is responsible for evaluating whether a goal is reached and providing an appropriate reward $r_t(g)$ to the controller. So, the objective function for the meta-controller is to maximize the cumulative external reward $F_t = \sum_{t'=t}^{\infty} \gamma^{t'-t} f_{t'}$, where γ is the reward discount factor. Similarly, the objective of the controller is to optimize the cumulative intrinsic reward $R_t(g) = \sum_{t'=t}^{\infty} \gamma_t^{t'-t} r_{t'}(g)$.

During a dialogue, in a given timestep t, the system receives a user utterance $x = \langle x_1, x_2, \ldots, x_m \rangle$ and the user identifier $u \in U$. Each word x_i is encoded in a vector representation (embedding) $\boldsymbol{x}_i$ by using a lookup operation on the word embedding matrix $\boldsymbol{W}_w \in \mathbb{R}^{|V| \times d_w}$ and the user identifier u is encoded in an embedding $\boldsymbol{u}$ by using a lookup operation on the user embedding matrix $\boldsymbol{W}_u \in \mathbb{R}^{|U| \times d_u}$, where d_w is the word embedding size and d_u is the user embedding size. The sequence of word embeddings $\boldsymbol{x}_i$ is encoded using a bidirectional *Recurrent Neural Network (RNN)* encoder with *Gated Recurrent Units (GRU)* as in [26] which represents each word x_i as the concatenation of a forward encoding $\overrightarrow{\mathbf{h}}_i \in \mathbb{R}^h$ and a backward encoding $\overleftarrow{\mathbf{h}}_i \in \mathbb{R}^h$. From now on, we denote the contextual representation for the word x_i by $\tilde{\mathbf{x}}_i \in \mathbb{R}^{2h}$. In order to allow the system to keep track of the relevant information until the dialogue turn t, we equip it with an *RNN* with *GRU* units which encodes $\tilde{\boldsymbol{x}_m}$ to generate a representation of the dialogue turn called dialogue state $\boldsymbol{d} \in \mathbb{R}^{d_d}$.

We define the *meta-controller* policy π_{MC} as a feedforward neural network which receives in input the dialogue state $\boldsymbol{d}$ to predict the goal $g \in G$. Formally, the meta-controller is defined by the following equation:

$$\pi_{MC} = P(g|x, u) = \text{softmax}(\boldsymbol{d}W_{MC}), \tag{1}$$

where softmax(y) is the *softmax* activation function applied to the vector y to obtain a probability distribution over the set of possible goals G and $W_{MC} \in \mathbb{R}^{d_d \times |G|}$ is a weight matrix.

Due to the various requirements of each goal, differently from [12], we design a *goal-specific representation module* which represents relevant aspects of the current state exploited by the agent to complete the current goal. Given the current goal g, the system encodes it in $\boldsymbol{g}$ by using a lookup operation on the goal embedding matrix $\boldsymbol{W}_g \in \mathbb{R}^{|G| \times d_g}$, where d_g is the goal embedding size. After that, the system asks the *goal-specific representation module* ϕ_g for a score vector $\boldsymbol{z} \in \mathbb{R}^{|V|}$ which represents the agent attention towards specific tokens in the vocabulary V. In the implementation of the framework we support two different goals which belong to the set G namely *chitchat* and *recommendation*. Therefore, we suppose that each conversation can be divided in turns which can be associated to one of the two available goals. For each of them, we provide a *goal-specific representation module* which generates the score vector $\boldsymbol{z}$ according to a defined strategy. The *chitchat* module is intended to support general conversation utterances (e.g., "Hey", "My name is John", etc.) so it simply returns a vector of zeros as a result of the fact that it has not focused its attention on any token. In order to complete the *recommendation* goal, we have designed a module called *IMNAMAP* presented in [9] and inspired to [26], which is able to generate a score vector by applying an attention mechanism over multiple documents retrieved from a knowledge base to uncover a possible inference chain that starts at the query and the documents and leads to the attention scores.

In order to fully support the user during the conversation, the system should be able to exploit information gathered during previous turns that can be useful in subsequent turns. For instance, during a given turn an agent may know the preferred movie director by the user and in a successive turn needs to leverage it in order to suggest relevant items to him. For this reason, the system applies an *intra-dialogue attention mechanism* to refine the score vector z_t according to z_k where $k = 1, \ldots, t$. In particular, each z_k is concatenated with g_t and d_t and given in input to a feedforward neural network in order to estimate a relevance score $r_{t,k}$. Then, a probability distribution over the score vectors is generated using $\tilde{r}_t = softmax([r_{t,1}, \ldots, r_{t,t}])$. Finally, the refined score vector is evaluated as $\tilde{z}_t = \sum_{k=1}^{t} \tilde{r}_{t,k} z_k$. In this way, we give to the agent the capability to understand the most relevant information extracted during the conversation.

The *controller* exploits the refined score vector $\tilde{z}_t$ to generate a sequence of tokens $a = \langle a_1, \ldots, a_n \rangle$ leveraging the *Sequence-to-sequence* framework [28] (also called *Encoder-Decoder* [6]). The *Sequence-to-sequence* framework consists of two different modules: an *RNN encoder* which represents the input sequence and an *RNN decoder* able to decode the output sequence using a context vector c. In this work, the context vector c is represented by the final state of the encoded user utterance x_m^-. The RNN decoder generates latent representations $\langle \tilde{a}_1, \ldots, \tilde{a}_n \rangle$ for the system response using *Persona-based GRU* units [13] to exploit the user preferences in the text generation task. A 2-layer feedforward neural network receives in input $\tilde{a}_i$ and $\tilde{z}_t$ to generate a probability distribution over the tokens of the vocabulary V, for each token a_i. Formally, the feedforward neural network is defined by the following equation:

$$\tilde{a}_i = softmax([a_i, (\tilde{z}_t W_{ih})] W_{ho}), \tag{2}$$

where $W_{ih} \in \mathbb{R}^{|V| \times d_{ih}}$ and $W_{ho} \in \mathbb{R}^{(h+d_{ih}) \times |V|}$ are weight matrices, d_{ih} is the input-to-hidden layer size and $[\cdot, \cdot]$ is the concatenation operator.

Inspired by [25,33], we develop a two-stage training strategy for our conversational agent composed by a preliminary *Supervised Learning (SL)* stage and a successive *Reinforcement Learning (RL)* stage. The motivation behind the adoption of the above-mentioned training strategy is to take into account historical data collected from previous interactions between a user and a system, which can be used to learn an initial effective policy for the meta-controller and the controller which can be further improved by the successive RL stage.

In the SL stage, the agent learns to replicate the conversations which belong to a given dataset by minimizing a loss function which takes into account both the meta-controller and the controller errors with regard to the training data. Given a dataset D_{MC} which consists of N dialogs, each of them composed by T turns $(x_{i,j}, u_i, g_{i,j})$, we define the supervised loss function for the meta-controller policy π_{MC} as follows:

$$L_{MC}(D_{MC}) = \frac{1}{N} \sum_{i=1}^{N} \sum_{j=1}^{T} CE(g_{i,j}, \pi_{MC}(x_{i,j}, u_i)), \tag{3}$$

where CE is the cross-entropy loss function which is used in order to evaluate the error in the meta-controller prediction $\pi_{MC}(x_{i,j}, u_i)$ with regard to the target goal $g_{i,j}$. Given a dataset D_C which consists of N dialogs, each of them composed by T turns $(x_{i,j}, u_i, g_{i,j}, (a_{i,j,1}, \ldots, a_{i,j,n}))$, we define the supervised loss function for the controller policy π_C as follows:

$$L_C(D_C) = \frac{1}{N} \sum_{i=1}^{N} \sum_{j=1}^{T} \sum_{k=1}^{n} \omega(a_{i,j,k}) CE(a_{i,j,k}, \pi_C(x_{i,j}, u_i, g_{i,j})) \qquad (4)$$

where CE is the cross-entropy loss function and $\omega(y_{i,k,j})$ is a function which defines a weight associated to a token $a_{i,j,k}$ equal to 2 if the position j refers to the last utterance in position $T - 1$ and $a_{i,j,k} \in E$, where E is the set of entities defined in the dataset (e.g. movies, actors, ...), 1 otherwise. The function ω weights more errors done on generated suggestions. The meta-controller and the controller are jointly trained by minimizing a loss function L_a which linearly combines the two loss functions and applies L_2-regularization on it as follows:

$$L_a(D_{MC}, D_C) = L_{MC}(D_{MC}) + L_C(D_C) + \alpha L_2(\boldsymbol{W}_w, \boldsymbol{W}_u, \boldsymbol{W}_g). \qquad (5)$$

A joint training has the benefit to refine the shared representations employed by the agent to represent the user utterances, the user embedding and the goal embedding in order to obtain good performance in both tasks.

Given a set of experiences D_{MC} which consists of N dialogs, each of them composed by T turns $(x_{i,j}, u_i, g_{i,j}, R_{i,j})$, we define a loss function based on *REIN-FORCE* [31] for the meta-controller policy π_{MC} as follows:

$$\lambda(i, j) = \varepsilon_{MC} E(\pi_{MC}(g_{i,j}|x_{i,j}, u_i))$$

$$L_{MC}(D_{MC}) = -\frac{1}{N} \sum_{i=1}^{N} \sum_{j=1}^{T} \log(\pi_{MC}(g_{i,j}|x_{i,j}, u_i))$$

$$\cdot (R_{i,j} - b(x_{i,j}, u_i)) + \lambda(i, j) \qquad (6)$$

$$+ \alpha L_2(\boldsymbol{W}_w, \boldsymbol{W}_u, \boldsymbol{W}_g),$$

where $R_{i,j}$ is the discounted cumulative reward for the current state, ε_{MC} is a weight associated to the entropy regularizer $E(\pi_{MC})$ and $b(x_{i,j}, u_i)$ is the *baseline* implemented as a feedforward neural network which estimates the expected future return from the current state received by the agent. Given a set of experiences D_C which consists of N dialogs, each of them composed by T turns $(x_{i,j}, u_i, g_{i,j}, (R_{i,j,1}, \ldots, R_{i,j,n}), (a_{i,j,1}, \ldots, a_{i,j,n}))$, we adopt the loss function proposed in [34] for the controller policy as follows:

$$\rho(i, j, k) = \log(\pi_C(y_{i,j,k}|(y_{i,j,k-1}, \ldots, y_{i,j,1}), x_{i,j}, u_i, g_{i,j}))$$

$$\sigma(i, j, k) = (R_{i,j,k} - b(y_{i,j,k}, x_{i,j}, u_i, g_{i,j}))$$

$$\lambda(i, j, k) = \varepsilon_C E(\pi_C(y_{i,j,k}|(y_{i,j,k-1}, \ldots, y_{i,j,1}), x_{i,j}, u_i, g_{i,j}))$$

$$L_C(D_C) = -\frac{1}{N} \sum_{i=1}^{N} \sum_{j=1}^{T} \sum_{k=1}^{n} \rho(i, j, k)\sigma(i, j, k) + \lambda(i, j, k) \qquad (7)$$

$$+ \alpha L_2(\boldsymbol{W}_w, \boldsymbol{W}_u, \boldsymbol{W}_g)$$

where $R_{i,j,k}$ is the cumulative reward for the current state, ε_C is a weight associated to the entropy regularizer $E(\pi_C)$ and $b(y_{i,j,k}, x_{i,j}, u_i, g_{i,j})$ is the *baseline* implemented as a feedforward neural network which estimates the expected future return from the current state received by the agent. The entropy regularization is considered in the RL community as another relevant optimization trick for Policy-based methods which is applied in order to prevent premature convergence to sub-optimal policy and improve exploration [32].

3   Experimental Evaluation

The experimental evaluation aim is to evaluate the performance of the developed agent in the generation of accurate suggestions and appropriate response to the user utterances. In order to achieve our objective, we defined a general procedure that can be used on classical recommender system datasets to generate a goal-oriented dialogue (Table 1) exploiting user preferences. The details of the defined procedure are reported in [27].

Table 1. Dialogue generated from the *MovieLens 1M* dataset. To help reading, *Wikidata* ids have been replaced with the corresponding entities.

Agent	Utterance	Goal
user	Hey	chitchat
bot	What is your name?	chitchat
user	I am Sofia	chitchat
bot	How old are you?	chitchat
user	I am 25	chitchat
bot	What is your occupation?	chitchat
user	sales/marketing	chitchat
bot	Which are your favourite movies?	recommendation
user	I love Speed	recommendation
bot	I suggest you Erin_Brockovich Witness Pocahontas Four_Weddings_and_a_Funeral Anna_and_the_King. Do you like them?	recommendation
user	I hate them	chitchat
bot	What are your favourite directors?	recommendation
user	I like John_Waters	recommendation
bot	What are your favourite actors?	recommendation
user	I like Josef_Sommer Wade_Williams Marg_Helgenberger Jeroen_Krabb	recommendation
bot	What genres do you like?	recommendation
user	My favourite genres are teen_film romance_film biographical_film	recommendation
bot	I suggest you Erin_Brockovich Witness Ever_After Simply_Irresistible Hairspray. Do you like them?	recommendation
user	I like them	chitchat
bot	I am glad that you like them	chitchat

We applied the dialogue generation procedure on two well-known recommender system datasets such as *Movielens 1M (ML1M)* [10] and *Movie Tweetings (MT)* [8]. For *ML1M* we leveraged the available demographic information associated to the user in order to extend the generated conversation with useful contextual questions about the user name, age and occupation. For each dataset, we retrieved information associated to the properties *director (wdt:P57)*, *cast member (wdt:P161)* and *genre (wdt:P136)* associated to the items coming from the *Wikidata* knowledge base. The generated datasets *ML1M* and *MT* are composed of $157, 135$ and $48, 933$ dialogs whose mean lengths are 14.78 and 6.64, respectively. In addition, ML1M contains $19, 039$ tokens, while MT contains $53, 988$ tokens.

In order to assess the effectiveness of the two-stage training strategy, we designed an evaluation procedure in which we first evaluated the *CEI* model after the SL training and then we evaluated the trained model after the successive RL training to demonstrate the improvement of the model performance.

3.1   Supervised Learning Setting

In the SL stage the *CEI* model was trained on a dataset obtained by removing the utterances corresponding to the "refine" step from the generated dialogues because it should replicate the dialogues ignoring the additional "refine" steps. Intuitively, we want that the model avoids to learn from incorrect dialogue turns.

The effectiveness of the model was evaluated against some baselines such as Random, which is a random hierarchical agent which generates random goals and utterances composed by random tokens, and Seq2seq, which is an agent able to generate a response exploiting the popular *Sequence-to-sequence* framework trained through SL on the generated dialogues. The comparison with Random was performed in order to prove that the designed agent is able to learn to replicate the training dialogues, while the comparison with Seq2seq was designed to demonstrate the effectiveness of the proposed architecture with respect to a classical *Sequence-to-sequence* model which has been adopted in different conversational agents [30]. The current implementation of the Seq2seq model had all the weights initialized from a normal distribution $\mathcal{N}(0, 0.05)$, employed a bidirectional RNN with *GRU* units to encode the user utterance and applies a dropout of 0.5 on the RNN encoder input and output connections [35]. The word embedding size d_w was fixed to 50 and the GRU output size was fixed to 256. The model was trained using the *Adam* optimizer [11] using a learning rate of 0.001 and applying gradient clipping considering as the maximum L_2 norm value 5, as suggested in [22]. An L_2 regularization factor was applied on the word embedding matrix $\boldsymbol{W}_w$ weighted by a constant value of 0.0001. The training procedure exploited mini-batches of size 32 for both the datasets and we decided to apply an early stopping procedure considering the loss function value on the validation set. In particular, we stopped the training of the model when the validation loss function was higher than the lowest value obtained for 5 consecutive times. Otherwise, we interrupted the training at the epoch 30. This work used the official *TensorFlow* implementation of the Seq2seq model[1].

---

[1] https://www.tensorflow.org/api_docs/python/tf/contrib/seq2seq.

In order to demonstrate the appropriateness of the meta-controller and controller implementation, we evaluated both the ability of the meta-controller to select specific goals and the ability of the controller to generate personalized responses. Particularly, to assess the effectiveness of the meta-controller implementation we evaluated the *Precision* of the trained model on the test set leveraging the goal associated to each turn of the conversation. For the controller we used two different metrics to assess the effectiveness of the proposed suggestions for a specific user and the goodness of the generated system responses from a "linguistic" perspective. Specifically, we used the F_1-measure, which gives an idea of the goodness of the list of suggestions according to the ground truth suggestions present in the test set related conversation. Moreover, a *per-user* F_1-measure was evaluated considering all the unique proposed suggestions by the trained model in the test set dialogues with regard to all the positively rated items of a given user present in test conversations. The system responses have been evaluated using the *BLEU* [21] measure by comparing the generated sequences with the corresponding ones present in the test set. In particular, we exploited the *sentence-level BLEU* with smoothing function presented in [14] and whose effectiveness has been confirmed in [5].

As regards the *CEI* model parameters, we fixed the embedding size d_w, d_u e d_g to 50. In addition, due to the complexity of the model, we applied dropout of 0.5 on all the GRU cell input and output connections, a dropout of 0.2 on the *IMNAMAP* search gates and a dropout of 0.5 on all the hidden layers in fully connected neural networks employed in the architecture. The batch size was fixed to 32 and we applied the same early stopping procedure employed in the *seq2seq* model. The training procedure exploited the *Adam* optimizer with a learning rate of 0.0001 and we decided, due to the different datasets sizes, to apply a lower L_2 regularization weight α equal to 0.0001 on the *ML1M* dataset whereas we fixed α to 0.0001 on *MT*. To stabilize the training procedure and avoid that the model converges to poor local minima, we applied gradient clipping considering as the maximum L_2 norm value 5. We exploited the same procedure used in [9] to manage all the facts related to the given user query. In particular, the search engine returns at most the top 20 relevant facts for the user query. All the tokens which compose the knowledge base facts are stored in the vocabulary V as well as all the other tokens which belong to the dataset. The conversations which belong to the dataset were tokenized using the *NLTK* default tokenizer[2]. The model was implemented using the *TensorFlow* framework [1].

Firstly, we evaluated different configurations of the *CEI* model in order to find the best configuration on a specific dataset. In the evaluation, we have tried different values for a limited set of parameters while all the others are fixed to the above-mentioned values. In particular, the *GRU* output size can assume a value in the set $\{128, 256\}$, the *inference GRU* output size s in the *IMNAMAP* model can assume a value in the set $\{128, 256\}$, the output representation of the dialogue state RNN q can assume a value in the set $\{256, 512\}$ and the hidden layer size r in the controller RNN decoder can assume a value in the set $\{1024, 2048\}$.

---

[2] NLTK word tokenizer documentation: https://goo.gl/L4Y1Rc.

Thanks to the preliminary comparisons, we have selected the best configuration of the CEI model on the two datasets, which is the one that has the higher average score between all the evaluated measures (in the tables of results the best configurations are highlighted in bold). After that, we compared the best CEI model with the proposed baselines. Table 2 shows the experimental comparison between the best performing configuration and the other baselines according to the evaluation measures. An *NA* value in the table is associated to a configuration for which, due to its implementation constraints, it is not possible to evaluate the measure (i.e., the *seq2seq* model it is not equipped with a meta-controller so it is not possible to evaluate its effectiveness).

In the final experimental evaluation we can observe that all the values associated to the measures related to the effectiveness of the suggestions are pretty satisfying compared to the one obtained by *Random* and *Seq2seq*. In particular, on both the *MT* and the *ML1M* dataset, there is a marked difference in terms of *per-user* F_1 and F_1 measure between *CEI* and the baselines which is justified by the ability of the *intra-dialogue attention mechanism* to propagate the attention scores collected during the conversation to the controller which exploits them in the response generation procedure. It is worth noting that on the *MT* dataset the *BLEU* measure evaluated for the *Seq2seq* model is higher than the one for our model. This is a relevant factor which calls for further investigation on the real ability of the RNN decoder with *Persona-based units* to understand when to generate a token exploiting the RNN latent representation and when to use the score vector generated from the *intra-dialogue attention mechanism*.

Table 2. Evaluation between the best performing CEI model and all the baselines on MT and ML1M.

Configuration	MC precision		C BLEU		C F1		C per-user F1	
	MT	ML1M	MT	ML1M	MT	ML1M	MT	ML1M
Random	0.332	0.333	0	0.001	0	0	0	0.002
Seq2seq	NA	NA	**0.791**	0.839	0.022	0.01	0.044	0.029
CEI SL	**1.0**	**1.0**	0.784	**0.851**	**0.110**	**0.07**	**0.170**	**0.108**

3.2   Reinforcement Learning Setting

For the RL stage, a particular *OpenAI Gym* [4] environment called *Recommender System Environment (RSEnv)* is designed to let a hierarchical agent interact with a simulated user according to his/her preferences extracted from the dialogue datasets. For each user we build the user profile by composing the available information collected during the dialogue generation procedure concerning his/her name, age, occupation and preferences. For each simulated dialogue, the environment selects a random user that will interact with the bot. The environment checks the presence of particular keywords in the bot utterance and generates the appropriate answer by exploiting the user profile. When the agent generates a sequence of tokens, it receives a reward which is evaluated by the *BLEU* metric so that, in the long-term, it should be able to understand which are the appropriate tokens that should be generated in specific states. Therefore, the agent keeps answering the user until a list of suggestions is proposed to him/her and, according to the current user preferences, a reward is generated as the mean between the F_1-measure and the *BLEU* which represents the user satisfaction for the proposed suggestions. Depending on the value of the evaluated reward signal, the user answers with a positive utterance (i.e., "I like them") or a negative utterance (i.e., "I hate them"). It is in this moment that the system receives a supplementary reward signal for the meta-controller – extrinsic reward – which is equal to 50 if the user satisfaction score is over 0.5, -5 otherwise. There are some limit cases that the environment should be able to manage in order to support an effective training procedure. In particular, if the system accidentally generates a sequence of tokens which does not contain a recognized keyword, a special tag "unknown" is used to notify to the agent that the environment is not able to process its utterance. In this case, a reward signal of -5 is returned for the meta-controller and a reward equal to 0 is returned to the controller. Another case that the environment should manage is when the agent asks the environment for information which are not present for the current user. In this case, the environment notifies the agent that it does not know the answer and returns a "nothing" message. Furthermore, in order to prevent that the agent is trapped in a loop in which the environment answers always with the same utterance, we interrupt the interaction between the agent and the environment after 10 turns. If the system is not able to complete the dialogue in a number of turns which is less than the predefined threshold value, it is penalized with a reward of -5 for the meta-controller and receives 0 for the controller.

For each dataset, we selected only the best configuration in the SL training phase for the successive RL training stage. In this way, we expect to assess, thanks to a quantitative evaluation, if the system is able to improve its performance by learning from its own experiences with users. We exploited the *REINFORCE* algorithm for the meta-controller and the controller in order to fine-tune their policies directly from the experiences collected by the agent. The model is trained using the SL training procedure is used in the RL training procedure during which it interacts with the environment by exploiting the meta-controller and the controller policy to collect experiences from which it can learn from.

The adopted training procedure starts by loading the pre-trained model obtained from the SL stage and uses it in a RL scenario so it selects actions according to a state given by the environment and observes a reward according to their goodness. The model parameters are the same as the ones used in the SL training procedure so the parameters are used as they are in the RL setting. The only difference relies in the optimization method employed and in the loss function exploited to optimize the model parameters. We run the training process in the RL scenario for a fixed number of experiences e and we used mini-batches of them to update the model parameters. The advantages of this strategy are twofold: first we are able to obtain more accurate gradient approximation and second we are able to exploit the power of the GPU leveraged in our experiments to compute simultaneously multiple matrix operations. The batch size is fixed to 8 on the *MT* dataset and to 32 on the *ML1M* dataset. The entropy regularization weights ε_{MC} and ε_C are fixed to 0.01, the number of experiences is fixed to 10,000 for each dataset and we apply a discount factor on the meta-controller rewards equal to 0.99. In the RL scenario we do not design a joint training procedure because the loss functions of the meta-controller and the controller are updated in different moments, as described in [12]. Moreover, they represents different behaviour strategies that cannot be easily mixed together as they are. We also changed our optimization algorithm from *Adam* to the vanilla *SGD* because we observed during our experiments with *Adam* catastrophic effects on the effectiveness of the policies due to the aggressive behaviour of the algorithm in the early stages of the training. Indeed, according to our experience, it upsets the learned policies making them completely useless for our tasks.

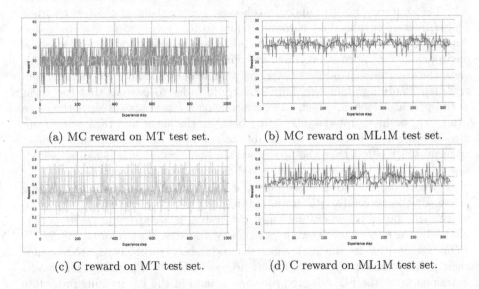

(a) MC reward on MT test set.   (b) MC reward on ML1M test set.

(c) C reward on MT test set.   (d) C reward on ML1M test set.

Fig. 1. Results of the RL experimental evaluation on the MT and ML1M datasets.

As described before, when the RL training stage is completed, we evaluate the performance of the learned model on a test environment which contains users data that the agent have not seen in the SL and RL training stages. The learned model resulting from the training procedure is evaluated according to a similar procedure that is used during the training stage. Particularly, we exploit the user profile information related to the users present in the test set of each dataset and we monitor how the system behaves in terms of two different measures collected during the system interaction with the environment: *MC rewards*, which is the meta-controller mean reward obtained in a mini-batch, and *C rewards*, which is the controller mean reward obtained in the mini-batch. Analyzing the graphs

Fig. 1b, d related to the *ML1M* dataset, we can observe how the meta-controller and the controller are able to interact with the environment. The performance is stable for each batch of examples underlining the capability of the model to generalize quite well over the training experiences. The same trend is observed in the charts Fig. 1a, c for the *MT* dataset which is promising because, despite the significantly different dimensions of the two datasets, the agent performance is still reliable and satisfying.

4 Related Work

In the literature CRSs have been classified under different names according to the strategy adopted in order to extract relevant information about the user and provide recommendation to him/her. *Case-based Critique* systems finds cases similar to the user profile and elicits a critique for refining the user's interests [20,23] throughout an iterative process in which the system generates recommendations in a ranked list and allows the user to critique them. The critique will force the system to re-evaluate its recommendations according to the specified constraints.

A limitation of classical CRSs is that their strategy is typically hard-coded in advance; at each stage, the system executes a fixed, pre-determined action, notwithstanding the fact that other actions could also be available for execution. This design choice negatively effects the flexibility of the system to support conversation scenarios which are not expected by the designer. In fact, despite the effectiveness of these systems in different complex scenarios, as reported in [20], they always follow a predefined sequence of actions without adapting to the user requirements. Moreover, typically they uses a representation for the items that is hand-crafted which is incredibly labour-intensive for complex domains like music, movies and travels. For instance, in the work presented in [3] is exploited a first-order logic representation of the items by an attribute closure operator able to refine the attribute set of the items considered in the current conversation.

To overcome these limitations the work first presented in [15] and then extended in [16–18], proposes a new type of CRS that by interacting with users is able to autonomously improve an initial default strategy in order to eventually learn and employ a better one applying RL techniques. It was first validated in off-line experiments to understand which were the state variables required by the system and then it was evaluated in an online setting in which the system had the task to support travellers. Another relevant work is the one presented in [7]. It exploits a *probabilistic latent factor model* able to refine the user preferences according to a fully online learning recommendation approach.

5 Conclusions and Future Work

CEI represents a framework for a *goal-oriented conversational agent* whose objective is to provide a list of suggestions according to the user preferences. Our intuition is that a dialogue can be subdivided in fine-grained goals whose achievement allows the agent to successfully complete the conversation with the user. The framework leverages a combination of *Deep Learning* and *Hierarchical Reinforcement Learning* techniques and is trained by using a two-stage procedure.

As regards with the answer generation module we plan to understand if the current implementation is well suited to take into account the score vector weights generated by the intra-dialogue attention mechanism in order to effectively exploit them in the recommendation phase. In addition, we think that allowing the model to leverage multiple information sources can give it the possibility to grasp different views of the items that can be used to provide more accurate suggestions according to the user preferences.

References

1. Abadi, M., Agarwal, A., Barham, P., Brevdo, E., Chen, Z., Citro, C., Corrado, G.S., Davis, A., Dean, J., Devin, M., et al.: Tensorflow: large-scale machine learning on heterogeneous distributed systems. arXiv preprint arXiv:1603.04467 (2016)
2. Bellman, R.: A Markovian decision process. Technical report, DTIC Document (1957)
3. Benito-Picazo, F., Enciso, M., Rossi, C., Guevara, A.: Conversational recommendation to avoid the cold-start problem. In: Proceedings of the 16th International Conference on Computational and Mathematical Methods in Science and Engineering, CMMSE 2016 (2016)
4. Brockman, G., Cheung, V., Pettersson, L., Schneider, J., Schulman, J., Tang, J., Zaremba, W.: OpenAI gym (2016)
5. Chen, B., Cherry, C.: A systematic comparison of smoothing techniques for sentence-level BLEU. In: ACL 2014, p. 362 (2014)
6. Cho, K., Van Merriënboer, B., Gulcehre, C., Bahdanau, D., Bougares, F., Schwenk, H., Bengio, Y.: Learning phrase representations using RNN encoder-decoder for statistical machine translation. arXiv preprint arXiv:1406.1078 (2014)
7. Christakopoulou, K., Radlinski, F., Hofmann, K.: Towards conversational recommender systems. In: Proceedings of the 22nd ACM SIGKDD International Conference on Knowledge Discovery and Data Mining, KDD 2016, pp. 815–824. ACM, New York (2016)
8. Dooms, S., De Pessemier, T., Martens, L.: Movietweetings: a movie rating dataset collected from Twitter. In: Workshop on Crowdsourcing and Human Computation for Recommender Systems, CrowdRec at RecSys, vol. 2013, p. 43 (2013)
9. Greco, C., Suglia, A., Basile, P., Rossiello, G., Semeraro, G.: Iterative multi-document neural attention for multiple answer prediction. In: Proceedings of the AI*IA Workshop on Deep Understanding and Reasoning: A Challenge for Next-generation Intelligent Agents 2016 co-located with 15th International Conference of the Italian Association for Artificial Intelligence (AIxIA 2016), Genova, Italy, 28 November 2016, pp. 19–29 (2016)
10. Harper, F.M., Konstan, J.A.: The movielens datasets: history and context. ACM Trans. Interact. Intell. Syst. (TiiS) **5**(4), 19 (2016)
11. Kingma, D., Ba, J.: Adam: a method for stochastic optimization. arXiv preprint arXiv:1412.6980 (2014)

12. Kulkarni, T.D., Narasimhan, K., Saeedi, A., Tenenbaum, J.: Hierarchical deep reinforcement learning: integrating temporal abstraction and intrinsic motivation. In: Advances in Neural Information Processing Systems, pp. 3675–3683 (2016)

13. Li, J., Galley, M., Brockett, C., Spithourakis, G.P., Gao, J., Dolan, B.: A persona-based neural conversation model. arXiv preprint arXiv:1603.06155 (2016)

14. Lin, C.Y., Och, F.J.: Automatic evaluation of machine translation quality using longest common subsequence and skip-bigram statistics. In: Proceedings of the 42nd Annual Meeting on Association for Computational Linguistics, p. 605. Association for Computational Linguistics (2004)

15. Mahmood, T., Ricci, F.: Learning and adaptivity in interactive recommender systems. In: Proceedings of the Ninth International Conference on Electronic Commerce, pp. 75–84. ACM (2007)

16. Mahmood, T., Ricci, F.: Adapting the interaction state model in conversational recommender systems. In: Proceedings of the 10th International Conference on Electronic Commerce, p. 33. ACM (2008)

17. Mahmood, T., Ricci, F.: Improving recommender systems with adaptive conversational strategies. In: Proceedings of the 20th ACM Conference on Hypertext and Hypermedia, pp. 73–82. ACM (2009)

18. Mahmood, T., Ricci, F., Venturini, A., Höpken, W.: Adaptive recommender systems for travel planning. Inf. Commun. Technol. Tour. **2008**, 1–11 (2008)

19. Maisto, D., Donnarumma, F., Pezzulo, G.: Divide et impera: subgoaling reduces the complexity of probabilistic inference and problem solving. J. R. Soc. Interface **12**(104), 20141335 (2015)

20. Mc Ginty, L., Smyth, B.: Deep dialogue vs casual conversation in recommender systems (2002)

21. Papineni, K., Roukos, S., Ward, T., Zhu, W.J.: BLEU: a method for automatic evaluation of machine translation. In: Proceedings of the 40th Annual Meeting on Association for Computational Linguistics, pp. 311–318. Association for Computational Linguistics (2002)

22. Pascanu, R., Mikolov, T., Bengio, Y.: On the difficulty of training recurrent neural networks. In: ICML, vol. 3, no. 28, pp. 1310–1318 (2013)

23. Ricci, F., Nguyen, Q.N.: Acquiring and revising preferences in a critique-based mobile recommender system. IEEE Intell. Syst. **22**(3), 22–29 (2007)

24. Rubens, N., Elahi, M., Sugiyama, M., Kaplan, D.: Active learning in recommender systems. In: Ricci, F., Rokach, L., Shapira, B. (eds.) Recommender Systems Handbook, pp. 809–846. Springer, Boston, MA (2015). doi:10.1007/978-1-4899-7637-6_24

25. Silver, D., Huang, A., Maddison, C.J., Guez, A., Sifre, L., Van Den Driessche, G., Schrittwieser, J., Antonoglou, I., Panneershelvam, V., Lanctot, M., et al.: Mastering the game of go with deep neural networks and tree search. Nature **529**(7587), 484–489 (2016)

26. Sordoni, A., Bachman, P., Trischler, A., Bengio, Y.: Iterative alternating neural attention for machine reading. arXiv preprint arXiv:1606.02245 (2016)

27. Suglia, A., Greco, C., Basile, P., Semeraro, G., Caputo, A.: An automatic procedure for generating datasets for conversational recommender systems. In: Proceedings of Dynamic Search for Complex Tasks - 8th International Conference of the CLEF Association, CLEF 2017, Dublin, Ireland, 11–14 September 2017 (2017)

28. Sutskever, I., Vinyals, O., Le, Q.V.: Sequence to sequence learning with neural networks. In: Advances in Neural Information Processing Systems, pp. 3104–3112 (2014)

29. Sutton, R.S., Precup, D., Singh, S.: Between MDPs and semi-MDPs: a framework for temporal abstraction in reinforcement learning. Artif. Intell. **112**(1), 181–211 (1999)
30. Vinyals, O., Le, Q.: A neural conversational model. arXiv preprint arXiv:1506.05869 (2015)
31. Williams, R.J.: Simple statistical gradient-following algorithms for connectionist reinforcement learning. Mach. Learn. **8**(3–4), 229–256 (1992)
32. Williams, R.J., Peng, J.: Function optimization using connectionist reinforcement learning algorithms. Conn. Sci. **3**(3), 241–268 (1991)
33. Wu, Y., Schuster, M., Chen, Z., Le, Q.V., Norouzi, M., Macherey, W., Krikun, M., Cao, Y., Gao, Q., Macherey, K., et al.: Google's neural machine translation system: bridging the gap between human and machine translation. arXiv preprint arXiv:1609.08144 (2016)
34. Zaremba, W., Sutskever, I.: Reinforcement learning neural turing machines-revised. arXiv preprint arXiv:1505.00521 (2015)
35. Zaremba, W., Sutskever, I., Vinyals, O.: Recurrent neural network regularization. arXiv preprint arXiv:1409.2329 (2014)

Attentive Models in Vision: Computing Saliency Maps in the Deep Learning Era

Marcella Cornia[(✉)], Davide Abati, Lorenzo Baraldi, Andrea Palazzi,
Simone Calderara, and Rita Cucchiara

University of Modena and Reggio Emilia, Modena, Italy
{marcella.cornia,davide.abati,lorenzo.baraldi,andrea.palazzi,
simone.calderara,rita.cucchiara}@unimore.it

Abstract. Estimating the focus of attention of a person looking at an image or a video is a crucial step which can enhance many vision-based inference mechanisms: image segmentation and annotation, video captioning, autonomous driving are some examples. The early stages of the attentive behavior are typically bottom-up; reproducing the same mechanism means to find the saliency embodied in the images, i.e. which parts of an image pop out of a visual scene. This process has been studied for decades in neuroscience and in terms of computational models for reproducing the human cortical process. In the last few years, early models have been replaced by deep learning architectures, that outperform any early approach compared against public datasets. In this paper, we propose a discussion on why convolutional neural networks (CNNs) are so accurate in saliency prediction. We present our DL architectures which combine both bottom-up cues and higher-level semantics, and incorporate the concept of time in the attentional process through LSTM recurrent architectures. Eventually, we present a video-specific architecture based on the C3D network, which can extracts spatio-temporal features by means of 3D convolutions to model task-driven attentive behaviors. The merit of this work is to show how these deep networks are not mere brute-force methods tuned on massive amount of data, but represent well-defined architectures which recall very closely the early saliency models, although improved with the semantics learned by human ground-truth.

Keywords: Saliency · Human attention · Neuroscience · Vision · Deep learning

1 Introduction

When humans look around the world, observing an image or watching at a video sequence, attentive mechanisms drive their gazes towards salient regions. Attentional mechanisms have been studied in psychology and neuroscience since decades [17], and it is well assessed that the attentional mechanism is mainly bottom-up in its early stages, although influenced by some contextual cues, and

F. Esposito et al. (Eds.): AI*IA 2017, LNAI 10640, pp. 387–399, 2017.
https://doi.org/10.1007/978-3-319-70169-1_29

guided by the salient points in the scene which is scanned very quickly by the eyes (in about 25–50 ms per item). If the person has a task-driven behaviour, e.g. when one drives a car, top-down attentive process arise; they are slower (at least 200 ms of reaction in humans) and due to the learned semantics of the scene. In general, the control of attention combines some stimuli processed in different cortical areas to mix spatial localization and recognition tasks, integrating data-driven pop outs and some learned semantics. It has also a temporal evolution, since some mechanisms such as the inhibition of return and the control of eye movements allow humans to refine attention during time.

Reproducing the same attentional process in artificial vision is still an open problem. In the case of a static image, researchers have shown that salient regions can be identified by considering discontinuities in low-level visual features, such as color, texture and contrast, and high-level cues as well, like faces, text, and the horizon. When watching a video sequence, instead, static visual features have lower importance while motion gains a crucial role, motivating the need of different solutions for static images and video. In both scenarios, computational models capable of identifying salient regions can enhance many vision-based inference mechanisms, ranging from image captioning [11] to video compression [13].

Since the seminal research of Kock, Ulman and Itti [18,23], traditional prediction models have followed biological evidences using low-level features and semantic concepts [14,22]. With the advent of Deep Learning (DL), researchers have developed data-driven architectures capable of overcoming many of the limitations of previous hand-crafted models. This is not only due to the brute-force of DL architectures, with their capability of being trained by supervised data. This is one area where these architecture are particularly suitable since they recall precisely the neural biological models. Still, it is surprising to see how much today's models share with those early works.

Motivated by these considerations, we present an overview of different solutions that we have developed for saliency prediction on images and video with DL, which represent now the state-of-the-art in public available benchmarks. We compare the neural network model with the early models of computational saliency map, to show similarities and differences. The main contribution of this work is a discussion on why the model of attention prediction with Deep Learning is useful. The paper will show that today's models, based on Convolutional Neural Networks (CNNs) share many of the principles of early models, while at the same time solving many of their drawbacks. Different convolutional architectures will be presented, to deal with features extracted at multiple levels, and to refine saliency maps in an iterative way. Eventually, a solution for video saliency prediction will be discussed and analyzed in the case of driver attention estimation.

2   Related Work

2.1   Saliency Prediction on Images

Early works on saliency prediction on images were based on the Feature Integration Theory proposed by Treisman and Gelade [32] in the eighties. Itti *et al.* [18], then, proposed the first saliency computational model: this work, inspired by Koch and Ullman [23], computed a set of individual topographical maps representing low-level cues such as color, intensity and orientation and combined them into a global saliency map. The saliency map is a scalar map, as large as the image, where each point represents the visual saliency, irrespective of the feature dimension that makes the location salient. The *locus* of highest activity in the saliency map is the most probable eye fixation point or is the point where the focus of attention should be localized.

After this work, a large variety of methods explored the same idea of combining complementary low-level features [5,14] and often included additional center-surround cues [38]. Other methods enriched predictions exploiting semantic classifiers for detecting higher level concepts such as faces, people, cars and horizons [22].

In the last few years, thanks to the large spread of deep learning techniques, the saliency prediction task has achieved a considerable improvement. First attempts of predicting saliency with convolutional networks mainly suffered from the absence of fine-tuning of network parameters over a saliency prediction dataset and from the lack of sufficient amount of data to train a deep saliency architecture [25,33]. The publication of the large-scale attention dataset SALICON [20] has contributed to a big progress of deep saliency prediction models and several new architectures have been proposed.

Huang *et al.* [16] introduced a deep neural network applied at two different image scales trained by using some evaluation metrics specific for the saliency prediction task as loss functions. Kruthiventi *et al.* [24] proposed a fully convolutional network called *DeepFix* that captures features at multiple scales and takes global context into account through the use of large receptive fields. Pan *et al.* [27] instead presented a shallow and a deep convnet where the first is trained from scratch while some layers of the second are initialized with the parameters of a standard convolutional network. Finally, Jetley *et al.* [19] introduced a saliency model that formulates a map as a generalized Bernoulli distribution and they used these maps to train a CNN trying different loss functions.

2.2   Saliency Prediction in Video

When considering video inputs, saliency estimation is quite different with respect to still images. Indeed, motion is a key factor that strongly attracts human attention. Accordingly, some video saliency models pair bottom-up feature extraction with a further motion estimation step, that can be performed either by means of optical flow [39] or feature tracking [37]. Somehow differently, some models have been proposed to force the coherence of bottom-up features across time. In this setting, previous works address feature extraction both in a supervised [30] and unsupervised [34] fashion, whereas temporal smoothness of output maps can be achieved through optical flow motion cues [39] or explicitly conditioning the current map on information from previous frames [28].

As previously discussed for the image saliency setting, the representation capability of deep learning architectures, along with large labeled datasets, can yield better results. However, deep video saliency models still lack, being the work in [4] the only meaningful effort that can be found in the current literature. Such model leverages a recurrent architecture iteratively updating its hidden state over time, and emitting the saliency map at each step by means of a Gaussian Mixture Model.

3   Saliency Prediction with Deep Learning Architectures

In this section we provide a detailed discussion of different deep learning architectures for saliency prediction on images and video. We will introduce a convolutional model for images, which incorporates low and high level visual features, and which, conceptually, extends the seminal work by Itti and Koch [18] by means of a modern neural network. A discussion on the similarities and differences between these two models will follow, and forerun the presentation of a second model, in which a recurrent convolutional architecture is used to refine saliency maps in a way which is roughly similar to the human scanpath. Finally, we will present an architecture for saliency prediction on video, and show how this particular domain differs from that of images in the case of driver attention prediction.

3.1   Incorporating Low-Level and High-Level Cues in a Multi-Level Network

In [8], we proposed a Deep Multi-Level Network (ML-Net) for saliency prediction. In contrast to previous proposals, in which saliency maps were predicted from a non-linear combination of features coming from the last convolutional layer of a CNN, we effectively combined feature maps coming from three different levels of a fully convolutional network thus taking into account low, medium and high level cues. Moreover, to model the center bias present in human eye fixations, we incorporated a learned prior map by applying it to the predicted saliency map. Figure 1 shows the overall architecture of our ML-Net model.

More in details, the first component of our architecture is a CNN based on a standard convolutional network originally designed for image classification and then employed in several other computer vision tasks. This network, named VGG-16 [29], is composed by 13 convolutional layers, divided in 5 different blocks, and 3 fully connected layers. Since we aimed at producing a 2-dimensional map (*i.e.* the predicted saliency map), we removed the fully connected layers thus obtaining a fully convolutional architecture. Several other deep saliency

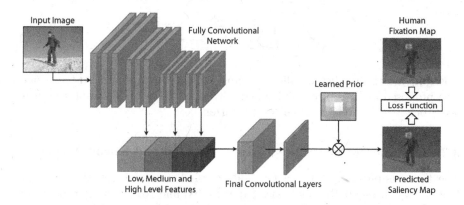

Fig. 1. Overview of our Multi-Level Network (ML-Net) [8].

models [9,16,19,27] employ the VGG-16 as starting point for their architectures and almost each of them combines feature maps coming only from the last convolutional layer of the VGG-16 network differentiating from each other by designing specific saliency component or by using different training strategies. In contrast to this approach, the second component of our model took as input feature maps coming from three different levels of the VGG-16 network: the output of the third, fourth and fifth convolutional blocks. Our model effectively combined these feature maps through two specific convolutional layers that merge low, medium and high level features and then produce a temporary saliency map. Finally, we decided to incorporate an important property of human gazes in our model. In fact, when an observers looks at an image its gaze is biased toward the center of the scene. To this end, the last component of our architecture was designed to model this center bias through a learned prior map which was applied to the predicted saliency map thus giving more importance to the center of the image.

It is well known that at training time a deep learning architecture has to minimize a given loss function that, in the saliency prediction task, aims at effectively approaching the predicted saliency map to the ground-truth one obtained from human fixation points. Previous deep saliency models were trained with different strategies by using a saliency evaluation metric as loss function or, more commonly, a square error loss (such as the euclidean loss). We instead designed a specific loss function inspired by three different objectives: predicted saliency maps should be similar to ground-truth ones, therefore a square error loss was a reasonable choice. Secondly, predictions should be invariant to their maximum, and there is no point in forcing the network to produce values in a given numerical range, so predictions were normalized by their maximum. Third, the loss should give the same importance to high and low ground-truth values, even though the majority of ground-truth pixels are close to zero. For this reason, the deviation between predicted values and ground-truth values was weighted by a linear function, which tends to give more importance to pixels with high ground-truth fixation probability. The overall loss function was thus

$$L(\mathbf{w}) = \frac{1}{N} \sum_{i=1}^{N} \frac{\left\| \frac{\phi(\mathbf{x}_i)}{\max \phi(\mathbf{x}_i)} - \mathbf{y}_i \right\|^2}{\alpha - \mathbf{y}_i} \tag{1}$$

where $\mathbf{x}_i$ are the predicted saliency maps while $\mathbf{y}_i$ are the ground-truth ones. The proposed architecture was trained with mini-batch of N samples by using the Stochastic Gradient Descent as optimizer.

3.2   Deep Learning Architectures vs. the Itti and Koch's Model

The first computational model for saliency prediction, and probably the most famous, was presented in a seminal paper by Itti and Koch [18]. It proposed to extract multi-scale low-level features from the input image which were linearly combined and then processed by a dynamic neural network with a winner-takes-all strategy to select attended locations in decreasing order of saliency. As we have shown in the previous section, nowadays saliency prediction is generally tackled via CNN architectures, therefore giving more importance to learning than to hand engineering of features. However, today's models share a lot with that influential work.

The model in [18] extracted three kinds of features from input images: color (as a linear combination of raw pixels in color channels), intensity (again, computed as a linear combination of color channels), and orientation, by means of oriented Gabor pyramids [12]. It should be noted that all these features can be easily extracted by a single convolutional layer, and, indeed, visualization and inversion techniques [36] showed that filters learned in the early stages of a CNN roughly extract color and gradient features. Also, the linear combinations of color channels in [18] can be computed via a single convolutional layer with channel-wise uniform weights or with a 1×1 kernel.

One detail, however, is missing in current convolutional architectures: authors of [18] extracted the same features at multiple scales, and then validated them by performing central differences between adjacent scales. In a CNN, instead, features are always computed at a single scale, even though the overall architecture extracts (different) features at different scales thanks to pooling stages. Of course the multi-scale validation of features was also motivated by the need of extracting robust features, something which comes almost for free in modern architectures. Moreover, many state of the art CNN models are multi-scale by construction, feeding a pyramid of images to the same convolutional stack. Even in our model, we combine different features extracted at different scales to form the final prediction, instead of taking only those produced by the last layer.

Conversely, the most evident characteristic that the Itti and Koch model misses with respect to today's architectures is the ability to extract higher level features, and to detect objects and part of objects. This is achieved, in today's networks, by increasing the depth of the network (e.g. 152 layers in the ResNet model [15]). This, given the big performance gap, clearly highlights the need of high-level features for saliency prediction.

Table 1. Comparison results on the MIT300 dataset [21].

	SIM ↑	CC ↑	sAUC ↑	AUC ↑	NSS ↑	EMD ↓
Infinite humans	1.00	1.00	0.80	0.91	3.18	0.00
ML-Net	0.59	0.67	0.70	0.85	2.05	2.63
Itti	0.44	0.37	0.63	0.75	0.97	4.26

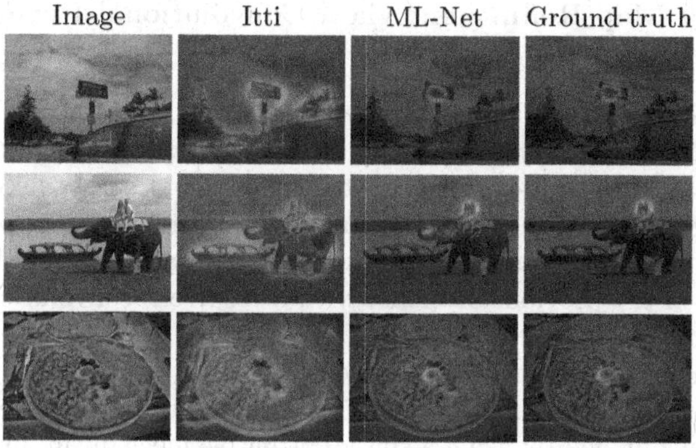

Fig. 2. Qualitative comparisons between the Itti [18] and ML-Net [8] models. Images are from the SALICON dataset [20].

As a proof of concept, in Table 1 we compare the results of the model in [18][1] with those of our method. We use the standard performance indicators for saliency: the Similarity, the Linear Correlation Coefficient (CC), the Area Under the ROC Curve (AUC) and its shuffled version (sAUC), the Normalized Scanpath Saliency (NSS) and the Earth-Mover Distance (EMD). We refer the reader to the work by Bylinskii *et al.* [7] for a detailed discussion on these metrics. It can clearly be seen that CNNs overcame that early model by a big margin, with respect to all metrics, and this experimentally confirms the need of high-level features for saliency prediction, rather than just employing low-level cues such as in [18]. To give a better insight of the performance gain, we also report some qualitative results on images randomly chosen from the SALICON dataset. We show them in Fig. 2, along with the ground-truth saliency map computed from human eye fixations. While the model of [18] tends to concentrate on color and gradient discontinuities, which often do not match with the human fixation map, our model can clearly guess most of the saliency maps in a way which is almost indistinguishable from the ground-truth. The middle image, showing a pizza, is also a good example to show the role of the center prior: when there is no a clear object which stands out in the scene, human eyes tend to fix the center of

---

[1] Numerical and qualitative results of the Itti-Koch model have been generated using the re-implementation of [14], which is also the one reported in the MIT Saliency Benchmark [6].

the image, as our model has learned to do. Also, predictions from our ML-Net are particularly focused on small areas, similarly to the SALICON ground-truth. This is due to the fact that, in absence of a task-driven attentive mechanism, the focus tends to be directed on what is *a-priori* known, such as a person, a face, a traffic sign. The architecture, trained on similar data, does not overfit specific points, but tends to replicate the same semantic-based attentive behaviour.

3.3   Saliency Map Refinement via a Convolutional Recurrent Architecture

Models for saliency prediction can also go beyond feed-forward neural networks and include recurrent components. Recurrent neural networks are usually employed to deal with time-varying input sequences, but can be used, in general, to process any kind of sequence. Following this intuition, we proposed a second model [10] in which we combined a fully convolutional network (similar to the one described in the previous sections) with a recurrent convolutional network, endowed with an attention mechanism. The recurrent network, instead of looping on a time sequence as in the case of video captioning [3], performs an iterative refinement of the saliency map by focusing on different part of the image. This behaviour is encouraged by using a spatial attentive mechanism, inspired by the machine translation literature [2]. We called the overall architecture SAM, i.e. *Saliency Attentive Model*.

Figure 3 shows, for some images taken from the SALICON dataset, the prediction from the model of Itti and Koch [18], that from our previous model [8], and the output of the attentive network at each step, for $t = 1, ..., 4$, as well as the ground-truth map. As it can be noticed, the refinement strategy carried out by the network results in a progressive improvement of the prediction, which overcomes the performance of a feed-forward neural network like the one in the ML-Net model.

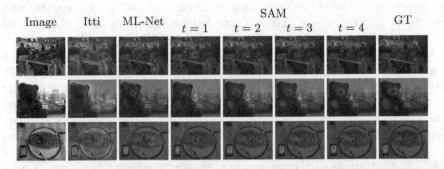

Fig. 3. Qualitative comparison between the Itti [18], ML-Net [8] and SAM [10] models on images taken from the SALICON dataset [20]. For the SAM model, we show predictions given by the recurrent attentive network at different steps.

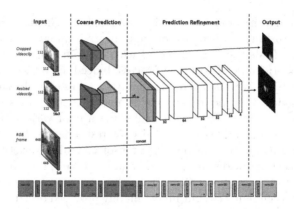

Fig. 4. Illustration of the COARSE+FINE model depicting the both streams guiding the optimization during training. Please note that in test stage the cropped stream is not used. At the bottom, the architecture of the COARSE module is illustrated.

3.4   Estimating Task-Driven Saliency in Videos

In [26], we described a model devised for predicting saliency on the DR(eye)VE dataset [1], and capable of replicating human attentional behavior while driving. The need for a different model tailored for this specific context is twofold: first, as anticipated, objects motion in videos tends to capture human attention. Moreover, fixations recorded during the dataset acquisition in [1] are strongly related to the driving activity, and call for a task-driven model and training procedure.

Motivated by the insight that a small temporal window holds sufficient information meaningful for the task of driving, our model captures short-term correlations by means of 3D convolutions, which also stride along time axis. Accordingly, it takes as input samples holding 16 consecutive frames (called *clips* from now on) and provides a dense saliency probability map for the last (current) frame of the clip. The network is jointly trained with two input streams (Fig. 4), in order to tackle the central bias that usually affects saliency benchmarks in general, and is even more noticeable in the driving task. Both streams rely on the same backbone encoder, that we name COARSE module as provides a rough, harsh saliency estimate. Such model is based on the work by Tran *et al.* [31] and employs their C3D architecture to map pixels into a 512-dimensional encoding space. Being interested in spatially coherent feature maps, we drop the top fully connected classification module. Moreover, we discard the deepest convolutional layer, which encodings are strongly tailored to the original action recognition task, retaining only the most general features provided by previous layers. Eventually, we modify the last pooling layer to cover the whole time axis, and therefore squeeze out the temporal dimension from the output features. The resulting map, which is reduced by a 16x factor along spatial dimension and lacks the temporal axis due to pooling layers, is then processed to produce a saliency estimate as big as the original image and featuring a single probability channel. This is achieved by means of a series of upsampling followed by convolutions.

During training, the model is fed with two streams. The first stream encourages the model to learn saliency estimation given visual cues rather than prior spatial bias, and feeds the COARSE model with random crops. Cropping is also employed in the original C3D training process. Indeed, in [31] authors perform a tensor resize to 128×128 and then a random 112×112 crop. In our experience, this cropping policy is too polite, and yields models strongly biased towards the image center since ground-truth maps still suffer a poor variety. The policy we employ is immoderate, and features a 256×256 resize before the crop. This way, samples cover a small portion of the input tensor and allow variety in prediction targets, at the cost of a wider attentional area. Intuitively, the smaller crops are, the larger the attentional map will appear. Thus, the trained model was able to escape the bias when required, but unfortunately provided over-rough estimates. To address this issue, we feed the COARSE model with a second stream providing images resized to match the crop size. The prediction, after being resized and concatenated with the last frame of the clip, than undergoes a further block of convolutional layers (FINE module) that refine the map. Estimates from both streams are modeled as a probability density P over pixels, and optimized jointly against a ground-truth map Q by means of the Kullback-Leibler divergence:

$$D_{KL}(P,Q) = \sum_i Q_i \, \log \left(\epsilon + \frac{Q_i}{\epsilon + P_i} \right) \tag{2}$$

where the summation index i spans across image pixels and ϵ is a regularization constant.

Evaluation. Here we discuss the experiments performed in order to assess the design choices of our architecture for video saliency. As common in public benchmarks, we first compare our model against two central baselines. The first one represents the central bias as a Gaussian $\mathcal{N}(\mu, \Sigma)$, being μ the image center and Σ a diagonal covariance matrix whose variances are coherent with the image aspect ratio. A more precise, task-driven baseline is obtained by averaging all training ground-truth maps, and two unsupervised state-of-the-art video saliency models [34,35] are also included in the comparison. The evaluation has been carried out comparing the shift between predicted and ground-truth maps both in terms of Pearson's correlation coefficient (CC) and Kullback-Leibler divergence (D_{KL}). We report such measures evaluated both in the whole test set and in the attentive subsequences only[2] in Table 2. Moreover, we report the results of the ML-Net model, that was originally proposed for image saliency and has been properly trained from scratch on the DR(eye)VE dataset.

Several conclusions can be drawn from this evaluation. Firstly, from the poor performances of unsupervised models emerges the peculiar nature of the driving context, that demands for task-driven supervision. Moreover, it can be

---

[2] *Attentive subsequences* in DR(eye)VE are clips in which the driver is looking far from the image center due to a peculiar maneuver he is performing. We refer the reader to [26] for details.

Table 2. Evaluation of the proposed models against central baselines, both on the test and attentive sequences of DR(eye)VE.

	Test seq		Att. seq	
	$CC \uparrow$	$D_{KL} \downarrow$	$CC \uparrow$	$D_{KL} \downarrow$
Baseline (gaussian)	0.33	2.50	0.22	2.70
Baseline (mean train GT)	0.48	1.65	0.17	2.85
Wang *et al.* [35]	0.08	3.77	–	–
Wang *et al.* [34]	0.03	4.24	–	–
ML-Net	0.41	2.05	0.29	2.49
COARSE	0.44	1.73	0.19	2.74
COARSE+FINE	0.55	1.42	0.30	2.24

Frame	GT	COARSE+FINE	ML-Net

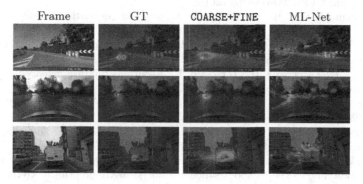

Fig. 5. Representation of differences in the video saliency estimation. This qualitative assessment indicates the suitability of the COARSE+FINE model in encoding temporal information. On the other hand, the ML-Net model processes still images and is more influenced by low-level non temporal features.

noticed that the attentive subset of samples is crucial for the evaluation, as simple input-agnostic baselines perform positively overall. Finally, an important remark is revealed by the superior performance of the proposed model w.r.t ML-Net. The gap in performance is due to the temporal nature of video data: indeed, COARSE+FINE profitably learned to extract temporal features that are meaningful for video saliency prediction, whereas the design of ML-Net cannot capture such precious dependencies. A qualitative illustration of the difference in predictions is illustrated in Fig. 5.

4   Conclusions

In this work we presented different deep learning architectures for saliency prediction on images and video, showing the importance of multi-level features and the ability of recurrent architectures to enhance saliency prediction results.

We also shown, with experiments on a driving dataset, that dealing with video sequences requires ad-hoc architectures due to the need of extracting motion features. The comparison between today's models and the early model by Itti and Koch [18] revealed several similarities in the way feature are extracted, and motivated the gap in performances with current models, which is not merely due to the their brute-force nature, but also to their ability to recall very closely early saliency and biological models, although improved with the semantics learned on the ground-truth.

References

1. Alletto, S., Palazzi, A., Solera, F., Calderara, S., Cucchiara, R.: DR(eye)VE: a dataset for attention-based tasks with applications to autonomous and assisted driving. In: CVPR Workshops (2016)
2. Bahdanau, D., Cho, K., Bengio, Y.: Neural machine translation by jointly learning to align and translate. arXiv preprint arXiv:1409.0473 (2014)
3. Baraldi, L., Grana, C., Cucchiara, R.: Hierarchical boundary-aware neural encoder for video captioning. In: CVPR (2017)
4. Bazzani, L., Larochelle, H., Torresani, L.: Recurrent mixture density network for spatiotemporal visual attention. In: ICLR (2017)
5. Bruce, N., Tsotsos, J.: Saliency based on information maximization. In: ANIPS, pp. 155–162 (2005)
6. Bylinskii, Z., Judd, T., Borji, A., Itti, L., Durand, F., Oliva, A., Torralba, A.: Mit saliency benchmark. http://saliency.mit.edu/
7. Bylinskii, Z., Judd, T., Oliva, A., Torralba, A., Durand, F.: What do different evaluation metrics tell us about saliency models? arXiv preprint arXiv:1604.03605 (2016)
8. Cornia, M., Baraldi, L., Serra, G., Cucchiara, R.: A deep multi-level network for saliency prediction. In: ICPR (2016)
9. Cornia, M., Baraldi, L., Serra, G., Cucchiara, R.: Multi-level net: a visual saliency prediction model. In: Hua, G., Jégou, H. (eds.) ECCV 2016. LNCS, vol. 9914, pp. 302–315. Springer, Cham (2016). doi:10.1007/978-3-319-48881-3_21
10. Cornia, M., Baraldi, L., Serra, G., Cucchiara, R.: Predicting human eye fixations via an LSTM-based saliency attentive model. arXiv preprint arXiv:1611.09571 (2017)
11. Cornia, M., Baraldi, L., Serra, G., Cucchiara, R.: Visual saliency for image captioning in new multimedia services. In: ICME Workshops (2017)
12. Greenspan, H., Belongie, S., Goodman, R., Perona, P., Rakshit, S., Anderson, C.H.: Overcomplete steerable pyramid filters and rotation invariance. In: CVPR (1994)
13. Hadizadeh, H., Baji, I.V.: Saliency-aware video compression. IEEE Trans. Image Process. 23(1), 19–33 (2014)
14. Harel, J., Koch, C., Perona, P.: Graph-based visual saliency. In: ANIPS, pp. 545–552 (2006)
15. He, K., Zhang, X., Ren, S., Sun, J.: Deep residual learning for image recognition. In: CVPR (2016)
16. Huang, X., Shen, C., Boix, X., Zhao, Q.: SALICON: reducing the semantic gap in saliency prediction by adapting deep neural networks. In: ICCV (2015)
17. Itti, L., Koch, C.: Computational modelling of visual attention. Nat. Rev. Neurosci. 2(3), 194–203 (2001)

18. Itti, L., Koch, C., Niebur, E., et al.: A model of saliency-based visual attention for rapid scene analysis. IEEE TPAMI **20**(11), 1254–1259 (1998)
19. Jetley, S., Murray, N., Vig, E.: End-to-end saliency mapping via probability distribution prediction. In: CVPR (2016)
20. Jiang, M., Huang, S., Duan, J., Zhao, Q.: Salicon: saliency in context. In: CVPR (2015)
21. Judd, T., Durand, F., Torralba, A.: A benchmark of computational models of saliency to predict human fixations. MIT Technical report (2012)
22. Judd, T., Ehinger, K., Durand, F., Torralba, A.: Learning to predict where humans look. In: ICCV (2009)
23. Koch, C., Ullman, S.: Shifts in selective visual attention: towards the underlying neural circuitry. In: Vaina, L.M. (ed.) Matters of Intelligence, pp. 115–141. Springer, Dordrecht (1987). doi:10.1007/978-94-009-3833-5_5
24. Kruthiventi, S.S., Ayush, K., Babu, R.V.: Deepfix: a fully convolutional neural network for predicting human eye fixations. arXiv preprint arXiv:1510.02927 (2015)
25. Kümmerer, M., Theis, L., Bethge, M.: DeepGaze I: Boosting saliency prediction with feature maps trained on ImageNet. In: ICLR Workshops (2015)
26. Palazzi, A., Solera, F., Calderara, S., Alletto, S., Cucchiara, R.: Learning to attend like a human driver. In: Intelligent Vehicles Symposium (2017)
27. Pan, J., Sayrol, E., Giro-i-Nieto, X., McGuinness, K., Giró-i, N.X.: Shallow and deep convolutional networks for saliency prediction. In: CVPR (2016)
28. Rudoy, D., Goldman, D.B., Shechtman, E., Zelnik-Manor, L.: Learning video saliency from human gaze using candidate selection. In: CVPR (2013)
29. Simonyan, K., Zisserman, A.: Very deep convolutional networks for large-scale image recognition. CoRR abs/1409.1556 (2014)
30. Mathe, S., Sminchisescu, C.: Actions in the eye: dynamic gaze datasets and learnt saliency models for visual recognition. IEEE TPAMI **37**(7), 1408–1424 (2015)
31. Tran, D., Bourdev, L., Fergus, R., Torresani, L., Paluri, M.: Learning spatiotemporal features with 3D convolutional networks. In: ICCV (2015)
32. Treisman, A.M., Gelade, G.: A feature-integration theory of attention. Cogn. Psychol. **12**(1), 97–136 (1980)
33. Vig, E., Dorr, M., Cox, D.: Large-scale optimization of hierarchical features for saliency prediction in natural images. In: CVPR (2014)
34. Wang, W., Shen, J., Porikli, F.: Saliency-aware geodesic video object segmentation. In: CVPR (2015)
35. Wang, W., Shen, J., Shao, L.: Consistent video saliency using local gradient flow optimization and global refinement. IEEE Trans. Image Process. **24**(11), 4185–4196 (2015)
36. Zeiler, M.D., Fergus, R.: Visualizing and understanding convolutional networks. In: Fleet, D., Pajdla, T., Schiele, B., Tuytelaars, T. (eds.) ECCV 2014. LNCS, vol. 8689, pp. 818–833. Springer, Cham (2014). doi:10.1007/978-3-319-10590-1_53
37. Zhai, Y., Shah, M.: Visual attention detection in video sequences using spatiotemporal cues. In: ACM MM (2006)
38. Zhang, J., Sclaroff, S.: Saliency detection: a boolean map approach. In: ICCV (2013)
39. Zhong, S.H., Liu, Y., Ren, F., Zhang, J., Ren, T.: Video saliency detection via dynamic consistent spatio-temporal attention modelling. In: AAAI (2013)

Philosophical Foundations, Metacognitive Modeling and Ethics

Supporting Organizational Accountability Inside Multiagent Systems

Matteo Baldoni[1]([✉]), Cristina Baroglio[1], Katherine M. May[2],
Roberto Micalizio[1], and Stefano Tedeschi[2]

[1] Dipartimento di Informatica, Università degli Studi di Torino, Turin, Italy
{matteo.baldoni,cristina.baroglio,roberto.micalizio}@unito.it
[2] Università degli Studi di Torino, Turin, Italy
{katherine.may,stefano.tedeschi}@edu.unito.it

Abstract. We present and analyze the problem of realizing an accountability-supporting system in multiagent systems technology. To this aim and to avoid ambiguities, we first characterize the concept of accountability, which we later work to realize computationally, particularly in relation to the partially overlapping notion of responsibility. Then, with the aim of achieving accountability as a design property, we provide a few principles that characterize an accountability-supporting multiagent system. We provide an accountability protocol to regulate the interaction between an agent, willing to play a role in an organization, and the organization itself. Finally, we show as a case study how the use of such a protocol allows multiagent systems, realized with JaCaMo, to support accountability.

Keywords: Computational ethics · Accountability · Multiagent systems · Sociotechnical systems

1 Introduction

In the field of multiagent systems (MAS), individual and organizational actions have social consequences, which require the development of tools to trace and evaluate principals' behaviors and to communicate good conduct. This concerns the value of accountability. The main contribution is to provide a notion of when an organization of agents supports accountability by investigating the process of construction of the organization itself as well as to give the definition of a protocol to be followed in order to design and build an organization that supports accountability. The core of the analysis is the notion of role and the action of role adoption (or enactment). Indeed, the concept of role has been studied in many different fields of computer science like software engineering, databases, security and, of course, artificial intelligence. Despite several proposals have been made about a characterization of such a concept, there is little consensus about its properties and purposes. A reason for this lack is the diversity of scopes and applications that such a general concept could have in different disciplines. If seen

© Springer International Publishing AG 2017
F. Esposito et al. (Eds.): AI*IA 2017, LNAI 10640, pp. 403–417, 2017.
https://doi.org/10.1007/978-3-319-70169-1_30

from an organizational point of view, roles should describe the way individuals can interact with and act upon an organization.

Continuing our work on accountability as presented in [3], in this study we wish to present a more nuanced view of the concept, particularly in relation to its close sibling, responsibility, and offer an initial exploration of platform requirements for a software-based, accountability-attribution process. Building on our previous characterizations of accountability, this study adds considerations that consequently impact implementation decisions on our chosen platform. We also attempt to tie our work more closely to work in the field of ethics so as not to diminish the rich meaning behind accountability and avoid cheapening the concept to the point of a definitional equivalence with traceability. We offer ethical dilemmas to force our hand into programming difficult decisions and form a more conceptually complete system of accountability. With some conceptual modifications, we believe JaCaMo [5] a particularly apt platform for building in an accountability mechanism.

2   A Characterization of Accountability and Responsibility

As a potentially wide-ranging concept, accountability can take on many different characteristics and meanings, especially depending on the discipline in which discussion takes place. Our own approach relies on a more mechanistic view in which accountability is a backward-looking, institutional process that permits one entity to be held to account by another. The accountability process activates when a negative (or positive) state is reached and an authoritative entity wishes to hold to account those behind said state. The process itself is divided into three primary phases: (1) an investigative entity (forum) receives all information regarding agents' actions, effects, permissions, obligations, etc. that led to the situation under scrutiny, (2) the forum contextualizes actions to understand their adequacy and legitimacy, and finally (3) the forum passes judgment on agents with sanctions or rewards [7]. Our goal consists in automating the entire process for use in a MAS, although we will presently leave out the sanctioning piece of the third phase due to its organization-specific application. In order to realize our goal, we begin by looking at the reasoning process behind accountability to identify points of adaptation into the software world.

Three conditions for accountability attribution are identified in [8]: agency, causal relevancy, and avoidance opportunity. The agency condition expresses not only an individual's independence and reasoning capacity, but also that entity's ability to distinguish right and wrong. Because software agents have no independent ethics, we maintain that their moral compass, so to speak, only emerges in and is unique to a given software organization. An agent's "ethics" will be expressed through adherence to norms and commitments. The causal relevancy condition expresses the necessity of causation linking a given agent to a situation under scrutiny. The avoidance opportunity condition specifies that an "agent should have had a reasonable opportunity to have done otherwise" [8]. The condition does not imply that in absence of the agent's action, the situation would not have come to pass. That is, an agent can be held accountable for a causal contribution even in the presence of the inevitable. To illustrate, we can consider the example from [8] in which we find ourselves in the presence of two murderers who simultaneously shoot someone, their bullets piercing the victim's heart in the same moment. Should one of the murders have chosen not to shoot, the victim would still have died, yet we would naturally hold both accountable. They both had an opportunity to avoid causally contributing to the victim's death.

The accountability attribution process, due to its quality of determining the parties who causally contributed to a given situation, necessarily uses of a backward-looking approach. Its domain lies in the past, uncovering intrigue and revealing causal mystery. Responsibility attribution, as accountability's temporal mirror sibling, instead looks to the future and places its definitional weight on parties deemed capable and worthy of realizing a certain goal or goals. Both concepts, divided only by time, work towards the common purpose of situational deconstruction in order to distribute responsibility or accountability in a reality-reflecting fashion among a situation's atomic agents. Their common purpose gives rise to a strong working relationship between the concepts. Their complementary nature permits considerations and evaluations to flow between the two, which can, at the very least, inform their respective investigations. As expressed in [9], "When I am responsible for my actions now, I may be held accountable later".

Despite their close relationship, one concept cannot directly implicate the other. Even if a responsible entity's task was not completed as planned, that does not automatically indicate that fault lies with said entity. Likewise, if an entity is deemed accountable, that entity was not necessarily designated responsible in planning stages. As an example, should a person be named responsible for task A but then be coerced to realize *"not A"*, that person cannot be, at the very least, wholly accountable. We would rather name the coercer partially accountable if not solely accountable for her/his role in causing *"not A"*. However, even beyond the extreme example of coercion, other forces can also impact an individual's ability to realize a task. For example, say we have an organization consisting of two members: one to prepare a wall, *wall-preparer*, and another who paints the wall, *painter*. The encompassing organization would give both access rights and distribute responsibility to *wall-preparer* for prepping the wall, and to *painter* for painting the wall. Then come execution time, *wall-preparer* fulfills her/his task by spackling the wall but, having a whimsical side, unexpectedly paints a black stripe down the middle. Unfortunately, due to the unexpected action, *painter* has not the correct amount of materials and cannot fulfill her/his task. Though not coerced, *painter* cannot proceed due to the actions of another.

If we assume the complete absence of unplanned influences in a given context, responsibility directly maps to accountability. Though one might be hard-pressed to justify such an assumption in an organization with human actors, its absurdity diminishes in a world of software agents. Simply put, we must be able to adequately plan for the unexpected. To illustrate, we can take the previous example and imagine it unfolding in a multiagent setting. Before agreeing to be the organization's painter, *painter* would stipulate provisions for its role goals, in this case, *white wall*. An organization, accepting *painter*'s provisions, would then add *white wall* as a goal condition to the job description of *wall-preparer*. *Wall-preparer* would in turn accept its new goal condition. Come execution time, when *wall-preparer* adds the black stripe, not only will *painter*'s provisions not be met, but *wall-preparer* will also have violated its own goal conditions. Since *wall-preparer* knows what it did was wrong thanks to goal conditions, causally contributed to an adverse situation of work failure, and could have avoided causally contributing, it will be held accountable for the adverse state. A direct correlation between responsibility and accountability presents other advantages for accountability. As discussed in [9], when it comes time to assess an event, an investigative forum analyses who was involved, at what level, and whether those involved acted correctly or the presence of mitigating circumstances if not. If, however, we exclude the possibility of unplanned actions, any deliberations a forum would make would be already programmed in and accounted for in the very definitions of roles and groups. The deliberation would, thus, take the form of tracing violated pre and post conditions to their source.

An exclusion of unexpected actions fulfills both the positive and negative approaches to accountability. The positive approach means that an agent will be held accountable if it doesn't fulfill its job, while the negative approach means that it will not negatively affect the organization independently of its own designated job. While a realization of the positive approach implies a careful interaction pattern between an organization and its agents to keep an agent to its post conditions should its provisions hold, the negative approach implies a more temporally independent mechanism for the entire lifecycle of an organization to hold its members to correct behavior. This study concentrates firstly on the positive approach with the negative approach to follow in future studies.

Difficult ethics questions on moral responsibility and accountability present us with critical decision points wherein we must choose the "ethics" of our software agents. The famous Frankfurt example [16] confronts us with such a choice. Consider an individual who performs an action. Unknowingly, a mechanism in her/his brain would cause her/him to perform the action anyway, even should she/he choose not to act. The example complicates the assumption for moral responsibility of the alternate possibilities condition. As difficult a question the example raises, we find a comfortingly simpler scenario when we translate the example to software. Suppose an organization contains a certain agent who performs an action. That same agent by design cannot have a hidden mechanism because quite simply it knows its own plans. Plans it does not know it cannot execute. However, if the same agent finds itself in that troublesome state whatever action it performs, should the agent be held accountable for the adverse state when that state is inevitable? We adopt the incompatibilist position to moral responsibility and conclude in a software setting that an agent cannot be held accountable in causal determinism. That said, due to our distributed approach to accountability in which agents declare their provisions and goals, the burden of discovery of inevitable states lies with the agents. If an agent stipulates provisions for an inevitable adverse state, that same adversity would be represented to some degree in its provisions due to its inevitable nature. The agent would still be held accountable for the state, because it effectively declares responsibility for a goal through its accepted stipulated conditions.

. Likewise as a consequence of building up provisions and goal conditions dynamically in part through agent declarations, an organization effectively excludes goal impossibilities. If an agent offers to realize a goal in the presence of a certain provisions, it is declaring for all intents and purposes that the goal is possible under certain conditions. Should that agent offer up an incorrect assessment and the goal be effectively impossible even with stipulations, the agent will nevertheless be held accountable, because the organization "believes" an agent's declaration. We therefore conclude, thanks to the distributed nature of our vision of accountability, that an organization can consider absent both impossibilities and inevitabilities.

Another ethical dilemma concerns knowledge of the consequences of one's actions. That is, can one be held accountable for an unforeseeable outcome? In software this particular ethical dilemma can take on various forms. As an initial observation, thanks to the principles of information hiding, a software agent by design cannot, and indeed should not, know all the effects of its actions in an organizational setting. In our case the modularity of software makes it possible for us to address the ethical dilemma. For instance, in the context of JaCaMo [5], an agent can see organizational goals and roles and, therefore, knows nothing beyond its own place in a chain of goals. An agent can, therefore, be accountable for interrupting its own goal, and consequently the executions of future-dependent goals, but cannot be accountable for causing an error that crashes the server. Only if an organization were to communicate to its agents that a certain state crashes the server would agents be accountable for a crash-causing state.

3   Organizational Accountability as a Design Property

As a consequence of our ethical dilemmas and general considerations of the intricacies surrounding responsibility and accountability, we conclude the concepts require the presence of a number of attributes. Because a direct mapping between responsibility and accountability requires the absence of unplanned actions, an agent must be aware of future expectations, that is, must be able to plan for all required future actions. Thus, if an organization requires an agent to realize a certain goal, the agent must be made aware before taking on its corresponding responsibility. Since goals only take on meaning in a given context, the assumption of responsibility also only meaningfully occurs within a specific context. A general acontextual responsibility assignment cannot indicate a later potential accountability due to lack of situatedness. To talk about accountability in a MAS we need to trace such a characterization back to the notions upon which MASes are traditionally built, like agents, roles, organization, environment, and interaction. To this end, we distill the following few founding principles at the basis of the way to achieve organizational accountability *as a design property*.

Principle 1. *All the collaborations and communications subject to considerations of accountability among the agents occur within a single scope that we call organization.*

This principle derives from the observation that accountability is a relationship between principals, and this is meaningful only within a specific context, i.e., the organization. The organization is a social structure in the sense given by Elder-Vass [14], i.e. an entity that is made up of parts (entities themselves), with which given relationships hold. Accountability in this perspective is a synchronically emergent property of the organization, that is a property that holds because of its parts and their relationships. The parts (or relationships) taken by themselves would not show it.

Placing an organizational based limit on accountability determinations serves multiple purposes. It isolates events and actors into more manageable pieces so that when searching for causes/effects, one need not consider all actions from the beginning of time nor actions from other organizations. Agents are reassured that only for actions within an organization will they potentially be held accountable. Actions, thanks to agent roles, also always happen in context.

Principle 2. *An agent can enroll an organization only by playing a* role *that is defined inside the organization.*

Related to the need to set a context to agent interaction, roles, which we see as an organizational and contextual aid to accountability, attribute social significance to an agent's actions and can, therefore, provide a guide to the severity of non-adherence.

Principle 3. *An agent willing to play a role in an organization must be aware of all the powers associated with such a role before adopting it.*

Following Hohfeld [18], a power is "one's affirmative 'control' over a given legal relation as against another." The relationship between powers and roles has long been studied in fields like social theory, artificial intelligence, and law. Here we invoke a knowledge condition for an organization's agents, and stipulate that an agent can only be accountable for exercising the powers that are publicly given to it by the roles it plays. Such powers are, indeed, the means by which agents affect their organizational setting. An agent cannot be held accountable for unknown effects of its actions but, rather, only for consequences related to an agent's known place in sequences of goals. By definition, accountability operates in the context of relationships between, borrowing terms from [11], an account-giver and an account-taker. To give it a computational form, it is necessary to start from the relationship-describing stipulations, for both account-giver and account-taker, of conditional expectations on account-giver's behavior. Thus, an agent will not be held accountable for an unknown goal that the organization attaches to its role, and this leads us to the next principle.

Principle 4. *An agent is only accountable, towards the organization or another agent, for those goals it has explicitly accepted to bring about.*

This means that a rational agent has the possibility to take on the responsibility for a goal only when it knows it possesses the capabilities for achieving the goal. In other words, not only is the autonomy of an agent is not constrained by accountability, it is even improved since the agent can apply forms of practical reasoning to determine whether to join an organization and under what conditions. Indeed, accountability's very domain lies in contextual dynamics and situational complication. In our own societies we are very familiar with the complexities within which accountability operates: certainly no person would agree to be held unconditionally accountable for any goal because, simply put, context matters. So too must the participating agents in a MAS have the opportunity to stipulate their own provisions, as expressed in the next principle.

Principle 5. *An agent must have the leeway for putting before the organization the provisions it needs for achieving the goal to which it is committing. The organization has the capability of reasoning on the requested provisions and can accept or reject them.*

Thinking about the use of accountability in the world of artificial agents, one might rightfully ponder accountability's potential role. From the extensive history of moral responsibility, we find two such justifications for the attribution of praise/blame: (1) because individuals deserve the feedback, and (2) in order to influence change in an individual (and indeed attribution is only appropriate when such a change occurs) [15]. Naturally, we find our own purpose in the latter. With our concept of computational accountability we strive towards a general goal of teaching agents correct behavior in the context of a particular organization. Our goal consists in realizing a fully automized system of accountability. We wish to directly program accountability in a MAS platform, specifically JaCaMo, while maintaining the most integral pieces of the concept, namely autonomy balanced with traceability and culpability.

4   An Accountability Protocol

We turn now to a MAS design-phase application of the above-mentioned accountability principles. Chopra and Singh explored a similar approach of design-phase accountability in [11]. In their work, Chopra and Singh suggest that an actor can legitimately depend on another to make a condition become true only when such a dependency is formalized in an *institutionalized expectation*, whose structure describes expectations one actor has of another and whose inherently public nature wields normative power. To tackle accountability as a design property, Chopra and Singh introduce the notion of *accountability requirement* as a special case of institutionalized expectation. An accountability requirement is a relation involving two principals, an account giver (a-giver) and an account taker (a-taker). The a-giver is accountable to the a-taker regarding some conditional expectation; namely, the expectation involves an antecedent condition and a consequent condition. Usually, the consequent condition is pursued only when the antecedent condition is true. In principle, if an accountability requirement is violated, the a-taker has a legitimate reason for complaint. The notion of accountability requirement can be further refined in terms of *commitments*, *authorizations*, *prohibitions*, and *empowerments* [11]. Each of these relations has specific implications in terms of who is accountable and for what reason. It is worth noting that an a-giver is normally accountable for a specific condition towards the whole group of agents in a MAS. That is, in an agent society, agents are accountable for their actions towards the society as a whole. Rather than creating an accountability requirement between each possible pairs of a-giver and a-taker, it is convenient to adopt the perspective by Chopra and Singh, i.e. to consider both the agents and the organization as principals, among which mutual expectations can be defined.

In other words, an organization is considered as a *persona iuris* [11], a legal person that, hence, can be the a-giver or a-taker of an accountability requirement, as any other principal represented by an agent. In addition, an organization will also be the conceptual means through which complex goals are articulated in terms of subgoals, and distributed among a set of *roles*. An organization is, therefore, a design element that allows one to specify: (1) what should be achieved by the MAS (i.e., the organizational goals), and (2) what roles are included in the organization and with what (sub)goals. Concerning accountability, an organization that shows the above features naturally satisfies Principles 1 and 3.

Our intuition is that in order to obtain accountability as a design property of a MAS, the agents who are willing to be members of an organization enroll in the organization by following a precise *accountability protocol*. The organization provides the context in which accountability requirements are defined. To define such an accountability protocol, we rely on the broad literature about commitment-based protocols and focus our attention on the accountability requirements that can be expressed as (practical) commitments. Commitments have been studied at least since the seminal works by Castelfranchi [10] and Singh [22]. A social commitment is formally represented as $C(x, y, p, q)$, where x is the debtor (a-giver, in our case), that commits to the creditor y (a-taker) to bring about the consequent condition q should the antecedent condition p hold. From the accountability point of view, the a-giver is accountable when the antecedent becomes true, but the consequent is false.

The gist of the accountability protocol is to make explicit the legal relationships between the agent and the organization. These are expressed as a set of (abstract) commitments, directed from organizational roles towards the organization itself, and vice versa. The first step captures the adoption of a role by an agent. Let $pwr_{i,1}, \ldots, pwr_{i,m}$ be the powers that agent Ag_i, willing to play role R_i, will get. Ag_i will commit towards the organization to exercise the powers, given to it by the role, when this will be requested by the legal relationships it will create towards other agents. In this way, the agent stipulates awareness of the powers it is endowed with, becoming accountable, not only towards some other agent in the same organization but also towards the organization itself, of its behavior:

$cpwr_{i,1}::$ $\mathsf{C}(Ag_i, Org, \mathsf{C}(Ag_i, Z_1, pwr_{i,1}), pwr_{i,1})$

$\ldots$

$cpwr_{i,m}::$ $\mathsf{C}(Ag_i, Org, \mathsf{C}(Ag_i, Z_m, pwr_{i,m}), pwr_{i,m})$

above Z_j, $j = 1, \ldots, m$ represent some roles or some (not necessarily different) agents in the organization. These commitments represent the fact that, from an accountability-based point of view, an agent, when exercising a power because of a social relationship with some other agents, has some duties towards the social institution which provides that power, too. Indeed, when an employee is empowered by a manager to perform a given task on behalf of the company, the result is not only a commitment of the employee with the manager, but also a commitment of the employee with the company. An agent willing to play a role is expected to create a commitment that takes the form:

$cpwr_{R_i}::$ $\mathsf{C}(Ag_i, Org, \mathsf{accept\_player}_{Org}(Ag_i, R_i), cpwr_{i,1} \wedge \cdots \wedge cpwr_{i,m})$

where $\mathsf{accept\_player}_{Org}(Ag_i, R_i)$ is a power of the organization to accept agent, Ag_i, as a player of role R_i. Org, then, has the power to assign goals to the agents playing the various roles through $assign_{Org}$. This is done through the creation of commitments by which the organization promises to assign some goal to some agent should the agent accept to commit to pursue the goal:

$cass_{i,1}::$ $\mathsf{C}(Org, Ag_i, cg_{i,1}, \mathsf{prov}_{i,1} \wedge \mathsf{assign}_{Org}(Ag_i, goal_{i,1}))$

$\ldots$

$cass_{i,n}::$ $\mathsf{C}(Org, Ag_i, cg_{i,n}, \mathsf{prov}_{i,n} \wedge \mathsf{assign}_{Org}(Ag_i, goal_{i,n}))$

Above, $cg_{i,k=1,\ldots,n}$ denote the commitments by whose creation the agent explicitly accepts the goals and possibly asks for provisions $\mathsf{prov}_{i,k=1,\ldots,n}$. Here, $goal_{i,k}$ is a goal the organization would like to assign to the agent Ag_i. The antecedent condition of $cg_{i,k}$ has the shape $prov_{i,k} \wedge assign_{Org}(Ag_i, goal_{i,k})$, where $prov_{i,k}$ stands, as said, for a provision the agent requires for accomplishing the task, and the consequent condition has the shape $achieve_{Ag_i}(goal_{i,k})$:

$cg_{i,1}::$ $\mathsf{C}(Ag_i, Org, \mathsf{prov}_{i,1} \wedge \mathsf{assign}_{Org}(Ag_i, goal_{i,1}), \mathsf{achieve}_{Ag_i}(goal_{i,1}))$

$\ldots$

$cg_{i,n}::$ $\mathsf{C}(Ag_i, Org, \mathsf{prov}_{i,n} \wedge \mathsf{assign}_{Org}(Ag_i, goal_{i,n}), \mathsf{achieve}_{Ag_i}(goal_{i,n}))$

Provisions are to be instantiated with those prerequisites that Ag_i discloses as necessary for it to complete its job and that Org is expected to provide. On the agent side, these commitments are the means through which the agent arranges the boundaries of its accountability within the organization. For instance, *painter*, in our example above, is an agent hired in a painting organization including also *wall-preparer*. A provision for *painter* to paint a wall could be *wall-prepared*, a condition that is to be achieved by another agent from the same organization, and that appears in the accountability requirements of its role.

Should *wall-preparer* behave maliciously (as in our example), *painter* would not be accountable for not painting the wall as provision *wall-prepared* would be missing. On the organization side, provisions are part of the information used to decide whether to assign the goal to the agent (the internal decision processes of an organization are outside the scope of the paper). An agent becomes obliged to achieve a goal only after this assignment so as to not violate the accountability requirement. Finally, $achieve_{Ag_i}(g_{i,j})$ denotes that goal $goal_{i,j}$ is achieved.

We can now introduce the protocol that regulates the enrollment of an agent, Ag_i, in an organization, Org, as a player of role R_i, and the subsequent assignment of goals to Ag_i carried out by Org.

(1) create($cpwr_{R_i}$)

(2) accept_player$_{Org}(Ag_i, R_i)$

(3) create($cpwr_{i,1}$), ..., create($cpwr_{i,m}$)

(4) create($cass_{i,k}$), $k = 1, \ldots, n$

(5) create($cg_{i,k}$), $k = 1, \ldots, n$

(6) assign$_{Org}(Ag_i, goal_{i,k})$, $k = 1, \ldots, n$

(7) prov$_{i,k}$, $k = 1, \ldots, n$

(8) achieve$_{Ag_i}(goal_{i,k})$, $k = 1, \ldots, n$

An agent Ag_i, willing to play role R_i, makes the first step by creating the commitment, $cpwr_{R_i}$ (1). By doing so it proposes itself as role player. It is worth noting that the creation of $cpwr_{R_i}$ is possible only as a consequence of Principle 3, by which an organization must disclose the powers associated with its roles. The organization is free to decide whether to accept an agent as role player (2). In case of acceptance the agent creates the commitments by which it becomes accountable with the organization of the use of its powers (3). Step (4) allows the organization to communicate the goals it wishes to assign to the agents. The agents are expected to accept them by creating the corresponding commitments of Step (5), thereby knowing which goals it may be asked to achieve at Step (6). Steps (7) and (8) respectively allow the organization to satisfy the provisions, and the agent to communicate goal achievement.

Principle 1 finds an actualization in the fact that all the mentioned commitments are created within a precise organization instance. When Org accepts Ag_i as a player for role R_i, the enrollment of the agent is successfully completed. After this step, the agent operates in the organization as one of its members. This satisfies Principle 2, for which an agent is a member of an organization only when it plays an organizational role. Principles 4 and 5 find their actualization in terms of the commitments $cg_{i,k}$'s. Principle 4 demands that an agent is accountable only for those goals it has explicitly accepted to bring about. The creation of one of the commitments $cg_{i,k}$ represents the acceptance of being responsible, and hence accountable, for the goal occurring in the commitment consequent condition. Principle 5 states that an agent must have the leeway to negotiate its own duties, which we obtain in two ways. First, the agent creates its own commitments, which means that the mission commitments might cover just a subset of the goals. Second, the agent can make explicit provisions for each role goal.

5   Case Study: Accountability in JaCaMo

JaCaMo [5] is a conceptual model and programming platform that integrates agents, environments, and organizations. It is built on the top of three platforms, namely Jason [6] for programming agents, CArtAgO [21] for programming environments, and Moise+ [20] for programming organizations. The aim of the framework is both to integrate the cited platforms, and to integrate the related programming meta-models to simplify the development of complex MASs. The presence of an actual programming platform fills the gap between the modeling level and the implementation level. According to [19], the Moise+ organizational model, adopted in JaCaMo, explicitly decomposes the specification of an organization into three different dimensions. The *structural* dimension specifies roles, groups and links between roles in the organization. The *functional* dimension is composed of one (or more) scheme(s) that elicits how the global organizational goal(s) is (are) decomposed into sub-goals and how these sub-goals are grouped in coherent sets, called missions, to be distributed to the agents. Finally, the *normative* dimension binds the two previous dimensions by specifying the roles' permissions and obligations for missions. One important feature of Moise+ [20] is to avoid a direct link between roles and goals. Roles, indeed, are linked to missions by means of permissions and obligations. In this way, the functional and the structural specifications are kept somehow independent. This independence, however, is the source of some problems when reasoning about accountability. The reason is that schemes can be dynamically created during the execution, and assigned to groups within an organization, when agents are already playing the associated roles. This means that agents, *when entering into an organization* by adopting an organizational role, *have no information about what they could be obliged to do in the future* because this information, related to a specific scheme, could be not available or even not present at all at that time. *This contradicts Principle* 4.

Let's now consider an excerpt of the *building-a-house* example presented in [5]. An agent, called Giacomo, wants to build a house on a plot. In order to achieve this goal he will have to hire some specialized companies, and then ensure that the contractors coordinate and execute in the right order the various tasks and subgoals. We will focus on the second part of the work, namely the *building phase*. A company that is to be hired needs to adopt a role in the organization. Roles are gathered in a group that is responsible for the house construction. After goal adoption, a company agent could be asked (through an obligation issued by the organization) to commit to some "missions." Now, let's suppose that Giacomo is a dishonest agent and wants to exploit the contracted companies in order to achieve some purposes that are unrelated to house construction. In particular, let's suppose he wants to delegate a `do_a_very_strange_thing` goal to the agent who is playing the `plumber` role. This would be possible because an agent, when adopting a role, has no information about the kind of tasks that it could be assigned. These are, indeed, created in an independent way w.r.t. roles, and are associated with them only later. In the example, the `plumber` agent reasonably will not have a plan to achieve the `do_a_very_strange_thing` goal. Consequently, when the corresponding obligation is created, it will not be fulfilled.

Given the above scenario, who could we consider accountable for the inevitable goal failure of `do_a_very_strange_thing`? The agent playing the `plumber` role? Indeed, the agent is violating an obligation. Giacomo, because it introduced the new goal? Perhaps the system itself, since it permits such unfair behavior? The system, however, doesn't know the agents' capabilities, and cannot consequently make a fair/unfair judgment call. Our inability to attribute accountability stems from the lack of adherence to the Principles 4 and 5. Goal assignment is, in fact, without replication and is performed thorugh schemes, which can even be dynamically created and associated with an existing group. Moreover, the very independence between roles and goals violates Principle 4: when enacting a role in JaCaMo, agents make no claim about what kind of goals they are willing to have assigned (indeed, they could even not have the possibility to do so). For this reason they cannot be held accountable later for some organizational goal they haven't achieved. Finally, since agents do not explicitly commit to any goal while adopting a role, they cannot specify any provision needed in order to achieve a particular state of affairs. This contradicts Principle 5.

Our work with JaCaMo highlights a conceptual challenge in the concept of role and role's central place in responsibility and accountability (in the form of "role-following responsibility") as illustrated by [12]. To a certain degree, decoupling a role from an organizational execution essentially negates the role's function to limit its operational domain. As illustrated in our tinkering with building-a-house, without prior agreement of what exactly a role means in a particular organizational context, we can force a role to mean whatever we want so long as the language matches. This is in contrast with Principle 4. The consequent dynamism of roles makes automatic considerations of accountability impossible to conclude. In our construction of computational accountability, roles represent a division of responsibility and pattern of interaction that serve the investigative forum to assign accountability. The accountability protocol allows achieving accountability by design by excluding that the organization assigns goals beyond the powers the agents acquire by enacting a role. Moreover, the protocol allows agents to make their provisions explicit. As one way to enforce a behavior that respects the protocol, one could modify the conceptual model of JaCaMo (and its implementation) so that it follows the five principles. Another way is to introduce proper monitors that, if needed, can check that the protocol is respected. This calls for the realization of a kind of artifact that can monitor the interaction, represent the social state (made of the existing commitments), and track its evolution. A proposal based on [1] can be found in [2].

6   Conclusions

If we adapt the approach to roles developed in [4], in which roles essentially define an organization, accountability takes on functional implications for the very definitional existence of the organization. Should some roles remain unfulfilled, an organization would correspondingly find itself in definitional crisis. As illustrated in [17], role fulfillment means continual realization of role relationships, that is, a role's duties and obligations. Accountability allows an organization some recourse in crisis and a method of expressing the relative importance its roles play. Armed with the knowledge of relative responsibility and therefore importance in the collective, an organization enables role-playing agents to make informed decisions should conflicts arise and to make their own cost/benefit analysis should one wish to not perform its function.

A mechanism based on commitments presents numerous conceptual advantages for accountability. An agent is able to specify the exact social context in which it can fulfill the specified goal. It effectively announces to the organization that should its requirements become true, it will be accountable for fulfilling the goal. Essentially the commitments require pre-execution knowledge of expectations and requirements both on the part of the organization and of the agent, which satisfies accountability's foreknowledge requirement. Commitments can therefore provide indications of responsibility, as a pre-execution assignment, which will then, thanks to the exhaustive definitions of pre and post conditions, provide a direct mapping to accountability post execution. Since the agent by design creates the commitment to the organization, the agent, not the organization, specifies its requirements to satisfy the goal. Casual determinism and impossibilities are consequently absent at an organizational level because each agent stipulates the exact social circumstances in which it can operate and realize the goal. Moreover, role relationships become explicit through the provision stipulation, which will later provide basis for role-adherence determination. The commitment structure therefore provides the necessary characteristics for beginning to speak of accountability.

Based from our beginning discussion of accountability, responsibility plays a key role in building out our accountability system. Based on work like [13], we will need to associate levels of responsibility with roles in an organization, which will serve to later implicate accountability. In order to justify a direct mapping between responsibility and accountability, in future studies we will also work to fulfill the negative approach to accountability.

Acknowledgments. This work was partially supported by the *Accountable Trustworthy Organizations and Systems (AThOS)* project, funded by Università degli Studi di Torino and Compagnia di San Paolo (CSP 2014). The authors warmly thank the reviewers for their constructive and helpful comments which helped revising the paper.

References

1. Baldoni, M., Baroglio, C., Capuzzimati, F., Micalizio, R.: Commitment-based agent interaction in JaCaMo+. Fundam. Inf. (2017, to appear). http://www.di.unito.it/argo/papers/2017_FundamentaInformaticae.pdf
2. Baldoni, M., Baroglio, C., May, K.M., Micalizio, R., Tedeschi, S.: ADOPT JaCaMo: accountability-driven organization programming technique for JaCaMo. In: Prin-

ciples and Practice of Multi-Agent Systems, PRIMA 2017. Lecture Notes in Computer Science. Springer, Cham (2017)

3. Baldoni, M., Baroglio, C., May, K.M., Micalizio, R., Tedeschi, S.: Computational accountability. In: Proceedings of the AI*IA WS on Deep Understanding and Reasoning: A Challenge for Next-Generation Intelligent Agents 2016. CEUR Workshop Proceedings, vol. 1802. CEUR-WS.org (2017). http://ceur-ws.org/Vol-1802/paper8.pdf

4. Boella, G., van der Torre, L.: The ontological properties of social roles in multi-agent systems: definitional dependence, powers and roles playing roles. Artif. Intell. Law 15(3), 201–221 (2007)

5. Boissier, O., Bordini, R.H., Hübner, J.F., Ricci, A., Santi, A.: Multi-agent oriented programming with JaCaMo. Sci. Comput. Program. 78(6), 747–761 (2013)

6. Bordini, R.H., Hübner, J.F., Wooldridge, M.: Programming Multi-Agent Systems in AgentSpeak Using Jason, vol. 8. Wiley, Hoboken (2007)

7. Bovens, M., Goodin, R.E., Schillemans, T. (eds.): The Oxford Handbook of Public Accountability. Oxford University Press, Oxford (2014)

8. Braham, M., van Hees, M.: An anatomy of moral responsibility. Mind 121(483), 601–634 (2012)

9. Burgemeestre, B., Hulstijn, J.: Designing for accountability and transparency: a value-based argumentation approach. In: van den Hoven, J., Vermaas, P.E., van de Poel, I. (eds.) Handbook of Ethics, Values, and Technological Design: Sources, Theory. Values and Application Domains. Springer, Dordrecht (2015). doi:10.1007/978-94-007-6970-0_12

10. Castelfranchi, C.: Commitments: from individual intentions to groups and organizations. In: ICMAS, pp. 41–48. The MIT Press (1995)

11. Chopra, A.K., Singh, M.P.: The thing itself speaks: accountability as a foundation for requirements in sociotechnical systems. In: IEEE 7th International Workshop RELAW, p. 22. IEEE Computer Society (2014)

12. Conte, R., Paolucci, M.: Responsibility for societies of agents. J. Artif. Soc. Soc. Simul. 7(4) (2004)

13. Yazdanpanah, V., Dastani, M.: Distant group responsibility in multi-agent systems. In: Baldoni, M., Chopra, A.K., Son, T.C., Hirayama, K., Torroni, P. (eds.) PRIMA 2016. LNCS (LNAI), vol. 9862, pp. 261–278. Springer, Cham (2016). doi:10.1007/978-3-319-44832-9_16

14. Elder-Vass, D.: The Causal Power of Social Structures: Emergence, Structure and Agency. Cambridge University Press, Cambridge (2010)

15. Eshleman, A.: Moral responsibility. The Stanford Encyclopedia of Philosophy (2014)

16. Frankfurt, H.G.: Alternate possibilities and moral responsibility. J. Philos. 66(23), 829–839 (1969)

17. Guarino, N., Welty, C.: Evaluating ontological decisions with OntoClean. Commun. ACM 45(2), 61–65 (2002)

18. Hohfeld, W.N.: Some fundamental legal conceptions as applied in judicial reasoning. Yale Law J. 23(1), 16–59 (1913)

19. Hübner, J.F., Boissier, O., Kitio, R., Ricci, A.: Instrumenting multi-agent organisations with organisational artifacts and agents. Auton. Agent. Multi-Agent Syst. 20(3), 369–400 (2010)

20. Hübner, J.F., Sichman, J.S., Boissier, O.: Developing organised multiagent systems using the MOISE+ model: programming issues at the system and agent levels. Int. J. Agent-Oriented Softw. Eng. 1(3/4), 370–395 (2007)

21. Ricci, A., Piunti, M., Viroli, M., Omicini, A.: Environment programming in CArtAgO. In: El Fallah Seghrouchni, A., Dix, J., Dastani, M., Bordini, R. (eds.) Multi-Agent Programming, pp. 259–288. Springer, Boston (2009). doi:10.1007/978-0-387-89299-3_8
22. Singh, M.P.: An ontology for commitments in multiagent systems. Artif. Intell. Law **7**(1), 97–113 (1999)

Providing Self-aware Systems with Reflexivity

Alessandro Valitutti[1](✉) and Giuseppe Trautteur[2]

[1] University of Bari, Bari, Italy
alessandro.valitutti@gmail.com
[2] University of Naples Federico II, Naples, Italy
trau@na.infn.it

Abstract. We propose a new type of self-aware systems inspired by ideas from higher-order theories of consciousness. First, we discuss the crucial distinction between introspection and reflexion. Then, we focus on computational reflexion as a mechanism by which a computer program can inspect its own code at every stage of the computation. Finally, we provide a formal definition and a proof-of-concept implementation of computational reflexion, viewed as an enriched form of program interpretation and a way to dynamically "augment" a computational process.

Keywords: Computational reflexivity · Computational augmentation · Self-aware systems · Self-representation · Self-modification · Self-monitoring

1 Introduction

Self-aware computing is a recent area of computer science concerning autonomic computing systems capable of capturing knowledge about themselves, maintaining it, and using it to perform self-adaptive behaviors at runtime [1,13,24]. Almost all self-aware systems share one or more of three properties dealt with extensively in the AI literature: *self-representation*, *self-modification*, and *persistence*. Examples of self-aware behaviors are the introspection and reflection features implemented in some programming languages such as Java. Type introspection is the ability of a program to examine the type or properties of an object at runtime, while reflection[1] additionally allows a program to manipulate objects and functions at runtime.

However, neither of them have all of the above three properties. In fact, introspection implies self-representation but not self-modification. Moreover, reflection is temporally-bound, since it occurs in a small portion of the program execution. Even self-monitoring, considered as a periodic sequence of introspective events, implies persistence but not self-modification. We may wonder if we could have a type of computational self-awareness in which persistent self-representation and self-modification would occur simultaneously and yet being functionally distinct.

---

[1] The term *reflection* should not be confused with the term *reflexion*, which will be discussed in Sects. 2.3 and 3.

© Springer International Publishing AG 2017
F. Esposito et al. (Eds.): AI*IA 2017, LNAI 10640, pp. 418–427, 2017.
https://doi.org/10.1007/978-3-319-70169-1_31

In this paper, we address this issue and present a computational architecture provided with this property, which we call *computational reflexivity*. Specifically, we propose to introduce introspection and reflection at every step of the execution, enriching the interpretation loop with additional instructions aimed to represent the program at a meta level, combine local and global information, and perform a second-order execution. The enriched interpreter is thus capable of running a program and, concurrently, generating and executing a corresponding modified (or "augmented") version.

This separation between "observed" (or *target*) and "observing" (or *augmented*) process allows the system to perform self-modification at a virtual level (i.e., on the augmented process). As a consequence, the system can choose whether and when the modification should be applied to the target process. In addition to the formal definition of computational reflexivity, we provide a proof-of-concept prototype, implemented through the modification of a well-known meta-circular interpreter. It allows us to demonstrate that the proposed mechanism is computationally feasible and even achievable with a small set of instructions.

In our definition of computational reflexivity, we have been inspired by several concepts discussed in the literature on consciousness studies. Some of them will be reported in the following sections. Our main source of inspiration is, however, the notion of self-conscious reflexivity, as discussed in higher-order theories of consciousness, and the attempts to describe it in neuroscientific [6] and computational [25] terms.

The rest of the paper is organized as follows. In the next section, we present an overview of self-awareness, introspection, and reflexion in the context of both computer science and consciousness studies. Section 3 introduces the formal definitions of computational reflexion, and Sect. 4 introduces the prototype. Finally, we present a short discussion in Sect. 5 and draft possible applications and next research steps in Sect. 6.

2   Background

2.1   Procedural Introspection

In the context of the present work, we use the term *computational introspection* to indicate a program capable of accessing itself, create a self-representation, and manipulate it. However, a preliminary distinction should be made between different meanings of 'knowledge' underlying the notions of 'representation' and 'manipulation'. We distinguish between *procedural knowledge* and *declarative knowledge*, the former based on computable functions, and the latter on logical statements. Depending on which meaning of 'knowledge' is adopted, there are two different ways to define computational introspection, called here *procedural introspection* and *declarative introspection*, respectively.

Batali [3] claims that "introspection is the process of thinking about one's own thoughts and feelings. [...] To the degree that *thoughts* and *feelings* are computational entities, computational introspection would require the ability of a process to access and manipulate its own program and its current context" (See Valdemir and Neto [26] on *self-modifying code*). In other words, computational introspection corresponds to the ability of a program to process its own code as data and modify it[2].

By contrast, in declarative introspection, the *access* corresponds to the generation of a set of logical statements, while their *manipulation* is performed by logical inference [14,28]. Batali [3] says that "The general idea is that a computational system (an agent preferably) embodies a theory of reasoning (or acting, or whatever). This is what traditional AI systems are – each system embodies a theory of reasoning in virtue of being the implementation of a program written to encode the theory."

As discussed by Cox [5], "From the very early days of AI, researchers have been concerned with the issues of machine self-knowledge and introspective capabilities. Two pioneering researchers, Marvin Minsky and John McCarthy, considered these issues and put them to paper in the mid-to-late 1950s. [...] Minsky's [17] contention was that for a machine to adequately answer questions about the world, including questions about itself in the world, it would have to have an executable model of itself. McCarthy [14] asserted that for a machine to adequately behave intelligently it must declaratively represent its knowledge. [...] Roughly Minsky's proposal was procedural in nature while McCarthy's was declarative." On the basis of these ideas, Stein and Barnden performed a more recent work to enable a machine to procedurally simulate itself [21].

Interestingly, Johnson-Laird [10], inspired by Minsky, proposes a definition of procedural introspection closer to the concept of computable function. He claims that "Minsky's formulation is equivalent to a Turing machine with an interpreter that consults a complete description of itself (presumably without being able to understand itself), whereas humans consult an imperfect and incomplete mental model that is somehow qualitatively different." According to Smith [20], "the program must have access, not only to its program, but to fully articulated descriptions of its state available for inspection and modification." [...] Moreover, "the program must be able to resume its operation with the modified state information, and the continued computation must be appropriately affected by the changes."

Unlike the use of 'procedural' discussed above, actually consisting of a "declarative" representation of the "procedural knowledge", we employ the term in a more restrictive way. *Procedural introspection* is here limited to program code access and modification, without any logical modeling and inference. In this way, we want to avoid the possible dependence of a particular declarative modeling from the choices of the human designer, instead focusing on aspects connected to program access and modification.

---

[2] In this definition, we put together self-representation and self-modification and, thus, the *introspection* and *reflection* features mentioned in Sect. 1.

2.2   Introspection in Consciousness Studies

Historically, all the uses of the term 'introspection' in computer science have been influenced by the meaning of the same term in philosophy of mind and, later on, neurosciences and cognitive science. In consciousness studies, introspection is often discussed in the context of the so-called *higher-order (HO)* theories, based on the assumption that there are different "levels" or "orders" of mental states. Perceptions, emotions, and thoughts are instances of first-order mental states. Higher-order mental states are mental states about other mental states. For example, a thought about thinking something. Introspection is considered as "an examination of the content of the first-order states" [18]. It is not clear, however, if introspection itself is a high-order state or it is involved in the occurrence of first-order states.

2.3   Self-conscious Reflexivity

Introspection is not generally considered the main characteristic of conscious states. By contrast, as claimed by Peters [19], "consciousness is reflexivity", where *reflexion* is the "awareness that one is perceiving". Unlike other defining characteristics, such as intentionality, reflexivity is the only one that is considered unique to consciousness. Trautteur remarked that Damasio was the first scientist to describe reflexion in the context of neuroscience [25]. Damasio's definition of reflexion (referred to by the term *core self*) is reported in the following statement:

- It is the process of an organism caught in the act of "representing its own changing state as it goes about representing something else" ([6, p. 170]).

This definition is meant to be based on biological (and, thus, physicalist, objective) terms since the term 'representation' here denotes specific neural patterns. The next statement expresses the attempt by Trautteur to translate the above "metaphorical" definition in computational terms:

- [It] is the process of an agent "processing its own processing while processing an input[3]."

In this version, the *organism* is reformulated as a computational *agent* and *representation* as a computational *process*. Both the above statements present a logical issue. We refer to it as the *identity paradox*. It consists of the fact that the object and the subject of the experience are perceived as the same entity. It is a *violation of the identity principle*, also detectable in other expressions used by the same and other authors such as "presence of the self to itself" or "the identity of the owner (of experience) and the owned" [25].

---

[3] This statement is extracted from unpublished notes by Trautteur.

2.4 Elements of Inspiration and Informal Definition of Computational Reflexivity

To overcome this logical contradiction, we moved the focus from *identity* to *simultaneity*. This frame shifting was inspired by Van Gulick [27], which emphasizes the simultaneity of observed and observer: "what makes a mental state M a conscious mental state is the fact that it is accompanied by a simultaneous and non-inferential higher-order (i.e., meta-mental) state whose content is that one is now in M". The above statement triggered the insight that reflexion can be seen as the simultaneous occurrence of two *distinct* and *synchronized processes*. It implies three underlying assumptions in it: *temporal extension* (i.e., 'state' means that we are dealing with *processes*), *distinction* (i.e., we have *two* separate processes), and *synchronicity* (i.e., the two processes are *simultaneous*). Because of the temporal extension, the term 'simultaneity' is employed here in the sense of *interval simultaneity*, which refers to sequences of events [9]. Interval simultaneity does not necessarily imply, here, the simultaneity of the single events. Our assumption of synchronicity requires that each step in one of the two processes must occur only after a corresponding step in the other one. As shown in the next section, each pair of steps are part of the same interpretation loop.

Therefore, we informally define *computational reflexion* as the concurrent (i.e. at every step of the interpretation loop) and synchronized execution of a computer program and manipulation of its code. Correspondingly, an interpreter capable of performing computational reflexion is said to be provided with *computational reflexivity*. This definition implies that computational reflexivity is a characteristic of a particular class of universal machines.

3 Formal Definition of Computational Reflexion

In this section, we provide, a step a time, all building blocks for the formal definition of computational reflexion. We assume reflexivity as a property applicable to the execution of any computer program, instead of a property of a single program. For this reason, it must rely on a particular type of program interpretation. From the point of view of an interpreter, the execution of a program can be reduced to a number of iterations of the same *interpretation loop*. We use the term *step* to denote a single occurrence of the interpretation loop, despite its internal complexity. We unravel below the definition of computational reflexivity as a sequence of incremental enrichments of the interpretation loop. Each enrichment, referred by both a textual symbol and a graphic mark, is meant to induce a corresponding modification at the process level.

1. **Lower Step and Standard Execution.** The original computational step (i.e., the unmodified interpretation loop) is called here *lower step*, indicated by the symbol (S_L) and the graphic mark $\rightarrow$. At the process level, we call *target process* the overall program execution.

2. **Single Introspection and Tracing.** In this modified step, the interpreter executes a *local procedural introspection* on the current step, returning the code of the current instruction. It is called *single introspection*, indicated by the symbol (S_L, I_S) and the graphic mark of the interpretation loop is ⌐⌐ . At the process level, the system generates a trace of execution, similar to the one produced by a debugger.

3. **Single Upper Step and Mirroring.** The interpreter executes the instruction just extracted by introspection. We call it *upper step*, denoted by (S_L, I_S, S_{SU}). The overall loop is graphically represented as ⌐⌐ . At the process level, we have two identical programs simultaneously executed. We use the term *mirroring* to indicate this real-time duplication of the target process.

4. **Double Upper Step and Augmentation.** Here the interpretation loop is enriched with two further operations: the modification of the current step of the "mirrored program" by introduction of an additional instructions, and the next step execution[4]. The term *double upper step*, with the symbol (S_L, I_S, S_{DU}), indicates the execution of the "mirrored" instruction and the additional one. The overall loop is graphically represented as ⌐⌐ . We call *computational augmentation* the modification of the interpretation loop performed so far. Correspondingly, we have two simultaneous processes: the target process and the augmented process. The latter one is based on the former but modified *at the step level*.

5. **Double Introspection and Reflexion.** Now, we consider a particular type of computational augmentation, in which the additional instruction of the *double upper step* is a further operation of *global procedural introspection*. While the local introspection returns the code of the current instruction of the target program (i.e., the lower step defined above), the global introspection returns the code of the entire target program or a subset of it. In this case, the upper step consists of an execution of the mirrored instructions of the target program *plus* additional *global* instructions about it. We call *double introspection* this type of double upper step, and denote it by the symbol (S_L, I_D, S_{DU}). The overall loop is represented by the graphical mark ⌐⌐ . Finally, we define *computational reflexion* as the process generated by the loop composed by *lower step, double introspection* and *double upper step*.

Table 1 summarizes the schema of all components. Each row reports the symbolic representation, the graphical mark, and the corresponding terminology at both step and process level. In summary, the addition of specific groups of instructions to the interpretation loop underlies the generation of different processes, each built on the previous one: *standard execution, tracing, mirroring, augmentation*, and *reflexion*. Given a target process, the enriched interpreter executed the related program and a concurrent version executed, at every step,

---

[4] Although a more general class of code modification is conceivable, we limit the focus on the modification by instruction insertion. As explained in the next point, the aim is to enrich the second process with information about the target process.

Table 1. Different versions of the interpretation loop, with the addition of step components, and related computational processes.

Symbol	Step Components	Process Creation	Process
(S_L) →	*Lower Step*	*Standard Execution*	*Target Process*
(S_L, I_S)	*+ Single Introspection*	*Tracing*	*Execution Trace*
(S_L, I_S, S_{SU})	*+ Single Upper Step*	*Mirroring*	*Mirror Process*
(S_L, I_S, S_{DU})	→ *Double Upper Step*	*Augmentation*	*Augmented Process*
(S_L, I_D, S_{DU})	→ *Double Introspection*	*Reflexion*	*Reflexive Process*

with its own code. Our definition of computational reflexion is thus a formal specification of the informal one reported in Sect. 2.4.

4 Prototypical Implementation

As a proof of concept of the feasibility to implement computational introspection, as defined in the previous section, we developed a prototypical version. Specifically, we employed and modified the code of a Lisp meta-circular interpreter [8,12] (i.e., an interpreter of the Lisp programming language, implemented in the same language), called here *Lisp in Lisp*. The main reason for using *Lisp in Lisp* is that it is one of the simplest ways to implement a general-purpose interpreter. Indeed, it is a specific model of computation based on Church's Lambda Calculus [4,15]. As reported by McCarthy [16], "Another way to show that Lisp was neater than Turing machines was to write a universal Lisp function and show that it is briefer and more comprehensible than the description of a universal Turing machine. This was the Lisp function eval [...]" The program is just a few lines of code and the definition of its main function, *eval*, is based on the composition of a few primitive operators. The *eval* function is what is performing the interpretation (or *evaluation*) process.

In this case, we call *computational step* (and, equivalently, interpretation loop) the *Lisp in Lisp* execution between two next calls of the *eval* function. Therefore, using the sequence of steps described in the previous section, we modified the definition of *eval* adding additional function calls. For example, the single introspection event correspond to a call of the function *quote*, which returns the code of the argument (i.e. the instruction under execution). Respect to the original version of *Lisp in Lisp* the modified version was reformulated as a continuation-passing interpreter [7] with two additional arguments: one representing the "future of the computation" (i.e., the *continuation*) and the other representing the "past of the computation" (i.e., the *history*).

In the same way proceeded in the previous section, we focused on the interpretation loop and gradually enriched to obtain the version implementing computational reflexion.

1. **Lower Step.** It is equivalent to the interpretation loop defined above.
2. **Single (Local) Introspection.** The current *eval* call returns the code of the current instruction, consisting of a function call.
3. **Single Upper Step.** The code of the current function call, produced by the local introspection, is in turn executed (i.e. *eval* is called on it).
4. **Double Upper Step.** The code generated by local introspection is enriched with additional instructions. As an example, we added a *print* call to the output of the current call. In this way, the interpreter will display on the terminal the trace of execution.
5. **Double Introspection.** Finally, the interpretation loop is enriched with the instruction for global introspection. In other words, it returns the code of the entire program.

In summary, at any stage of the computation, the interpreter accesses and executes the code both locally and globally. In particular, the program code could be modified at each step and, thus, influence the next execution. The complete code of the program and applied examples of executions are free available for research purpose[5].

5   Discussion

The intuitions formalized in this paper are aimed to envision a new type of self-aware systems. While almost all state-of-the-art systems are based on introspection, we propose to consider reflexion as the main aspect of self-awareness. We could intuitively define computational reflexion as *"a mechanism for making a computational process continuously self-informed"*. The expression *"mechanism of making"* expresses the fact that is the property of a particular type of interpreter. Indeed, we focused on the interpretation loop and modified it. Reflexivity is not the feature of a specific class of computer programs but, instead, something that can be provided to any executable programs through this form of interpretation. Through reflexion, the standard program execution (i.e., the *target process*) is dynamically "reflected" into the execution of its augmented counterpart (i.e., the *reflexive process*).

As explained in Sect. 3, each instruction of the target program is executed twice: the first time (as sequence of *lower steps*) to achieve the standard execution (and generate the target process), and the second time (as sequence of *upper steps*) as part of the reflexive process. In the term *'self-informed'* used in the above definition, the prefix *'self'* is not referring to a single entity but to a couple of mutually interactive entities. This *duality* between the two synchronized processes is the way we addressed the *identity paradox* introduced in Sect. 2.3.

---

[5] Available at the URL http://valitutti.it/papers/reflexion/index.html.

6   Possible Applications and Future Work

The specific nature of computational reflexivity, summarized in the previous section, allows us to imagine a variety of applications. For example, we could see the execution of the target program and the corresponding reflexive augmentation as performed by two separate but synchronized devices. Specifically, we could have an autonomous agent (e.g. a robot in a physical environment) and an interfaced web service implementing reflexion. Therefore, computational reflexivity could be used as a way to provide a system with a temporary "streaming of self-awareness".

The aimed next steps of our research are focused on the following aspects. Firstly, we intend to further develop the proposed formalization and achieve possible interesting implications as formal theorems. Secondly, we aim to study the degree to which the reflexive process should give feedback to the target process and modify the related program. In other words, we would like to investigate aspects of run-time "virtual" self-modification, not yet taken into account, at this stage of the research, in our prototype.

A crucial issue is about efficiency. We need to investigate to what degree the combination of step-level local and global introspection and corresponding execution can be feasible performed. If the target program is sufficiently complex, there is a limitation in the number of instructions capable of being executed along the duration of the interpretation loop. In this case, the procedural modeling of the target process should be optimized. It would also interesting to compare the notion of computational reflexivity with the metacognitive mechanisms employed in general cognitive architectures such as CLARION [22,23], SOAR [11], or ACT-R [2]. Finally, we intend to explore the extent to which computational reflexivity could be employed to achieve a form of self organization, using the information gathered by the step-level introspective acts to train a self-reinforcement system.

References

1. Amir, E., Anderson, M., Chaudhri, V.K.: Report on DARPA workshop on self-aware computer systems. Technical report, Artificial Intelligence Center SRI International, Washington DC (2004)
2. Anderson, J.R., Bothell, D., Byrne, M.D., Douglass, S., Lebiere, C., Qin, Y.: An integrated theory of the mind. Psychol. Rev. **111**(4), 1036–1060 (2004)
3. Batali, J.: Computational introspection. Technical report AI-M-701, Massachussetts Institute of Technology (MIT), Cambridge, MA, US (1983)
4. Church, A.: The Calculi of Lambda-Conversion. Princeton University Press, Princeton (1941)
5. Cox, M.T.: Metacognition in computation: a selected research review. Artif. Intell. **169**(2), 104–141 (2005)
6. Damasio, A.: The Feeling of What Happens: Body and Emotion in the Making of Consciousness. Harcourt Brace, New York (1999)
7. Friedman, D.P., Wand, M.: Essentials of Programming Languages. The MIT Press, Cambridge (2008)

8. Graham, P.: The roots of lisp, 18 January 2002. http://lib.store.yahoo.net/lib/paulgraham/jmc.ps
9. Jammer, M.: Concept of Simultaneity: From Antiquity to Einstein and Beyond. The Johns Hopkins University Press, Baltimore (2006)
10. Johnson-Laird, P.N.: A computational analysis of consciousness. Cogn. Brain Theory **6**, 499–508 (1983)
11. Laird, J.: The Soar Cognitive Architecture. MIT Press, Cambridge (2012)
12. Landauer, C., Bellman, K.L.: Self-modeling systems. In: Laddaga, R., Shrobe, H., Robertson, P. (eds.) IWSAS 2001. LNCS, vol. 2614, pp. 238–256. Springer, Heidelberg (2003). doi:10.1007/3-540-36554-0_18
13. Lewis, P.R., Chandra, A., Faniyi, F., Glette, K., Chen, T., Bahsoon, R., Torresen, J., Yao, X.: Architectural aspects of self-aware and self-expressive computing systems: from psychology to engineering. Computer **48**(8), 62–70 (2015)
14. McCarthy, J.: Programs with common sense. In: Proceedings of the Teddington Conference on the Mechanization of Thought Processes, London (1959)
15. McCarthy, J.: Recursive functions of symbolic expressions and their computation by machine, part I. Commun. ACM **3**, 184–195 (1960)
16. McCarthy, J.: History of LISP. ACM SIGPLAN Not. - Special Issue: Hist. Program. Lang. Conf. **13**(8), 217–223 (1978)
17. Minsky, M.: Matter, mind, and models. In: Minsky, M. (ed.) Semantic Information Processing, pp. 425–432. MIT Press, Cambridge (1969)
18. Overgaard, M., Mogensen, J.: An integrative view on consciousness and introspection. Rev. Phil. Psych. **8**, 129–141 (2016). doi:10.1007/s13164-016-0303-6
19. Peters, F.: Theories of consciousness as reflexivity. Philos. Forum **44**, 341–372 (2013)
20. Smith, B.: Reflection and semantics in a procedural language. Technical report 272, MIT Laboratory of Computer Science (1982)
21. Stein, G., Barnden, J.: Towards more flexible and common-sensical reasoning about beliefs. In: Cox, M., Freed, M. (eds.) Proceedings of the 1995 AAAI Spring Symposium on Representing Mental States and Mechanisms, pp. 127–135. AAAI Press, Menlo Park (1995)
22. Sun, R.: The clarion cognitive architecture: extending cognitive modeling to social simulation. In: Sun, R. (ed.) Cognition and Multi-Agent Interaction, pp. 79–99. Cambridge University Press, New York (2006)
23. Sun, R., Zhang, X., Mathews, R.: Modeling meta-cognition in a cognitive architecture. Cogn. Syst. Res. **7**, 327–338 (2006)
24. Torresen, J., Plessl, C., Yao, X.: Self-aware and self-expressive systems. Computer **48**(7), 18–20 (2015)
25. Trautteur, G.: Some remarks about consciousness. Networks **3–4**, 165–172 (2004)
26. Valdemir, A., Neto, J.: Adaptivity in programming languages. Trans. Inf. Sci. Appl. **4**(4), 779–786 (2007)
27. Van Gulick, R.: Consciousness. In: Zalta, E.N. (ed.) The Stanford Encyclopedia of Philosophy. The Metaphysics Research Lab, Spring 2014 edn. (2014)
28. Weyhrauch, R.: Prolegomena to a theory of formal reasoning. Artif. Intell. **13**(1), 133–176 (1980)

Towards a Cognitive Semantics of Types

Daniele Porello[✉] and Giancarlo Guizzardi

Free University of Bozen-Bolzano, Bolzano, Italy
danieleporello@gmail.com

Abstract. Types are a crucial concept in conceptual modelling, logic, and knowledge representation as they are an ubiquitous device to understand and formalise the classification of objects. We propose a logical treatment of types based on a cognitively inspired modelling that accounts for the amount of information that is actually available to a certain agent in the task of classification. We develop a predicative modal logic whose semantics is based on conceptual spaces that model the actual information that a cognitive agent has about objects, types, and the classification of an object under a certain type. In particular, we account for possible failures in the classification, for the lack of sufficient information, and for some aspects related to vagueness.

Keywords: Types · Conceptual spaces · Sortals · Identity · Vagueness

1 Introduction

Conceptual Modelling is a discipline of fundamental importance for several areas in Computer Science, including Software Engineering, Enterprise Architecture, Domain Engineering, Database Design, Requirements Engineering and, in particular, for several subareas of Artificial Intelligence, most notably, Knowledge Representation and Ontology Engineering [7].

From a cognitive point of view, without types, we would not be able classify objects and, without classification, our mental life would be chaotic. As [21] puts it: *Categorization [...] is a means of simplifying the environment, of reducing the load on memory, and of helping us to store and retrieve information efficiently.* If we perceived each entity as unique, we would be overwhelmed by the sheer diversity of what we experience and unable to remember more than a minute fraction of what we encounter. Furthermore, if each individual entity needed a distinct name, our language would be staggeringly complex and communication virtually impossible. In contrast, if you know nothing about a novel object but you are told it is an instance of X, you can infer that the object has all or many properties that Xs have [20].

Frequently, monadic types used in conceptual models have as their instances *objects*, i.e., entities that persist in time, possibly undergoing qualitative changes, while keeping their identity throughout most of these changes. On the one hand, the importance of object types is well recognized in the aforementioned areas,

© Springer International Publishing AG 2017
F. Esposito et al. (Eds.): AI*IA 2017, LNAI 10640, pp. 428–440, 2017.
https://doi.org/10.1007/978-3-319-70169-1_32

as basically all conceptual modelling, ontology design, and knowledge representation approaches have as first-class citizens modelling primitives to represent them. On the other hand, in most of these approaches, the notion of object types taken is equivalent to the notion of a unary predicate in first-order logical languages. As a consequence, these approaches ignore a number of fundamental ontological and cognitive aspects related to the notion of object type. These include the following.

Not all types have the same ontological nature, hence, not all types classify objects in the same manner and with the same force. In particular, whilst all types provide a *principle of application* for deciding whether something fall under their classification, only types of a particular sort (termed *sortals*) provides also a *principle of persistence, individuation, counting and trans-world identity* for their instances [12,16]. In particular, a specific type of sortal termed a *kind* is fundamental for capturing the *essential properties* of the objects they classify. Hence, kinds classify their instances *necessarily* (in the modal sense), i.e., in all possible situations. In fact, there is a large amount of empirical evidence in cognitive psychology supporting the claim that we cannot make any judgment of identity without the support of a kind [16,22]. This, in turn, should have direct consequences to our formal understanding of types. For instance, given that there is no identity and no counting of individuals without a kind, then we should not quantify over individuals of our domains without the support of a kind. On a second aspect, from a cognitive point of view, our judgment of both the qualities and attributes of an object as well of which objects fall under a certain type are *vague*.

In this paper we make a contribution towards a new logical system designed to capture important ontological and cognitive aspects of types. Firstly, we propose a view of types that is grounded in the information that a cognitive agent has about the type, the object that may be apt to be classified under the type, and about the act of classification. In order to ground this view on a cognitively motivated account of types, we place our modelling within the theory of conceptual spaces proposed by Gärdenfors [6]. Briefly, Gärdenfors models the qualities of an objects by means of multidimensional space, a *conceptual space*, endowed with a distance that is intended to represent similarity between qualities. An example is the space of colours, composed by a three dimensions (brightness, chromaticness, hue) that are capable of explaining the similarity perceived by a cognitive agent among colours, by means of the methodology of multidimensional scaling [10].

Secondly, this system is compatible with philosophical view of objects and types, which focuses on the crucial distinctions between sorts of types, in particular, differentiating between sortals and ordinary predicates and between essential (kinds) and inessential sortals. In order to characterize these distinctions, a system must heavily rely on a modal treatment of objects and types. For this reason, it is compelling to understand how the modal view can be combined with the idea of the classification captured by conceptual spaces.

A combination of modal logic and conceptual spaces has been developed in [8] where the semantics of types may be given in terms of *concepts* in the sense of Gärdenfors, i.e., suitable subsets of a conceptual space. In this paper, we aim to extend the conceptual view of types by introducing a number of elements that better account for possible failures, partiality, and vagueness of the task of classification that cognitive agents might face. In order to achieve that, a number of significant points of departures from Gärdenfors' view has to be embraced.

On the one hand, we shall view the semantics of types as *rough sets* rather than mere sets. Rough sets are a generalisation of sets that allows for indeterminacy in the classification [17]. A rough set is intuitively composed by three regions: its positive part, containing the case of certain classification, its negative part, containing the cases of non-classification, and a boundary of undetermined classification. Rough sets are then a viable tool for representing partiality, vagueness, or uncertainty in the task of classification.

On the other hand, the view of objects in conceptual spaces is problematic both from a cognitive and a philosophical perspective [15]. Objects in the view of Gärdenfors are identified with points in a conceptual space. From a cognitive perspective, that amounts to viewing the information about a certain object as fully determined. For instance, an agent must know the precise shade of colour, the exact weight, the sharp length of any recognisable object. This is indeed cognitively unrealistic. From a philosophical perspective, by identifying objects as points in a conceptual space, we are identifying the reference of a proper name with its specified sensible qualities and this aspect poses serious problems to the modalisation of the view of objects. In particular, we lose the rigid designation of proper names, as it is hard to assume that the qualities of an object are stable across possible worlds, time, circumstances. Abandoning the rigid designation of proper names entail facing a serious amount of complications effectively highlighted by Kripke [11]. For that reason, we prefer to embrace rigid designation of proper names (i.e. the individual constants in our logical language) and abandon the identification of objects with points in a conceptual space.

To cope for this two aspects, the cognitive and the philosophical perspective, we shall assume that individual constants are interpreted in a separated set of objects that is distinguished by the conceptual space. The denotation of constants is then rigid, in any possible world the denotation of individual constants is the same. However, the amount of information about the object may vary. For this reason we shall also associate the individual constants to the amount of information that an agent has about the qualities of the objects. The information associated to the individual constants plays the role of the *intension* in a Fregean perspective: roughly, the intension captures the amount of information that is required in order to access or recognise the extension, or the denotation, of the constant [5]. In a similar way, we shall introduce the intension of a type as the amount of information that the agent has about the type and we shall define the extension of a type as set of objects classified by the type. According to a Fregean perspective, as we shall see, the intension of a type will allow for determining its extension.

The contribution of this paper is the following. We present a three-valued logic to reason about the classification of objects under possibly rough types emerging form concepts in a conceptual space. For this reason, we extend the treatment of classification of [8] to account for partial and vague information. Moreover, we develop a modal logic on top of the three-valued logic in order to formally capture the significant definitions of kinds of types, therefore extending [14,15] to account for modalities. The remainder of this paper is organised as follows. The next section presents a simplified formulation of conceptual spaces. Section 3 presents a three-valued logic for rough sets that is adequate to represent classification under the assumption of vague or partial information. Section 4 discusses the proof-theory of the proposed system. Section 5 presents an applications of our framework to the classification of types. Section 6 concludes.

2   Conceptual Spaces

We present our formal framework that relies on previous work on conceptual spaces. Our definition of conceptual spaces is inspired by the formalizations based on vector spaces provided in [1,19]. A *domain* Δ is given by a number of n quality dimensions $Q_1, \ldots, Q_n$ endowed with a distance d_Δ that usually depends on the distances defined on its quality dimensions. Following [1], we assume that every domain contains the distinguished point $*$.[1] A conceptual space is defined by Gärdenfors as a set of domains $\{\Delta_1, \ldots, \Delta_n\}$. We simplify the model by putting the following definition:

Definition 1. *A conceptual space is a subset of the cartesian product of n domains:* $\mathcal{C} \subseteq \Delta_1 \times \cdots \times \Delta_n$.

Our definition is weaker than the one proposed by [1], as we are taking any subset of the cartesian product as a conceptual space. This is motivated just as a simplifying move. Stronger definitions, that express, for instance, separability and integrality of the domains, can be retrieved by putting suitable constraints on $\mathcal{C}$.

A point of a conceptual space with n domains is an element $x \in \mathcal{C}$, that is, $x = \langle x_1, \ldots, x_n \rangle$ is a vector of values in each domain, i.e., we do not explicitly consider the dimensions of the domains and the reduction of the distances d_{Δ_i} to the ones of the dimensions. These aspects are not relevant to the present treatment.

Gärdenfors represents *concepts* as regions in conceptual spaces. In addition, he assumes that *natural* concepts correspond to sets of convex regions (that represent natural properties) in a number of domains with a salience assignment. We leave salience for future work and, to provide an interpretation to disjunctions and negations of concepts, we do not concentrate on what Gärdenfors terms natural concepts, e.g., the union or the complement of convex regions, in general, is not convex. A *sharp concept* is then represented just as a subset $R \subseteq \mathcal{C}$. By contrast, we represent *rough concepts* by *rough sets* [17]. Following [2], a rough set of $\mathcal{C}$ is specified by means of a pair of sets $\langle A, B \rangle$ such that $A \subseteq B \subseteq \mathcal{C}$: A

---

[1] $*$ means here that a certain quality is not applicable to a certain object.

represents the interior of the rough set, B is its exterior, and $B \setminus A$ its boundary. The intuition behind a rough concept C is that one does not have a sharp definition of C, i.e., only the properties that belong to its interior are necessary for all the instances of C. The properties that belong to its boundary are, in general, satisfied only by some instances of C. Therefore, for the objects placed at the boundary of C, one can neither conclude that they are C-instances nor that they are not C-instances. This aspect relates to *prototype theory*, where one can consider a *graded membership* with two thresholds, one associated with A, the other with B. These thresholds can also be defined on the basis of the distances d_Δ defined on the relevant dimension. Finally, note that sharp concepts are just a special case of rough ones, i.e., they can simply be represented by particular rough sets with form $\langle A, A \rangle$.

3   A Logic for Types

We introduce a predicative language $\mathcal{L}$ by specifying the alphabet that contains a countable set of individual constants $\mathbf{C} = \{c_1, c_2, \dots\}$ and a countable set of variables $\mathbf{V} = \{x_1, x_2, \dots\}$. The set of unary predicates (i.e. types) is split into two sorts of predicates: *kind* $\mathbf{K} = \{K_1, K_2, \dots\}$ and *regular*, or common, predicates, $\mathbf{P} = \{P_1, P_2, \dots\}$ that have, as we shall see, distinct interpretations. We focus on unary predication in this paper, thus we do not introduce relations at this point, besides the identity $\{=\}$, which we shall discuss in a dedicated section. In particular, we also assume a set of (relative identity) relations $\{=_{K_1}, \dots, =_{K_n}\}$, where K_i are kinds. As we shall see, the relative identity relations apply only to objects of the same kind.

Moreover, we assume the following set of logical connectives $\{\neg, \wedge, \vee, \rightarrow\}$. For quantification, we assume as in [8] only a restricted form of quantification that depends on a kind, that is, we assume the following set of restricted quantifiers $\{\forall_{K_1}, \forall_{K_2}, \dots, \}$ where $K_i \in \mathbf{K}$. Moreover, we assume a modal operator on propositions $\{\Box\}$.

The set of formulas is defined by induction in the usual way. Assume that $c_i, c_j \in \mathbf{C}$, $Q \in \mathbf{S} \cup \mathbf{P}$, $\star \in \{\neg, \wedge, \vee, \rightarrow\}$, and $\phi(x)$ denotes the formula ϕ with x as the sole free variable[2].

$$\mathcal{L} ::= c_i =_{K_i} c_j \mid Q(c_i) \mid \phi \star \phi \mid \forall_{S_j} \phi(x) \mid \Box \phi$$

We introduce now the structure that we use to define the models of our language [15].

Definition 2. *A conceptual* structure for $\mathcal{L}$ *is a tuple* $S = \langle \mathcal{C}, \mathcal{O}, \epsilon, \iota, \sigma \rangle$ *where:*

- $\mathcal{C}$ *is a conceptual space;*
- $\mathcal{O}$ *is a non empty set of* objects;
- ϵ *is a function that maps individual constants into objects,* $\epsilon : \mathbf{C} \rightarrow \mathcal{O}$;

---

[2] Since we deal with restricted quantification, we define the predicative language without open formulas.

- ι *is a function that maps predicates into rough sets of* $\mathcal{C}$, $\iota : \mathbf{P} \to \mathcal{P}(\mathcal{C}) \times \mathcal{P}(\mathcal{C})$;
- σ *is a function that maps objects into regions of* $\mathcal{C}$, $\sigma : \mathcal{O} \to \mathcal{P}(\mathcal{C})$.

A *conceptual model* M is then obtained by adding a valuation function $||\cdot||_M$ that maps formulas to a suitable set of truth-values. $||\cdot||_M$ depends on ϵ, ι, σ but also on the choice of the set of truth-values that captures the possible classifications. To capture reasoning about rough sets, we assume three truth-values $\{t, u, f\}$, representing truth, false, and undetermined.

The modal structure of the logic is then captured by means of the following definitions.

Definition 3. *A constant domain frame* $\langle W, R, \mathcal{C}, O \rangle$ *is given by a set of possible worlds* W, *an accessibility relation* R, *a conceptual space* $\mathcal{C}$ *and a domain of interpretation of the individual constants, that is in our case, the set of objects* O.

An interpretation $\mathcal{I}_w$ specifies, for each $w \in W$, a conceptual model M for w. That is, a conceptual structure $S = \langle \mathcal{C}, \mathcal{O}, \epsilon, \iota_w, \sigma_w \rangle$ such that $\mathcal{C}$, O, and ϵ are fixed for every possible world w. What indeed can change through possible worlds is the intension of individual constants σ_w and of predicates ι_w and therefore, as we shall see, their extension when varying w.

Formally, the objects in $\mathcal{O}$ provide the denotation of the individual constants in $\mathbf{C}$. The function ϵ, called *extension*, associates individual constants to objects, thus it plays the role of the interpretation function in a standard first-order model. In Fregean terms, ϵ provides the denotation, or the reference, of the individual constant.

The σ function locates objects in $\mathcal{C}$, i.e., it characterises an object in terms of its properties, represented as regions of $\mathcal{C}$. In this sense, the view of the meaning of individual constants defined here is similar to their treatment in terms of individual concepts proposed in [8]. Different objects may then have the same associated properties, allowing us to deal with the problem of coincidence and separate it from identity. In addition, the partial or vague information about objects can be represented by locating them in regions (rather than points) of $\mathcal{C}$, in case the exact (fully determinate) properties of an object are not known. To capture the case of fully determinable objects, it is always possible to assign all the objects to singleton subsets of $\mathcal{C}$. Again, in Fregean terms, σ provides the intension of the individual constant, the amount of information about the object that is required in order to understand its denotation.

The (rough) concepts of $\mathcal{C}$ provide the semantics of both kinds and regular predicates of $\mathcal{L}$. The function ι_w, called *intension*, maps a predicate $P \in \mathbf{P}$ into a (rough) set of $\mathcal{C}$ that we indicate by $\langle \underline{\iota_w}(P), \overline{\iota_w}(P) \rangle$.[3] Given a rough set, we

---

[3] Note that we are using a concept of intension that differs from the standard view of modal logics, i.e. the Carnap view of intensions as functions form possible worlds to extensions of predicates. Here the intension of a type, in a Fregean perspective, is the relevant information associated to the type. This information may or may not change through possible worlds. This is an open question that requires further investigation. In this paper, we prefer not to commit to either assumption.

can define three regions (that depend on the interpretation of P in w): $POS_P^w = \underline{\iota_w}(P)$, $NEG_P^w = \mathcal{C} \setminus \bar{\iota_w}(P)$, and $BN_P^w = \bar{\iota_w}(P) \setminus \underline{\iota_w}(P)$.

The (rough) extension of a predicate P in the world w—the set of objects that (roughly) satisfy P in w—can be defined on the basis of how an object is positioned in $\mathcal{C}$ (via σ_w) with respect to the intension of P in w. This is captured by means of the following definition:

$$\epsilon_w(P) = \{o \in \mathcal{O} \mid \sigma_w(o) \subseteq \iota_w(P)\} \tag{1}$$

The extension of a predicate in w is given by the set of objects that are classified by $\iota_w(P)$. This view embraces a Fregean perspective on predicates and on predication: the intension of a predicate (its *Sinn*) is a mean to obtain, or compute, its extension, cf. [5]. In this way, we partially capture the intension of predicates, i.e., their meaning is not reduced to a mere set of objects, rather it is given by the amount of information that is required to perform the classification [18].

Since fully determinate objects are associated to points and sharp sets are a special case of rough sets, our modelling generalises the case of classification defined in [6,8].

3.1 Semantics of Predication

We start by presenting the semantics of atomic sentences. We denote by $||\phi||_w$ the valuation of a formula ϕ in w, meaning that ϕ has value $||\phi||_w$ at w. Since objects are associated to regions in $\mathcal{C}$ and predicates are mapped to rough sets of $\mathcal{C}$, we have to decide how to view the amount of information about the object and the concept [15]. Among the viable readings, we choose the following definition.

$$||P(a)||_w = t \text{ iff } \sigma_w(\epsilon(a)) \subseteq POS_P^w \tag{2}$$
$$||P(a)||_w = u \text{ iff } \sigma_w(\epsilon(a)) \nsubseteq POS_P^w \text{ and } \sigma(\epsilon(a)) \nsubseteq NEG_P^w \tag{3}$$
$$||P(a)||_w = f \text{ iff } \sigma_w(\epsilon(a)) \subseteq NEG_P^w \tag{4}$$

True means that all the points in $\sigma(\epsilon(a))$ are certainly P, that is, they are in the positive part of P. The case of falsity means that all the points of $\sigma(\epsilon(a))$ are certainly not P, that is, they are in the negative part of P. The case of $||P(a)||_w = u$ does not entail that $\sigma(\epsilon(a))$ is fully included in BN_P^w, $\sigma(\epsilon(a))$ may spread across all the three regions POS_P^w, NEG_P^w, and BN_P^w, cf. Fig. 1.

3.2 Kinds vs Regular Types

We define kinds as predicates that are rigid and that provide an identity criterion. To capture the distinction between kinds and regular predicates, we restate the previous definition as follows. For $P \in \mathbf{P}$, $||Q(a)||_w$, is exactly as in (2), (3), and (4). For $K \in \mathbf{K}$, we fix the interpretation of K across possible worlds:

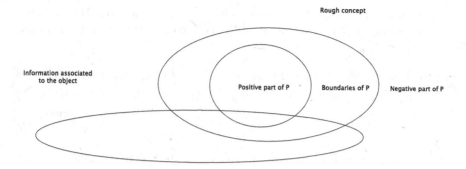

Fig. 1. Undertermined truth-value of classification

$$||K(a)||_w = t \text{ iff for all } w, \sigma_w(\epsilon(a)) \subseteq POS_K^w \qquad (5)$$

$$||K(a)||_w = u \text{ iff for all } w, \sigma_w(\epsilon(a)) \nsubseteq POS_K^w \text{ and } \sigma(\epsilon(a)) \nsubseteq NEG_{K_w} \qquad (6)$$

$$||K(a)||_w = f \text{ iff for all } w, \sigma_w(\epsilon(a)) \subseteq NEG_K^w \qquad (7)$$

The definition of kinds amounts to assuming that their extension is fixed in any possible worlds. For instance, an object that is classified as (of the kind) person cannot cease to be a person. In principle, we could also fix the intension of each kind for every world, that would amount to assuming that the information associated to a kind is the same in any possible world.

A second crucial feature of kinds is that they provide identity criteria. That is, identity is only defined across individuals classified by the same kind (either directly classified under the same kind or classified under sortals that specialize the same kind). For this reason, we present now the treatment of the identity relation.

3.3   Identity

We can in principle add a standard identity relation to the first order language. The semantics is given by the following definition. For any two terms τ and τ', we have that:

- $||\tau = \tau'||_w = t \text{ iff } \varepsilon(\tau) = \varepsilon(\tau').$
- $||\tau = \tau'||_w = f \text{ iff } \varepsilon(\tau) \neq \varepsilon(\tau').$

As the definition shows, the truth-value of every identity statement only depends on ε. This view of identity is *ontological*, in the sense that it does not depend on any data about τ and τ'. Moreover, identity statements are determined, there is indeed no room for the third truth-value u.

This view entails, due to the constant domain assumption, that if an identity statement is true at a world, then it is necessary true. In this sense, that notion of identity captures an ontological view of identity.

In our language, instead, we assume that ontological identity is always relative to a kind. That is why we assumed the set of relative identity relations $\{=_{K_1}, \ldots, =_{K_n}\}$.

$$||\tau =_{K_1} \tau'||_w = t \text{ iff } \sigma(\varepsilon(\tau)) \subseteq POS_{K_l}^w, \sigma(\varepsilon(\tau')) \subseteq POS_{K_l}^w \text{ and } \varepsilon(\tau) = \varepsilon(\tau'). \quad (8)$$
$$||\tau =_{K_l} \tau'||_w = f \text{ iff } \sigma(\varepsilon(\tau)) \subseteq POS_{K_l}^w, \sigma(\varepsilon(\tau')) \subseteq POS_{K_l}^w, \varepsilon(\tau) \neq \varepsilon(\tau'). \quad (9)$$
$$||\tau =_{K_1} \tau'||_w = u \text{ iff otherwise} \quad (10)$$

In case we also have a standard identity predicate, the relative identity relations can be defined as follows.

$$- \tau =_{K_i} \tau' \leftrightarrow K_i(\tau) \wedge K_i(\tau') \wedge \tau = \tau'$$

As we have seen, the standard identity is always determined. Relative identity is not, this is due to the possible uncertainty in classifying an object under a kind, e.g. the truth-value of $K_i(\tau)$ may be u. For this reason, the relative identity has a cognitive note, it depends on the actual information that are available about the relata and their classification under a kind.

3.4 Semantics of Logical Operators

The definition of logical connectives follows the following truth tables of Kleene logic plus the Lukasiewicz definition of implication, which is suited for treating a semantics based on rough sets [2] (Table 1).

¬	t u f
	f u t

∧	t u f
t	t u f
u	u u f
f	f f f

∨	t u f
t	t t t
u	t u u
f	t u f

→	t u f
t	t u f
u	t t u
f	t t t

The semantic definition of restricted quantifiers is the following. Denote by $Q(x/c_j)$ the substitution of the variable x with constant c_j.

$$||\forall_{K_l} x\, Q(x)||_w = t \text{ iff for all } c_j \text{ such that } \sigma(c_j) \subseteq POS_{K_l}^w, ||Q(x/c_j)||_w = t \quad (11)$$

$$||\forall_{K_l} x\, Q(x)||_w = f \text{ iff there is a } c_j \text{ such that } \sigma(c_j) \nsubseteq POS_{K_l}^w, ||Q(x/c_j)||_w = f \quad (12)$$

$$||\forall_{K_l} x\, Q(x)||_w = u \text{ iff otherwise.} \quad (13)$$

The true clause of restricted quantification means that a universal statement is true if for any constant c_j whose interpretation satisfies the kind K_l (i.e. $\sigma(c_j) \subseteq POS_{K_l}$), $Q(x/c_j)$ is true at w. The false clause only required that there is a counterexample to $\forall_{K_l} x\, Q(x)$ among those c_j that fall under the kind K_l. In any other case, the value of $\forall_{K_l} x\, Q(x)$ is undetermined.

Table 1. Axioms and rule for modal Lukasiewicz logic

Axioms

1. $A \rightarrow (B \rightarrow A)$
2. $(A \rightarrow B) \rightarrow ((B \rightarrow C) \rightarrow (A \rightarrow C))$
3. $(A \rightarrow (B \rightarrow C)) \rightarrow (B \rightarrow (A \rightarrow C))$
4. $((A \rightarrow B) \rightarrow B) \rightarrow ((B \rightarrow A) \rightarrow A)$
5. $(((A \rightarrow B) \rightarrow A) \rightarrow A) \rightarrow (B \rightarrow C) \rightarrow (B \rightarrow C)$
6. $A \wedge B \rightarrow A$
7. $A \wedge B \rightarrow B$
8. $(A \rightarrow B) \rightarrow ((A \rightarrow C) \rightarrow (A \rightarrow B \wedge C))$
9. $A \rightarrow A \vee B$
10. $B \rightarrow A \vee B$
11. $(A \rightarrow C) \rightarrow ((B \rightarrow C) \rightarrow (A \vee B \rightarrow C))$
12. $(\neg B \rightarrow \neg A) \rightarrow (A \rightarrow B)$
13. $\forall x A(x) \rightarrow A(\tau)$
14. $\forall x (A \rightarrow B) \rightarrow (A \rightarrow \forall x B)$ (where x is not free in A).
15. $\forall x \Box A(x) \leftrightarrow \Box \forall x A(x)$
16. $\Box(A \rightarrow B) \rightarrow (\Box A \rightarrow \Box B)$

Rules

- *Modus Ponens*: if $\vdash A$ and $\vdash A \rightarrow B$, then $\vdash B$.
- *Generalisation*: if $\vdash A$, then $\vdash \forall x A(x)$.
- *Necessitation*: if $\vdash A$, then $\vdash \Box A$

The semantics of the $\Box$ modality is then the following:

$$||\Box \phi||_w = t \text{ iff for all } w' \text{ such that } wRw', ||\phi||_w = t \tag{14}$$
$$||\Box \phi||_w = f \text{ iff there is a } w' \text{ such that } wRw', ||\phi||_w = f \tag{15}$$
$$||\Box \phi||_w = u \text{ iff otherwise.} \tag{16}$$

In a similar fashion as the case of universal quantification, we assume that a $\Box \phi$ is true if for every accessible world, ϕ is true there, $\Box \phi$ is false if there is an accessible world that falsifies ϕ, and it is undetermined in the other cases. Note that, in case we want to maintain a standard modal logic setting, kinds and restricted quantification can be defined by maintaining the following axioms. Denote by $A(x)$ a formula with x among its free variables.

$$K(x) \leftrightarrow \Box K(x) \tag{17}$$
$$\neg K(x) \leftrightarrow \Box \neg K(x) \tag{18}$$
$$\forall_K x A(x) \leftrightarrow \forall x (K(x) \rightarrow A(x)) \tag{19}$$

The first two axioms fix the extension of a kind in every possible world, while the third axiom defines the relative identity relations.

4   A Hilbert System

We can introduce a Hilbert system for capturing reasoning in our proposed system. The first-order Lukasiewicz three-valued logic is defined by means the following list of axioms and two inference rules developed in [3,9]. For the modal part, since we are assuming a constant domain for the interpretation of the individual constants (via σ), we shall assume the Barcan formula and its converse [4]. Moreover, we assume the principle K, i.e. axiom 16, and the necessitation rule.

The concept of derivation in $\vdash$ is defined by induction as usual [3]. We leave the proof of soundness and completeness for a dedicated future work.

In this calculus, the distinction between kinds and regular predicates, the restricted quantifications, and the relative identity relations can be defined as we have seen in Definitions (17), (18), and (19).

5   Sortal, Rigid, Anti-rigid Types

We defined a kind K as a predicate that is rigid and that provides an identity criterion, by enabling to define a relative identity relation $=_K$. For the sake of example, we present how to define a few other important notions of types. Firstly, we define the concepts of rigidity, non-rigidity, and anti-rigidity.

- We say that a predicate P is *rigid* if $\Box\forall x(P(x) \rightarrow \Box P(x))$
- We say that a predicate P is *non-rigid* if $\neg\Box\forall x(P(x) \rightarrow \Box P(x))$
- We say that a predicate P is *anti-rigid* if $\forall x(\neg\Box P(x))$

We define a *sortal* type S as the conjunction (i.e. the specialisation) of a kind K by means of a predicate that may not be rigid.

A predicate S is a *sortal* iff $S(x) \leftrightarrow (K(x) \wedge P(x))$ where P is any predicate
$$\tag{20}$$

That is, a sortal is logically equivalent to the specialisation of a kind by means of any predicate. Even if K is rigid, since P may be any predicate, the sortal S may or may not be rigid (there may be worlds in which $P(x)$ is not true while $K(x)$ is). The sortal S inherits however the identity criterion provided by the kind K: two elements of S must be elements of K, therefore the identity criterion provided by $=_K$ applies to them. Notice that in case also P is a kind, we have that the sortal S is also rigid. Therefore, in this case, the sortal is also a kind. In this case, the sortal is a kind that is logically equivalent to the conjunction of two other kinds.

Moreover, we define what the philosopher David Wiggins [21] terms a *phased sortal* as the specialisation of a kind by means of an anti-rigid predicate.

A predicate S is a *phased sortal* iff $S(x) \leftrightarrow (K(x) \wedge P(x))$ where P is anti-rigid
$$\tag{21}$$

For instance, the type *student* can be defined as the specialization of the kind *person* by the anti-rigid property of being enrolled in some course of study.

For completeness, we can also define types that are provided by the specialisation of a kind by means of a non-rigid predicate.

Further properties of kinds can be added by means of logical constraints. For instance, the assumptions that individuals are partitioned into kinds can be easily expressed in this language. We leave that for a dedicated future work.

6 Conclusion

We have introduced a logic for types that combines a cognitively inspired semantics and a modal treatment. We embraced a Fregean perspective in separating, for individual constants and types, their intension, which provides the actual amount of information available, and their extension. By using rough sets on a conceptual space, we modelled the possibly vague intension of types and, by associating regions in conceptual spaces to objects, we modelled the possibly vague or partial information about the objects. As we have seen, the logic that is adequate to model predication under this assumptions requires three truth values. We extended this treatment with modalities in order to capture the fundamental classifications of types, e.g. kinds, sortals, phased sortals.

Future work concerns two directions. On the one hand, we are interested in establishing the adequacy and the computational complexity of the proposed logical system to the reasoning about possibly uncertain classifications under types and in investigating its viable extensions. On the other hand, we intend to use this framework to provide an cognitively motivated exhaustive classification of the variety of types actually used in Conceptual Modelling and Knowledge Representation.

References

1. Aisbett, J., Gibbon, G.: A general formulation of conceptual spaces as a meso level representation. Artif. Intell. **133**(1), 189–232 (2001)
2. Akama, S., Murai, T.: Rough set semantics for three-valued logics. In: Nakamatsu, K., Abe, J. (eds.) Advances in Logic Based Intelligent Systems. Frontiers in Artificial Intelligence and Applications, vol. 132, pp. 242–247. IOS press, Amsterdam (2005)
3. Avron, A.: Natural 3-valued logicscharacterization and proof theory. J. Symb. Log. **56**(01), 276–294 (1991)
4. Fitting, M., Mendelsohn, R.L.: First-Order Modal Logic. Springer Science & Business Media, Dordrecht (2012). vol. 277
5. Frege, G.: On function and concept. In: Translations from the Philosophical Writings of Gottlob Frege, 3rd edn., pp. 1–128. Blackwell, Oxford (1980)
6. Gärdenfors, P.: Conceptual Spaces: the Geometry of Thought. MIT Press, Cambridge (2000)
7. Guizzardi, G.: Ontological patterns, anti-patterns and pattern languages for next-generation conceptual modeling. In: Yu, E., Dobbie, G., Jarke, M., Purao, S. (eds.) ER 2014. LNCS, vol. 8824, pp. 13–27. Springer, Cham (2014). doi:10.1007/978-3-319-12206-9_2

8. Guizzardi, G.: Logical, ontological and cognitive aspects of object types and cross-world identity with applications to the theory of conceptual spaces. In: Zenker, F., Gärdenfors, P. (eds.) Applications of Conceptual Spaces. SYLI, vol. 359, pp. 165–186. Springer, Cham (2015). doi:10.1007/978-3-319-15021-5_9

9. Hájek, P.: Metamathematics of Fuzzy Logic. Springer Science & Business Media, Dordrecht (1998). doi:10.1007/978-94-011-5300-3. vol. 4

10. Jones, S.S., Koehly, L.M.: Multidimensional scaling. In: Keren, G., Lewis, C. (eds.) A Handbook for Data Analysis in the Behavioral Sciences, pp. 95–163. Lawrence Erlbaum Associates, New Jersey (1993)

11. Kripke, S.: Naming and Necessity, rev. edn. Harvard University Press, Cambridge (1980)

12. Lowe, E.: Kinds of Being: A Study of Individuation, Identity and the Logic of Sortal Terms. Blackwell, Oxford (1989)

13. Markman, E.: Categorization and Naming in Children. MIT Press, Cambridge (1989)

14. Masolo, C., Porello, D.: A cognitive view of relevant implication. In: Lieto, A., Battaglino, C., Radicioni, D.P., Sanguinetti, M. (eds.) Proceedings of the 3rd International Workshop on Artificial Intelligence and Cognition, pp. 40–53. CEUR, Turin (2015)

15. Masolo, C., Porello, D.: Understanding predication in conceptual spaces. In: Formal Ontology in Information Systems - Proceedings of the 9th International Conference, FOIS 2016, Annecy, France, 6–9 July 2016, pp. 139–152 (2016). https://doi.org/10.3233/978-1-61499-660-6-139

16. Mcnamara, J.: Logic and cognition. In: The Logical Foundations of Cognition, 3rd edn., pp. 1–128. Blackwell, Oxford (1994)

17. Pawlak, Z.: Rough Sets: Theoretical Aspects of Reasoning About Data. Springer, Netherlands (1991). doi:10.1007/978-94-011-3534-4. vol. 9

18. Porello, D.: Modelling equivalent definitions of concepts. In: Christiansen, H., Stojanovic, I., Papadopoulos, G.A. (eds.) CONTEXT 2015. LNCS, vol. 9405, pp. 506–512. Springer, Cham (2015). doi:10.1007/978-3-319-25591-0_40

19. Raubal, M.: Formalizing conceptual spaces. In: Formal ontology in information systems. In: Proceedings of the Third International Conference, FOIS 2004, vol. 114, pp. 153–164 (2004)

20. Smith, E., Medin, D.: Categories and Concepts. Harvard University Press, Cambridge (1981)

21. Wiggins, D.: Sameness and Substance Renewed. Cambridge University Press, Cambridge (2001)

22. Xu, F., Carey, S., Quint, N.: The emergence of kind-based object individuation in infancy. Cogn. Psychol. 40, 155–190 (2004)

Planning and Scheduling

On the Evolution of Planner-Specific Macro Sets

Mauro Vallati[1]([✉]), Lukáš Chrpa[2,3], and Ivan Serina[4]

[1] School of Computing and Engineering, University of Huddersfield, Huddersfield, UK
m.vallati@hud.ac.uk
[2] Artificial Intelligence Center, Czech Technical University in Prague,
Prague, Czech Republic
[3] Faculty of Mathematics and Physics, Charles University,
Prague, Czech Republic
[4] Dipartimento di Ingegneria dell'Informazione, Universitá degli Studi di Brescia,
Brescia, Italy

Abstract. In Automated Planning, generating macro-operators (macros) is a well-known reformulation approach that is used to speed-up the planning process. Most of the macro generation techniques aim for using the same set of generated macros on every problem instance of a given domain. This limits the usefulness of macros in scenarios where the environment and thus the structure of instances is dynamic, such as in real-world applications. Moreover, despite the wide availability of parallel processing units, there is a lack of approaches that can take advantage of multiple parallel cores, while exploiting macros.

In this paper we propose the Macro sets Evolution (MEvo) approach. MEvo has been designed for overcoming the aforementioned issues by exploiting multiple cores for combining promising macros –taken from a given pool– in different sets, while solving continuous streams of problem instances. Our empirical study, involving 5 state-of-the-art planning engines and a large number of planning instances, demonstrates the effectiveness of the proposed MEvo approach.

1 Introduction

Macro-operators ("macros" for short) are a well-established problem reformulation technique for encapsulating sequences of planning operators in the same format as original planning operators. Macros can be thus seen as state space "short-cuts": they can reduce the number of steps needed to reach the goal, at the cost of an increased branching factor.

In the last decades, numerous techniques have been proposed for extracting macros. These techniques are usually either planner-independent such as MUM [3] and BLOMA [5], or planner-specific such as SOL-EP version of MacroFF [2] or Wizard [11]. The former approaches are designed to perform well in general regardless of planning techniques, while the latter approaches are tailored to a specific planning technique.

Most of the existing macro generation techniques rely on a training phase, where training plans, solutions of simple problems, are analysed. Doing so gives useful insights into structure of plans that can be exploited (in form of macros)

F. Esposito et al. (Eds.): AI*IA 2017, LNAI 10640, pp. 443–454, 2017.
https://doi.org/10.1007/978-3-319-70169-1_33

for solving harder problems in the same domain. On the negative side, training might unintentionally introduce a bias towards a specific subclass of problems. This is because training instances are believed to be representative of the testing problems. The problem is exacerbated by the fact that generated macros cannot be modified, and are used on any instance of the considered domain: instances where the generated macros are not helpful therefore become hard to solve. Aforementioned issue can be partially overcome by online macro generation techniques such as Marvin [6], OMA [4], or DHG [1]. However, limited information is available online and, for the sake of efficiency, the extraction process can not be too sophisticated.

Remarkably, although numerous techniques exist for extracting macros, no work has been done in the area of the realtime evaluation of usefulness of macros, possibly generated by different approaches, and in their automatic combination in suitable macro sets, which would allow to deal with continuous streams of differently-structured problem instances. To the best of our knowledge, there is also a lack of approaches for exploiting macros in parallel planning, where more than one processing unit can be exploited for solving a given problem instance.

In this work we propose **MEvo** –**M**acro sets **E**volution– that, given a pool of macros and a domain-independent planner, can automatically combine macros in suitable sets to be used for solving a stream of problem instances from a given domain and, more importantly, can evolve the composition of such sets according to observed performance. Therefore, we can deal with situations where problem structure changes, and can select macros that "comply" with a given planning engine. MEvo is based on the following pillars: (i) nowadays, multi-core machines are widely available and cheap; (ii) multi-core planning engines are not as well engineered as traditional planners (as observed in [10,15]); and (iii) given the large number of existing techniques, macros can be collected from various sources, and even hand-coded. The idea is that when a new problem instance arrives, several parallel runs of the solver attempt to solve it. One run is exploiting the original problem encoding, while each of the other runs incorporates different sets of macros. As soon as one run solves the instance, all the others are terminated and the usefulness evaluation of each macro is then updated accordingly. Because the original domain model is considered among the parallel runs, a lower bound on performance can be guaranteed, thus macros do not have a detrimental effect on overall performance. Furthermore, in case new macros are discovered, they can be added to MEvo pool and will be taken into consideration for solving upcoming instances.

A large-scale experimental analysis demonstrates the usefulness of MEvo, and provides valuable insights into structure and size of macro sets whose impact on the performance of particular planning engines is considerable.

2   Background

Classical planning deals with finding a partially or totally ordered sequence of actions to transform the environment from an initial state to a desired goal state,

---

Algorithm 1. Components of the MEvo algorithm

1: **procedure** MEvo(M,I,D,p,n)
2:     E = initialiseMacroScores(M)
3:     **for** i in I **do**
4:         S = getMacroSets(E,M,n)
5:         r = solveInstance(S,D,i,p)
6:         E = updateMacroScores(r,E)
7:     **end for**
8: **end procedure**

---

with a static and fully observable environment and deterministic and instantaneous actions [8]. In the Planning Domain Description Language (PDDL) representation the environment is described by predicates. *States* are defined as sets of grounded predicates. We say that $o = (name(o), pre(o), eff^-(o), eff^+(o), cost(o))$ is a *planning operator*, where $name(o) = op\_name(x_1, \ldots, x_k)$ (op_name is an unique operator name and $x_1, \ldots x_k$ are variable symbols (arguments) appearing in the operator) and $pre(o), eff^-(o)$ and $eff^+(o)$ are sets of (ungrounded) predicates with variables taken only from $x_1, \ldots x_k$ representing o's precondition, negative and positive effects, and $cost(o)$ is a numerical value representing o's cost. *Actions* are grounded instances of planning operators. An action a is *applicable* in a state s if and only if $pre(a) \subseteq s$. Application of a in s (if possible) results in a state $(s \setminus eff^-(a)) \cup eff^+(a)$.

A *planning domain model* is specified by a set of predicates and a set of planning operators. A *planning problem* is specified via a domain model, a set of objects, initial state and set of goal predicates. A *solution plan* of a planning problem is a sequence of actions such that their consecutive application starting in the initial state results in a state containing all the goal predicates.

Macros are encoded in the same way as ordinary planning operators, but encapsulate sequences of planning operators. Technically, an instance of a macro is applicable in a state if and only if a corresponding sequence of operators' instances is applicable in that state and the result of application of the macro's instance is the same as the result of application of the corresponding sequence of operators' instances. Macros can be added to the original domain models, which gives the technique the potential of being *planner independent*.

3   The MEvo Approach

The core of the proposed MEvo approach can be abstracted to Algorithm 1, taking five parameters: a domain model D, a stream of problem instances I, a solver p, a pool of macros M and the maximum number of macros in a set n. Firstly, a vector of scores E is initialised. Each macro is associated to a *score* in the range $[0, 100]$, where 0 indicates that the macro has never improved the performance of the planner, while 100 indicates a very useful macro, that always had a positive impact on the performance of the considered solver. Initially, the score can be assigned randomly, or it can rely on some previously observed performance or on some experts' knowledge. In our implementation the initial score has been set to 10: this can be seen as a defensive strategy, as it relies on the fact that macros are expected to provide a very limited speed-up to the planning process.

Solving the stream of problem instances I one at a time, four sets of macros S (including the empty set) are generated according to scores E. Each set S must not include more than n macros. This limit is needed because the number of instances of macros is often high, because they usually have a large set of parameters, that derives from the parameters of the original operators that are encapsulated: as a result, the branching factor in the search space is increased, and this can dramatically slow down the planning process.

The macro sets are then used for creating four different domain models which are exploited in four parallel runs of the solver p. As soon as one run finishes solving the instance, all of them are terminated and corresponding results are recorded in r. Finally, macro scores are updated according to observed performance. It is of critical importance to stop all runs as soon as one finds a solution: otherwise, MEvo would be as slow as its slowest run, thus wasting a lot of valuable CPU-time. As a drawback, this does not allows to exploit any information on relative performance of the considered sets.

In Algorithm 1, the *getMacroSets* procedure provides four different sets of macros (*average* is an average score of all the macros in M):

- **Original:** an empty set, i.e. the original domain model;
- **Random:** a set including between 1 and n randomly selected macros;
- **Best:** the best set of macros identified so far; it includes the top $\min(k, n)$ macros (k stands for the number of macros whose score is higher than *average*)
- **AlmostBest:** a set of macros including top j macros from the best set where j is (strictly) smaller than the size of the best set, and top l macros ($l \geq 1$) that were not included in the best set. The values of j and l are randomly chosen, but $j + l \leq n$ must hold.

The use of the original model guarantees that, in the case in which all the sets of macros have a detrimental impact, the problem will be solved as if running without knowledge. The random set allows to explore the space of macros. The best set exploits the set of macros believed to be the most suitable. Finally, the almost best set includes (with some probability) part of the best set and part of the "nearly best" macros, so it aims at exploring possibly useful macros that might not (yet) qualify to the best set.

In Algorithm 1, procedure *updateMacroScores* consider the results of runs on an instance i for updating macro scores E. Macros (if any) which were in the set that achieved the best performance for i have their score c_V incremented as follows (*size* is the number of macros included in the set, *average* is the average score of all the macros in M):

$$c_V = c_V + \frac{100 - c_V}{size} * (1 - \frac{|c_V - average|}{100}) \qquad (1)$$

Conversely, macros that are involved in the other sets, which did not achieved the best performance, have their score c_V decremented as follows ($size$ and $average$ have the same meaning as before):

$$c_V = c_V - \frac{c_V}{size} * (1 - \frac{|c_V - average|}{100}) \qquad (2)$$

If none of the considered runs (including Original) solved instance i, all scores remain unchanged. That is because no information is available.

Evidently, the introduced scoring method is strongly based on the average value of all the macros. The underlying idea is that macros scoring close to the average should get larger score increments/decrements in order to categorize their potential usefulness early in the process. Considering the $size$ of the set allows, at the same time, to keep the same score for macros that "work well together", or to reward more macros that singularly gives a boost in performance (this results in the best set including only such macro). Also, it is worth emphasising that the scoring method cannot rely on information about the relative performance –such as speedup– of the parallel runs, because as soon as one run finds a solution, all the others are terminated for the sake of performance. Moreover, given the fact that MEvo is planner-independent, information about the search performed by the different runs –such as visited states– is unavailable.

The proposed MEvo framework can easily accommodate changes to the macros M while solving instances from the stream I: new macros can be added, for instance, because a new macro generating technique has been developed. The initial score for a newly added macro can be randomly initialised, fixed at the average of other macros or defined according to expectations.

The described technique is modular: while the proposed version is focused on a typical quad-core machine, it is straightforward to exploit additional cores by considering different macro sets.

4   Experimental Analysis

The experimental analysis main aims are: (i) assessing the usefulness of the MEvo approach in the depicted scenario; (ii) checking the ability of MEvo to cope with sudden changes in the planning instances structure; and (iii) comparing MEvo with state-of-the-art parallel planners.

4.1   Experimental Settings

We considered instances from the following domains: Barman, Blocksworld, Depots, Matching-BW, Parking. Domains were selected due to the large availability of differently structured macro actions, thus providing an interesting challenge for the approach MEvo. For each of the considered domain models, macros have been generated by BLOMA [5], Wizard [11], MUM [3], MacroFF

[2] on some disjointed set of training instances. Also, manually crafted macros have been considered; such macros encode the human expertise (intuition) of the domain. Around 15 different macros have been considered per domain model, and between 100 and 200 problems have been generated using existing randomised generators, and considering the size of instances used in recent learning tracks of the international planning competition. Problems have been ordered according to their size (from simplest to the most complex), in order to simulate an environment in which problem instances evolve over time.

As benchmarking planners we chose Jasper [17], LPG-td [7], Mp [12,13], Probe [9], Yahsp [16]. All the planners competed in International Planning Competitions (IPCs), with remarkable results; moreover they exploit very different techniques for finding satisficing plans. All of them have been used in the configuration for finding one satisficing plan (no incremental search for improving plan quality) and, whether possible, seeds have been fixed.

A runtime cutoff of 900 CPU seconds (15 min, as in learning tracks of IPC) was used. IPC score (time metrics), as defined for the learning track of the IPC 2011 has been considered: for a planner $\mathcal{C}$ and a problem p, $Score(\mathcal{C}, p)$ is 0 if p is unsolved, and $1/(1 + \log_{10}(T_p(\mathcal{C})/T_p^*))$ otherwise (where T_p^* is the minimum time required by compared systems to solve the problem). The IPC score on a set of problems is given by the sum of the scores achieved on each instance.

We fixed the maximum size of macro sets (n in Algorithm 1) to $n = 3$: this has been empirically observed to be a good upper bound (see, e.g., [2,3]). All the experiments were run on a quad-core 3.0 GHz CPU, with 4 GB of RAM made available for each run. Presented results are averaged across three runs, in order to take –to some extent– randomness into account. Overhead due to macro selection and scores update is negligible (few milliseconds).

4.2 Performance on Considered Benchmarks

Table 1 shows the results achieved by the considered planners, in terms of accumulated IPC score and percentage of solved instances, when exploiting the Original domain model (O), the Best macro set –according to MEvo– (B) and the AlmostBest set (A). The overall performance of the proposed approach is shown; clearly, they should not be directly compared with performance of O, B and A sets, since MEvo subsumes them. Results of planners exploiting the random sets are not shown, due to space constraints and also because they are only focused on exploring the space of macros. It should be noted that –given a stream of instances on a specific domain– Best and AlmostBest sets contain different macros, according to the evolution of scores of considered macros. As a baseline –not shown in Table 1– we run experiments where the domain models were extended using all the available macros; none of the considered planners was able to solve any instance. Naively, these results support the need of selecting good quality macros, from the available pool.

From Table 1 three main conclusions can be derived. First, the same macros can have a very different impact on planners exploiting different approaches. This behaviour, even though well-known, is confirmed by the variability of the relative

Table 1. Accumulated IPC score (percentage of solved instances) of the considered planners exploiting the Original domain model (O), the Best macro set (B) and the AlmostBest set (A) on the selected domains. The MEvo row reports the overall performance achieved by the planner when exploiting the proposed approach. Bw stands for Blocksworld. The number of testing instances is indicated on top of each column. Bold indicates best IPC score among O, B and A sets for a given planner.

Set		Domains				
		Barman 150	Bw 160	Depots 165	Matching-Bw 150	Parking 140
Jasper	O	94.3 (69.3)	57.2 (36.9)	84.6 (55.2)	**36.8** (26.7)	0.0 (0.0)
	B	113.6 (80.7)	**86.2** (55.0)	**86.1** (56.3)	34.7 (26.0)	0.0 (0.0)
	A	**115.1** (80.7)	40.3 (31.3)	78.9 (52.1)	34.3 (26.)	0.0 (0.0)
	MEvo	130.0 (86.7)	97.0 (60.6)	120.0 (72.7)	49.0 (32.7)	0.0 (0.0)
LPG	O	0.0 (0.0)	70.2 (76.9)	**146.2** (100.0)	**24.2** (17.3)	0.0 (0.0)
	B	0.0 (0.0)	**158.4** (100.0)	107.6 (95.2)	22.5 (18.7)	0.0 (0.0)
	A	0.0 (0.0)	98.7 (63.1)	111.6 (100.0)	23.2 (19.3)	0.0 (0.0)
	MEvo	0.0 (0.0)	160.0 (100.0)	165.0 (100.0)	33.0 (22.0)	0.0 (0.0)
Mp	O	13.5 (10.7)	0.0 (0.0)	147.8 (100.0)	**1.2** (1.3)	1.0 (0.7)
	B	**15.5** (11.3)	**98.5** (62.5)	**162.8** (100.0)	1.1 (1.3)	1.0 (0.7)
	A	14.5 (10.7)	47.8 (31.3)	159.9 (98.8)	1.0 (0.7)	0.0 (0.0)
	MEvo	24.0 (16.0)	106.0 (66.3)	165.0 (100.0)	3.0 (2.0)	1.0 (0.7)
Probe	O	89.6 (68.0)	106.6 (77.5)	**164.5** (100.0)	37.8 (27.3)	2.0 (1.4)
	B	**98.4** (73.3)	**140.8** (88.8)	159.0 (100.0)	**42.2** (32.7)	2.0 (1.4)
	A	93.5 (71.3)	135.2 (86.3)	157.6 (100.0)	34.7 (27.3)	0.0 (0.0)
	MEvo	128.0 (85.3)	144.0 (90.0)	165.0 (100.0)	64.0 (42.7)	2.0 (1.4)
Yahsp	O	0.0 (0.0)	0.0 (0.0)	0.0 (0.0)	6.9 (4.7)	0.0 (0.0)
	B	0.0 (0.0)	0.0 (0.0)	3.7 (2.4)	7.0 (4.7)	0.0 (0.0)
	A	0.0 (0.0)	0.0 (0.0)	**8.0** (4.8)	7.0 (4.7)	0.0 (0.0)
	MEvo	0.0 (0.0)	0.0 (0.0)	11.0 (6.7)	7.0 (4.7)	0.0 (0.0)

performance between the Original and the Best sets, and indicates the need for systems that can automatically identify the best set of macros to exploit –if any–. The second observation we derived from the results is that the best set of macros that outperforms the original encodings is usually established after solving a relatively small number of instances; see, for instance, the performance of Yahsp in Gripper domain. Third, Table 1 clearly indicates that the MEvo algorithm can effectively exploit the speed-up given by macros, but still guaranteeing a minimum level of performance (see MEvo rows).

Figure 1 (coloured) shows a typical pattern of the evolution of the accumulated IPC score of the four sets of macros considered by the MEvo. Specifically, the example shows the performance of the Probe planning system on a continuous stream of instances taken from the Blocksworld domain. Initially, the performance of Original and Best sets are exactly the same: there is no available information about promising macros –i.e., no macro has a score higher than the average– therefore an empty set is used also by the Best set. As soon as some exploration has been performed by the Random set, and some useful macros

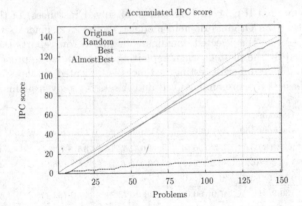

Fig. 1. Accumulated IPC score of Probe exploiting the four considered sets of macro on instances from the Blocksworld domain. (Color figure online)

have been identified, the performance of the Best set improves and the gap between Original and Best set increases. At the same time, the AlmostBest set also shows performance improvement due to the exploitation of a subset of the most promising macros set. At some point, in Fig. 1 this happens approximately after that 125 instances has been processed, the problem instances are too large to be solved by the planner exploiting the original domain model. Conversely, macros are still very helpful, thus allowing Probe to solve such large instances.

With regards to the size of Best macro sets that are identified by MEvo, and to the macros included, it is worth noting that both aspects vary among considered planners. For instance, Yahsp and Mp usually exploit sets composed by a single macro. Conversely, Probe shows a significant performance improvement when exploiting set composed by 2–3 macros. In terms of structure of exploited macros, Mp can better exploit short macros, i.e. those encapsulating a small number of original operators (2–3), while Probe can also exploits macros encapsulating 4–5 operators.

We noticed that in cases where the accumulated IPC score of the Original and Best sets are very similar –with regard to Table 1– this is due to: (i) no macros are improving the performance of the planner; (ii) macros speed-up is limited; (iii) there is a large number of macros that are, in turn, providing limited improvement on different instances. In principle, the performance of the Best MEvo set can be improved by introducing a threshold (currently, only the average value is considered). However, given the fact that the Original set guarantees a lower bound on performance, we preferred to give some freedom to the Best set; this can potentially lead to better overall performance of the MEvo framework.

Finally, in order to shed some light on the usefulness and importance of the *size* and *average* aspects in Eqs. 1 and 2, we re-run MEvo on the considered benchmarks using modified equations, where such aspects were in turn removed. Unsurprisingly, MEvo exploiting such modified equations performs similar to the original system when the Best set for the selected planner includes a single macro, and such macro allows to improve the performance of the planner in most of the considered instances. Otherwise, original equations allows MEvo to perform better because: (i) they allow a faster convergence to a good set of macros; and (ii) they limit the impact of cases in which macros perform very differently than usual on very few instances.

4.3 Comparison with the State of the Art of Parallel Planning

As previously discussed, the MEvo approach exploits four cores in parallel. It is therefore important to investigate how it performs when compared with the state of the art of multi-core parallel planning engines. As a baseline for this comparison, we considered the winner of the sequential multi-core track of the deterministic part of the 2014 edition of the International Planning Competition, ArvandHerd-14 [14]. In that competition track, planners were allowed to exploit four cores in parallel for solving a single planning instance, exactly as MEvo does.

In our experimental analysis, ArvandHerd-14 were run on the same benchmark instances considered in Table 1, with a cutoff of 900 wall-clock CPU seconds. Since we are evaluating the runtime of planners, ArvandHerd-14 was stopped as soon as the first solution was found. It is worth remarking that the MEvo framework, when running a given domain-independent planner, exploits some additional domain-specific knowledge, under the form of macros. Therefore, we expect the planners empowered by the MEvo system to achieve better performance, in terms of runtime, than ArvandHerd-14.

Table 2 shows the IPC scores achieved on the benchmark instances by ArvandHerd-14 and the five planners considered in this experimental analysis, exploiting the MEvo framework. The overall results (last row of Table 2) indicate that all the considered planners, except Yahsp, shows performance that are similar to those of ArvandHerd-14 on the considered benchmarks domains. As observed in Table 1, Yahsp is generally unable to solve a vast majority of

Table 2. IPC score of the parallel planner ArvandHerd-14 (ArHerd), and of the five considered sequential planners when exploiting the MEvo framework. Bw stands for Blocksworld. Bold indicates best IPC score. Results shown for the MEvo approach are averaged over 3 runs.

	ArHerd	MEvo				
		Jasper	LPG	Mp	Probe	Yahsp
Barman	46.0	84.1	0.0	10.9	**126.8**	0.0
Bw	43.1	48.1	**156.5**	66.9	73.8	0.0
Depots	22.7	37.0	**147.9**	132.7	78.9	3.1
Matching-Bw	**88.9**	29.1	29.2	0.8	41.3	3.1
Parking	0.0	0.0	0.0	1.0	**2.0**	0.0
Total	200.7	198.3	**333.6**	212.3	322.8	6.2

the testing instances. Furthermore, most of the considered sequential planners outperform ArvandHerd-14.

From a domain perspective, results in Table 2 show that in most of the considered domains, all the planners (ignoring Yahsp) running on the MEvo framework are able to achieve considerably better results than ArvandHerd-14. In Matching-BW, ArvandHerd-14 clearly outperforms MEvo. This is because the considered planners are not very efficient in this domain. As we recognise that MEvo is also exploiting some additional domain-specific knowledge, which is not available for ArvandHerd-14, we believe that the results of the performed comparison suggest that running differently extended domain models –according to identified promising macros– can be a fruitful way for exploiting multiple cores. This is particularly true if we take into account that, out of the four cores used by MEvo, only two are "smartly" exploiting the additional knowledge: Original and Random sets are, respectively, used for backup and exploration of macro sets purposes.

Results presented in Table 2 suggest that considering different domain model formulations, wisely extended with promising macros, can be a fruitful way for exploiting additional cores. This observation is of particular interest for the future development of the area. Specifically, in the light of the fact that most of the works in parallel planning focused mainly on the "reasoning" side, by running different algorithms, or the same algorithm investigating different areas of the search space, on each available core.

5   Conclusion

In this paper we proposed MEvo, an approach for improving performance of domain-independent planners by dynamically combining and evolving suitable sets of macros, given a pool of macros and a continuous stream of problem instances. MEvo can cope with one of the major drawbacks of existing macros extraction approaches: the fact that impact of extracted macros, when used on instances very different from those used for training or with different planners, is unknown. Remarkably, the pool of macros can be modified while instances are solved: newly-identified macros can be immediately exploited by MEvo.

Our large experimental analysis: (i) demonstrates the usefulness of MEvo as a framework for improving the performance of domain-independent planners; (ii) confirms the ability of MEvo in evolving suitable macro sets, also in case of sudden structural changes of the stream of instances; (iii) indicates that MEvo outperforms the state of the art of multicore planning; and (iv) provides insights into the size of macro sets and structure of macros, that allows improving the performance of different planners. Planner-specific knowledge about macros' structure, gained by using MEvo, can be useful for improving macro generation processes.

The results of the comparison between sequential planners exploiting the MEvo tool and the winner of the sequential multicore track of last IPC, are of particular interest. Specifically, in the light of the fact that most of the works in parallel planning focused on the "reasoning" side, by running different algorithms, or by investigating different areas of the search space, on available cores. Our results suggest that also considering different domain model formulations, wisely extended with promising macros, can be a fruitful way for exploiting additional cores.

Future work includes an analysis of smarter ways for generating the Random set of MEvo, and the use of online macro-generation approaches (e.g., [1,6]) for increasing over time the pool of considered macros.

Acknowledgements. Research was partially funded by the Czech Science Foundation (project no. 17-17125Y).

References

1. Armano, G., Cherchi, G., Vargiu, E.: Automatic generation of macro-operators from static domain analysis. In: Proceedings of ECAI, pp. 955–956 (2004)
2. Botea, A., Enzenberger, M., Müller, M., Schaeffer, J.: Macro-FF: improving AI planning with automatically learned macro-operators. J. Artif. Intell. Res. (JAIR) **24**, 581–621 (2005)
3. Chrpa, L., Vallati, M., McCluskey, T.L.: Mum: a technique for maximising the utility of macro-operators by constrained generation and use. In: Proceedings of the International Conference on Automated Planning and Scheduling, ICAPS, pp. 65–73 (2014)
4. Chrpa, L., Vallati, M., McCluskey, T.L.: On the online generation of effective macro-operators. In: Proceedings of IJCAI, pp. 1544–1550 (2015)
5. Chrpa, L., Siddiqui, F.H.: Exploiting block deordering for improving planners efficiency. In: Proceedings of the Twenty-Fourth International Joint Conference on Artificial Intelligence, IJCAI, pp. 1537–1543 (2015)
6. Coles, A., Fox, M., Smith, A.: Online identification of useful macro-actions for planning. In: Proceedings of ICAPS, pp. 97–104 (2007)
7. Gerevini, A.E., Saetti, A., Serina, I.: Planning through stochastic local search and temporal action graphs. J. Artif. Intell. Res. (JAIR) **20**, 239–290 (2003)
8. Ghallab, M., Nau, D., Traverso, P.: Automated Planning, Theory and Practice. Morgan Kaufmann, Burlington (2004)
9. Lipovetzky, N., Ramirez, M., Muise, C., Geffner, H.: Width and inference based planners: SIW, BFS(f), and probe. In: The Eighth International Planning Competition. Description of Participant Planners of the Deterministic Track, pp. 6–7 (2014)
10. López, C.L., Celorrio, S.J., Olaya, Á.G.: The deterministic part of the seventh international planning competition. Artif. Intell. **223**, 82–119 (2015)
11. Newton, M.A.H., Levine, J., Fox, M., Long, D.: Learning macro-actions for arbitrary planners and domains. In: Proceedings of the International Conference on Automated Planning and Scheduling, ICAPS, pp. 256–263 (2007)
12. Rintanen, J.: Engineering efficient planners with SAT. In: Proceedings of ECAI, pp. 684–689 (2012)
13. Rintanen, J.: Madagascar: scalable planning with SAT. In: The Eighth International Planning Competition. Description of Participant Planners of the Deterministic Track, pp. 66–70 (2014)

14. Valenzano, R., Nakhost, H., Müller, M., Schaeffer, J., Sturtevant, N.: Arvandherd 2014. In: The Eighth International Planning Competition. Description of Participant Planners of the Deterministic Track (2014)
15. Vallati, M., Chrpa, L., Grzes, M., McCluskey, T.L., Roberts, M., Sanner, S.: The 2014 international planning competition: progress and trends. AI Mag. **36**(3), 90–98 (2015)
16. Vidal, V.: YAHSP3 and YAHSP3-MT in the 8th international planning competition. In: Proceedings of the 8th International Planning Competition, IPC 2014, pp. 64–65 (2014)
17. Xie, F., Müller, M., Holte, R.: Jasper: the art of exploration in greedy best first search. In: Proceedings of the 8th International Planning Competition, IPC 2014 (2014)

A Tool for Managing Elderly Volunteering Activities in Small Organizations

Amedeo Cesta[(✉)], Gabriella Cortellessa, Riccardo De Benedictis, and Francesca Fracasso

CNR - Italian National Research Council, ISTC, Rome, Italy
{amedeo.cesta,gabriella.cortellessa,riccardo.debenedictis,
francesca.fracasso}@istc.cnr.it

Abstract. This paper describes a pilot application developed by the authors within a project in the area of elders assistance. Specifically, the work addresses the problem of assigning scheduled activities to a set of volunteers by means of an interactive tool that considers both users' needs/preferences and constraints posed by the organization that manages the volunteers. Particular emphasis is given to the problem of assigning a group of seniors to the "right task" so as to obtain a positive outcome of the services offered by the volunteering association while maximizing the volunteers' level of satisfaction perceived, in this domain, as a relevant requirement. This paper describes the design of a complete application for supporting this process focusing, in particular, on the back-end functionalities where a formalization as a generic optimization problem and a heuristic, developed to serve the time constants required in the domain, have been integrated. Experimental results, conducted with realistic data, support the particular design of the solution and encourage future work.

1 Introduction

The *Active and Assistive Living* (AAL) Joint Program is a European funding initiative aiming at promoting the synthesis of new ICT solutions for helping people to age well. The program (active since 2008 with the previous extended name of *Ambient Assisted Living*) is now strongly focusing on the fact that elderlies should remain active as long as possible in order to preserve their role in the society longer. The program Call for project proposals number 6 (2013) specifically asked for "the development of ICT-based solutions which enable elderlies to continue managing their occupation at work in an office, a factory or any working environment; in a first or subsequent career, in paid or voluntary occupation including local social activities while preserving health and motivation to remain active". Additionally, the specific call was looking for solutions that promote, enhance and sustain both paid (including for example professional,

Authors work is partially funded by the Active and Assisted Living Joint Program under the SpONSOR project (AAL-2013-6-118 - http://sponsor-aal.eu/).

© Springer International Publishing AG 2017
F. Esposito et al. (Eds.): AI*IA 2017, LNAI 10640, pp. 455–467, 2017.
https://doi.org/10.1007/978-3-319-70169-1_34

entrepreneurial/small business and self-employment) and unpaid activities (e.g., volunteering, knowledge sharing, counseling).

The SPONSOR project [4] aims at developing, testing and implementing an ICT platform that facilitates the posting, browsing and exchange of key information between competence-offering elderlies and search-based requests, from competence-demanding organizations both in the public, private and volunteering sectors. Figure 1 shows the taken perspective pursued in SPONSOR. The goal consists in supporting Organizations that favor occupation (upper part of the figure) creating a software platform that help them in the task of facilitating contact between people who offer their work and people in need of support (lower part). Indeed, during the development of the project, we have mostly focused on the relation between organizations and the older workers. The third group of people (those in need for a support) will be *de-facto* mediated by the role of the organizations.

Within the project, the authors were responsible for the assessment of the Italian situation and the development of an Italian case study. In the first part of the project they focused on the understanding of the situation of the Italian older adults who either lose their jobs or retire. In particular, we discovered how realities which help elderlies in finding again a job are really very few and, in most of the cases the older adult is left alone to face a very frustrating problem. However, it has been confirmed that also in Italy volunteering organizations play an important role in retaining elderlies occupied. Thanks to these associations, elderlies feel

Fig. 1. The context in which the SPONSOR system operates.

more useful to the society and less abandoned, resulting in a better attitude in searching new activities on a regular basis. One of the major problems of volunteering work is the high level of abandonment. Hence, the main objective of these organizations is to allocate tasks to volunteers in a way that spurs them in giving continuity to their collaboration over time. Keeping persons motivated is a challenging aspect that also depends on the level of satisfaction that the volunteers have while performing the assigned activities. In this light, a feature of this problem is that doing a volunteer is not only a question of skills (hard and soft) but also of the adequacy of the activities to the predisposition of those who have to do them.

This paper focuses on the experience in developing the Italian pilot for SPONSOR. The case, called *S4AMT* (for "SPONSOR for Activity Matching and Timetabling"), is devoted to the problem of allocating elderly volunteers to a set of activities proposed by an organization. The pursued overall aim is to find the best match that respects the tasks' constraints while maximizing the level of satisfaction of elderly users, thus contributing to increase their level of motivation in performing volunteering work. The paper particularly describes the work done for formalizing the problem and for creating an effective problem solving module that fits the computational time constants required in the given environment, for a decision support system suited for a small organization.

The paper is organized as follows: Sect. 2 presents in details the problem of one volunteering association that manages around 120 volunteers (all retired people), highlighting the current practice for performing the best match between volunteers and activities; Sect. 3 presents the formalization of the problem as Binary Integer Programming; Sect. 4 presents the proposed approach for solving the problem as well as a domain dependent heuristic aimed at helping the reasoning process; Sect. 5 presents an experimental evaluation of the whole work. Section 6 shortly describes the complete application where the presented work has been integrated, while some final considerations close the paper.

2   Using SpONSOR at Televita

Televita[1] is a volunteering association which is active since 1993 within the 2nd and 3rd municipalities of Rome. Among the activities carried out by the organization we can mention tele-assistance services (tele-friendship) and a 24 h active helpline devoted to lonely elderlies who need support. Beside this, there are several laboratories that involve elderlies both as attendees and conductors. Examples include a computer lab, a tailoring lab, an Italian language teaching for foreign people, etc. Furthermore, even if not very often, the association organizes cultural events as concerts, museum visiting, theater, etc. The overall objective is to maintain the elderlies active and motivated, leveraging upon individual aptitudes and/or competencies. Televita's volunteers, in fact, are, themselves, elderlies who want to keep active by offering their abilities and competences to the organization.

A peculiar aspect of Televita, compared to other volunteering organizations, consists in the evaluation of their volunteers which, rather than just considering their skills, takes into account, also, their attitude and their adequacy in performing specific tasks. As said before, one of the main problems of volunteering organizations is related to the volunteers resignation rate, which might be interpreted as the consequence of assigning unsatisfying tasks to the volunteers, making feel them inadequate. The idea pursued by Televita is to select the volunteers according to their own inclinations and to assign them the "most suitable" activities. This will presumably increase the level of satisfaction and accomplishment of the volunteers and, hence, the likelihood of avoiding drop out.

At present time, the Televita's objective is pursued through the periodic screening of volunteers by means of customized questionnaires (see Fig. 2) that assess their psychological aspects. The idea is that such questionnaires allow the detection of aspects of the volunteers which make them best suited for some activities. Specifically, the answers to the questionnaires are construed so as to

---

[1] http://www.televita.org.

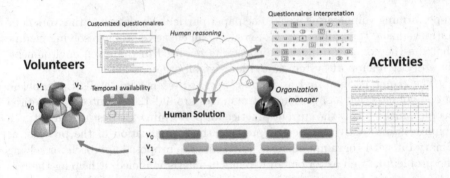

Fig. 2. The Televita current modalities in managing the organization. Volunteers answer a customized questionnaire and managers, by interpreting the results of the questionnaires, assign activities to them.

extract behavioral and emotional aspects characterized by the following relevant features:

- The **President, (P)** coordinates common efforts so as to achieve the ultimate goals.
- The **Structurer, (S)** represents the leader of the working group.
- The **Brilliant, (B)** is the source of original ideas, suggestions and proposals for the team.
- The **Evaluator, (Ev)** contributes at producing precise and unbiased evaluations.
- The **Concrete, (C)** is the practical organizer.
- The **Explorer, (Ex)** is the member of the team who goes outside of the organization so as to capture information and ideas, developing them for the common interest.
- The **Worker, (W)** is the most sensitive of the team.
- The **Objectivist, (O)** worries about what might end up badly.

After the answers construing process, for each volunteer, a value is associated to each of the above features. By observing these values and, in particular, the highest ones, it is possible, for a Televita manager, recognize some peculiar characteristics of the volunteer which make him/her adequate at performing some specific tasks. The vector $\langle P = 21, S = 5, B = 11, Ev = 12, C = 5, Ex = 8, W = 7, O = 1 \rangle$ describes, for example, a person with a dominant *president* trait. This characterizes the person as suitable to carry out decision-making tasks. The same person is, nevertheless, evaluated as *brilliant* and as an *evaluator*, hence, suitable (albeit with less relevance) in performing other tasks. At the same time, the organization has a set of activities, distributed over a quarterly planning horizon, to be carried out. These activities are characterized by a temporal span and by a set of required skills. An "Animation" activity, for example, might require that the "animator" volunteer is a structurer, brilliant, explorer and objectivist. The task of the organization manager becomes, therefore, to find the most appropriate person, among the available volunteers, to carry out this task, seeking for the right compromise between people's availability, as well as their abilities and desires. It is worth noting that a volunteer who caters to a volunteering association, does so in order to feel useful and to help the society. It is, therefore, responsibility of the organization not to leave him/her without any activity to be carried out. On the other hand, the organization has some activities that must be carried out by someone and volunteers, with their skills, constitute a "limited resource", hence the idea of exploiting AI techniques so as to optimize the matching process.

Challenges. The relatively high number of volunteers, along with the high number of activities to be carried out, however, makes it extremely difficult to perform, optimally, the above matching problem. Specifically, Televita currently manages the work of 126 persons partitioned according to

Table 1. The current Televita volunteers and high-level tasks

Number of volunteers	Activity type
65	Helpline
8	Psychological/Spiritual support
30	Animation/Socialization
15	Coordination/Organization
3	Training
5	Technological support

the schema in Table 1. The organization and the management of such a number of users makes manual coordination impracticable. Additionally, the assignment of volunteers to activities based on the analysis of users' features is currently made by a single person who is particularly expert in this kind of analysis. The challenge for this specific domain is therefore to build a support system that helps the human organizer in finding this "best match" while helping not expert people at performing an effective assignment.

3   Formalizing the Problem as Optimization

In this section we produce a formalization of the Televita problem that we call the *S4AMT* problem. The problem mainly consists in assigning a set of activities to a set of volunteers while taking into account behavioral and emotional aspects. Specifically, at the core of the model there is a set V *volunteers* whose activities should be decided. Each volunteer $v \in V$ has his/her own *temporal availability* $\mathbb{T}_v = \{[lb_1^v, ub_1^v], \ldots, [lb_i^v, ub_i^v]\}$ representing the temporal intervals within which the volunteer has provided willingness in performing activities. Furthermore, each volunteer v has associated a *psychological profile vector* $\mathcal{P}_v = \langle p_0^v, \ldots, p_7^v \rangle$ representing the 8 values resulting from the interpretation of his/her questionnaire. As an example, the following expression describes both the temporal availability and the psychological profile vector of a specific volunteer.

$$\mathbb{T} = \{[8:00, 11:00], [13:00, 15:00], [32:00, 35:00]\}$$
$$\langle P = 15, S = 5, B = 8, Ev = 14, C = 5, Ex = 8, W = 10, O = 5 \rangle \quad (1)$$

At the same time, a set A *activities* should be carried out by the above volunteers. Each activity $a \in A$ has its own *execution interval* $t_a = [lb^a, ub^a]$ representing the span of time within which the activity is carried on. In addition, each activity a has associated a *skill vector* $\mathcal{S}_a = \langle q_0^a, \ldots, q_7^a \rangle$ of boolean values representing the relevant skills needed to perform the activity. As an example, the following expression describes the execution interval and the required skills vector for one of such activities.

$$t = [8:30, 10:30]$$
$$\langle P = 0, S = 1, B = 0, Ev = 1, C = 0, Ex = 1, W = 1, O = 0 \rangle \tag{2}$$

For each of the $\langle v, a \rangle$ couples we introduce a binary integer variable $d_{v,a} \in [0, 1]$ and give it the following semantic: $d_{v,a} = 1$ if and only if the volunteer v performs the activity a. The task of the solver will be to assign values to such variables while guaranteeing that (i) each volunteer performs at least one activity (we recall that volunteers should feel useful), (ii) each of the activities should be performed by someone (more specifically, by exactly one volunteer), (iii) volunteers' temporal availability should be compatible with the assigned activities temporal span and (iv) each volunteer can perform at most one activity at a time.

Additionally, in order to consider the volunteers' attitudes and preferences, we introduce the concept of *adequacy* $w_{v,a} = \mathcal{P}_v \times \mathcal{S}_a^T$, representing how much a volunteer v is "adequate" in performing the activity a. As an example, assigning the activity described by expression 2 to the volunteer described by expression 1 would result in an adequacy of $15 \times 0 + 5 \times 1 + 8 \times 0 + 14 \times 1 + 5 \times 0 + 8 \times 1 + 10 \times 1 + 5 \times 0 = 37$. We can thus introduce the objective function of the optimization problem:

$$\sum_{v \in V, a \in A} w_{v,a} d_{v,a}$$

Maximizing the above expression, given the premises, guarantees an optimal assignment, in terms of the *adequacy*, of the activities to the volunteers.

General Constraints. Once the decision variables have been introduced, it is possible to enforce constraints among them. Specifically, guaranteeing that each volunteer performs at least one activity, can be expressed by means of the expressions $\sum_{a \in A} d_{v,a} \geq 1 \quad \forall v \in V$. Analogously, guaranteeing that each activity is performed by exactly one volunteer can be expressed as $\sum_{v \in V} d_{v,a} = 1 \quad \forall a \in A$. The expression $[\neg \exists t_k \in \mathbb{T}_v : t_k \subseteq t_a] \Rightarrow d_{v,a} = 0 \quad \forall v \in V, a \in A$, where $t_k \in \mathbb{T}_v$ represents the temporal availability of the volunteer v, t_a the temporal span of the activity a and $t_k \subseteq t_a$ is true if the interval t_k *contains* the interval t_a (i.e. $[lb(t_k) \leq lb(t_a)] \wedge [ub(t_a) \leq ub(t_k)]$), guarantees that the temporal availabilities are met. Finally, the constraints $\sum_{a \in O} d_{v,a} \leq 1 \quad \forall v \in V, O \in Overlaps$, where O represents the i-th set of all the temporally overlapping activities *Overlaps* within the foreseen plan's horizon, forbid the assignment of more than one activity at a time to the volunteers. Notice that a viable strategy for computing the O sets consists in adapting the "collecting peaks" procedure described in [5].

It is worth noting that, conversely to a standard Assignment Problem (refer to [1] for a comprehensiveness introduction at the Assignment Problem) the

S4AMT problem allows the assignment of more than one activity to each volunteer, provided that they do not temporally overlap, rather than exactly one. Furthermore, the temporal availability, omitted in the case of the Assignment Problem, guarantees that a single volunteer does not performs those activities which are carried on when he/she is unavailable. It follows that the *S4AMT* problem can be seen as an Assignment Problem enhanced with temporal constraints. Conversely, the presence of the temporal constraints could suggest a Staff Scheduling and Rostering problem (see, for example, [2,7]). Nonetheless, unlike these kinds of problems, the *S4AMT* problem takes into account the adequacy measure. In conclusion, the *S4AMT* problem mixes aspects of an Assignment Problem and of a Staff Scheduling and Rostering problem. Finally, it is worth specifying that those activities which require more than one volunteer can be modeled by means of concurrent, separated, activities each requiring a volunteer.

Additional Constraints for a More Realistic Modeling. From the interaction with the volunteering organization, further constraints have emerged for guaranteeing the generation of solutions that can be feasibly enacted by both the organization and the volunteers. These additional constraints are intended to refine the produced solutions, taking into account further factors which are not considered by the previous modeling.

A first constraint, for example, is aimed at limiting the working hours of people in order to improve the fairness. In particular, the organization tries to avoid more than l (typically one) weekly activity for each single volunteer. Furthermore, the organization aims at reducing the job demand on public holidays (e.g. Sundays) implementing a simple turnover strategy. It turns out that any volunteer who performs a task on a Sunday, will not perform tasks in the other Sundays of the month – formalized as $\sum_{a \in W} d_{v,a} \leq l \quad \forall v \in V, W \in Weeks$, where W represents the i-th set of the activities that fall within the i-th week of all the *Weeks* of the foreseen plan's horizon. Notice that these sets can be easily built from the execution intervals of the activities. Analogously, the following formula $\sum_{a \in H} d_{v,a} \leq 1 \quad \forall v \in V, H \in Months$, enforces that the sum of the activities within all the holidays of each month of the whole plan's horizon must be lower or equal than one. H represents the i-th set of the activities that fall on the holidays of the i-th month among all the *Months* of the foreseen plan's horizon. Similarly to the W sets, the H sets can be easily built from the execution intervals of the activities.

A further constraint, unlike the previous ones, deals with managing particular cases. Some activities, indeed, can only be carried out by some people having some specific skill or authorization. A visit to a museum, for example, requires the use of a bus that can be driven only by a volunteer with the appropriate driving license. Given a set of volunteers $S \subseteq V$, sharing some specific skill, and a set of activities $D \subseteq A$, it is possible to define new constraints characterized by the following form $\sum_{v \in S, a \in D} d_{v,a} \geq 1$. Notice that the above constraint covers the most general case in which an activity requires more than one person to be carried out (D, in this case, contains the activities in which the shared activity is decomposed). In the particular case in which the set D contains a single element (i.e. the activity requires a single person), the previous constraint can be replaced by a more intuitive (and, as well, more efficient) constraint which prevents those users, not having the required feature, to perform the activity: $\sum_{v\in\{V\}/\{S\},a\in\{A\}/\{D\}} d_{v,a} = 0$.

4   The *S4AMT* Solver

As a first step, aimed at quickly arriving to a complete solution, we have developed a system based on two pre-packaged solvers, namely Z3 [6] and Choco [8]. This initial solution relied on the pure solvers abilities while capturing the earlier small size instances provided by Televita. As the problem size increased, however, being it an NP-Hard problem, it quickly resulted as intractable forcing us to use more sophisticated techniques. In fact, with the increase of the number of users and activities, aimed at fulfilling the real needs of the Televita pilot, general solvers resulted insufficient, alone, to efficiently solve the combinatorial optimization problem. Local consistency techniques like, for example, arc-consistency, implemented in standard solvers, find inconsistencies "too late", resulting in an inefficient resolution process, rather slow even in finding a first feasible solution. Random restart and no-good learning techniques partially improve the performance of the resolution process which, however, preserves its slowness resulting to be inadequate for real usage. It is worth reminding that our goal is the one of delivering a complete tool to the volunteering association that is working with us. Suggesting strategies like "leave the solver running during the night" were not among the possible solutions given that also the Televita managers are volunteers themselves and should take the maximum advantage from their time. Hence the need for exploring domain dependent heuristics.

The Domain-Dependent Heuristic. The efficiency issue has been addressed by introducing a domain-dependent heuristic, taking into account the underlying structure of the problem, into the Choco solver with the aim of allowing the solving process to make smarter choices. The idea behind the heuristic simply consists in associating to the volunteer who carries out less activities the activity that is more suited to him/her which is not yet carried out by anybody else. Specifically, for each volunteer $v \in V$, we maintain an integer variable $load_v = \sum_{a\in A} d_{v,a}$, called the *workload* of the volunteer, representing the number of assigned activities. When choosing a decision variable $d_{v,a}$ we search for the less committed volunteer v_i, i.e. the one having the smallest lower bound for the $load_{v_i}$ variable and, among the $d_{v_i,a}$ variables, we chose the one, d_{v_i,a_j}, which is both not instantiated and has the greatest adequacy w_{v_i,a_j}. Finally, we assign d_{v_i,a_j} the value 1 and perform propagation.

Algorithm 1 presents the pseudo-code of our heuristic. This relatively simple technique allows us to find a feasible solution reducing the need of backtracking. Furthermore, the above heuristic creates solutions which, although suboptimal according to our objective function, are relatively fair from a workload point of

---

Algorithm 1. The domain-dependent heuristic for SPONSOR$_T$

---

function SELECTNEXTVAR($users, activities, l$)
    int $c\_load \leftarrow \inf$
    volunteer $v_i \leftarrow null$
    int $c\_adequacy \leftarrow -\inf$
    activity $a_j \leftarrow null$
    for all $v \in volunteers$ **do**   ▷ we select the less committed volunteer
        if $lb(load(v)) < c\_load$ **then**
            $c\_load \leftarrow lb(load(v))$
            $v_i \leftarrow v$
        end if
    end for
    for all $a \in activities$ **do**   ▷ we select the best activity for v_i
        if $\neg instantiated(d_{v_i,a}) \wedge w_{v_i,a} > c\_adequacy$ **then**
            $c\_adequacy \leftarrow w_{v_i,a}$
            $a_j \leftarrow a$
        end if
    end for
    return d_{v_i,a_j}
end function

---

view. Starting from this solution, Choco applies standard techniques for improving the quality of the found solutions according to a branch-and-bound procedure while allowing the user to interrupt the resolution process when satisfied with the best solution found so far.

5   Experimental Results

This section introduces an experimental evaluation produced during the development of the SPONSOR solution. The SPONSOR system, indeed, could impact in different ways with the current Televita management. Two particularly important aspects, on which we concentrated most, consist in (a) the improvement of the time spent by the Televita managers in generating a solution to their management problem and (b) the quality of the generated solution. From a technical point of view the application could, therefore, be evaluated on these measures.

Specifically, in an effort to simulate different organizations, so as to guarantee that the platform is accessible from the widest possible number of different realities, we have generated some benchmark problems[2]. In order to characterize the instances, two parameters are introduced: the *VA* coefficient, a value between 0 and 1, representing the ratio between the number of volunteers and to the number of scheduled activities, and the *AR* coefficient, a value greater than 1, representing the ratio between the total amount of time that the volunteers make available and the total amount of time required by the activities. Table 2 provides some overall statistics about the generated benchmark problems. The

---

[2] We plan to make these problems publicly available to enable their use from others.

created problems are characterized by a growing complexity that is obtained through the progressive increasing of the number of users and activities.

Notice that the *VA* and the *AR* parameters are intended more to show a certain distribution over the various instances of possible problems rather than establishing some kind of correlation with the actual complexity. We have exploited these parameters to generate benchmarks that have different characteristics so that, once the software is distributed to the organizations, it may result robust in the highest number of real cases.

Table 2. Description of the benchmark problems.

Name	Nr. Volunteers	Nr. Activities	VA	AR
#0	3	17	0.176	3.661
#1	6	25	0.24	5.268
#2	12	30	0.4	8.907
#3	23	33	0.697	15.92
#4	21	22	0.954	22.909
#5	26	27	0.963	22.554
#6	27	41	0.658	15.18
#7	28	62	0.452	10.5
#8	30	70	0.429	8.606
#9	30	70	0.428	7.793

Table 3 compares the performances, both in time (measured in seconds) and quality (i.e., the value of the objective function), of the different solvers. Specifically, the different abbreviations are described hereafter:

- **ChF**, first solution of the Choco solver
- **HChF**, first solution of the Choco solver enhanced with the domain-dependent heuristic
- **Z3F**, first solution of the Z3 satisfability solver
- **ChO**, the optimal solution of the Choco solver
- **HChO**, the optimal solution of the Choco solver enhanced with the domain-dependent heuristic
- **Z3O**, the optimal solution of the Z3 optimization solver

We impose a timeout of 5 min (represented, in Table 3, by means of the "to" acronym) and, for those instance for which the timeout is not reached, we compute the average value among ten measurements. It is worth noticing that the introduction of the domain-dependent heuristic, as described in Sect. 4, allows finding a first solution in (sometimes, significantly) faster times. In case of benchmark #5, for example, Choco reaches the timeout even before the first

Table 3. Experimental results.

Name	ChF time	ChF quality	HChF time	HChF quality	Z3F time	Z3F quality	ChO time	ChO quality	HChO time	HChO quality	Z3O time	Z3O quality
#0	0.3454	530	0.3249	644	0.2226	707	2.8343	749	2.5254	749	0.2249	749
#1	0.3905	869	0.3496	884	0.6778	999	to	978	to	1,003	0.2967	1,098
#2	0.3719	1034	0.3409	1051	9.995	1,128	to	1,127	to	1,153	166.3888	1,314
#3	5.2358	1221	0.3578	1210	44.9755	1,220	to	1,248	to	1,286	to	to
#4	1.075	721	0.35	767	10.5638	757	to	772	to	780	to	to
#5	to	to	0.3576	976	28.8545	925	to	to	to	984	to	to
#6	0.4811	1432	0.371	1518	133.3643	1,574	to	1,492	to	1,601	to	to
#7	0.4269	2232	0.3997	2316	to	to	to	2,289	to	2,390	to	to
#8	0.4961	2,521	0.4563	2,646	to	to	to	2,575	to	2,722	to	to
#9	0.4311	2,485	0.4037	2,648	to	to	to	2,553	to	2,723	to	to

solution is found. Similarly, Z3 is not able to find a feasible solution for the #7, #8 and #9 cases within the timeout. From a user interaction point of view, the use of Choco with the domain-dependent heuristics is the best choice as it generates, within a short time, an admissible solution to be presented to the user. Except in some cases, the quality of the first solution found thanks to the heuristic is better than the quality of the first solution, on the same instance, found by the other solvers. In those cases where other solvers are able to find a better solution, they do it spending higher times.

As concerns the optimization process, in those cases where the table shows a value for the quality of the solution but does not show the time it takes to calculate it, we are showing the best solution found before the timeout has been reached. Specifically, while the two instances of Choco (with and without the heuristic) are able to demonstrate the optimum of the first benchmark only, Z3, configured as an optimization solver, is able to demonstrate the optimum of the first three benchmarks. In other words, exception made for the first three instances, we do not know which is the optimal value. Since Z3 was able to demonstrate the optimum for a greater number of instances, fostered by its by its simplex-based implementation, initially, we used it as the only solver. Unfortunately, however, we were not able to retrieve intermediate solutions by Z3, thus affecting the interactivity with the end user who has no chance to settle for a suboptimal solution. The definition of new heuristics, as well as the introduction of different search strategies, also appears to be prohibitive from an implementation point of view, thus making Z3, for the moment, a second choice. At the moment, using Choco with the heuristic is, again, the best choice, allowing the organization manager to find good quality solutions in a reasonable amount of time.

6 The Complete System and Its Current Status

The present paper is focalized on the formalization of the addressed problem as the *S4AMT* and the synthesis of a solver for meaningful instances of that problem. We have currently implemented a complete system, the SPONSOR$_T$ system (standing for "SPONSOR for Televita") that is based on the described algorithm.

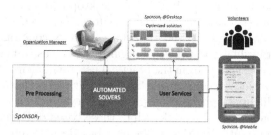

Fig. 3. The SPONSOR$_T$ end-to-end system.

SPONSOR$_T$ represents an end-to-end product suited to serve the small organizations with similar structures.

Figure 3 sketches the applied approach and the three developed functionalities: (a) a Pre-Processing module that supports data gathering (e.g., the questionnaires from the different volunteers, the periodic formulation of the problem, etc.); (b) a Solving module implementing the solver as described in Sect. 4; (c) a Run-Time Interaction module, that offers a combination of front-ends to guarantee support for continuous use by different classes of users: specifically the SPONSOR$_T$@Desktop allows the organisation managers to look for solutions and communicate them to volunteers; the SPONSOR$_T$Mobile is devoted to volunteers who can see their assigned tasks by means of an app downloadable on their mobile. For the sake of space the interaction capabilities of modules (a) and (c) are not part of this paper, their current design principles are described in the paper [3]. The system is currently in the transition from laboratory testing to an extensive test with users. A preliminary test with a restricted group of Televita managers has been more than encouraging.

7   Conclusions and Future Work

The SPONSOR project has exposed the authors to a perspective of becoming elderly that is particularly complex and to a social problem not easy to be solved. As always, when addressing problems of frail segments of the population it is better to avoid broad statements like "we have solved a relevant social problem with AI" and we will not make such a statement here. Nevertheless with the current work we have identified a particular class of problems where the use of AI techniques can help the human users to find better solutions with respect to an hand-made current practice. It is worth reminding the main aspect of our current approach: we have studied the practice at Televita and integrated their approach in our pre-processing phase to be used as an input of the solving procedure. The key assumption is the choice of the objective function that uses the *adequacy* metric to associate people to activities. After having formulated the *S4AMT* problem, this paper presents an exploration of the use of different solvers for a well characterized set of instances for the problem. An heuristic approach is then proposed that guarantees good quality in acceptable computational time so as to be integrated in a simple desktop based system. The experimental section demonstrates how this result has been achieved.

The agenda for the immediate future is constrained by the need to perform a user evaluation in the real organization so as to make sure that also the various soft constraints from the practical use are implemented in SPONSOR. Indeed from the strictly technical side we would like to perform some additional exploration of different optimization procedures ranging, for example, from those based on Large Neighborhood Search to those based of Genetic Algorithms. Furthermore, some multi-objective strategies, based on Pareto frontier, can be adopted by including, also, the overall workload of the volunteers in the objective function, with the aim of producing fairer solutions, as well as possible preferences on the volunteers' temporal availabilities.

Acknowledgments. Authors would like to thank Sergio Cametti for his enthusiastic participation in the project, for offering us the Televita case and for believing in what we are doing notwithstanding the difficulties of a dialogue between our so different worlds.

References

1. Burkard, R., Dell'Amico, M., Martello, S.: Assignment Problems, Revised Reprint: Other titles in applied mathematics. Society for Industrial and Applied Mathematics (SIAM), Philadelphia (2009)
2. Burke, E.K., De Causmaecker, P., Berghe, G.V., Van Landeghem, H.: The state of the art of nurse rostering. J. Sched. **7**(6), 441–499 (2004)
3. Cesta, A., Coraci, L., Cortellessa, G., De Benedictis, R., Fracasso, F.: Do the right task! supporting volunteers timetabling with preferences through SpONSOR platform. In: ForItAAL, Proceedings of the 8th Italian Forum on Ambient Assisted Living, Genova, June 2017
4. Cesta, A., Cortellessa, G., De Benedictis, R., Fracasso, F., Baumann, D., Cuomo, S., Doyle, J., Imeri, A., Khadraoui, D., Rossel, P.: Personalizing support to older adults who look for a job with the SpONSOR platform. In: Bandini, S., Cortellessa, G., Palumbo, F. (eds.) AI*AAL 2016, Proceedings of the Artificial Intelligence for Ambient Assisted Living AI*IA Workshop (Ceur Ws 1803), pp. 105–122 (2016)
5. Cesta, A., Oddi, A., Smith, S.F.: A constraint-based method for project scheduling with time windows. J. Heuristics **8**(1), 109–136 (2002). doi:10.1023/A:1013617802515
6. de Moura, L., Bjørner, N.: Z3: an efficient SMT solver. In: Ramakrishnan, C.R., Rehof, J. (eds.) TACAS 2008. LNCS, vol. 4963, pp. 337–340. Springer, Heidelberg (2008). doi:10.1007/978-3-540-78800-3_24
7. Ernst, A., Jiang, H., Krishnamoorthy, M., Sier, D.: Staff scheduling and rostering: a review of applications, methods and models. Eur. J. Oper. Res. **153**(1), 3–27 (2004). http://www.sciencedirect.com/science/article/pii/S037722170300095X. Timetabling and Rostering
8. Prud'homme, C., Fages, J.G., Lorca, X.: Choco Documentation. TASC, INRIA Rennes, LINA CNRS UMR 6241, COSLING S.A.S. (2016). http://www.choco-solver.org

An Advanced Answer Set Programming Encoding for Nurse Scheduling

Mario Alviano[1], Carmine Dodaro[2(✉)], and Marco Maratea[2]

[1] DEMACS, University of Calabria, Rende, Italy
alviano@mat.unical.it
[2] DIBRIS, University of Genova, Genoa, Italy
{dodaro,marco}@dibris.unige.it

Abstract. The goal of the Nurse Scheduling Problem (NSP) is to find an assignment of nurses to shifts according to specific requirements. Given its practical relevance, many researchers have developed different strategies for solving several variants of the problem. One of such variants was recently addressed by an approach based on Answer Set Programming (ASP), obtaining promising results. Nonetheless, the original ASP encoding presents some intrinsic weaknesses, which are identified and eventually circumvented in this paper. The new encoding is designed by taking into account both intrinsic properties of NSP and internal details of ASP solvers, such as cardinality and weight constraint propagators. The performance gain of CLINGO and WASP is empirically verified on instances from ASP literature. As an additional contribution, the performance of CLINGO and WASP is compared to other declarative frameworks, namely SAT and ILP; the best performance is obtained by CLINGO running the new ASP encoding.

Keywords: Answer Set Programming · Knowledge representation and reasoning · Nurse Scheduling

1 Introduction

The Nurse Scheduling Problem (NSP) consists of generating a schedule of working and rest days for nurses working in hospital units. The schedule should determine the shift assignments of nurses for a predetermined window of time and must satisfy requirements imposed by the Rules of Procedure of hospitals. A proper solution to NSP is crucial to guarantee the high level of quality of health care, to improve the degree of satisfaction of nurses, and the recruitment of qualified personnel. Given its practical relevance on the quality of hospital structures, NSP has been widely studied in the literature and several variants have been considered [14,18]. Such variants are usually grouped according to several factors, as the planning period, the different types of shifts considered, and requirements on the preferences of hospitals and nurses.

The NSP variant considered in this paper concerns a planning period fixed to one year with three different types of shifts (morning, afternoon and night) and

© Springer International Publishing AG 2017
F. Esposito et al. (Eds.): AI*IA 2017, LNAI 10640, pp. 468–482, 2017.
https://doi.org/10.1007/978-3-319-70169-1_35

requirements on nurses and hospitals provided by an Italian hospital. Specifically, such requirements concern restrictions to the number of working hours per year and to the number of times nurses are assigned to a specific shift.

Recently, the aforementioned variant of NSP has been modeled by means of an Answer Set Programming (ASP) [13] encoding presented in [21]. The encoding resulted to be natural and intuitive, in the sense that it was designed by applying the standard modeling methodology, yet it obtained reasonable performance on solving the analyzed instances.

On the other hand, it turned out that the encoding presented in [21] shows some limitations and intrinsic weaknesses, mainly due to *aggregates* [7], i.e. operations on multi-sets of weighted literals that evaluate to some value. The encoding of [21] presents some aggregates with a quite large number of literals and few different weights, resulting to be counterproductive for the performance of modern ASP solvers [27], since they deteriorate their propagation power. In this paper, we circumvented such limitations by taking into account only combinations of values that can lead to admissible schedules. Interestingly, the new encoding did not require to significantly sacrifice the readability of the encoding, which remains intuitive and clear.

The performance of the ASP solvers executed on the new encoding has been empirically evaluated on the same data and settings used in [21], showing a clear improvement on the performance of state of the art ASP systems CLINGO [26] and WASP [5]. As an additional contribution, the ASP-based approaches have been compared to other declarative frameworks, namely Propositional Logic Satisfiability (SAT) [8] and Integer Linear Programming (ILP) [1]. Results show that CLINGO and WASP executed on the new encoding outperform their counterparts executed on the original encoding. Moreover, CLINGO executed on the new encoding is considerably faster than all other tested approaches.

The contributions of the paper can be summarized as follows:

1. We formalize the variant of NSP considered in this paper and in [21] (Sect. 2.2).
2. We propose a new ASP-based solution to NSP overcoming some limitations of the encoding presented in [21] (Sect. 3.3).
3. We present an experimental analysis comparing the ASP solution proposed in this paper with the previous one as well as with SAT and ILP based solutions (Sect. 4). Results show a significant improvement of the performance of ASP solvers and, specifically, CLINGO performs better than all other alternatives.

2   Description and Formalization

We start this section by providing a description of the problem as posed by an Italian hospital (Sect. 2.1). In the description we identify parameters that allow to reuse the proposed solution even if part of the specification given by the hospital will change. The formalization presented in Sect. 2.2 in fact considers these parameters as part of the input.

2.1   Nurse Scheduling Problem

NSP amounts to the totalization of partial schedules assigning nurses to working and rest days over a predetermined period of time, which is fixed to one year in this paper. Usually, partial schedules to be totalized involve few data concerning already authorized vacations. Admissible schedules must satisfy a set of requirements dictated by the rules of the hospital units. In the following, we report the requirements specified by an Italian hospital.

Hospital requirements. For every working day, nurses can be assigned to exactly one of the following shifts: *morning* (7 A.M.–2 P.M.), *afternoon* (2 P.M.–9 P.M.), *night* (9 P.M.–7 A.M.). Thus, the morning and the afternoon shifts last 7 h, whereas the night shift lasts 10 h. In order to ensure the best assistance program for patients, the number of nurses in every shift $x \in \{morning, afternoon, night\}$ must range from x_{min}^{nurse} to x_{max}^{nurse}.

Nurses requirements. In order to guarantee a fair workload, each nurse must work a number of hours ranging from $work_{min}$ to $work_{max}$. Additional requirements are also imposed to ensure an adequate rest period to each nurse: *(a)* nurses are legally guaranteed 30 days of paid vacation; *(b)* the starting time of a shift must be at least 24 h later than the starting time of the previous shift; and *(c)* each nurse has at least two ordinary rest days for every window of fourteen days. In addition, nurses working on two consecutive nights deserve one special rest day in addition to the ordinary rest days.

Balance requirements. The number of morning, afternoon and night shifts assigned to every nurse should range over a set of acceptable values, that is, from x_{min}^{day} to x_{max}^{day} for each $x \in \{morning, afternoon, night\}$.

2.2   Formalization

According to the above requirements, we define the following decisional problem NSP^d: Given a set N of nurses, a partial schedule

$$s' : N \times [1..365] \nrightarrow \{morning, afternoon, night, special\text{-}rest, rest, vacation\} \tag{1}$$

natural numbers $work_{min}$, $work_{max}$, and x_{min}^{nurse}, x_{max}^{nurse}, x_{min}^{day}, x_{max}^{day} for $x \in \{morning, afternoon, night\}$, check the existence of a schedule

$$s : N \times [1..365] \rightarrow \{morning, afternoon, night, special\text{-}rest, rest, vacation\} \tag{2}$$

extending s' and satisfying the following conditions:

$$x_{min}^{nurse} \leq | \{n \in N : s(n, d) = x\} | \leq x_{max}^{nurse} \tag{3}$$

for all $x \in \{morning, afternoon, night\}$, and all $d \in [1..365]$;

$$work_{min} \leq 7 \cdot | \{d \in [1..365] : s(n, d) \in \{morning, afternoon\}, n \in N\} | \\ + 10 \cdot | \{d \in [1..365] : s(n, d) = night, n \in N\} | \leq work_{max}; \tag{4}$$

$$| \{d \in [1..365] : s(n, d) = vacation\} \,|= 30 \tag{5}$$
$$| \{d \in [2..365] : s(n, d) = morning, \; s(n, d - 1) \in \{afternoon, night\}\} \,|= 0$$
$$| \{d \in [2..365] : s(n, d) = afternoon, \; s(n, d - 1) = night\} \,|= 0 \tag{6}$$

for all $n \in N$;

$$| \{d' \in [d..d + 13] : s(n, d') = rest\} \,|\geq 2 \tag{7}$$

for all $n \in N$, and all $d \in [1..352]$;

$$s(n, d) = special\text{-}rest \text{ if and only if } s(n, d - 1) = night \text{ and } s(n, d - 2) = night \tag{8}$$

for all $n \in N$, and all $d \in [3..365]$;

$$x_{min}^{day} \leq | \{d \in [1..365] : s(n, d) = x\} \,|\leq x_{max}^{day} \tag{9}$$

for all $n \in N$, and $x \in \{morning, afternoon, night\}$.

Optimal balance requirements. In addition to the above requirements, the hospital reported some further requirements to guarantee a balance in the assignment of shifts. Indeed, the number of morning, afternoon and night shifts assigned to every nurse should be *preferably* fixed to some desired values, that is, x^{day} for each $x \in \{morning, afternoon, night\}$.

According to the above additional requirement, we define the following *optimization* problem NSP^o: Given a set N of nurses, natural numbers $work_{min}, work_{max}$, and $x_{min}^{nurse}, x_{max}^{nurse}, \; x^{day}, x_{min}^{day}, x_{max}^{day}$ for $x \in \{morning, afternoon, night\}$, check the existence of a schedule s of the form (2) satisfying (3)–(9), and minimizing

$$\sum_{x \in \{morning, afternoon, night\}, \, n \in N} abs(x^{day} - | \{d \in [1..365] : s(n, d) = x\} \,|). \tag{10}$$

3   ASP Encodings

In Sect. 3.3 we present the new advanced encoding, improving on the existing one introduced in [21] and briefly recalled in Sect. 3.2. We assume that the reader is familiar with basic knowledges of Answer Set Programming and ASP-CORE-2 input language specification [15] (some minimal notions are given in Sect. 3.1).

3.1   ASP Evaluation Strategies

In the following a summary of the evaluation strategies of ASP programs are reported in order to provide a better insight on the properties of the new encoding. The evaluation of an ASP program is usually made in two steps, called *grounding* and *solving*. First, the ASP program with variables is evaluated by the grounder, which is responsible to produce its variable-free (propositional) counterpart.

Example 1 (Grounding). Consider as example the following rules:

```
a(1..5). b(1..10). c(1..3).
{output(X,Z,Y) : c(Z)} = 1 :- a(X), b(Y).
```

The grounder produces 50 (i.e. 5×10) propositional rules of the following form:

$$
\begin{aligned}
p_1 : \quad & \{\texttt{output(1,1,1); output(1,2,1); output(1,3,1)}\} = 1. \\
p_2 : \quad & \{\texttt{output(1,1,2); output(1,2,2); output(1,3,2)}\} = 1. \\
p_3 : \quad & \{\texttt{output(1,1,3); output(1,2,3); output(1,3,3)}\} = 1. \\
& \qquad\qquad\qquad \vdots
\end{aligned}
$$

Intuitively, the choice rule p_1 enforces that exactly one atom between output(1,1,1), output(1,2,1) and output(1,3,1) must be true in an answer set. Similar considerations hold for other ground rules generated. ◁

The resulting propositional program is evaluated by the solver, whose role is to produce an answer set. Modern ASP solvers implement the algorithm CDCL [27], which is based on the pattern *choose-propagate-learn*. Intuitively, the idea is to build an answer set step-by-step by starting from an empty interpretation, i.e. all atoms are initially undefined. Then, the algorithm heuristically *chooses* an undefined atom to be true in the answer set, and the deterministic consequences of this choice are *propagated*, i.e. new atoms are derived true or false in the answer set candidate. The propagation may lead to a *conflict*, i.e. an atom is true and false at the same time. In this case, the conflict is analyzed and a new constraint is added to the propositional program (*learning*). The conflict is then repaired, i.e. choices leading to the conflict are retracted and a new undefined atom is heuristically selected. The algorithm then iterates until no undefined atoms are left, i.e. an answer set is produced, or the incoherence of the propositional program is proved, i.e. no answer sets are admitted.

Example 2 (Propagation). Consider the propositional rule p_1 reported in Example 1 and assume that atoms output(1,1,1) and output(1,2,1) have been heuristically assigned to false. Then, the solver derives output(1,3,1) to true because it is the only way to satisfy the rule p_1. ◁

3.2 Existing Encoding

Instances of NSP^d and NSP^o are represented by means of ASP facts and constants. Specifically, the interval [1..365] of days is encoded by facts of the form day(d), for all $d \in [1..365]$, and the number of days is fixed by the fact days(365). The nurses are encoded by facts of the form nurse(n), for all $n \in N$. Available shifts are encoded by facts of the form shift(id_x, x, h), where $id_x \in [1..6]$ is a numerical identifier of the shift, $x \in \{morning, afternoon, night, special\text{-}rest, rest, vacation\}$, and h is the number of working hours associated to the shift. Natural numbers x_{min}^{nurse}, x_{max}^{nurse} for $x \in \{morning, afternoon, night\}$ are represented by facts of the form nurseLimits($id_x, x_{min}^{nurse}, x_{max}^{nurse}$), where id_x is the identifier of the shift x.

```
        % Choose an assignment for each day and for each nurse.
r₁ :    {assign(N,S,D) : shift(S,Name,H)} = 1 :- day(D), nurse(N).

        % Limits to nurses that must be present for each shift.
r₂ :    :- day(D), #count{N : assign(N,S,D)} > Max, nurseLimits(S,Min,Max).
r₃ :    :- day(D), #count{N : assign(N,S,D)} < Min, nurseLimits(S,Min,Max).

        % Each nurse works at least Min and at most Max hours per year.
r₄ :    :- nurse(N), #sum{H,D : assign(N,S,D), shift(S,Na,H)} > Max, workLimits(Min,Max).
r₅ :    :- nurse(N), #sum{H,D : assign(N,S,D), shift(S,Na,H)} < Min, workLimits(Min,Max).

        % Exactly 30 days of holidays. The ID 6 corresponds to the vacation.
r₆ :    :- nurse(N), #count{D : assign(N,6,D)} != 30.

        % Each nurse cannot work twice in 24 hours (based on the order on the IDs).
r₇ :    :- nurse(N), assign(N,T1,D), assign(N,T2,D+1), T2 < T1, T1 <= 3.

        % At least 2 rest days each 14 days. The ID 5 is associated to rest.
r₈ :    :- nurse(N), day(D), days(DAYS), D <= DAYS-13,
             #count{D1 : assign(N,5,D1), D1 >= D, D1 <= D+13} < 2.

        % After two consecutive nights there is one rest day.
        % The ID 3 is associated to the shift night, while 4 is associated to special rest.
r₉ :    :- not assign(N,4,D), assign(N,3,D-2), assign(N,3,D-1).
r₁₀:    :- assign(N,4,D), not assign(N,3,D-2).
r₁₁:    :- assign(N,4,D), not assign(N,3,D-1).

        % Balance requirements.
r₁₂:    :- nurse(N), #count{D : assign(N,S,D)} > Max, dayLimits(S,T,Min,Max).
r₁₃:    :- nurse(N), #count{D : assign(N,S,D)} < Min, dayLimits(S,T,Min,Max).

        % Added only in the optimization variant.
r₁₄:    :~ nurse(N), X=#count{D : assign(N,S,D)}, dayLimits(S,T,Min,Max),
             X >= Min, X <= Max. [|X-T|@1,N]
```

Fig. 1. ASP encoding introduced in [21] for NSP^o (and for NSP^d if r_{14} is removed).

Natural numbers $x^{day}, x^{day}_{min}, x^{day}_{max}$ for $x \in \{morning, afternoon, night\}$ are represented by $\texttt{dayLimits}(id_x, x^{day}, x^{day}_{min}, x^{day}_{max})$, while $work_{min}, work_{max}$ by $\texttt{workLimits}(work_{min}, work_{max})$. Hence, according to the specification given by the hospital, the following facts and constants are considered in our setting:

```
day(1..365).            days(365).                nurses(1..41).
shift(1,morning,7).     shift(2,afternoon,7).     shift(3,night,10).
shift(4,specialrest,0). shift(5,rest,0).          shift(6,vacation,0).
nurseLimits(1,6,9).     nurseLimits(2,6,9).       nurseLimits(3,4,7).
dayLimits(1,78,74,82).  dayLimits(2,78,74,82).    dayLimits(3,60,58,61).
workLimits(1687,1692).
```

The computed schedule is encoded by atoms of the form $\texttt{assign}(n, x, d)$, representing that nurse n is assigned shift x on day d, that is, $s(n, d) = x$. The same predicate $\texttt{assign}$ is used to specify the partial schedule s' in input. x

The ASP encoding introduced in [21] is reported in Fig. 1. It implements the *Guess&Check* programming methodology: Choice rule r_1 is used to guess the schedule $s : N \times [1..365] \rightarrow [1..6]$ extending s' and assigning each day of each nurse to exactly one shift, and rules r_2–r_{13} are used to discard schedules not satisfying some of the desired requirements. Specifically, hospital requirements, formalized as property (3), are enforced by the integrity constraints r_2 and r_3, which filter out assignments exceeding the limits. Regarding nurse requirements, property (4) is enforced by integrity constraints r_4 and r_5, property (5) by integrity constraint r_6, property (6) by integrity constraint r_7, property (7) by integrity constraint r_8, and property (8) by integrity constraint r_9-r_{11}. Note that r_7 takes advantage of the numerical identifiers associated with shifts, and in particular by the fact that morning has ID 1, afternoon has ID 2, and night has ID 3. Concerning balance requirements, formalized as property (9), they are enforced by integrity constraints r_{12} and r_{14}. Rules r_1-r_{13} encode NSP^d, while for NSP^o we also need weak constraint r_{14}: It assigns a cost to each admissible schedule measured according to function (10). Optimum schedules are those minimizing such a cost.

3.3   Advanced Encoding

The aim of this section is to introduce a new encoding, shown on Fig. 2, which improves the encoding reported in the previous section. First of all, note that many constraints of the encoding in Fig. 1 only involve assignments to working shifts, that is, morning, afternoon and night. The *Guess* part of the encoding (i.e., rule r_1) can thus be replaced by two different choice rules, r'_{1a}, r'_{1b}, where r'_{1a} guesses among one of the working shifts or otherwise marks nurses as *not working*, and r'_{1b} eventually guesses among rest, special-rest and vacation for each nurse marked as not working. To achieve such a behavior, an additional *meta-shift* is added to the set of facts, namely shift(7,notworking,0).

Table 1. Number of working hours assigned to nurse n, that is, $7 \cdot (M + A) + 10 \cdot N$, where $M =| \{d \in [1..365] : s(n, d) = morning\} |$, $A =| \{d \in [1..365] : s(n, d) = afternoon\} |$, and $N =| \{d \in [1..365] : s(n, d) = night\} |$. Admissible values, that is, those in the interval $[1687..1692]$, are emphasized in bold.

N	$M + A$																
	148	149	150	151	152	153	154	155	156	157	158	159	160	161	162	163	164
58	1616	1623	1630	1637	1644	1651	1658	1665	1672	1679	1686	**1693**	1700	1707	1714	1721	1728
59	1626	1633	1640	1647	1654	1661	1668	1675	1682	**1689**	1696	1703	1710	1717	1724	1731	1738
60	1636	1643	1650	1657	1664	1671	1678	1685	**1692**	1699	1706	1713	1720	1727	1734	1741	1748
61	1646	1653	1660	1667	1674	1681	**1688**	1695	1702	1709	1716	1723	1730	1737	1744	1751	1758

A second improvement is obtained by combining the knowledge represented by Eqs. (4) and (9) with some observations on how rules r_4 and r_5 are evaluated. In fact, during the solving phase, rules obtained by instantiating r_4 and r_5 comprise aggregates with relatively large aggregation sets and few different weights. Specifically to our setting, where morning and afternoon shifts are fixed to 7 h, and night shifts to 10 h, each aggregation set contains 365 elements with weight 7, and 365 elements with weight 10. It turns out that several schedules result into exactly the same sum value. The question is now how many

```
     % Choose an assignment for each day and for each nurse.
r'₁ₐ:  {assign(N,S,D):shift(S,Name,H), S != 4, S != 5, S != 6} = 1 :- day(D), nurse(N).
r'₁ᵦ:  {assign(N,S,D):shift(S,Name,H), S >= 4, S <= 6} = 1 :- day(D), nurse(N), assign(N,7,D).

     % Limits to nurses that must be present for each shift.
r'₂:   :- day(D), #count{N : assign(N,S,D)} > Max, nurseLimits(S,Min,Max).
r'₃:   :- day(D), #count{N : assign(N,S,D)} < Min, nurseLimits(S,Min,Max).

     % Nurses requirements.
r'₄:   valid(Nu) :- nurse(Nu), admissible(N,M+A),
           countGE(1,Nu,M), not countGE(1,Nu,M+1),
           countGE(2,Nu,A), not countGE(2,Nu,A+1),
           countGE(3,Nu,N), not countGE(3,Nu,N+1).
r'₅:   :- nurse(N), not valid(N).

     % Exactly 30 days of holidays. The id 6 corresponds to the vacation.
r'₆:   :- nurse(N), #count{D : assign(N,6,D)} != 30.

     % Each nurse cannot work twice in 24 hours (based on the order on the IDs).
r'₇:   :- nurse(N), assign(N,T1,D), assign(N,T2,D+1), T2 < T1, T1 <= 3.

     % At least 2 rest days each 14 days. The id 5 is associated to rest.
r'₈:   :- nurse(N), day(D), days(DAYS), D <= DAYS-13,
           #count{D1 : assign(N,5,D1), D1 >= D, D1 <= D+13} < 2.

     % After two consecutive nights (ID 3) there is one rest day (ID 4).
r'₉:   :- not assign(N,4,D), assign(N,3,D-2), assign(N,3,D-1).
r'₁₀:  :- assign(N,4,D), not assign(N,3,D-2).
r'₁₁:  :- assign(N,4,D), not assign(N,3,D-1).

     % A nurse should be assigned to the shift S at least Min and at most Max days.
r'₁₂:  :- dayLimits(S,T,Min,Max), nurse(N), not countGE(S,N,Min).
r'₁₃:  :- dayLimits(S,T,Min,Max), nurse(N), countGE(S,N,Max+1).

     % Added only in the optimization variant. The ID 7 corresponds to notworking.
r'₁₄:  :~ nurse(N), countGE(S,N,X), not countGE(S,N,X+1),
           dayLimits(S,T,Min,Max), S != 7, V = |X-T|. [V@1,N,S]

     % Admissible pairs of nights and morning+afternoon shifts, and limits for nonworking
     % days.
r'₁₅:  admissible(N,M+A) :-
           dayLimits(1,T1,MinM,MaxM), dayLimits(2,T2,MinA,MaxA), dayLimits(3,T3,MinN,MaxN),
           M = MinM..MaxM, A = MinA..MaxA, N = MinN..MaxN,
           V = 7*(M+A) + 10*N, workLimits(MinW, MaxW), MinW <= V, V <= MaxW.

r'₁₆:  dayLimits(7,null,Min,Max) :- days(DAYS), Min = #min{DAYS-MA-N : admissible(N,MA)},
           Max = #max{DAYS-MA-N : admissible(N,MA)}.

     % countGE(S,N,V) is derived when a nurse N is assigned to the shift S at least V days.
r'₁₇:  countGE(S,N,V) :- nurse(N), dayLimits(S,T,Min,Max), V = Min..Max+1,
           #count{D : assign(N,S,D)} >= V.

     % The derivation of countGE(S,N,V) implies the derivation of countGE(S,N,V-1).
r'₁₈:  :- dayLimits(S,T,Min,Max), V > Min, countGE(S,N,V), not countGE(S,N,V-1).
```

Fig. 2. Advanced ASP encoding for NSP^o (and for NSP^d if r'_{14} is removed).

of these schedules actually satisfy both (4) and (9). Restricting to the specification given by the hospital, that is, $morning_{min}^{day} = afternoon_{min}^{day} = 74$, $morning_{max}^{day} = afternoon_{max}^{day} = 82$, $night_{min}^{day} = 58$, and $night_{max}^{day} = 61$, the possible sum values are those reported in Table 1, where we also highlight admissible values in the interval $[work_{min}..work_{max}] = [1687..1692]$. The new encoding therefore determines the admissible pairs of the form $(N, M + A)$, where M, A, N are the number of morning, afternoon and nights assigned to a given nurse, by means of rule r_{15}'. These pairs are then used to check whether the assignment of working shifts is valid for each nurse by means of rules r_4' and r_5'.

Actually, rules r_4' and r_5' take advantage from a third improvement of the advanced encoding. The number of morning, afternoon and night shifts that can be assigned to a nurse must adhere to Eq. (9), and are therefore limited to a few different values. The possible values of these aggregations are therefore encoded by means of atoms of the form $\mathtt{countGE}(x, n, v)$, being true whenever $|\{d \in [1..365] : s(n, d) = x\}| \geq v$. It turns out that any answer set satisfies the following property: for each shift x and for each nurse n, there is exactly one value v such that $\mathtt{countGE}(x, n, v), \mathrm{not}\ \mathtt{countGE}(x, n, v + 1)$ is true. In the advanced encoding, predicate $\mathtt{countGE}$ is defined by rule r_{17}'. Moreover, rule r_{18}' is used to enforce truth of $\mathtt{countGE}(x, n, v - 1)$ whenever $\mathtt{countGE}(x, n, v)$ is true; it is not required for correctness, but convenient to prune the search space in case $\mathtt{countGE}(x, n, v)$ is assigned to true during the computation even if $|\{d \in [1..365] : s(n, d) = x\}| \geq v$ does not yet hold (for example, in case $\mathtt{countGE}(x, n, v)$ is selected as a branching literal).

The fourth improvement is obtained by noting that rules r_{12}–r_{14} aggregate on sets $\{d \in [1..365] : s(n, d) = x\}$ for $x \in \{morning, afternoon, night\}$. It is therefore convenient to rewrite these rules in terms of predicate $\mathtt{countGE}$, hence obtaining rules r_{12}'–r_{14}'. Finally, a further improvement is obtained by checking the number of nonworking days assigned to each nurse. For the specification given by the hospital it must range between 149 and 150, and in general the admitted range can be determined by rule r_{16}'. The check itself is then performed by rules r_{12}' and r_{13}' (for $\mathtt{S}$ being 7). Note that also this last check is not required to guarantee correctness of the encoding.

4 Empirical Evaluation

In this section the results of the empirical evaluation conducted on the same setting of [21] is reported. The experiments consider real data provided by the Italian hospital unit, which comprises a set of 41 nurses and holidays selected using the preferences of nurses of the year 2015. Moreover, the scalability of the approach has been evaluated by considering different number of nurses. In particular, an additional experiment was run by considering 10, 20, 41, 82 and 164 nurses without fixed holidays. We consider both the decisional (NSP^d) and the optimization (NSP^o) variants of NSP. Concerning the decisional variant, we compared our new ASP-based approach with the previous ASP encoding, with a solution based on SAT and one based on ILP.

The ASP encodings have been tested using the system CLINGO (v. 5.1.0) [24] and the solver WASP (v. 996bfb3) [5] combined with the grounder GRINGO [25], both configured with the core-based algorithms [4] for NSP^o. Solvers LINGELING (v. bbc-9230380-160707) [12], GLUCOSE (v. 4.1) [8] and CLASP (v. 3.2.2) have been executed on the SAT encoding, while the commercial tool GUROBI (v. 7.0.2) [1] on the ILP encoding. Concerning the optimization variant, the same tools for ASP and ILP have been used, whereas LINGELING and GLUCOSE have been replaced by the MaxSAT tools MSCG [32] and MAXINO [6], both binaries taken from MaxSAT Competition 2016.

In order to test SAT and ILP solutions, we created a pseudo-Boolean formula based on the ideas of the advanced ASP encoding. The pseudo-Boolean formula was represented using the OPB format, which is parsed by the tool GUROBI. Concerning the SAT-based solutions, we use the tool PBLIB [33] to convert the pseudoBoolean formula into a CNF. The running time of PBLIB has not been included in the analysis.

Time and memory were limited to 1 h and 8 GB, respectively. All the material can be found at http://www.star.dist.unige.it/~marco/Data/material.zip.

Results. The results of the run on the instance provided by the Italian hospital are reported in Table 2. The best result overall is obtained by CLINGO executed on the advanced encoding for both NSP^d and NSP^o, which is able to find a schedule in 42 and 70 s, respectively. This is a clear improvement with respect to the original encoding. Indeed, CLINGO executed on the original encoding was able to find a schedule in 22 and 7 min for the decisional and optimization variant, respectively. However, the advanced encoding does not help the other ASP solver WASP: its bad performance seems related to the branching heuristic, which is not effective on this particular domain. SAT-based (and MaxSAT-based) approaches are also not able to find a schedule within the allotted time and memory. In this case their performance can be explained by looking at the large size of the formula to evaluate (approximately 65 millions of clauses), which makes the solvers exceed the allotted memory. The tool GUROBI obtained good performance on both NSP^d and NSP^d instances. In particular for NSP^d GUROBI is faster than CLINGO executed on the original encoding. On the contrary, GUROBI is slower than CLINGO on NSP^o instances.

Scalability. We also performed an analysis about the scalability of the encoding, considering different numbers of nurses. In particular, for both NSP^d and NSP^o we considered five instances containing 10, 20, 41, 82 and 164 nurses, respectively. For each instance, we proportionally scaled the number of working nurses during each shift and holidays are randomly generated, whereas other requirements are not modified. Results are reported in Table 3.

The best results overall is obtained again by CLINGO executed on the advanced encoding, which outperforms all other tested approaches. Concerning ASP-based approaches, their performance is much better when they are executed on the advanced encoding. Indeed, the running time of CLINGO decreases considerably for all tested instances in both NSP^d and NSP^o. Moreover, Fig. 3

Table 2. Results of the experiment with 41 nurses and fixed holidays.

NSP^d		NSP^o	
Solver	Solving time (s)	Solver	Solving time (s)
CLINGO (ORIG ENC)	1352	CLINGO (ORIG ENC)	431
CLINGO (ADV ENC)	43	CLINGO (ADV ENC)	70
WASP (ORIG ENC)	-	WASP (ORIG ENC)	-
WASP (ADV ENC)	-	WASP (ADV ENC)	-
GLUCOSE (SAT ENC)	-	MSCG (MAXSAT ENC)	-
LINGELING (SAT ENC)	-	MAXINO (MAXSAT ENC)	-
CLASP (SAT ENC)	-	CLASP (MAXSAT ENC)	-
GUROBI (ILP ENC)	1018	GUROBI (ILP ENC)	1073

Table 3. Scalability of the approach. Solving time (s) for each solver.

Solver		Nurses				
		10	20	41	82	164
NSP^d	CLINGO (ORIG ENC)	155	117	738	1486	2987
	CLINGO (ADV ENC)	4	9	70	351	1291
	WASP (ORIG ENC)	-	-	-	-	-
	WASP (ADV ENC)	5	20	-	-	-
	GLUCOSE (SAT ENC)	-	-	-	-	-
	LINGELING (SAT ENC)	-	-	-	-	-
	CLASP (SAT ENC)	-	-	-	-	-
	GUROBI (ILP ENC)	62	172	1018	-	-
NSP^o	CLINGO (ORIG ENC)	37	94	339	798	1689
	CLINGO (ADV ENC)	4	13	72	482	1590
	WASP (ORIG ENC)	-	-	-	-	-
	WASP (ADV ENC)	4	-	-	-	-
	MSCG (MAXSAT ENC)	-	-	-	-	-
	MAXINO (MAXSAT ENC)	-	-	-	-	-
	CLASP (MAXSAT ENC)	-	-	-	-	-
	GUROBI (ILP ENC)	113	411	2004	-	-

shows a comparison among the number of conflicts found by CLINGO executed on the original and on the advanced encodings. The new encoding takes advantage of the better propagations, thus it is able to find a solution with a smaller number of conflicts. Concerning NSP^o, it can also be observed that the performance of the two versions of CLINGO are comparable on the instance with 164 nurses, even if the number of conflicts are much lower when CLINGO is executed on the advanced encoding. To explain this discrepancy we analyzed the number of branching choices performed by CLINGO, which are around 128 millions for the original encoding, and around 300 millions for the advanced encoding. Thus, for this specific instance, the branching heuristic of CLINGO seems to be more effective when the original encoding is considered. Moreover, WASP executed on the advanced encoding is able to find a schedule for NSP^d when 10 and 20 nurses are considered whereas WASP executed on the original one does not terminate the computation in 1 h. The performance of SAT (and MaxSAT) solvers are also in this case not satisfactory since they cannot solve any of the tested instances. GUROBI can solve instances up to 41 nurses, whereas it is not able to find a schedule when 82 and 164 nurses are considered.

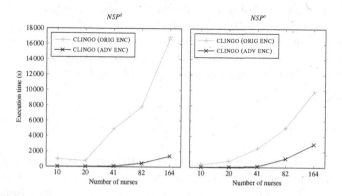

Fig. 3. Comparison of the number of conflicts (in thousands) of CLINGO executed on the original and on the advanced encodings for both NSP^d and NSP^o with different number of nurses.

5 Related Work

In recent years, several approaches to solve NSP have been proposed. The main differences concern (i) the planning periods; (ii) the different type of shifts; (iii) the requirements related to the coverage of shifts, i.e. the number of personnel needed for every shift; and (iv) other restrictions on the rules of nurses (see [14] for more detailed information). In this paper a one-year window of time has been considered as in [17], where however the same requirements on nurses and hospitals were not reported. Concerning the shifts, we considered three different shifts (morning, afternoon and night) with no overlapping among shifts, whereas in the literature other approaches were based on one single shift only (see e.g. [31]). Other requirements depend on the different policies of the considered hospitals. Thus, this makes the different strategies not directly comparable with each other.

Concerning other solving technologies reported in the literature, they range from mathematical to meta-heuristics approaches, including solutions based on integer programming [9,11], genetic algorithms [3], fuzzy approaches [35], and ant colony optimization algorithms [28], to mention a few. Detailed and comprehensive surveys on NSP can be found in [14, 18].

The approach described in this paper represents an enhancement of the one proposed in [21]. The two encodings mainly differ with respect to how the constraints related to hospital and balance requirements are modeled. Indeed, the new encoding takes into account only combinations of parameters values that can lead to a valid schedule.

Finally, we report that ASP has been already successfully used for solving hard combinatorial and application problems in several research areas, including Artificial Intelligence [10, 20], Bioinformatics [22, 29], Hydroinformatics [23], Databases [30] and also in industrial applications [2, 19]. ASP encodings were proposed for scheduling problems other than NSP: *Incremental Scheduling Problem* [16], where the goal is to assign jobs to devices such that their executions do not overlap one another; and *Team Building Problem* [34], where the goal is to allocate the available personnel of a seaport for serving the incoming ships. However, to the best of our knowledge, the only ASP encodings for NSP are those shown in Sect. 3.

6   Conclusion

In this paper an advanced ASP encoding for addressing a variant of NSP has been proposed. The new encoding overcomes the limitations of the one proposed in [21] by taking into account intrinsic properties of NSP and internal details of ASP solvers. The resulting approach has been compared with the previous one and with other declarative approaches on real setting provided by an Italian hospital. Results clearly show that CLINGO executed on the new encoding outperforms all alternatives, being able to solve all instances within 30 min, even with more than 100 nurses.

Acknowledgments. We would like to thank Nextage srl for providing support for this work. Mario Alviano has been partially supported by the Italian Ministry for Economic Development (MISE) under project "PIUCultura – Paradigmi Innovativi per l'Utilizzo della Cultura" (no. F/020016/01-02/X27), and under project "Smarter Solutions in the Big Data World (S2BDW)" (no. F/050389/01-03/X32) funded within the call "HORIZON2020" PON I&C 2014-2020, and by Gruppo Nazionale per il Calcolo Scientifico (GNCS-INdAM).

References

1. The website of Gurobi. http://www.gurobi.com
2. Abseher, M., Gebser, M., Musliu, N., Schaub, T., Woltran, S.: Shift design with answer set programming. Fundam. Inform. **147**(1), 1–25 (2016). https://doi.org/10.3233/FI-2016-1396
3. Aickelin, U., Dowsland, K.A.: An indirect genetic algorithm for a nurse-scheduling problem. Comput. OR **31**(5), 761–778 (2004). https://doi.org/10.1016/S0305-0548(03)00034-0

4. Alviano, M., Dodaro, C.: Anytime answer set optimization via unsatisfiable core shrinking. TPLP **16**(5–6), 533–551 (2016). https://doi.org/10.1017/S147106841600020X

5. Alviano, M., Dodaro, C., Leone, N., Ricca, F.: Advances in WASP. In: Calimeri, F., Ianni, G., Truszczynski, M. (eds.) LPNMR 2015. LNCS (LNAI), vol. 9345, pp. 40–54. Springer, Cham (2015). https://doi.org/10.1007/978-3-319-23264-5_5

6. Alviano, M., Dodaro, C., Ricca, F.: A MaxSAT algorithm using cardinality constraints of bounded size. In: IJCAI 2015, pp. 2677–2683. AAAI Press (2015)

7. Alviano, M., Faber, W.: The complexity boundary of answer set programming with generalized atoms under the FLP semantics. In: Cabalar, P., Son, T.C. (eds.) LPNMR 2013. LNCS (LNAI), vol. 8148, pp. 67–72. Springer, Heidelberg (2013). https://doi.org/10.1007/978-3-642-40564-8_7

8. Audemard, G., Simon, L.: Extreme cases in SAT problems. In: Creignou, N., Le Berre, D. (eds.) SAT 2016. LNCS, vol. 9710, pp. 87–103. Springer, Cham (2016). https://doi.org/10.1007/978-3-319-40970-2_7

9. Azaiez, M.N., Sharif, S.S.A.: A 0–1 goal programming model for nurse scheduling. Comput. OR **32**, 491–507 (2005). https://doi.org/10.1016/S0305-0548(03)00249-1

10. Balduccini, M., Gelfond, M., Watson, R., Nogueira, M.: The USA-advisor: a case study in answer set planning. In: Eiter, T., Faber, W., Truszczyński, M. (eds.) LPNMR 2001. LNCS (LNAI), vol. 2173, pp. 439–442. Springer, Heidelberg (2001). https://doi.org/10.1007/3-540-45402-0_39

11. Bard, J.F., Purnomo, H.W.: Preference scheduling for nurses using column generation. Eur. J. Oper. Res. **164**(2), 510–534 (2005). https://doi.org/10.1016/j.ejor.2003.06.046

12. Biere, A., Fröhlich, A.: Evaluating CDCL variable scoring schemes. In: Heule, M., Weaver, S. (eds.) SAT 2015. LNCS, vol. 9340, pp. 405–422. Springer, Cham (2015). https://doi.org/10.1007/978-3-319-24318-4_29

13. Brewka, G., Eiter, T., Truszczynski, M.: Answer set programming at a glance. Commun. ACM **54**(12), 92–103 (2011). https://doi.org/10.1145/2043174.2043195

14. Burke, E.K., Causmaecker, P.D., Berghe, G.V., Landeghem, H.V.: The state of the art of nurse rostering. J. Sched. **7**(6), 441–499 (2004). https://doi.org/10.1023/B:JOSH.0000046076.75950.0b

15. Calimeri, F., Faber, W., Gebser, M., Ianni, G., Kaminski, R., Krennwallner, T., Leone, N., Ricca, F., Schaub, T.: ASP-Core-2 Input Language Format (2013). https://www.mat.unical.it/aspcomp.2013/files/ASP-CORE-2.01c.pdf

16. Calimeri, F., Gebser, M., Maratea, M., Ricca, F.: Design and results of the fifth answer set programming competition. Artif. Intell. **231**, 151–181 (2016). https://doi.org/10.1016/j.artint.2015.09.008

17. Chan, P., Weil, G.: Cyclical staff scheduling using constraint logic programming. In: Burke, E., Erben, W. (eds.) PATAT 2000. LNCS, vol. 2079, pp. 159–175. Springer, Heidelberg (2001). https://doi.org/10.1007/3-540-44629-X_10

18. Cheang, B., Li, H., Lim, A., Rodrigues, B.: Nurse rostering problems - a bibliographic survey. Eur. J. Oper. Res. **151**(3), 447–460 (2003). https://doi.org/10.1016/S0377-2217(03)00021-3

19. Dodaro, C., Gasteiger, P., Leone, N., Musitsch, B., Ricca, F., Schekotihin, K.: Combining answer set programming and domain heuristics for solving hard industrial problems (application paper). TPLP **16**(5–6), 653–669 (2016). https://doi.org/10.1017/S1471068416000284

20. Dodaro, C., Leone, N., Nardi, B., Ricca, F.: Allotment problem in travel industry: a solution based on ASP. In: Cate, B., Mileo, A. (eds.) RR 2015. LNCS, vol. 9209, pp. 77–92. Springer, Cham (2015). https://doi.org/10.1007/978-3-319-22002-4_7

21. Dodaro, C., Maratea, M.: Nurse scheduling via answer set programming. In: Balduccini, M., Janhunen, T. (eds.) LPNMR 2017. LNCS (LNAI), vol. 10377, pp. 301–307. Springer, Cham (2017). https://doi.org/10.1007/978-3-319-61660-5_27
22. Erdem, E., Öztok, U.: Generating explanations for biomedical queries. TPLP 15(1), 35–78 (2015). https://doi.org/10.1017/S1471068413000598
23. Gavanelli, M., Nonato, M., Peano, A.: An ASP approach for the valves positioning optimization in a water distribution system. J. Log. Comput. 25(6), 1351–1369 (2015). https://doi.org/10.1093/logcom/ext065
24. Gebser, M., Kaminski, R., Kaufmann, B., Ostrowski, M., Schaub, T., Wanko, P.: Theory solving made easy with Clingo 5. In: ICLP TCs. OASICS, vol. 52, pp. 2:1–2:15. Schloss Dagstuhl - Leibniz-Zentrum fuer Informatik (2016). https://doi.org/10.4230/OASIcs.ICLP.2016.2
25. Gebser, M., Kaminski, R., König, A., Schaub, T.: Advances in *gringo* series 3. In: Delgrande, J.P., Faber, W. (eds.) LPNMR 2011. LNCS (LNAI), vol. 6645, pp. 345–351. Springer, Heidelberg (2011). https://doi.org/10.1007/978-3-642-20895-9_39
26. Gebser, M., Kaufmann, B., Kaminski, R., Ostrowski, M., Schaub, T., Schneider, M.T.: Potassco: the Potsdam answer set solving collection. AI Commun. 24(2), 107–124 (2011). https://doi.org/10.3233/AIC-2011-0491
27. Gebser, M., Kaufmann, B., Schaub, T.: Conflict-driven answer set solving: from theory to practice. Artif. Intell. 187, 52–89 (2012). https://doi.org/10.1016/j.artint.2012.04.001
28. Gutjahr, W.J., Rauner, M.S.: An ACO algorithm for a dynamic regional nurse-scheduling problem in Austria. Comput. OR 34(3), 642–666 (2007). https://doi.org/10.1016/j.cor.2005.03.018
29. Koponen, L., Oikarinen, E., Janhunen, T., Säilä, L.: Optimizing phylogenetic supertrees using answer set programming. TPLP 15(4–5), 604–619 (2015). https://doi.org/10.1017/S1471068415000265
30. Marileo, M.C., Bertossi, L.E.: The consistency extractor system: answer set programs for consistent query answering in databases. Data Knowl. Eng. 69(6), 545–572 (2010). https://doi.org/10.1016/j.datak.2010.01.005
31. Miller, H.E., Pierskalla, W.P., Rath, G.J.: Nurse scheduling using mathematical programming. Oper. Res. 24(5), 857–870 (1976). https://doi.org/10.1287/opre.24.5.857
32. Morgado, A., Dodaro, C., Marques-Silva, J.: Core-guided MaxSAT with soft cardinality constraints. In: O'Sullivan, B. (ed.) CP 2014. LNCS, vol. 8656, pp. 564–573. Springer, Cham (2014). https://doi.org/10.1007/978-3-319-10428-7_41
33. Philipp, T., Steinke, P.: PBLib – a library for encoding pseudo-boolean constraints into CNF. In: Heule, M., Weaver, S. (eds.) SAT 2015. LNCS, vol. 9340, pp. 9–16. Springer, Cham (2015). https://doi.org/10.1007/978-3-319-24318-4_2
34. Ricca, F., Grasso, G., Alviano, M., Manna, M., Lio, V., Iiritano, S., Leone, N.: Team-building with answer set programming in the Gioia-Tauro seaport. TPLP 12(3), 361–381 (2012). https://doi.org/10.1017/S147106841100007X
35. Topaloglu, S., Selim, H.: Nurse scheduling using fuzzy modeling approach. Fuzzy Sets Syst. 161(11), 1543–1563 (2010). https://doi.org/10.1016/j.fss.2009.10.003

Automated Planning Techniques for Robot Manipulation Tasks Involving Articulated Objects

Alessio Capitanelli[1], Marco Maratea[1]($^{(\boxtimes)}$), Fulvio Mastrogiovanni[1],
and Mauro Vallati[2]

[1] DIBRIS, Univ. degli Studi di Genova, Viale F. Causa 15, 16145 Genoa, Italy
{alessio.capitanelli,marco.maratea,fulvio.mastrogiovanni}@unige.it
[2] University of Huddershield, Huddersfield, West Yorkshire HD1 3DH, UK
M.Vallati@hud.ac.uk

Abstract. The goal-oriented manipulation of articulated objects plays an important role in real-world robot tasks. Current approaches typically pose a number of simplifying assumptions to reason upon how to obtain an articulated object's goal configuration, and exploit *ad hoc* algorithms. The consequence is two-fold: firstly, it is difficult to generalise obtained solutions (in terms of actions a robot can execute) to different target object's configurations and, in a broad sense, to different object's physical characteristics; secondly, the representation and the reasoning layers are tightly coupled and inter-dependent.

In this paper we investigate the use of automated planning techniques for dealing with articulated objects manipulation tasks. Such techniques allow for a clear separation between knowledge and reasoning, as advocated in Knowledge Engineering. We introduce two PDDL formulations of the task, which rely on conceptually different representations of the orientation of the objects. Experiments involving several planners and increasing size objects demonstrate the effectiveness of the proposed models, and confirm its exploitability when embedded in a real-world robot software architecture.

1 Introduction

The manipulation of non rigid objects, including *articulated* or *flexible* objects, such as strings, ropes or cables, is one of the most complex tasks in Robotics [11,20]. Apart from issues related to grasping and dexterity, and differently from rigid objects, the *configuration* of an articulated or flexible object (i.e., the set of relative *poses* of its constituent parts) varies due to the relative position of its constituent parts with respect to each other. This induces a representation problem for such objects, which, on the one hand, is tightly connected with robot perception capabilities and their accuracy, and on the other hand impacts on processes reasoning about configuration changes and the associated robot manipulation actions.

© Springer International Publishing AG 2017
F. Esposito et al. (Eds.): AI*IA 2017, LNAI 10640, pp. 483–497, 2017.
https://doi.org/10.1007/978-3-319-70169-1_36

In the literature about the manipulation of non rigid objects, this problem did not receive sufficient attention, nor a principled formalisation is available. Indeed, it is possible to find examples in which robots exhibit the capability of manipulating ropes [25], tying or untying knots [19] and operating on mobile parts of the environment, such as handles of different shapes [5], home furniture [12] or valves in search and rescue settings [17]. However, in all these cases, manipulation actions are directly grounded on perceptual cues, such as the peculiar geometry of the object to deal with [1], assumed to be easy to identify in a robust way, or based on *a priori* known or learned information about the object to manipulate, e.g., its stiffness or other physical features [6,7]. As a result, every time either the element that has to be manipulated or the manipulator changes, a new reasoner has to be developed from scratch.

A structured approach to perception, representation and reasoning, as well as execution, seems beneficial: on the one hand, we can decouple perception and representation issues, thus not being tied to specific perception approaches or *ad hoc* solutions; on the other hand, domain knowledge and reasoning logic can be separated, with the advantages of an increased maintainability, and the possibility to interchange reasoners and models in a modular way.

In this paper, we investigate the use of automated planning techniques for manipulation tasks involving articulated objects. Such techniques assume an abstract model of the object to manipulate, a clear separation between knowledge representation and reasoning, and the use of standard languages, such as PDDL [16], and widely available domain-independent planners. Language standard and planners' efficiency have been fostered by the International Planning Competition series (see, e.g., [22]). Our contribution is at the problem formalisation and modelling levels. It should be noted that the representation of an articulated object can be modelled using two alternative approaches, which differ on how link orientations are expressed: *relative*, with respect to each other (e.g., any link with respect to the previous one, assuming an ordering among links), or *absolute*, with respect to an external, possibly robot-centered, reference frame. In this context, it is evident that we are not trying to generate joint trajectories to achieve a desired object configuration, but rather determine a series of model-defined actions towards such goal. Roboticists are familiar with numerical methods and motion control strategies for articulated structures, what the planner should provide is a series of intermediate reference joint states to be fed to those lower level systems.

From a robotics perspective, a relative representation is very sensitive to perception issues: *small* perception errors in link orientations can lead to dramatically *huge* errors in the estimate of the object's configuration, since it is necessary to compute forward all the robot-centred orientations to support manipulation actions: this seems to suggest that an absolute representation would be preferable, but also the efficiency of planners on the related formulations must be taken into account.

In this respect, starting from the relative and absolute representations of link orientations, we propose two planning models: the first, which we refer to as *basic*, assumes pairwise relative link orientations and primary features of PDDL; the second, which is termed *conditional*, treats orientations as absolute and employs also conditional statements. Experiments have been performed using an architecture integrating a modified ROSPlan framework [4] on a dual-arm robot manipulator. They show that our approach (*i*) efficiently solves tasks with a realistic size, in terms of number of links constituting the object and the resolution of their orientations, and (*ii*) scales in a satisfactory way with increasingly more complex problems, which is of particular relevance since it provides a challenging benchmark for the planning community, and can be seen as an important step toward the manipulation of flexible objects.

The paper is structured as follows. Section 2 provides the reader with needed preliminaries about our scenario and automated planning, whereas Sect. 3 introduces the problem statement. Then, Sect. 4 presents the two models, whose evaluation with automated planners is shown in Sect. 5. Conclusions follow.

2   Background

In this section we provide the necessary background on the reference scenario, and on automated planning.

2.1   The Reference Scenario

The tabletop scenario we consider involves a Baxter dual-arm robot manipulator from Rethink Robotics (see Fig. 1). Each arm has 7 degrees of freedom and is equipped with a standard gripper. An RGB-D device located on the Baxter's *head* and pointing downward is used to perceive the robot's frontal workspace. The workspace is constituted by a table, on which articulated objects can be manipulated by rotating its constituting parts. Given our reference scenario, the granularity of rotations can not be small. We employ wooden objects, which have been purposely hand crafted to minimise perceptual errors: the first has three 40 cm long links (and two loose joints), whereas the second has seven 20 cm long links (and six stiff joint). On the second object we fixed a QR tag to each link, in order to quickly determine its orientation.

A software architecture has been developed, based on the well known ROS framework and integrating ROSPlan, which allows sensory-based knowledge representation, action planning and execution via a number of nested control loops. A point cloud or link poses (determined using QR tags) are obtained either continuously or *on demand* from the RGB-D device. Perception data are processed in order to obtain a model-based representation of the scene [3], for instance the configuration of an articulated object, which is maintained within an OWL-based ontology [13]. The ontology is updated whenever a new perception is available. In order to obtain a new object's goal configuration, the information within the ontology can be accessed by a planner, which can extract information to build the initial state of the planning problem. Since the planner is treated as a

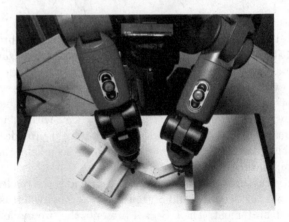

Fig. 1. The reference robotic framework.

ROS service, any suitable planner can be used as long as it adheres to a well-defined communication interface. If a plan is found, each manipulation action therein is executed. After each execution a new perception is obtained, whereas the scene representation in the ontology is updated, and compared with the expected effects of the action: if they are compatible, the execution continues, otherwise re-planning occurs. The execution continues until the final state of the plan is reached, or aborted as per designer's instructions.

2.2 Automated Planning

Automated planning, and specifically classical planning, deals with finding a (partially or totally ordered) sequence of actions, which modify a static, deterministic and fully observable *environment* from an initial state to a desired goal state [9].

In classical planning, the environment is represented as an appropriate set P of $|P|$ First Order Logic *predicates*, $p_1, \ldots, p_{|P|}$, whereas *states* $s_1, \ldots, s_{|S|}$ are defined as appropriate sets of ground predicates $\bar{p}_1, \ldots, \bar{p}_{|P|}$.

An *operator* $o = \big(name(o), pre(o), eff^-(o), eff^+(o)\big)$ is defined such that $name(o) = o\_name(x_1, \ldots, x_K)$, where o_name is a unique operator name and $x_1, \ldots, x_K$ are its K arguments, $pre(o)$ is the set of predicates P_{pre} representing the operator's preconditions, whereas $eff^-(o)$ and $eff^+(o)$ are, respectively, the sets of predicates P_{eff-} and P_{eff+} representing the operator's negative and positive effects. As a consequence, *actions* $a_1, \ldots, a_{|A|}$ are ground instances of planning operators. An action $a = (pre(a), eff^-(a), eff^+(a))$ is *applicable* in a state s if and only if $pre(a) \subseteq s$. If allowed, the application of a in s results in a new state such that $\big(s \setminus eff^-(a)\big) \cup eff^+(a)$.

A *planning domain* $\mathcal{D}$ is specified via sets of predicates $P_{\mathcal{D}}$ and operators $O_{\mathcal{D}}$, such that $\mathcal{D} = (P_{\mathcal{D}}, O_{\mathcal{D}})$. A *planning problem* $\mathcal{P}$ is specified via a planning domain $\mathcal{D}$, an initial state s_i and set of goal atoms $\bar{P}$ (both made up of ground predicates), such that $\mathcal{P} = (\mathcal{D}, s_i, \bar{P})$. A *solution plan* $\mathcal{S}$ is a sequence of I actions $a_1, \ldots, a_I$ such that, starting from the initial state s_i, a consecutive application of the actions in the plan results in a final state s_f that satisfies the goal $\bar{P}$.

3   Problem Statement

In general terms, the problem we consider in this paper can be stated as follows: given an articulated object, determine a solution plan that modifies the initial object's configuration to a specified goal configuration, where the solution plan is made up of a number of manipulation actions to be executed by a robot. In order to better specify the boundaries of the problem we consider, let us pose the following assumptions:

1. We consider articulated objects as *simplified* models for fully flexible objects. These can be modelled as articulated objects with a huge number of links and joints. This assumption is widely accepted [25].
2. We do not consider the effects of gravity on the object being manipulated, nor those of any external force but manipulation actions. For this reason, the object is considered as laying on a horizontal plane (large enough to accommodate it). As a consequence, we consider articulated objects which lay strictly on the plane.
3. We assume sensing and representation to be decoupled, the latter assuming *perfect* sensing. On the basis of the features extracted from sensing data, this leads to different problem formulations.
4. The object can be easily manipulated by standard Baxter's grippers. The specific object we use has been purposely manufactured to that aim, and therefore we do not consider issues related to grasping or dexterity.

More formally, an articulated object α is defined as an ordered set $\mathcal{L}$ of $|L|$ links and an ordered set $\mathcal{J}$ of $|J|$ joints, such that $\alpha = (\mathcal{L}, \mathcal{J})$. Each link l is characterised by a length λ_l and an orientation θ_l on the plane, whose meaning depends on the considered planning model, namely basic or conditional. Therefore, a configuration C_α is a $|L_\alpha|$-ple such that $(\theta_{l_1}, \ldots, \theta_{l_{|L|}})$, i.e., the orientations of all the links. Obviously enough, since $\mathcal{L}$ and $\mathcal{J}$ are ordered sets, links and joints are pairwise correlated, such that a link l_l is bounded upstream by j_l and downstream by j_{l+1}, apart from $l_{|L|}$.

Configurations change as a consequence of manipulation actions. In our case, we only consider rotations of a given link l_l around the corresponding joints j_l or j_{l+1}. If we refer to δ as the *granularity* associated with variations in orientations, then a manipulation action a operating on a link l_l can either increase or decrease its orientation θ_l by δ, with respect to an axis perpendicular to the horizontal plane. In doing so, and given the stiffness of α, the robot needs the use of two grippers: the first is used to keep the upstream (resp. downstream) l_{l-1} (resp. l_{l+1}) link still, which is a non modelled action in the solution plan (nonetheless executed by the robot when needed), whereas the second is used to rotate l_l around j_l (resp. j_{l+1}).

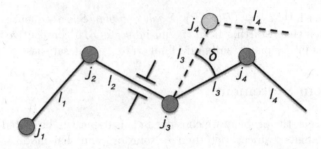

Fig. 2. An example of rotation: l_3 rotates around j_3 of an angle δ while l_2 is kept still, which induces l_4 to rotate.

An example can be found in Fig. 2, where a 4-link, 4-joint articulated object is shown. The initial state s_i corresponds to link poses in black, whereas in the final state s_f links l_3 and l_4 must be rotated by δ, i.e., l_3 must rotate around j_3. The expected sequence of manipulation actions includes: grasping and keeping l_2 still, grasping l_3, rotating l_3 counter clockwise around j_3 of about δ, releasing l_3 and releasing l_2. However, the first action, which is a necessary prerequisite for the rotation to occur, need not to be explicitly modelled, but can be delegated to the robot action execution system.

4   Proposed Formulations

In order to tackle the problem introduced above, and to evaluate the two possible semantics associated with link orientations, we designed two PDDL formulations, which exploit different sets of language features. The *basic* formulation employs the :STRIPS subset of PDDL, extended with equalities and negative-preconditions, whereas the *conditional* version requires also the use of conditional-effects. Notably, the precision limits of most manipulators requires the granularity discretisation of angular movements, hence there is no practical necessity for continuous or hybrid planning models. Therefore, PDDL provides an appropriate level of abstraction.

On the one hand, in the basic formulation, given a link l_l, its orientation θ_l must be considered as being relative, for instance, to the orientation of the upstream link l_{l-1}. From a planning perspective, each manipulation action changing θ_l does not affect any other upstream or downstream link orientations, since all of them are relative to each other, and therefore the planning process is computationally less demanding. However, since manipulation actions are expected to be based on link orientations grounded with respect to a robot-centred reference frame, i.e., absolute in terms of pairwise link orientations, a conversion must be performed, which may be greatly affected by perceptual noise, therefore leading to inaccurate or even inconsistent representations. On the other hand, in the conditional formulation, θ_l is considered as absolute, and therefore it can be associated directly with robot actions. Unfortunately, this means that each manipulation action changing θ_l does affect numerically *all* other upstream or downstream link orientations, depending on which side of the object is kept still, in the representation, which must be kept track of using conditional effects in the planning domain.

It is noteworthy that the use of advanced PDDL features, such as conditional effects, may allow for a more accurate representation of the domain but, at the same time, it may reduce the number of planners able to reason on the model.

4.1 Basic Formulation

As described in Sect. 3, an articulated object α is represented using two ordered sets of joints and links. We use a `connected` predicate to describe the sequence of links in terms of binary relationships involving a joint j_{l+1} and a link l_l, which induces a pairwise connection between two links, namely l_l itself and l_{l+1}, since they share the same joint j_{l+1}. We assume that each joint j_l is associated with an angle θ_j, which ranges between 0 and 359 *deg*, through the predicate `angle-joint`. Obviously enough, in such a range it holds that $\theta_j = \theta_{l+1} - \theta_l$. As we anticipated, this formulation assumes that link orientations are expressed as pairwise relative to each other. This means that the robot perception system is expected to provide the representation layer with the set of joint angles $\theta_1, \ldots, \theta_{|J|}$ as primitive information, whereas the set of link orientations $\theta_1, \ldots, \theta_{|L|}$ is not directly observable, but must be computed applying forward kinematics formulas to the object's configuration C_α. As we discussed already, if noise affects the perception of joint angles, as it typically does, the reconstruction of the object's configuration may differ from the real one, and it worsens with link lengths. This position significantly simplifies the planning model's complexity: from a planner's perspective, the modification of any link orientations does not impact on other relative joint angles, and therefore manipulation actions can be unfolded *in any order* the planner deems fit.

Angles are specified using *constants*, which are then ordered using the `angle-before` predicate. The difference between constant values is the *granularity* δ of the resolution associated to modelled orientations. For example, `d45` and `d90` are used as constants representing, respectively, a 45 and a 90 *deg* angle. Then, a predicate (`angle-before d45 d90`) is used to encode the fact that `d45` is the granularity step preceding `d90`, i.e., in this case $\delta = 45$ *deg*.

The domain model includes two planning operators, namely `increase-angle` (shown in Fig. 3) and `decrease-angle`. Intuitively, the former can be used to increase the angle of a selected joint of a δ step, while the latter is used to decrease the joint's angle, by operating on the two connected links. As an example, if $\delta = 45$ *deg* and a joint angle $\theta_j = 135$ *deg*, `increase-angle` would produce $\theta_j = 180$ *deg*, whereas `decrease-angle` $\theta_j = 90$ *deg*. In the operator's definition, `?link1` and `?link2` represent any two links l_l and l_{l+1}, `?joint` is the joint j_{l+1} between them, whereas `?a1` and `?a2` are the current and the obtained joint angles, respectively. If `?joint` connected two different links `?link1` and `?link2`, the angle `?a1` of such joint would be increased of a δ step and become `?a2`. A similar description could be provided for `decrease-angle`.

```
(:action increase-angle
   :parameters (?link1 ?link2 - link
   ?joint - joint ?a1 ?a2 - angle)
   :precondition (and
      (connected ?joint ?link1)
      (connected ?joint ?link2)
      (not (= ?link1 ?link2))
      (angle-joint ?a1 ?joint)
      (angle-before ?a1 ?a2))
   :effect (and
      (not (angle-joint ?a1 ?joint))
      (angle-joint ?a2 ?joint)))
```

Fig. 3. The *basic* formulation of `increase-angle`.

A problem is defined by specifying initial and final states. The former includes the *topology* of the articulated object in terms of `connected` predicates, and its initial configuration using `angle-joint` predicates; the latter describes its goal configuration using relevant `angle-joint` predicates.

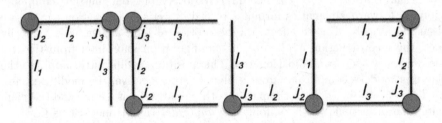

Fig. 4. Without end point joints, the basic formulation cannot discriminate among these four configurations.

It is noteworthy that, as shown in Fig. 2, we add one seemingly unnecessary joint to the configuration, as one of the *end points* of the link chain. As a matter of fact, from a representation perspective, the use of relative angles leads to issues in discriminating between some configurations of the articulated object. Let us consider, for instance, the case of an articulated object made up of 3 links, namely l_1, l_2 and l_3, which are connected by two joints, namely j_2 (connecting l_1 and l_2) and j_3 (connecting l_2 and l_3). Then, let us set both joint angles to 90 *deg*. If j_2 and j_3 were treated as relative, in the planning process it would be impossible to distinguish between configurations $C_\sqcap$, $C_\sqsubset$, $C_\sqcup$ and $C_\sqsupset$ in Fig. 4. In order to deal with this drawback, the end point joint j_1 and a related "hidden" link l_0 (not shown in the Figure) can be added to one of the articulated object's extremes. This hidden link defines an *ad hoc* reference frame that allows for discriminating among configurations characterised by the same shape, but with different orientations. Such hidden links must be added to problem definitions.

4.2 Conditional Formulation

The *conditional* formulation differs from the *basic* one in that joint angles θ_j originate from link orientations expressed with respect to a unique, typically robot-centred, reference frame, and as such are absolute. Therefore, the set of link orientations $\theta_1, \ldots, \theta_{|L|}$ is assumed to be directly observable by the robot perception system. However, if a manipulation action is planned, which modifies a given joint angle θ_j, not only the related link orientations θ_l or θ_{l+1} (depending on whether the upstream or downstream link is kept still) must be updated, but it is necessary to propagate such changes to all the upstream or downstream link orientations. As a consequence, such a representation increases the complexity of the planning tasks but is more robust to perception errors: in fact, perceiving independent link orientations induces an *upper bound* on the error associated with their inner angle.

```
(:action increase-angle
   :parameters (?link1 ?link2 - link
   ?joint - joint ?a1 ?a2 - angle)
   :precondition (and
     (connected ?joint ?link1)
     (connected ?joint ?link2)
     (not (= ?link1 ?link2))
     (angle-joint ?a1 ?joint)
     (angle-before ?a1 ?a2))
   :effect (and
     (not (angle-joint ?a1 ?joint))
     (angle-joint ?a2 ?joint)
     (forall (?js - joint ?a3 ?a4 - angle)
       (when (and
       (affected ?js ?link1 ?joint)
       (not (= ?js ?joint))
       (angle-joint ?a3 ?js)
       (angle-before ?a3 ?a4) )
       (and
           (not (angle-joint ?a3 ?js))
           (angle-joint ?a4 ?js))))))
```

Fig. 5. The *conditional* version of `increase-angle`.

The `connected`, `angle-joint` and `angle-before` predicates are the same as in the *basic* formulation, subject to the different semantics associated with joint angles. Also in the *conditional* formulation two planning operators are used, namely `increase-angle` (shown in Fig. 5) and `decrease-angle`. However, with respect to the *basic* formulation, the effects of the operator differ. In particular, the model assumes that we can represent which joints are affected when a link is rotated around one of its associated joints. This is done using the `affected` predicate, i.e., a ternary predicate (`affected ?joint1 ?link1 ?joint2`), where ?link1 is the link that is rotated, ?joint2 is the joint around which ?link1 rotates, and ?joint1 is a joint affected by this rotation. So, if ?joint1 were affected, its angle would be changed as well in the conditional statement and, as such, it would affect other joints via its corresponding link.

With reference to `increase-angle`, as in the previous case, the joint angle ?joint, located between ?link1 and ?link2, is increased by δ, according to the `angle-before` predicate. If rotating ?link2 around ?joint affects ?js, the latter is updated and affects in cascade all other joints upstream or downstream.

In terms of problem definitions, it is necessary to include the list of appropriately defined `affected` predicates.

5   Experimental Evaluation

The aim of this experimental evaluation is to assess the computational performance of the *basic* and *conditional* models, and in particular whether the proposed planning-based approach can be effective in a real-world robot software architecture. First we discuss the experimental settings, then we show how the two planning models scale with increasingly difficult problems (in terms of the number of joints in the articulated object and the granularity δ associated with link orientations).

Settings. We selected 4 planners, based on their performance in the agile track of the 2014 International Planning Competition: Madagascar (Mp) [18], Probe, SIW [15], and Yahsp3 [23]. We also included Lpg [8] due to its widespread use in real-world planning applications. Both Yahsp3 and Lpg do not support conditional effects.

Experiments have been performed on a workstation equipped with 2.5 Ghz Intel Core 2 Quad processors, 4 GB of RAM and the Linux operating system.

Synthetic problem instances have been randomly generated parameterised on the number of joints j^* (the same as the number of links) and the number of allowed orientations g^* (which induces certain granularity values), which both affect the problem's size. Once j^* and g^* are defined, a configuration C^* is determined by normally sampling, for each link, among the finite set of possible orientations induced by g^*. The cutoff time has been set to 300 CPU-time seconds. Generated plans have been validated using the well-known VAL tool [10], in order to check their correctness with respect to the planning models, and also to verify the presence of flaws.

Computational Performance. In a first series of tests we analyse the sensitivity of planning models with respect to increasing values for j^*. It is noteworthy that in the literature there is hardly evidence of objects manipulated by robots made up of more than four or five joints at best. However, it seems reasonable to model flexible objects as articulated objects with a huge number of links. In that case, the higher the number of links, the better the approximation given by the model. We generated problem instances in which j^* ranges between 3 to 20, fixing $g^* = 90\ deg$. As such, only four orientations are possible. For each value of j^*, three instances have been generated and the results averaged.

Unsurprisingly, the *basic* model is faster than the *conditional* model. When using the *basic* model, j^* has no significant impact on a planner running time. In all cases, valid plans have been found in less than 1 CPU-time second. This is due to the fact that, in the *basic* model, each rotation is independent, and the final state can be quickly reached by focusing on one joint at a time. Instead, the *conditional* model requires the planner to consider the impact a rotation has on other links. Moreover, the size of the *conditional* problem model exponentially increases with j^*, due to the presence of `affected` predicates that need to be specified.

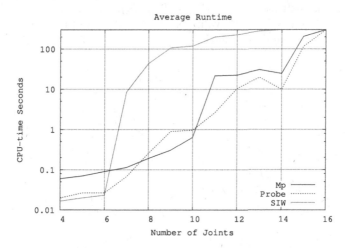

Fig. 6. Average CPU-time seconds needed by Mp, Probe, and SIW to solve instances with j^* from 4 to 16 using the *conditional* model.

Figure 6 shows, for the three planners able to cope with conditional effects, how the average runtime is affected by j^*. SIW is the most negatively affected, while Mp and Probe share a similar trend. According to the Wilcoxon test [24], the performance of SIW is statistically significantly worse than those of Mp and Probe. Furthermore, Probe has statistically better performance than Mp. None of the planner solved, within the 300 CPU-time seconds cutoff, any instance with j^* greater than 15.

When assessing the quality of plans generated using the *basic* model, empirical evidence indicates that Mp, Probe and SIW generate plans of similar length (approx. 10 actions). Yahsp3 and Lpg find plans consistently worse than those found by the above mentioned planners: on average, LPG (Yasp3) finds plans that are 85% (25%) longer than those found by Mp, Probe and SIW. Instead, when using the *conditional* model, SIW typically provides the shortest plans on average, followed by Probe (17% longer) and Mp (50% longer). Interestingly, when comparing the quality of plans generated by the same planner, on the two considered models, we can identify two different behaviours. Mp and Probe seem to suffer the way conditional effects propagate rotations: plans generated with the *conditional* model are significantly longer. An in-depth analysis suggests that such planners use many actions to *fix* joint angles affected by previous manipulation actions. On the contrary, SIW seems to exploit the additional information leveraged by conditional effects, and this is reflected by shorter plans.

In a second series of tests we investigate how g^* affects a plan's feasibility and size. Intuitively, a high value for g^* (e.g., 90 *deg*) implies a low number of possible orientations (e.g., 4), thus a small number of manipulation actions must be planned, and *viceversa*. We generated problem instances in which j^* is set to 5, 10, 15, or 20. For each size, we modelled the problem with three different values for g^*, namely 90 *deg*, 60 *deg* and 30 *deg*, thus leading to 4, 6 and 12 possible orientations. For each value of j^* and g^*, three instances have been generated and the results averaged.

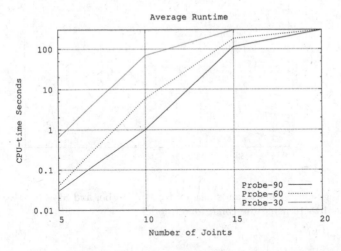

Fig. 7. Average CPU-time seconds needed by Probe to solve instances with j^* equal to 5, 10, 15, or 20, and g^* equal to 90, 60, and 30 *deg*, using the *conditional* model.

As expected, also in this case, the *basic* model allows all the planners to generate solution plans. As in the previous case, all instances are solved in less than 1 CPU-time second. When considering the *conditional* model, the observed results show that Probe has the best scalability. SIW and Mp run out of time also for small values of j^*, when $g^* = 30$ *deg*. Figure 7 presents the impact of the considered values for g^* on the average runtime performance of Probe. It is apparent that the granularity has a very strong impact on planning performance: on instances with the same number of joints, the runtime can increase up to two orders of magnitude for different granularities in link orientations.

Finally, we executed some of the plans obtained by Probe when considering objects with j^* of 3 and 7 and $g^* = 90$ *deg*, on the actual Baxter manipulator shown in Fig. 1, which was controlled using the ROSPlan framework [4]. All plans were successfully executed by the robot, which was able to manipulate the object in order to provide the required goal configuration.

6 Conclusion

This paper presented the use of automated planning to plan for robot manipulation of articulated objects, which is one of the most complex tasks in robotics. We introduced two PDDL models, based either on *relative* or *absolute* representation of links orientation. The former model requires the robotic framework to be able to provide an accurate perception of the position of the articulated object, while the latter is more robust to perception errors, at the price of a higher complexity.

Our experimental analysis, which involved four state-of-the-art planning engines and objects of different sizes, performed on synthetically generated problem instances and by using the ROSPlan framework for controlling a Baxter manipulator, shows that: (*i*) both models allow to generate plans that are executable by a typical robotics manipulator; (*ii*) both the models allows considered planners to efficiently solve tasks with a realistic size; and (*iii*) the basic model can be fruitfully exploited when very large objects are considered, as an approximation of flexible objects. We also observed that the conditional model can be exploited as a challenging benchmarks for testing the capabilities of planning engines: the number of conditional effects per grounded action can be extremely large.

We see several avenues for future work. We plan to investigate how to extend the proposed models in order to represent multi-dimensional joint movements. We are also interested in testing the proposed approach using different manipulators, and to test its feasibility for representing flexible –rather than articulated– objects such as ropes. Finally, we also envisage to study knowledge processing mechanisms to possibly improving the flexibility of control processes (see, e.g., [2,14,21]).

References

1. Berenson, D.: Manipulation of deformable objects without modelling and simulating deformation. In: Proceedings of the 2013 IEEE-RSJ International Conference on Intelligent Robots and Systems (IROS 2015), Tokyo, Japan, November 2013

2. Borgo, S., Cesta, A., Orlandini, A., Umbrico, A.: A planning-based architecture for a reconfigurable manufacturing system. In: Coles, A.J., Coles, A., Edelkamp, S., Magazzeni, D., Sanner, S. (eds.) Proceedings of the Twenty-Sixth International Conference on Automated Planning and Scheduling, ICAPS 2016, pp. 358–366. AAAI Press (2016)

3. Buoncompagni, L., Mastrogiovanni, F.: A software architecture for object perception and semantic representation. In: Proceedings of the Second Italian Workshop on Artificial Intelligence and Robotics (AIRO 2015), Ferrara, Italy, September 2015

4. Cashmore, M., Fox, M., Long, D., Magazzeni, D., Ridder, B., Carrera, A., Palomeras, N., Hurtós, N., Carreras, M.: ROSPlan: planning in the robot operating system. In: Proceedings of the Twenty-Fifth International Conference on Automated Planning and Scheduling, ICAPS, pp. 333–341 (2015)

5. Dang, H., Allen, P.: Robot learning of everyday object manipulations via human demonstrations. In: Proceedings of the 2010 IEEE-RSJ International Conference on Intelligent Robots and Systems (IROS 2010), Taipei, Taiwan, October 2010

6. Elbrechter, C., Haschke, R., Ritter, H.: Folding paper with anthropomorphic robot hands using real-time physics-based modeling. In: Proceedings of the 2012 IEEE-RAS International Conference on Humanoid Robotics (HUMANOIDS 2012), Osaka, Japan, October 2012

7. Frank, B., Schmedding, R., Stachniss, C., Teschner, M., Burgard, W.: Learning the elasticity parameters of deformable objects with a manipulation robot. In: Proceedings of the 2010 IEEE-RSJ International Conference on Intelligent Robots and Systems (IROS 2010), Taipei, Taiwan, October 2010

8. Gerevini, A.E., Saetti, A., Serina, I.: Planning through stochastic local search and temporal action graphs in LPG. J. Artif. Intell. Res. **20**, 239–290 (2003)

9. Ghallab, M., Nau, D., Traverso, P.: Automated Planning, Theory and Practice. Morgan Kaufmann Publishers, Burlington (2004)

10. Howey, R., Long, D., Fox, M.: VAL: automatic plan validation, continuous effects and mixed initiative planning using PDDL. In: 16th IEEE International Conference on Tools with Artificial Intelligence (ICTAI), pp. 294–301 (2004)

11. Jimenez, P.: Survey on model-based manipulation planning of deformable objects. Robot. Comput.-Integr. Manuf. **28**(2), 154–163 (2012)

12. Knapper, R., Layton, T., Romanishin, J., Rus, D.: Ikeabot: an autonomous multi-robot coordinated furniture assembly system. In: Proceedings of the 2013 IEEE International Conference on Robotics and Automation (ICRA 2013), Karlsruhe, Germany, May 2013

13. Krotzsch, M., Simancik, F., Horrocks, I.: A description logic primer. arXiv:1201.4089v3 (2013)

14. Lemaignan, S., Ros, R., Mösenlechner, L., Alami, R., Beetz, M.: Oro, a knowledge management platform for cognitive architectures in robotics. In: 2010 IEEE/RSJ International Conference on Intelligent Robots and Systems, pp. 3548–3553. IEEE (2010)

15. Lipovetzky, N., Ramirez, M., Muise, C., Geffner, H.: Width and inference based planners: SIW, BFS(f), and PROBE. In: Proceedings of the 8th International Planning Competition (IPC 2014) (2014)

16. McDermott, D.: The 1998 AI planning systems competition. AI Mag. **21**(2), 35–55 (2000)

17. Newman, W., Chong, Z.H., Du, C., Hung, R., Lee, K.H., Ma, L., Ng, T., Swetenham, C., Tjoeng, K., Wang, W.: Autonomous valve turning with an Atlas humanoid robot. In: Proceedings of the 2014 IEEE-RAS International Conference on Humanoid Robotics (HUMANOIDS 2014), Madrid, Spain, November 2014

18. Rintanen, J.: Madagascar: scalable planning with SAT. In: Proceedings of the 8th International Planning Competition (IPC 2014) (2014)
19. Schulman, J., Ho, J., Lee, C., Abbeel, P.: Learning from demonstrations through the use of non-rigid registration. In: Inaba, M., Corke, P. (eds.) Robotics Research. STAR, vol. 114, pp. 339–354. Springer, Cham (2016). doi:10.1007/978-3-319-28872-7_20
20. Smith, C., Karayiannidis, Y., Nalpantidis, L., Gratal, X., Qi, P., Dimarogonas, D., Kragic, D.: Dual arm manipulation: a survey. Robot. Auton. Syst. **60**(10), 1340–1353 (2012)
21. Tenorth, M., Beetz, M.: Representations for robot knowledge in the KnowRob framework. Artif. Intell. **247**, 151–169 (2017)
22. Vallati, M., Chrpa, L., Grzes, M., McCluskey, T., Roberts, M., Sanner, S.: The 2014 international planning competition: progress and trends. AI Mag. **36**(3), 90–98 (2015)
23. Vidal, V.: YAHSP3 and YAHSP3-MT in the 8th international planning competition. In: Proceedings of the 8th International Planning Competition (IPC 2014) (2014)
24. Wilcoxon, F.: Individual comparisons by ranking methods. Biom. Bull. **1**(6), 80–83 (1945)
25. Yamakawa, Y., Namiki, A., Ishikawa, M.: Dynamic high-speed knotting of a rope by a manipulator. Int. J. Adv. Rob. Syst. **10**, 1–12 (2013)

PLATINUM: A New Framework for Planning and Acting

Alessandro Umbrico[1], Amedeo Cesta[1], Marta Cialdea Mayer[2],
and Andrea Orlandini[1(✉)]

[1] Istituto di Scienze e Tecnologie della Cognizione,
Consiglio Nazionale delle Ricerche, Roma, Italy
{alessandro.umbrico,amedeo.cesta,andrea.orlandini}@istc.cnr.it
[2] Dipartimento di Ingegneria, Università degli Studi Roma Tre, Roma, Italy
cialdea@ing.uniroma3.it

Abstract. This paper presents a novel planning framework, called PLATINUM that advances the state of the art with the ability of dealing with temporal uncertainty both at planning and plan execution level. PLATINUM is a comprehensive planning system endowed with (i) a new algorithm for temporal planning with uncertainty, (ii) heuristic search capabilities grounded on hierarchical modelling and (iii) a robust plan execution module to address temporal uncertainty while executing plans. The paper surveys the capabilities of this new planning system that has been recently deployed in a manufacturing scenario to support Human-Robot Collaboration.

1 Introduction

The continuous improvements in robotics in terms of efficacy, reliability and costs are fostering a fast diffusion in a large variety of scenarios where *robots* are required to demonstrate more flexible and interactive features like, e.g., those for supporting and interacting with humans. For instance, during the last decade *lightweights robots* are being increasingly used in manufacturing cells to support human workers in repetitive and physical demanding operations. The co-presence of a robot and a human in a shared environment while operating actively together entails many issues that must be properly addressed requiring the deployment of *flexible controllers* capable of preserving *effectiveness* while enforcing *human safety*. In manufacturing, Human-Robot Collaboration (HRC) challenges concern both *physical interactions*, guaranteeing the *safety* of the human, and *coordination* of activities, improving the productivity of cells [7].

In such scenarios, the presence of a human, which plays the role of an *uncontrollable* "agent" in the environment, entails the deployment of control systems capable of evaluating *online* the robot execution time and continuously adapt its behaviors. Namely, deliberative control systems are required to leverage temporal flexible models (such as in [6]) as a key enabling feature both at planning and execution time. In this sense, standard methods are not fully effective as current

© Springer International Publishing AG 2017
F. Esposito et al. (Eds.): AI*IA 2017, LNAI 10640, pp. 498–512, 2017.
https://doi.org/10.1007/978-3-319-70169-1_37

approaches do not foresee/estimate the actual time needed by robots to perform collaborative tasks (i.e., tasks that directly or indirectly involve humans). Indeed, robot trajectories are usually computed *online* by taking into account the current position of the human and, therefore, it is not possible to know in advance the time the robot will need to complete a task. Thus, it is not possible to plan robot and human tasks within a long production process and take into account performance issues at the same time.

Some plan-based controllers rely on temporal planning mechanisms capable of dealing with coordinated task actions and temporal flexibility e.g., T-REX [17] or IxTeT-eXeC [10] that rely respectively on EUROPA [1] and IxTeT [8] temporal planners. It is worth noting how both these systems do not have an explicit representation of *uncontrollability* features in the planning domain. As a consequence, the resulting controllers are not endowed with the *robustness* needed to cope with *uncontrollable dynamics* of domains such as, for instance, the one needed in HRC scenarios.

This paper presents a new Planning framework, called PLATINUM, which integrates temporal planning and execution capabilities that both explicitly deal with temporal uncertainty, thus resulting as well tailored for flexible human-robot collaborative scenarios. The system has been developed and deployed within the FOURBYTHREE research project[1] [12]. The PLATINUM planning and acting capabilities have been integrated in a software environment that facilitates the adaptation of a new robotic arm in different HRC manufacturing scenarios. The proposed planning system has been completely deployed in a realistic case study [16] demonstrating its ability to support a productive and safe collaboration between human and robot. In particular, PLATINUM has been able to find well suited task distribution between human and robot increasing the productivity of the working cell, without affecting the safety of the operator.

2   Human-Robot Collaboration: Needs from a Case Study

In manufacturing, HRC scenarios consist of a human operator and a robot that interact and cooperate to perform some common tasks. Namely, the human and the robot represent two *autonomous agents* capable of performing tasks, affecting each other behaviors and sharing the same working environment.

The motivations of this work rely on a research initiative related to the FOUR-BYTHREE project funded by the European Commission. FOURBYTHREE is a research project [12] whose main aim is to realize new robotic solutions that allow human operators to safely and efficiently collaborate with robots in manufacturing contexts. Specifically, the project outcomes will be a new generation of collaborative robotic solutions based on innovative hardware and software. The envisaged solutions present four main characteristics (*modularity, safety, usability* and *efficiency*) and take into account the co-presence of three different actors (the *human,* the *robot* and the *environment*). In this context, the

---

[1] CNR authors are partially supported by EU project FOURBYTHREE (GA No. 637095 – http://www.fourbythree.eu).

solution proposed by FOURBYTHREE is a combination of several hardware and software components for implementing safe and effective HRC applications. On the one hand, a brand new collaborative robotic arm has been designed and is under validation. On the other hand, a set of software modules spanning from very high level features, such as, e.g., voice and gesture commands detection, to low-level robot control have been developed. The resulting complex integrated robotic solution implements two possible robot-human relationships in a given workplace without physical fences: (i) *coexistence* (the human and the robot conduct independent activities); (ii) *collaboration* (the human and the robot work collaboratively to achieve a shared productive goal). Validation tests are ongoing in four pilot plants, covering different types of production process, i.e., assembly/disassembly, welding operations, large parts management and machine tending.

In this paper, one of the pilots in FOURBYTHREE is considered as a relevant HRC scenario for manufacturing. In such a scenario a robot and a human must cooperate in the assembly/disassembly of metal dies for the production of wax patterns. Some tasks of the process can be performed by both the robot and the human while other tasks that require a special dexterity can be performed only by the human. The robot is endowed with a screwdriver and therefore it can support the human in all the screwing/unscrewing operations of the process. Such HRC scenario can be addressed deploying Planning and Scheduling (P&S) technology [4], i.e., modeling the control problem as a time-flexible planning problem and, then, solving it by means of a hierarchical timeline-based application [20]. The hierarchical approach provides a description of the problem at different levels of abstraction ranging from the process definition level to the robot task implementation level. Then, timelines coordinate the behaviors of the human and the robot over time in order to achieve the desired production goals.

2.1 Planning with Timelines Under Temporal Uncertainty

The formal characterization of the timeline-based approach defined in [6] is well-suited to model HRC scenarios thanks to its capability of representing *temporal uncertainty*. Indeed, temporal uncertainty plays a relevant role in HRC where the human represents an *uncontrollable* element of the environment with respect to the robot. Thus, it is crucial to properly represent and handle such uncertainty in order to produce *robust* plans and dynamically adapt the behavior of the robot to the *observed* behavior of the human. According to [6], a domain specification is composed by a set of *multi-valued state variables*. Each state variable models the allowed temporal behaviors of a particular feature of the domain that must be controlled over time. A state variable is formally defined by the tuple (V, D, T, γ) where: (i) V is a set of values the feature can assume over time; (ii) $D : V \rightarrow \mathbb{R}_{>=0} \times \mathbb{R} \cup \infty$ is a duration function specifying for each value the allowed non negative minimum and maximum duration; (iii) $T : V \rightarrow 2^V$ is a transition function specifying the allowed sequences of values over the timeline; (iv) $\gamma : V \rightarrow \{c, u\}$ is a controllability tagging function

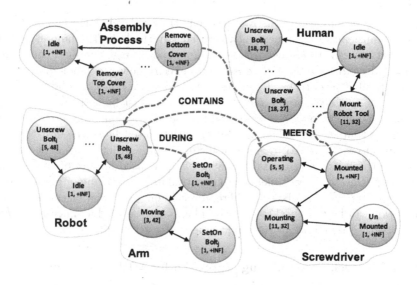

Fig. 1. A partial timeline-based domain specification for a HRC scenario

specifying for each value whether it is controllable or not. State variables model a single feature of a domain by describing the local constraints that must be satisfied in order to build valid temporal behaviors (i.e., valid timelines). *Synchronization rules* specify additional (temporal) constraints that coordinate the behavior of different state variables in order to realize complex tasks or achieve goals.

For instance, Fig. 1 partially shows the domain specification for the collaborative assembly/disassembly process in FOURBYTHREE. An *Assembly Process* state variable models the high-level tasks that must be performed in order to carry out the desired collaborative process. A *Robot* and a *Human* state variables model the possible behaviors of the robot and the human in terms of the low-level tasks they can perform over time. Finally, *Arm* and *Screwdriver* state variables model respectively robot motion tasks and tool management. It is worth to underscore the capability of the formal framework to allow the modeling of uncontrollable dynamics in the considered scenario. The human agent is modeled as an element of the environment and therefore all human tasks are tagged as uncontrollable. In addition, a human may indirectly affect the behavior of the robot in such a working scenario because the robot can slow-down or even interrupt motion tasks in order to guarantee free-collision trajectories. Thus, the actual duration of motion tasks is not under the control of the control system and, therefore, such tasks are also tagged as uncontrollable. The dotted arrows in Fig. 1 represent temporal constraints entailed by a synchronization rule defined for the value *Remove Bottom Cover* of *Assembly Process* state variable. Such constraints specify operational requirements needed to carry out a high-level task (*Remove Bottom Cover*) of the assembly/disassembly process.

A set of *contains* temporal constraints specify the low-level tasks the human and the robot must perform. Specifically, they specify the bolts the human and the robot must unscrew to remove the cover. Then, additional temporal constraints (*during* and *contains* temporal constraints) specify how the robot must implement related low-level tasks. To successfully unscrew a bolt the robot arm must be set on the related location and the screwdriver must be activated.

In such a context, a *plan* is composed by a set of *timelines* and a set of *temporal relations* that satisfy the domain specification and achieve the desired goals. Each timeline is composed by a set of flexible temporal intervals, called *tokens* describing the possible temporal behavior of the related feature of the domain. *Temporal flexibility* allows timelines to encapsulate an envelope of possible temporal behaviors. Such a rich temporal representation together with controllability information can be exploited to generate plans that can be dynamically adapted to the observed dynamics of the environment at execution time.

2.2 A Hierarchical Modeling Approach for HRC Scenarios

In general, the design of effective models is a crucial issue in the development of plan-based controllers. Indeed, a planning model must capture the information about the system to be controlled and the environment in which it works. A planning model is to capture such complexity and to allow a Planner to make decisions at different levels of abstraction. To this aim, hierarchical modeling approaches have been successfully applied in real world scenarios. They support the planning process by *encoding* knowledge about a particular problem to address. HRC scenarios are complex problems that require to take into account several aspects from different perspectives. Thus, hierarchies are well-suited in such a context as they allow to model a complex problem from different levels of abstraction and decompose the related complexity in sub-problems.

Pursuing the hierarchical modeling approach described in [4,20], it is possible to model a HRC scenario by identifying three hierarchical levels. A *supervision level* models the process and the high-level tasks that must be performed. At this level of abstraction the model specifies the operational constraints that must be satisfied to carry out the process regardless of the *agent* that will perform the tasks. The state variable *Assembly Process* in Fig. 1 is the result of such a level. A *coordination level* models the decomposition of high-level tasks of the process into low-level tasks that the human or the robot can directly handle. At this level of abstraction the model specifies the possible assignments of tasks to the robot and therefore the possible interactions between a human and a robot. The state variables *Human* and *Robot* in Fig. 1 model the low-level tasks that the robot and the human may perform and the synchronization rules connecting these values with state variable *Assembly Process* model possible assignments. An *implementation level* models the operations and the related requirements that allow a robot to perform assigned tasks. The state variables *Arm* and *Screwdriver* in Fig. 1 and the synchronization rules connecting their values with the state variable *Robot* model the motion tasks and the tool activations needed to carry out robot tasks.

3   A Framework for Planning and Execution Under Uncertainty

The modeling and solving approaches described above have been implemented in a general framework called EPSL (*Extensible Planning and Scheduling Library*) [20]. EPSL complies with the formal characterization given in [6] and initial steps have been done in order to compare it with other state-of-the-art frameworks [19]. Nevertheless, EPSL was not fully suited to address the needs related to task planning problems in FOURBYTHREE. Most importantly, handling temporal uncertainty both at planning and execution time results as a key capability for effectively and safely deploy P&S robot control solutions. Thus, a new system, called PLanning and Acting with TImeliNes under Uncertainty (PLATINUM), is presented here constituting a uniform framework for planning and execution with timelines with (temporal) uncertainty[2].

The capability of handling temporal uncertainty both at planning and execution time allows the framework to address problems where not all the features of a domain are under the control of the system. Moreover, the "combination" of temporal flexibility and temporal uncertainty allows P&S controllers to generate *flexible* and *temporally robust* plans that can be dynamically adapted at execution time without generating new plans from scratch. Robust plan execution is particularly relevant in HRC scenarios in order to avoid to continuously generate a new plan every time an unexpected behavior of the human is detected (e.g., human execution delays).

Recent results [16] have shown the capability of a PLATINUM instance to realize flexible collaborations by dynamically adapting the behavior of a robot to the observed/detected behavior of a human. Before describing the deployment of PLATINUM in a realistic collaborative assembly scenario, next sections provide a description of how the P&S framework has been extended in order to deal with temporal uncertainty at both planning and execution time.

3.1   Solving Timeline-Based Problems with Uncertainty

Given a domain specification and a particular problem to solve, the role of a timeline-based planner is to synthesize a set of flexible timelines that satisfy domain constraints and achieve some goals. A plan includes a set of timelines each of which describes the allowed temporal behaviors of a particular domain feature (i.e., state variables). In such a context, a plan represents an envelope of possible solutions. Indeed, *temporal flexibility* allows timelines to encapsulate an envelope of possible temporal behaviors. Given the considered HRC scenario, a plan consists of a set of coordinated human and robot beahviors that carry out a particular production task. The solving process of a P&S application can be generalized as a plan refinement search. Basically, a solver iteratively refines an initial partial plan until a valid and complete plan is found. The refinement of a plan consists in detecting and solving a set of *flaws* that affect

---

[2] https://github.com/pstlab/PLATINUm.git.

either the validity or the completeness of the plan. However, the *validity* of a plan with respect to the domain specification does not represent a sufficient condition to guarantee its *executability* in the real world. The *uncontrollable dynamics* of the environment may prevent the complete and correct execution of plans. Thus, from the planning perspective, it is important to generate plans with some properties with respect to the *controllability problem* [13, 21]. *Dynamic controllability* is the most relevant property with respect to the execution of a plan in the real world. Unfortunately, it is not easy to deal with such a property at planning time when the temporal behaviors of domain features are not complete. Typically, such a property is taken into account with post-processing mechanisms after plan generation [3, 5, 13, 21]. Another property worth to be considered at planning time, is the *pseudo-controllability* property which represents a necessary (but not sufficient) condition for dynamic controllability [13].

The pseudo-controllability property of a plan aims at verifying that the planning process does not make hypotheses on the actual duration of the uncontrollable activities of a plan. Specifically, pseudo-controllability verifies that the planning process does not *reduce* the duration of uncontrollable values of the domain. Consequently, a timeline-based plan is pseudo-controllable if and only if all the flexible durations of uncontrollable tokens composing the timelines have not been changed with respect to the domain specification. Although pseudo-controllability does not convey enough information to assert the dynamic controllability of a plan, it represents a useful property that can be exploited for *validating* the planning domain with respect to temporal uncertainty. Indeed, if the planner cannot generate pseudo-controllable plans, then it cannot generate dynamically controllable plans either. Thus, the general solving procedure of EPSL has been now extended in PLATINUM aiming at dealing with temporal uncertainty at planning time. Algorithm 1 shows the new PLATINUM planning procedure.

Hierarchy-Based Flaw Selection Heuristics. The behavior of the planning procedure shown in Algorithm 1 is determined by the particular search strategy S and the flaw selection heuristic $\mathcal{H}$. Specifically, flaw selection can strongly affect the performance of the planning process even if it does not represent a backtracking point of the algorithm. Indeed, each solution of a flaw determines a branch of the search tree. A flaw selection heuristic is supposed to encapsulate smart criteria for suitably evaluating flaws during planning. A good selection of the next flaw to solve can *prune* the search space by cutting off branches that would lead to *unnecessary* or *redundant* refinements of the plan. In addition, leveraging the hierarchical modeling approach presented in Sect. 2.2, a suitable heuristics to guide the selection of flaws can be defined by means of the domain knowledge. The work [20] has shown that it is possible to define a hierarchy-based heuristic capable of leveraging such information and improve the planning capabilities of timeline-based applications.

Algorithm 2 depicts the *SelectFlaws* procedure in Algorithm 1 (row 14) according to such hierarchy-based heuristic. The heuristic takes into account the hierarchical structure of the domain and select flaws that belong to the most

Algorithm 1. A general pseudo-controllability aware planning procedure

```
 1: function SOLVE(𝒫, 𝒮, ℋ)
 2:     F_pc, F_≠pc ← ∅
 3:     π ← InitialPlan(𝒫)
 4:     // check if the current plan is complete and flaw-free
 5:     while ¬IsSolution(π) do
 6:         // get uncontrollable values of the plan
 7:         U = {u_1, ..., u_n} ← GetUncertainty(π)
 8:         // check durations of uncontrollable values
 9:         if ¬Squeezed(U) then
10:             // detect the flaws of the current plan
11:             Φ^0 = {φ_1, ..., φ_k} ← DetectFlaws(π)
12:             // apply the heuristic to filter detected flaws
13:             Φ^* = {φ_1^*, ..., φ_m^*} ← SelectFlaws(Φ^0, ℋ)
14:             // compute possible plan refinements
15:             for φ_i^* ∈ Φ^* do
16:                 // compute flaw's solutions
17:                 N_{φ_i^*} = {n_1, ..., n_t} ← HandleFlaw(φ_i^*, π)
18:                 // check if the current flaw can be solved
19:                 if N_{φ_i^*} = ∅ then
20:                     Backtrack(π, Dequeue(F_pc))
21:                 end if
22:                 for n_j ∈ N_{φ_i^*} do
23:                     // expand the search space
24:                     F_pc ← Enqueue(n_j, 𝒮)
25:                 end for
26:             end for
27:         else
28:             // non pseudo-controllable plan
29:             F_¬pc ← Enqueue(makeNode(π), 𝒮)
30:         end if
31:         // check the fringe of the search space
32:         if IsEmpty(F_pc) ∧ ¬IsEmpty(F_¬pc) then
33:             // try to find a non pseudo-controllable solution
34:             π ← Refine(π, Dequeue(F_¬pc))
35:         else if ¬IsEmpty(F_pc) then
36:             // go on looking for a pseudo-controllable plan
37:             π ← Refine(π, Dequeue(F_pc))
38:         else
39:             return Failure
40:         end if
41:     end while
42:     // get solution plan
43:     return π
44: end function
```

Algorithm 2. The hierarchy-based flaw selection heuristic

```
 1: function SELECTFLAWS(π)
 2:     // initialize the set of flaws
 3:     Φ ← ∅
 4:     // extract the hierarchy of the domain
 5:     H_π = {h_1, ..., h_m} ← extractHierarchy(π)
 6:     for h_i = {sv_{i,1}, ..., sv_{i,k}} ∈ H_π do
 7:         if Φ = ∅ then
 8:             // detect flaws on state variables composing the hierarchical level h_i
 9:             for sv_{i,j} ∈ h_i = {sv_{i,1}, ..., sv_{i,k}} do
10:                 // select detected flaws
11:                 Φ ← detctFlaws(sv_{i,j})
12:             end for
13:         end if
14:     end for
15:     // get selected flaws
16:     return Φ
17: end function
```

---

independent state variables of the domain (i.e., flaws concerning state variables that come first in the hierarchy). The rationale behind the heuristic is that the hierarchical structure encapsulates dependencies among the state variables composing a planning domain. Thus, the resolution of flaws concerning state variables at the *higher* levels of the hierarchy (i.e., the most independent variables) can simplify the resolution of flaws concerning state variables at the *lower* levels of the hierarchy (i.e., the most dependent variables).

3.2   Timeline-Based Plan Execution

The most innovative aspect in PLATINUM is its ability to perform also plan execution relying on the same semantics of timelines in the pursued planning approach [6]. Therefore, PLATINUM executives leverage information about *temporal uncertainty* in order to properly manage and adapt the execution of plans. In general, the execution of a plan is a complex process which can fail even if a plan is valid with respect to the domain specification. During execution, the system must *interact* with the environment, which is *uncontrollable*. Such dynamics can affect or even prevent the correct execution of plans. A *robust* executive system must cope with such exogenous events and dynamically *adapt* the plan accordingly during execution.

Controllability-Aware Execution. The execution process consists of *control cycles* whose frequency determines advancement of time and the discretization of the temporal axis in a number of units called *ticks*. Each *control cycle* is associated with a *tick* and realizes the execution procedure. Broadly speaking, the execution procedure is responsible for detecting the actual behavior of the system (*closed-loop* architecture), for verifying whether the system and also the environment behave as expected from the plan and for starting the execution of the activities of the plan.

Algorithm 3. The PLATINUM executive control procedure

1: **function** EXECUTE(Π, $\mathcal{C}$)
2:      // initialize executive plan database
3:      $\pi_{exec} \leftarrow$ *Setup* (Π)
4:      // check if execution is complete
5:      **while** $\neg CanEndExecution$ (π_{exec}) **do**
6:          // wait a clock's signal
7:          $\tau \leftarrow$ *WaitTick* ($\mathcal{C}$)
8:          // handle synchronization phase
9:          *Synchronize* (τ, π_{exec})
10:          // handle dispatching phase
11:          *Dispatch* (τ, π_{exec})
12:      **end while**
13: **end function**

Algorithm 3 shows the pseudo-code of the general PLATINUM executive procedure. The procedure is composed by two distinct phases, the *synchronization phase* and the *dispatching phase*. At each tick (i.e., control cycle) the synchronization phase manages the received execution feedbacks/signals in order to build the current status of the system and the environment. If the current status is valid with respect to the plan, then the dispatching phase *decides* the next activities to be executed. Otherwise, if the current status does not fit the plan, an *execution failure* is detected and *replanning* is needed. In such a case, the current plan does not represent the actual status of the system and the environment and therefore replanning allows the executive to continue the execution process with a new plan, which has been generated according to the *observed* status and the executed part of the *original plan*.

Algorithm 4 shows the pseudo-code of the synchronization procedure of the executive. The synchronization phase monitors the execution of the plan by determining whether the system and the environment are aligned with respect to the expected plan. Namely, at each iteration the synchronization phase builds the current situation by taking into account the current execution time, the expected plan and the feedbacks received during execution. A *monitor* is responsible for propagating observations concerning the actual duration of the dispatched activities and detecting discrepancies between the real world and the plan. The executive receives feedbacks about the successful execution of dispatched commands or failure. The monitor manages these feedbacks in order to detect if the actual duration of tokens comply with the plan. If the feedbacks comply with the plan, then the execution of the plan can proceed. Otherwise, a *failure* is detected because the current situation does not fit the expected plan and the executive reacts accordingly (*replanning*).

Algorithm 4. The PLATINUM executive procedure for the synchronization phase

```
 1: function SYNCHRONIZE(τ, π_exec)
 2:     // manage observations
 3:     O = {o_1, ..., o_n} ← GetObservations (π_exec)
 4:     for o_i ∈ O do
 5:         // propagate the observed end time
 6:         π_exec ← PropagateObservation (τ, o_i)
 7:     end for
 8:     // check if observations are consistent with the current plan
 9:     if ¬IsConsistent (π_exec) then
10:         // execution failure
11:         return Failure
12:     end if
13:     // manage controllable activities
14:     A = {a_i, ..., a_m} ← GetControllableActivities (π_exec)
15:     for a_i ∈ A do
16:         // check if activity can end execution
17:         if CanEndExecution (τ, a_i, π_exec) then
18:             // propagate the decided end time
19:             π_exec ← PropagateEndActivity (τ, a_i)
20:         end if
21:     end for
22: end function
```

Algorithm 5 shows the pseudo-code of the dispatching procedure of the executive. The dispatching phase manages the actual execution of the plan. Given the current situation and the current execution time, the dispatching step analyzes the plan π_{exec} in order to find the tokens that can start execution and dispatches the related commands to the underlying system. Namely, the dispatching step allows the executive to advance execution and decide the next tokens to execute. Thus, a *dispatcher* is responsible for making dispatching decisions of plan's tokens. For each token, the dispatcher checks the related *start condition* by analyzing the token's scheduled time and any dependency with other tokens of the plan. If the start condition holds, then the dispatcher can decide to start executing the token (i.e., the dispatcher propagates the scheduled start time into the plan).

3.3   Token Lifecycle

A plan and its temporal relations encapsulate a set of execution dependencies that must be taken into account when executing timelines. Besides the scheduled temporal bounds, such dependencies specify whether the executive can actually start or end the execution of a token. Let us consider for example a plan where the temporal relation A *before* B holds between tokens A and B. Such a temporal relation encapsulates an execution dependency between token A and token B.

Algorithm 5. The PLATINUM executive procedure for the dispatching phase

```
 1: function DISPATCH(τ, π_exec)
 2:     // manage the start of (all) plan's activities
 3:     A = {a_i, ..., a_m} ← GetActivities (π_exec)
 4:     for a_i ∈ A do
 5:         // check if activity can start execution
 6:         if CanStartExecution (τ, a_i, π_exec) then
 7:             // propagate the decided start time
 8:             π_exec ← PropagateStartActivity (τ, a_i)
 9:             // actually dispatch the related command to the robot
10:             SendCommand (a_i)
11:         end if
12:     end for
13: end function
```

The executive can start the execution of token B if and only if the execution of token A is over. In addition, the executive must take into account *controllability properties* of tokens. Different controllability properties entail different execution policies of tokens and therefore different *lifecycles*.

Controllable tokens are completely under the executive control. In this case the executive can decide both the start time and the duration of the execution of this type of tokens. Both decisions are controllable. *Partially-controllable tokens* are not completely under the control of the executive. Tokens of such a type are under the control of the *environment*. The executive can decide the start time (i.e., the dispatching time) while it can only *observe* the actual execution and update the plan according to the *execution feedbacks* received from the environment. Finally, *uncontrollable tokens* are completely outside the control of the executive. The executive can neither decide the start nor the end of the execution. Both "events" are under the control of the environment. *Execution feedbacks* concern both the start time and the end time of the execution and therefore the executive can only update/adapt the controllable part of the plan accordingly.

4   Deployment in a Real Scenario

A separate work [16] describes how an instance of PLATINUM has been deployed in a manufacturing case study integrating the task planning technology described above with a motion planning system for industrial robots [15]. In that integration, PLATINUM and its features are leveraged to implement an integrated task and motion planning system capable of selecting different *execution modalities* for robot tasks according to the expected *collaboration* of the robot with a human operator. This is the result of a tight integration of PLATINUM with a motion planning system. Indeed, the pursued approach realizes an *offline analysis* of the production scenarios in order to synthesize a number of collision-free *robot motion trajectories* for each collaborative task with different *safety* levels. Each trajectory is then associated with an expected temporal execution bound and represents a tradeoff between "speed" of the motion and "safety" of the human. The integrated system has been deployed and tested in laboratory on an assembly case study similar to collaborative assembly/disassembly scenario described above. In [16], an empirical evaluation is provided in order to assess the overall productivity of the HRC cell while increasing the involvement of the robots (i.e., increasing the number of tasks the robot is allowed to perform). The results show the effectiveness of PLATINUM in finding well suited distribution of tasks between the human and the robot in different scenarios with an increasing workload for the control system. Specifically, the PLATINUM instance results as capable of increasing the productivity of the production process without affecting the safety of the operator.

Before concluding the paper it is worth underscoring that for lack of space this paper does not concern an experimental evaluation of PLATINUM features. Some focalized experiments are contained in [16] while a wider experimental campaign is undergoing and will constitute an important pillar for a future longer report.

5   Conclusions

In this paper, a recent evolution of a timeline-based planning framework has been presented. In particular, taking also advantage of the needs coming from the FOURBYTHREE project, the EPSL planner has been endowed of novel features for structured modeling, synthesizing plans under uncertainty and plan execution functionality. The obtained framework, called PLATINUM, is currently supporting the need of adaptability in new domains. The table below summarizes the main features and capability introduced in PLATINUM and points out differences with respect to EPSL.

	EPSL	PLATINUM
Representation	Temporal flexibility	Temporal flexibility with uncontrollability
Solving	Hierarchical	Hierarchical with uncertainty
Execution	Not supported	Plan execution with uncertainty

PLATINUM represents a uniform framework for planning and execution with timelines under uncertainty. It relies on a well-defined formalization of the timeline-based approach [6] and has proven to be particularly suited for addressing HRC scenarios. It is worth underscoring how PLATINUM enters in the current state of the art in a sub-area of planning systems for robotics together with CHIMP [18], HATP [9], meta-CSP planner [11], FAPE [2] that creates a *current generation* of planners for robotics whose goal is to evolve with respect to classical temporal frameworks such as, for instance, EUROPA [1] and IxTeT [8]. Finally, leveraging the work in [14], a current research effort is related to the extension of the knowledge engineering framework for PLATINUM to enable use by *non specialist* planning users. Our goal, as already said, is to enable the use of our technology in different industrial settings. To this aim, creating a tool for non specialists for modelling, configuring and implementing plan-based controllers is an important goal to pursue.

References

1. Barreiro, J., Boyce, M., Do, M., Frank, J., Iatauro, M., Kichkaylo, T., Morris, P., Ong, J., Remolina, E., Smith, T., Smith, D.: EUROPA: a platform for AI planning, scheduling, constraint programming, and optimization. In: The 4th International Competition on Knowledge Engineering for Planning and Scheduling, ICKEPS 2012 (2012)
2. Bit-Monnot, A.: Temporal and hierarchical models for planning and acting in robotics. Ph.D. thesis, Doctorat de l'Université Federale Toulouse Midi-Pyrenees (2016)
3. Cesta, A., Finzi, A., Fratini, S., Orlandini, A., Tronci, E.: Validation and verification issues in a timeline-based planning system. Knowl. Eng. Rev. **25**(3), 299–318 (2010)
4. Cesta, A., Orlandini, A., Bernardi, G., Umbrico, A.: Towards a planning-based framework for symbiotic human-robot collaboration. In: 21th IEEE International Conference on Emerging Technologies and Factory Automation (ETFA). IEEE (2016)
5. Cialdea Mayer, M., Orlandini, A.: An executable semantics of flexible plans in terms of timed game automata. In: The 22nd International Symposium on Temporal Representation and Reasoning (TIME). IEEE (2015)
6. Cialdea Mayer, M., Orlandini, A., Umbrico, A.: Planning and execution with flexible timelines: a formal account. Acta Informatica **53**(6–8), 649–680 (2016)
7. Freitag, M., Hildebrandt, T.: Automatic design of scheduling rules for complex manufacturing systems by multi-objective simulation-based optimization. CIRP Ann. Manuf. Technol. **65**(1), 433–436 (2016)
8. Ghallab, M., Laruelle, H.: Representation and control in IxTeT, a temporal planner. In: 2nd International Conference on Artificial Intelligence Planning and Scheduling (AIPS), pp. 61–67 (1994)
9. Lallement, R., de Silva, L., Alami, R.: HATP: an HTN planner for robotics. CoRR abs/1405.5345 (2014). http://arxiv.org/abs/1405.5345
10. Lemai, S., Ingrand, F.: Interleaving temporal planning and execution in robotics domains. In: AAAI 2004, pp. 617–622 (2004)
11. Mansouri, M., Pecora, F.: More knowledge on the table: planning with space, time and resources for robots. In: 2014 IEEE International Conference on Robotics and Automation, ICRA 2014, Hong Kong, China, 31 May–7 June 2014, pp. 647–654. IEEE (2014)
12. Maurtua, I., Pedrocchi, N., Orlandini, A., Fernández, J.D.G., Vogel, C., Geenen, A., Althoefer, K., Shafti, A.: FourByThree: imagine humans and robots working hand in hand. In: 2016 IEEE 21st International Conference on Emerging Technologies and Factory Automation (ETFA), pp. 1–8, September 2016
13. Morris, P.H., Muscettola, N., Vidal, T.: Dynamic control of plans with temporal uncertainty. In: International Joint Conference on Artificial Intelligence (IJCAI), pp. 494–502 (2001)

14. Orlandini, A., Bernardi, G., Cesta, A., Finzi, A.: Planning meets verification and validation in a knowledge engineering environment. Intell. Artif. **8**(1), 87–100 (2014)
15. Pellegrinelli, S., Moro, F.L., Pedrocchi, N., Tosatti, L.M., Tolio, T.: A probabilistic approach to workspace sharing for human-robot cooperation in assembly tasks. CIRP Ann. Manuf. Technol. **65**(1), 57–60 (2016)
16. Pellegrinelli, S., Orlandini, A., Pedrocchi, N., Umbrico, A., Tolio, T.: Motion planning and scheduling for human and industrial-robot collaboration. CIRP Ann. Manuf. Technol. **66**(1), 1–4 (2017)
17. Py, F., Rajan, K., McGann, C.: A systematic agent framework for situated autonomous systems. In: AAMAS, pp. 583–590 (2010)
18. Stock, S., Mansouri, M., Pecora, F., Hertzberg, J.: Online task merging with a hierarchical hybrid task planner for mobile service robots. In: 2015 IEEE/RSJ International Conference on Intelligent Robots and Systems (IROS), pp. 6459–6464, September 2015
19. Umbrico, A., Cesta, A., Cialdea Mayer, M., Orlandini, A.: Steps in assessing a timeline-based planner. In: Adorni, G., Cagnoni, S., Gori, M., Maratea, M. (eds.) AI*IA 2016. LNCS, vol. 10037, pp. 508–522. Springer, Cham (2016). doi:10.1007/978-3-319-49130-1_37
20. Umbrico, A., Orlandini, A., Mayer, M.C.: Enriching a temporal planner with resources and a hierarchy-based heuristic. In: Gavanelli, M., Lamma, E., Riguzzi, F. (eds.) AI*IA 2015. LNCS, vol. 9336, pp. 410–423. Springer, Cham (2015). doi:10.1007/978-3-319-24309-2_31
21. Vidal, T., Fargier, H.: Handling contingency in temporal constraint networks: from consistency to controllabilities. JETAI **11**(1), 23–45 (1999)

Author Index

Printed in the United States
By Bookmasters